CAPE TOWN

The Story of Cape Town, Robben Island and the Cape Peninsula

T.V. BULPIN

SUNBIRD PUBLISHERS

An imprint of Jonathan Ball Publishers

Sunbird Publishers (Pty) Ltd, P O Box 6836, Roggebaai, 8012, South Africa
Registration number: 1984/003543/07

First Edition published as *Tavern of the Seas* by TV Bulpin, 1995
Second Edition published as *Tavern of the Seas* 2003
Third Edition 2009
Reprinted in 2010

Editor Peter Joyce
Design concept Peter Bosman
DTP layout Mandy McKay
Reproduction by Resolution Colour, Cape Town. Printed and bound by Tien Wah Press (Pte) Ltd, Singapore

ISBN 978-1-920289-10-2

Front cover Table Mountain as seen from Bloubergstrand.
Previous page The peaks of the Twelve Apostles rise behind Camps Bay.
Above Table Mountain and the Waterfront buildings are reflected in the waters of the Victoria Basin.
Opposite The protea family, including Leucospermum cordifolium, flourishes on Table Mountain.
Back cover Aerial view of the Cape Peninsula.

CONTENTS

CHAPTER ONE

THE BIRTH OF A CITY

APE TOWN IS FORTUNATE. There are few other cities so splendidly displayed, so influenced by a benign setting of mountains which, by their presence, sowed its seeds, nurtured its roots, directed its growth and provided it with so handsome a background.

The city and the mountains belong to one another. Cape Town without the mountains would not be quite so interesting. The mountains – Table Mountain, Devil's Peak, Lion's Head and Signal Hill – would still be superb without the city, but their offspring provides them with an animated contrast of capricious moods, an unfolding drama of events, an agreeable mix of sounds, aromas, scandals, all taking place beneath the overlooking piles of rock, like children playing at the feet of indulgent parents.

Look down upon Cape Town from the mountain heights, one of the great views of the world. It is spectacular by day, exquisite by night, especially beautiful in the early evening when a golden glow lingers from the sunset and, one by one, countless lights start to appear like stars descending from the Milky Way to dance and play in the city all night.

STORY OF A MOUNTAIN

How did it all start? As mountains go, Table Mountain is no giant. It is only 1 086 m high but, standing next to the sea, every metre of it is visible. It is one of the most renowned shipping landfalls on Earth. It stands on the southwest end of Africa, its distinctive shape looming up as a gigantic beacon halfway on one of the globe's principal trade-routes, the sea lane around Africa linking east to west.

In making this mountain and positioning it so strategically, nature revealed a piquant sense of humour and sympathy to human needs. Not only was the mountain so positioned as to be seen from far out to sea, but its unique shape made it easily identifiable. To make it even more distinctive, nature provided it with a cloud table-cloth, a phenomenon created by the action of the southeasterly wind, which carries a heavy load of moisture, picked up in its passage over the warm waters of the

Right The Delville Wood memorial in the Gardens commemorates the battle of the Somme in 1916.

Mozambique-Agulhas Current which reaches the end of its flow in False Bay. Orographic condensation turns this moisture into cloud as the wind is forced to rise over the mountain top and suddenly cools. Tumbling over the northern edge of the tabletop, the wind falls immediately back to a lower and warmer level. The cloud disappears at this level and Table Mountain is left with its table-cloth.

Who were the first human beings to see the majestic spectacle of Table Mountain and its cloud? Fossils and artefacts at least 15 000 years old have been found in caves in the Cape Peninsula. Until recently examples of rock art on the walls of cave shelters on Table Mountain itself were reminders, until they faded away, of the presence in former years of people of the Later Stone Age.

Legends tell that Phoenician and Arab sailors, 2 000 and more years ago, were the first to reach the mountain from the sea. The Phoenicians, circumnavigating Africa for the first time from Europe, are said to have landed at the foot of the mountain to rest, repair their ships, and replenish their food by planting and reaping crops of wheat. The Arab sailors, exploring the east coast of Africa, described Table Mountain as a magic place, with a magnetism which drew ships to doom.

The Phoenicians were looking for a way around the southern end of the African continent; the Arabs more particularly for an extension of their slave, ivory and gold trading enterprises on the east coast. To both the pioneer groups and the countless seafarers who followed them, Table Mountain became the eagerly looked-for beacon at the end of Africa. Fresh water could always be obtained there from the mountain streams. Meat could be bartered from the nomadic pastoral people of unknown name who grazed their herds in the area.

A MEETING OF CULTURES

It is not known who were the first of the modern European seafarers to see Table Mountain and its bay. The records of the discovery of the Cape of Good Hope by Bartholomeu Dias in 1488 are incomplete and make no mention of it.

The written story started in 1503 when the Portuguese admiral, António de Saldanha, on his way to the East with a fleet of three ships, mislaid his position and found himself quite inadvertently sailing into Table Bay. After anchoring, Saldanha left his men on the shore to replenish water casks while he and a party followed the freshwater stream to the foot of the mountain and then up the Platteklip Gorge, which provides the only relatively easy climb to the summit. From the top he could see the whole of the Cape Peninsula as far as the Cape of Good Hope, and this grand view of the classic peninsula shape cleared the confusion in his mind about his whereabouts.

Back on the shore, Saldanha found his men trying to bargain for livestock with the resident pastoral people. The discord of two completely different languages made such bargaining extremely difficult. The haggling deteriorated into a squabble. The first recorded encounter of African and

Opposite The Victoria and Alfred Waterfront is a busy, working harbour as well as a place of recreation.

of Saldanha. In 1591 the English admiral, George Raymond, with James (later Sir James) Lancaster as captain of one of his three ships, sailed into the bay in search of fresh water and meat. The Englishmen traded as many animals as they wanted – two knives for an ox and one knife for a sheep were considered to be fair prices.

Raymond also sailed over to the kidney-shaped island in the bay, known today as Robben Island ('Island of seals'), where he found an unexpected bounty. There were so many sea birds, eggs and seals that the seafarers recorded that 'there can be no other island in all the world as full of fowl and seal as this. It is astounding'. The Englishmen replenished their food-store and sailed on, leaving behind on the island a number of sheep which were too thin and sickly to withstand a voyage.

From the earliest days Robben Island – just 3,5 km long, 2 km wide – played a peculiarly important role in the story of Cape Town. This importance derived from three characteristics: its strategic position commanding the entrance to Table Bay; its isolation and thus its immunity from mainland predators, and thirdly its shales and deposits of marine shells (limestone), both valuable building materials, and its wildlife – penguins and other sea birds nested on the place in prodigious numbers while seals lolled around completely tame and still to learn of man's rapacity.

Dutch sailors also made considerable use of Robben Island. In 1601 Joris van Spilbergen named it *Cornelia* after his mother. He had visited Dassen Island as he came down the west coast and named it *Elizabeth*. On that odd island he had been surprised, as all visitors have been, at the presence of the dassies (coneys) which have given the island its name. The origin of these little animals on an island so isolated from the mainland (where they are common) would have slightly puzzled Charles Darwin. Captain Van Spilbergen captured a number of them for food and released a few on his Cornelia Island as some exchange for the plump sheep which he found there, now running wild.

Leaving some surplus livestock on Robben Island to fatten in safety, and then be replaced in exchange with thinner animals by later voyagers, became a courteous habit no matter whether the seafarers were friends or enemies. Another habit which started at this time, on both the island and the mainland, was to inscribe stones with the name of a ship and the date of its visit. Underneath these stones letters were placed with requests that they be carried forward, east or west as required, by other ships. The courtesy was granted even in times of war. The so-called 'Post-Office Stones' became a custom of visitors to Table Bay and those letters which survive tell engrossing stories of sea fights, storms, wrecks, adventures, hopes, disappointments and the hardship of long voyages in

European on the site of the future city of Cape Town ended in bloodshed. António de Saldanha was slightly wounded himself. The Portuguese were driven back to their ship and they sailed off in disgruntled mood.

From thence on the bay was known to the Portuguese as the Aguada de António de Saldanha ('Watering place of António de Saldanha). Seven years later Dom Francisco de Almeida, returning to Portugal after a bloody five year spell as the first Portuguese Viceroy of India, put into Table Bay with a fleet of three ships. The crew replenished drinking water from the mountain stream and started a trade for livestock with a group of pastoralists somewhere on the site of the present suburb of Woodstock. Everything seemed to be going well, with the Africans friendly, killing a sheep and inviting the Portuguese to a feast.

Then a fight developed - for obscure reasons, but said to have begun when the Portuguese attempted to take a man by force either as a hostage or to meet their commander. The language barrier was impenetrable. The Portuguese were driven to the beach. Almeida decided that the prestige of Portugal demanded retaliation. A few days later he landed on the beach with 150 men and marched to the African village. In a sur-

prise attack the Portuguese seized a number of children and cattle. There were only about 80 African males but they rallied to rescue their children and livestock. Sheltering behind bullocks trained for combat, they charged at the Portuguese, throwing stones and spears in a barrage. It was the turn of the Portuguese to be surprised. They retreated to the beach and were dismayed to find that the sailors who had conveyed them from the anchored ships had moved further eastwards.

There was a running battle as the Portuguese, many of them already wounded, retreated along the beach. Reinforcements reached the Africans, and now 170 men harassed the heavily armed Portuguese. Almeida died with a spear through his throat. Seventy-five of his men, including eleven officers, died with him. The fact that 170 primitive African people could so overwhelm 150 well-armed European soldiers was considered to be one of the worst disasters in Portuguese history, especially as several of the casualties were members of illustrious families and Almeida was a nobleman of high rank. Few Portuguese ships ventured into the bay at the foot of Table Mountain after this disaster.

ISLAND OF SEALS

Towards the end of the 16th century, seafarers of other nations started to sail around the Cape and they had no qualms in visiting the watering place

itors overcame the difficulty by applying a nickname to the pastoralists, Hottentot, said by some to mean a stammerer, from the odd sounds in their speech and by others to have originated from a rhythmic word sounding like *huttentutton*, which the pastoralists are said to have repeated constantly while they danced. The smaller and less numerous hunter-gatherer people were eventually given by the Dutch the name of Bosjesmans (Bushmen) because they seemed to lurk in the cover of the shrubs. The pastoralists referred offhandedly to these people as *Sonkwa*. The origin and ancestral relationship of the hunter-gatherers and the pastoralists remains unknown. Their languages were similar but their lifestyles very different. They were both, however, essentially nomadic, wandering about in groups or small tribes, each group having its own name and not recognising any paramount power or generic name.

The seafarers had some peculiar ideas of winning friends and influencing the local inhabitants. They couldn't have had it much better. Scrap metal and junk trinkets bartered for enough fat slaughter animals to provision one whole fleet; 39 fat oxen and 115 sheep in exchange for 'a little brass which we cut from two or three old kettles'. This was in 1612.

The English felt that things could be still better if they had a resident middleman who could ensure trade. To this purpose, in 1613, the chief of the local pastoralists (whose name sounded like Cory), together with another man, was lured on board a homeward-bound ship and kidnapped. One man died on the voyage but Cory reached England, where the plan was to teach him English and for the company to learn from him something of the possibilities of the Cape country for trade. Cory was even dressed in clothes of the current English fashion. He was accommodated in London in the home of Sir Thomas Smythe, the founder of the English East India Company. He would lie on the ground crying and pleading 'Cory home go, Souldana go, home go', over and over.

Smythe eventually relented and sent Cory back to the Cape. As soon as he landed he bolted for home, tore off his English clothing and reverted to traditional dress. The English were disgruntled. They complained that the bottom line bargaining price for livestock went up sharply after Cory's return, although it was still cheap enough.

THE DEEP DIVIDE

It was on the shores of Table Bay that, at this time, a development was taking place with consequences which were to bedevil the whole turbulent story of Southern Africa. A plural society was being spawned from complete misunderstanding between persons of African and non-African origin. The division was not caused so much by colour, as by a barrier of

appalling conditions, with bad water, worse food, dismal living conditions, and the ships haunted by the dreadful curse of scurvy, 'a disease which rots the flesh and makes the mouth like an open sore'.

NAMES AND NICKNAMES

With the launching in 1600 of the English East India Company and in 1602 of the Dutch East India Company there was a considerable increase of shipping calling in Table Bay. Only the Portuguese continued to bypass the Cape, using as their refreshment place the islet of Mozambique, 3 000 km further north.

The Cape was extolled by nearly all the English and Dutch seafarers who called there. It was halfway on what could be a terrible journey. The climate was healthy, the water from the Fresh River (as it was called) tast-

ed exquisitely pure and sweet. There was no malarial fever; and, as Thomas Aldworth, senior merchant for the English East India Company reported to his superiors, he arrived there 'with many of our people sick, they all regained their health and strength within twenty days'. As for the local pastoralists, Aldworth found 'the natives of the country to be very courteous and tractable folk, and they did not give us the least annoyance during the time we were there'.

Nobody knew what to call these indigenous African inhabitants. The clicks and odd sounds in their language made it extremely difficult for visitors to understand them or pronounce any word or name. The Dutch vis-

Above The Foreshore area was under water until the 1930's, when a land reclamation scheme was commenced.

Opposite Cape Town city centre and Table Bay, seen from Tafelberg Road on Table Mountain.

separate cultures and languages, each with sounds extremely difficult for the other group to learn or pronounce. The two divisions in the Cape simply could not communicate or comprehend each other's life-style or ethos. They had to formulate assessments of each other by superficial observation during casual encounters.

To the Africans, seafarers of whatever origin, Asian or European, were, at first, just curiosities and no threat because they did not stay long. But as traders they were demanding – and it was inevitable that the rubbish they offered for livestock would soon become unacceptable. The newcomers' obvious disdain of the African's clothing, eating habits and hygiene was irritating. African clothing suited the climate and was the product of available dress materials. Their eating habits were to the taste of the Africans and, as for hygiene, the rancid fat they rubbed into their bodies might stink to the visitors but it drove away bugs. It was the visitors who looked sick near to death when they arrived, recovered in the healthy environment and then sailed away leaving behind such scourges as the smallpox and venereal disease which caused heavy mortality to the indigenous people.

As for culture, the Africans had their music, traditions, legends and religion. The seafarers considered them to be barbarians with no schools or buildings better than huts, no signs of parliament, government, tax collections, churches or the evident signs of religion in the form of vestments, ceremonies, services, attendance registers and promises of rewards to come in another world. The Africans were bemused by this; they had not much belief in paradise to come and soon discovered the fact, particularly important for them, that none of the foreign religions had the least condemnation of slavery. The Ten Commandments and the golden rule of not doing to others that which you would not have them do to you were indeed preached but definitely not much practised. The vaunted superiority of Eastern and Western civilisations, to the Africans, amounted to nothing against the barbarous murders, wars, inhumanity and ruthless exploitation of the environment, which were so integral a part of the life-style of the newcomers.

Finally, there was the matter of land. The visitors saw no sign of fences, cultivation or private ownership. The African concept of collective ownership was completely contrary to the ideas of European and Asian people. Private property, to them, was sacrosanct, but here, beneath Table Mountain, there was no sign of any such thing. The whole land seemed to be wide open, up for the taking.

COLONIAL OVERTURE

Notwithstanding their disappointment in Cory, the director of the English East India Company decided on establishing a permanent presence at the Cape. His method of effecting this presence was rather peculiar. From King James I he obtained a reprieve for seventeen condemned prisoners, who were offered the choice of the gallows or the Cape. With some hesitation they accepted the Cape. They were joined voluntarily by three other convicts. On 5 June 1615, Cory and his people were somewhat disconcerted to see landed on the shores of Table Bay nine of these felons led by a celebrated highwayman and former yeoman of the Royal Guard known as Captain James Crosse. This little band was supposed to start a plantation, be grateful to their king for saving their lives, behave like Christians, and explore the country to see if they could discover anything which might be beneficial to England and to their honourable employers.

The means given to the men to enable them to effect these miracles were pitiful: a tent, some turnip seeds and spades, two knives, a short pike, a sword and a knapsack for each man, a store of bread, dried Newfoundland fish and, as an act of charity, a little wine and 'strong water'. They also had use of a ship's whaleboat, which allowed them to make their base in security on Robben Island. The idea was to stock the island with livestock bartered from the mainland pastoralists. Visiting ships could be provided with a dependable supply of fresh meat.

The idea was interesting but, in view if the type of men involved, it never had a real chance. The islanders found additional interests on the mainland, and Captain Crosse had his throat slit in a quarrel over women. The whaleboat was wrecked on the island's rocky coast and the men were marooned. After eight months, a ship was seen on the horizon but seemed to have no intention of venturing into Table Bay. The islanders, by then, were 'almost mad by reason of their several pressing wants and extremities'. They had made a raft from the wreckage of the whaleboat. On this, four of the men attempted to paddle to the ship. They were overturned in a swell and drowned.

The next day the ship, homeward-bound to England, entered Table Bay. The surviving islanders begged to be taken away. Within a few hours of landing in England, the three were arrested for stealing a purse. They were hanged by special warrant of the Lord Chief Justice who, without further trial, simply revived their original condemnation.

On 3 July 1620 two English commanders, Commodore Andrew Shillinge and Captain Humphrey Fitzherbert, annexed the Cape to King James, hoisted the flag of St George and erected a cairn of stones on what they called 'King James his Mount' (now Signal Hill).

Nothing resulted from this annexation. The English government and the East India Company were on friendly terms with the Dutch and quite happy to let them have the Cape if they wanted it.

Meanwhile, Cory had died and the English visitors tried to find a replacement middleman. About 1631 one of their ships bound for the East took aboard a beachcomber who they named Harry. He was given a round trip, taught some English on the journey, well treated, and returned safely to Table Bay. Unfortunately he was not esteemed by the pastoral tribes. He and his people were lowly *strandlopers* (beach-combers, so named by the Dutch) who lived largely on dead whales and the sea creatures washed up on shore. The superior pastoral people would have none of him.

To save Harry from being killed, the English removed him and a number of his clan to Robben Island where they could live safely, and where Harry could continue his career as interpreter and negotiator. Some such arrangement was very needful. In March 1632, just before Harry returned to the Cape, 23 of the crew of a Dutch ship had been killed when, it is said, they tried to seize cattle without payment to the owners.

THE HAPPY CASTAWAYS

Notwithstanding such disasters, the reputation of the Cape as a place of refreshment grew. In 1647 this reputation received a considerable boost. On 25 March of that year the homeward-bound Dutch ship *Haarlem* had the misfortune of being blown by a southeast gale on to the beach at Blouberg on the northern end of Table Bay. Nobody was drowned but the ship stuck fast and it was carrying a valuable cargo. Most of the crew and passengers were taken aboard two other Dutch ships anchored in the bay, while 40 others were given passage to Europe aboard two English ships. The 60 men who remained, led by a junior merchant, Leendert Janssen, stayed to salvage the cargo. They built a small fort on shore and, in the months they stayed there, worked, planted a vegetable garden, fished, hunted and rowed over to Robben Island to gather penguins, eggs and to club seals to secure oil for their lamps.

A few beachcombers were the only local inhabitants they at first encountered, but after five months a group of pastoralists wandered into the area and were quite happy to trade cattle and sheep for what they considered to be fair exchange in items from the shipwreck. The ship-wrecked men lived well and were even able to supply meat and vegetables to ships that called. In March 1648 a homeward-bound fleet of twelve Dutch ships arrived. The salvaged cargo, 60 healthy men and ample stocks of food were taken aboard and conveyed in good order to the Netherlands. The report compiled by Janssen and Nicolaas Proot, a fellow member of the shipwrecked party, to the Dutch East India Company eulogised the Cape, its health, peaceful inhabitants, and possibilities of profit from seals, whales, fishing, and supplying food to passing ships. As a consequence of this report, the Company, on 20 March 1651, finally decided to establish a victualling station at the Cape. It was a momentous decision for Southern Africa.

Two ships, *Dromedaris* and *Reiger*, and a yacht *Goede Hoop* were commissioned to convey to the Cape a party of 70 men. The command was offered to Nicolaas Proot. When he declined the position, it was offered to 33-year-old Johan (Jan) van Riebeeck, who had already seen

Above The reconstructed Dolphin Pool within the Castle courtyard, much as it was in Lady Anne's time.

service in the East with the Company as an under-surgeon and then as assistant clerk. After some trouble over private trading at Tonkin he had been recalled to Holland in 1648. He left the Company, married Maria Quevellerius (also known as Maria de la Queillerie), made trading voyages to Greenland and the West Indies and then rejoined the Company with the rank of merchant at the pay of £4. 11s. 8d a month. He accepted the offer to lead the venture to the Cape.

On his first return voyage from the East, Van Riebeeck had lived on shore at the Cape for three weeks while the cargo of the wrecked *Haarlem* was being loaded on the homeward-bound ships. He shared the opinion that the Cape was suitable for a permanent refreshment station.

THE FIRST SETTLERS

The instructions given to Van Riebeeck and the captains of the three ships were to proceed directly to Table Bay. The materials for a wooden building were included in the loading of the ships and, on arrival, this was to be erected close to the all-important watering place at the mouth of the Fresh River. A site for a fort had then to be selected and the stronghold built as quickly as possible. It was designed to accommodate about 80

his clan of beachcombers. Van Riebeeck learned that Harry's people, a very small clan, had a name which the Dutch wrote as 'Goringhaikona', the nearest they could get to recording the clicks and exotic sounds. Two larger clans of pastoralists habitually used the area for grazing when the rains came. They were the (Dutch spelling) Goringhaikwa and the Gorachoukwa. At least eight other pastoral clans had their grazing areas in what is now the province of the Western Cape. All these clans were nomadic, wandering about in search of the best grazing. They were generally peaceful, the country was large and there were not many of them. They could avoid one another. These were the people nicknamed Hottentots by the Dutch. They had no generic name for themselves.

Work started the next day, 8 April, on erecting a wooden house and store shed close to the mouth of the Fresh River. The site for the fort was selected where the fruit stalls stand today on what is known as the Grand Parade in the centre of modern Cape Town. One hundred men were selected from the three vessels to work on construction on shore and were housed in tents.

On 24 April, Van Riebeeck and his family removed from the *Dromedaris* to the shore. On the previous evening a hippopotamus had been killed in the swamp and on this animal the whole party feasted. They likened the flesh to veal and craved for more, but hippos were difficult to kill with the muskets and balls of the period. For some time the principal items on the Cape menu were the fish which swarmed in huge shoals in Table Bay and were described by Van Riebeeck and his people as the most delicious they had ever tasted. These fish made a hard, cold, wet, miserable winter bearable. Everything else was in short supply.

There was, though, a silver lining: the rains transformed the vegetation and softened the soil. Hendrik Boom, the gardener, made haste to plant seeds and soon health-restoring vegetables were growing. Great herds of game animals also appeared in the area on what was apparently their seasonal migration. The sight of these wild animals made the longing for fresh meat almost an obsession but the inexperienced hunters had little success with their simple weapons. In the whole winter season, only one young hartebeest was run down by dogs. For the rest, the wild animals outwitted marksmen, traps and pitfalls with agile impunity.

Van Riebeeck looked to Robben Island for a solution, for that little place always seemed to be productive of something interesting. The yacht was sent over and came back with over 100 carcasses of sea birds and 3 000 penguin eggs, a very welcome addition to food supplies. He also decided it was time to examine the possibilities of the country behind Devil's Peak. This beautiful and fertile agricultural land delighted him. He thought that if a population of Chinese settlers could be introduced to farm this area (now known as Constantia) an unlimited supply of vegetables and other produce could be obtained for supply to shipping. But nothing came of

men. Four small cannon of the type known as culverins were to be mounted on the fort's angles. Once secure in this fort, Van Riebeeck and his men had to take possession of a fertile extent of arable land suitable for vegetable and fruit cultivation. A professional gardener, Hendrik Boom and his family, were members of Van Riebeeck's party.

The party was instructed not to injure any of the local inhabitants or their cattle but to endeavour to win friendship. The instruction did not indicate how this goodwill could be obtained and maintained if select sites for occupation, agriculture and grazing were also to be set up without negotiation or suggested payment. All nations except Portugal would be welcome to trade and even to occupy areas of the country for themselves beyond the Company's boundaries.

On Sunday, 24 December 1651, a fine easterly wind blew from the mainland of Europe. Like a flock of birds waiting to migrate, a whole fleet of

Above The lovely Disa uniflora, known as 'Pride of Table Mountain', still grows on shady river banks.

Dutch merchant ships set sail for many far ports of trade. Amongst these vessels were the two ships and the yacht *Goede Hoop* conveying Van Riebeeck and his party to the Cape. The voyage was uneventful and, for those days, speedy, and on 5 April 1652, about the fifth glass of the afternoon watch, the chief mate of the *Dromedaris* saw Table Mountain rise just above the horizon.

Captain Coninck of the *Dromedaris* was the first to go ashore with six armed soldiers and a party of sailors. They landed just after dawn, caught delicious fish in a seine net, collected some herbs and found a box containing three letters left on 26 February by the admiral of a homeward-bound fleet. Later that afternoon, Van Riebeeck went ashore with a party to select the best site for the fort.

The area of the future city of Cape Town had been well dehydrated by the summer season of the southeast wind. Wildlife as well as the pastoralists had abandoned the place until the winter rains came to refresh it. In a swamp close to the present Church Square, a few hippos garumphed at the intruders. The only human inhabitants were Harry and the scheme. Hendrik Boom, the gardener, was left with the assistance of a few labourers supplied from the garrison to slowly create the Company's vegetable garden close to the fort.

Living conditions in the primitive fort were miserable. The feeling of isolation and insecurity made the men quarrelsome and insubordinate. Many would have deserted if there was any place where they could go. Discipline in the fort was severe, while outside there was a vast continent filled with unimaginable dangers. Lions seemed to be crowding around the fort, even attempting to assault the place. 'This night,' wrote Van Riebeeck 'it appeared as if the lions would take the fort by storm, that they might get at the sheep, they made a fearful noise, as if they would destroy all within but they could not climb the walls ...'

THE COMING OF THE CAPE PEOPLE

The annual migration of the Goringhaikwa people to the Cape, with their flocks and herds, took place at the beginning of October. On the 9th of the month two of their men arrived at the fort. They were far stronger looking than the beachcombers of Harry. They were armed with spears and sticks, naked except for a well-prepared skin draped down over one of their arms as European gallants affected a mantle. Their arms and legs were decorated with ivory and copper ornaments. They were friendly, informed Van Riebeeck that their people would soon be coming to graze their livestock on the spring growth of fresh grass and herbs. Van Riebeeck was delighted. He showed them his stock of trade goods – copper, brass and other metals, tobacco and alcohol, gave them samples and entertained them hospitably before they returned to their people. The rest of the Gorinkhaikwa arrived a few days later and camped on the sites of the future suburbs of Rondebosch and Claremont. Harry acted as interpreter, assisted by his niece, a bright child of about 11 years who was named Eva by the Europeans. She took up residence in the fort, was taught Dutch, Christianity, assorted European skills and industry and dressed like a young lady from Holland. The pastoral tribes were becoming known to Van Riebeeck and his party by the colloquial name of 'Kaapmans' ('Cape people'), abbreviated at times to Capeys.

Not all went according to plan, though. Through the interpreters, Harry and his young niece, the Cape people repeatedly asked when the English were coming. They were reluctant to part with any large numbers of their livestock. The settlers became aggrieved and thought that Harry had somehow prejudiced the Cape People against the Dutch because they had settled permanently on the traditional grazing grounds of the tribe. Van Riebeeck candidly recorded his thoughts in his diary: 'What would it

Above Some 6 000 plant species, including proteas, flourish on the Peninsula mountains.

matter if we took at once from them 6 000 or 8 000 cattle, there is opportunity enough for it, as we do not perceive that they are very strong in number, but indeed very timorous, coming often only two or three men driving 1 000 cattle under our guns.' The directors in the Netherlands, however, prohibited such action.

Meanwhile, visitors to the Cape were captivated by the scenery and the lovely flora of one of the Earth's principal domains of wild flowers. It was a vast natural garden in a superb scenic setting. As the intended Tavern of the Sea expanded its facilities and reputation for hospitality so visitors would be attracted, if not to settle, then at least to see so remarkable a place. The first stirrings of a future tourist industry were taking place.

ANXIOUS TIMES

Restraints by the parent authority in Europe on the headstrong doings of its colonial offspring were destined to become increasingly contentious as the years passed. Van Riebeeck'd superiors, however, approved at least

one of his urgent desires – his demand for labour. The Cape people were not much tempted into work for the newcomers. Nor were they physically suited to slavery, and they would find it too easy to run away. Imported slaves were regarded as the answer. The Cape settlement therefore became one more market for slave traders to dispose of their wares. The slaves came mainly from the nearest source of supply, Angola, and they supplied the human material for the system of forced labour management which was considered to be normal in the world at that time.

These were anxious days for Van Riebeeck. On 18 January 1653, the galiot *Zwarte Vos* arrived with the news that war had broken out between the Netherlands and the Commonwealth of England under Oliver Cromwell. This was very bad news. The Netherlands was already at war with Portugal and Van Riebeeck in his fort had little defence against any attack by either of the hostile maritime powers. The fort was just about capable of keeping at bay the marauding lions and leopards, the available cannon were feeble and, to worsen matters, the local pastoral people were increasingly resentful of the Netherlanders' occupation of the grazing lands. Even Harry and his beachcombers with young Eva sneaked away one day while the garrison was in church, stole 42 of the herd of 44 cattle then in the possession of the Company and murdered the young Dutch herdsman. For the European settlers, times were hard and the future looked bleak.

But ships continued to call for supplies. The vegetable garden was increasingly productive. If beef was in short supply, then penguins and their eggs from the islands provided good eating and the sheep on Robben Island fattened in security.

The anniversary (6 April) of the arrival of Van Riebeeck and his party in the Cape was treated as a day of thanksgiving. At that date there was not much to give thanks for but four months later, with the spring flowers blossoming, there was a change for the better. On 15 August the yacht *Vlieland* arrived with the good news from the Netherlands that there was peace with the English. The oppressive sense of threat and isolation, which had gathered over the settlement, simply vanished away like the storm clouds of winter. International shipping returned to Table Bay, one of the ships bringing the first vine stocks all the way from the vineyards of the Rhine. The indefatigable gardener, Hendrik Boom, soon had them settled in the local soil along with a varied collection of fruit trees and the flourishing fields of vegetables. To the visiting ships, some with more than half of their crew dead or half dead from scurvy, Van Riebeeck's garden, orchard and vineyard at the Cape offered a new chance of life, a little cheer and the beginning of what became the famed cuisine of the Cape.

Cape Classic Cuisine, as it is called, is based on the essential foundation of fresh, tasty local produce, a good contribution from the vineyards and a subtlety of cookery which came from the blending of the skills of Europe, Africa and the East. The Dutch had acquired a liking in Indonesia

for the exotic tastes of that country. These tastes were brought to the Cape to an increasing extent from 1654 onwards. It was in that year that four Indonesians were sentenced by the Dutch court of justice in Batavia to banishment, and hard labour for life. Their crime was resistance to Dutch seizure of their homeland. Three of the men were left on the island of Mauritius. The fourth was landed at the Cape. He was the first of many people to be banished from the East to spend their lives in Southern Africa. Most were from Indonesia; nearly, but not all, were Muslims. For some reason they were indiscriminately known in the Cape as Malays. Their influence on cooking, architecture, building and industry became notable in the story of the Cape.

DOING DEALS WITH THE BLACK CAPTAIN

Trading conditions at the fort improved suddenly in June 1655 when Harry the prodigal reappeared, accompanied by 50 strangers who brought 40 cattle for trade. Harry flatly denied having anything to do with the recent murder and theft of cattle. Van Riebeeck considered it wise to at least pretend to believe the man. Harry even volunteered to lead a party to the shores of False Bay in search of people prepared to trade their cattle. Particularly gratifying was the arrival of a large group of pastoralists under a chief named Gonnema, nicknamed the Black Captain because he used soot as a facial cosmetic instead of the red clay favoured by the Cape people. The newcomers built on the site of the future suburb of Rondebosch an encampment of two hundred huts, linked with a palisade and containing a huge corral (or 'kraal') in which they secured their livestock at night. Van Riebeeck had the satisfaction of trading copper scrap for nearly 400 head of cattle and about the same quantity of sheep. The sheep were taken over to Robben Island for fattening in safety.

Two other local men did duty as interpreters, a beachcomber known as Klaus Das because he had learned Dutch working with the seal hunters on Dassen Island, and a Cape man nicknamed Doman because his demeanour seemed as grave and transparent as a dominee (parson). He was so highly regarded that Van Riebeeck sent him on a round trip to Batavia to expand his knowledge of the Dutch and their language. He returned two years later not quite as angelic as he had seemed when he left the Cape, as will be seen later in this story.

PUTTING DOWN ROOTS

A momentous change to the nature of the Cape settlement came that same year (1655). The directors in Holland revised their plan to have Company employees stationed in what was intended as a simple trading

Left A family celebration in a cosy Bo-Kaap homestead. Bo-Kaap is sometimes known as the Malay Quarter.

station. They decided that employees on completion of their service contracts in the Cape, if they did not wish to return to Europe or be posted to the East, could be settled as freemen on ground close to the fort and earn a living by producing food or by some other industry.

With this decision, the Cape became a colony rather than just a service station on the East-West route.

The directors of the Dutch East India Company unfortunately had much to learn about the peculiar nature of a colony. Their hope was to see the transplant into new soil of the same industrious peasantry that farmed smallholdings in Holland. They failed to appreciate that the contagious cancer of slavery persuaded a 'freeman' or 'free burgher' to take others into bondage, to become a squire, patron or slave master rather than a worker himself. Work was for slaves; the landowner automatically became a gentleperson in the local social scale, craving ever larger land holdings as the means to rise still higher in popular esteem, clamouring for more slave workers whose labour would reward the master with the profits to support an ever more demanding lifestyle.

The facilities offered to shipping were improved in 1656 with the opening of a hospital. A strong wooden jetty was also completed and this was a great convenience to the loading of fresh water casks and general supplies. The first two inns were also opened, one by the wife of Sergeant van Harwarden, the other by Annetje de Boerin, wife of the gardener Hendrik Boom, an enterprising lady who already had secured the right to lease the company-owned herd of dairy cows and supply the community with fresh milk. Industrious Annetjie also raised eight children, and the pioneer family eventually returned to the Netherlands.

Four years after its establishment, the Cape settlement, transforming to a colony, presented a bustling scene. Practically every garden crop of that age was flourishing. Only potatoes and maize had still to be successfully introduced. The genius and industry of Hendrik Boom had created a garden so productive that it now even provided luxuries such as strawberries and blackberries and all things in such quantity that an export business to Batavia of high quality seeds had commenced. Oak and fir trees had been introduced; domestic livestock were flourishing, the wild animals were being driven away by professional hunters and the quality of their venison was much appreciated as an alternative to the meat of domestic animals.

Wheat and barley at first proved difficult to cultivate, for their ripening time unfortunately coincided with the season of the desiccating southeasterly wind. Crops simply withered. Van Riebeeck then discovered that the southeaster was not nearly so venomous on the western side of

Opposite Groote Schuur, once a barn, was the home of Cecil Rhodes and also a prime-ministerial residence.

Devil's Peak. An experimental crop was grown in the area known as Ronde Doorn Bossien, from a round grove of thorn trees which grew there. The results were excellent. Rondebosch, as the area came to be known, was developed as a wheat farm. A substantial building, known as the Groote Schuur ('Great barn'), was erected to store the grain, as well as a redoubt to shelter a small guard of soldiers.

The whole question of the security of the expanding settlement, especially now that families, under the freeman scheme, would be granted land beyond the protection of the fort, was causing concern. There was even a notion of digging a moat or canal from Table Bay to False Bay. This would act as a barrier between the indigenous tribes and the settlers. The projected separation of people was based rather on religion than anything else. Christians would live within the area on the western side of the 20 km long moat. Non-believers would live on the eastern side. The possessions of heathens could be seized without sin, and they could be enslaved. Professing Christians, whatever their colour or ethnic origin, could not be kept in bondage or discriminated against in any way. Intermarriage in the slow-growing settlement was common.

The idea of the moat was discarded as being too expensive. Alternative schemes were then considered, including building a line of forts connected by a strong palisade or a thick hedge of wild almond trees running from the banks of the stream known as the Liesbeek, (the name was taken from a kind of water plant) where it flows from the heights of the .

Above The hills and well-drained slopes of Constantia have carried vineyards for more than 300 years.

Bosbergen, along the summit ridge of the Bosheuwel ('Bushy slopes'), below the cluster of granite boulders known from their shape as the Hen and Chickens, and across the flatlands to the mouth of the Salt River. It took some time for this defensive scheme to mature.

The first two groups of freemen, five in one group and four in the second, chose land for themselves on the outer side of the Liesbeek River. They were each gifted by the company with plots about 28 acres (or 13 morgen) in extent and were free of the burden of taxes for twelve years. The prospects looked good. More men decided to take their freedom in the Cape from company service and become property or business owners at no cost to themselves. Not all wanted to be farmers. Wouter Mostert had been a miller in the Netherlands. He set up a water-mill in the upper reaches of the Fresh River. Others became carpenters, tailors, wagonmakers, fishermen, hunters or innkeepers. A straggling little town started to grow in the afternoon shadow of Table Mountain.

PRISON ISLAND

Robben Island also gained in importance. On its highest point a pole, and later a platform, was erected on which pitch rings were set alight each night as a navigational beacon. The hill was named Vuurberg ('Fire mountain') and this was, in its simple way, the first lighthouse on the coast of Southern Africa.

Van Riebeeck found still another use for the island. It was a very handy place to have right on the doorstep of the Cape settlement. All manner of problem human beings could be sent to it and there accommodated well concealed from public view. Van Riebeeck was convinced at that time that Harry the interpreter was playing a treacherous game, pretending friendship but plotting with the Cape people to destroy the settlement before it entirely enveloped their traditional grazing fields. He considered Harry, as interpreter, was now expendable. If Europeans found it almost impossible to learn the local language with its clicks and exotic sounds, some of the Cape people found it relatively far easier to learn Dutch in the form of a local version which started to develop as a convenient medium of communication. People such as Doman and the girl Eva could take over duties of interpretation and negotiation. If Robben Island was difficult to reach for people who had no boats then it would obviously be just as difficult for boatless people to leave. The stone quarries and lime-making industries on the island provided ideal hard labour employment for prisoners.

Accordingly, as Van Riebeeck cynically noted in his diary (July 1658), 'The ex-interpreter, or as the English call him, King Harry, was removed in a sheep boat out of his kingdom in this furthest corner of Africa to Robben Island with two of his companions'. These three Cape men, with some political prisoners exiled in chains from Batavia, were the first to obtain

what Van Riebeeck considered secure quarters where the massed arum lilies wave so freely in the wind on Robben Island. The irrepressible Harry, however, was to prove Van Riebeeck wrong – he was the first prisoner to escape from Robben Island. Very few other prisoners had the same audacity and good fortune in the years to follow.

RUMOUR, GREED AND SLAVERY

Life in the infant Cape Town might have been on the rough side but it was certainly eventful and a place of interesting rumours. The legendary land of Monomotapa, the golden Ophir of Solomon and Sheba, was reported to be within easy reach to the north. Friendly cattle-rich tribes were said to live just beyond the mountains. Parties set off in search of this wealth.

No quick wealth in gold or cattle rewarded these explorers. News of their travels, however, fascinated the stay-at-homes in the Cape settlement and provided relief from the continuous rumours of attack from the dispossessed original inhabitants. Eva, the young lady interpreter, was a great source of such assorted tales of riches and troubles to come. She treated listeners to elaborate accounts of the Nama people who she said had white skins, long hair, wore clothing and owned black slaves who tilled the soil, worked mines and built stone houses for their masters. Such tales of gentlemanly living in Africa were beguiling to employees of the Dutch Company. These people of various nationalities had a background in Europe of hard living and poorly rewarded labour. It seemed to them that by being posted for duty to the southwesterly end of Africa, they had escaped from a humdrum existence into a new era of prosperity, of generous land grants, the award of monopolies in trading and professional occupation, of rights to own slaves, of the whole prospect ahead of them of a fat-cat society.

They were all transformed into land owners and moneygrubbers, wanting only lawyers, stock exchange manipulators, developers, promoters, usurers, speculators and swindlers to complete the social strata of the Cape. Even Van Riebeeck was in the real estate business. He was granted land on the southeastern side of the Liesbeek River, and here he planted grapevines, naming the place Wynberg ('Wine mountain'). The name was later transferred to adjoining high ground and Van Riebeeck's farm was renamed Boscheuwel ('Bushy slopes').

The basic contradictions of a slave-based society became apparent when the first substantial number of slaves reached the Cape. On 28 March 1658, the *Amersfoort* brought 170 black Africans to the Cape. On the way from Holland, the *Amersfoort* had captured a Portuguese ship bound from Angola to Brazil with over 500 slaves. The ship was too

Opposite Rockbound Robben Island has lured many ships to their doom, despite the presence of a lighthouse.

home. How many of them, if any, ever managed to reach their homes is unknown. It would make an epic story.

There was also a feeling that the Cape people sympathised with the slaves and aided their escape. Ill feeling, attacks on farmers, theft of livestock and rumours of war bedevilled the Cape settlers. Even the young girl, Eva, left the settlement with some of her people, wishing Van Riebeeck goodbye with the ominous warning 'Mynheer Van Riebeeck, take good care. I shall not return for a long time, your land will now be full of war.' It was a prophecy that held for centuries.

THE BATTLE FOR THE LAND

When the Cape people returned in 1659 to their traditional grazing grounds, they found them sprinkled with neat farmhouses and tilled fields, all the largesse of the Dutch East India Company showing gratitude to its employees by generous gifts to them of other people's land. The Cape people were enraged.

The Tavern of the Seas was now far too strong to be overrun by force. Doman, the angelic-looking interpreter, had returned to the Cape in 1658 from his visit to Batavia. Abandoning his European clothes, he deserted the fort one night, became an adviser to the Cape people and leader of an aggressive band of cattle thieves. His advice to his followers was to avoid any confrontation with superior European firearms but to harass them at night and in the rain when the old flint firelock guns were almost useless. He had observed that the principal motivation of white people was to make money and he felt that the best way to drive them away was simply to ruin them.

Van Riebeeck organised the freemen and the garrison into a militia and, by indefatigable action, rallied them to strengthen the farmhouses, keep their powder kegs dry, their weapons at the ready and to hold prayer meetings every Wednesday to ask God to withdraw his rage against them. Various reasons were given for this wrath of God, principally the goings-on in the taverns. Van Riebeeck and his superiors had no doubt, however, that the cause of the trouble with the Cape people was the direct result of the occupation of their land. They could no longer even get their livestock to the river to drink without trespassing on private property.

A bounty of 137 shillings and 6 pence was put on the head of Doman, 55 shillings for each of the Cape people taken prisoner, and 27 shillings and 6 pence for each one killed. Vengeance and profit stimulated the militia. Van Riebeeck made plans to build watch houses along the outer line of the settlement.

Early in 1660 the Cape people wished to make their customary journey to the Cape, but they had lost their spirit to fight, and consented to a peace treaty. Another was signed with the upcountry Gorachoukwa. Neither group, however, received much advantage from the agreements:

decrepit to be a worthwhile prize. The Netherlanders relieved the slaver of 250 of the best of the Angolans and then allowed the Portuguese to continue their voyage to Brazil. Of the 250 slaves, 80 died before the *Amersfoort* reached the Cape and the remaining 170 were in a very miserable state. Two weeks later, the *Hasselt* arrived in Table Bay with 228 slaves. Before this influx there were only about twelve individuals in bondage in the Cape and these were from Indonesia and Madagascar.

Eighty-nine of the newcomers were sold off to the local freemen, and the Company put a number into its own bondage. A surplus of 172 was sent on to Batavia. In the Cape the slave owners reconditioned their new acquisitions by feeding them on seal meat, sea birds and eggs from the

islands. The *Hasselt* had brought with the slaves seeds of their staple food, maize, but it would take at least a year before crops could be produced.

A chain of events now began which baffled the slave owners. As soon as the slaves recovered their strength individuals took the first opportunity to run away. They knew vaguely that their homeland was north up the West Coast. They had no idea how far they would have to go or through what dangers of wild animals, hostile people, or the harshness of the desert country they would have to traverse. They simply wanted to go

Above Sun-dappled Government Avenue leads through the Company's Garden.

the Europeans retained possession of the land. The total number of individuals in the pastoral tribes living near the Cape was not more than about
15 000 and of the whole of their race in Southern Africa about 40 000 at
most, fragmented and widely scattered. They had to accept the fact of
occupation by a stronger power.

Thus ended the first war between African and European people fought
in the Cape. Van Riebeeck was delighted. The trade in livestock revived. In
the general atmosphere of peace, four successive parties of explorers
were sent northwards in search of the Nama people and the city of
Davagul or Vigita Magna where the legendary Monomatapa ruled in gold-
en splendour. The Nama people were reached in their arid homeland.
Some of them were induced to visit the Cape and peace, friendship and
trade were established. Davagul, Vigita Magna and the Monomatapa
remained in legends.

THE CHANGING OF THE GUARD

As for Jan van Riebeeck, he had done his best, worked hard and been a
loyal servant to his employers. He dreamed of promotion to a position of
importance in the East, working with what he called the more orderly
people of Asia as a change from the primitive tribes of the Cape. He had
been the midwife at the birth of the city of Cape Town but his directors
in Holland had little appreciation of this. They often listened to carping
accounts by visitors that the Cape was a dreary place, the anchorage
exposed to violent gales, the meat tough, the little town a place of lodg-
ing and tap houses where strong liquor was sold by persons not having
the fear of God before their eyes when they made their charges. In 1660
the directors decided to transfer him to India.

His successor, however, Gerrit Harn, died on the way to the Cape from
Holland. It took months before his successor, Zacharias Wagenaar, arrived.
In the meantime Van Riebeeck cleared up his effects.

It is interesting to read that when he handed back to the company the
farm of Bosheuwel; the improvements included 1 162 young orange,
lemon and citron trees, five apple, two pear, nineteen plum, two olive,
three walnut, forty-one other fruit trees and several thousand vines.
Wagenaar took over the government of the Cape in a ceremony in the
fort on 6 May 1662.

Early on the morning of 8 May, Van Riebeeck and his family sailed for
Batavia where he was appointed head of the Company's trading station at
Malacca. In the three years he remained there as commander, his wife
died. He then went to Batavia, married again and was employed by the
Company as secretary of the Council of India. He died in 1677.

The fort built by Van Riebeeck has vanished entirely, replaced by the
later Castle. It stood on the site of the stalls on the southern side of the
Grand Parade. The original vegetable garden, 18 ha in extent, cultivated by
Hendrik Boom with the aid of 300 slaves, is now a botanical garden

reduced in size to less than 6 ha. The rest of the former garden is occupied by the buildings of the Houses of Parliament, the town residence of
the President of South Africa, the Anglican cathedral of St George the
Martyr, the National Library of South Africa, the National Gallery, the South
African Museum, the first synagogue in South Africa, built in 1862, and a
cluster of buildings housing several departments of the University of Cape
Town. An avenue of oak trees 1 km long, known as Government Avenue,
traverses the site of the original garden and provides a pleasant walk.
Capetonians call it simply 'The Avenue'.

Above Artists and performers hold sway in the traffic-free surrounds
of St George's Mall.

In a curious way, the only still living link with Van Riebeeck is a remnant
of the almond hedge he planted with the intention of separating the Cape
settlement and civilisation, as Van Riebeeck knew it, from primitive Africa.
Portions of the hedge still flourish and produce nuts.

There is no known authentic portrait in existence of Van Riebeeck or
his wife. The two portraits thought to be of them and often reproduced
on postage stamps, bank notes and in books, were proved (in 1984) to be
of Bartholomeus Vermuyder and Catharina Kettingh. The two were not
even related to each other. They were painted by Dirck Graey and are
exhibited in the Amsterdam Rijks Museum. Just how they were palmed off
on South Africa as authentic portraits of the Van Riebeecks would make
an interesting story.

GROWING UP

A T THE TIME HE TOOK OVER AT THE CAPE, Zacharias Wagenaar was a conservative servant of the Dutch East India Company, elderly and in poor health. After the volatile Van Riebeeck, the new Commander was not disposed to promote change or development. He was happy to find the Cape peaceful, with deputations from the local tribes visiting the fort to wish him well and cement their friendship by enjoying free jollification. In return, he visited them, dispensing gifts of tobacco and strong drink, and confirming the barter trade for sheep and cattle.

But these were fluid times in Europe; international alliances were constantly changing; indeed the local people never knew whether a visiting ship was friend or foe until it anchored. In this uncertain atmosphere, the Company decided that Van Riebeeck's earth fort was in need of replacement by a more robust stronghold. Plans were drawn up in Holland for a proper stone castle; Wagenaar was empowered to recruit 300 soldiers from passing ships to work on the new fortress while an assortment of convicts and slaves were to be sent to Robben Island to quarry stone and make lime from shells in kilns fired by wood from Houtbaai ('Wood bay'). Commissioner Goske arrived from Holland on 18 August 1665. After eight days of inspections and discussions he selected a site 227 metres southeast of the old fort.

Then began the largest constructional activity so far undertaken in the Cape settlement.

Saturday, 2 January 1666, was a gala day . Practically every resident as well as the crews of visiting ships, soldiers and merchants, all dressed in their best, gathered to see four heavy pieces of stonework lowered into the foundation trench for the massive walls of the projected castle. Tables were spread within the area marked by the foundation trenches, and heavily laden with beef, mutton, vegetables, fruit and eight heavy casks of Cape ale to toast the castle, which had been named Good Hope. There was music and jollification, and the recital of a poem specially composed for the occasion..

Right Time and shade for refreshment in St George's Mall, now free of all vehicular traffic.

THE MIXED SOCIETY

Commander Wagenaar was a sick man at that time. He had already asked the company to relieve him of his post. His successor, Cornelis van Quaelberg, reached the Cape in August 1666 after a dreary voyage lasting eight months, much impeded by weather and the war between Holland and the England of King Charles II. At least the Cape was peaceful when he took over. The pastoral tribes had willy-nilly accepted the reality of their ineffectiveness against the expanding settlement. In any case, their ability to resist had waned. About a fifth of them had died by this time from some unidentified disease. Many of the survivors had moved away to the interior; others took servuce with the settlers or the company and started to merge with the population of slaves of various ethnic origins and especially with the progeny of slave women.

About three-fourths of the children from the slave mothers were from European fathers. White females remained in short supply in the Cape and there was in any case no colour bar. In this mix of humanity the future

ethnic group of the so-called Cape Coloureds had their origin. The slave owners and their conservative allies considered that a directive, issued by the Company and the Church, that all these children be baptised, brought up in the Christian faith, and, as Christians, be free persons even if their fathers disowned them, to be scandalous. The slave mothers, if they became Christian, would also be released from bondage. This threat to the vested interests in slave ownership created a deep schism in the established Dutch Reformed Church. There were unpleasant scenes of protest when slave women brought their half-breed children to be baptised. Cant and great argument split even families into contentious divisions, but Cape slavery endured for almost two centuries.

From its beginning in the first Church in the infant Cape Town, this squabble persisted through the whole story of Southern Africa.

Eva, the young lady interpreter, was the first of the Cape people to become a Christian. Known also as Krotoa, she was baptised early in the regime of Commander Wagenaar. A short while later, on 2 June 1664, she married Pieter van Meerhof, the Danish mercenary soldier and amateur surgeon. There was a bridal feast in the residence of the commander and a wedding gift from the Company of £10. This was the first marriage in the Cape between a couple of African and European origin. Van Meerhof was promoted to the rank of surgeon and overseer of Robben Island. Here the couple made their home and it was here that Eva presented her husband with their first child.

WAR AND PEACE

Work on the new castle proceeded slowly, and then halted – the threat of attack by the English had so diminished following the destruction of their shipping by Admiral De Ruyter in the Thames, that the expense of building a castle at the Cape was no longer a priority. Quarrying on Robben Island was also suspended. Van Meerhof was appointed head of an expedition to Madagascar, where he and eight of his men were killed

Opposite Greenmarket Square was once the city's produce market, and is now a fascinating tangle of craft stalls.

in a clash with the Malagasy at Antongil Bay. Eva, left a widow on Robben Island, went to pieces, became an alcoholic, alternating between loose living on the mainland and disciplinary removals to the Island. She eventually died (in July 1674) and was buried within the church of the castle. A sad ending for an interesting person.

Commander Van Quaelberg also came to grief in the Cape. On 18 June 1668 he was summarily dismissed from his position and relieved by Jacob Borghorst, an invalid who had no desire to remain in the colony. His successor, Peter Hackius, was another sick man – his health had been ruined by long service to the Company in the East. At this stage in his life he was not much inclined to launch new ventures or to do much except keep out of trouble.

The growing town was simply left to its own devices, its buildings increasingly taking on the so-called 'Cape-Dutch' appearance created by the number of Muslims banished from the East and employed as convict or slave builders, aided by the African slaves. They gave subtle variation to the architectural ideas of their European masters.

There was peace with England. The French, however, continued to cause some anxiety by sending fleets around the Cape, anchoring in Table Bay, requesting water and provisions and going into Saldanha Bay to reclaim the old islands of their seal hunters.

In this setting Commander Pieter Hackius died on 30 November 1671 and was buried beneath the floor of the rough building used as a church within the area of the unfinished castle. Until a successor arrived, the Cape was governed by a committee of senior officials, who were instructed to complete the castle to its original design as quickly as possible in order to confront what the Netherlands now considered the inevitability of a war with England and France. These two states had combined in order to seize the rich trade with the East.

THE LEGAL THEFT OF THE CAPE

Since its founding ten years previously, 370 of the Company's ships, 26 French, 9 English and 2 Danish ships were recorded as having visited Cape Town for supplies, having on board over 7 000 crew and passengers. All had drunk of the sweet waters of Table Mountain and replenished their stores from the produce of Van Riebeeck's Tavern of the Seas. The Company now regarded their Cape settlement, not as an infant but as an adolescent in its growth, and upgraded its administration. Even before news of the death of Commander Hackius reached the Netherlands, his

Left The minaret of Mosque Shafee looks over Bo-Kaap. It is one of five mosques in the area.

Opposite Cape minstrels and their colourful costumes are an old tradition, with origins that go back to the days of slavery.

successor had been appointed – Isbrand Goske, the man who had originally selected the site of the castle. He was to have the rank of Governor with a monthly salary of £25, a generous table allowance, formal quarters in the castle as soon as it was ready, and a pleasure house in a garden setting at Rondebosch, where he could relax and entertain visitors. It would be named Rustenburg ('Place of rest'). Two senior officials were appointed at the same time to the posts of Secunde, or second in command and law enforcement officer.

Before the new Governor arrived to take office a ship came in from Batavia bearing one Arnout van Overbeke, a justice of the high court at Batavia and admiral of the return fleet of 1672, who had been commissioned, while the fleet was in Cape Town, to investigate local affairs. His immediate concern was to devise some legal basis for the creation, by the Dutch East India Company, of a colony in the Cape. The area had never been conquered. The settlement had grown unofficially, without the native inhabitants being able to do anything about it. The earliest known hunter-gatherer occupants of the area had been driven out by the pastoral people before Van Riebeeck's arrival. Both these groups were too weak to resist any invader and had no permanent vested interest in the Cape save hunting or grazing.

Since Van Riebeeck's time, Gogoswa, the chief of the principal clan of Cape people, had died. His son Osingkima, known to the Dutch as Prince Schacher, had succeeded him but the local pastoralists had largely disintegrated into small clans. Nevertheless, for want of a more paramount power, Commissioner Van Overbeke offered Prince Schacher £800 worth of assorted goods for the whole of the area from the Peninsula to Saldanha Bay. The pastoralists could graze their animals only where the Company or the freemen did not require the area. Peace was to prevail between the pastoralists and the settlers. The Company would protect Prince Schacher's followers if they were attacked.

Prince Schacher accepted the offer without demur. There was nothing else he could do. His people had already lost the Cape Peninsula to the Company; other parts, such as the area of Saldanha Bay, were the grazing grounds of different groups, but they were not considered. Trade goods of the value of just £2 16s 5d were actually handed over to Prince Schacher to consummate the 'sale'. A similar agreement was signed with the Chainoukwa for the Hottentots Holland area and the False Bay coast. Again the terms were £800 worth of goods for everything, but only £6 16s 4d changed hands, plus assorted junk, liquor and tobacco. The legal gobbledegook of the two agreements, and the cynical complacency of the report to the directors in the Netherlands about the value of the goods actually given to the two pastoral tribes, emphasise the reality of the old proverb, 'a man is not a slave of his word', the basis of so many similar documents drawn up in pretentious legal language.

THE FRONTIER FORTRESS

Governor Goske arrived from Holland on 2 October 1672. News had already reached the Cape that war had commenced between the Netherlands and the combined forces of England, France and two powerful ecclesiastical princes, the elector of Cologne and the Bishop of Munster. It was a formidable force for a small country such as the Netherlands to confront. Moreover, the Dutch were divided by feuds. They were, however, a hardy people and stubborn by nature. The castle being built at the Cape was now considered by the Dutch to be the frontier fortress of India. While they held it they could defy any attempt by their enemies to challenge their dominance in the East.

Governor Goske exerted every effort to complete the castle, meanwhile repairing the earth walls of the old fort. An outpost was also established in the newly acquired Hottentots Holland to which the people of Cape Town could retreat in the event of a successful onslaught on the town by the enemy. There were, at that time, about 600 Europeans resident or stationed in the Cape and times were exciting. An expedition was even organised to capture the British-held island of St Helena. Four ships then in Table Bay were fitted out and their crews augmented with men from the Cape garrison. On 10 January 1673 this pugnacious little force captured St Helena, driving the small British garrison away. Four months later, the British recaptured the island but at least they were aware that an attack on the Cape would require a more considerable force than they had available in the area.

The castle at this time was sufficiently advanced in its construction to allow the garrison to move into it but,. curiously, the urgency diminished – word arrived that the English had made peace with the Dutch. The French at that time lacked the naval power to be regarded as a threat.

Governor Goske had been sent to the Cape expressly to guide it through the troubled times of war, and his task was completed. His successor, Johan Bax, promoted from his post as second officer on the island then known as Ceylon (Sri Lanka), relieved him on 14 March 1676. The new Governor inherited an exuberant little town, full of hope for the future and with only one problem, a 'war' which had been raging in desultory fashion for the previous four years between the neighbouring pastoral tribes. In due course a treaty ended hostilities. The various pastoral chiefs found Governor Bax to be a likable and friendly man.

The castle by then needed only a moat and some finishing touches. As the Company was no longer interested in financing work on the structure, the Governor promulgated a regulation that required everyone, of any rank or sex, to contribute labour towards the digging of the moat. To set an example, Bax, his wife and little son, all the Company's officers and the leading inhabitants of the town, gathered together and spent some time in excavation. Over the next months work steadily extended the moat but

unhappily the Governor, although young and healthy, did not live to see its completion. He caught a cold during the hard winter and died on 29 June 1678, leaving the second in command to control affairs until the Company appointed a successor.

GOVERNOR SUPREME

The new man only reached the Cape from the Netherlands on 12 October 1679. He was rated only as a Commander, for peace made the Cape less important, but he was to prove one of the most energetic men ever to be head of affairs anywhere in Southern Africa. His name was Simon van der Stel. He was the eldest son of Adriaen van der Stel of Dordrecht, Commander of the Dutch East India Company troops then engaged in the conquest of Ceylon (Sri Lanka). Shortly after his arrival in Ceylon, Adriaen was captured in battle, decapitated, and his head displayed on a spear to the Dutch troops and his family. Simon's mother was Maria Lievens, born in Batavia from a slave mother. .

The Dutch East India Company had an obligation to the families of their employees. In 1659, Simon van der Stel was sent to the Netherlands to complete his education. When he finished his schooling he was employed by the Company and on 23 October 1663 married Johanna Jacoba Six, daughter of a well-to-do Amsterdam family. Over the next thirteen years he showed great competence in his work and was then rewarded with the offer of the post as Commander of the Cape. It was a big career opportunity at a far superior salary and he accepted with enthusiasm. His wife declined to accompany her husband to the Cape. Her health was poor and she remained in the comfort of Amsterdam until her death in 1700. Van der Stel's four sons, Willem, Adriaan, Hendrik and Frans, and his daughter Catharina, together with his wife's younger sister Cornelia, sailed with him, so he was well supported on the voyage.

When they landed on 12 October 1679 they were received with such pomp as the Cape could mount to honour a new Commander – discharges of cannon and musketry, the cheers of onlookers who saw their new head of government as a short, dark-complexioned man, refined of manner, courteous, highly intelligent and very alert. For the next twenty years Simon van der Stel was to control the colony. He was destined never to leave the Cape that he loved.

Shortly after his arrival Van der Stel rode out to examine the countryside, encamping on the banks of a small tributary to the Eerste ('First') River, the principal watercourse draining one of the loveliest and most fertile parts of Africa, a domain of wild flowers destined to rank among the principal wine and fruit farming lands of the Western Cape. It was then

Opposite Trails of black mussel shells mark the tidal flow at Blouberg beach, where a British army stormed ashore in 1806.

empty of people, free of any pollution and serenely beautiful. For five days Van der Stel explored this wild garden of infinite charm, following the Eerste River towards its source in the bosom of the mountains, a place which captivated him completely. Here there was no sign of other human beings. In his mind he saw a picture of a thriving agricultural community, of rich crops and fat cattle grazing on the green pastures, drinking their fill of the amber coloured water of the streams. He returned to the castle and began to fulfil his dreams of a new Holland on the southern part of the vast continent of Africa.

Before the year ended the first settler had occupied ground at Stellenbosch. Next year eight families followed this; all had been tempted by the offer of as much free land as they could cultivate, selected by themselves, and only to be reclaimed by the Company if they ceased to cultivate it. The sole obligation to the Company was a tithe of the grain grown by the farmers. There was free grazing on all uncultivated land.

Cape Town also received Van der Stel's beneficial attention. The Company garden was replanned, divided into separate plots, some devoted to vegetables, others to fruit, still others experimental plantations of timber trees collected from all over the world. The wild flowers, herbs and trees of the Cape were also planted and studied to discover their special uses. Van der Stel enlarged the garden on its southern side and, on the north, eventually built a large hospital and a lodge in which the Company slaves were housed. A pleasure lodge made its appearance on the site of the present statue of Queen Victoria. Pathways and an avenue were laid out. Many visitors told Van der Stel that nowhere else in the world was there a more varied display of trees and plants in so beautiful a setting.

Wide, straight streets were laid out, while trees in great number were planted to provide shade, rest the eye, and beautify a town where the buildings were mainly a dazzling white from the use of the limewash which protected walls.

THE MAGIC CIRCLE

Increasingly, the buildings carried in their design a touch of the East as well as of Africa and Europe. Prisoners and political exiles from Indonesia and India, many of them cultured and highly intelligent men, were being sent to the Cape. These personages, generally accompanied by a handful of followers and family members, at first felt themselves dreadfully detached from their familiar Eastern society. But they received a little comfort when one of them, a man of great influence, Khardi Abdusalem, urged them to hold their faith without fear for they would one day live protected by a holy circle of kramats (saintly places) which would come into being at the tombs of holy men who would constantly intercede on their behalf with Allah. A line drawn connecting these kramats would form a magic ring. Within it the residents of Cape Town, not only Muslims, would live safe

from fire, famine, plague, earthquake, tidal wave or attack by hostile forces. Among high-born exiles from Java was the revered Sheik Yussuf of Macassar, a man of powerful influence and a thorn in the flesh to the Dutch colonists in the East. He died, on the then isolated farm Zandvliet, in May 1677. His burial place was the first and most important of the kramats of the magic circle around Cape Town.

Sheik Yussuf's tomb is now an impressive memorial, built in 1925 by Hadji Sullaiman Shah. The kramat is on a low hill with a grand view of mountains and farmlands. It is close to the banks of the Eerste River, for the sound of running water is not only pleasant but is said to have magical curative powers. Five other kramats complete the magic circle around Cape Town. Close to the road followed by countless people to the viewsite on the summit of Signal Hill, there is a pretty little domed building, resting place of Sayed Muhammad Hassan Gaibi Shah. On the slopes of Signal Hill, above the old quarry at the top of Strand Street, is the third Kramat, where lie the bodies of four holy men: Khardi Abdusalem, Tuan Syed, Tuan Guru and Tuan Nurman.

The magic circle then leads to Oudekraal where, from the scenic drive of Victoria Road, a concrete stairway rises beneath the trees to a kramat where lies buried Nureel Mobeen, who is said to have been banished to Robben Island. He escaped by swimming to the mainland supported on a plank. For the rest of his life he hid in the bush of Oudekraal. In his time he is said to have performed many miracles.

The fifth kramat in the magic circle is on Robben Island – the tomb of Sayed Abdurahman Matura, Prince of Ternate, an island in the Molucca sea of Indonesia. He was banished to Robben Island in January 1744 and died there in 1755. The sixth kramat is on the slopes of Islam Hill in the Constantia valley, close to the stream known as the Spaanschemat. Nearby, at the entrance gate to the farm Klein Constantia, again beside a running stream, there is the tomb of Abdumaah Shah.

The paths to these places are well trodden, and have not been forgotten. To 'make the circle', to visit each one of the kramats, is much desired by all devout Cape Muslims.

SLAVERY, CRIME AND PUNISHMENT

In October 1684, the Company's governing body, the Assembly of Seventeen, appointed one of its members, Hendrik Adriaan van Rheede, the Lord of Mydrecht, to head a commission to examine the affairs of the Cape and those of Ceylon and Hindustan. According to the colonial norms of the time the Cape was doing well. It was not only feeding itself and profiting handsomely from supplying ships but even starting to export food to the East. As far as its social system went, it was amazing how readily people from Europe adjusted their thinking to a slave-based colonial society. In their home countries slavery might be repugnant but by simply

crossing an ocean they could walk ashore into a new world of buying, selling and ruthless exploitation of human beings. Such a society, in fact, perfectly revealed man's inhumanity to man with not the slightest awareness of any wrong to it.

The Lord of Mydrecht found nothing too objectionable in slavery in the Cape, though he tried to improve things with a law that offered freedom to imported slaves (of both sexes) after 30 years of bondage, and to slaves born in the Cape on reaching the age of 40. In contradiction, though, these men and women could be freed only as a favour on the part of the owner. As a rule owners were reluctant to free slaves until they were so old as to be useless. In order to save feeding them they were then emancipated, and driven out to fend for themselves, usually by begging or as vagrants living in destitution in caves or crude shelters on the mountain slopes, where they were known as 'Bergies'. His lordship also made it a law that slave children under the age of twelve were to be sent to school, where they were to be taught the principles of Christianity, to read, write and conduct themselves respectfully to their superiors.

Some restrictions, too, were placed on punishment. Excessive retribution drove slaves to desert and turn criminal. Fugitives who were captured were to be flogged and chained as a warning to others, but such punishment could only be inflicted with the consent of the authorities. Punishment generally, to law breakers of any colour, remained severe. Robben Island was always accommodating. The slight rise at Green Point called Gallows Hill possessed a gibbet capable of hanging seven or more condemned persons at a time. Around it were the grim means for torture and execution by impalement or breaking at the wheel, sometimes from the feet up in order to prolong agony. There were ten wheels used for this limb-breaking.

So far as relations with the indigenous population were concerned, the original inhabitants had either dispersed or fragmented to insignificant numbers. The local Sonkwa (or Bushmen) were nearly extinct. The pastoral tribes living further from the Cape, such as the Hessekwa, the Inkwa and the Outenikwa along the coast to the east, were friendly and prepared to trade significant amounts of their livestock for the usual junk.

From the west coast, the Namakwa sent several representatives to meet the Commissioner. They came riding into town seated on trained oxen. Some of these oxen also carried on their backs the simple skin huts which these nomads were accustomed to take with them as they wandered with their herds and flocks in search of pasture. Even more interesting were the fine samples of copper ore which they showed the Dutch authorities. Where there was copper there might be gold.

Opposite The kramat or burial place of a Muslim holy man on Signal Hill is one of several such places.

The Lord of Mydrecht was pleased that Van der Stel had already sent three expeditions (unfortunately abortive) up the west coast to reach what were called the copper mountains. Prospectors were also busy fossicking through the mountains of the Cape Peninsula hoping to find such precious metals as gold and silver. One prospect shaft in the Steenberge (present-day Silvermine) had already yielded a strange ore which the people of Cape Town excitedly thought was silver. This was eventually identified in Holland as manganese but the discovery at least stimulated what was the beginning of systematic prospecting in Southern Africa. Van der Stel was authorised to personally lead an expedition to the copper mountains of the Nama people.

COLONIAL PROGRESS

The Lord of Mydrecht also approved of the foundation of Stellenbosch and the generous grants of free land there to stimulate settlement. In Holland every effort was already being made by the Company to attract immigrants to the Cape, with particular attention to females. Van der Stel himself was rewarded with a superbly situated piece of ground beyond the last farm then occupied at Wynberg. He named it Constantia, presumably in honour of the young daughter of Commissioner Rijkloff van Goens, who had that name, or simply because the name meant 'constancy'.

Van der Stel now launched himself into a considerable programme of work. In August 1685 he set out, with about 100 men, on an exploratory journey northwards to Nama country, which everyone hoped was a venture leading to the discovery of vast wealth, not only of copper, but of many precious metals and gemstones. The explorers, after many adventures, reached the Copper Mountains on 21 October and, guided by the Nama people, found copper ore of great richness and quantity. But the two months it had taken to reach the area had seen the explorers forced to penetrate such rugged, arid country that there could be no way of carrying heavy ore all the way to Cape Town on the transport of the day. The dream of a huge and instant profit for the Company, which had obsessed every commander of the Cape since Van Riebeeck, still proved elusive. The richness of the samples of copper ore tantalised everybody who saw them but it was to be 200 years before the copper mines of Namaqualand were to come into production.

Van der Stel was always a great man for trees. The Cape was not well wooded, except in the mountain gorges, where the forests were fragile and already over-exploited for fuel and timber. Experimental work in the

Left The manor house and vineyards of Buitenverwachting nestle below Constantiaberg.
Opposite Buitenverwachting wears the classic symmetry of the Cape Dutch style of architecture.

Company's garden indicated that imported oaks would do best in local conditions. Van der Stel launched an extensive programme of cultivation, and by the spring of 1687 there were over 50 000 oaks in the nurseries and 5 000 planted out.

Stellenbosch, in the short time of its existence, was already showing signs of its future destiny as the prettiest town in Southern Africa. An annual fair was inaugurated in the town in 1686. Each year, from the 1st to the 14th of October, became a holiday season for the people of the Cape. They travelled to Stellenbosch to buy and sell without any restriction, to feast and drink the products of the country, to play games and compete in gun shooting at a target traditionally shaped like a parrot. A church, courthouse, residence for the magistrate and a mill all made their appearance in 1686.

Van der Stel also undertook experimentation in agriculture. Crops such as rice, cassava, hops and olives were all tried without success. Vines were doing well but the wine was poor. The quality from the Stellenbosch farms was better than from anywhere else in the Cape but not up to the wines of Europe. Van der Stel planted vines obtained from many countries, even from Iran (Persia), the reputed home of the grape.

Immigrants arrived, and were settled in the Drakenstein valley – 23 families in 1687 and, in the following year, the first batch of a stream of French Protestant Huguenot refugees who had fled religious persecution in France. Van der Stel was delighted, although he would have preferred them to be Dutch. The Huguenots were, however, fine farming stock, a few of them were experienced viticulturists and, importantly, most of them were married. They established themselves on glorious farmlands in what became known as Franschhoek ('French glen'), at the upper valley of the Berg River.

CAPE TOWN'S PROBLEMS

The Cape prospered, notwithstanding the shortage of marriageable females, which continued to be a source of social problems. Each year saw more shipping anchoring in Table Bay, and in the bay close to Cape Point around which Simon's Town would develop. The growth of the colony generally, and the esteem in which Simon van der Stel was held by his directors in Holland, was marked on 1 June 1691 when the Commander was elevated to the dignity of a Governor.

But Cape Town had its problems. Garbage collection was left to the hyenas and other scavengers which came down each night from lairs on the mountain slopes and wandered at will through the dark streets. Heavy drinking and gambling in the taverns led to fights and murders. There was no police force. The shortage of females was the cause of violent brawls. Even slave women were in short supply, and their men's immorality was a source of concern to the authorities..

Lions and leopards still frequented the countryside, occasionally venturing into the little town and dragging away the odd drunkard who had fallen asleep on the roadside. Gangs of runaway slaves provided a hard-core criminal element. These last were a community of the lost. Their destitution and hopeless future gave them no alternative but to resort to robbery while the brutality of punishment when they were caught made them desperate. To die on the gallows was at least a quick way out but sentences of torture 'close to death', impalement, or to be broken on the rack or wheel was the more usual punishment, with the mangled wretch dumped to die on Gallows Hill. The only possible mercy came from one of their comrades creeping into the town at night to put them out of their misery by strangulation.

Pollution of drinking water was becoming a health hazard. Even the once pure Fresh River on which the shipping depended was carrying down to the sea unpalatable run off from dirty streets and the dirtier habits of human beings using it for washing their persons, clothes, utensils and as a form of waterborne sewage disposal. The southeast wind of summer, known as the Cape Doctor, fortunately blew most of the stinks, miasmas and assorted bugs, insects and bacteria away and kept the town healthier than its population deserved.

An endless stream of thirsty and amorous sailors called at the Cape. Most of them were the crews and passengers of the Dutch East Indiamen. Amongst this motley company the majority were reasonably honest merchants, but others were pirates. Slave traders also frequented Table Bay, mainly taking human cargoes from East Africa, Mozambique and Madagascar to the West Indies, but always prepared to oblige local demand for what were advertised as sturdy, stout Negroes, male or female. Auctions of slaves were periodically held on what became known as Church Square, a piece of waste land, once a marsh, which adjoined the grounds of the present Groote Kerk with its pleasant, leisurely sounding two-note clock chime marking the passing of the hours. A small monument in Bureau Street marks the site.

Governor Van der Stel did nothing to ease the degradation of slavery. The dual morality of the time made the lot of those in bondage of little concern to the rest of the community. The development of the Governor's own estate of Constantia was based on slave labour and there was no available substitute. At least, however, he made Cape Town, for all of its people, a far more agreeable place in which to live. The Heerengracht was improved; a new road was constructed along the line of the canal known as the Keisersgracht (which took water from the Fresh River to the castle moat) and much later named after C.H. Darling, the British Lieutenant-Governor of the Cape from 1852 to 1854. On the seaward side of this road, work began in 1697 on levelling the ground and this became the Grand Parade.

Most important of all was the building of the new hospital, larger, far better and more suitably located on a site between the upper end of the Heerengracht and Berg Street (now St George's Street). This was the last work by Van der Stel in his capacity as Governor. In 1696 he requested permission to resign his office and retire to his estate of Constantia. The directors gave him a final honour when they appointed his eldest son, Willem Adriaan, born in 1664, as his successor.

THE PASSING OF A GOVERNOR

On 11 February Van der Stel left the castle and removed to his estate, Constantia. For the next thirteen years he lived there, farming, ranching cattle, planting thousands of oak trees and vines and producing fine wine. His reputation for hospitality, good food and wine attracted innumerable visitors to what was regarded as one of the most beautiful properties in the world. He obtained more grants of land, and grazing rights for his cattle until he controlled practically the entire Cape Peninsula outside the settled area of Cape Town. He ran a fishing and sealing industry at Saldanha Bay and was altogether a man for all seasons and activities. His one great disappointment came from his son, whose governance foundered in accusations of oppression and venality. Willem was recalled to Holland on 3 June 1707.

Simon van der Stel was left in the Cape without the companionship of any of his family. As death approached he became despondent. In his last will and testament, his scribe wrote: 'His excellency was overcome with the evil and weakness of human life, passing away like a shadow, knowing that nothing is more certain than death and, in contrast, nothing more uncertain than man's time and span upon this earth.'

He bequeathed Constantia to his five children. None of them was interested in the estate, other than as a source of financial inheritance. Simon van der Stel died at Constantia on 24 June 1712.

After the estate was wound up it was divided into three sections in order to make it more saleable. Over the decades there was a succession of owners; the property went into decline until it was sold, in 1778, to Hendrik Cloete of Stellenbosch. A glorious revival then took place.

There is no known completely authentic portrait of Van der Stel. A canvas showing a man thought to have been him, in a hunting party and considered nine-tenths authentic, was unfortunately destroyed in 1963 in a fire in the Napier collection in Ireland. Only a photograph of this painting remains. A second portrait, also of a huntsman, but of less authenticity, is in the The Hague's Rijksdienst Beeldende Kunst. This portrait, however, is only considered one-tenth possible and nine-tenths of dubious authenticity.

Opposite On Wednesday and Saturday mornings the Grand Parade is a bustling marketplace.

CHAPTER THREE

CITY, BAY AND ISLAND

As cities go, CAPE TOWN, compared with those ancient places of Asia and Europe, is still a mere juvenile. In its relatively brief three and a half centuries, however, it has experienced interesting, sometimes dramatic times and gathered memories of odd events and diverse people who have come to the Tavern of the Seas, dallied for perhaps just a little while or, beguiled by its beauty and atmosphere, remained for the rest of their lives.

Many of those who landed on the shores of Table Bay did so involuntarily. They were wrecked there. During the winter months when the prevailing wind was the northwester, the bay could become a death trap for shipping. There was simply no shelter from this wind, which can blow gale force for a merciless hour then deceptively lull, while it recovers breath for another big blow. Over 200 ships have come to grief in Table Bay.

A particularly famous wreck occurred during a storm on 1 June 1773. The Dutch East Indiaman *De Jonge Thomas* ran aground and began breaking up in the pounding of heavy surf. Employed as a dairyman by the Dutch East India Company was 65-year-old Wolraad Woltemade, who saw that the crew of the ship were almost helpless against the power of the sea. He rode his horse through the waves seven times, each time returning with two men holding on. On the eighth attempt he and his horse were themselves overwhelmed by a huge wave and drowned.

THE STRUGGLE FOR A HARBOUR

The loss of life, ships and cargo from winter storms was the principal disadvantage of the Cape victualling station. With the means available at that time it was very difficult to do anything about this problem. Engineering on a massive scale was the answer but this would demand a lot of expenditure. After the disastrous storms of May 1737, attempts were made to create a breakwater (or mole) at what became known as Mouille Point on the western side of Table Bay, but although a lot of work was done (farmers bringing wagon-loads of produce for sale in Cape Town were required

Right The view from Robben Island shows the peaks of the Twelve Apostles next to Table Mountain.

to use their empty vehicles to transport one load of stones to the site), nothing came of the venture.

No further progress was made in providing artificial shelter in Table Bay although periodic northwesterly winds continued to create havoc. In 1831 six ships were wrecked and the British government, who then controlled the Cape, were sufficiently disturbed to appoint the first Harbour Board, directed to construct a stone pier from the bottom of Bree Street. This was completed but it proved to be almost useless. A second stone pier was then built from the foot of Adderley Street, together with a wooden pier near the site of the original stone jetty built by Van Riebeeck in 1656. None of these works provided any shelter for ships.

It was only in 1856 that Captain James Vetch, harbour surveyor to the British Admiralty, produced a plan for an enclosed harbour in Table Bay. The plan included an inner and an outer basin, protected by two breakwater piers – a scheme subsequently modified to save money. John Coode was appointed engineer-in-chief. The following year a prodigious

gale stormed into the bay. For three days a northwest wind blew at overwhelming force. Sixteen large ships and seven smaller boats were wrecked. The storm died, the sun shone, but five days later, on 14 June, the storm returned and wrecked two more big ships.

After a disaster of this magnitude construction of a proper harbour had to start, no matter the cost. It had an auspicious beginning. On 17 September 1860, Prince Alfred, the 16-year-old second son of Queen Victoria, at the start of a tour of the Cape Colony and Natal, pulled a silver trigger to tip the first truckload of stones into 1,8 metres of water to start the new breakwater. A bronze plaque on a stone pillar on East Pier road marked this construction which eventually, with the help of convict labour, resulted in the man-made harbour of Table Bay, a major engineering accomplishment by any world standard. The Prince was a fitting man to launch so considerable a work. At the time of his visit to Cape Town he was a midshipman on the steam frigate *Euryalus* with ahead of him a distinguished lifelong career in the Royal Navy. His tour, the first royal tour of South Africa, was undertaken mainly on horseback, from Cape Town along the coast to Durban, then over the Drakensberg to the Orange Free State where he was entertained to the greatest hunt known in history with the shooting on the farm Bainsvlei west of Bloemfontein of several thousand head of antelope in one afternoon of 'sport'. The prince shot 24 of the animals.

Prince Alfred visited Cape Town on three more occasions. In 1867, as captain of the steam frigate *Galatea*, he laid the foundation stone of what was named the Alfred Dock. After the ceremony he travelled to Knysna, where he hunted elephants in the forest in company with the well-known Rex family, the Governor of the Cape Colony, Sir Philip Wodehouse, and a considerable party of staff and dignitaries. He was back in December 1868 and again in 1870, at which time officially opened the completed Alfred Basin and, at the same time, laid the foundation stone for a drydock that was to be named, in 1881, after Sir Hercules Robinson, Governor

Opposite The Tavern of the Seas offers safe and sheltered anchorage to vessels plying the East-West trade route.

of the Cape. The attractive clock and signalling tower at the entrance to the basin was built in 1883. The entrance is so narrow that it was from the beginning a problem to pilots and shipmates. It was known as the Cut. A small flat-bottomed double-ended ferryboat known as the Penny Ferry provided a service for pedestrians wishing to cross the Cut. The first ferryman, Abdul, spent his lifetime working the boat and was estimated at the time of his retirement to have covered a distance equal to twice around the world.

DREDGING DEEP

In 1890, 1000 labourers and 600 convicts, housed in what was called the Breakwater Prison, commenced work on extending the breakwater to 1 430 metres in order to protect a water area of 27 hectares, creating what was named the Victoria Basin, with jetties and a new south pier. It took five years of work to complete this phase of development. Larger ships could then call at Table Bay and be berthed in safety, but the outbreak of the Anglo-Boer war and a massive increase in shipping made the whole new facility inadequate within four years.

The end of the war in 1902 provided some relief from the pressure on the harbour but by 1925 the situation was impossible with ever-larger ships demanding deeper water and bigger berths. Work on a new basin on the southeastern side of the Victoria Basin began in 1926. There was, however, a limit to the size of the new basin. In 1913 the Cape Town municipality had constructed a recreation pier projecting from the foot of Adderley Street. For the time being, new harbour works were confined to the northwest side of this pier. The new basin was opened in 1932. It was 75 hectares in extent. It had a wide entrance to allow larger ships to berth in sheltered conditions, but a serious problem was soon revealed.

On 25 January 1936, the biggest ship so far to visit South African waters, the 43 000 ton *Empress of Britain*, arrived at dawn in Table Bay after a record-breaking run from Madeira. The liner was carrying 387 wealthy passengers, including 30 millionaires, on a cruise around the world and their arrival was considered to be of major publicity value in the development of a South African tourism industry.

The ship was docked at B berth without difficulty. Entertainment and tours around the Cape Peninsula and inland had been arranged for the passengers until the planned sailing time at noon on 28 January. A vicious southeaster, however, blew up and gleefully showed its power. The big ship was pressed so firmly against the quay that all the port's tugboats and all the port's men could not get the *Empress of Britain* out to sea again. At least, not until the southeaster died down. It took its own time.

The great liner left 30 hours late and this was a sad embarrassment to the Table Bay harbour. The battle between man and ship against the wind had been well reported around the world. A big audience of spectators watched every effort by the tugboats. At 6.37 pm on 29 January there was a little lull. The tugboats were waiting for the chance. They managed to get the ship out just in time. By 8 pm the wind was back at over 100 km an hour but the liner was far gone by then, heading around the Cape of Good Hope at full speed for Durban and India.

A new harbour scheme was launched involving major engineering construction and dredging work. Time was of the essence: World War II loomed; the navies of the free world would need a bigger and better port of call at the southern tip of Africa. The municipal pier had to be demolished together with most of the abortive new basin construction. Two new quay walls parallel to each other, 1 000 metres long and 670 metres apart, had to be built extending from the Woodstock beach towards the Victoria Basin; massive dredging of the area between the two walls yielded a spoil which had to be pumped by pipeline and deposited on the land (south) side of the project, completely burying the original shore and the historic landing place of Roggebaai. The spoil provided 140 hectares of landfill, known as the Foreshore, as a brand-new and very welcome addition to the available building space of the city area of Cape Town, already feeling somewhat compressed between sea and mountains.

It was a spectacular engineering concept. The dredging operation started on 15 May 1935. By the outbreak of the war on 3 September 1939, 117 hectares of what was named the Duncan Dock, after Sir Patrick Duncan, Governor-General of the Union of South Africa, was in use. The contract originally intended the whole new harbour to be completed by 8 July 1941 but the war delayed completion until 1 July 1945. The new harbour included a small craft harbour presided over by the Royal Cape Yacht Club, and the largest graving dock – it was named the Sturrock Dock – in the southern hemisphere, 360 metres long, 47,6 metres wide and 13,7 metres deep. Bulk storage space for coal and liquid fuel was provided, as well as a 27 220 ton grain elevator and pre-cooling stores for 29 000 tons of fruit for what is the third-largest fruit export harbour in the world. There is also a floating dock capable of lifting 1 016 tons.

In 1966, a new bulk tanker berth on the northeastern (seaward) mole of the Duncan Dock was opened. It is connected by three pipelines to the oil refinery at Milnerton. The containerisation of maritime cargoes has resulted in further development, both in the harbour and inland at Paarden Eiland. Progress has also meant the complete disappearance of Woodstock Beach, once a cherished Cape Town amenity.

Left The elegant Clock Tower was once the Port Captain's office, from which he could overlook the entire harbour.

Opposite The Waterfront is once of Cape Town's most visited venues, and first in a survey of tourist destinations.

BIRTH OF THE WATERFRONT

Table Bay is the principal passenger and mail harbour of Southern Africa, and a haven for repairing, revictualling and refuelling passing ships. Its fishing industry is enormous, as nine-tenths of the fish eaten in South Africa is landed, processed and railed from Cape Town. From the harbour, South African trawlers work the Agulhas Bank; while fishing fleets from many foreign countries, far outnumbering the local ships, use Table Bay as a base, trans-shipping their catches onto refrigerated vessels for transport to their home countries, replenishing their own stores and fuel, and allowing their crews spells of shore leave.

In 1969, the contracts were awarded for a new outer basin especially for the use of container ships. Heavy blasting of the rock of the seabed was needed to provide this new harbour with 22 deep-water berths. It was completed in 1975 and named after Ben Schoeman, the then Minister of Transport who opened it on 1 July 1977. The spoil from the dredging of

Above The Royal Cape Yacht Club has its home in a well-occupied corner of the Duncan Dock.

this massive work provided the material for a new foreshore area of 180 hectares which buried the original coastline of Table Bay on the southeast side of the new harbour. This area is known as Paarden Eiland, which means island of horses: back in the 1780s Arend van Kielligh, contractor of wagons and horses to the Dutch East India Company, grazed his livestock here. It was loosely defined as the area between the mouths of the Salt River and the Diep River, which flows south from Rietvlei and forms the Milnerton lagoon. Sailors from the stranded *Haarlem* set up their camp in this vicinity in 1647 and demonstrated the potential of Table Bay as a European settlement. It remains at least something of an island, completely overgrown not with lush vegetation but with a hodgepodge of factories.

After all these large-scale harbour works, the historic Alfred Basin, still in use mainly by fishing vessels, with the waterfront facing into the Victoria Basin, was starting to look somewhat woebegone, its warehouses and other structures, architecturally interesting but showing their Victorian age. Their neglect put them in peril of demolition and there was some controversy as to what would replace them if they were sold off to the tender mercies of property speculators. In the end it was decided that the Victoria and Alfred working harbours be maintained as a colourful, animated, lively centre-piece for the revitalisation of the waterfront buildings for tourism, entertainment and related uses. The concept was largely the vision of Mike Myburgh, the Assistant General Manager of SA Harbours. It was brilliant.

In November 1988, Transnet established its first private company, Victoria & Alfred Waterfront (Pty) Ltd. Brian Kantor, head of the School of Commerce of the University of Cape Town, was appointed chairman with David Jack as managing director. In the first five years of the ongoing project, the fading waterfront was transformed like a Cinderella. Prince Alfred and his revered mother would have been more than delighted to have their names attached to such a glittering princess. Restaurants, cafés, cinemas, theatres, hotels, a waterfront brewery, innumerable speciality shops, the headquarters of the National Sea Rescue Institute, a mineral world with wonderful displays of gemstones and a scratch patch with finders keepers for all manner of lovely things, arts and crafts, a vast sea world aquarium, boat trips, the SA Maritime Museum, a giant Imax cinema, the endless movement of shipping, the old Breakwater Prison converted into the University of Cape Town's Graduate School of Business, seals basking on ledges as a lazy contrast to the coming, going, promenading, meandering and search by human beings for fun and food, day and night, in what has become one of the major tourism and recreational attractions of Southern Africa. The story of the man-made harbour of Table Bay has gone far from the very first attempt to provide a sanctuary for shipping.

Opposite Still waters belie the bustle within the graceful buildings of the Waterfront.

THE ISLAND

The ferry for Robben Island has its base in the Victoria Basin. It is fitting at this stage in the story of the Tavern of the Seas to take the 13 km journey across Table Bay to Murray's Bay, the island's neat, modern little harbour.

In 1806 the new British administration at the Cape was just starting to appreciate the varied charms and values of Robben Island. Its convenience

Above Bontebok, once an endangered species, are among the contented exiles of Robben Island.

as an isolation centre was obvious. In 1807 a superintendent was appointed and unwanted persons were thenceforth ferried over to be placed under his charge. These persons included young army officers who had got themselves into debt or some personal trouble, and were sent to the island to hunt rabbits and be kept out of mischief. But most of the other arrivals were human wrecks of various sorts. Very little money was provided to maintain this growing population of outcasts. Government authority had the happy notion that such people could simply be swept away, dumped with little prospect of ever returning, or of seeing their

friends and relatives again. They were considered to be the living dead, and only rarely were relatives allowed to visit them.

At that time it was a wretched place. The sick, mad and criminal were herded together in a number of shacks. They had nothing to do save look longingly at the distant Table Mountain and potter about the shore, fishing and gathering shellfish from the rocks and fishing. Then the superintendent hit upon a scheme to set one person to watch another, which provided the outcasts with occupation, and created such dissent and mutual suspicion that there was little prospect of rebellion or escape.

Persons banished to the island for political reasons formed a special group. They were generally individuals of some stature and intelligence. They found conditions on the island particularly intolerable with escape constantly on their minds. Several tried, some succeeded, but the sea was bitterly cold and the currents hazardous. Makhanda, the revered Xhosa mystic who led his followers on an abortive, bloody attack on Grahamstown on 22 April 1819, was one of the political prisoners. On the night of 9 August 1828 he led 30 other prisoners in a resolute attempt to escape. They overpowered their guards, seized the whaling boats on the beach of Murray's Bay and set out for the mainland. Reaching the shore, the excited men, sensing freedom, plunged into the surf and made for the beach. Only Makhanda failed to reach the shore. He was drowned. The rest of the men scattered in several parties. Three of them were captured, others were shot, and some escaped. The three captured men, including one named John Smith, were hanged, their heads then fixed on stakes and mounted on Robben Island as a warning to others.

As for Makhanda, such was his mystic reputation that for over 50 years the Xhosa people refused to accept that he was dead. They called him Nxele and affirmed that one day he would return to lead them to victory against the whites. His personal mats, clothes and ornaments, were carefully kept for him. When, at last, all hope for his return was abandoned, a proverb found a lasting place with the Xhosa people, *Kukuza kuka Nxele* (the coming of Nxele), said to anybody who longed for something which would never happen.

In 1843 a considerable change came to Robben Island when it was proposed that all the common convicts be brought back to the mainland and set to work building roads. The accommodation vacated by the convicts would be available for the housing of lepers, lunatics, beggars, paupers, chronically and terminally ill people, cripples and the blind. Political prisoners would remain on the island. Quite a considerable exchange of island population took place, which prompted new construction. A substantial house was built for the superintendent, quarters for the military personnel who did tours of guard duty, a bakery, butchery, blacksmith's shop and other conveniences. A neat little Anglican church had been built in 1841 by Captain R.J. Wolfe, who later settled at Wynberg. A 200 metre long jetty made its appearance in 1847, and a regular village started to grow as a centre for the island.

Conditions for the sick remained primitive. The lepers, particularly, lived in complete squalor. Their hospital was hopelessly overcrowded, with the kitchen acting after meals as a bathroom. Perhaps understandably, the lepers were described as a parcel of desperate characters, idle, insolent, insubordinate and, knowing the then incurable nature of their disease, reckless to a degree. Without adequate funds the succession of medical superintendents could do little and some of them were not particularly notable for their ability. The island cemetery grew larger year by year.

Conditions improved after 1861 when, following a government inquiry, Dr William Edmunds was appointed as medical superintendent and more money was provided. The island was cleaned up; its 'capital' grew into a pretty village unofficially known as Irishtown because most of the nurses and officials stationed there came from Ireland. With such a community it could only be lively. There were dances and romances, picnics among the arum lilies or next to one of the great rock pools. Edmund's Pool was a favourite with its underwater forests of marine vegetation, anemones of exquisite colour and quaintly patterned little fish so tame that at the first sign of a picnic they rose to the surface in eager anticipation of a share of at least the crumbs of the good things of life. The main street of Irishtown had a tramway with mule-drawn trolleys. Schools were built as well as a library, recreation hall, fire station and general dealer. A second church, constructed from island stone and designed by the celebrated architect Herbert Baker, was built in 1895 by the lepers and named the 'Church of the Good Shepherd'.

On the summit of Vuurberg (now Minto Hill), the highest point of the island and the site of the first navigation beacon on the South African coast, a neat, permanent lighthouse was erected in 1864. It was much needed. The rocky north, south and western shores are well littered with at least 27 shipwrecks.

One of the wrecks endowed Robben Island with the aura of a genuine treasure island and gave it a sad little ghost story. In 1693 the Dutch East Indiaman *Goude Buys*, outward bound from the Netherlands with a rich cargo of gold and other valuables for the trading stations in the East, came to grief on the west coast about 24 km north of St Helena Bay. Of the 190 individuals who had set out on the ship, there were fewer than a dozen who had not already died or were in process of dying from scurvy. Leaving the ship at anchor, seven men set off along the shore in search of assistance. Five of these died of hunger; one was found by the local Africans and safely taken to the Dutch East India Company post at Saldanha Bay; the other was eventually rescued after seven weeks of aimless wandering.

The *Goude Buys*, meanwhile, drifted ashore and could not be salvaged. Only one person was found alive in the ship and he died soon after the

rescuers arrived. The cargo, however, could be retrieved. The Cape yacht *Dageraad* was employed on that task. Heavily laden, the yacht, in the misty early hours of 20 January 1694, ran ashore on the western side of Robben Island. Sixteen of the crew drowned while all the salvaged cargo and the treasure scattered among the kelp and rocks. Only fragments have since been retrieved.

Above Robben Island's lighthouse, on Minto Hill, was built in 1864. The light is 47 metres above sea level.

The shipwrecked men were buried on the island. Among them was the skipper, and of him there is an island folk tale. Over his grave is a ship's anchor. It is said that his ghost used to roam about, frightening everyone by its wailing. The anchor was put on the grave to hold down the restless spirit, which was thenceforth allowed to wander only as far away as the anchor cable length. The spirit guards the wreck, sitting on the rocks at night at the scene of the disaster, bewailing the mishap.

In 1913 the lunatics were removed from the island to mainland asylums, and in 1931 the lepers were transferred to Pretoria. After all the years of

and an anti-aircraft battery. Several thousand servicemen – and service-woman – did their wartime duty on Robben Island.

At the end of the war came another era in the story of the island. The South African Navy established a base and training centre for seamen on what they called SAS *Robbeneiland*. During the war and immediate post-war years a one-mile security zone was imposed, which allowed the marine population to flourish. Line fish, abalone and rock lobster increased to at least something like the numbers which must once have found a home in a typical West Coast kelp-bed ecosystem.

MONUMENT AND MUSEUM

In 1960 control of the island passed to the Department of Prisons. A new maximum-security jail was erected and the first political prisoners were sent to the island two years later, by a regime intent on reviving the historic use of the place as a dumping ground for individuals the politicians considered best out of sight and out of mind. The intake included most of the then leadership of the African National Congress, headed by the revered Nelson Mandela. They remained on the island, doing hard labour in such occupations as rock quarrying, until the last of them were transferred to mainland jails on 15 May 1991. About 600 common criminals replaced them.

This dismal period produced one minor compensation. As a maximum-security jail the wildlife of the island and the surrounding sea was stringently protected from the usual depredations of fishermen, treasure seekers and assorted looters of nature. The fish flourished, the bird population increased spectacularly with even mainland birds such as cattle egrets and black-crowned night herons arriving to breed in security. Penguins, locally extinct following which their mass slaughter, made a welcome return. In the 1970s the South African National Foundation for the Conservation of Coastal Birds (SANCCOB) found it convenient to release on the island penguins which they had cleaned of pollution from oil spills. At first the penguins simply used the island as a staging post on their return to their homes on islands such as Dassen, but in 1983, nine breeding pairs made their nests. The colony is now well established.

In 1996 the island was declared a national heritage site and museum. Control passed to the Department of Arts, Culture, Science and Technology. In January 1997 the first parties of tourists visited the island on conducted tours, including the prison and the cell occupied for so long by Nelson Mandela. On 1 December 1999 Robben Island was declared a World Heritage Site by UNESCO.

Visitors to the island catch the ferry from Jetty 1 in the Victoria & Alfred Waterfront. During the 30 minute voyage they enjoy a video showing the history of the island. Tour guides, who are former political prisoners, show guests around the maximum security jail, and then a bus takes them on a

their isolation, it had been found that salt-sea air was actually deleterious to their condition. The wards they had occupied were destroyed by fire. Irishtown went into decline. From a peak population of 2 000 in the 1920s, the place became something like a ghost town. Houses and hospi-tal wards stood empty. A green tangle of vegetation grew over the ceme-tery. For a time the lighthouse keepers and their families were about the only inhabitants.

Then, with World War II looming, a new activity commenced. The South African Defence Force took over the island and prepared it as a fortress to guard the entrance to Table Bay. Construction work included a harbour at Murray's Bay, an airstrip, emplacements for three large cannon

Above The Robben Island ferry is by far the busiest boat on the Victoria and Alfred Waterfront.

circular trip, stopping at the house where Robert Sobukwe was held, the lime quarry where the political prisoners worked, the Leper Church and several other landmarks before stopping at the village.

FORESHORE AND ADDERLEY

To explore Cape Town it is fitting to start from the docks. The two main dock gates both face Table Mountain from slightly different angles and take the traveller on to what is known as the Foreshore. This is the 145 ha level area reclaimed from the sea during the vast dredging operations which, as mentioned, were necessary for the construction of the Duncan Dock.

When the dredging and pumping were over, Cape Town found itself separated from its harbour by a wide, open, windswept Foreshore which, once the dust had settled, had great potential to provide the city, already compressed between mountain and sea, with a unique face-lift. Today the Foreshore comprises a grid of wide streets and a hotchpotch of buildings. The original anchorage of Roggebaai is buried deep beneath the reclamation; traversed by the main thoroughfare known as the Heerengracht ('Gentleman's canal'), the name given in former years to the canalised lower section of the Fresh River. The traffic junction of this thoroughfare outside the dock gates is the unmarked beginning of one of the most romantic highways in the world – the Cape-to-Cairo road, followed by countless travellers using many different forms of transport.

Further up the Heerengracht, there is a traffic circle around a fountain and ornamental pools where a happy and garrulous squawk of sea-birds habitually disport themselves. The site of the pools roughly marks the original shoreline. Growing in the vicinity are a few palm trees, displaced relics of a once-handsome row of palms standing along a vanished marine promenade. Looking across the pools at the mountain are the graceful bronze statues of Jan van Riebeeck and his wife Maria, standing very near to the spot where this founder of Cape Town must have been happy to step ashore from his little ship on 7 April 1652.

The statues and pools mark the end of the Foreshore. Among the various buildings standing on it is the Artscape complex, containing an opera house and theatre, both well equipped, with excellent acoustics and seating. Each year many performances of ballet, opera, music, drama and other theatrical entertainments take place at these two venues. Facing this complex is the massive Civic Centre.

Beyond the statues of Van Riebeeck and his wife is the main street of Cape Town, Adderley Street, named after C.B. Adderley, a member of the British House of Commons who, in 1850, gave considerable support to the people of the Cape Colony in their struggle to dissuade the British

Right Visitors to Signal Hill have this panoramic view of city and bay, extending to the cloud-decked Koeberg hills.

Government from turning the colony into a convict settlement. At the beginning of Adderley Street is an imposing bronze monument to those who fell in the two World Wars and the Korean War. It was sculpted by Vernon March, who modelled it on the famous Winged Victory (the Nike of Samothrace) in the Louvre.

On the right-hand side of the street in front of the Medical Centre, just

Above The Castle courtyard is a refuge from the busy life of the city. The gabled arch is the main entrance.

before the war memorial, there is a small bronze ship mounted on a pedestal erected in memory of Robert Falcon Scott, the explorer of the Antarctic. On the left-hand side of the street, opposite the monument, are the extensive buildings housing the Cape Town railway station, airways and coach terminus.

Adderley Street, lined with commercial buildings, leads for nine blocks towards the mountain. It is the city's main shopping thoroughfare and is an animated scene during the week. New arrivals from overseas are immediately aware that there is a peculiar quality to the air in Southern

Africa that seems to make everything a little brighter than it really is. Certainly Adderley Street on a clear morning has an attractive sparkle, with everybody on the run and fast-moving pedestrians and traffic showing an alarming tendency to ignore each other. The pedestrian traffic is interestingly cosmopolitan, a many-hued throng presenting a well-dressed, amiable, perhaps overfed picture, with African ladies flaunting bright colours to particular advantage.

After commercial hours the city area tends to become deserted as Capetonians abandon it for homes and entertainment in the suburbs. Cafés with open doors become hard to find. However, for the young late-night reveller, there is a wide choice of clubs, discos and live music.

The buildings of Adderley Street are attractive, without any particularly noteworthy examples of modern architecture. The railway station is connected to the opposite side of Adderley Street by an underground shopping mall. Between the General Post Office and the railway station there is the extensive Golden Acre development, a massive complex housing shops, restaurants, cinemas and offices on the site of Cape Town's first railway station. The Golden Acre is on the site an early reservoir, built in 1663, the walls of which were salvaged, carefully removed and preserved in the precincts of the new building. At this reservoir, old-time seafarers filled their water casks and bartered for food.

Just up Adderley Street from the Golden Acre, there is a roofed alley known as Trafalgar Place. This is the centre for Cape Town's flower sellers, where loquacious ladies and men of varied temperament offer wonderful blooms for sale, and combine any transaction with a colourful commentary on life in general.

THE CASTLE OF GOOD HOPE

The Grand Parade Centre building and the post office were built on what was originally part of the military parade-ground in front of the castle. It's now, mainly, a parking area with a row of stalls at the western end – site of Van Riebeeck's first earthwork fort. Nothing remains of this. The Castle of Good Hope, which replaced it, was built on the northern end of the parade between 1666 and 1679. In it there is an interesting military museum containing uniforms and medals as well as other items relating to the Cape's military history. The defensive cross wall known as the Kat, built in 1691 across the interior grounds of the Castle, once contained the official quarters of the Governor and his staff. The ornamental balcony in front of the Kat was the scene of important proclamations and the swearing in of new governors. Today the Kat houses a fine collection of paintings, furniture and ceramics of the Cape, known as the William Fehr Collection. The Castle is open to the public; the changing of the guard takes place at 12h00 daily. The ceremony of the keys takes place at 10h10 daily, and re-enacts the ceremonial of the 17th century..

Overlooking the Grand Parade is the City Hall, a massive sandstone building in the Italian style, completed in 1905. The clock tower contains, apart from an excellent clock, the first and largest carillon (44 bells) in South Africa. The hall was the home for several years of the Cape Town Symphony Orchestra, a body of professional musicians giving concerts of a first-class standard often under the baton of international guest conductors. The orchestra is now based at the Artscape Centre and carries on the tradition of good music. It also goes out into the community and plays at venues throughout the Greater Cape Town area.

ADDERLEY STREET TO BO-KAAP

Above the intersection with Darling Street, Adderley Street continues towards the mountain. On the left-hand side stands one of its most notable buildings, the Groote Kerk ('Great church'). This, the mother church of the Dutch Reformed Church is Southern Africa, is also the oldest surviving church, completed in 1704 and enlarged twice since. It contains a magnificent pulpit carved by Anton Anreith.

Beyond the Groote Kerk, on the same side of Adderley Street, stands the old Slave Lodge, originally the quarters for slaves employed in the great vegetable garden founded by Van Riebeeck and maintained by the Dutch East India Company to provide fresh food for ships. In later years, when slavery came to an end, the lodge became the building housing the Supreme Court. Previously known as the South African Cultural History Museum, the Slave Lodge contains an interesting collection of furniture and articles from Cape Town's past. The customs and art of the Islamic people in the Cape are well presented.

Adderley Street ends with the Slave Lodge. A sharp right-hand turn takes traffic into the beginning of Wale Street (Waale or Walloon Street, where two individuals of that nationality used to live), which then climbs the lower slopes of Signal Hill to reach what is known as the Bo-Kaap ('High Cape') or Malay Quarter, an interesting area largely inhabited by Muslims. Many of the neat little cottages here have recently been restored; there are several pretty mosques, and the call to prayer can be heard at all proper hours.

The various annual festivals, such as the Feast of the Orange Leaves held on the birthday of the Prophet (the date varies in the non-Muslim calender) and Ramadan (in the ninth lunar month from new moon to new moon) are all devoutly observed. Weddings, funerals and Tamat (when a Muslim boy completes his study of the Koran) are all practised in the Malay Quarter. One of the restored houses, 71 Wale Street, has been converted into the Bo-Kaap Museum.

Above Cape Town's flower sellers, and their wares, at Trafalgar Place, have been famous for decades.

THE CULTURAL MIX

A very diverse population of human beings made their homes in what become simply known, without formal naming, as Cape Town. Retired soldiers, sailors, time-expired employees of the Dutch East India Company, mercenaries, adventurers and wanderers of many different nationalities made their homes there. A fair sprinkling of retired pirates too, who, having made fortunes from their nefarious trade, 'turned honest' and settled within the blue afternoon shadow of Table Mountain. There were slaves – brown, black and yellow – from Indonesia, Mozambique, Madagascar, and West and East Africa. To communicate with one another, a new language of convenience was created, basically the official Dutch from the Netherlands, but modified by words and pronunciations derived from many other sources. It was a language increasingly spoken first by slaves, farmers and labourers, and then, willy-nilly, by the officials, clergy, traders and aristocrats – the language eventually recognised as Afrikaans.

The culture of Cape Town, predictably, developed as an interesting blend, a major element of which is the irrepressible cheerfulness and joy of living expressed in the Cape Minstrels' Carnival held annually on 1 and

2 January. On these days there is great celebration. The origin of the carnival is uncertain. Some say that it started as an annual reminder of the ending of slavery in the Cape. To others it is simply a colourful way of starting the new year. For several months before the end of the year, groups of individuals form minstrel troupes, each with its own costume, colours, songs and musicians. On the days of the carnival, the troupes pour through the streets of Cape Town and converge on the stadium at Green Point, where they compete with one another in singing, music and colourful costumes that are new every year.

AROUND THE GARDEN

The hospitality of Cape Town was integral with its reputation as the Tavern of the Seas. The descendants of the slaves as well as the freemen and the time-expired soldiers, sailors and officials who chose to remain in the area at the end of their contracts with the Dutch East India Company, created between them a notable industry in the provision of food and good cheer for the passing ships. Farmers, butchers, bakers, vintners and fishermen all worked to contribute to the bill of good fare on offer. To supply the fresh vegetables and fruits so essential for the repair of the ravages of scurvy and malnutrition of long periods at sea, the Company created the great vegetable garden, founded in 1652 and nourished by the same mountain stream which provided good drinking-water. The Company's Garden is now a botanical showcase covering less than 6 ha of the original area, and planted with flowers, trees and shrubs collected from many parts of the world. In this pleasant place there are delightful walks, an open-air tea-room, aviaries, lily ponds and statues of public figures. The bell tower next to the aviary was built in the style of the Cape-Dutch slave bell towers.

The oldest tree in the Garden is a saffron pear (*Pyrus communis*), believed to date from Van Riebeeck's time. The original trunk is dead. The present four arms arose as suckers around the parent. Aloes flower in winter. Demonstrations of rose pruning are given at the end of each July. The various ponds are cleaned in September and surplus goldfish are sold to the public. These fish and a lantern made of white granite were presented to Cape Town in 1932 by Japan as a token of appreciation for kindness shown to Japanese immigrants when passing Cape Town on their way to South America. The sundial bears the date 1787, but its history and it's origin are unknown.

The area of the old Company's Garden steadily diminished over the years as buildings were erected on much of it. Most important of the structures are the South African Houses of Parliament, originally built in 1885 and since much enlarged. Each January the National Assembly commences its sitting with some pomp and ceremony. A second session starts at the beginning of August. In the basement of the Parliament building there is a magnificent library of Africana, the Mendelssohn Library. The grounds and buildings of the Houses of Parliament are immaculately maintained, and there is a graceful statue of Queen Victoria among the trees on the lower side. Guided tours of the Houses of Parliament take place throughout the year .

Immediately across Government Avenue from the terracotta brick Parliament buildings is the sandstone Anglican cathedral of St George the Martyr, designed by Sir Herbert Baker to replace an older cathedral on the same site.

Between the cathedral and the Garden is the building complex of the National Library of South Africa housing a massive collection of books dealing with Africa. Among them is the Grey Collection, donated to the

Left A graceful 19th century memorial fountain in the Company's Garden commemorates an early Cape politician.

library by Sir George Grey, a former governor of the Cape Colony. The collection is housed in the annexe and comprises about 5 000 volumes, including many medieval manuscripts, early printed books and first editions of famous works. There is a first folio Shakespeare (1623), easily the most valuable volume, and a copy of the second folio (1632), as well as a 15th century copy of Dante's *Divine Comedy* and a 14th century copy of Mandeville's *Travels* (in Flemish). The library also contains the oldest book in South Africa, the four Gospels, a manuscript authentically dated about the year 900. The Library is open to the public on weekdays.

Further up Government Avenue, on the same side as the Parliament buildings, stands De Tuyn Huys ('The garden house'), surrounded by beautifully kept formal gardens. Today this is the town residence of the President of South Africa. It was built in 1699 as a pleasure lodge in the Garden for the Governor, Willem Adriaan van der Stel, who used it to escape the confines of his more formal residence in the Castle. Later British governors resided there permanently, and many illustrious guests have graced its spacious rooms.

Government Avenue is itself a renowned feature of Cape Town. It is a fine kilometre-long promenade through a shady tunnel of oak trees inhabited by a permanent population of doves, pigeons and American squirrels (introduced by. Cecil Rhodes more than a century ago). All live comfortably on handouts of bread and peanuts from a benevolent public. A discord of vagrant cats lives agreeably on the hand-fed doves, pigeons and an occasional unwary squirrel. A walk through the Avenue, feeding the animals or lolling on the numerous benches, are all pastimes which Capetonians and visitors have enjoyed for many years.

THE ODDBALLS OF THE AVENUE

It is on Government Avenue, too, that the characters of the town, the eccentrics and dropouts, spend much of their time. Such individuals come and go in all cities, and they add a touch of spice to an otherwise staid, humdrum world. Cape Town has known some marvellous and attractively quaint characters among this community of bench sitters and Avenue promenaders. There was old 'Professor' Herbst with his long white beard and seafarer's attire, who sold love potions for a living; there was a woman who wore the same dress every day for years, it is said, to spite her husband who had once accused her of extravagance in buying clothes. Towards the end of her life the dress was an incredible garment made up of threads and patches. Then there was a mystery man, always dressed in knickerbockers and carrying a paper shopping carrier; and a rabbinical character who slept on benches and snored loudly; and a man who lived

Right Tuynhuys was once the residence of English governers, and is now the President's home.

well for years by coaxing plump doves and pigeons into a paper bag containing titbits; and Cape Town Charlie, who earned a living as a snake charmer and conjurer; and many more.

In modern times we had Cas Lucas, a happy-go-lucky individual who claimed to have achieved his life's ambition by becoming Cape Town's top tramp. A frequently photographed pair were Iris Theodora Holmes and her son Anthony, who, for 48 years, fed the birds and squirrels in the Avenue each day. Around 1980, the reigning characters were a brother-and-sister team, Giesbert and Dagmar Westphal, known locally as the 'Sack People' on account of their strange attire made up of sacks. They

spent their time strolling the streets deep in conversation or sitting on benches in the Avenue, tapping a collection plate with a gentle request to passers-by to give them 'something'. And always there is a new face, a new story among the familiar characters of the Avenue.

GALLERIES AND MUSEUMS

The upper portion of the present Garden is crossed by an open space containing ornamental ponds and a number of statues and monuments of persons and events, the most notable being a memorial to South African soldiers killed in the Battle of Delville Wood during the First World War. On the southeast side of this open space is the South African National Gallery, which exhibits a collection of European and South African art. The European collection includes works representative of the main schools of English and Dutch paintings. Perhaps the best known is Gainsborough's 'Lavinia', and there are good specimens of the work of Raeburn, Reynolds, Romney and Morland. The Dutch pictures include works by Heremans, Vijtmens, Van der Kessel and other 17th and 18th century artists. There are paintings of the 17th and 19th century French schools, and works of such English painters of the early 20th century as Wilson Steer, Sickert, Rothenstein and John. A highlight of the collection is the Sir Abe Bailey Collection of sporting pictures – one of the most distinguished of its kind in the world. It includes paintings and drawings by George Stubbs, Herring senior and junior, James Pollard and Munnings, among others. There is also a collection of leading South African and African artists.

On the opposite side of the open space stand the buildings of the South African Museum which has a notable collection of San rock art, the mysterious Lydenburg Heads, the only example of a quagga foal (the species is extinct) and 250 million-year-old Karoo mammal-like reptiles. The Whale Well with its skeleton of a blue whale is well worth a visit. A planetarium, attached to the main building, presents shows daily including an evening show once a week.

Just above the art gallery loom the twin towers of the Great Synagogue, built in 1905 alongside the original synagogue, the first in South Africa (opened in 1862). The picturesque old synagogue housing the Jewish Museum has now been linked by a walkway to a new specially designed museum building erected behind it. The Cape Town Holocaust Museum, the first and only Holocaust Centre in Africa, stands next door to the Great Synagogue in the Albow Centre in Hatfield Street. It contains a permanent exhibition on the Holocaust, including text and photo panels, archival documents and film footage, multimedia displays, artefacts, recreated environments and survivor testimonies. Both museums are open Sundays to Fridays.

Further along Government Avenue are a pair of ornamental gateways guarded by stone lions (the work of the sculptor Anton Anreith). The gateways were once the entrance to a menagerie established by Governor Adriaan van der Stel. A beasts-of-prey park was situated on the right-hand side and a bird and antelope park on the left. The right-hand gateway now leads to a cluster of buildings housing the Michaelis School of Fine Art, the Little Theatre and other cultural and educational institutions, one of which is constructed in neo-Egyptian style. It was built for the South African College (later the University of Cape Town) in 1839 as the city's first building erected for higher education. Near to it is Bertram House, a Georgian brick edifice constructed in the 1830s as a town house and now serving as a museum displaying the British contribution to life at the Cape.

Government Avenue ends where it is bisected by Orange Street. The imposing pillared entrance just across Orange Street leads to the Mount Nelson Hotel with its beautiful grounds, private property for the enjoyment of the hotel's guests.

Besides the main artery of Adderley Street, the city area of Cape Town has many other interesting streets. Plein Street, named after Stal Plein ('Stable square'), is a busy shopping thoroughfare, at the top of which, at the square, there is an equestrian statue of military hero and first Union prime minister Louis Botha, the Roman Catholic Cathedral of St Mary, and the Lodge de Goede Hoop, the first Masonic lodge in South Africa.

St George's, Burg and Long are also commercial streets. Burg bisects Greenmarket Square, the site of the original open-air vegetable market, is now the scene of a fleamarket. On one side stands the attractive Old Town House, built in 1761, originally the Burgher Watch House and later the civic centre and council house of Cape Town. It was replaced by the present city hall in 1905 and is now preserved as a national heritage site housing the Michaelis Collection of old Dutch and Flemish paintings. The pride of the collection is a woman's portrait painted by Frans Hals and probably the most valuable in Southern Africa.

Unfortunately modern buildings have replaced most of the older structures in Cape Town. The few that remain are hemmed in by aggressive new developments. In Strand Street, after it bisects Burg Street, stands a handsome Lutheran church, built surreptitiously in 1774 by Martin Melck, a wealthy Lutheran merchant who erected it ostensibly as a store-room in the days when no religion was tolerated in the Cape other than the Dutch Reformed. The sexton's house adjoining this Lutheran church was built in 1787 and is now occupied by the Netherlands Consulate. On the south side of the church is the Martin Melck House, a fine specimen of an 18th century Cape-Dutch townhouse and now a business centre.

On the opposite side of Strand Street stands another graceful old house, built in 1702 and named the Koopmans-de Wet House after the family who acquired it at the beginning of the 19th century. It is now a historical monument and museum, containing an interesting collection of period furniture, antiques and prints.

TOWARDS THE MOUNTAIN

Between the top of Government Avenue and the slopes of Table Mountain lie the oldest residential suburbs of Cape Town. Gardens is a popular place for boarding-houses and rooms for business people. Vredehoek ('Peaceful corner') and Kloof (cleft) are also populated by working and business people of the city; Oranjezicht ('Orange view'), originally a farm, was so named because the farmhouse had a view of the Oranje bastion of the Castle of the Cape of Good Hope.

Tamboerskloof ('Drummer's ravine') is further west, against the slopes of Lion's Head; Devil's Peak, University Estate and what used to be a picturesquely decrepit slum area, District Six, all lie on the slopes of Devil's Peak. District Six, now demolished, once enjoyed an atmosphere of great vitality and gaiety, despite its conditions of anguished poverty. There are plans to rebuild District Six as a residential area.

The eastern boundaries of the farm on which the suburb of Oranjezicht now stands were along the banks of the Fresh River. Although this river has been forced underground in the lower reaches of its flow through the modern city, the stream in its upper reaches remains on the surface; and, in the winter rainy season when there is a flow of water, it is pleasant to walk along its shady banks and find lingering there something of the atmosphere of Cape Town long ago.

To reach the beginning of this still-unspoilt upper valley of the Fresh River, go up what was once the outlying street of Cape Town, Buitenkant ('Outer side') Street, which passes the lovely old rococo house Rust en Vreugd ('Rest and peace'), now a national heritage site and gallery for fine water-colours collected by William Fehr. Among these paintings are a number by the famous wildlife artist, Edmund Caldwell.

Beyond Rust en Vreugd, the street continues up the hill in the direction of Table Mountain. Passing the Gardens Shopping Centre, one reaches the imposing building and grounds of Highlands House, the Jewish old age home.

It is here that the Fresh River is free from its conduit and flows merrily down the lower mountain slopes through a beautiful, tree-filled valley, nowadays called the Van Riebeeck Park, attractively laid out with picnic spots and shady glades. Many lovely, perfectly maintained homes such as Rheezicht nestle among the trees on both sides of the valley. In former years a cobbled pathway known as the 'slave walk' made its way up this portion of the valley to wash houses where the clothes of Cape Town were laundered.

Further up, on a steep slope of the tongue of land between the river and its tributary stream, stood a house whose ruins, more than half buried

Above A cloudy tablecloth starts to form on the mountain above the city. This is a characteristic of the South-east wind.

ASCENDING THE HEIGHTS

Climbers have found over 350 separate routes, ranging from easy to very difficult, to the summit of Table Mountain. This great pile of sandstone, a mountain playground in the backyard of a city, is also a National Heritage site, National Park and recreational area belonging to all, with wild flowers in astonishing profusion, sizes and colours, ranging from the giant protea to the fragile disa, to be seen somewhere on the mountain throughout the year.

The level but rough and rocky summit has many points of interest. It is 3 km long, east to west, with its highest point, the 1 086 m Maclear's Beacon (Sir Thomas Maclear was a one-time Astronomer Royal), on the eastern end.

The western end of the narrow table plateau supports the distinctive concrete 'pimple' of the upper cable station, where the engines are housed which safely lift over 500 000 people to the summit each year.

The cableway was opened in October 1929 and, notwithstanding many hazards, nobody had been killed in the its construction and no serious accident ever marred its operation. It was replaced with a new cableway in 1997. The upper and lower cable stations were rebuilt to accept larger, circular shaped cable cars, weighing 13 tons each and holding 65 passengers. They are similar to the cable cars used on mountains in Switzerland, and they carry 890 passengers an hour instead of the old 250.

There are two carrying (or track) cables, 1 220 m long and 46,5 mm thick. They have a breaking strain of 168 tons and are minutely inspected once each month. The two cabins counterbalance each other. One goes up as the other goes down, taking about 6 minutes to do the journey. The breaking strain of the hauling rope is over 36 tons. The driving engine is powered by electricity from Cape Town. If the power supply failed, the cabin would remain stationary until an auxiliary power supply was switched on.

The experience of going up the Table Mountain cableway is unique. There is tremendous drama in the great rock mass of the mountain. The cable cars revolve slowly as they travel and the view expands with every metre the car climbs, revealing the whole of Cape Town, with Table Bay and a long view northwards to the mountain ranges on the far horizon. It is always best to check with the cableway office as to whether they are running or not as, often, the wind can come up at short notice. It is also possible to pre-book tickets.

Climbing the mountain by foot and hand should not be attempted without expert advice, as several people are killed on it each year. The Mountain Club of South Africa is happy to advise prospective climbers, and publishes an excellent guide and map for walkers and climbers, with all climbs rated.

The narrow tabletop falls away sharply into the back table, a walker's rugged paradise, with gorges, wild flowers, pine forests, and a set of reservoirs supplying water to Cape Town. This back table eventually ends precipitately in the south in Orange Kloof. Its eastern precipices, beautifully

---

in shrubbery, still overlook the valley through a tangle of oak and fir trees. The view stretches as far as the distant waters of Table Bay. There are many legends about this house, which was called De Grendel van de Platteklip Kloof ('The bolt of the flat stone cleft') because it blocked access to the upper reaches of the valley. Its isolated situation, the shadows of the trees and the tumbling rush of a waterfall beside it, certainly make it an ideal home for ghosts. Here, legend has it, lived Antjie Somers, the favourite bogeyman (or woman) of the Cape Coloured people. Antjie is a mystical character who appears in many rhymes and tales, especially those told by mothers to frighten naughty children. In this area too, according to folklore, stood Verlatenbosch ('Abandoned bush'), where the leprous son of a former governor lived in solitude. He had apparently

been infected by playing a flute he had picked up, once owned by a leper and deliberately placed by an enemy of the governor where his son could find it. The sound of the flute is said still to haunt the area.

Just above the ruins of the abode of Antjie Somers, the Fresh River comes racing down over a series of flat rock surfaces. These give the name of Platteklip ('Flat stone') to the higher reaches and the great diagonal gorge which cleaves the front of Table Mountain, providing the easiest (but dullest) scramble up to the summit where the busy little river has its source.

Above The cable cars revolve during their short journey between bottom and top.

wooded, overlook the southern suburbs of Cape Town. The twelve sun-drenched and bare buttresses of its western precipices, known as the Twelve Apostles, dominate the Atlantic Ocean suburbs such as Camps Bay.

THE MOUNTAIN'S NEIGHBOURS

The actual western edge of the table, with the upper cable station and restaurant on its top, falls away almost alarmingly to the saddle of land known as Kloof Nek. This saddle links Table Mountain to one of its satellites, the 669m high Lion's Head, a striking sugarloaf-shaped peak connected by a long body to a rump known as Signal Hill, which overlooks the docks. Signal Hill has on it the ceremonial cannons of Lion's Battery which, by firing a shot at noon each day, prompt the pigeons of Cape Town to take fright and the human populace to check their time. Lion's Head was once known as the Sugarloaf. The reason for the change of name is apparently either its shape, or the shooting there of the last Cape lion. For many years a look-out man was stationed on its summit to warn Cape Town merchants, and the military, with a small signal cannon and flags of the approach and identity of ships.

A well trodden pathway spirals to the summit through sparkling groves of silver trees and lovely spring displays of watsonias, its final stretch up steep rocks facilitated by chains. The climb is not unduly demanding and the 360-degree panorama is, if anything, aesthetically superior to the higher but more directional view from the top of Table Mountain.

The road which climbs the lower slopes of Lion's Head runs past the domed kramat (tomb) of Mohammed Gasan Gaibbie Shah and leads to the summit of Signal Hill. There is a picnic site nearby, on top of the saddle of land linking Lion's Head to Signal Hill. A pair of old signal cannons are mounted on a look-out just above the tomb. Countless sightseers have travelled this road to view the scene at night, when the whole city lies glittering like a fairyland necklace elegantly suspended around the smoothly curved neck of Table Bay. Midnight on the last day of the year is a memorable time to be on this wonderful vantage-point. The glow of lights, firing of rockets, distant sounds of revelry, hooting of ships, whistling trains, the sound of bells, all rising from the city and echoing and reflecting from the watching face of Table Mountain, provide an almost dream-like prelude to the coming year. Table Mountain is floodlit.

From the Signal Hill observation point it is pleasant to drive back to Kloof Nek and then along Tafelberg Road which, with its constantly changing views, is lovely by day and night. It follows the 350 m contour below the cliffs of Table Mountain, past the lower cable station to the slopes of the 1 001 m high Devil's Peak, which stands guard on the flank of Table Mountain opposite to Lion's Head.

Devil's Peak was originally known as the Wind Mountain. The reason for

Above Lion's Head, to the right of Table Mountain was once called 'The Sugarloaf'.

its two names is not only interesting but also explains several local weather peculiarities. An oft-told local legend introduces us to a retired pirate named Van Hunks. This rugged character, it appears, was accustomed to spend his days sitting beneath a clump of trees at what is known as Breakfast Rock on the summit of the saddle of land connecting Devil's Peak to Table Mountain. There he passed his time smoking a potent mixture of rum-soaked tobacco and viewing the shipping in the bay, speculating on the wealth of their cargoes. One day the Devil visited Van Hunks and the two began a smoking contest. This contest continues throughout the summer months. (In winter Van Hunks has rheumatism and cannot climb the mountain.) Proof of the competition is the marvellous, billowing, smoke-like cloud which in the summer season seems to begin at the clump of trees at Breakfast Rock, grows, expands and then rolls over the summit of Table Mountain to produce the phenomenon of the table-cloth.

The scientific explanation for the table-cloth is equally fascinating (see page 4), and is closely associated with Cape Town's famous southeast wind. This is the prevailing wind during the summer, appearing towards the end of October and petering out in February, leaving just before the most idyllic months at the Cape, March and April. In May the northwest wind appears, far less venomous in its impact, but the bringer of cool weather and up to 1524 mm of rain during winter, turning the Cape into a green garden.

Chapter Four

The Central Peninsula

For the tourist, the exploration of the Cape Peninsula is one of the most rewarding travel experiences in the world. The Peninsula is strikingly varied, combining scenery that is both dramatic and charming with a piquant atmosphere.

Centuries ago the serenely beautiful hook-like finger of land, with its interesting ocean currents, its marine fauna and its unique scents and flavours, was accepted as a merging place of East, West and the great dividing continent of Africa. For the indigenous wildlife and people of Africa this was the cul-de-sac of their migration routes from north to south. Later, exotic folk from both East and West joined them in a veritable maelstrom of human cultures, activities and aspirations, enriching the ambiance of this most renowned and strategic Cape.

The drive around the Cape Peninsula, starting and ending at the statues of Jan van Riebeeck and his wife, where Adderley Street merges with the Heerengracht, is 143 km long. It requires at least one full day but no day could be better spent. A more agreeable medley of scenes, atmospheres, experiences, aromas, colours, interesting people, stories, myths and legends, it would be difficult to find anywhere else. Let's be off, then, on a journey of discovery from the city to the Cape of Good Hope and then back with our thoughts full of a day never to be forgotten.

One block from Van Riebeeck's statue, down the Heerengracht towards the docks, there is a turn right into Hertzog Boulevard and then up to the interchange which marks the beginning of National Road N2, the coastal highway which connects Cape Town to Durban and the country of the Zulu . Below this elevated dual carriageway (known here as the Eastern Boulevard), the docks and central city area of Cape Town provide a handsome sight. Table Mountain and its companions, Devil's Peak on the left, Lion's Head and Signal Hill to the right, dominate the scene. Immediately to the right of the road is the area once known as District Six. This was a shabby but vibrantly atmospheric home for the poorer folk of the city – until the whole community was summarily driven out of what

Right The main campus of the University of Cape Town is situated on the slopes of Devil's Peak.

they sometimes called 'fairyland'. District Six was levelled to the ground in the name of apartheid. Its population was dispersed to distant areas, where it would be out of sight and out of mind to an uncaring political regime, just like the old days of Robben Island. The area is being rebuilt. After 3 km there is a turn-off to the first of the southern suburbs of the Cape Town metropole ...

WOODSTOCK AND NEIGHBOURS

The heavily built-up suburb of Woodstock was once a pleasant residential area known as Papendorp but in 1881, when the place was granted a village management board, the name Papendorp sounded slightly odd. The majority of its inhabitants, who were all satisfied customers of the local pub, The Woodstock, arranged a change of name in honour of their favourite place of recreation. Whether the social downfall of the neighbourhood dated from this change of name is unknown, but nonetheless Woodstock became thenceforth a lot less select and more congested.

Beyond the turn-off to Woodstock, Eastern Boulevard joins De Waal Drive, which has come around the slopes of Devil's Peak from the upper portion of the city. At this junction the route has reached its highest level and from this point onwards there is generally a distinct reduction in temperature (especially in summer). The road leaves the built-up area below. On the left there is a fine view over the Cape Flats towards the mountain ranges on the near horizon. On the right, beautifully wooded slopes rise upwards to the Peak's jagged summit.

De Waal Drive has been cut into the slopes in finely graded curves, its verges planted with indigenous flowering species which provide many visitors with their first sight of the wonderful flora of Southern Africa. At the junction, the combined roads take on the name of Rhodes Drive, which sweeps down the slopes of Hospital Bend. On the left is the vast complex of Groote Schuur Hospital, the buildings of the Medical School and, in perhaps unfortunate if convenient proximity, a cemetery. This coincidental grouping of interrelated human activities and inactivities should provide motorists with food for thought, but it seems to have little noticeable effect on the local brand of demon drivers. Hospital Bend is a favourite place for accidents. Groote Schuur Hospital was founded in 1932 and became world famous when Professor Chris Barnard performed the first heart transplant operation there on 3 December 1967. The theatre he used for this renowned operation is now an historical monument.

Below the hospital, to the north and east, the unbeautiful city jumble of concrete and bricks gropes upwards as though trying to engulf the unspoilt mountain heights.

The story of the preservation of this lovely area is interesting. The mountain slopes were part of the farm Welgelegen ('Well situated') owned by the Van Reenen family. On this property Sybrandt Mostert had erected (in 1796) a windmill known as Mostert's Mill and this is maintained today in good working order as a national heritage site. In 1891, Cecil Rhodes, Prime Minister of the Cape Colony, then only 38 years of age but

Opposite Indigenous fynbos, including the Protea family, share the mountain slopes with long established but alien pine trees.

master of the Kimberley diamond mines and one of the most powerful financiers in the world, bought the estate and began acquiring control of the mountain slopes all the way to Constantia Nek far to the south. On his death in 1902 this whole area was bequeathed to the people of South Africa. The brooding spirit of a remarkable man is an indefinable presence guarding this legacy from any spoliation.

Beyond Hospital Bend, 5 km from the start of our journey, the N2 road branches off as Settlers Way and begins its long journey along the southern coast, and De Waal Drive undergoes a change of name. As Rhodes Drive, it swings southwards, passing Mostert's Mill on the left, with its four arms held up to embrace the sun and the wind. The mill is open to the public. Close to it a gracefully designed footbridge takes walkers over Rhodes Drive to a path leading beneath the stone pines, which Rhodes introduced to the Cape from their home in Italy. The path leads through their shade and up the slopes of the mountain., where antelope of a number of species graze, eventually reaching the memorial to Rhodes on a site he particularly loved. From here one can see the whole of the Cape Flats from Table Bay on the left to False Bay on the right, from the built-up suburbs below to the mountain ranges on the northern horizon.

The Rhodes memorial was built by public subscription and unveiled on 5 July 1912. It is an impressive work. It was designed by Francis Masey and Sir Herbert Baker, mainly using granite, Rhodes's favourite stone. The centrepiece is the first cast of the famous bronze statue by G.F.Watts: 'Physical Energy', the original of which stands in Hyde Park, London. The statue faces north, where Rhodes dreamed and schemed of so many things. It is set on a granite base at the foot of a granite stairway guarded by bronze lions. At the top of the stairway, in what resembles a Doric temple, there is a bust of Rhodes inscribed with Kipling's words:

Living he was the land and dead
His soul shall be her soul.

Silver trees, proteas and other species of the Cape floral kingdom flourish around the memorial. Stone pines provide shade to the parking area; a tea-room provides refreshment, while paths lead upwards to join the contour path which wanders through the trees high on the slopes of Devil's Peak. The remains of three blockhouses still stand on these slopes, where they were erected by the British during the time of their first occupation of the Cape (1795-1803). This was the period of the French Revolution,

Left The statue of 'Physical Energy' is a centrepiece of the memorial to Cecil Rhodes.
Opposite The silver tree, Leucadendron argenteum, is one of the delights of Table Mountain.

and the British took over in order to control the Cape's strategic situation and prevent the spread of French revolutionary ideas, which were anathema to the conservative English ruling class. The forts, or blockhouses, were small but sturdily built. A number of the cumbersome cannon of the period were dragged with considerable effort to positions of vantage from which it was hoped any invading Frenchmen, along with their ideas of liberty and equality, could be blown away. No onslaught by the French ever occurred.

OBSERVATORY

From the seats below the Rhodes memorial, a site where Rhodes himself was reputedly fond of sitting, there is a panoramic view over the suburbs built on the eastern side of Rhodes Drive and De Waal Drive. To the northeast lies the suburb of Observatory.

In 1821 the British Admiralty established a southern hemisphere branch of the Royal Observatory. The site selected, on the banks of the Liesbeek River, was then pleasantly rural and free from the glare of modern electric lighting. The purpose of the observatory was to set time and longitude. Many important research tasks were also given to this observatory and many distinguished scientists worked in it. Its principal instruments were the 1m Elizabeth reflecting telescope and the 0,6m Victoria refracting telescope. Apart from its observations, the observatory was given the task of setting standard time for Southern Africa; and later, by remote electrical control, it fired the noon gun on Signal Hill.

But the steady encroachment of urban areas, atmospheric pollution and floodlighting prompted the establishment, in 1972, of a new observatory near Sutherland in the Karoo, where the skies are unpolluted and, for much of the year, unaffected by clouds. The main instruments from the Cape Town, Johannesburg and Pretoria observatories were moved to the site. The Royal Observatory in Cape Town remains the administrative centre. The astronomical staff spend about one week in every six at Sutherland, the rest of the time in Cape Town analysing their data and preparing new programmes. Much routine and technical service activity, as well as the measurement of stellar distances, continues in the old Royal Observatory. Guided tours are organised on the second Saturday evening of each month (weather permitting).

MOWBRAY TO RONDEBOSCH

South of Observatory lies the suburb of Mowbray which, like Woodstock, grew up around a roadside tavern, though it began life with a different and much more gruesome name. In 1724 Johannes Beck decided to build a wayside hostelry, and while it was under construction, three slaves, in vengeance for some grievance, murdered a farm foreman named Behr and his wife on a farm close by. It is said that a baby of the murdered cou-

ple survived when its slave nurse hid the infant in the kitchen oven. The slaves were captured, condemned and executed in the usual barbarous manner. They were first broken on the wheel, then beheaded with their heads exhibited on stakes at the scene of the crime. The name Drie Koppen ('Three heads') was attached to the tavern, with a signboard displaying the heads, and the name was passed on to the village which grew around it. Much later the name was changed to Mowbray, the name of a local estate owned by a man from Melton Mowbray in England. The three heads were still depicted on the coat of arms of the municipality which was established in 1890. Three cups, presumably in memory of rollicking times in the tavern, were also included in this rather odd emblem.

Above Rondebosch Common, set beneath jagged Devil's Peak, was once a military camp-ground.

South of Mowbray and immediately east of the Rhodes Memorial is the suburb of Rosebank, much used as a dormitory area for students of the University of Cape Town. In Cecil Road you'll find the Irma Stern Museum, devoted to the work of that outstanding South African artist. The attractive Baxter Theatre complex, part of the University of Cape Town, stands on Main Road.

Originally named Ronde Doorn Bosjen ('Round thorn bushes'), after a long-vanished landmark – a circle of thorn trees – Rondebosch is now covered with attractive residences, schools such as the Diocesan College (Bishops), Rondebosch Boys (high and primary), Westerford (high), Rustenburg Girls Junior and High, in whose grounds stand the original summer residence of the Dutch governors (hence the name, which means 'Place of Rest'). Rondebosch Common, a large open space much used as a camping ground by the Dutch and British military during the long

drawn -out Napoleonic wars, is now a protected space graced by several species of wild flowers. Overlooking it on the eastern side is the Red Cross War Memorial Children's Hospital. In the centre of Rondebosch stands a cast-iron fountain built about 1884 as a drinking trough for horses and which later became the support for the first electrically generated street light in Cape Town.

Rhodes Drive continues from Mostert's Mill, passing (on the right) the creeper-covered walls of the main cluster of University buildings. They are magnificently situated, with the serrated summit of Devil's Peak and the rugged cliffs of the back of Table Mountain forming a backdrop.

A statue of Rhodes, a great benefactor of the place, sits on the steps in front of the university, looking in pensive mood at the playing fields and beyond. The imposing site is on Rhodes's gift of his Groote Schuur estate. The University of Cape Town is the oldest in Southern Africa. It had its

origin in 1829 as a private enterprise named the South African College, housed in the city area. The college became a public venture in 1837 and then, as a university, was transferred to its present situation in 1925, when the foundation stone of the first building was laid by the Prince of Wales, later King Edward VIII.

On the left stands the one-time summer-house of the British governors, known as The Belvedere. Beyond it the dual carriageway curves around the end of the university campus and passes, on the left, the gateway leading to the lovely homestead of Groote Schuur ('Great barn'). This was originally built by Jan van Riebeeck as a grain store. It was converted by later English owners into a residence called The Grange, and then purchased by Rhodes as the nucleus of his great estate along the slopes at the back of Table Mountain and Devil's Peak. A disastrous fire practically destroyed the house in 1896. It was then remodelled for Rhodes in the

Cape-Dutch style by the famous architect, Sir Herbert Baker. From the fire-blackened ruins rose the stately Groote Schuur manor-house of today. It is full of treasures, for Rhodes was a great collector of antiques and curiosities. The garden outside became famous for its hydrangeas, passion flowers and plumbago, all planted in great banked masses which he felt were appropriate to the prodigious scale of the African continent. A pleasant tradition was that each Christmas the hydrangeas were cut, and taken, literally by the truckload, to decorate the wards of Groote Schuur and other hospitals.

Rhodes bequeathed his home as the official residence of the Prime Minister of the Cape (later South Africa). He also built a second house on the estate, The Woolsack, as a summer home for his friend, Rudyard Kipling. This later became the official residence of the Deputy Prime Minister, and is now part of the university. Across the way from Groote

Schuur is Westbrooke, originally bought (in the early 1800s) by Judge William Westbrooke Burton and today the country residence of the State President. The name was changed in 1995 to Genadendal ('the dale or valley of grace').

LADY ANNE'S WORLD

Just beyond the entrance to Groote Schuur, the road reaches the Princess Anne traffic interchange. From here there is a branch leading right to the Rhodes Memorial and to the University of Cape Town. To the east (left) there is a turn leading down to Rondebosch and to Newlands Avenue which takes you beneath a fine avenue of oak trees, past the South African College Schools and through the northwestern side of the suburb of Newlands, one of the choicest of the city's residential suburbs.

From the Princess Anne traffic interchange Rhodes Drive changes its name to Union Avenue and provides a splendid drive with the forest-covered mountain slopes dominating it on the right-hand side. The verges and central islands of the road are lineal gardens of indigenous flowers, while the attractive houses of Newlands drowse their days away in the shade of trees on the left. There is a turn-off to a picnic and barbecue site just after the interchange. At intervals along the length of the forest are parking places, marking the start of paths which wander to many parts of this lovely domain of trees.

In 1706 a part of this forest was granted to Willem ten Damme, who succeeded his father as chief surgeon to the Dutch East India Company in the Cape. He named his possession Paradijs, and built a cottage as a farmhouse, close to a perennial mountain stream flowing down into a deep valley known as De Hel ('The abyss'). It was to this 'paradise' amidst the trees that there came, for a little while, one of the more romantic couples in the Cape story. In 1797, when the British occupied the Cape for the first time, they sent out as governor an Irish gentleman, George Earl Macartney, recently raised to the peerage as reward for many years of diligent service to the British as an ambassador and governor. His wife declined to accompany him to the Cape but amongst the staff he brought with him from England was Andrew Barnard, appointed to the position of Colonial Secretary. Barnard brought with him his wife Lady Anne, daughter of the Earl of Balcarres. She took over the duties of the first lady of the British administration, charged with the organising of social functions and the making of friends with the Kapenaars (Cape people). With her husband she was allotted the Castle Residency for accommodation. This she furnished with tasteful informality. In the Council Room of the castle she held drawing-room receptions and dances with a band of six black fiddlers.

Above This whimsically shaped pool at Kirstenbosch was built in the 19th century by Colonel Bird.

Lady Anne's personal history was interesting. Born in 1750, she was an artist of repute and author of the famous ballad 'Auld Robin Grey'. She became involved in an unfortunate and lengthy love affair with Henry Dundas (later Viscount Melville, Secretary for War and the Colonies). His political ambitions required that he form an alliance with another powerful family, and Lady Anne became something of an embarrassment. She was intelligent, attractive and artistic but at 43 years of age she was still dreaming of an impossible marriage to her lover. There must have been a great deal of hard talking behind the scenes.

The upshot was that Lady Anne was married off to Andrew Barnard, a man thirteen years her junior with little hope of professional advancement without influential friends. What he got was Lady Anne and the appointment to Lord Macartney's staff as Colonial Secretary, a plum job for so young a man. So off he sailed with his talented wife, many horizons away from Henry Dundas, to Cape Town.

The Barnards enjoyed a good living in the Cape. Barnard proved efficient in his position and Lady Anne was a brilliant success as first lady of the administration. The Cape benefited from their presence. Lady Anne endeared herself not only to contemporary local society but also to posterity, through a sequence of letters she wrote to Henry Dundas, recording an amusing, perceptive and most readable picture of life in Cape Town. As a rural escape from their official duties, Lady Anne and her husband were allocated the cottage in the woodlands of Paradijs estate. They found the cottage 'too old and crazy to be safe any longer' (as Lady Anne described it). Barnard therefore set to work and built a 'wee cottage' on an 8-ha plot on the banks of the Liesbeek River. This estate the Barnards named 'The Vineyard'. They moved there in 1800 and spent their spare

Above The Vineyard Hotel enjoys the same view that delighted Lady Anne Barnard.

time in creating a dream garden, digging out the palmiet reeds and planting fruit trees and vegetables. The pity was that time was short. There were changes in the Cape colonial hierarchy, and Lady Anne returned to Britain at the beginning of 1802, never to come back.

The Vineyard at first was abandoned to dilapidation. Then the Governor, Lord Charles Somerset, restored the place as his country retreat. Later it passed into private hands. Fruit, grapes, flowers and vegetables, with pumpkins described as 'big as a barrel of beef' were grown there. Then it became a hotel. The house was enlarged and new buildings constructed but in some indefinable way the amiable, hospitable and romantic personalities of the Barnards remain attached to it. The proud owner of The Vineyard today, has carefully maintained its atmosphere and has preserved within the body of the place something of the elegance and charm of bygone days. The garden is superb, the river still flows along the boundary, while the hospitality is a legacy from Lady Anne.

BEER AND CONVICTS

The pleasant climate, fertility and plentiful fresh water from rainfall, mountain streams and springs not only attracted residents, but provided Newlands with a commercial property of considerable value. The possibilities of reticulating the pure water for domestic use and for the production of aerated drinks and beer were obvious.

Jacob Letterstedt, a Swedish merchant who settled in the Cape in 1822, entered the brewery business. In 1840 Letterstedt built a new mill, with a huge cast-iron water wheel, which he named the Josephine Mill after Crown Princess Josephine of Sweden. Things went well for him until a problem started to develop in the late 1840s. The British Government, in May 1841, proposed that Europeans condemned to long terms of imprisonment in India, particularly soldiers, be sent to Robben Island and, after serving their sentence, be liberated in Cape Town.

There was a public outcry in Cape Town. But the British government seemed obsessed with the idea of clearing out their crowded jails of surplus individuals and proposed various other schemes, which they always withdrew when the local people reacted. The controversy seemed to be dying down. But then, in March 1849, news reached Cape Town that, without further consideration of local feelings, a ship, the *Neptune*, had sailed

from Britain with a load of convicts from Pentonville prison, some of them Irishmen serving sentences for trifling offences committed during the potato famine. They were certainly not hardened criminals but the Cape people still wanted none of them.

There was a considerable public disturbance. An anti-Convict association organised a pledge declaring that the undersigned inhabitants of the Cape of Good Hope would not employ or knowingly admit, provide work for, assist, associate with or support convicted felons. Petitions to the Queen, parliament and the people of England were drawn up. The country people supported the town people in a united opposition to the Cape as a convict settlement. Nevertheless, on 19 September 1849 the good ship *Neptune* anchored in Simon's Bay with 282 convicts on board. Mass public meetings were held in Greenmarket Square and on the Grand Parade. The Governor, Sir Harry Smith, was informed that any person, company or government department in any way supplying the *Neptune* would be boycotted.

Weeks passed with the unfortunate ship lying at anchor and nobody allowed to land. On 10 October the names were published in the press of twelve men who were denounced as supplying provisions and aid for the ship. Among these names was that of Jacob Letterstedt. He found his

businesses boycotted, and he was (with others) personally assaulted, abused, threatened, his effigy burned and his business premises damaged. The whole dismal affair dragged on until a dispatch from Earl Grey reached Cape Town in February 1850 instructing the Governor to send the *Neptune* on to Van Diemen's Land (Tasmania). There the convicts would receive pardon and be liberated. There was jubilation in the Cape. The ship was provisioned, a small sum of money collected to be given to the convicts, and the *Neptune* sailed away after five dreary months at anchor.

Cape Town relaxed. The principal street, the Heerengracht, was renamed in gratitude after C.B. Adderley, a member of the House of Commons who had ably championed the cause of the Cape in Britain. Those individuals who had supported the government, especially the twelve men who had been denounced in the press and suffered losses by boycott, damage or physical violence, attempted to get some compensation. One of them, Captain Robert Stanford, was knighted for his services in breaking the boycott of supplies and received £5 000, but the rest received nothing. Jacob Letterstedt was particularly aggrieved at the ingratitude of the authorities. He felt that he had supported a government which did not support him. He decided to quit the Cape and move to France.

Letterstedt's Josephine Mill and his brewery in Newlands were eventually sold to Ole Anders Ohlsson, a Swede who had emigrated to the Cape in 1860 and who built the business up into the largest manufacturing enterprise in South Africa.

Newlands is still a supplier of water to the southern suburbs of Cape Town. The springs near the brewery (now owned by South African Breweries) are still used. One of them, the Albion springs, was for long the basis of the softdrinks bottled there by Schweppes until they moved elsewhere.

The Josephine Mill was restored. A fully operational milling museum was incorporated into the building and this is open to the public. The commodious building is also used for concerts. The museum of the South African Rugby Board is housed at the Sports Science Institute, opposite the mill. The entrance to the Newlands rugby ground, home of the Western Province Rugby Union, is close to the mill, with the playing fields of the Western Province Cricket Club and the Kelvin Grove Sports Club on the eastern side of the suburban railway line. Ohlssons Brewery stands across the road from the Josephine Mill.

Union Avenue continues its pleasant way between forest and suburb and then, with a turn eastwards, reaches a crossroads 9,5 km from the

Left Like spectators at a show, the carved wooden faces of Africa gaze back at tourists.
Opposite Cape Town's elegant Italianate City Hall overlooks the Grand Parade and its market stalls.

tion in the park and always provide a colourful show.

At the important intersection of Union Avenue with Newlands Avenue and Paradise Road (9,5 km from the city), turn sharp right off the double carriageway and follow the continuation of Rhodes Drive up the avenue (now called Rhodes Avenue) along the bottom of the slopes at the back of Table Mountain. The road is a scenic delight and leads through what is without doubt one of the most attractive residential areas to be found anywhere in the world – the green and fertile expanse of the lands of Van Riebeeck's old farm Boschheuwel ('Bushy hill'), now known more generally as Bishopscourt, after the official residence there of the Anglican archbishop of Cape Town.

Boschheuwel was laid out in the sheltered valley of the upper Liesbeek River. The southeastern rise took the name of Wynberg from Van Riebeeck's farm vineyard. The valley is now covered with lovely homes, and a drive through the estate is a thoroughly enjoyable diversion from the main route of Rhodes Avenue. An especially pleasant little road to explore is Boshof Avenue, the first turn-off to the right down Paradise Road. It passes through the gates of the old Boshof Estate, shaded by a fine avenue of oaks, and continues past many a handsome home including, on the right, the original Boshof homestead with the date 1776 on its gable. Further on is the beautiful and secluded Fernwood (now simply the pavilion of the Parliamentary sports club). In its commodious grounds is contained what is surely one of the most delightful cricket fields to be found anywhere that the game is played.

After 2 km Rhodes Avenue passes the entrance to Kirstenbosch, one of the most famous botanical gardens in the world. In 1811 the area of the future garden became the property of Henry Alexander, the Colonial Secretary in the British administration. He was quite an individualist. He built a homestead with windowless bedrooms, as he considered such rooms would only be used at night. This interesting establishment was unfortunately burned down. Another intriguing construction in 1811 was the exquisite sunken bath in one of the springs of the Liesbeek River. It was built by a Colonel Christopher Bird, in the shape of a bird, and became known as Lady Anne Barnard's Bath in memory of that notable lady. Some visitor started the custom of throwing a coin into the bath and making a silent wish to Lady Anne. The men who service this bath of crystal-clear spring-water appreciate the custom.

Cecil Rhodes bought the whole of Kirstenbosch in 1895 and presented it to the people of South Africa with the intention that it become the site of a botanical garden. In 1911 Professor Harold Pearson confirmed its suitability, and in 1913 it was proclaimed as the Kirstenbosch National Botanical

start of our journey. To the left Newlands Avenue leads through lines of oak trees. Ahead, Union Avenue changes its name for a short distance to Paradise Road. It bridges over the Liesbeek River and then divides into Protea Road, which leads eastwards as a boundary between Newlands and the suburb of Claremont. The other branch, known as Edinburgh Drive, twists southwards, climbs Wynberg Hill past Bishopscourt on the right and then down the southern slopes, with the suburb of Wynberg on the left. Constantia lies on the right, while ahead is a distant view of False Bay and the end of the Cape Peninsula.

CLAREMONT AND KIRSTENBOSCH

Claremont, which has an important commercial centre, is still sometimes referred to as the 'village' and its rugby team is known as the Villagers. But today it is more like an infant city, with a major shopping centre and one of the most beautiful public parks in Southern Africa, the Arderne Gardens. The garden was originally part of the estate known as The Hill, in the halcyon days when Claremont was still a village in the centre of a quiet rural area. In 1840 an English immigrant, Ralph Arderne, acquired this estate. He was a lover of trees, and on the site he planted one of the finest tree collections in Southern Africa. He acquired about 325 species from all over the world, including magnificent Norfolk Island pines, Indian rubber trees, Atlas Mountain cedars, North American swamp cypresses and many others. All flourished. The Black River has its source here; the spring was converted by Arderne into a delightful Japanese garden with bridges, ferns and water-fowl. Azaleas, rhododendrons and roses grow to perfec-

Above A cool dell at Kirstenbosch where all plants are indigenous to South Africa.

Opposite Spring at Kirstenbosch is the season for bright displays of flowering annuals.

Gardens. Professor Pearson became its first director. The garden encompassed an area of 497 hectares, including the entire overlooking slopes and back summit of Table Mountain right up to the highest point, Maclear's Beacon (1 066 m). In this virgin area Pearson set to work to make a home for the collection, preservation and study of the indigenous flora of Southern Africa. The success of his efforts is gloriously self-evident. Over 4 000 of the 18 000 species of the flora of Southern Africa are happily gathered there with an all-year-round display of flowers amidst a magnificent collection of shrubs, plants and trees. Pearson died in 1916. His grave in the garden has a fitting epitaph: 'All ye who seek his monument look around.'

Pearson's successor was Professor R.H.Compton who, from 1919 to 1953, carefully guided the garden until it became one of the world's principal botanical showcases. The headquarters and shop of the Botanical Society of South Africa are in the gardens. The Compton Herbarium provides an ultimate authority in the identification and classification of the flora of Southern Africa.

INTO THE CONSTANTIA VALLEY

From Kirstenbosch, Rhodes Avenue climbs the southern slopes of the Liesbeek Valley, providing changing views of the fashionable residential area of Bishopscourt. Reaching the top of the slope, it swings sharply right over the Boschheuwel at the junction with Klaassens Road which leads eastwards through the trees to the suburb of Wynberg. A portion of Van Riebeeck's hedge of wild almonds still flourishes on the left-hand side of the road. The route winds through an avenue of chestnut trees, which give way to a lovely tunnel formed by oak trees. This area was acquired by Cecil Rhodes in order to preserve its beauty and to build a scenic drive around the mountain slopes above the estate Bel Ombre all the way to Constantia Nek. The forest above the road is named Cecilia, and through it meander several paths and tracks leading to such beauty spots as the Cecilia Waterfall, and up to the reservoirs on the back of Table Mountain.

Rhodes Avenue continues its way and 5 km from its beginning reaches the end of its journey at the traffic circle on the summit of the divide over Constantia Nek. The avenue merges there with the road from Constantia to Hout Bay. The road to Hout Bay descends through an avenue of oaks while on the eastern side the road makes a curving descent to the green and pleasant area of Constantia. It is this road which we will follow.

Half a kilometre down the eastern side from the summit of Constantia Nek, the main road passes on its left side a bus stop at a small parking place. From here there is a fine walk down the tree-covered valley known

Left Vineyards at Constantia are sheltered by the mountain spine of the Cape Peninsula.

as De Hel ('The abyss'). This circular path, down one side of the valley, crosses the stream at its bottom and back on the far side has rewarded countless walkers with the moderately strenuous pleasure of exploring an unspoilt example of a Cape ravine forest surviving from the past.

From the parking place at De Hel, the main road continues its curving descent through the tall trees. The road is now descending the southeast slopes of the mountain ridge of the Cape Peninsula and passing through the estate of Witteboomen ('Silver trees'). The area has had a succession of owners since Lambert Symonsz bought it in 1697, and the record of sales makes interesting reading. At the one held in 1833 the slaves were the first to be sold. The most valuable, Abraham, a blacksmith, fetched 2 000 rixdollars. Neptune, a Mozambican slave had absconded but was sold in absentia, with the buyer gambling on his apprehension. Ontang, from Batavia, asked if he could buy his own freedom. This was allowed. Nobody else bid for him as he was very old, so he bought himself for four stuyvers (about two cents).

The main road we are following passes, at one point, between the estates of Silverhurst on the left and High Constantia on the right. High Constantia has an imposing manor-house of a design rather surprising to see in an area so essentially associated with Cape-Dutch architecture. The building looks as though it belongs to an illustration to a Walter Scott novel. Its occupants are just as unusual in this setting of vineyards and cellars, for High Constantia is the home in the Cape of the religious order of the Schoenstatt Sisters of Mercy, founded in Germany in 1914 by Father Joseph Kentenich. This lay movement was dedicated to Mary, the Mother of Christ. Members are active in professions, working as doctors, social workers, teachers and nurses. The movement has retreats, and retirement and holiday homes for its members in several parts of the world.

High Constantia also passed through the hands of a succession of owners. Originally the place consisted of a simple thatched house, but in 1902 it was sold to Robertson Fuller Bertram, who had made a fortune on the Witwatersrand gold-fields as a stockbroker, speculative land owner and developer. The suburb of Bertrams in Johannesburg is named after him. Bertram planned to retire at High Constantia and he intended to do it in style. First of all he set out to rebuild the farmhouse, but it fell to pieces. The only thing was to pull it down. The new manor-house was planned on sumptuous lines. Money was no object. There was granite from Scotland, English oak, with a grand staircase carved in England and dominating an entrance hall fit for the reception of a king.

The Bertrams entertained celebrities and aristocrats. The Prince of Wales once danced all night there. Musicians, actors and actresses

Right A sugar bird is among the many species that feed on insects and nectar found on proteas.

enjoyed the Constantia hospitality. Because the guests were such a thirsty lot, Bertram is said to have decided to start making his own wine and, in association with a professional wine-maker, Walter Stokes, he founded Bertrams Wines, producing a variety of alcoholic drinks, including liqueurs such as the traditional Van der Hum.

Where did all the fine wines and glamorous guests go, and the fortune made on the Witwatersrand? Bertram went bankrupt. It was a classic case of the dread Constantia Blight. He died a very sad man in 1942. His wife and son died shortly afterwards. High Constantia fell under the auctioneer's hammer but the imposing mansion was difficult to sell. The farmlands were separated from the house and sold in sections. Somebody tried to turn the house into a hotel but the building wasn't too suitable for the purpose. The usual quick succession of owners followed. Then, in 1957 it was sold to the Schoenstadt Sisters of Mary, who remain there today in this idyllic setting.

The estate opposite High Constantia, on the main road, was originally named Frankengift, then changed to New Constantia and, finally, to Silverhurst because of the silver trees growing there. On this residentail estate memories of the wine-making past linger on. The slave bell dated 1815 stands quiet but remindful of the labours of the past. Across the main road from the entrance to Silverhurst, 3 km from the divide where Rhodes Avenue ended, there is a small cluster of shops, including an outdoor-restaurant. From here a short approach road leads to the manor-house of the estate of Groot Constantia, home to the renowned governor Simon van der Stel.

GROOT CONSTANTIA

The story has been told, in Chapter 2, of the beginning of this estate and of its fragmentation when Van der Stel died in 1712. In 1778 Hendrik Cloete of Nooitgedacht farm in Stellenbosch bought the portion on which stood the manor-house and gave it to his son, also named Hendrik. The Cloete family, who have been so intimately a part of the history of Constantia, came to the Cape with Jan van Riebeeck. Jacob Cloeten was a mercenary soldier from Cologne in Germany; in the Cape they became known by the name of Cloete.

The new owner of Constantia found the place half in ruin, and set to work with a will on restoration. A handsome new cellar was built, said to have been designed by the French architect, Louis Thibault. The sculptor, Anton Anreith, a friend of Cloete, gave him as a gift the famous pediment. The manor-house was almost completely rebuilt, converted from a double-storeyed building to its Cape Dutch style elegance of today. The vine-

yard had been as much neglected as the house. Cloete planted 10 000 new vines and launched a search for the ideal cultivar for the area. A relative of Cloete, Johannes Colyn, had married a widow who owned De Hoop op Constantia ('The Hope of Constantia'), a fragment of the original estate. Colyn had already begun a systematic testing of each of the soil types and climatic micro-areas on this property. He and Cloete shared results, and the same ambition to establish the Constantia area as a world leader in wine. They succeeded brilliantly, producing on their sections of the original estate two of the most celebrated of all wines – the legendary red and white Constantias.

The two men left posterity no details of the making of these wines. Laboratory tests of the contents of a few surviving bottles found in the cellars of such collectors as the Duke of Northumberland reveal that it was a natural, unfortified wine, the flavour that of a luscious raisin-like liqueur with a subtle aroma. The two wines were a drink for the gods as well as for ordinary mortals. They were carried all over the world, and eulogised in the writings of many celebrated authors. Charles Dickens wrote in *The Mystery of Edwin Drood* of 'the support embodied in a glass of Constantia and a home made biscuit'. Jane Austen in *Sense and Sensibility* advised her heroine Elinor Dashwood to try a glass of Constantia for it had 'healing powers on a disappointed heart'. Alexander Dumas and Henry Longfellow and many others wrote fondly of these wines. Baudelaire, in his poem 'Les Fleurs du Mal' wrote 'Even more than Constantia, than opium, than Nuits I prefer the elixir of your mouth'. They were sipped with appreciation by the captains and the kings. Princess Alice of Athlone liked to reminisce that her grandmother, Queen Victoria, drank a man-sized glass of Constantia wine every evening after dinner. Frederick the Great, Bismarck, the kings of Holland, France and England drank the wine and beguiled their guests at state banquets with its taste and fragrance.

Napoleon, in his exile on St Helena Island, found solace in drinking a bottle a day. On his deathbed, it is reputed that the last thing he asked for was a glass of Constantia.

Strangely enough, the production of this and other wines was made possible in the Cape by the presence over the vineyards of a remarkable bird. Each year in November the steppe buzzards of Russia escape the approaching Siberian winter by migrating across Africa to the Cape. Until the end of March these raptors keep guard over the Cape vineyards, gliding, wheeling and coursing incessantly, killing or driving away fruit-eating birds such as the starlings which are capable of destroying an entire harvest. The buzzards do not eat grapes themselves. By the time they return to Siberia, the grapes have been safely harvested and the wine is maturing in the cellars.

What happened to the two Constantia wines, the most celebrated wines ever made in Southern Africa? Henry Cloete, fourth generation of the Cloetes to own Groot Constantia, was not much interested in a farming life. He liked France and spent most of his time there. He returned to Groot Constantia in 1885 to find the estate in ruins, with the vineyards destroyed by the fungal disease oidium and the root parasite phylloxera. He sold the farm at a public auction. It was bought by the Cape government and converted to a training and experimental farm under the direction of a German viticulturist, Baron Carl von Babo, who knew nothing of the two celebrated old wines. The South African government took over the estate in the early 1960s. In 1976 the estate was transferred to the Groot Constantia Control Board who, although still government owned, ran it as a viable commercial wine producer.

In 1993 ownership of the estate was again transferred, this time from the government to the Groot Constantia Trust. Today, a range of fourteen estate wines are produced and sold *in situ*; tours of the cellar are conducted each hour on the hour between 10h00 and 16h00. The historic farmyard, which includes the famous manor-house, the Jonkershuis complex and the beautiful Cloete cellar, is open to visitors. Some leisurely walks under oak-lined avenues may be enjoyed with a lovely ornamented bath a short walk from the main house. Furthermore the estate offers two restaurants where the wines may be enjoyed as a pleasant accompaniment to good food, including traditional Cape cuisine. Vineyards have been established to produce the famed Constantia wines of yesteryear.

ALPHEN AND THE REMARKABLE JAMES BARRY

From the entrance to Groot Constantia, the main road continues through the residential area, past the Constantia Village shopping centre and, after

3 km, reaches the Alphen interchange with the Simon van der Stel freeway. Just before this interchange there is a turn left onto the Alphen road which leads past the Alphen Hotel, one of the finest and most elegant of South African hostelries.

This area was originally the Alphen farm whose manor-house, built in 1753 by Abraham Leever (known as 'the Monsieur from Amsterdam'), is in the Cape Dutch style but unusual in that it is double-storeyed, the upper floor supported on massive walls, insulating it from the extremes of heat and cold. Tall windows and high-beamed ceilings ensure ventilation from the winds of the Cape. The front and rear parts of the house are divided by a superb screen of yellowwood and stinkwood. The teak front door has elegant baroque arhitecture. The house faces a large oak-shaded square with, on its sides, two cellars in Cape-Dutch style, a Victorian double-storey block known as the Dower House, and the Jonkershuis, which now houses an atmospheric pub.

In 1801 Alphen was bought by Thomas Frederick Dreyer, a great friend of Lord Charles Somerset, Governor of the Cape. Lord Charles and Mr Dreyer were lovers of horses and hunting. Alphen became the base for the Constantia Hunt, complete with all its social trimmings of balls, dinners and entertainments. The Governor was a frequent visitor to Alphen and with him came that remarkable and enigmatic individual, Dr James Miranda Stuart Barry, whose portrait, a copy of the only one known, graces the sitting room at Alphen today.

Dr Barry was born around 1790 of unknown parentage. He was brought up by two individuals he always referred to as his uncle and aunt, the Royal Academician James Barry and his sister Mrs Mary Anne Bulkerley. James Barry died in 1806, a distinguished artist. Two of his patrons, General Francisco de Miranda and David Stuart Erskine, the Earl of Buchan, took an interest in the youth and in 1809 Mrs Bulkerley took him to Edinburgh, where he entered the university and studied medicine, graduating as a doctor in 1812. His thesis was dedicated to his two patrons.

In October 1812, young Dr Barry entered the United Hospitals (Guys and St Thomas's) in London and there qualified as a regimental surgeon. In this capacity he served in Plymouth and London and then was posted to Cape Town, arriving there on 1 August 1816 at the beginning of a remarkable career. Lord Charles Somerset was the Governor of the Cape at that time and Barry had a letter of introduction to him from the Earl of Buchan. Barry, apart from his regimental duties, was appointed physician to the Governor's family.

In appearance Dr Barry was small in stature, red haired with a rather high-pitched voice, prominent eyes, no hair on face and hands, and a notably effeminate disposition, manner, appearance and gait. There were rumours that he was really a female but, of whatever sex, there was no doubting the competence of the individual as a surgeon. In 1819 Barry was ordered to Mauritius to deal with an epidemic of cholera. Back in the Cape in 1822 he was appointed colonial medical inspector. On 25 July 1826 he made medical history when he delivered the wife of T.C. Munnik of a son by the first successful Caesarean operation in Southern Africa. The grateful parents named their son James Barry Munnik. Years later these three names were given as Christian names to a godson of James Barry Munnik. This infant, James Barry Munnik Hertzog, became prime minister of South Africa.

Dr Barry could be brusque and even offensive in his speech. He made enemies of powerful officials by his insistence on more humane treatment of convicts, lepers and the outcasts on Robben Island and the old leper colony at Hemel-en-Aarde. He stopped unqualified persons from acting as doctors and clashed several times with the authorities over the appalling conditions in the Cape Town jail. In June 1824 placards were posted overnight in the streets alleging an unnatural relationship between Dr Barry and the Governor. Notwithstanding the offer of a reward of 5 000 rixdollars nobody was apprehended for the scurrilous attack.

Dr Barry regarded Alphen as something of a home from home and he showed considerable interest in one of the winsome daughters of Mr Dreyer, who had fourteen children. Josias Cloete was also attracted by the young lady and the two fought a formal duel over her on the back steps of the manor-house. Neither of the contestants was injured. They shook hands and became the firmest of friends. What Miss Dreyer thought of the proceedings it would be interesting to know. Barry continued his career at the Cape. The feud with the authorities became more bitter. In 1824 he found a man named Elliot in the jail, lying filthy and verminous, without bed, pillows, blankets or any comfort, and with a broken leg. When the jailer was asked if there were any other prisoners with broken bones, he replied 'Only one'. He showed Barry a convict from Robben Island, Jan Kiser, who had one leg fractured and the other surrounded by a heavy chain. The climax came when Dr Barry ordered a mentally deranged man to be treated in hospital and not simply thrown into the asylum. Barry stated that the man's state might be 'the result of bad treatment he had received in the jail'. This criticism really upset the applecart.

Barry was summoned to give evidence on 15 September 1825. He refused to take the oath or to answer questions and was ordered to be imprisoned for one month for contempt of court. The Governor then intervened and overruled the sentence. Barry remained stubbornly persistent in his criticism of conditions. On 12 January 1826 he resigned all his official appointments. Public esteem for him was high but the administrative officials hated him. To settle what was becoming an awkward situation,

Opposite The Jonkershuis was originally built as the home of the landowner's eldest son.

he was promoted to staff surgeon and in 1828 transferred to Mauritius.

Promotions and transfers followed in steady succession, the West Indies, St Helena, Malta, deputy inspector of hospitals stationed at Corfu, and in 1858 to one of the highest medical ranks in the British Army, inspector-general stationed in Canada. There his health broke down. He was used to living in warmer climates. Bronchitis and influenza forced him to retire in 1859. He returned to London and died on 15 July 1865. Rumours about the sex of Dr Barry had intrigued so many people that the military authorities ordered an examination of the corpse. The person who laid out the body stated that Barry was a woman and, moreover, had given birth. To finally settle the mystery, the army surgeons reported to the registrar-general of Somerset House that Dr Barry was 'neither male nor female, but rather an imperfectly developed man'. There was no evidence to support the story that as a woman she had given birth. Dr Barry, she or he, died still an enigma.

The Cloetes were a fruitful family. One of them, Dirk, acquired Alphen in 1850. The house was already well furnished but to it the new owners took many of their own treasures, including a magnificent 17th century kist which had contained the family effects from Europe when they sailed with Van Riebeeck. They settled in and Dirk began planting vines. One of his sons, Louis, was sent to France to study wine-making. On his return he built the great cellar, renovated the manor-house, and started making wine.

The oldest son, Henry, inherited the estate but he was an advocate in Johannesburg and he left the running of Alphen to his younger brother, Louis. In the difficult political period leading to the Anglo-Boer war, Henry was pro-British. He served as British agent in Pretoria when the British diplomatic mission was withdrawn. When the war was imminent, Henry returned to stay in Alphen until peace came. With him came his wife Christina Deliana, daughter of Nicholaas van Warmelo who had brought the Nederduitse Hervormde Kerk to South Africa from Holland. She was very pro-Boer in the conflict and, unknown to her husband, set up a spy network based on Alphen. It was an excellent base, a great resort of high-ranking British officers such as Lord Kitchener and Lord Roberts. She found eavesdropping on their after-dinner conversations particularly informative. This information she placed in a hollow oak on the farm, where it was collected by undercover couriers and conveyed to Pretoria concealed in cases with false bottoms and hand-made dolls with hollow porcelain heads.

Apart from her espionage work, Mrs Cloete performed her wifely duties. She had four daughters and then at last came the longed-for son. Henry threw a great dinner to celebrate the birth of his heir. At the height of proceedings the nurse rushed in asking for a little brandy for the baby. There were roars of laughter from the guests and comments about a young chip off the old block. The next morning, however, the baby was dead, and a period of gloom settled on the house.

THE BERGVLIET ESTATE

Groot Constantia, with its manor-house, cellars and vineyards, is the classic wine estate of the Cape. It is hospitable and proud to display its treasures to visitors. It is a provider of good food and fresh grapes, especially of the muscatel varieties, picked and sold from February to June. Wine of course is available throughout the year, in several varieties and vintages, its cellars open for inspection and the sale of their contents direct to the public. If no other of the great wine estates in the Cape are visited, Groot Constantia must not be missed. It is a unique part of the history of the people of South Africa.

Several other parts of the fragmented original Groot Constantia estate of Simon van der Stel are also open to visitors. A tour through the Constantia Wine Route, as it is known, is very rewarding, full of beguiling scenes and interest. Start this journey from the entrance to the Groot Constantia estate on the main Constantia-Hout Bay road. A kilometre down this road, just before it reaches the Constantia Village centre, turn right at a traffic light into an oak-shaded street known as Ladies Mile and Ladies Mile Extension. Follow this road for one kilometre until it reaches another traffic light where it crosses the road named after the Spaanschemat ('Spanish rushes') River.

The Ladies Mile road leads over the Simon van der Stel freeway and then continues for 2 km until it ends by joining the lower main road. The Ladies Mile passes through a completely built-up area. In 1714 this was one of the three divisions of Groot Constantia sold at auction. One of the sections was Bergvliet ('Mountain stream').

When the British occupied the Cape in 1795, they found Bergvliet, then owned by Hendrik Oostwald Eksteen, to be in a very prosperous condition. Eksteen, however, was a supporter of current French revolutionary ideals. This made him very suspect by the conservative British, who regarded ideas of liberty, equality and fraternity as akin to the pox. Thus, when Eksteen sent out invitations to his daughter's wedding at Bergvliet and addressed them to Citizen so-and-so, Lord Macartney sent a party of rough-and-ready dragoons to arrive on the scene at the height of festivities, shoulder their way to the food and devour it with the manners of a pride of lions. The practice of 'quartering' dragoons on persons of known sympathies to revolutionary ideals became common. Feeding and accommodating such rowdy men subdued many farmhouses in the Cape, with young women sent far away for safety.

A climax came in the story of Bergvliet when the wealthy widow, Leanora Colyn of De Hoop op Constantia, built a house, as a present for one of her sons, on a portion of the original Bergvliet which she had pur-chased. She called it Sweet Valley. This farm lay on the south side of Bergvliet and was reached by a rough farm road crossing part of Bergvliet. When the Colyn family had bought De Hoop op Constantia, the original deed of sale dividing the property from Bergvliet gave the owners of De Hoop op Constantia rights in perpetuity to the use of this and other roads.

Hendrik Oostwald Eksteen didn't like the widow Colyn and she didn't care a fig for him. They disagreed in politics and practically everything else. She deliberately made full and flamboyant use of her right of way on the road across Bergvliet, galloping backwards and forwards each day to see her son, and sending wagons and carts to convey building materials for the new house and bring back thatching material for her own home. Eksteen seethed with rage. One day he put his slaves to work digging a deep ditch directly across the road. Leonora Colyn promptly appealed to the court and judgement was against Eksteen.

Thus began the so-called 'battle of Constantia'. It was a lawyer's delight, two wealthy people determined to fight each other to the bitter end no matter what the cost. Advocates were briefed. The judge tried to arrange an out-of-court settlement but the contestants were adamant. Advocate Olof Bergh, for Eksteen, pleaded that the deed of sale gave the widow rights to use the paths and roads of Bergvliet but not to go across it. Advocate Johannes Truter, for Leonora Colyn, responded that Eksteen, in personal pique, was simply trying to deny a right which had been enjoyed without argument for a hundred years.

Eksteen won the case. The widow appealed to the King in Council, the first time this had been done by a resident of the Cape. In 1827 His Majesty ruled in favour of Leonora Colyn. 'Ladies Mile', the road which runs through Bergvliet, was thenceforth named after this celebrated and costly squabble. It proved to be the ruination of Eksteen. Costs were awarded against him. They were murderous and he went insolvent.

So far as Leonora, the redoubtable lady of the Ladies Mile was concerned, she died in 1839. Her son, Johannes Nicolaas, inherited De Hoop op Constantia. Eventually, the Board of Management of Groot Constantia bought the manor-house and the remaining thirteen hectares of ground; the rest of De Hoop op Constantia estate is lost under housing development. But at least a little was saved.

KLEIN CONSTANTIA

To discover the fate of the other portions of the original Constantia estate, let us go back to the crossroads where Ladies Mile extension crosses the Spaanschemat River road. From this point, instead of continuing straight, turn right down this road. After another kilometre the road diverges left

Opposite Although closely pressed by suburbia, Constantia retains its rural atmosphere.

slightly, while the Klein Constantia road branches off diagonally on the right. For an all-too-short 3 km this road leads through trees and past gardens of flowers. The estate known as De Hoop op Constantia lies on the right with a glimpse of its lovely manor-house peeping through the trees. Passing a turn-off to the left leading to the estate of Buitenverwachting, the road enters the grounds of Klein Constantia.

Klein Constantia was part of Simon van der Stel's original Groot Constantia. When Hendrik Cloete acquired the estate in 1772 and set out to revive its sagging agricultural industry, he soon discovered that some of the best wine-producing grapes flourished on this portion of Constantia and on the adjoining portion of De Hoop op Constantia. Both areas came under considerable cultivation of the grape varieties, Pontac and Muscat de Frontinac, used in the production of the famous red and white Constantia wines. There was no manor-house on Klein Constantia then, but on a particularly pleasant site, Cloete planted a grove of oak trees close to a mountain stream which was directed to feed a dam. A secluded guest-house was built in this pleasant area and named Marlbrook, the popular name of the renowned British general, the Duke of Marlborough, whose powerful support put on the throne of England, William of Orange, defender of the Protestant faith. Both men were much admired by Hendrik Cloete. The death of Hendrik brought a decline in the fortune of Groot Constantia from the golden years of the famed Constantia wines. His widow, Anna Catharina, had the task of controlling what seemed like a Cloete tribe of children and grandchildren.

Anna Catherina was a tough matriarch who seemed to revel in incessant family feuds. One of her sons, Johan Gerhard, in 1819, bought the 195 ha portion of the old estate known as Klein Constantia. He built the manor-house but failed to achieve notable success in farming. Thereafter Klein Constantia declined under a succession of owners. Some tried their best, but for so beautiful a place there seemed to be a blight. The Van der Byl family had it from 1890 to 1909. During this period the pioneer fruit nurseryman, Harry Pickstone, rented Marlbrook and planted there experimental orchards of fruit and beds of strawberries.

In 1913, however, Klein Constantia was acquired by a couple who at least gave it some renown in the social life of the Cape. The couple were Mr and Mrs Abraham Lochner de Villiers. He had been a milliner in Paarl and was nicknamed 'La Mode' from the name of his shop. He saved enough money from his business to take a holiday in Europe. Before departing he jocularly told his friends that he intended marrying a millionairess. He did. Clara Hussey, whose money came from the Pittsburgh steel mills, was the lady.

Back in the Cape the millinery shop was soon sold. Clara purchased Klein Constantia and, with her husband, set out to convert the somewhat run-down manor-house into a romantic scene of parties, balls, banquets,

fun and games and all manner of social occasions. Some farming was also undertaken, but not much.

Clara made spacious additions to the manor-house, including a chapel, a ballroom with a gallery for an orchestra and a swimming-pool renowned for what the servants discreetly described as 'moonlight frolics'. Clara often had 600 guests at her all-night parties, sometimes inviting all the passengers and officers of passing cruise-liners to join in a grand jollification. A ghostly whisper of giggling and the popping of champagne corks is still said to be heard from the pool on some warm summer nights. The couple had no children. Lochner died in 1930 aged 61. Clara was four years older than him but she lived to the ripe age of 90 before dying in 1955. Jan de Villiers, nephew of Lochner, inherited the estate but he had insufficient finance to run the place.

In 1980 Douglas Jooste, after the merger of his family-owned company, Sedgwick Tayler, with Stellenbosch Farmers' Winery, bought Klein Constantia. He set out to revive its capability of producing fine wines. One of his dreams was to recreate at least one of the two legendary Constantia wines of the days of Hendrik Cloete. Supported by the advice of Professor Chris Orffes, the authority on wine varieties, the viticulturist Ernst le Roux, the master wine-maker Ross Gower, and his own enthusiastic son Lowell, he began a ten-year period of experimentation.

All that was certain was that some unspecified areas of the estate had produced the grapes needed in producing the two Constantia wines, Muscat de Frontinac for the white and Pontac for the red wine.

Both these cultivars had fallen out of favour in Cape viticulture but some relics of the original vines were found still growing where Van der Stel or Cloete had planted them. These were cloned and a vineyard planted with Muscat de Frontinac vines. The steppe buzzards then obliged by doing their job as guardians. The ripening grapes were selectively pruned and the remaining berries were left to a slow ripening until they had the appearance almost of shrivelled raisins with a taste like honey gathered by bees from the wild flowers and aromatic shrubs of the Cape. The first harvest was picked and crushed in 1986 and the young wine put into wood for a leisurely period of reflection and maturation. To the winemakers this was the most difficult part of the operation, as Ross Gower said, 'waiting for it, just waiting for it'.

In 1989 the first bottle was opened and they tasted it. Was it exactly the same as the famed Constantia white wine of the past days? It is impossible to know. Taste it yourself. Vin de Constance, as it is named, has a luscious sweetness, a lingering fragrance of the Cape mountains, a taste which could only come from a combination of the soils, winds and lush vegetation of the floral kingdom of the Cape. The great experiment has now started with a vineyard planted with Pontac grapes. The objective is a red Vin de Constance.

BUITENVERWACHTING

The neighbouring estate to Klein Constantia is Buitenverwachting ('Beyond expectations'), reached by a turn-off from the Klein Constantia road a little less than a kilometre before it enters the Klein Constantia estate. From this turn-off it is another kilometre to the manor-house, cellars and restaurant.

The estate with its werf (farmyard) in a magnificent garden setting has had, for so lovely a place, a curious history of disappointment. Originally the area was part of the estate of Bergvliet, itself a portion of Groot Constantia. In 1793 Hendrik Oostwald Eksteen, owner of Bergvliet, sold 200 morgen of the estate to Cornelis Brink, who sold most of it to his brother Arend in 1794.

Arend Brink gave his estate its name in 1796 and built the manor-house. He planted vines and had high hopes of fortune, but beauty is sometimes treacherous. A cheque-book farmer can only last as long as his bank balance. In 1797 Brink sold the farm to Ryk Arnoldus Mauritius Cloete, a brother of Hendrik Cloete of Groot Constantia. Ryk was a lot different from Hendrik. His farming industry seemed to consist principally of borrowing money and speculating in slaves. He bought, sold, long-term leased and short-term hired human beings. He lived too well on the proceeds. Ryk Cloete went bankrupt. He moved to the family refuge of Marlbrook and left the mess to a liquidator to handle. The whole property and all its chattels was auctioned off and sold to another Cloete (Pieter Lourens). Of the roster of slaves it is interesting to see that their value ranged around 350 rixdollars for a skilled worker. The lowest was 6 rixdollars for a three-year-old boy who was bought by a free maid, Betjie by name, who bid from the crowd and, it is hoped, had the sympathy of the assembly who failed to run up the price, realising that the woman had so little to her name and wanted to possess what was apparently her son.

Over the following years seventeen successive owners attempted to farm the estate with little success and several bankruptcies. One of the owners, the abovementioned Pieter Lourens Cloete, went so far as to change the name of the estate to Plumstead in the hope that this would bring better luck. It didn't, not to him.

In 1981, Richard Müller bought the estate and launched a comprehensive plan to realise, at last, its potential as a producer of fine wine. In the midst of a considerable investment in capital and creativity, the new owner, however, found himself in an awkward position. It was the time of the so-called 'Cold War'. Richard Müller was accused of complicity in supplying the Soviet Union with high-tech computers. He found it expedient to leave South Africa and make his home in East Europe, continuing his proj-

Opposite Buitenverwachting came close to destruction before being restored to its original gabled splendour

ects on Buitenverwachting through a management trust. The work continued with complex three-directional ploughing. The clay and the top soils were mixed to a depth of one metre. This ensured that moisture be maintained in the soil and provided the depth necessary for root development. It was the intention that natural rainfall would be the sole source of moisture. Organic farming techniques were introduced with no artificial fertilisers, herbicides or pesticides.

In May 1989, Richard Müller's wife, Sieglinde, took over the estate from the trust and ambitious development continued under her direct management. Today the modern state-of-the-art cellar produces a range of fine wines. Visitors are welcome. There are tours, tastings and direct sale of wine to visitors during normal business hours. A considerable dairy industry is also maintained on the estate, and there is a restaurant of high repute. It is interesting to see that a small block of hanepoot table grapes, about 100 years old, has been left in the midst of the modern cultivars and still rewards the owner for continued life by yielding great bunches of delicious grapes.

UITSIG AND TOKAI

To the right of the Spaanschemat River is a cricket oval complete with a Victorian pavilion – a surprising sight in so intense an agricultural setting. Constantia Uitsig ('Constantia view') is the delight of David McCay, a Johannesburg banker with a passion for cricket, wine, and Constantia. When he bought the property in 1988, together with a 60 ha portion of neighbouring Nova Constantia, it was little more than a neglected vineyard, a broken-down old cellar and a forlorn atmosphere – a little lost dog of a place, waiting to be put down by some real-estate speculator. The assets were a panoramic view and a rambling Victorian farmhouse in a lovely garden shaded by trees.

The new owner, supported by an enthusiastic staff, set to work to reinvigorate the estate. A comprehensive planting of new vines transformed the vineyards. Constantia Uitsig may be the smallest of the wine farms but the resolve was to make it one of the best. From past years, only the wonderful old hanepoot dessert grapes were left untouched and each season they are still sold from a stall beside the Spaanschemat road. The farmhouse has been converted into a restaurant featuring traditional Cape cuisine with vegetables, herbs, salads and artichokes grown on the estate, and is rated among the most popular restaurants of South Africa. Twelve luxurious guest cottages have also been built in the shady garden.

Beyond the entrance to Constantia Uitsig, the Spaanschemat River road continues southwards. After one kilometre it enters the area of the estate named Tokai, after the hills in Hungary where the decorative, subtly flavoured Tokai grapes had their original home and still produce a famous wine. In 1792 a German mercenary soldier, Johan Andreas Rauch, bought

the land but sold it in the same year to another German soldier, Andreas Georg Teubes, who in 1796 built the manor-house, designed for him by that indefatigable architect Louis Thibault. The house was a picture but within twelve months Herr Teubes put it up for auction, along with 70 000 growing vines, wagons, bullocks, wine caskets empty and full, good slaves and furniture of different kinds.

Johan Caspar Loos, a deacon to the German Lutheran community, became the next owner and he kept it until 1814. Then it was bought by Petrus Michiel Eksteen, son of the litigious Hendrik Oostwald Eksteen of Bergvliet. Wild times came to Tokai. Eksteen was a high roller, a rake and a profligate seemingly determined to ruin himself and his family. He wined, dined and lived on borrowed money and time. His wife was a Cloete, his sister the mistress of Alphen. In the beginning his credit was good. The parties he threw in the manor-house were famous. At one of them, on a New Year's eve, a celebrated ghost story of the Cape had its origin.

A vainglorious young man, said by some to have been one of the numerous Eksteens, accepted a bet on a boast he had made that he could ride his horse up the steps, into the dining-room, around the table and then down the steps again. Egged on by his friends the young man called for his horse to be saddled, rode up the steps into the dining-room, around the table, had a drink of brandy from the saddle, poured a good tot into the horse's mouth and then, to loud applause and cheers, galloped off out of the room, across the stoep and took off over the high flight of curving steps. Horse and rider were killed. The ghosts of the two are said to come galloping out of the surrounding trees each New Year's eve and repeat the performance.

Above Constantia Uitsig (Constantia view) has so-called 'holbol' (concavo-convex) end gables.

Petrus Michiel Eksteen went bankrupt, and eventually, in 1883, the Tokai estate was bought by the Cape government and given to the Forestry Department. Joseph Storr Lister, the man regarded as the pioneer of forestry in Southern Africa, moved into the manor-house with his wife Georgina and created the foundation forestry nursery for the government policy of reforestation in the Cape and later throughout South Africa. Lister was appointed as the first Superintendent of Woods and Forests. His salary was £10 a month for himself and £5 for his horse. Both were granted free accommodation in the Tokai manor-house and stables.

Lister had learned the art and science of forestry in India, where he had gone after completing schooling in Cape Town. At Tokai he planted an arboretum of trees, collected from many parts of the world, in his search for those species most suited to South Africa, a country where timber trees, especially quick-growing soft-woods, were in short supply. He cultivated great numbers of pine and eucalyptus on the slopes of Prinseskasteel (Constantiaberg); the lower areas he devoted to American vine cuttings, which were resistant to phylloxera, and which he supplied to the Cape wine estates to revive the vineyards destroyed by the disease.

It was all a lot of work, but to Joseph Lister a labour of love. His dedication to the lovely world of trees and plants drew, perhaps, a little inspiration from the knowledge that Robert Brown, the Scottish botanical scientist so famous in later years, had walked the same good Tokai earth decades before. Brown's ship, on its way to Australia, called in at Simon's Bay in October 1802. Brown and his party wanted exercise and the chance to see something of the Cape. They set out to walk to Cape Town. Caught by a rainstorm and lost, they arrived at Tokai. The owner, then, was Johan Loos. He was away in Cape Town but a pleasant young lady received them graciously, fed them and persuaded them to stay the night, bedded snug on feather mattresses while the rain pelted down all night on the thatched roof. The next morning they walked on, climbed Table Mountain and then, with a load of botanical specimens, walked back to Tokai.

Forester Lister, after only three years' happy stay in Tokai, was transferred to King William's Town and eventually took charge of the Cape Province's forestry department. The plantation he created at Tokai flourished and today is the setting of a school of forestry. The reserve provides pleasant walking, riding and picnicking for the public. It is open daily from dawn to dusk.

STEENBERG

The Spaanschemat River road, changing its name to Orpen Road, leads through the Tokai forest for 2 km and then crosses the Tokai main road

Opposite Tokai and the farmlands of Constantia valley, seen from Ou Kaapse Weg.

and eventually, after a right turn, and after changing its name to Steenberg Road, continues southwards with the great estate of Steenberg ('Stone mountain') on the right and the sombre Pollsmoor Prison on the left. The prison was built on the site of a former Grand Prix motor-racing track created just before the Second World War on the farm owned in the 1870s by Hendrik van der Poll and his wife Johanna Kirsten, after whose family Kirstenbosch is named. After 2 km the Steenberg road passes the entrance to the Steenberg estate, with the manor-house and original farm building still standing in superb condition.

Steenberg originally had the name Swaaneweide ('Feeding place of swans'). Its first owner was an extraordinary young woman named Catharina Ustings who arrived in the Cape in 1662, a 22-year-old widow from Lübeck on the Baltic coast of Germany. What her short history had been it would be interesting to know. She survived the appalling conditions of a sea voyage from Europe to the Cape, landed just ten years after Jan van Riebeeck's founding of the Tavern of the Sea, and considered it wise to get herself safely married as soon as possible. A young, single woman could experience rather rough handling in those times and parts. Her choice of husband was Hans Ras. He was a former soldier who had become a free burgher settled in the valley of the Liesbeek River on property he had acquired from Jacob Cloete.

The marriage started with an uproarious wedding day. On the way home from the church the two wagons conveying guests and the married couple were raced against each other by highly intoxicated drivers. There was a collision. The incensed bridegroom received a knife between his ribs while he was involved in a brawl with the drivers. His wife pulled the knife out of her husband and managed to get him home but there was little joy in the marriage night.

Hans Ras survived the knife wound and had time to father several children before he was killed by a lion. Catharina married again but the new husband was murdered by one of the locals. Catharina tried again but husband number three was trampled to death by an elephant. Catharina was persistent. A woman on her own faced many hazards in those days. She selected Matthys Michelse as number four. By that time she had also reputedly become the part-time mistress of Simon van der Stel. She persuaded the Governor to grant her the farm she named Swaaneweide. Van der Stel was pleased to oblige. In 1682 Catherina and her husband built their first house on this farm. By the time Simon van der Stel retired to his estate of Groot Constantia, Catherina was well established and a personality of some renown in the Cape. When the commissioner, Baron van Rheede tot Drakenstein, rode on inspection through the lowlands below the Steenberge, he and his party lunched with her, finding the food excellent but having some views about the lady. 'She rides bare-back like an Indian,' the baron wrote, 'and her children resemble Brazilian cannibals.'

In 1695 Catharina sold the farm to Frederick Russouw and moved to the valley of the Berg River. Russouw's wife, Christina Diemer, was a woman in the same resolute mould as Catharina. While her husband farmed, she provided a continuity of effective management which saw the farm develop, especially after 1741 when the horrific wrecks in Table Bay induced the Dutch East India Company to make Simon's Bay a winter refuge for shipping. She became the principal supplier of provisions for ships anchoring off Simon's Town. She also acquired the grant of additional land from Baron von Imhoff, Governor-General of the Netherlands East Indies, including what she named Imhoff's Gift, the site of the modern village of Kommetjie. She and a gentleman friend, Carol Georg Wieser, a wealthy farmer, built two seaside cottages at what was destined to become a popular resort next to the natural tidal pool, the kommetjie ('Little basin') which gave the place its name.

Over the decades the estate changed hands two or three times, but there was continuity – it remained more or less within the family – and it was generally well managed. It prospered. Finally, in 1990, it was sold to the Johannesburg Consolidated Investment Company, Limited (JCI). Under this ownership a vast transformation has come to Steenberg. The lower-lying portion, with soil of less agricultural potential, has been converted into an 18-hole golf-course directly fronted by 210 residential erven as homes for wealthy golf-lovers. The design of the central clubhouse is harmonious with the historic architecture of the estate. A state-of-the-art wine cellar is surrounded by new vineyards with cultivars selected to suit the chemical nature of the soils, micro-climate and altitude of the slopes of the Steenberge.

DEATH OF A PRINCESS

The wine estates of Constantia all lie with their backs resting against the narrow spinal range of sandstone mountains which run southwards from Table Mountain down the Peninsula to its tip at Cape Point, where the Cape of Good Hope provides the south-western end to the continent of Africa. A number of springs have their source on these mountains. Of some of these there is a curious legend concerning the final decline of the pastoral tribes who had once grazed their herds and flocks in the area of the Cape Peninsula and the Hottentots Holland.

After the 'purchase' by the Dutch East India Company in 1672 of the Cape Peninsula, the Hottentots Holland and most of the interior as far as what were called the Mountains of Africa, the once dominant tribes, who had themselves supplanted the earlier inhabitants, and now been themselves swindled out of the area, fell to petty squabbling and dissipating their remaining wealth in livestock by bartering for trinkets, scrap metal, alcohol and tobacco.

The Chainoukwa had been persuaded into selling their homeland of the Hottentots Holland to the Dutch East India Company for £6 16s 4d worth of junk. The tribe had then fragmented under two contentious leaders, Prince Dorha (the original paramount chief known as Klaas to the Dutch) and a rival chieftain known as Koopman. Dorha was married to the daughter of Goukou, the ruler of the powerful and wealthy tribe of the Hessekwa, who lived in the area of the river known as the Riviersonderend ('River without end'). Goukou supported his son-in-law and, at first, so did the Dutch until there was a quarrel over cattle trading.

A punitive force of 100 soldiers and 100 burghers was sent from Cape Town to settle the matter. Koopman gleefully joined in the attack on his rival. Dorha and two of his leading men were arrested, and all their cattle were seized and shared among the attackers. Booty included the wife of Dorha, known as the Prinses ('Princess'). Dorha and his two companions were sent to Robben Island on 8 August 1683. Appeals on their behalf were made by several of the Dutch colonists who were friendly with Dorha, and by his father-in-law.

The authorities in Cape Town relented. Dorha and his companions were allowed to return to the mainland and settle near the site of modern Muizenberg. He begged for the return of his wife but the Prinses said she preferred to remain with Koopman. The two chiefs became mortal enemies. They both wanted the Prinses and to get her were prepared to ruin themselves and their people.

In the midst of this bloodshed, the Prinses changed her mind and ran away to rejoin her husband. Koopman pursued her. He claimed to have killed her but legend says that she feigned death and escaped to hide in the great cave known from its shape as the Elephant's Eye below the summit of the 928 m high Prinseskasteel ('Castle of the princess'), nowadays less romantically known as Constantiaberg.

In the cave the Prinses remained, hoping that the fighting would come to an end. Instead, in June 1701, Dorha was killed. Koopman was ruined and the Chainoukwa tribe dispersed. In her cave the Prinses is said to have wept bitterly at the death of her husband and the dissipation not only of the tribe but of her entire race. She committed suicide, and legend says that the springs on the mountain are forever reinforced with the magical sadness of her tears. They flow to the sea, replenishing on the way lakes which fill the hollows in the flat land below the mountains, Prinsesvlei ('Princess marsh'), Klein Prinsesvlei ('Little princess marsh'), Zandvlei ('Sandy marsh'), Rondevlei ('Round marsh;) and Zeekoevlei ('Hippopotamus marsh'). These lakes today provide recreation for the people of the Cape Peninsula. Perhaps the tears still shed today by the sad Prinses are as much for the degeneration of her lakes through pollution as for the dissipation of her people.

Above Silvermine – these alien pines have since been felled and fynbos, in the foreground, now flourishes throughout.

CHAPTER FIVE

THE SOUTHERN PENINSULA

THE MAIN DUAL CARRIAGEWAY ROAD known as Paradise Road, after passing the turn-off to Claremont, takes on the name of Edinburgh Drive and eventually climbs the slopes of what Van Riebeeck named the Wynberg ('Wine mountain'). As it tops the rise, there is a fine view over the Cape Flats and towards False Bay, with a first glimpse in the distance of the tip of the Cape Peninsula, which is the principal objective of this pleasant journey.

On the summit of the hill, 12 km from city centre, there is a turn-off left past the stone pines, oaks and silver trees of Wynberg Park. By turning left here and again after passing the second traffic-light, the traveller enters the suburb of Wynberg.

FROM WYNBERG TO THE OLD CAPE WAY

Wynberg is a substantial and very congested commercial centre, but it does have its charming side – many of its old cottages have been restored in what is locally known as 'Chelsea' style. In these a community of artists, craftspeople and would-be artists have made their homes and studios. The park and the open-air theatre of Maynardville are also in the Chelsea area of Wynberg.

James Maynard, after whom the park is named, was a 19th-century timber merchant and member of the Cape Legislative Assembly. His daughter's son, William Maynard Farmer, who inherited the estate in 1874, accumulated wealth in the exciting days of the diamond rushes, lived in style and created a colourful ornamental garden of oleanders, hydrangeas, fountains and lawns (his gardener was trained at London's Kew). In due course the property came under municipal control to become a park and an open-air theatre, venue of an annual summer Shakespeare production in an idyllic setting. The original homestead has been demolished, but several ghosts of its grand days reputedly linger on. These include a cast-off, unwed daughter with babe in arms and rapidly receding horse's hooves, said to be either the culprit fleeing or the father in pursuit.

Right Boat trips to Seal Island are run from Kalk Bay harbour. The island also attracts numerous sharks.

Mining magnates also raised mansions in Wynberg. The controversial Sir Joseph ('J.B.') Robinson built Hawthornden in the style of a French country house, with elegant balconies and cast iron, including a greenhouse to supply his kitchen with fresh vegetables. Also in Herschel Walk is Trovato, a stone-built mansion described as being in the 'millionaire institutional tradition' and erected as the Cape home of Carl Jeppe to the design of Sir Herbert Baker.

Back to the double carriageway, which continues southwards across an undulating, green and pleasant landscape. There are turn-offs to suburbs such as Diep River, Bergvliet and Meadowridge. At 20 km from the city, a road to the left leads to the suburb of Retreat and, on the right, to the forest area of Tokai. Retreat was always closely connected with the British army, which established two camps there – Pollsmoor and Westlake, both used as marshalling and resting-places for troops in transit to Asia or Europe, especially during the two world wars. With the interminable movement of manpower during those years, countless numbers of men

found themselves quartered in Retreat, and it remains an address remembered by many.

From the turn-off to Retreat and Tokai, the Simon van der Stel freeway continues for 1,5 km and then reaches an intersection. To the left are Lakeside and Muizenberg, to the right the scenic Ou Kaapse Weg (old Cape way), a superb drive that begins with a steady climb up the Steenberg ('Stony mountain'), reaching a grand viewsite on the summit. A turn-off leads to a parking area and, further on, to a toll-gate providing entry into a magical land of pine forests and picnic sites. The whole area is known as the Silvermine Nature Reserve, now part of the Cape Peninsula National Park, and it is rich in indigenous flora. Even the verges of the road are gardens of wild flowers, brilliant with colour, especially in spring. Pause awhile at the viewsite and look down at the tidal wave of housing relentlessly pressing the fertile farmlands of Constantia back against the stony mountains. You can almost see, and certainly sense, the dynamics of this movement, of humanity trampling to oblivion the good earth which sustains them.

There are many pleasant picnic places in the nature reserve and the walks are delightful. One of them takes you to the great cave of the Elephant's Eye with its memories of the sad princess (see page 74). Notable, too, is the circular route up the forest road which leads from the reservoir to the summit of the mountain and then down to the other side of the reservoir. Near the highest point of the road, a short walk away, the stone beacon on top of Noordhoek Peak (756 m above sea-level) may be seen. From this beacon there is a spectacular view of Hout Bay and the sea, surrounded by beach and mountain.

One kilometre further along the Ou Kaapse Weg, beyond the turn-off to the summit viewsite and toll-gate, there is another digression, this one on the left-hand side of the road. A gate, open during daylight hours, allows access to another popular picnic area close to a waterfall which, in the wet winter months, presents an attractive spectacle. From here there are walks to the Kalk Bay and Muizenberg mountains with their caves,

Opposite From sheltered Table Bay, the Peninsula extends south to far distant Cape Point.

some perhaps still to be discovered, wild flowers and glorious views over False Bay.

At the turn-off to the Ou Kaapse Weg, the main double carriageway of the Simon van der Stel freeway comes to an end. Turn left (the right turn, as we've noted, takes you to the Silvermine reserve) and in due course you're in the seaside suburb of Muizenberg, 26 km from city centre.

FALSE BAY

The coastal road is narrow and congested, especially on holidays and sunny weekends when half of the population of Cape Town seems to be travelling along it to reach their chosen recreational areas on the False Bay coast. Muizenberg is justly ranked as one of the world's more famous seaside resorts. The glory of the place is its beach, the finest and most spacious on the coast of Southern Africa. The offshore waters are warm, and safe for bathing.

Above A black-headed heron finds abundant food in the shallows. The Cape Flats lakes are a haven for bird-life.

The town lies on the northwestern end of False Bay, a 30 km by 30 km inlet of the sea held between the mountainous arms of the Cape Peninsula. During the summer months, when the prevailing wind is the powerful southeaster, the warm Mozambique-Agulhas Current from the Indian Ocean flows down as far as the Cape of Good Hope. False Bay lies at the end of its journey down the east coast. The bay fills with sparkling blue water, warmed to about 22°C and well populated with Indo-Pacific species of fish. This is in the summer-holiday time – False Bay is at its best from November to April. The splendid beach stretches east to west for 35 unbroken kilometres. Rudyard Kipling, who knew and loved the place, was a regular summer visitor, swam with his friend Cecil Rhodes in the azure water, strolled bare-foot along the beach and, in 1895, wrote his poem 'The Flowers', which contains the oft-quoted line 'White as the sands of Muizenberg, spun before the gale'. Rhodes, whose lungs were weakened by years of tuberculosis, bought (in 1899) a seaside cottage beside the coastal road and spent as much time as he could in this unpretentious little place, and the fresh air he loved to breathe in long, deep breaths seemed to be his last links to his fragile life.

The magnificent beach stretches off eastwards to the mountain range of the Hottentots Holland. Baden-Powell Drive follows the shoreline, providing an attractive panorama of glistening sands and restless surf. There are kilometres of safe and enjoyable bathing, surfing and fishing stretches, such as those at Strandfontein; Mnandi and Swartklip, 18 km from Muizenberg. From Swartklip the road veers inland to join Settlers Way.

Strandfontein has been developed as a recreational area for suburbs such as Mitchell's Plain, and has a large tidal pool, caravan park, some bungalows and wind-protected picnic grounds, as well as the Strandfontein Snake, Crocodile and Reptile Park.

At Mnandi there is a large pool with slides and boat rides; at Swartklip a resort known as Monwabisi (which means 'The one which makes others happy') with the largest tidal pool in the southern hemisphere plus picnic spots, camping and caravanning grounds and shops. Swartklip has been developed, particularly, as a resort for the residential area named Khayelitsha ('New home').

Close to the shores of False Bay lie several lakes, fed by streams which have sources mainly in the mountains of Constantia and Tokai. On reaching the level ground of the Cape Flats, these streams half lose themselves in the sandy former sea bed in depressions which trap their flow and become shallow lakelets such as Sandvlei ('Sandy marsh'), beloved by canoeists, owners of small yachts, windsurfers and by numerous birds. Around Sandvlei's shores is Marina da Gama, an extensive luxury housing project with waterside sites opening on to a series of artificial canals – an imaginative residential concept, built on what was originally a garbage dump and wasteland.

The Diep River supplies water from the two connected lakelets known as Little Princess Vlei and Big Princess Vlei, valued for the size of the carp living in their waters. Two other lakelets fed by water from the mountains and from other sources are Zeekoeivlei ('Hippopotamus marsh'), the largest of them all and a favourite haunt of yachtsmen, and Rondevlei ('Round marsh'), a famous bird sanctuary established in 1952 as the first ornithological field station in South Africa. In this 105 ha sanctuary some 200 bird species make their home or are occasional visitors, including flamingos and pelicans. The birds are systematically studied in relation to one another, to food and to climatic conditions, and are at their most prolific around midsummer. Visitors have access to observation towers and a hide, and to an interesting museum. Hippos were reintroduced to Rondevlei in 1981 in order to control the growth of vegetation.

Close to Rondevlei lie the extensive artificial lakes of the Strandfontein sewage disposal area. In these nutrient-rich waters live an array of water birds rivalling that of any of the world's famous bird sanctuaries. Flamingos (both the greater and lesser species), pelicans, avocets, stilts, innumerable ducks and other birds visit the area seasonally or live there permanently. Rondevlei is open to the public all year round.

False Bay, as the terminal of the Mozambique-Agulhas Current, is of great significance to marine biologists: there is constant seasonal change in the nature of its marine life. From April to June, for example, the rare and remarkable argonauts drift in, strange little creatures which have no powers of self-locomotion and are entirely at the mercy of wind, current and tide. Their exquisite, fragile shells, are easily damaged, especially those of the larger, more mature animals. If they are washed up in daylight the seabirds swoop on them, destroying the shells in order to feed on the animal inside. A large, undamaged argonaut shell is a valuable item – shells are sold to collectors and shops all over the world. To walk on the False Bay beach at night with a torch and to see an argonaut washed up unbroken at your feet is a real thrill, and rewards you with a real treasure.

The winter months in False Bay bring a profound change. The northwest wind replaces the summer southeaster. The warm Mozambique-Agulhas Current is pushed back with all its varied life-forms. The cold Benguela Current, a spin-off of the Antarctic Drift, flows into the bay. The water temperature drops to around 15°C. Cold-water species of marine life displace the warm-water species. Swimmers need to be of a hardier breed but surfers, protected in their wetsuits, find wave conditions to be far more exciting. The waves are larger, although the shallow water of the False Bay littoral acts as a brake – it slows them down, making the coast particularly safe for swimmers as well as novice surfers, who regard the area as their nursery. The

Opposite The suburb of Lakeside takes its name from the waters of Sandvlei.

only current in False Bay is a leisurely clockwise movement along the coast. Sharks, including the Great White, although present in the bay (as they are in all oceans), prefer deep water and, in any case, feed on the copious supply of seals who have their home on Seal Island in the middle of the bay.

STORY OF A TOWN

Muizenberg grew up as the principal recreational area for the Cape Peninsula, but its origins are more serious: it started life as a military stronghold intended to defend the narrow passage where the coastal road leads between the sea and the slopes of the mountain. The Oudepost (old post) building, erected there in 1743, still survives.

Imagine the place as it was in those days. To the south there stretched a rocky coast overlooked by towering cliffs. Only wild creatures such as baboons lived there and these were so numerous that the soldiers, we are told, dared not go out unless they were in parties of five or six. The post building looked eastwards over False Bay with it beach stretching away to the hotizon, at that period a place only of birds, of basking seals and the endless murmur of the surf.

Northwards, the post was linked to Cape Town by a sandy track, only 25 km long but, by its roughness, involving quite a difficult journey for the soldiers and their carts. Close to this road lay the shallow lake of Sandvlei, a place of pelicans, flamingos, coots, wild ducks and wonderful reflections from the water – of the dawns and sunsets and the distant shapes of Devil's Peak and Table Mountain. Wax-berries, milkwood trees and reeds grew around the lake while great shoals of baby fish found their way in from the sea via the estuary. The nutrient-rich waters of the lake acted as a nursery where the young fish could grow in safety until such time as instinct drew them to swim out once more into the open ocean.

The Muizenberg area has quite a dramatic place in the annals of the Cape. It was here that, in 1795, British troops led by Major-General J.H. Craig landed from a fleet of warships commanded by Admiral Sir George Elphinstone. This was the time of the French Revolutionary wars; the French had occupied the Netherlands, and the British, worried about the security of their vital sea-lane to the East, decided to pre-empt a possible invasion. There was some skirmishing around the outpost, the invaders were reinforced, and the Dutch forces (an infantry regiment plus artillery, mounted bughers and the 'coloured' Pandour Corps), led by Colonel Robert Gordon, a Dutchman of Scottish descent, retreated towards Cape Town, fighting a running battle that ended with the formal surrender of the Cape to the British.

Shortly afterwards Colonel Gordon committed suicide in the garden of his Cape Town home. It was said that he could not bear the jibe that the only time he had drawn his sword had been when he led his men out of the castle and commanded them to lay down their arms.

After the surrender there was perhaps an understandable tendency to celebrate amongst the British forces. The Cape Town taverns did a roaring trade.

Along the track from Muizenberg most of the farmhouses were looted, wine drunk, livestock stolen and some damage done. Even the grand manor-house of Groot Constantia, home of the renowned wine master, Hendrik Cloete, was visited by a stray party of roistering sailors who destroyed furniture, broke open several barrels of good wine and drank until they were incapable of any further activity. It is said that to make amends to the hospitable Mr Cloete, they later presented him with a collection of cannonballs fired during the battle of Muizenberg. These cannonballs may still be seen at Groot Constantia ornamenting the pillars of the lower vineyard.

In those days the track from Cape Town to Simon's Town was a long one for thirsty men. The few wayside farmhouses were not places of refreshment, and inns could only be established with profit when there was a steady demand by increased traffic along a better road. Such a state of affairs came about after the second British occupation of the Cape in 1806. Simon's Town in 1814 then became a Royal Navy base, and although the road from Cape Town still remained unmade it carried such a stream of travellers that wayside inns became viable.

One of the most celebrated of these inns was Merckel's Halfway House hotel, established by George Merckel at Diep River. After Merckel's death in 1839 his widow Hester married a renowned character of the Cape, Johan Georg Rathfelder, a big burly man who had been born in Stuttgart in 1811, emigrated to the Cape in 1835 and, through his marriage, became the host of what was renamed as Rathfelder's Halfway House. Dressed in black leather, shell jacket ornamented with chains, jackboots and helmet, riding a big bay horse, he maintained, at the hotel, the hounds of the Cape Hunt and, riding hard, he was almost the prototype in Southern Africa of the Hell's Angels. Known as the 'King of the Landlords', he kept an excellent table and good order in the establishment, with a clientele of Anglo-Indians on recuperative leave, enthusiasts of the hunt, passing sailors and many distinguished guests including Prince Alfred of England (in 1860). Rathfelder died in the hotel in 1873 and the building eventually became part of the former Eaton Convalescent Home.

Further along the road an equally famous wayside inn was established in Muizenberg in 1825 by two immigrants from Britain, the brothers Henry and Simon Peck. Farmer Peck's Inn, as it was called, was a rambling, thatched, white-walled building which stood on the site of the present town's tallest building, Cinnabar. A sign on the front showed the gentle shepherd of Salisbury Plain, a benevolent-looking rustic with a lamb under his arm. Above the sign was another board displaying an atrocious piece of verse, an effusion said to have been concocted by two midshipmen

who, unable to pay their bill after a night in the place, presented the hosts with the poem and painted the inn sign instead of paying cash. In the pub there was another sign which read:

This is a home for all those who haven't a home of their own, and a refuge for all who have one'.

The Pecks were reputed to be smugglers and purveyors of strong drink which had not known the revenue collector's seal of blessing. They were occasionally in trouble with the law but around their inn the seaside resort of Muizenberg had its start. Simon died in 1850 and Henry in 1857. Rathfelder from the Halfway House then bought the inn and it was run by his daughter, an enormously fat woman whose contented appearance was considered a considerable advertisement for the place. Apart from eating, she spent much of her time dozing in a double-sized rocking chair in a corner of the bar. Nothing remains of the building. The name Peck's Valley lingers on in a vale above Muizenberg.

MUIZENBERG TODAY

The village which developed around the inn started with a few fishermen's cottages, gradually attracted holidaymakers and became the rather atmospheric place of today. It is worth strolling through the narrow streets of what is known as the 'ghetto', and then, in Beach Road along 'Millionaires Row', the imposing line of mansions that were mostly built in Edwardian times as holiday homes for the wealthy of Johannesburg.

A magnificent feature of Beach Road are four adjoining houses designed by the celebrated architect, Herbert Baker. These houses – Crawford Lea, Rokeby, Sandhills and Swanbourne – became the possession of Joan St Leger Lindbergh, great granddaughter of Frederick St Leger, founder of the *Cape Times* newspaper and daughter of A.V. Lindbergh, a Rand financier and creator, amongst other enterprises, of the Central News Agency. His daughter was a poet and philanthropist. She consolidated the four houses and Swanbourne was opened on 28 August 1996 as the Joan St Leger Lindbergh Arts Foundation. In this handsome setting there are art exhibitions, lectures, readings and musical occasions. It is a fine cultural asset. There is a tea-room, reference library and conference facilities.

Muizenberg has a pavilion, swimming pools, miniature golf, children's playgrounds, a promenade, water slides and a pond for small motor boats. Trek fishermen still bring in hauls of harders (mullet), yellowtail, and other table fish. The beach stretches far away, inviting a swim, a paddle in the tidal zone, a night-time chance of finding an argonaut,

Opposite Majestic rollers advance in line, like disciplined battalions, upon 'the white sands of Muizenberg'.

tribute, dies disgraced', disbursed over £70 000 000 for the benefit of his fellow man. He died in 1919, aged 84.

The Carnegie Library building later became the police station, while the post office became the magistrate's court. The two eventually fell out of use but in June 1990 they were opened as the Police Museum, the first of its kind in the Western Cape. The various aspects of police life are depicted in displays of antique furniture and memorabilia of police duties in the field. In the office, there are photographs of old stations, chief magistrates, officials and detachments; historical snippets reflecting the development of the Cape police force prior to Union; and displays of uniforms and kits, arms and equipment. Also on view are authentic reconstructions of police single quarters, a police inspector's office of about 1948, a charge office, a periodical court-room, and police cells, complete with one prisoner trying to escape and another trying to set the building alight! The full gamut of the world of crime is well represented in the displays portraying notorious crimes of the past and of weapons used by criminals.

Next along the coastal road stands the elegant building named The Fort, built between 1929 and 1930 as the home of Count Natale Labia, who came to South Africa in 1916 as Italian Consul in Johannesburg and later his country's first minister plenipotentiary in South Africa. Count Labia married Ida, second daughter of the mining magnate, Sir J.B. Robinson. Their Muizenberg home was designed, on a grand scale, as the official residence of the Italian legation and became a renowned social and diplomatic centre with receptions, parties and the visits of innumerable celebrated people in the world of diplomacy and the arts. Count Labia died in 1936. The title of Prince was conferred upon him posthumously in recognition of distinguished service to his country. His wife, Princess Ida, died in 1961, and the house was leased as an embassy to the Canadian Government and then to the Argentinian Government. In 1983 it was presented by Prince Labia's son, Count Labia, with its treasures of art and design, to the people of South Africa, and is . now known as the Natale Labia Museum. The building, a national heritage site, was adapted for use as a museum and gallery in 1988. With its lecture rooms, gallery, restaurant and garden, it is an exquisite asset to the cultural life of the Cape.

Continuing down the Historic Mile, there are several interesting houses such as Canty Bay, Graceland, Knights, and Rust en Vrede, the mansion built in 1903 by the mining magnate Sir Abe Bailey. Graceland was the home of John Garlick, merchant prince and philanthropist. It is a superbly furnished and most elegant home in a garden which extends behind the house up the slopes of the mountains almost to the level of Boyes Drive. Paths take walkers through what is a sanctuary of wild flowers and beautiful trees.

Perhaps the most interesting of all the buildings of the Historical Mile is the small, almost insignificant, thatched Barkly Cottage, bought in 1899 by Cecil Rhodes as a seaside retreat with a small bedroom and a living-room.

The main coastal road continues its way southwestwards, passing the railway station built in 1913 to serve the suburban line opened in 1882. Several interesting and contrasting buildings line the right hand side of the road and provide what is known as the Historical Mile of Muizenberg. First after the railway station is the simple little building of De Post Huys ('The post house') which has been restored in modern times and is preserved as an historic monument. When the British occupied the Cape, the old building became the quarters of the commanding officer of the Muizenberg garrison, with three batteries, a powder magazine close to the sea, and a barracks on the site of the later Muizenberg park.

Just beyond De Post Huys stand two buildings. The first housed the original post office, erected on the site of the old toll house where all passing traffic had to stop and pay their dues for the use of the road. Next to this building stands the Carnegie Library, built in 1911 from a grant made by Andrew Carnegie, the great Scottish philanthropist who made a vast fortune in America, then returned to Scotland and, in accordance with his belief that 'a man who dies possessed of wealth which he was free to dis-

Above Colouful cubicles, locally known as 'bathing boxes', line the beach at St James.

It was there that Rhodes spent as much of his remaining life as he could, and there he died, on 26 March 1902. His close friends and associates were gathered to see him for the last time. From his deathbed he concluded the planning of and paperwork for the creation of the Rhodes Fruit Farms, destined to transform the entire fruit-growing and exporting industry of South Africa. He was only 49 years of age. It is said that his last words were 'So much to do, so little done'. His doctors could only despair – there was so much the matter with this man that it was only his indomitable will that had kept him alive so long. From birth he had suffered from a hole in the heart; His lungs were shattered by tuberculosis, and a drastic surgical procedure to arrest this wasting disease, which had travelled the length of his spinal column, left him, at the age of 17, a eunuch. He panted rather than breathed. The southeaster with its rush of pure, fresh air, actually seemed to sustain him in the last months of his life. A hole was knocked through the wall of his house to allow the wind to sweep in to his sickbed. Physically he was a wreck but he had achieved so much and left so much to Southern Africa and the world that his memory will long linger.

Rhodes Cottage, which is open to the public, is maintained with its original furniture and many interesting personal possessions and photographs concerned with the eventful life of a remarkable man.

THE KALK BAY AREA

On 5 October 1858 the foundation stone of a small church was laid to provide a place of worship for the Catholic community living along the coast between Muizenberg and Kalk Bay. A number of Filipino fishermen, survivors of a shipwreck, had settled in the area. They were Catholics and the nearest church to them was at Simon's Town. They supported the building of the new church. It was named in honour of the apostle and fisherman St James, who was also the patron saint of Spain. Spanish was the language of the Filipino fishermen. A priest rode from Wynberg each week to the church to say Mass.

On 1 June 1874, Father John Duignan, an Irish priest who could speak Spanish, was sent to serve the community. He was supposed to relieve only for six months but remained for 50 years. the St James Mission School was established close to the church, with Father Duignan and Francis Hilario as teachers to the children of the fisherfolk of Kalk Bay.

More people settled along the coast. The Cape Government Railways decided in 1900 that a proper station was needed to replace a simple whistle-stop, and they needed the site of the church for this station. John Duignan only assented on condition that the station be named St James. The indefatigable Duignan, supported by the Filipinos and other inhabitants of the coast, then set about building the handsome sandstone church of today. A larger school was also needed and this, with the aid of

Italian stonemasons, was also built of sandstone. The new convent school, named Star of the Sea, was opened at the beginning of 1908.

St James has a beach and tidal swimming pool sheltered from the southeast wind. An attractive residential area has made its appearance on

Above left The view from Boyes Drive encompasses Kalk Bay and distant Simon's Town.

the overlooking mountain slopes with grand views of False Bay. A walkway close to the sea links St James to Muizenberg 1,5 km away. Beyond St James the coastal road continues for a further 1,5 km and then, at the entrance to Kalk Bay harbour, joins the road coming down the slopes from the scenic sweep of Boyes Drive.

Kalk Bay ('Lime bay') takes its name from former years when kilns were burned to produce lime from shells for painting buildings. Quite a num-

THE MOUNTAINS AND THEIR CAVES

Perhaps the area's most intriguing venues are the many remarkable caves, about which there is a story. In 1924 a schoolmaster by the name of Johannes Meyer spent a holiday at Kalk Bay, and on learning that there were caves in the mountains he followed the paths meandering up to the heights. His experiences entranced him so much that his holiday became a period of joyful discovery. The paths which made their way upwards, some steep and direct, others gradual and diagonal, rewarded him with memorable views. At his feet were gaily coloured wild flowers – heaths, proteas, everlastings, watsonias, scarlet-coloured flames and countless other lovely shrubs.

The caves added a touch of drama and adventure to this natural beauty. Several were already well known in the 1920s. Muizenberg Cave, with its enchanting moss-grown entrance, its low caverns and deep, mysterious well, had not yet been totally disfigured by morons with their idiotic name painting; but the process had started – the first graffito date was 1873. Clovelly Cave, with its labyrinth of passages and chambers, was sufficiently well known to be considered haunted by the local 'coloured' folk. Apparently a half-demented old mountain hermit had once made his home there and had amused himself by stealthily approaching visitors on the mountains and scaring them out of their wits with his sudden chuckle. Eventually he was found dead in his cave, and the sinister echo of his laughter is reputed to linger on. It's also said that a cold hand touches any interloper's shoulder the moment his light goes out.

The amazing Boomslang Cave, penetrating right through a ridge for 146 m, was discovered in 1911, and it was here that Meyer met a fellow explorer. It was an amusing chance meeting. Meyer started his cave journey from the low northern entrance, wriggling in on his stomach. At the same time, J.C.W. Moore started from the southern side, where the entrance is high and overlooks the Fish Hoek glen. The two men met in one of the chambers in the middle reaches of the cave and, with a candle burning on a ledge of rock, they enjoyed a chat about the mountains and the wonders of the caverns. Moore was a Kalk Bay man who knew the area well, and his knowledge stimulated Meyer to learn more about this fascinating place. As a result of his holiday explorations, Meyer was privileged to discover two new caves which he named Central Grotto and Johles Cave, the latter a combination of his own name and that of a companion, Leslie van Blerk. He never forgot the pleasure of these pioneer explorations. In 1935 he retired, a sick man, but he returned to Kalk Bay and made his home there, determined to devote what time he had left to a study of the mountains and to the discovery of more caverns. During the following

ber of the white-walled homes of the Cape owed their smart appearance to the area's lime. The village had its beginning as a simple outspan along the rough coastal track, but in 1806 Abraham Kloppers, who had started trek fishing in Muizenberg, acquired some ground, built a home and started to catch and dry fish as slave rations. A number of the Filipino sailors also settled at Kalk Bay.

In the days before refrigeration, the making of bokkems (kippers), the drying and salting of snoek and other suitable catches was the only means of preserving fish. The harbour is always a busy place, but around June and July, the peak of the snoek season, it is especially bustling. Catches of 40 000 snoek, landed in a single day in this compact little har-

bour, are not uncommon. Fresh fish is sold in the harbour. There are two small tidal pools.

The mountain massif dominating the Muizenberg to Kalk Bay coastal stretch is a superb recreational area for the energetic walker, cave explorer and nature lover. It is like a gigantic rock garden, ingeniously devised by Nature to shelter a vast variety of flowering plants that display their lovely blooms against a background of splendid views across False Bay. There are paths to most places of interest in these mountains.

Above Kalk Bay, named for former lime ('kalk') kilns, is both a flourishing suburb and working harbour.

Opposite Sturdy line-fishing boats harvest the waters of False Bay, and the catch is sold on the jetty.

months he wandered over the heights and the more he explored, the more he found. The exercise and fresh air gave him a new lease on life.

A small band of friends gathered around Meyer, for he was a most amiable companion on the mountains. Knowledgeable, communicative, humorous, he knew many good yarns and was a fine hand at brewing coffee and grilling a chop. Through their activities, Meyer and his friends became known as the Moles. Meyer was recognised as First Mole. A certificate was awarded to his companions who had explored at least the dozen principal caves of the 95 assorted grottoes, caverns, pits and other exciting places that had been discovered and named, most of them by the energetic Meyer.

The pleasure the Moles had in their various outings is reflected in the names: Rest-a-Bit, Light and Gloom, Six Moles Cave, Moss and Diamonds, Drip-Drop, Sunbeam Cave, Noonday Rest, Mirth Parlour and many more. Some of these have vanished from modern maps but most remain, many painted on the rock walls. Countless later visitors have enjoyed pleasant days of adventurous exercise in rediscovering these interesting places.

The heights of this sandstone mass consists of a number of parallel ridges. The ceaseless dripping and washing of water during the wet months of winter has eroded the rocks into curious shapes (such as the remarkable head overlooking Devil's Pit, which resembles that of a latter-day South African prime minister) and modelled numerous caverns. Of these, the most extensive so far found is Ronan's Well, a cave known before Meyer's time but for many years thought to be only 68 m long. Then a modern cave explorer (or speleologist), Michael McAdam, followed a draught of air coming through a narrow crack and, with some difficult scrambling and a tight 2,5 m long squeeze, opened the way into an involved series of underground chambers, halls and crevices stretching for 365 m into the depth of what is known as Ridge Peak and thence out through two other caves, Aladdin and Robin Hood. Ronan's Well is not a cave for a beginner to explore: even the entrance is tricky – a rather sinister-looking grotto with a dark hole 5,5 m up its inner wall, which takes the explorer into the heart of the mountain.

Boomslang Cave, the second most extensive cave so far found is a safe, exciting 146 m passage through the ridge known as Cave Peak. There are several impressive chambers, a 9 m crawl on the northern end, and an impressive southern exit high over Fish Hoek. It was at the pool on the floor of this exit that the original discoverers disturbed a boomslang ('Tree snake') – hence the name. The third largest cave in these mountains was found by Meyer in 1941, and exploring it must have been thrilling. The first entrance he found was a narrow 9,5 m deep pit, and to descend he needed a rope ladder. At the bottom end of the pit the cave stretches out in a succession of passages and chambers for 132 m. At the southeastern end an easier entrance was later found; a 3,6 m deep chimney connected,

Above View from Kalk Bay mountainside, which is riddled with caves. Some may yet be undiscovered.

through a low cavern and a narrow passageway, with Annie's Hall, the first of the large caverns. Meyer, who named several of his cave discoveries after figures in classical mythology, called the whole remarkable cave sequence Oread Hall, after the Oreads, the nymphs of caverns and mountains in Greek legend.

Among the numerous parties which Meyer conducted through the caves was one consisting of twenty lady teachers. Getting them through

the section of Boomslang Cave, where explorers are forced to crawl, must have taken some coaxing, but generally he seems to have enjoyed having women accompany him on explorations. Several of his discoveries carry names of these friends and acquaintances, such as Pollie's Cave, Beatrice Cave, Nellie's Pool and Dolly's Doorway.

The last cave Meyer and his Moles found was a small cavern rather wistfully named Me Too. After that his health deteriorated and, in 195, broke down completely. He recovered partially, made two more climbs and then died of lung cancer on 9 September 1952. He was 78 years old; the mountains had given him the gift of nineteen healthy years during which his diary records 1 700 climbs into the Kalk Bay mountains. Memories of him will linger over the uplands. In later days Jose Burman and S. MacPherson found a cave on the Red Afrikaner Ridge and fittingly named it Meyer's Memorial.

From Kalk Bay the coastal road continues past the entrance to the harbour and curves around the slopes of the mountains. After 1,5 km a fine view of Fish Hoek and its glen is revealed, with (on the northern side) the residential suburb of Clovelly.

FISH HOEK

Fish Hoek is almost unique in Southern Africa. It's a striking example of non-town-planning, and for nearly two centuries it's been 'dry'! The original grant of the farm Vischhoek ('Fish glen') was made by the Governor, Lord Charles Somerset, to Andries Bruins in 1818. There were conditions to this grant. The farm lay directly on the road to the naval station of Simon's Town and some very thirsty sailors on shore leave. The prudent Somerset therefore stipulated that no public wine house be kept on the farm, a condition perpetuated in the township created in 1919. The municipality grew up as one of the country's few teetotaller centres. You could drink in Fish Hoek from your own supplies but, in the absence of bottle stores and bars, the town boasted a minimal crime rate.

Nowadays there are still no liquor outlets but restaurants and sports clubs are licensed.

The place grew up as a residential area connected by railway to Cape Town. Despite its congested and unbeautiful layout, its dismal absence of trees, and its principal commercial street doubling up as the main coastal road carrying heavy traffic to the southern end of the Cape Peninsula, it is a relaxed, self-contained seaside centre with a safe bathing beach.

The glen in which Fish Hoek lies cuts right across the Cape Peninsula. In comparatively recent geological times (Cretaceous: 65-125 million years ago) the sea washed through, leaving the southern portion of the Peninsula an island. The sandy floor of the glen was once the sea bed. In a great rock shelter overlooking its northern side, prehistoric people once lived and dined on marine molluscs, fish and the tidal life which teemed

in the shallow waters below them. The rock shelter became known as the Schildersgat ('Painter's cave') from the rock art left on its walls by the early inhabitants. It is now more generally known as Peers Cave after Victor Peers and his son Bertram, who in 1926 began a painstaking exploration of the place, which yielded the skull of Fish Hoek Man, a representative of the community which inhabited this part of Southern Africa 15 000 years ago, or perhaps even earlier.

Peers Cave may be reached by following the road from Fish Hoek through the glen to the western side of the Peninsula. At 3,5 km from the centre of Fish Hoek, there is a sign indicating the turn-off to the sports ground and to the cave. From the end of this road there is a path through

a forest of Port Jackson trees, then over glistening white sand dunes and up the slopes of the ridge to Peers and to the remarkable Tunnel Cave, in which interesting artefacts have also been found.

The beach at Fish Hoek slopes gently and provides safe swimming. The pleasant Jager Walk winds its way through the rocks at the water's edge. In the beach restaurant there is an interesting memento of the trek fishermen of yesteryear: the 19th century Filipino fishermen who started the industry. The first boat they used, the *Bonita*, was overturned in a False Bay

Above left Trek fishermen and passersby discuss prospects on the wide expanse of Fish Hoek beach.

storm and the crew were drowned. The prow of the boat now stands as the centrepiece of the restaurant, a mute memorial to a sad tragedy, kept in a place that specialises in seafood.

SIMON'S TOWN

From Fish Hoek, the main road passes the small residential area of Glencairn, a kilometre beyond which is the Dido Valley Road turn-off. A short way along this road is Topstones, more familiar to Capetonians and visitors as The Scratch Patch, the world's largest gemstone-tumbling factory. It has interesting origins: in 1967 Bruce Baines finished his training as a lawyer in Cape Town, but decided not to enter practice. His interest lay in gemstones and in the creation of beautiful things. He went to London and established a gemstone manufacturing and distributing business.

Then fate took a hand in the game. Bruce secured a contract to provide Mobil Europe with 40 million gemstones for use in a free-gift promotional scheme in garages. To produce these Bruce, his brother and two other partners had to set up a factory. The contract called for the gemstones known as tiger's eye to be a substantial part of the 40 million stones. Tiger's eye is of South African origin, and a law forbade its export in unfinished form. There had to be a tumbling plant in South Africa, and Simon's Town was the choice.

Such was the beginning of Topstones. Since its creation countless thousands of beautiful gemstones have been tumbled, polished and mounted in the factory. Outside there is a treasure-hunter's delight, a patch where fossickers have a real chance of finding all manners of lovely things amongst thousands of fragments of gemstones. The Scratch Patch also has a branch at the Waterfront.

The main coastal road, after another kilometre, reaches Simon's Town, spectacularly situated beneath a 678 m high ridge of mountains. Governor

Simon van der Stel recommended its development, in 1687, as an alternative winter sanctuary to Table Bay, which was exposed to northwesterly storms, and it was named Simon's Bay in his honour. A wooden pier, barracks and two small forts were built in 1743, and in 1814 it became a naval base for the British South Atlantic Squadron. Substantial workshops and a dry dock were constructed , and it is from this time that Simon's Town, with its narrow, twisting streets, acquired something of the special naval atmosphere of a small English seafaring centre. The handsome Admiralty House, which had initially done duty as lodgings, was taken over by the British as the residence of the Commander-in-Chief. The South African Navy assumed control of the naval base in 1957.

Simon's Town is the home port for over 200 private ocean-going yachts and power boats, many used by their owners to pursue big game-fish (tunny and marlin) during the summer season off the Cape of Good Hope. The False Bay Yacht Club, which incorporates the South African Marlin and Tuna Club, has its quarters close to the harbour. The South African record bluefin tunny stands at 361 kg, and was caught by Brian Cohen in December 1968.

Simon's Town is the terminus of the suburban railway from Cape Town, and a stroll down the main street is a rewarding experience: like Muizenberg, it has its Historic Mile of period buildings and heritage sites. The Simon's Town Museum, in the original Residency used by the Governor on his periodic visits, contains a varied collection of intrguing relics from Simon's Town's past. One section is devoted to the celebrated dog 'Just Nuisance', who was a great friend of the British sailors during the Second World War. He died in Simon's Town in April 1944 at the age of just seven and is buried above the town. A bronze memorial to him stands in Jubilee Square in the centre of the town, where he often helped collect money for charity. The original police cells, including a 'black hole' (punishment cell), are in the museum's basement. Next door is the South African Naval Museum, where you can see ship models, a hands-on operations room, the bridge of a submarine and of a minesweeper.

Another interesting building is the Martello Tower, built in 1796 by the British who, after seizing the Cape, needed to guard it against possible invasion by Napoleon's forces. The tower was a copy of a French fortification which had caused the British no little grief when, in 1794, they set out to capture the bay of Florenzo in Corsica as a base for their blockade of port of Toulon. The British had never encountered such a fortification. It was deceptively simple, just a circular tower of stone garrisoned by two grenadiers, twenty seamen and armed with two cannon. Two British warships were soundly repelled by the fortification, which stood on Cape Mortella. The two ships were severely damaged before the disgruntled British withdrew from the resolute little fort. It took a land attack, launched the next morning, to subdue the tower, and then only by smoking the defenders out by setting fire to damp wood piled around the sides.

The Martello Tower stands on naval property but may be visited by arrangement. A stone wall with a gate surrounds the tower. On the slopes overlooking Simon's Town stand several historic old gun batteries, including the Scala Battery of three 9,2 inch (23,2 cm) calibre guns, capable of firing a projectile for nearly 40 km. Even older is the Zoutman Battery with a 9 inch (22,8 cm) muzzle-loading gun built in 1890. Numerous ruins of old fortifications can be seen.

THE ROAD SOUTH

The main coastal road leaves Simon's Town (and the last petrol point for 55 km) and continues to the end of the Peninsula along a stretch of coast that is best described as one long ocean playground. Here are delectable

Left A colony of endemic African (previously Jackass) penguins at home on the beach at Boulders.
Opposite Simon's Town was fondly known as 'Snoekie' by the Royal Navy, which occupied it from 1814 until 1957.

little bathing places such as Seaforth and Boulders, which are sheltered from the winds of summer. Seaforth was named by an early settler, Captain Harington, whose wife was a niece of the Earl of Seaforth.

A pathway links Seaforth to Boulders, where a protected colony of penguins lives among the gigantic granite boulders and mixes on sociable terms with human beings. Other delightful bathing places in this area include Windmill Beach, Water's Edge Beach, Fisherman's Beach, Foxy Beach and Froggy Pond.

Above A profusion of flowering fynbos covers the windswept flats near Cape Point.

The highlight of this stretch of coast comes 8 km from Simon's Town, at Miller's Point. In 1828 this beautiful locality was acquired by Edmund Miller, who built a seaside cottage there called Elsemere. Until 1850 his family had the whole place to themselves and he conducted whaling operations in False Bay, mainly during the winter months when female southern rights and humpback or fin whales habitually come into False Bay to calve. Then the estate passed into other hands. Today Miller's Point is a fine public coastal resort. In this superb setting, the then Cape Divisional Council imaginatively created a caravan park, with vehicles deployed on terraces that enjoy a view of sea and distant mountains which no luxury hotel could surpass. Playgrounds, boat-launching facilities, a restaurant, a large tidal swimming-pool, green lawns, innumerable picnic spots and a profusion of wild flowers are among the attractions of this recreational area. For the canoeist and underwater swimmer there is a glorious garden beneath the ocean, with anemones and sea urchins of brilliant hues set in waving forests of seaweed, among which shoals of lively fish wander like butterflies in a magical world.

From Miller's Point the road continues south along the coast for a further 5 km, passing many picnic spots and viewsites until, gaining steadily in height, it climbs diagonally along the cliffs 91 m above the bay known as Smitswinkel ('The blacksmith's shop'), a name suggested by a pair of rocks in the sea, one shaped like an anvil, the other like a bellows. Smitswinkel Bay is a favourite fishing spot, with a cluster of informal shacks built on the water's edge, where their owners enjoy a happy privacy. Troops of baboons frequent this portion of the road. Human visitors are warned that it is an offence to feed wild animals. Baboons are amusing to watch but they can become nasty if they are tempted to climb onto cars by handouts of food.

The road now swings away from the coast, and after 8 km reaches a junction with a turn-off to the left, taking the traveller for the final 13 km southwards to Cape Point. This final stretch leads through the Cape of Good Hope Nature Reserve.

THE CAPE OF GOOD HOPE

A visit to the Cape of Good Hope Nature Reserve at the tip of the Peninsula makes a most fascinating outing. The area has excellent roads and is easily accessible at all seasons of the year. The summer months (November to March) are inclined to be windy. The winter months (May to August) are pleasant, as the rainfall is hardly sufficient to disturb visitors for more than a few days each year. Spring (September and October), when the countryside is strewn with wild flowers, is particularly lovely.

Top Engagingly human-like baboons may also be vicious and resentful. Do not feed!

Walking trails lead to many pleasant and secluded places. At Buffel's Bay and Bordjiesrif there are enclosed tidal swimming-pools and at Buffel's Bay a launching ramp for boats. Other amenities include picnic spots and a field museum. Most tourists to the region visit the reserve. The end of the road at Cape Point, in fact, is one of the most famous coach terminuses in the world.

At this stage it is perhaps appropriate to clarify a persistent controversy about the waters washing the two sides of the Peninsula. Are they those of the Indian Ocean or those of the Atlantic Ocean? In actual fact the sea knows no oceans. Man, for the sake of geographical convenience, has applied a variety of names to portions of the sea, but the straight lines he draws between them are just as imaginary as the thread stretched across the lens of a telescope by sailors and shown as the equator to gullible passengers when they first cross the famous 'line'.

The sea knows only the differences of temperature and currents in its various parts, and these are the decisive influences affecting all forms of marine life. When the first sailors came down the west coast searching for an end to Africa and a sea route to the east, they discovered that the peninsula of the Cape of Good Hope was the most southwesterly point. It was not the most southerly point – that is Cape Agulhas, 170 km eastwards – but it was to them the most important, for on doubling it, they not only began the great swing eastwards, but changes in water temperature and marine life confirmed that they were entering a new world. No such significant changes were discernible on either side of Cape Agulhas at any season of the year. It was the Cape of Good Hope, which marked the blending of the cultures and life forms of East and West. It is here that two powerful currents of this part of the sea – the warm Mozambique-Agulhas coming down the east coast and the cold Antarctic Drift which forms the Benguela Current running up the west coast of Africa – have their collision course. The warm waters of the east finally lose themselves, but by their pressure ensure that the cold waters sweep on up the west coast and do not penetrate eastwards.

Few fish or other forms of marine life can tolerate a temperature change of 5°C or more in water. To the warm-water Indo-Pacific species living on the east side of Africa, and the cold-water species living on the southwest side, the difference between the two currents provides a barrier as impenetrable as a garden wall.

The Cape of Good Hope is always the beacon. It is one of the great landmarks of the world, proclaiming that this is where the two halves of the globe, East and West, merge; where two ways of life have their frontiers and blend with the culture of the great dividing continent of Africa. It

Opposite The old Cape Point lighthouse was replaced by another, closer to sea level.

is here that two major ocean currents, each with an enormous influence on all forms of life, climate and scenery in their proximity, have a rendezvous and, simultaneously, a parting of the ways.

Luis de Camões, the poet genius of Portugal, tells of the legendary origin of the Cape Peninsula in the majestic verse of his *Lusiads*. The monstrous Adamastor ('The untamed') was one of the 100 giants who rebelled against the gods of ancient Greece and attempted to take Mount Olympus by storm. Defeated by Hercules and Vulcan at the head of all the gods, the giants were condemned to eternal punishment. They were banished to the far places of Earth and buried under volcanoes and mountains.

Adamastor, the personification of the perceived barbarism of ancient Africa, was consigned to a special transmutation. It is his body 'turned to rocks all rough and strange' which forms the peninsula of the Cape of Good Hope. His spirit forever haunts this tomb. With Table Mountain as his workshop for storms and thunderbolts, he roams the surrounding seas in the form of howling gales and dark storm-clouds, roaring dire vengeance on the sailors who disturb his seclusion. The pioneer Portuguese explorers were the sailors who first dared Adamastor's rage. The vengeance which he cursed upon them persists, as may be seen in the strange tale of the *Flying Dutchman*.

THE STORY OF THE CAPE

Apart from leaving a few middens, prehistoric human beings played no significant part in the story of the Cape Peninsula. Their ancient garbage dumps may still be seen at places such as Batsata Cove, Cape Maclear, Bonteberg and Rooikrans, where there was some natural shelter from the winds and where drinking-water was available from springs.

Early human beings in these areas collected shellfish and lobsters, caught various fish species, foraged for bulbs, roots and edible vegetation, and hunted and trapped game in close competition with other resident predators, such as the now-extinct Cape lion and the lynx. There were probably not many game animals.

The winds of the Cape Peninsula made life unpleasant for the larger mammals and the absence in the soil of such essentials to their welfare as copper traces made the grazing unpalatable. Migrating animals which wandered about at will could visit the area seasonally but leave when they tired of the winds and poor grazing. Such migrants could have included Cape buffalo, elephant, black rhino and various antelope. Baboons were always present. They are today a source of amusement to all visitors and of interest to scientists in that they scavenge the beaches in search of sea foods in similar manner to prehistoric humans.

Opposite 'The Fairest Cape' with the cold Atlantic Ocean in the foreground, and False Bay in the distance.

Bird life was varied, with about 150 species resident at different seasons of the year. A variety of sea-birds was always the principal feature. Jackass penguins (now renamed African penguins) landed on the beaches, while albatrosses, giant petrels, gannets, black-backed gulls, Hartlaub's gulls and cormorants were all common around the coast. Of the land birds, the malachite and orange-breasted sunbirds were the most striking.

In the surrounding sea, Cape sea-lions, whales, porpoises, sharks, tunny, yellowtail and snoek were in abundance. On land, tortoises have always been common. The Cape of Good Hope Nature Reserve is, in fact, one of their great breeding grounds. A few Cape cobras, boomslangs, puffadders and other snakes also made their homes in the southern Peninsula.

The modern history of the Cape of Good Hope began in a howling gale, which blew in the last three weeks of January 1488 and which concealed, according to Luis de Camões, the sullen fury of the giant Adamastor. Down the west coast, probing, searching for the end of Africa, came the Portuguese explorer Bartholomeu Dias in a cramped cockleshell of a ship with a sick and frightened crew.

On 6 January 1488, off the southwest coast, they saw the lovely Cederberg range and named it 'Mountains of the Three Magi Kings'. Then another storm enveloped them. The tiny ship was blown far from land, with Dias pitting his own resolution against the full force of Nature. At last, as the storm abated, the sailors looked for land to the east, but found nothing save the swirling sea. The ship swung northwards. In the storm they had unknowingly rounded the tip of Africa. Only on 3 February 1488 did they reach land at what is now known as Mossel Bay. The unseen cape around which they had found their way they named the Cabo Tormentoso (Cape of Storms).

Dias sailed on, with his crew in a mutinous and sulky mood but beyond Algoa Bay, off the mouth of the Chalumna River, they were forced to turn back, leaving a stone pillar erected on a lonely headland known as the 'Rock of the Fountains'. At least the weather was fine, however. Keeping close to the coast, they discovered Cape Agulhas, naming it 'Cape St Brendan', as it was on the feast day of St Brendan (16 May), that they passed it.

A few days later they passed Cape Hangklip, looked into the spacious and lovely 'Gulf Within the Mountains' (False Bay); and then, in fair and gentle weather at last, the Portuguese historian Barros wrote, 'they beheld that great and remarkable Cape hidden for so many centuries, which when discovered revealed not itself alone, but another world of lands'. To this the Portuguese king eventually gave the new name Cape of Good Hope (applied to the whole cape, not simply to one point upon it). Dias spent a month anchored somewhere off its shores, resting his crew, writing his reports and perfecting a map of his voyage. Then, leaving

another stone cross (no trace of which has ever been found despite dedicated searching), he sailed for home.

In the renaming of the Cape of Good Hope, Dias conveniently forgot his earlier 'Cape of Storms', but it – and the vengeance of Adamastor – did not forget him. In 1500 he once again set out to double the Cape of Good Hope. Again he encountered a terrible storm and this time his ship and a companion vessel were overwhelmed. They both lie somewhere in the deep waters of the southern sea. Legend has it that in this disaster Adamastor had his revenge; and so the tale arose of a phantom sea captain and his ship, condemned forever in his attempt to round the Cape of Good Hope, but always frustrated by violent storms. The nationality of the unfortunate individual has varied with the telling through the years. Wagner, in his opera *The Flying Dutchman*, favoured the Dutch version, with Captain Van der Decken as the central character whose fate was redeemed by the constancy of a woman. But fundamentally the tale is rooted in the curse of Adamastor's fury and his vengeance on Bartholomeu Dias. This feud continues forever. It is in fact astonishing how many sailors navigating these waters have made serious reports about a sighting of the phantom ship. It is the world's most famous ghost story.

Since the time of its discovery, the Cape of Good Hope has remained a point of great interest to all voyagers. East- and west-bound travellers alike regard it as the half-way mark on their journreys. To double it in a storm is an achievement comparable to doubling Cape Horn. To sail around it in fair weather is a delightful experience. From the tiny 100 ton *Golden Hind*, Sir Francis Drake in the course of his round-the-world odyssey (1577 to 1580) saw it. In his log it is described as 'the fairest cape and the most stately thing we saw in the whole circumference of the globe'. Few disagree with this description.

A LIGHT IN THE DARKNESS

In the early years the southern part of the Peninsula was a windswept wilderness of wild flowers. A few fishermen and runaways from justice occasionally made their way down to the tip of the Cape, but there were no roads and no settlement in the area until the first quarter of the 19th century, when the British took control of the Cape and Simon's Town was developed as a naval base.

Farms were then allocated in the area. But nothing was done about a lighthouse for some years, although the need for a beacon became increasingly urgent as the volume of shipping around the Cape increased. In 1823 the coastline was properly surveyed by Royal Navy chartists, among them a Captain Owen, and names were given to the various rocks,

Opposite Dias Beach is named for an early explorer who sailed around the Cape.

including Bellows (the dangerous outlying rock, always covered in foam), Anvil, Whittle (in False Bay) and Dias Reef. Captain Owen, incidentally, also reported sighting the *Flying Dutchman*.

The first lighthouse, a prefabricated iron tower painted white with a red top, was erected in 1859 on Da Gama peak, the summit of Cape Point, 249 m above sea-level. Made by the Victoria Foundry Company in England, this was 9 m high with a 2 000 candlepower flashing light. The first lighthouse keepers soon found that their lamp was too high. When the mists swept in, the light was often well above the clouds and quite invisible to any shipping. This created a dangerous situation, but for some time nothing was done to rectify matters.

A few farmers had established themselves on land in the southern Peninsula, but little is remembered of them. With bad roads, thin soil and incessant wind, they were forced to live on a subsistence economy. Horses, however, flourished in the area. The farmers managed to grow some barley and wheat. Milk and vegetables were produced for the shipping at Simon's Town. A few homesteads were built of local sandstone cemented with lime made from shells in the kilns at Buffel's Bay and Bordjiesrif. Remnants of the homesteads may still be seen, but memories of the personalities who lived in them and the events which took place have long since been blown away with the winds.

Occasionally a shipwreck occurred somewhere around the coast, and there were sightings of the *Flying Dutchman*. One of the most famous of these was logged in 1881 by the future King George V when he was a midshipman on HMS *Bacchante*. The lighthouse keepers also reported sightings of odd vessels, with all sails set even in the worst weather, persistently trying to double the Cape. Even the coming of steamships did not end these tales of sea ghosts.

On the night of 18 April 1911 a major disaster occurred when the 5 557 ton Portuguese liner *Lusitania* struck Bellows Rock. The lighthouse of Cape Point was completely obscured by the mist. The ship was a total loss, although fortunately only four out of the 774 people aboard were drowned. This disaster tragically emphasised the urgency of a change to the lighthouse. It was recorded that in some years the light was obscured by mist for as much as 900 hours. This was an intolerable situation.

A new site was selected lower down on the tip of Cape Point, only 87 m above the sea and overlooking the strange column known as Dias Rock, which stands guard there as though watching eternally for a return of Dias's vanished ship. On 25 April 1914 the foundation was laid for the new lighthouse and in due course a 500 000 candlepower paraffin lamp installed. In 1936 this lamp was converted to electricity, with a giant reflector and lens providing 19 000 000 candlepower, making the lighthouse the most powerful in the world. This light was later reduced to 10 000 000 candlepower provided by a 1,5 kw lamp.

The light at Cape Point can justly be described as one of the greatest shipping beacons in the world. Countless sailors have been guided by its tremendous beam. The giant tankers which make their way around the Cape, rusty freighters, trim ocean liners, pugnacious warships, sneaky submarines on the prowl – all regard it as a massive landmark. During the Second World War German U-Boats lurked by day beneath the waters and by night lay on the restless surface just beyond the beam of light, waiting patiently for prey.

Several of these nocturnal prowlers reported sightings of the *Flying Dutchman*. Just before the war, in early 1939, crowds of holiday makers on False Bay beaches reported a weird-looking battered old sailing-ship making its way towards Muizenberg and then vanishing in a cloud of mist. This intriguing legend persists into modern times. It is a colourful part of the character and romantic atmosphere of the Cape of Good Hope, the commanding presence of which dominates one of the great strategic trade routes of the world.

THE MAKING OF A SANCTUARY

The idea of preserving the southern portion of the Cape Peninsula as a nature reserve originated in 1928, when the whole area was threatened with development – with seaside resorts complete with 'Trespassers will be Prosecuted' signs and forlorn, dilapidated holiday shacks deserted for months at a time.

Fortunately several public-spirited and influential Capetonians became interested in the area. Brian Mansergh, a Cape Town architect, had known it since his youth and had often discussed its conservation with local farmers. In November 1928 he wrote to the Minister of Lands, pleading for the establishment of a nature reserve. His plea was rejected on the grounds of cost. Mansergh continued to promote the idea of a reserve, supported by a number of friends, who gathered for a weekly informal lunch during which they discussed affairs in general and the southern tip of the Peninsula in particular. News of the formation of a syndicate to develop townships in the area particularly disturbed them. A patient spell of propaganda and some systematic agitation followed. Dr Stacy Skaife, Dr Leonard Gill, Anthony Leyds and Henry Hope concentrated on arousing public interest. The key property in the area was Smith's Farm, owned by Norman Smith and his family. This was actually the farm Buffelsfontein or Uiterstehoek, originally granted to John Osmond, extending across the end of the Peninsula. The Smith family was approached. They approved the idea of conservation and agreed to sell to the conservationists rather than to the land speculators.

The City Council was then approached, but the area was well outside their boundaries and individual councillors were not enthusiastic. One of them, A.Z. Berman, summed up resistance to the idea by stating flatly that

he would be against spending council money on an area where 'there was not enough vegetation to keep a scorpion alive'. Another councillor described it as 'wasteland, waterless and treeless'.

The enthusiasts were not dismayed. They started to make plans for raising the money to buy Smith's Farm, fence it in, and make it pay for its maintenance as a nature reserve by erecting a toll-gate on the road leading across it to the lighthouse and to resorts such as Buffel's Bay and the famous fishing ledges at Rooikrans, places much frequented by visitors.

At this stage Will and Percy Hare, owners of the farm Bloubergvlei, which was also in the area, offered their property to the projected nature reserve – provided that it would be maintained as a wilderness and that they would be allowed to live undisturbed in their seaside cottage at Brightwater, and that no road would ever be built across what had been their land. The whole concept of a nature reserve gained in stature. The Simon's Town municipality supported the idea. Its mayor, L.C. Gay, was particularly enthusiastic. The local morning newspaper, the *Cape Times*, gave it considerable editorial support. One memorable leader (23 November 1938) was amusingly specific: 'It seems almost treasonable to this stately peninsula of ours to think that its extreme end, now the only unspoilt part of our heritage, should fall into the hands of men who will cause it to pimple into a bungaloid acne'.

The City Council, however, remained hostile, although a poll of the people of Cape Town revealed overwhelming support. Charles Duminy, chairman of the Divisional Council of the Cape, and Jerwyn Owen, its secretary, had fortunately also been interested in the project for some time. They put it to their council and the idea was at last officially accepted. On 11 April 1939, a special meeting approved the purchase of Smith's Farm. The Cape of Good Hope Nature Reserve came into being, with the specific object of preserving for all time the 'fairest Cape' in the state in which it must have been seen by Bartholomeu Dias and Sir Francis Drake. Norman Smith was appointed first warden with £250 a year as salary and free occupation of his farmhouse.

The Divisional Council spent £16 000 in purchasing Smith's Farm with its homestead and three privately owned bungalows. Crown land was added by the State. In 1941 the farms Olifantsbos, Theefontein and Krommerivier were bought from the estate of D.C. de Villiers, as well as the Minicki family farm, Klaasjagers. Other land was acquired to consolidate the area. The last property to be purchased (in 1965) was a portion of Wildschutsbrand, owned by Mrs Jacoba Malherbe. This farm had been the first to be granted in the southern Peninsula – originally (in the 1660s) it had been the home of the first field-cornet, or district officer, appointed over the area. The homesteads of all these farms have vanished, including, unfortunately, the one known locally as Die Spookhuis ('The haunted house'), a building with quite a number of tales about its unorthodox residents.

With this acquisition, the Cape of Good Hope Nature Reserve attained its present dimension of 7 750 ha, obtained by the Divisional Council of the Cape at a total cost of £63 500. Completely protected and carefully maintained, it is a scenic and botanical delight. Game animals of the type which once roamed freely over the Southern Cape (eland, bontebok, hartebeest and mountain zebra) have been re-introduced. These, together with descendants of the indigenous population of grey rhebok, grysbok, steenbok, baboons, marine life, over 1 200 species of birds, dassies, tortoises (especially the Cape angulated tortoise) and other small wild creatures, live their natural lives in a setting which is peaceful, beautiful, and quite unique.

The original homestead of Smith's Farm was converted into a restaurant and gift shop to cater for an increasing stream of visitors. In 1994 the number of annual visitors reached 443 500. To cope with such numbers, a lease agreement was negotiated in 1995 with Concor Holdings (Pty) Limited for the self-financed construction and management of a modern complex of buildings and also the construction of a funicular railway to convey visitors from the road terminus to the viewsite on the summit of Cape Point. At the end of this lease, the ownership of this complex, including a restaurant, gift shop, information centre and funicular railway, reverts back to the Cape Metropolitan Council. The funicular track is 585 metres long and ascends 230 metres. The two coaches each have a capacity of 40 passengers and take three minutes to complete the journey. They replace a bus known as the *Flying Dutchman* which originally provided a service for those disinclined to do the walk. Utmost care was

Above The steel tower of Slangkop lighthouse has guided ocean traffic since 1914.

taken to preserve the environment during construction and many restrictions were placed on the developer with regards to the positioning of the funicular track, thus resulting in one of the most unique layouts accommodating varying gradients and curves.

In 1998 the number of visitors exceeded 750 000. It was apparent that a trip to the Cape of Good Hope was becoming an essential part of any tour of South Africa by international visitors.

There is also a good walkway to the summit, with viewsites and resting places en route. The original buildings, including the first lighthouse, have been restored. Since 1978 the South African Council for Scientific and Industrial Research (CSIR) have maintained on the summit an atmospheric trace gas research station with a laboratory, facilities and a 30 m high aluminium mask to provide experimental platforms and stratified air intakes. This facility is managed jointly by the CSIR and the IFU (Frauhofer Institute for Atmospheric Environmental Research) in Germany. It is part of the World Meteorological Organisation Global Atmosphere Watch Network. There are nineteen similar facilities maintained at strategic situations around the world. They keep a close, continuous watch on trace gases in the atmosphere, meteorological conditions and solar radiation.

Altogether the Cape of Good Hope Nature Reserve, with its fauna, flora, spectacular scenery, atmosphere and ongoing activity, is a very worthwhile place to visit and a credit to the staff who maintain it. The reserve forms part of the Cape Peninsula National park.

SCARBOROUGH AND KOMMETJIE

From the turn-off leading into the reserve, the main road commences its journey back to Cape Town up the west coast of the Peninsula. Carvings, crafts and curios are sold by wayside vendors. There are pleasant picnic sites beneath the trees on either side of the road and an ostrich show farm. At 8,5 km towards Cape Town, close to the junction with the road coming from Simon's Town over Red Hill, the farm Perdekloof ('Horse ravine') has been converted into a recreational area with shady trees and green grass, ideal for a picnic.

A further 3 km takes the road past Scarborough, which consists of a cluster of cottages close to the oddly shaped roadside landmark known as Camel Rock. There is a pretty beach. When the wind is not blowing, the picnic and camping sites are pleasant.

For 7,5 km beyond Scarborough the country is wild and bush-covered, with sandy bays such as Witsand ('White sands') and many picnic sites and camping grounds in sheltered places along the way. After 5 km there is a crossroads with a turn-off left which leads to the recreational area of Soetwater ('Sweet water'). A right turn provides a short cut through the housing estate of Ocean View to Fish Hoek. The main road now climbs to reveal a large stretch of coast with tidal pools, the Soetwater park and a

recreational area dominated by the graceful steel tower of Slangkop ('Snake peak') lighthouse.

The road now descends into the pleasant little resort known as Kommetjie ('Little basin'), which takes its name from a natural inlet in the rocks that has been developed into a large tidal pool. This area is a favourite place for surf riders, as is Long Beach, especially in the summer months when the southeaster is blowing. The view north towards Chapman's Peak and Hout Bay is particularly impressive from here. Swimming in the tidal pool is safe and the water is relatively warm.

Holidaymakers discovered the charms of the area, especially fishing and swimming, in the late 1800s. A few shacks were put up to provide more

Above Noordhoek's Long Beach is a great surfing beach when the south-easter blows.

substantial shelter than the milkwood trees, and then the inevitable developer arrived, determined that if the public showed signs of liking the area, they could be induced to buy plots. A company, Kommetjie Estate Ltd, was formed in 1902 by a Cape Town builder and contractor, who had the resort named Kommetjie laid out. A gravel road was built to Fish Hoek, its verges planted with the diverse-coloured flowering gums which make the route so beautiful in spring.

A few of the cottages built in those days still survive. Even a railway was planned, but after 85 years the first train has still to arrive. Visitors come by car through the avenue of flowering gums, with the modern tarmac road following substantially the same route as the original track from Fish Hoek. It is a pleasant and pretty drive.

Apart from fishing, surfing and swimming, attractions in the early days included shipwrecks. Back in May 1900 the *Kakapo* was steered directly on to Long Beach. The ship was brand-new and on its maiden delivery from British builders to New Zealand owners. It was named after the rare species of flightless owl parrot of New Zealand. The reason why the wreck occurred is a little obscure. The weather was fine. The navigator said that a sad error had been made: the Sentinel peak at Hout Bay had been mis-

taken for the Cape of Good Hope. But even if there had been no confusion, a similar sharp turn around the Cape of Good Hope would hardly have taken the ship to New Zealand. Knowing what goes on when crews of ships stop for refreshment in Table Bay, it is a wonder more of them don't end up on Long Beach!

The crew of the *Kakapo* experienced little hardship as a result of the wreck. The ship went straight onto thick sand; the crew jumped over the side and walked away. The vessel couldn't do the same, however, and was left to settle high and dry on that magnificent beach where surfers ride

Above Chapman's Peak Drive – an outstanding scenic coastal drive – will be reopened as a toll road.

the high waves today. The ship was cut down and stripped of its valuables and plates. The ribs, keel and boiler remain to form a picturesque scene, used in modern times as a set in several motion picture films, including *Ryan's Daughter*.

A wreck that attracted very large crowds to the salvage auctions held on the beach was the *Clan Monroe*, which struck the rocks just south of the basin on 2 July 1905. Fortunately the crew were all saved except for one man, a Lascar named Ormel Corsette, who was drowned while being taken ashore in a breeches buoy. He is buried on a sand dune near the Slangkop lighthouse. The ship carried a lethal amount of dynamite and cyanide destined for the mines, but there were other valuables aboard and these were auctioned on the beach.

The Slangkop lighthouse was built in 1914, a twin of the lighthouse on Dassen Island – a graceful steel tower in the classic lighthouse shape. The two towers were made in Britain and shipped out to South Africa in pieces. The Slangkop lighthouse was originally fitted with a lamp of 16 750 000 candlepower, making it the second most powerful on the coast of Africa after Cape Point.

During the Second World War a radar station was built on top of the Slangkop ridge, with a tracking leading to the concrete 'pillbox' buildings. The track can still be followed. As with the walk along the beach to the wreck of the *Kakapo*, the walk up to Slangkop ridge provides a pleasant outing. The wild flowers on the ridge are varied and very beautiful, especially in spring.

The route from the village up the ridge leads past St Joseph's Church in Rubbi Road. This charming little church was erected in 1948 as a memorial to Joseph Rubbi, an Italian builder who lived, worked and died in Kommetjie. The church is notable for its marble and mosaics. Behind it stands a building used as a retreat by Catholic nuns and priests.

North of Kommetjie the road leads, as noted, through an avenue of flowering gums. After 1 km it turns off to the left to the Imhoff Park caravan park and to the beach at Klein Slangkoppunt ('Little snake peak point'), from where there is a good walk up the beach of Chapman's Bay to the wreck of the *Kakapo*, now more than half buried in the sand.

NOORDHOEK AND CHAPMAN'S PEAK

After 7 km the road north reaches the suburb of Sun Valley and a junction with the Ou Kaapse Weg (see page 76). Bear left and you will get to Noordhoek ('North glen'), a rural settlement with two attractive little shopping centres – the Kakapo and Noordhoek Village – shaded by oak trees, and situated just below Chapman's Peak. From the main road a side road turns off through the trees, passes the tea-room and leads down to the beach. When the southeaster blows, there are superb surfing waves at De Hoek ('The corner'), where the beach ends on the steep slopes of

Chapman's Peak. There is some fine walking along the great beach which skirts the bay all the way up to Kommetjie. The name 'Chapman', applied both to the bay and to the dominant peak on the north side, originated on 29 July 1607 when the *Consort*, under Captain David Middleton, anchored off this coast. The master's mate, John Chapman, was sent in a boat to see if there was any anchorage.

In a lovely grove of milkwood and other shady trees there is a secluded cluster of mountainside cottages constructed in what is known as Monkey Valley. Each cottage is different, each has its own character. Each has a superb view of Chapman's Bay with its 8 km long beach. It is a private nature reserve with one of the finest of all forests of the protected milkwood tree permanently defended from the woodcutter's axe. A multitude of birds and a variety of small mammals find sanctuary in it.

The original owner of this 4-ha paradise was an immigrant from the Netherlands named Jan Hesterman. Tradition has it that one day he saw a troop of baboons gambolling up the ravine. Unaware of the difference between baboon and monkey, he called his farm Monkey Valley. In 1988 Monkey Valley was sold by his two sons to Jude Sole, who was enthralled with the beauty of it all, the murmur of the surf and the song of the birds, and determined that this beautiful place should not be defaced by any injudicious property development.

In this way was born the concept of an exclusive resort for a limited number of people sharing the pleasure of living in so sylvan a setting, each having the power to veto further development. Delightfully romantic log tree-houses and thatched brick cottages, all with spectacular views, were built in the forest overlooking the sea. Two private paths lead down to the unspoilt beach. Monkey Valley borders the world-famous Chapman's Peak scenic drive.

For the next 11 km the main road follows one of the world's most spectacular marine drives, cut into the cliffs around the 650 m high Chapman's Peak. This famous scenic road was the brainchild of Sir Frederic de Waal, the same energetic first Administrator of the Cape Province after whom De Waal Drive was named. Stimulated by his enthusiasm, the road was built between 1915 and 1922 and still remains an engineering feat of the first magnitude. It has been a toll road since 2004.

From this road, with its numerous look-out points and picnic places, there are incomparable views back over the great beach of Chapman's Bay and north across the handsome sweep of Hout Bay to the 330 m high Sentinel which looms over the busy fishing harbour. The road itself, for most of its journey around Chapman's Peak, has been cut into the junction line of the Cape granite and the sedimentary Table Mountain sandstone laid down on top of the granite and brilliantly coloured in layers of red, orange and yellow silt, with some dark lines of manganese ore appearing in between the layers.

HOUT BAY

At the end of this great drive the road descends with a grand sweep into the residential and fishing village of Hout Bay. 'Village', however, may be a misnomer: the place has grown enormously in recent years.

Soon after his arrival in the Cape in 1652, Jan van Riebeeck sent a party to explore the bay behind Table Mountain. The explorers found it to be a scenically beautiful, but dangerously exposed for shipping. In the valley there were mountain cypress trees (*Widdringtonia noeliflora*), and from their presence the bay was named Houtbaai ('Wood bay'). Over the years

Above Hout Bay village and harbour are tucked into the Peninsula's mountain chain.

the trees were cut down to supply timber for ships. In 1681 a lease was given over the area, a sawmill built and a wagon track made to the bay over Constantia Nek. A community of woodcutters settled in the area but for some years it remained remote and wild. The last two elephants there were shot in 1689. A few fishermen started to work from the bay, however, and it became regarded as an interesting possible expansion of the settlement at Cape Town.

During the American War of Independence, the French troops who garrisoned the Cape built a battery on the western end of the harbour to defend the place from any possible British invasion. A second battery was built on the eastern side in 1793. Two years later British troops occupied the Cape and built a blockhouse above the eastern battery. In 1804 the

The bronze leopard mounted on the rocks overlooking the bay is the work of the late sculptor, Ivan Mitford-Barberton, who lived in Hout Bay. There are daily launch trips around the bay and to the seals living on Duiker Island, together with sunset cruises to Cape Town and other sea trips on the pleasure launches and sailing craft. There are also some fine walks around Hout Bay, especially that from the harbour over the saddle of land connecting the Sentinel to the mainland. Duiker Island, with its resident population of seals, may be viewed from this walk. From the harbour, too, a disused road climbs steeply to the old radar station built during the Second World War on top of the 653 m high Karbonkelberg. The views are stunning. For the really hardy there is a rough and surprisingly long walk along the coast to Llandudno. With its crevices and hard going, this is a day-long outing, even though it looks short on the map. It is dangerous and should not be undertaken without a guide.

Hout Bay is renowned as the rock lobster capital of the world. During the oppressive apartheid years of sanctions, the place was jocularly proclaimed a 'republic', independent of the rest of South Africa, with its own benign president, an authentic-looking passport, border posts, and a viable economy based on seafoods and the tourists attracted by the excellent eating and the scenic beauty of the area.

Harbours, whatever their size, are fascinating places to visit. There is always something happening. Fishing and pleasure boats glide over waters so rich in reflections that they seem to be in a magical world of their own. Fishermen mingle with visitors strolling along the quays. Seals laze in the waters. Gossiping, squabbling seabirds fly just out of reach, always watchful for the handout of a fragment of food.

The Hout Bay harbour-front emporium of Mariner's Wharf was South Africa's first. Its world-famous fish market is built around the hull of the *Kingfisher*, an original 1940s trawler from the Cape Coast fleet. At the market the delicious local delicacy called snoek and other fish are smoked daily the old-fashioned way, live lobsters crawl around in the seawater tanks, and an incredible range of seafoods is available for the kitchen. The Wharf's own special souvenir wine, in a fish-shaped bottle, is also sold, a unique memento of a visit.

Then there is the excellent Wharfside Grill Restaurant with its private dining cabins displaying fascinating relics from ocean liners such as the *Queen Mary*, ships of the Union Castle Line and the Navy. The Grill is regarded as one of Africa's top seafood restaurants. Expect to get a glimpse of the rich and famous here – it has hosted celebrities from the likes of German Chancellor Helmut Kohl and Archbishop Desmond Tutu to royalty, sportspersons and filmstars.

There are also bars serving the grogs so beloved to seafarers from the days of yore. A restaurant, right in the water's edge, is also memorable and is known for the casual seafood and the singing of sea shanties.

Batavian administration also contributed to these varied military features with a battery. The ruins of these various structures still stand. A particularly beautiful architectural survival from this period is the homestead of Kronendal farm, built in 1800 in the Cape Dutch style and now a national heritage site. It houses a restaurant.

The Hout Bay fishing industry really started around 1867 when a German immigrant, Jacob Trautman, began catching and salting snoek to export to faraway places such as Mauritius. The presence in the area of vast numbers of rock lobsters was also noticed. In 1903 the hulk of a

Above The World of Birds is a busy and fascinating refuge for over 4 000 birds and a constant flow of visitors.

British barge, wrecked at Mouille Point, was bought, towed to Hout Bay and beached. It had been converted into a processing and canning factory before being towed to Hout Bay, and it continued as a factory until 1914, when an explosion in its refrigeration chamber killed seven people. The remnants of the hulk survived until after the Second World War, when they were removed to make way for the substantial fishing harbour and two large shore factories.

A museum in the village displays interesting exhibits on the history of Hout Bay, including such early activities as manganese mining, conducted from the 1880s until 1909. The ore was sent down a chute to a jetty, part of which is still standing. Guided walks to places of natural or historical importance are organised by the museum.

The Mariner's Chest, Shell, Shipwreck and Artifact Coves are where thousands of shells, ephemera and relics of shipwrecks gathered from the world's oceans are on sale; along with handmade sea-art, marine antiques, scrimshaw, nautical books, paintings, brassware and all kinds of fascinating fishing memorabilia.

Fish and chips are, inevitably, a speciality of the area. Alfresco meals on the quayside or on the upstairs decks offer great views of the surrounding bay and a beckoning harbour. Seabirds are always in attendance, approving companions to a pleasant way of satisfying appetites aroused by the ambiance and scenic settings.

Stanley Dorman is the man who created Mariner's Wharf. Coming from a family which settled in Hout Bay in the 1890s, he was prominent in and an integral part of the Hout Bay fishing industry for over 30 years prior to establishing South Africa's first harbourfront emporium, Mariner's Wharf. The beginnings were humble: way back in the 1970s he and his wife Pam started by selling smoked snoek over weekends from a makeshift kiosk outside their small factory. .

Stanley Dorman's enthusiasm for all things related to the sea permeates the whole enterprise. In the nearby village he created a craft village, aptly named Fisherman's World, where he re-ereced and rehabilitated its old fishermen's cottages, and even character buildings such as the original post office and the old gaol. A themed section devoted to the crafts, and special skills of fisherfolk, such as net-making and shipwrighting, encompasses the lifestyle and tools of trade of a traditional coastal community. Look out for the half boat on the rocks alongside the Main Road – preserved as a landmark for prosperity, in similar style to what Stanley has done in elevating old fishing boats into the roofline at Mariner's Wharf. This is his personal tribute to the fishing families whose home has been Hout Bay for over one hundred years. Their forefathers loved the quaint harbour as a sanctuary, long before the advent of today's suburban sprawl, when the village was still a distant outpost in Cape Town's countryside. A lovely grove of historical milkwood trees has likewise been thoughtfully preserved behind the attractive Mainstream Shopping Centre.

Immediately out of Hout Bay village the marine drive reaches a junction with the road which comes down through the shady avenues of oaks from Constantia Nek. The main road veers left, bridges the course of the Hout Bay River, also known as the Disa River, makes its way through an avenue of plane trees and then reaches a junction where a short road branches off left and leads to the fishing harbour.

THE WORLD OF BIRDS

On the right-hand side of Hout Bay's Valley Road is the World of Birds wildlife sanctuary, acknowledged to be the largest bird park in Africa, and the creation of Walter Mangold.

Dedicated to wildlife, Walter Mangold acquired land in Hout Bay and began breeding birds but, in 1974, was obliged to go into liquidation. He lost his land but kept his beloved birds. With no transport except a wheelbarrow, he moved his remaining possessions, birds and cages, to the new site lose, and it took a full year of labour to get the venture going, a year spent struggling to feed the birds, to pay innumerable bills. Then one night dogs broke into the cages and killed or maimed three quarters of the birds – a devastating and almost final blow. Only the kindness of neighbours gave him the strength to continue with his dream. They erected a

Above Owls, wide-eyed and alert, represent the nightlife at World of Birds, where activity is unending.

security fence for him and in its protection he worked long days and nights building cages and creating the substantial basis of the present World of Birds.

The setting is lush. Squirrel monkeys play with visitors, delightful families of meerkats pose for photos like slightly disapproving Victorians. The birds are elegant – black swans in pensive mood, solemn secretary birds apparently talking about money and management matters in the green forest. The aviaries are so large that visitors can walk freely through them, mingling with the inmates in a landscaped garden setting. Over 3 500 birds of 450 different species, South African and exotic, can be seen there along with a community of little mammals. Many of the birds are free to come and go as they please.

VICTORIA DRIVE

The main road veers sharp right as it leaves the Hout Bay valley and climbs the slopes of the 436 m high mountain known, from pronounced similarities in shape to Lion's Head overlooking Cape Town, as Little Lion's Head. To the right there are fine views of the valley of the Hout Bay River, while silver trees and many indigenous flowering shrubs adorn the estates on either side of the road.

At its highest point the road passes over the saddle of land connecting Little Lion's Head to the Twelve Apostles (the back of Table Mountain), and an entirely new vista of sea and mountain opens up. Immediately below lies the attractive little beach and residential area of Llandudno. From Llandudno there is a short walk south to Sandy Bay, a secluded nudist beach much liked by sunbathers. The wreck of a tanker, the *Romelia*, lay on the rocks for many years after it came to grief in 1977 while being towed to a scrap-yard in the Far East. The remains now lie in deep water at the base of Sunset Rocks.

Left Sandy Bay was the Peninsula's first 'full nudist' beach, and is reached only after a long trudge through the sand.
Above The white curve of Llandudno Beach offers shelter from the wind, but the sea is cold!.
Opposite The sugarloaf shape of Little Lion's Head overlooks Llandudno and distant Hout Bay.
Overleaf The peaks of the Twelve Apostles, really a face of Table Mountain, rise behind Camps Bay.

CAMPS BAY TO CLIFTON

The main marine drive is known as Victoria Road, for it was completed by Thomas Bain just before Queen Victoria's golden jubilee in 1887. It was a superb engineering feat by a master road builder and his last great work. Three kilometres from the Llandudno turn-off it sweeps around a bend and reveals one of the finest views of the Cape. Across a sparkling stretch of sea, Lion's Head can be seen in its most handsome aspect, with the houses of Camps Bay and Bakoven in pleasingly multicoloured disarray beneath it. The whole stretch of the Twelve Apostles provides a panorama on the right, while on the left the sea rolls in through a mass of granite boulders, with many little coves and inlets frequented by holidaymakers and fishermen.

One of these places, Hottentotshuisie ('Hottentot's shack'), developed over the years into the home of a curious community of permanent cave dwellers. Remnants of the wreck of the coaster *Bluff* lie on the rocks where it ran aground in 1965. Also on the rocks is the skeleton of the tanker *Antipolis*, wrecked in 1977 while being towed, along with the *Romelia*, to the ship-breakers.

Three kilometres along this interesting stretch of coast, the road leads past a path and stairway to the Bellsfontein kramat of the Muslim holy man Nureel Mobeen. It is said that about 13 000 Muslim slaves were buried in the protection of this sacred place, part of the original Oudekraal farm of the Van Bredas. The farmhouse is now the site of a five-star hotel.

The road enters the central suburbs of Cape Town at what is known as Bakoven ('Bake oven') from the shape of a large hollow rock on the coast. This area is now a place of bungalows built down to the water's edge, and through it Victoria Road leads directly into the suburb of Camps Bay. The place was named after Frederick von Kamptz, an invalid sailor who settled in the area in 1778. Camps Bay today is a well-to-do suburb built on the slopes of the Twelve Apostles overlooking a spacious beach, much used by sunbathers and picnickers. There is a large tidal pool and surfers find sport in a nearby cove (Glen Beach), though bathing is usually marred by very cold water and a frequent backwash. Camps Bay is the location of the attractive Theatre on the Bay.

From Camps Bay two roads lead up the slopes of the mountain, join at Kloof Nek and finally enter the city area. One of these, Geneva Drive, branches right from Victoria Road just after it passes the pavilion. The other, Kloof Road, branches right as Victoria Road leaves Camps Bay. This is a pleasant route around the slopes of Lion's Head past the Round House restaurant (an old shooting-box of the British governors), and The Glen picnic area, with fine views of Camps Bay through the trees.

Left The pocket-sized beaches of Clifton, renowned for their bikini beauties and sheltering granite boulders.

Camps Bay ends in a small headland preserved as a scenic and botanical reserve. Beyond this lie Clifton and its famous beaches (First, Second, Third and Fourth), all ideal for sunbathing and displays of feminine pulchritude, the coldness of the Atlantic Ocean providing bikini beauties with an excellent excuse not to swim. Informal (but expensive) little cottages (some not so little) are built on the cliffs overlooking the beach and are today very fashionable places in which to live. Several of these cottages were originally constructed as emergency housing after the First World War, and were regarded as temporary.

At Clifton, Lion's Head is much closer to the sea; and many of the houses along Victoria Road are built on stilts and piles. Roof-top parking is common. Before Bain made his Victoria Road, only a rough path provided a precarious way around the cliffs of what was then known as Skoenmakersgat ('Shoemaker's cave'), after a hermit who lived there and earned a living of sorts as a cobbler.

BANTRY BAY AND SEA POINT

From Clifton, Victoria Road is cut into the cliffs, winds tortuously around a mountain spur and passes through the heavily built-up area of Bantry Bay. Here, groups of apartment buildings cluster at the edge of a turbulent little bay, at the end of which is Sea Point. This suburb is crowded and unplanned with narrow, densely built-up streets. Its principal advantage is a handsome ocean front and some overwhelmingly beautiful sunsets. At the earliest opportunity a traveller should turn left out of Main Road into Beach Road, a far more relaxing route which follows the coast. An almost continuous cliff of expensive but nondescript apartment buildings lines the landward side. Sea Point has long been among Cape Town's most popular residential areas, with a vibrant night life.

Sea Point beachfront is laid out as a promenade with lawns, gardens, the Pavilion and tidal swimming-pools, including Graaff's Pool where men used to swim in the nude (the shoreline is too rocky for comfortable bathing). The pool was originally a quarry from which stone was blasted to provide ballast for the suburban railway which once connected with the city. A concrete causeway carried a trolley from the quarry to the railway line. A variety of hotels and restaurants flourish in the area. The ocean promenade is a favourite walk for people and their dogs taking the air on summer evenings.

The first building in Sea Point was a country club named the Heeren Huis ('Gentlemen's house'), erected in 1766 at the southern end. In front of the site of this long-vanished building there is an exposure of rocks of such great interest to geologists that it is marked by a plaque carrying

Right Sun-drenched Clifton is well sheltered from the summer south-easterly winds that rake the Peninsula.

the following inscription: 'The rocks between this plaque and the sea reveal an impressive contact zone of dark slate with pale intrusive granite. This interesting example of contact between sedimentary and igneous rock was first recorded by Clarke Abel in 1818. Since its discovery it has had an inspiring influence on the historical development of geology. Notable amongst those who have described it is Charles Darwin, who visited it in 1836.'

The suburb of Sea Point ends on its northeastern side at a small inlet known as Three Anchor Bay, after three anchors originally used during the Napoleonic war years to hold a defensive chain across the inlet. It is now used as a base for pleasure craft and the operations of private fishermen.

MOUILLE POINT AND GREEN POINT

From Three Anchor Bay the coast veers northwards for half a kilometre before reaching Green Point, where a lighthouse was built in 1824. From here the coast turns eastwards for a kilometre until it reaches Mouille Point, where it swings southeastwards at the beginning of the shoreline of Table Bay. It was at this point that the Dutch East India Company, between 1743 and 1746, attempted to build a *mouille* (mole or breakwater) to provide shelter for shipping in Table Bay. It was a forlorn effort – there was little money for a project which would have required massive engineering work to allow it to withstand the power of the sea.

Altogether this is a hazardous coast for shipping: misty, gale-swept and the scene of so many wrecks that a lighthouse was built in 1842 on Mouille Point to supplement the light on nearby Green Point and guide shipping entering Table Bay at night. Even with two lighthouses, however, there were still wrecks. The Mouille Point lighthouse was eventually demolished in 1908. The illumination provided by the Green Point lighthouse (often erroneously called the Mouille Point lighthouse) was increased in intensity to 850 000 candlepower and supplied with a deep-voiced foghorn.

On the southeast side of Mouille Point there is a small bay named Granger Bay, once a base for whaling. Then, in 1854, Captain Robert Granger, a merchant and shipping agent, made his home there and started a fishing industry. On a squally evening in February 1857 he saw a small schooner, the *Miner*, capsize as it was leaving Table Bay bound for Hondeklip Bay, and he rowed out alone to the distressed ship, rescuing five people. The remainder were brought to safety by another boat. The people of Cape Town paid formal tribute to Granger's gallantry. In 1964 Granger Bay became the site of the SA Merchant Navy Academy. A spec-

Left On the rocks at Bantry Bay, which was originally named Botany Bay, like the inlet in Australia.
Opposite Bantry Bay seafront under Lion's Head. A corner of Table Mountain is seen in the background.

tacular building development has converted the bay into a marina with luxurious apartments.

The coastal strip known as Mouille Point is simply what used to be called De Waterplaats ('The waterfront') of Green Point, the suburb which adjoins central Cape Town. Green Point Common is a large public area, immediately south of the Mouille Point coast and once a grazing area for the cattle of the Dutch East India Company. Here, In the 1850s the British created a horse-racing track (the grandstand was the area's first building).

Today it is the site of the Metropolitan golf course, the Green Point stadium, tennis courts and athletic track. Nearby are the City Hospital and the New Somerset Hospital (which houses the Cape Medical Museum), and the Fort Wynyard, an artillery battery that protected the anchorage.

Beyond Green Point the main road enters the city area of Cape Town and our circular drive around the Cape Peninsula comes to an end 143 km from where it began at the statue of Jan van Riebeeck, at the foot of the old road named Heerengracht.

Above Sea Point, where flat-dwellers enjoy a sea-front promenade past pocket beaches and tiny pools.

Opposite The attractions of Sea Point make it Cape Town's most densely populated suburb.

Caves and walks on the southern side of the Silver Mine Reserve

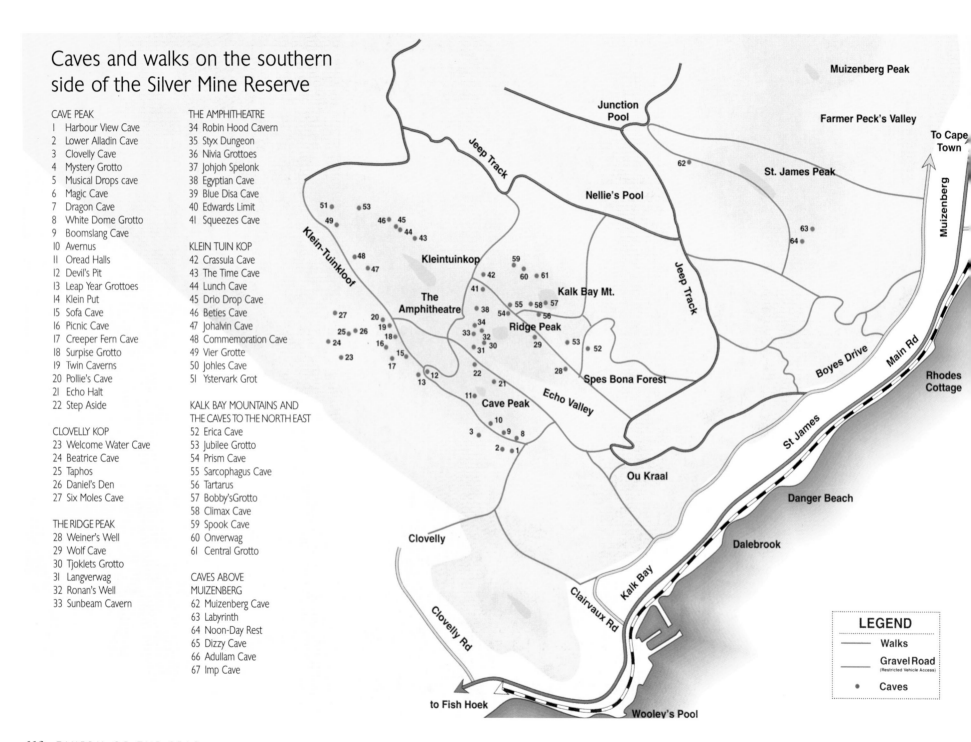

CAVE PEAK
1 Harbour View Cave
2 Lower Alladin Cave
3 Clovelly Cave
4 Mystery Grotto
5 Musical Drops cave
6 Magic Cave
7 Dragon Cave
8 White Dome Grotto
9 Boomslang Cave
10 Avernus
11 Oread Halls
12 Devil's Pit
13 Leap Year Grottoes
14 Klein Put
15 Sofa Cave
16 Picnic Cave
17 Creeper Fern Cave
18 Surpise Grotto
19 Twin Caverns
20 Pollie's Cave
21 Echo Halt
22 Step Aside

CLOVELLY KOP
23 Welcome Water Cave
24 Beatrice Cave
25 Taphos
26 Daniel's Den
27 Six Moles Cave

THE RIDGE PEAK
28 Weiner's Well
29 Wolf Cave
30 Tjoklets Grotto
31 Langverwag
32 Ronan's Well
33 Sunbeam Cavern

THE AMPHITHEATRE
34 Robin Hood Cavern
35 Styx Dungeon
36 Nivia Grottoes
37 Johjoh Spelonk
38 Egyptian Cave
39 Blue Disa Cave
40 Edwards Limit
41 Squeezes Cave

KLEIN TUIN KOP
42 Crassula Cave
43 The Time Cave
44 Lunch Cave
45 Drio Drop Cave
46 Beties Cave
47 Johalvin Cave
48 Commemoration Cave
49 Vier Grotte
50 Johles Cave
51 Ystervark Grot

**KALK BAY MOUNTAINS AND
THE CAVES TO THE NORTH EAST**
52 Erica Cave
53 Jubilee Grotto
54 Prism Cave
55 Sarcophagus Cave
56 Tartarus
57 Bobby'sGrotto
58 Climax Cave
59 Spook Cave
60 Onverwag
61 Central Grotto

**CAVES ABOVE
MUIZENBERG**
62 Muizenberg Cave
63 Labyrinth
64 Noon-Day Rest
65 Dizzy Cave
66 Adullam Cave
67 Imp Cave

Muizenberg Peak

Junction Pool

Farmer Peck's Valley

To Cape Town

Jeep Track

St. James Peak

Nellie's Pool

Muizenberg

Klein-Tuinkloof

Kleintuinkop

The Amphitheatre

Kalk Bay Mt.

Jeep Track

Ridge Peak

Spes Bona Forest

Boyes Drive

Main Rd

Rhodes Cottage

Echo Valley

Cave Peak

St James

Ou Kraal

Danger Beach

Clovelly

Dalebrook

Clairvaux Rd

Kalk Bay

Clovelly Rd

to Fish Hoek

Wooley's Pool

LEGEND
—— Walks
—— Gravel Road (Restricted Vehicle Access)
• Caves

PART 3

Paper 3.5

Strategic Business Planning and Development

ACCA Study Text

ACCA
Approved Publisher

ftc

FTC Foulks Lynch
A **Kaplan Professional** Company

British Library Cataloguing-in-Publication Data

A catalogue record for this book is available from the British Library.

FTC Foulks Lynch
Swift House
Market Place
Wokingham
Berkshire RG40 1AP

ISBN 1 84390 604 X

© The Financial Training Company Ltd, May 2005

Printed and bound in Great Britain by William Clowes Ltd, Beccles, Suffolk

Acknowledgements

We are grateful to the Chartered Institute of Management Accountants, the Association of Chartered Certified Accountants and the Institute of Chartered Accountants in England and Wales for permission to reproduce past examination questions. The answers have been prepared by FTC Foulks Lynch.

Contents

Introduction

This is the FTC Foulks Lynch Study Text for Paper 3.5 *Strategic Business Planning and Development*, and is part of the ACCA series produced for students taking the ACCA examinations.

This new edition, has been produced with direct guidance from the examiner. It covers the syllabus and study guide in great detail, giving appropriate weighting to the various topics. Targeted very closely on the examination, this study text is written in a way that will help you assimilate the information easily. Numerous practice questions and exam-type questions at the end of each chapter reinforce your knowledge.

DEFINITION

- **Definitions.** The text defines key words and concepts, placing them in the margin, with a clear heading, as on the left. The purpose of including these definitions is to focus your attention on the point being covered.

KEY POINT

- **Key points**. In the margin you will see key points at regular intervals. The purpose of these is to summarise concisely the key material being covered.

ACTIVITY 1

- **Activities**. The text involves you in the learning process with a series of activities designed to catch your attention and make you concentrate and respond. The feedback to activities is at the end of each chapter.

SELF-TEST QUESTIONS

- **Self-test questions**. At the end of each chapter there is a series of self-test questions. The purpose of these is to help you revise some of the key elements of the chapter. All the answers to these questions can be found in the text.

EXAM-TYPE QUESTIONS

- **End of chapter questions**. At the end of each chapter we include examination-type questions. These will give you a very good idea of the sort of thing the examiner will ask and will test your understanding of what has been covered.

Syllabus and study guide

Objectives of the study guide

This study guide is designed to help you plan your studies and to provide a more detailed interpretation of the syllabus for Paper 3.5 *Strategic Business Planning and Development*. It contains both the syllabus and the study guide, which you can follow when preparing for the examination.

The syllabus outlines the content of the paper. The study guide takes the syllabus content and expands it into study sessions of similar length. These sessions indicate what the examiner expects of candidates for each part of the syllabus, and therefore gives you guidance in the skills you are expected to demonstrate in the examinations.

Syllabus content

1   MODELS OF STRATEGIC MANAGEMENT

a   What is strategic management?
  i   corporate strategy
  ii   business strategy.

b   Why is strategic management important?

c   The process, content and context of strategic management.

d   Process of strategy development
  i   deliberate or prescriptive strategies
  ii   emergent and incremental strategies.

e   Strategic content
  i   strategic analysis
  ii   strategic choice
  iii   strategic implementation.

f   Strategic management in different contexts
  i   configuration
  ii   culture.

2   EXTERNAL ENVIRONMENTAL SCANNING

a   Analysis of the general environment
  i   SLEPT analysis
  ii   Porter's diamond
  iii   forecasting and scenarios.

b   Analysis of the customers and markets – marketing research.

c   Analysis of the competitive environment
  i   five forces model
  ii   competition and collaboration
  iii   competitor intelligence for business advantage
  iv   sustainable competitive advantage and critical success factors.

3   INTERNAL ASSESSMENT

a   Resource audit.

b   Analysis of capabilities and core competences.

c   Adding competitive value – value chain and value system.

d   Analysis of human resources.

e   Analysis of financial resources.

f   Analysis of operations resources.

4   THE NATURE OF STRATEGY ANALYSIS AND CHOICE

a   The purpose of the organisation
  i   stakeholder expectations
  ii   cultural context
  iii   mission, objectives and strategic intent.

b   Developing the strategy
  i   alternative directions for strategy development
    - resource based
    - market based
    - finance based
  ii   methods of strategy development
    - internal development
    - strategic alliances
    - mergers and acquisitions.

c   Strategy evaluation and selection
  i   analysis of suitability, feasibility and acceptability
  ii   corporate/business strategy selection.

5   THE NATURE OF STRATEGY IMPLEMENTATION

a   Marketing issues
  i   segmentation, targeting and positioning
  ii   strategies for market leaders, followers, challengers and nichers
  iii   development and application of marketing mix strategies.

b   Finance issues
   i   performance evaluation
   ii funding the implementation and the resource allocation.

c   Research and Development issues
   i   management of innovation
   ii management and control of quality.

d   IS/IT issues
   i   IT/IS as a strategic resource.
   Ii the management of information systems development.

e   HR issues
   i   recruitment and selection
   ii motivation and discipline
   iii appraisal and performance evaluation
   iv staff training and development.

f   Project management issues
   i   the project life cycle
   ii objectives of project management
   iii estimation of resource requirements
   iv tools and techniques of project management.

g   Management of change issues
   i   understanding the types of strategic change and their causes
   ii development of a strategic change programme
       • power influence
       • culture influence
   iii management roles in the strategy change process
   iv managing the strategic change process.

6   MATCHING STRUCTURES WITH STRATEGY

a   Types of organisation structures
   i   simple
   ii   functional
   iii divisional
   iv   matrix
   v   multinational
   vi   global
   vii strategic business unit.

b   Centralisation versus decentralisation.

c   Organisational configurations.

7   THE NATURE OF GLOBAL COMPETITION

a   The role of traditional international marketing.

b   The development of the global business
   i   market convergence
   ii   cost advantages
   iii government pressures
   iv   currency volatility and trade barriers
   v   the emergence of global competition.

c   Global strategies
   i   standardisation versus customisation
   ii   product positioning
   iii channel management
   iv   the development of global brands.

d   Managing a global company
   i   ethnocentric, polycentric or geocentric orientation
   ii   cross cultural management and leadership.

e   Reaching global customers
   i   international marketing research
   ii   international market segmentation.

8   OUTCOMES OF THE STRATEGIC MANAGEMENT PROCESS

a   Corporate versus business performance.

b   Sustainable competitive advantage.

c   A learning organisation.

d   Alternative performance measures:
   i   financial
   ii   non-financial
   iii strategic.

9   ETHICAL CONSIDERATIONS

a   The importance of social responsibility.

b   Corporate governance.

c   The attitude towards ethics on national and global scales.

Excluded topics

The syllabus content outlines the area for assessment. No areas of knowledge are specifically excluded from the syllabus.

Key areas of the syllabus

Although all the syllabus will be examined in some form, the core areas will be focused on the strategy formulation process. This comprises the identification of corporate objectives, strategic analysis, including internal and external reviews, strategy development, evaluation and implementation.

Study guide

OVERVIEW OF STRATEGIC MANAGEMENT

1   INTRODUCTION TO STRATEGIC MANAGEMENT   Chapter 1

a   Strategic management defined

   i   corporate strategy

     –   understand the strategic perspective

     –   evaluate the overall purpose and scope

     –   describe the expectations of owners

     –   describe the expectations of stakeholders

     –   explain the concept of added value

   ii   business strategy

     –   be aware of the role of business units

     –   identify market competition

b   The importance of strategic management

   –   define strategy and strategic thinking

   –   differentiate between policy, strategy, tactics

   –   understand the need for a long-term view

   –   define long-term objectives

   –   explain controlling the future

   –   understand long-term efficiency

c   The process, content and context of strategic management

   –   describe the present position of the organisation

   –   understand the external environment

   –   understand the organisation at present

   –   evaluate where does the organisation want to be

   –   demonstrate how is the organisation going to get there

d   The process of strategy development

   –   identify deliberate strategies

   –   identify prescriptive strategies

   –   identify emergent and incremental strategies

   –   understand strategic planning and strategic management

2   THE RATIONAL MODEL   Chapter 2

a   strategic analysis

   i   assess the strategic position

   ii   evaluate expectations and influence of stakeholders

b   strategic choice

   i   define underlying influences which guide strategy

   ii   evaluate strategic options

   iii   understand evaluation and selection procedures

c   strategic implementation

   i   define resource planning

   ii   define corporate strategy

   iii   define business strategy

   iv   define operational and financial strategy

3   STRATEGIC MANAGEMENT IN CONTEXTS   Chapter 2

a   strategic configuration

   i   understand logical incremental model

   ii   understand rational command model

   iii   understand cultural political influences

   iv   understand political choice

4   CULTURE   Chapter 3

a   define the meaning of culture

b   understand the determinants of culture: Schein

c   describe the cultural web: Johnson and Scholes

d   link culture with structure

e   discuss models of culture: Handy, Miles and Snow, Peters and Waterman, Mintzberg

f   understand changing organisational culture: Kanter, Lewin

g   evaluate the link between culture and strategic leadership

h   identify regional and national culture

5   EXTERNAL ENVIRONMENTAL SCANNING   Chapter 4

a   Analysis of the general environment

   i   SLEPT analysis

     –   be aware of the social impact on the organisation

     –   be aware of the legal issues and implications

     –   be aware of the role and influence of the economy

     –   be aware of the political environment

     –   be aware of the impact of technology

     –   be aware of complexity, dynamism and uncertainty

     –   understand systems thinking

     –   analyse the organisation as an open system

     –   understand the focal zone analysis

   ii   Porter's diamond

     –   explain firm strategy, structure and rivalry

     –   explain demand conditions

     –   explain factor conditions

     –   explain related and supporting industries

   iii   forecasting and scenarios

     –   understand strategic life cycles

     –   understand statistical forecasting techniques

     –   understand the Delphi technique

     –   understand scenario planning

6   ANALYSIS OF CUSTOMERS, MARKETS AND MARKETING RESEARCH   Chapter 5

a   Explain aggregate and sectoral concentration

b   Understand customer behaviour

c   Understand the principles of marketing research

d   Explain market research as a component of marketing research

e   Discuss social change and social trends

f   Discuss demographic factors

g   Discuss population size

h   Discuss demographic change

i   Discuss social structure

j   Discuss economic change

k   Analysis of the competitive environment

   i   the five forces model

     –   understand the general model

     –   discuss intensity of rivalry among existing competitors

     –   discuss bargaining power of suppliers

     –   discuss bargaining power of buyers

     –   discuss the threat of new entrants

     –   discuss the threat of substitutes

     –   evaluate the weaknesses of the model

     –   explain the threat of potential entrants

     –   understand the connection with market structure

     –   discuss the role of government and regulation

   ii   competition and collaboration

     –   review government regulation

     –   discuss the competition commission

     –   compare different market environments

     –   discuss cartels, oligopolies

7   COMPETITOR INTELLIGENCE FOR BUSINESS ADVANTAGE   Chapter 6

a   Understand the portfolio analysis approach

b   Describe the Boston Consulting Group model

c   Describe the Shell directional policy matrix/nine cell grid

d   Understand the importance of understanding portfolio analysis

e   Understand the product life cycle

f   Explain competitor benchmarking

g   Explain competitive positioning grid

h   sustainable competitive advantage

   i   define competitive advantage

   ii   explain competitive advantage

   iii   discuss generic strategies (Porter)

   iv   understand different approaches by management

   v   evaluate branding, patents, copyrights and trademarks

   vi   identify national advantage (Porter)

   vii   evaluate the strategic role of the marketing mix

i   critical success factors

   i   define how to measure success

   ii   compare actual and relative success factors

   iii   compare efficiency and effectiveness

   iv   evaluate financial measures

   v   contrast the expectations of stock holders and shareholders

   vi   discuss quality issues

   vii   evaluate success measurement for non profit making organisations

8   INTERNAL ASSESSMENT   Chapter 7

a   Resource audit

   i   identify quality, nature and extent of available resources

   ii   identify physical, human and financial resources

   iii   identify intangible resources

   iv   understand unique resources and competitive advantage

   v   evaluate internal control systems

   vi   analyse departmental organisation

b   Analysis of capabilities and core competences

   i   formulate a SWOT analysis

   ii   interpret a SWOT analysis

   iii   describe the product life cycle

   iv   understand the seven 'S' approach

   v   demonstrate threshold competences

   vi   demonstrate core competences

   vii   identify appropriate markets

   viii   review quality and reliability,

   ix   explain product attributes

9   ADDING COMPETITIVE VALUE   Chapter 8

a   understand the value chain

   i   link the value chain with organisational structure

   ii   explain the value system

   iii   discuss product and market differentiation

   iv   identify sources of differentiation

   v   assess innovation

   vi   understand technical development

   vii   identify new target markets

   viii   identify new distribution channels

   ix   identify new market segments

   x   be aware of sudden environmental shocks

10 HUMAN RESOURCE MANAGEMENT
Chapter 9

a   Analysis of human resources

   i   understand skills and competencies

   ii   discuss workforce adaptability

   iii   assess innovative capability

b   Analysis of operations resources

   i   evaluate the availability of resources

   ii   understand management information and control systems

   iii   understand production control systems

   iv   understand process control

   v   describe resource utilisation and costs

11 FINANCE RESOURCE MANAGEMENT
Chapter 9

a   Analysis of financial resources

   i   understand financial control systems

   ii   understand capital structure

   iii   understand liquidity and gearing

   iv   define the 'balanced scorecard': Kaplan and Norton

PURPOSE OF ORGANISATIONS

12 THE NATURE OF STRATEGY ANALYSIS
Chapter 10

a   stakeholder expectations

   i   understand stakeholder power and influence

   ii   be able to carry out stakeholder mapping: Mendelow

b   the cultural context

   i   identify national and local culture

   ii   understand organisational culture and objectives

13 CORPORATE MISSION AND STRATEGIC OBJECTIVES
Chapter 10

a   mission, objectives and strategic intent

   i   define policy, strategy and tactics

   ii   define strategic vision

   iii   define the mission statement

   iv   define strategic intent: Hamel and Prahalad

   v   define strategic scope

   vi   state implicit and explicit objectives

   vii   evaluate the prime organisational objective

   viii   evaluate the organisation's policy

   ix   understand marginalist theories of organisational objectives

   x   explain the accounting concept of profit

   xi   explain the economist concept of profit

   xii   explain behaviourist theories of organisational

   xiii   identify the expectations of the owners

   xiv   evaluate the role of stakeholders

14 DEVELOPING THE STRATEGY   Chapter 11

a   alternative directions for strategy development evaluate PIMS analysis

   i   understand resource based

   ii   understand product value and development

   iii   explain withdrawal strategy

   iv   explain consolidation strategy

   v   explain market based strategy

   vi   explain market development and extension strategy

   vii   explain market penetration strategy

   viii   explain market positioning strategy

   ix   understand growth vector analysis: Ansoff

   x   define the planning gap

   xi   define finance based strategies

   xii   understand the role of the budgetary process

15 METHODS OF STRATEGY DEVELOPMENT
Chapter 11

a   compare level one and level two strategies

b   evaluate internal development

c   evaluate organic growth: Greiner's growth model

d   analyse joint ventures and strategic alliances

e   review mergers and acquisitions

f   define concentric and conglomerate diversification

g   define forward and backward integration

h   be aware of the problems of diversification and acquisition

16 STRATEGY EVALUATION AND SELECTION
Chapter 12

Analysis of suitability, feasibility and acceptability suitability

a   Suitability

   i   understand life cycle analysis

   ii   understand life cycle/portfolio matrix

   iii   assess resources and competencies

   iv   discuss business profile analysis

   v   understand strategy screening

   vi   be aware of decision trees

b   Feasibility

   i   explain funds flow analysis

   ii   explain break even analysis

   iii   explain resource deployment analysis

c   Acceptability

   i   identify and justify expected performance outcomes

   ii   review profitability analysis

iii   review cost/benefit analysis

iv   review risk analysis

v   evaluate shareholder value

vi   assess expectation of stakeholders

d   corporate and business strategy selection

   i   formulate the role of planning

   ii   carry out a formal evaluation

   iii   analyse enforced choice

   iv   differentiate learning from experience

   v   be aware of dominant stakeholder selection

17 THE NATURE OF STRATEGY IMPLEMENTATION   Chapter 13

a   Marketing issues

   i   segmentation, targeting and positioning

   ii   understand strategic group analysis

   iii   define strategic groups and strategic space

   iv   describe market segmentation analysis

   v   explain segmentation by factor, market or organisation

   vi   describe targeting

   vii   distinguish between product and market positioning

b   Strategies for market leaders, followers, challengers and nichers

   i   understand the strategic clock: Bowman

   ii   understand the market options matrix

   iii   understand price based strategies

   iv   understand added value and differentiation strategies

   v   explain hybrid strategy

   vi   define focused differentiation

18 DEVELOPMENT AND APPLICATION OF MARKETING MIX STRATEGIES   Chapter 13

a   discuss product strategy

b   discuss price strategy

c   discuss place strategy

d   discuss promotion strategy

19 STRATEGIC SUPPORT FUNCTIONS   Chapters 14 and 15

a   Finance issues

   i   performance evaluation

     –   explain ratio analysis

     –   be aware of financial measures

     –   understand ROCE, ROI, profitability

   ii   funding the implementation and the resource allocation

     –   explain financial sources

     –   explain capital allocation

     –   explain shareholders funds

b   Research and Development issues

   i   management of innovation

     –   assess the role of research and development in strategy

     –   evaluate acquisition of new technologies

     –   discuss exploitation of existing technologies

     –   discuss innovation and existing products

     –   discuss innovation and new products

     –   explain innovation and intrapreneurship

   ii   management and control of quality

     –   discuss the role of quality in strategy

     –   describe quality procedures

     –   explain quality assurance

     –   explain total quality management

c   IS/IT issues

   i   IS/IT as a strategic resource

     –   understand organisation and control of the information strategy

     –   define usefulness and application of information technology

     –   assess monitoring advances and changes in information technology

     –   describe current good practice

     –   describe costs and benefits

     –   discuss information and organisational structure

20 HUMAN RESOURCE MANAGEMENT   Chapter 16

a   Recruitment and selection

   i   define the strategic role of human resources

   ii   formulate the human resource plan to identify and evaluate appropriate recruitment methods

   iii   advise on succession planning

b   Motivation and discipline

   i   understand the appropriate motivational and supportive policies

   ii   describe the links between objectives, appraisal, reward and motivation

c   Appraisal and performance evaluation

   i   assess organisational and individual objectives

   ii   assess appraisal methods

   iii   discuss appraisal and competence assessment

   iv   staff training and development

   v   understand the importance of the management of change

   vi   describe the management of diversity

   vii   evaluate the role of teamworking and empowerment

21 PROJECT MANAGEMENT   Chapter 17

a   define the project life cycle

   i   understand the objectives of project management

   ii   make an estimation of resource requirements

   iii   assess the efficient use of resources

   iv   understand operational research procedures

b   tools and techniques of project management

   i   understand statistical approaches

   ii   describe statistical process control

c   operations management

   i   assess the strategic significance of operations

   ii   link operations management and strategy

   iii   understand purchasing and inbound logistics

   iv   evaluate the manufacturing processes

   v   understand distribution and outbound logistics

   vi   describe quality and quality regimes

   vii   have knowledge of just-in-time supply management

   viii discuss business process re-engineering

22 MANAGEMENT OF CHANGE ISSUES   Chapter 18

a   assess the motivation to change

b   evaluate attitudes to change

c   link together culture and change

d   understand the managing of change: Lewin, System Intervention Strategy

e   Process of understanding types of strategic change and their causes

   i   identify external environmental change and shocks

   ii   identify internal environmental change

   iii   understand business relationships

   iv   understand transformational change

   v   discuss enforced change

   vi   identify technological change

   vii   evaluate people issues

f   development of a strategic change programme

   i   describe the Gemini 4Rs framework

   ii   describe force field analysis

   iii   describe power influence

   iv   understand culture influence

g   management roles in the strategy change process

   i   understand the importance of communication and education

   ii   evaluate collaboration

   iii   evaluate intervention

   iv   assess the importance of direction

   v   describe routine change

h   managing the strategic change process

   i   evaluate changing identity of the organisation

   ii   understand co-ordination and transition

   iii   appreciate the need for control

   iv   describe the role of change strategists

   v   describe the role of change implementers

   vi   describe the role of change recipients

ORGANISATIONAL STRUCTURE

23 MATCHING STRUCTURES WITH STRATEGY   Chapter 19

a   Types of organisation structures

   i   understand the determinants of structure

   ii   evaluate the meaning of structure

   iii   describe the simple organisation

   iv   describe the entrepreneurial organisation

   v   describe the functional organisation

   vi   describe the divisional organisation

   vii   describe the matrix organisation

   viii describe the multinational organisation

   ix   describe the global organisation

   x   understand the holding company

   xi   evaluate the role of the strategic business unit

   xii   assess intermediate and variations in structure

   xiii discuss advantages and appropriateness of different structures

   xiv   understand the process stage towards globalisation Kenichi, Ohmai, Keegan

b   Centralisation versus decentralisation

   i   evaluate issues in organisational structural change

   ii   understand organic and mechanistic structures: Burns and Stalker

   iii   describe contingency theory

   iv   describe the virtual organisation

c   Organisational configurations

   i   compare structural configurations: Mintzberg

   ii   make a comparison of organisational types

INTERNATIONAL BUSINESS

24 THE NATURE OF GLOBAL COMPETITION   Chapter 20

a   The internationalisation of business

   i   understand the motivations behind internationalisation

   ii   be aware of the concept of globalisation as distinct from international marketing

   iii   discuss the competitive advantage of nations: Porter

iv   understand absolute advantage and comparative advantage

v   evaluate implications for organisational success

vi   explain internationalisation strategies

vii   understand single markets and trading blocks

viii   explain multinational organisations: Bartlett and Ghoshal

b   The development of the global business

   i   discuss market convergence

   ii   explain cost advantages

   iii   explain government pressures

   iv   understand currency volatility and trade barriers

   v   understand purchasing power parity

   vi   understand the emergence of global competition

25 GLOBAL STRATEGIES   Chapter 20

a   evaluate market entry strategies

   i   compare standardisation versus customisation

   ii   understand product positioning

   iii   discuss international channel management

   iv   analyse the development of global brands

b   Managing a global company

   i   describe the international planning process

   ii   assess ethnocentric, polycentric and geocentric orientation

   iii   explain cross cultural management and leadership

c   Reaching global customers

   i   international marketing research

      –   be able to assess value of published statistics

      –   discuss comparability and reliability of data

      –   assess national and local information sources

      –   evaluate field sales force

   ii   international market segmentation understand the following:

      –   geographic

      –   ethnic

      –   economic

      –   technological capability

26 OUTCOMES OF THE STRATEGIC PROCESS
Chapter 21

a   Corporate and business performance

   i   discuss sustainable competitive advantage

   ii   evaluate critical success factors

b   A learning organisation

   i   assess shared purpose and vision

   ii   understand challenging experiences

   iii   explain the holistic view

c   Alternative performance measures

   i   understand performance standards

   ii   utilise financial indicators

   iii   utilise non financial indicators

   iv   formulate strategic success measurements

d   Strategic failure

   i   assess strategic drift: the Icarus Paradox

   ii   understand indicators of failure

   iii   analyse weak or inappropriate strategic leadership

   iv   discuss Z scores: Altman

27 ETHICAL CONSIDERATIONS   Chapter 22

a   The importance of social responsibility

   i   evaluate the meaning of social responsibility

   ii   discuss corporate social responsibility

   iii   review business ethics

   iv   review ethical dilemmas

b   Corporate governance

   i   assess corporate conduct

   ii   assess the governance framework

   iii   discuss governance change

   iv   distinguish between rights, duties and expectations of stakeholders

   v   understand the role of executive and non-executive directors

   vi   differentiate between the functions of a chairman and those of a chief executive office or managing director

c   The attitude towards ethics on national and global scales

   i   the ethical stance

   ii   discuss at the national and international level

   iii   explain at the corporate level

   iv   explain at the manager level

   v   evaluate the cultural context

28 REVISION

The examination

Format of the examination

	Number of marks
Section A: One compulsory scenario-based question	60
Section B: choice of 2 from 3 questions (20 marks each)	40
	———
	100
Total time allowed: 3 hours	——

Additional information

Primarily the subject – Strategic Business Planning and Development – will be considered at the strategic level. All aspects will be considered in terms of practical application. Wherever possible the subject will be integrated and not considered as isolated topics. Operational activities will only be introduced where they impinge upon strategic considerations.

The examination is a three hour paper in two sections. Section A is in the format of one major case study, usually with three to four parts worth between 10 and 20 marks each. This is compulsory and focuses on the core material, previously described, although other aspects of the syllabus could be introduced here. Questions will be mainly discursive but there will usually be some financial or other quantitative data included here to be analysed. Candidates are expected to closely relate all their answers to the case scenarios. Section B will consist of a choice of two questions from a total of three available. They will not be linked to the compulsory case scenario.

Examination tips

- Spend the first few minutes of the examination **reading the paper**.

- Where you have a **choice of questions**, decide which ones you will do.

- **Divide the time** you spend on questions in proportion to the marks on offer. One suggestion is to allocate 1½ minutes to each mark available, so a 10 mark question should be completed in 15 minutes.

- Unless you know exactly how to answer the question, spend some time **planning** your answer. Stick to the question and **tailor your answer** to what you are asked.

- **Fully explain** all your points but be **concise**. Set out all workings **clearly and neatly**, and state briefly what you are doing. Don't write out the question.

- If you do not understand what a question is asking, **state your assumptions**. Even if you do not answer precisely in the way the examiner hoped, you should be given some credit, if your assumptions are reasonable.

- If you **get completely stuck** with a question, leave space in your answer book and **return to it later.**

- Towards the end of the examination spend the last **five minutes** reading through your answers and **making any additions or corrections**.

- Before you finish, you must fill in the required information on the front of your answer booklet.

Answering the questions

- **Essay questions**: Make a quick plan in your answer book and under each main point list all the relevant facts you can think of. Then write out your answer developing each point fully. Your essay should have a clear structure; it should contain a brief introduction, a main section and a conclusion. Be concise. It is better to write a little about a lot of different points than a great deal about one or two points.

- **Case studies**: To write a good case study, first identify the area in which there is a problem, outline the main principles/theories you are going to use to answer the question, and then apply the principles/theories to the case. Include relevant points only and then reach a conclusion and, if asked for, recommendations. If you can, compare the facts to real-life examples – this may gain you additional marks in the exam.

- **Reports, memos and other documents**: Some questions ask you to present your answer in the form of a report or a memo or other document. Use the correct format – there could be easy marks to gain here.

Study skills and revision guidance

This section aims to give guidance on how to study for your ACCA exams and to give ideas on how to improve your existing study techniques.

Preparing to study

Set your objectives

Before starting to study decide what you want to achieve – the type of pass you wish to obtain. This will decide the level of commitment and time you need to dedicate to your studies.

Devise a study plan

- Determine which times of the week you will study.

- Split these times into sessions of at least one hour for study of new material. Any shorter periods could be used for revision or practice.

- Put the times you plan to study onto a study plan for the weeks from now until the exam and set yourself targets for each period of study – in your sessions make sure you cover the course, course assignments and revision.

- If you are studying for more than one paper at a time, try to vary your subjects, this can help you to keep interested and see subjects as part of wider knowledge.

- When working through your course, compare your progress with your plan and, if necessary, re-plan your work (perhaps including extra sessions) or, if you are ahead, do some extra revision/practice questions.

Effective studying

Active reading

You are not expected to learn the text by rote, rather you must understand what you are reading and be able to use it to pass the exam and develop good practice. A good technique to use is SQ3Rs – Survey, Question, Read, Recall, Review:

1 **Survey** the chapter – look at the headings and read the introduction, summary and objectives, so as to get an overview of what the chapter deals with.

2 **Question** – whilst undertaking the survey, ask yourself the questions that you hope the chapter will answer for you.

3 **Read** through the chapter thoroughly, answering the questions and making sure you can meet the objectives. Attempt the exercises and activities in the text, and work through all the examples.

4 **Recall** – at the end of each section and at the end of the chapter, try to recall the main ideas of the section/chapter without referring to the text. This is best done after a short break of a couple of minutes after the reading stage.

5 **Review** – check that your recall notes are correct.

You may also find it helpful to reread the chapter and try to see the topic(s) it deals with as a whole.

Note taking

Taking notes is a useful way of learning, but do not simply copy out the text. The notes must:

- be in your own words
- be concise
- cover the key points
- be well-organised
- be modified as you study further chapters in this text or in related ones.

Trying to summarise a chapter without referring to the text can be a useful way of determining which areas you know and which you don't.

Three ways of taking notes:

- **summarise the key points** of a chapter.

- **make linear notes** – a list of headings, divided up with subheadings listing the key points. If you use linear notes, you can use different colours to highlight key points and keep topic areas together. Use plenty of space to make your notes easy to use.

- **try a diagrammatic form** – the most common of which is a mind-map. To make a mind-map, put the main heading in the centre of the paper and put a circle around it. Then draw short lines radiating from this to the main sub-headings, which again have circles around them. Then continue the process from the sub-headings to sub-sub-headings, advantages, disadvantages, etc.

Highlighting and underlining

You may find it useful to underline or highlight key points in your study text – but do be selective. You may also wish to make notes in the margins.

Revision

The best approach to revision is to revise the course as you work through it. Also try to leave four to six weeks before the exam for final revision. Make sure you cover the whole syllabus and pay special attention to those areas where your knowledge is weak. Here are some recommendations:

- **Read through the text and your notes again** and condense your notes into key phrases. It may help to put key revision points onto index cards to look at when you have a few minutes to spare.

- **Review any assignments** you have completed and look at where you lost marks – put more work into those areas where you were weak.

- **Practise exam standard questions** under timed conditions. If you are short of time, list the points that you would cover in your answer and then read the model answer, but do try to complete at least a few questions under exam conditions.

- Also **practise producing answer plans** and comparing them to the model answer.

- If you are stuck on a topic find somebody (a tutor) to explain it to you.

- **Read good newspapers and professional journals**, especially ACCA's *Student Accountant* – this can give you an advantage in the exam.

- Ensure you **know the structure of the exam** – how many questions and of what type you will be expected to answer. During your revision attempt all the different styles of questions you may be asked.

Chapter 1

INTRODUCTION TO STRATEGIC MANAGEMENT

The objectives of this chapter are to explain the strategic management and business planning process. Strategic management is not an exact science; no organisation can apply strict rules. The 'best' strategy does not emerge from cookbook approaches and there are certainly no formulae for calculating the strategy. It is about the reading of signs and portents of the future and interpreting them in order to choose an appropriate direction for the future development of the organisation.

Objectives

When you have studied this chapter you should be able to:

- explain the purpose of strategic management and corporate and business planning

- understand why strategic management is important

- describe the process, content and context of strategy development.

1 Strategic management

1.1 What is strategic management?

Decisions about products, locations, structure, personnel and other resources are all major or strategic decisions.

These decisions will generally make an impact on the performance of the organisation. How these decisions are made and how they are implemented can be defined as the process of strategic management.

There are several definitions of strategic management.

- Ansoff sees it as 'a systematic approach to a major and increasingly important responsibility of general management to position and relate the firm to its environment in a way which will assure its continued success and make it secure from surprises'.

- Rowe et al describe it as 'the decision process that aligns the organisation's internal capability with the opportunities and threats it faces in the environment'.

Strategic management is concerned with matters that are important in that they affect the long-term welfare of the whole organisation. The environment with which strategists are wrestling is characterised by chaos, complexity, dynamism, turbulence and uncertainty. The strategic management process can be characterised as being complex with a long-term and external orientation and with a qualitative emphasis.

- A long-term orientation means that decisions taken in the present will be played out in the future. The length of the term depends on the type of business: a fast moving consumer goods manufacturer will have a time horizon of perhaps only a few months, while an organisation building aircraft will typically have a time horizon of years.

- An external orientation means that senior managers spend 50% or more of their time interacting with people and interests considering issues outside of their organisation.

- A qualitative emphasis means that detailed calculations are seldom called for. The emphasis is on the 'big picture' rather than on detail, making the determination of strategy qualitative in nature not quantitative.

Major strategic management concerns are with:

- Matching the organisation and its environment. This takes two forms - the organisation alters itself and the products and services it offers to match the needs of customers in its chosen marketplace (the market based approach) - or the organisation identifies where its strengths lie and chooses those activities that play to those strengths (the resource based approach)
- Initiating and handling both incremental and transformational change
- Managing the organisation's relationships with stakeholders, and
- Balancing short- and long-term considerations.

The strategy will be affected not only by environmental forces and resource availability, but also by the values and expectations of those who have power in and around the organisation. In some respects, strategy can be thought of as a reflection of the attitudes and beliefs of those who have most influence on the organisation - the stakeholders, e.g. shareholders, managers, employees and the economy. Each of these groups is looking for something different from the organisation and will therefore measure its performance differently.

1.2 The different levels of strategy

All organisations should carry out some form of strategic management. As the organisation becomes larger, and more complex, there is a greater need for involvement in the strategy process at all levels of the organisation. Consequently, much strategic activity will occur in a decentralised way, as each department or business unit attempts to carry out their own part of the strategy.

Johnson and Scholes identify three levels of strategic activity:

(a) **Corporate strategy** – what business or businesses the firm is in or should be in and how integrated these businesses should be with one another.

(b) **Business strategy** or competitive strategy – is concerned with how each strategic business unit (SBU) attempts to achieve its mission within its chosen area of activity. Here strategy is about which products or services should be developed and offered to which markets and the extent to which the customer needs are met whilst achieving the objectives of the organisation.

(c) **Functional or operational strategies** – are concerned with how the various functions of the organisation (marketing, production, finance, etc) contribute to the achievement of the corporate and competitive strategies. To improve performance in the organisation, functional strategies harness the activities, skills and resources available.

The distinction between corporate and business strategy is due to the development of divisionalised organisations, which typically have a corporate centre and a number of strategic business units (SBUs). A SBU is a unit within the overall corporate entity, which should have an identifiable and definable product or service range, market segment and competitor set. Porter suggests that these strategies are either cost leadership or differentiation of products and may encompass an entire market or be focused on a particular segment of it.

For all levels of strategy, the common purpose is to guide the use of the company resources in achieving the organisation's objectives. However, despite the points evaluated above, the boundaries between the three categories are very indistinct and much depends upon the circumstances prevailing and the kind of organisation.

2 Corporate and business strategy

2.1 Strategic perspective

A **strategic perspective** is a way of **being** in an organisation. The organisation is constantly scanning the internal and external environment in order to assess its role and impact and what it can learn through this process. It strives for organisational success and sustainability. This involves a **continuous process**, which helps guide the organisation on how it could change itself to deal with these constant changes. It requires constant strategic thinking and acting. To gain a strategic perspective of any business requires the use of frameworks or models, which enable the strategist to make sense of the complexity of the business and its environment by providing points of reference to improve awareness, identify position and locate opportunities and threats.

2.2 Corporate strategy

Corporate strategy is a set of policies adopted by senior management that guides the **scope** and **direction** of the entity, taking into account the environment in which the company operates. It is primarily concerned with the determination of ends, e.g. what business or businesses the firm is in or should be in, and how does it compete. For most organisations this means seeking ways to add value ie, where the value of the output is greater than the value (costs) of the inputs and the processes.

'**Scope**' used in this context relates to size and range; it concerns the way in which those responsible for managing the organisation conceive its boundaries. At this level the global objectives, e.g. growth, stability or retrenchment, and the general orientation to achieve them are defined. Corporate strategy consists of strategic planning at a corporate level and is not confined to one particular area – marketing, personnel, production/operational and financial implications are all taken into consideration.

The '**direction**' describes product/market positioning. Strategic decisions affect the long-term direction of the organisation. Once the wheels are set in motion it is often impossible to turn back.

2.3 Scope

Johnson and Scholes claim that corporate strategy is concerned with the scope of an organisation's activities eg, does it concentrate on one area of activity or many, and the matching of these to the organisation's environment, its resource capabilities and the values and expectations of its various stakeholders.

They have summarised the various aspects of strategic decisions:

- determining of the *scope* of the organisation's activities
- relating the organisation's activities to the *environment* in which it operates
- matching the organisation's activities to its *resource capability*
- the *allocation or re-allocation of resources*
- constraining and providing a framework for lower level *operational decisions*
- reflecting the *values and expectations* of the people in power within the organisation
- determining the *long-term direction* that the organisation takes
- often *implying change* in the organisation.

2.4   Expectations of owners (shareholders) and stakeholders

Argenti stresses that 'the sole purpose of a profit-seeking organisation is to make returns for its owners, the shareholders. They expect a fair financial return as payment of risk bearing and the use of their capital and wish to see a balance between current dividends and capital growth within the organisation. Argenti points out that there may be very many stakeholder groups and all with different demands on the organisation. In this confusion, he plumps for two sorts of stakeholder:

- the shareholders who are the intended beneficiaries, the people for whom the organisation was set up, and

- collateral stakeholders, the stakeholders who will also benefit from the operations of the organisation but have no rights to control it.

and this difference is enshrined in law: the legal position of shareholders is different to that of other stakeholders.

Organisational (or collateral) stakeholders are individuals or groups who have an interest in and/or are affected by the goals, operations or activities of the organisation or the behaviour of its members. They include employees, providers of finance, consumers, government, community and other organisations or groups.

Stakeholders have a wide variety of interests in the organisation. Managers are likely to have a particular interest in, and concern for, the size and growth of the organisation and its profitability and for their job security, status, power and prestige. Workers generally look for security of employment and increases in wages. Outside stakeholders may have a variety of interests concerning the quality of the product, the use of resources - particularly finance - and the effect of the business on the environment and society in general.

2.5   The concept of added value

Any business organisation can be viewed as a system for adding value to its inputs. The organisation takes various factors of production (land, labour, capital etc) and uses its expertise to combine them with a variety of activities. Where the end user is prepared to pay more than the cost of these activities, the organisation has created value. Businesses with a competitive advantage create value more effectively than their competitors. This value can then be distributed in a way that keeps financial stakeholders satisfied as well as the organisation investing in its own future.

Value creation is achieved using three key elements of strategic management, as shown below:

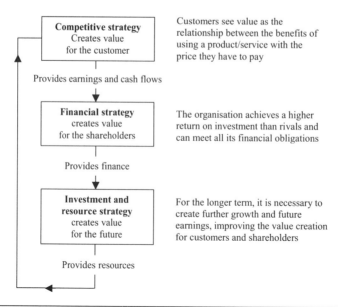

2.6   Business or competitive strategy

Business or competitive strategy is concerned with which products or services should be developed and offered to which markets; and the extent to which these meet the customer's needs in such as way as to achieve the objectives of the organisation - perhaps long-term profitability, market growth or measures of efficiency. So, whereas corporate strategy involves decisions about the organisation as a whole, business strategy is more likely to be related to a unit - a strategic business unit or SBU - within the whole.

A strategic business unit is a business within an organisation. It may be defined as a unit that:

- has a distinctive business mission, sensibly independent of that of any other business in the organisation

- offers a well-defined product or service in a well-defined market (and is not predominantly a supplier to other units in the organisation);

- is able to manage its strategy in a manner that is independent of other businesses within the corporation (although not of the strategy of the organisation itself);

- contains all the important components essential to the conduct of its business mission, for example technology, operations and marketing.

Thus in accounting terms an SBU corresponds to a profit centre - a unit that is responsible for the generation of profit. (The organisation is an investment centre - the unit that, among other things, decides what to do with the profits that the businesses have generated.) It can be seen that this definition of an SBU, although it includes reference to the organisation of which it is a part, is a definition that can easily be applied to 'stand-alone' businesses.

2.7   Market competition

While strategy may be about competing and surviving as a firm, one can argue that products (services), not organisations that compete and products are developed by business units. The role of the organisation then is to manage its business units and products so that each is competitive and so that each contributes to the organisation's purposes.

At the business unit level, the strategic issues are less about the coordination of operating units and more about developing and sustaining a competitive advantage for the goods and services that are produced. At this level, the strategy formulation phase deals with:

- positioning the business against rivals

- anticipating changes in demand and technologies and adjusting the strategy to accommodate them

- influencing the nature of competition through strategic actions such as vertical integration and through political actions such as lobbying.

ACTIVITY 1

A traditional manufacturer of diaries opened a publishing subsidiary. While the core business, diaries, declined, the publishing business was astonishingly successful. Classify the following strategic issues according to their level of strategy:

(a) Should the profits from the publishing company be used to rescue diaries, or grow the publishing company more quickly?

(b) Should the diaries move up market?

(c) How can the costs of the diaries be reduced, to improve the margin?

(d) Should the publishing company move into publishing novels?

(e) Should the diary business be sold to a rival, so that resources can be focused on the publishing company?

Feedback to this activity is at the end of the chapter.

3 The importance of strategic management

Organisations are groupings of people and resources created for a purpose. Running any organisation - your local newsagent or a multinational company - is a complex activity. It is complex because a lot of information from many sources needs to be considered in order to understand the organisation and the situation it finds itself in and take rational action. There are outside interests eg, for a college these include the interests of government, local education authorities, prospective students and their potential employers. There are the ambitions and skills of the students and staff, the suitability and state of repair of the buildings etc. There will also be concerns about what the organisation is aiming to do and the balance between carrying out present activities and preparing for future ones. Someone, or much more likely a group of people, must handle this complexity and the ambiguity that is often associated with information from multiple sources, and be responsible for the overall direction of the organisation, which sums up what strategic management is about. In small businesses this is a responsibility for the livelihood of the owners, the employees and their families. Large organisations are often faced with decisions related to acquisitions, mergers, takeovers, vertical or horizontal integration, internationalisation and the rationalisation of core activities to get back into the markets and customers they know best. This means responsibility for large financial investments and for the jobs and interests of maybe thousands of people, perhaps around the world, who might be affected directly by the organisation's operations. Thus strategic management truly is important, concerned as it is with the sustained well-being of the organisation and with the groups and individuals affected by its activities.

3.1 Definition of strategy

There is no universally accepted definition of strategy, and the word is used in different contexts to mean different things.

The following definition, although stated in a single sentence, provides a framework that can be expanded, shaped, applied and developed further.

DEFINITION

Strategy is a pattern of activities that seeks to achieve the objectives of the organisation and adapt its scope, resources and operations to environmental changes in the long term.

'**Strategy** is a pattern of activities that seek to achieve the objectives of the organisation and adapt its scope, resources and operations to environmental changes in the long term.'

The key ideas are the following:

- *Strategy is a pattern of activities* – it is not a strategic plan or the objectives of any plan. It is entirely possible to have a strategy without having a plan.

- *Strategy is concerned with achieving objectives* – invariably this involves gaining some advantage in the chosen areas of activity. For commercial organisations this is bound up with the notion of gaining a competitive advantage that will be used to achieve superior financial returns.

Strategy can also be considered as the *thinking*, the logic behind the actions. Drucker (1954) sees it as an indication of an organisation's positioning for the future, deciding *what* should be done rather than *how* it should be done. Strategy requires choices - deciding what particular kind of value an organisation wants to deliver to whom.

Henry Mintzberg suggests various definitions of strategy covering the five Ps.

- Strategy as a **plan**, which can be defined and followed.

- Strategy as a **ploy**, which can be seen as a move in a competitive business game. For example a firm might add unnecessary plant capacity. The intention is not to produce the goods but to discourage a competitor from entering the market. The strategy is not the activity but the deterrence.

- Strategy as a **pattern** of consistent behaviour, giving the impression of a logically thought out strategy. It is also relevant to Mintzberg's own ideas of emergent strategies, which result from unintended decisions, assuming a life of their own.

- Strategy as a **position** is a means of identifying where an organisation places itself in an environment or market. Hofer and Schendel believe that 'a critical aspect of top management's work today involves matching organisational competences (internal resources and skills) with the opportunities and risks created by environmental change in ways that will be effective and efficient'. Effectiveness is defined as the degree to which actual outputs correspond to desired outputs. Efficiency is the amount of output per unit of input.

- Strategy as a **perspective** consists not just of a chosen position but also of a unique way of perceiving the world. In this respect Mintzberg is suggesting that the organisation's strategy is similar to the individual's personality.

These five ways of discussing strategy are not mutually exclusive. Arguably they complement each other. In the right circumstances, any of the definitions will be the most apt. Nor is there a necessary hierarchy in which one comes before the other. A perspective can give rise to a plan. But the process of planning can result in an alteration of perspective.

3.2   Strategic thinking

The purpose of strategies is to determine and communicate through a system of major objectives and policies, a picture of the kind of enterprise that is envisioned. A strategist should be able to see beyond the present. Strategic thinking is a creative process and involves:

- flexible thinking - 'what if' questions

- avoiding wrongly-focused precision

- keeping details in perspective - especially *uncertain details*

- focusing on key factors and the essentials - or *distinctive competences* - of a business.

This process includes dissecting a problem or situation into its constituent parts; asking the right solution-oriented questions; constructing 'issue diagrams' and 'profit diagrams' to achieve the right diagnosis.

According to Ohmae, successful strategists 'have an idiosyncratic mode of thinking in which company, customers and competition merge in a dynamic interaction out of which a comprehensive set of objectives and plans for action eventually crystallises'. The challenge to strategic management is to try to reproduce this ability in organisational structures, forms and cultures.

Ohmae suggests that successful strategic thinking operates in the following way.

- Ask the right question - in other words, direct the question to finding a solution to a problem rather than a remedy to a symptom. An analogy is a headache caused by eyestrain. Although painkillers are a remedy to the symptom as they reduce the headache, they do not go to the underlying problem, which may be poorly made spectacles or bad lighting.

- To ask the right question, you have to observe the problem. If there are a variety of problems, a process of abstraction should allow them to be grouped under a number of headings. These groups of problems are then examined to see what is important about them, and what they signify. Only then can a new approach (concrete and specific) be determined.

- The process of abstraction is carried out by a variety of techniques eg, brainstorming to tap people's thoughts. So, it is important to identify the *key factors* underlying complex phenomena.

- Finally, a strategic thinker should be able to consider an 'ideal' state of affairs, so that constraints to achieving this vision are seen as surmountable obstacles rather than the natural laws of the business.

Ohmae identifies the 'four routes to strategic advantage':

1 strategy based on an organisation's key factors for success in its capability to increase market share and profitability

2 strategy based on exploiting any relative superiority

3 strategy based on aggressive initiatives which challenge accepted assumptions

4 strategy based on the development of innovations such as new markets or products.

3.3 Vision

The development of strategies can also be seen as the outcome of the influence of visionary leaders, especially where a charismatic leader dominates the organisation. These are generally organisations where the leader founded the company. There may be managers or other staff who may not be as dedicated to cause and effect strategies but may have very high intuitive skills and can identify new possibilities and ideas. These executives have a 'feel' for what makes sense in volatile environments where forecasting is useless.

The vision that a strategic thinker has is of what the business is and what it could be in an ideal world. Such an approach imparts a sense of direction to the company, even if there is not too much attention to detail. A vision is a sort of super-objective in that, like the Holy Grail, it may never be attained. Instead, it should provide continuous inspiration towards a desired end state. It should also encourage flexibility of thought within the context of a guiding idea.

A vision can be an ideal 'state of the world' ('a computer in every home') for the industry as a whole. It might provide the 'boundaries' for the firm's direction.

3.4 Overall purpose

The basic aim or objective of an organisation stems from why it was formed and provides the foundation upon which the formulation of policy is based. Originally, the founders will have set out the objectives to outline the aims to be achieved and the desired end results. In the case of limited companies, the basic objectives will be found in the objects clause of the memorandum of association and will generally aim to maximise shareholders' wealth. Clearly, this can be translated into more specific objectives, which then lend themselves to strategies. In a similar way, public sector organisations are often formed for the benefit of society as a whole. Thus the basic objective of the NHS is to provide a standard of health care for the population of the UK, irrespective of income.

Without clear objectives, managing is haphazard. No individual and no group can expect to perform effectively and efficiently unless there are objectives to give direction. Objective setting is primarily a political process: the objectives are formulated as a result of bargaining among the various interest groups - shareholders require profits, employees want wages and favourable working conditions, managers want power and customers demand quality products or services. The needs of these groups are often in conflict, making it difficult to maximise the objectives of any one particular group. Also, because the membership of these participating groups changes over time, the objectives are continually shifting to reflect the changes.

Managers at different levels in the organisational hierarchy are concerned with different kinds of objectives.

- The board of directors and top managers are very much involved in determining the purpose, mission and overall objectives of the organisation, as well as the more specific objectives in the key result areas.

- Middle level managers, eg the production manager, are involved in setting key result area objectives, division objectives and department objectives.

- Lower level managers are concerned with setting the objectives of departments and units, and also their subordinates.

Objectives are defined as the important ends towards which the organisational and individual activities are directed. In this sense objectives include missions, goals, purposes, tactics, policies, targets, quotas and deadlines.

Mission – describes the initiatives that will achieve the vision in ways deemed consistent with the organisation, its assumed market and the competitive, regulatory, social and technological environment.

The **mission statement** defines the basic reasons for the existence of an organisation and helps legitimise its function in society. It is the company's broad sense of purpose and will often define the industry the firm competes in and make comments about its general way of doing business, e.g:

- British Airways seek to be 'the world's favourite airline'

- Nokia speak of 'connecting people'

- DHL 'deliver your promises'.

Goal - this is a general statement of direction in line with the mission.

Objective - this is a more precise statement in line with the goal. It is more likely to be quantified. An overall objective of a government's road safety policy might be to reduce deaths and injuries. To this end, strategies to achieve the objective might include more stringent law enforcement, advertising and/or speed limits.

3.5 Strategies, policies and tactics

Strategies - are broad statements of intent that show the type of action required to achieve an objective. The term strategy (derived from the Greek word - strategos, meaning general) is treated in different ways, as we have already noted. One of the most comprehensive definitions refers to the determination of basic long-term objectives and of courses of action and allocations of resources to achieve these aims.

An explicit strategy for the business organisation is necessary for the following reasons.

- there is the need for people to co-operate together in order to achieve the benefits of mutual reinforcement.

- there are the effects of changing environmental conditions.

The absence of an explicit concept of strategy may result in members of the organisation working at cross-purposes.

Policies are general statements or understanding (they are often merely implied from the actions of managers), which guide or channel management thinking in decision-making. They do not usually require action but are intended to guide managers in their commitment to the decision they ultimately make. For example, the manager of a company may strictly follow the practice of promoting from within; this may then be interpreted as policy and carefully followed by subordinates.

Policies define an area within which a decision is to be made and ensure (that the decision will be consistent with, and contribute to, an objective. Policies help decide issues before they become problems, make it unnecessary to analyse the same situation every time it comes up, and unify other plans, thus permitting managers to delegate authority and still maintain control over what their subordinates do. The essence of policy is discretion. Strategy, on the other hand, concerns the direction in which human and material resources will be applied in order to increase the chance of achieving selected objectives. To be effective, strategies and policies must be put into practice by means of plans, increasing in detail until they get down to the nuts and bolts of operations.

Tactics are the action plans through which strategies are executed. For example, for road safety, tactics might include random breathalyser tests and the installation of street cameras.

3.6 Planning ahead

When deciding how far ahead to plan objectives, several factors should be taken into account.

- The organisation's horizon, ie, how long does it plan/expect to survive? - With most organisations that are owned by shareholders the answer is 'indefinitely', but in the case of small businesses its owners may set a short-term objective to sell the organisation, or may intend to wind up the business when they retire.

- Strategic lead-time - the longer the time it takes for an organisation to plan and implement a strategy (the 'lead-time') the further ahead it must set objectives. For example if it takes three years to develop a product and introduce it into the market, then the company will need to set objectives for at least that period of time ahead.

- Stability - if the objective is too short-term it will be unduly influenced by short-term cyclic fluctuations and may become meaningless.

- Estimated life of production facilities, measured either in terms of physical deterioration or technical obsolescence - if an organisation intends to invest in plant with a useful life expectancy of ten years, that period may need to be planned for if only in general terms.

- Estimated life of the product in its present form - if the present product has a foreseeable market further ahead than the estimated useful life of its production facilities, the organisation will need to plan for these to be upgraded or replaced.

- Reliability of forecasts - as an organisation plans objectives further into the future the forecasts become less reliable and the problem is much more difficult when the environment is dynamic and unpredictable.

3.7 The case for long-term corporate planning

The corporate planning disciplines concentrate management's attention on long-term matters, but not at the exclusion of short-term considerations. It is difficult to imagine managers making decisions, which have a degree of permanency, without some form of formalised strategic planning. Other benefits of strategic planning include the following.

- It demands a logical, deliberate and analytical approach to decision making, requiring the generation of alternative strategies, and the evaluation of the probable results of their execution. The planning helps to identify the risks involved in top management decisions and either prevents or mitigates their effects.

- It helps to develop a climate conducive to creative thinking, initiative and innovation.

- It aids in the formulation of organisational goals and objectives ensuring that performance is targeted rather than merely assessed against loose expectations. The process can be used to evaluate whether these objectives are achievable, given the organisation's resources and the nature of the changes occurring in its environment.

- The systematic survey of the environment involved in strategic planning can improve the basis of information on which trends are identified, projections made and strategic options interpreted and evaluated. The process can also identify product/market threats and resource weaknesses in time to bring in preventive or remedial measures.

- It quantifies long-term resource problems and produces a basis upon which resources can be planned and rationed between programmes.

- It helps to integrate long, medium and short plans and to harmonise the activities of different departments and functions. The plans formulated can be used as yardsticks against which actual performance can be judged.

4 Strategic management: process, content and context

In developing strategy, an important distinction needs to be drawn between the process, content and context within which strategy formulation takes place:

- *Context* refers to the environment within which the organisation operates/develops its strategies.

- *Content* refers to the substantive issues tackled in strategy formulation – the specific means by which corporate, business, or functional goals are to be achieved. (The different levels of strategy formulation typically refer to the content of strategies.)

- *Process* is the method by which strategies are derived, referring to specific steps or phases through which strategies are formulated and implemented (e.g. environmental, analysis, strategic thinking, strategic planning, implementation and control). The process indicates how the actions link together/interact as the strategy unfolds against a (changing) environment.

4.1   The present position of the organisation

Self-analysis identifies the present position of the organisation and aims to provide a detailed understanding of those aspects that are of strategic importance. In particular, it covers performance analysis, shareholder value analysis, product portfolio analysis and an examination of the key determinants of strategy such as strengths, weaknesses, and strategic problems. Self-analysis, like external analysis, usually has a strategic business unit (SBU) as a frame of reference but it can be productive at division or organisation level.

Performance analysis - profitability and sales provide an evaluation of past strategies and an indication of the current market viability of a product line. Return on assets, the most commonly used measure of profitability, can be distorted by the limitations of accounting measures-in particular, it ignores intangible assets such as brand equity .A key issue is to determine an appropriate target rate of return that takes into account the fact that not all strategies have the same degree of risk. Another performance measure is sales, which can reflect changes in the customer base with long-term implications.

Shareholder value analysis is based on generating a discounted present value of the cash flow associated with a strategy. It is theoretically sound and appropriately forward-looking (as opposed to current financials that measure the results of past strategies). However, it focuses attention on financial measures rather than other indicators of strategic performance. Developing the needed estimates is most difficult and subject to a variety of biases.

Other, non-financial performance measures are available that often provide better measures of long-term business health:

- Customer satisfaction/brand loyalty - how are we doing relative to our competitors at attracting customers and building loyalty?

- Associations - what do our customers associate with our business in terms of perceived quality, innovativeness, product class expertise, customer orientation, and so on?

- Product/service quality - is our product delivering value to the customer and is it performing as intended?

- Relative cost - are we at a cost disadvantage with respect to materials, assembly, product design, or wages?

- New product activity - have we a stream of new products or product improvements that have made an impact?

- Manager/employee capability and performance - have we created the type, quantity, and depth of management that are needed to support projected strategies?

DEFINITION

Product portfolio analysis considers the performance/ strength of each business area, together with the attractiveness of the business area in which it competes.

Product portfolio analysis - this analysis considers the performance/ strength of each business area, together with the attractiveness of the business area in which it competes. One goal is to generate a business mix with an appropriate balance between new and mature products. An organisation that lacks a flow of new products faces stagnation or decline. A balance also must exist between products generating cash and those using cash.

4.2 The external environment

KEY POINT

The external environment consists of factors that cannot be directly influenced by the organisation itself. These include social, legal economic, political and technological (SLEPT) changes that the firm must try to respond to, rather than control.

The external environment consists of factors that cannot be directly influenced by the organisation itself. These include social, legal economic, political and technological changes that the organisation must try to respond to, rather than control.

Demographic trends are important to many firms. Age patterns are crucial to those whose customers are in certain age groups, such as infants, students, or retirees.

The political environment can be especially important to multinationals that operate in politically sensitive countries. A luxury hotel chain may be interested in building codes and restrictions that might affect new hotels it is planning.

A technological development can dramatically change an industry and create difficult decisions for those who are committed to profitable 'old' technologies. For example, digital watches, transistors, and nylon all revolutionised industries. Technology can also make less dramatic but strategically important changes. The hotel business might be able to exploit visual as well as audio communication, allowing conferences to be held with participants in different cities.

Understanding the economic environment facing a country or an industry helps in projecting that industry's sales over time and in identifying special risks or threats. The hotel industry, for example, can see a link between the overall health of the economy in general and its primary customer segments in particular.

The cultural environment affects strategic judgments in many contexts. For example, the key success factor for many clothing industries is the capability to be 'right' with respect to fashion. Understanding the reasons behind the public's interest in nutrition and health is important to strategists in the frozen-novelty business.

4.3 Strategic content

KEY POINT

There are three elements to strategic management – strategic analysis, strategic choice and strategic implementation.

Johnson and Scholes suggest that there are three elements to strategic management – strategic analysis, strategic choice and strategic implementation. They stress that the process is not intended as a prescription of what strategic management should be, but it is a useful framework that can be used to structure strategic problems.

Strategic analysis – seeking to understand the strategic position of the organisation. Once management has generated a picture of the strategic possibilities then it requires techniques to assist in the evaluation of the available choices. **Strategic choice** – about the formulation of possible courses of action, their evaluation and the choice between them.

Strategic implementation – is concerned with the translation of strategy into action. Implementation of a chosen strategy is by making any necessary adaptations to structure, the systems and people of the organisation and managing the required acquisition and deployment of resources. We treat the process as having three parts. It may involve resource planning, changes in structure and strategic change.

4.4 Strategy in different contexts

This section shows how the strategic issues faced by managers in different organisations depend on their business context.

- The small business context - small businesses are likely to be operating in a single market with a limited range of products or services. The scope of the operation will be less of a strategic issue than in larger organisations. Decisions on competitive strategies will probably be strongly influenced by the experience of those running the business. Because they are likely to be private companies, small businesses are reliant on funding bodies such as banks to raise capital. This, combined with the founder's influence on choice of product or service, may mean the choices of strategy are significantly limited.

- The multinational - is likely to be very diverse in terms of both products and geographic markets. Any big multinational is intrinsically complex. It has multiple layers of managers and, in most cases, multiple businesses. It might develop products, manufacture and sell them and service them in many countries. In principle, a choice of strategy has to be embedded in a complex industrial and managerial structure so that the myriad choices made daily within the organisation fall into line with the chosen strategy orientation.

- Manufacturing and service organisations - there are differences between organisations providing services and those providing products, particularly with competitive strategy. For a manufacturing firm it is likely to be concerned with the product itself to a greater extent than in the case of service organisations. Senior managers in a manufacturing organisation can usually exercise more direct control over competitive strategy than can be exercised in a service firm, where factors that determine competitive advantage are more likely to be controlled by the people at the point of delivery.

- Public sector - where the government is the major stakeholder, and not the market, the motivation to meet customer needs is reduced. The consequences of failure to provide an appropriate level of service for the organisation and the individual are reduced. Being dependent on government policy also means that objectives may change rapidly as policy changes and this political dimension reduces the scope of management options and increases the time for decisions to be taken.

- Not for profit sector - includes charities, churches, private schools and foundations. The sources of revenue are different from most businesses and the influence from funding bodies may be high in terms of formulation of organisational strategies. Since the organisations are so dependent on funds that emanate from sponsors, there is a danger that managers become more concerned with resource efficiency than service effectiveness.

5 The process of strategy development

5.1 Strategic planning and strategic management

With the knowledge of the company's existing strengths and weaknesses and with all available forecasts of the environmental factors that may affect its future progress, the company will define a range of primary and secondary objectives and examine what opportunities are available, which might help to fulfil its ambitions. Of the opportunities reviewed, some will be eliminated by the constraints under which the firm exists; others will clearly be significant or peripheral to the main thrust of its advance. From those that remain it will be necessary to select, through some process of evaluation, a portfolio that represents a coherent, realistic and effective plan.

The above paragraph presents a simple, logical sequence of events. However, this is not in accordance with reality. For a large part of the manager's working life, he or she is bombarded with problems, forecasts and opportunities, which are perpetually rebuilt into a new perspective of the most promising strategic and tactical way ahead. The search for, and consideration of, new opportunities is a continuing process, and influences the way in which objectives are set as well as the strategies adopted in implementing those objectives.

Where a company has determined to take action to improve its profits (for example, by getting out of dying products or markets and changing its direction for survival or growth or wants to find weakly-managed companies and strip their assets or strengthen their management), it should be continually looking for threats to guard against, opportunities to overcome threats and opportunities to meet or improve on its objectives.

A search for opportunities needs to be conducted with a clear understanding of the company's objectives, the constraints and the current resources of the company resulting from a thorough analysis of past performances and a realistic appraisal of its strengths and weaknesses.

Areas for seeking new opportunities are considered under three main headings:

- current business ie, the better exploitation of existing products, markets and skills;

- product development;

- new business, outside the scope of the business as currently constituted.

5.2 Prescriptive - deliberate strategies

Prescriptive strategies are brought about by a top-down strategic approach and formal control processes. Supporters of the *prescriptive* approach view strategy to be a linear and rational process, starting with 'where-we-are-now' and then developing new strategies for the future. Objectives have been defined in advance and the main elements developed before the strategy commences. The objective may be adjusted if circumstances change significantly. They are the result of deliberate analysis and planning. This is the way we tend to visualise a strategy as being formulated; where the organisation's actual strategy comes about from deliberately devising and implementing plans. Prescriptive strategies want to *anticipate* how the environment will change in order to meet future needs ahead of competing organisations.

However, in many organisations where they attempt to formulate strategies in systematic ways, the intended strategies either do not become realised, or only a part of what was intended actually happens.

Drucker, in his book *Managing for Results*, discusses business strategies and states that whatever a company's programme it must include plans to help it make the following decisions:

(a) *what opportunities it wants to pursue and what risks it is willing and able to accept*

(b) *its scope and structure,* and especially the right balance between specialisation, diversification and integration

(c) *between time and money, between building its own or buying,* i.e. using sale of a business, merger, acquisition and joint venture to attain its goals

(d) *is the organisation structure appropriate* to its economic realities, its opportunities and its programme for performance.

There are three kinds of opportunities:

(a) **additive** – exploitation of existing resources

(b) **complementary** – involving structural changes in the company

(c) **breakthrough** – changing the fundamental economic characteristics of the business.

Risks can be placed in four categories:

(a) those that must be *accepted*

(b) those that can be *afforded*

(c) those that cannot be *afforded*

(d) those the company *cannot afford to miss.*

The right opportunities will not be selected unless the company attempts to maximise opportunities rather than to minimise risk. Quantitative techniques can be used to evaluate the likely outcomes of different decisions.

These ideas depend upon strategy and strategic management being a deliberate, rational process.

5.3 Emergent strategies

Another approach to formulating strategy is to recognise that you will never know how the environment will change and that the strategy should develop to take changing environmental conditions into account. Mintzberg (1987), one of the biggest critics of the prescriptive approach, developed the *emergent* approach to strategy formulation.

Emergent strategies – do not arise out of conscious strategic planning, but result from a number of ad hoc choices, perhaps made lower down the hierarchy. In this view, the final objective of the strategy is unclear and elements still develop as the strategy proceeds, continuously adapting to human needs -- the emergent strategy is evolving, incremental and continuous. Emergent strategies develop from patterns of behaviour; one idea leads to another, until a new pattern is formed and a new strategy has emerged. For example, a salesman visits a customer out in the field. The product isn't right, and together they work out some modifications. The salesman returns to the company and puts the changes through; after two or three more rounds, they finally get it right. A new product emerges, which eventually opens up a new market. The company has changed strategic course.

More recent approaches to emergent strategy (Pettigrew 1985; Mintzberg 1990) emphasise that people, politics and culture of organisations all need to be taken into account. Strategists such as Senge (1990) emphasise the learning approach to strategy, i.e. encouraging managers to undertake a process of trial and error to devise the optimal strategy. The organisation's strategy is derived as a result of negotiation, discussion, trial, repeated experimentation and small steps forward. Implementation does not follow strategy development, but is an integral part of the development

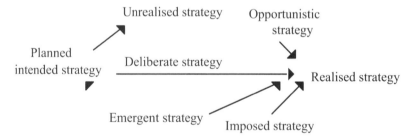

The diagram shows the organisation's actual (realised) strategy can come about from deliberately devising and implementing plans or the realised strategy can come about from a stream of decisions. The diagram also shows that strategies can come about in opportunistic ways. For example, as changes occur in the environment or new skills are recognised, the organisation may take advantage of them in an opportunistic manner, which leads to changes in the realised strategy.

Mintzberg argues that organisations can no longer rely solely on prescriptive strategies, such as profit maximisation. To cope with the turbulence, or even chaos, they have to revert to emergent approaches such as survival-based, uncertainty-based and human-resource-based theories and strategies, viewing human resources and their collective creativity as the most important assets of the organisation.

In practice, both deliberate and emergent strategies tend to be followed simultaneously and they combine to form the actual strategy.

Furthermore, whereas the prescriptive approach takes the view that the three core areas (process, content and context) are linked together sequentially, the emergent approach regards the three core areas as being interrelated.

5.4 Problems with deliberate models of strategy

There are critics who tend to reject deliberate models of strategy, and argue that strategy emerges as an often-unintended consequence of organisational behaviour.

Here we develop in greater detail the doubts about the deliberate approach that have been voiced by the emergent strategists.

Setting corporate objectives – a criticism frequently levelled at the practice of spelling out corporate objectives is that the exercise descends into the formulation of empty platitudes that offer no positive directional indicators for decision-making. It is too simplistic to suggest that the problem arises from poor planning. It is frequently the case that contradictory objectives are implied by the firm's long run strategy and the conflicting interests of key stakeholders – maximising profit for the shareholders may involve employee redundancy as a consequence of restructuring.

The difficulties of forecasting accurately – there are difficult problems associated with trying to accurately forecast for the long term:

- the fact that it is a long-term period
- the complexity of the environment that needs to be forecast
- the rapidity and novelty of environmental change
- the interrelationships between the environmental variables involved
- the limitations of the data available
- the amount and complexity of the calculations involved.

Several studies have shown that assessing the likelihood of future events is one of the hardest things that executives are asked to do, and most are not particularly good at it. However, this is only half the problem, even if strategists guess what is going to happen they still have to devise effective responses and implement them effectively.

Short-term pressure – the pressures on management are for short-term results and ostensibly strategy is concerned with the long term, e.g. 'What should we be doing now to help us reach the position we want to be in, in five years time?' Often it is difficult to motivate managers by setting long-term expectations when short-term problems can consume the whole working day. This is particularly true if senior managers are prone to changing their long-term strategy frequently, which may sound contradictory but is in fact rather common.

Rigidity – operational managers are frequently reluctant to specify their planning assumptions because the situations that their plans are designed to meet may change so rapidly that they can be made to look foolish. Even if a plan is reasonably accurate, the situation might change for reasons other than those forecast. Executives are often held prisoner by the rigidity of the planning process, because plans have to be set out in detail long before the period to which they apply.

The rigidity of the long-term plan, particularly in regard to the rationing and scheduling of resources, may also place the company in a position where it is unable to react to short-term unforeseen opportunities, or serious short-term crises.

Stifling initiative – if adherence to the strategy becomes all-important, it discounts flair and creativity. Operational managers can generate enthusiasm or dampen down potential trouble spots, and quick action may be required to avert trouble or improve a situation by actions outside the strategy. If operational managers then have to defend their actions against criticisms of acting '**outside the plan**', irrespective of the resultant benefits, they are likely to become apathetic and indifferent.

The cost – the strategic planning process can be costly, involving the use of specialists, sometimes a specialist department, and taking up management time. The process generates its own bureaucracy and associated paper or electronic data flow. Personal authorities are, to a greater or lesser extent, replaced by written guidelines.

Empirical evidence – if long range strategy really were as effective as its supporters claim, then it should be possible to produce evidence to demonstrate that companies that adopt a long range view and planning techniques consistently outperform those that do not.

Unfortunately, the result of a large number of studies is inconclusive, with some studies finding some evidence, but many finding none at all. Scott Armstrong's exhaustive review of all the evidence suggested that planning might give a small advantage in some manufacturing environments only, but other writers, Henry Mintzberg in particular, have been extremely critical of the theory and practice on planning.

5.5 Strategy development - incremental strategies

Mintzberg noted that most organisations that he studied were inclined to change incrementally with their strategies being formed gradually or through piecemeal change.

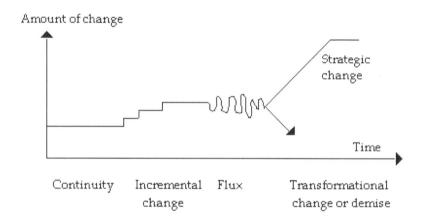

He noticed a tendency towards 'momentum' of strategy, where, once an organisation had adopted a particular strategy then it tended to develop from and within that strategy, rather than fundamentally changing direction. There were periods of continuity in which the established strategy remained unchanged and periods of fluctuation where the strategies did change but in no clear direction. Global or transformational change was infrequent, tending to occur at times of crisis in organisations when performance had declined significantly.

5.6 Models of strategy making

It must be realised at the outset that there is no one best way of managing the strategy of an organisation. A flexible, reactive style may suit a small firm in a rapidly changing environment, whereas a large company may need to take a long-term view and plan accordingly. Some methodologies are highly prescriptive and require rigid adherence to stages whilst others are highly adaptive allowing for creative use of their components. The former may be viewed as following a recipe and the latter as selecting suitable tools from a toolkit.

Strategies may come about in different ways and Mintzberg has identified various kinds of strategies, from very deliberate to mostly emergent.

- *Planned strategy* - precise intentions are formulated and articulated by a central leadership, and backed up by formal controls to ensure surprise-free implementation in an environment that is controllable. These strategies are extremely deliberate.

- *Entrepreneurial strategy* - intentions exist as the personal, unarticulated vision of a single leader, and so are adaptable to new opportunities. The organisation is under the personal control of the leader and located in a protected niche in its environment. These strategies are relatively deliberate but can emerge too.

- *Ideological strategy* - intentions exist as the collective vision of all the members of the organisation, controlled through strong, shared norms; the organisation is often proactive towards its environment. These strategies are rather deliberate.

- *Umbrella strategy* - leadership in partial control of the organisation's actions defines strategic targets or boundaries within which others must act. This strategy can be called deliberately emergent in that the leadership purposefully allows others the flexibility to manoeuvre and form patterns within the boundaries.

- *Process strategy* - the leadership controls the process aspects of the strategy, leaving the actual content of the strategy to others. Again, strategies are partly deliberate (concerning process) and partly emergent (concerning content) and deliberately emergent.

- *Disconnected strategy* - members of sub-units 'do their own thing' loosely coupled to the rest of the organisation. The strategies can be deliberate for those who make them and emergent for the organisation.

- *Consensus strategy*: through mutual adjustment, various members converge on patterns that pervade the organisation in the absence of central intentions. These strategies are rather emergent in nature.

- *Imposed strategy*: the external environment dictates patterns in actions, either through direct imposition or through implicitly pre-empting organisational choice. As we have already noted, government policies may have an impact on the strategy. Recession and threat of a takeover may force a strategy of cost cutting and retrenchment. Technological developments may cause an organisation to develop new products to replace obsolescent ones. These strategies are organisationally emergent, although they may be internalised and made deliberate.

- *Adaptive strategy* - is another mode of strategy making which fits the description that managers give of how strategies come about in their organisations. They see their role as strategists as being involved in a continual proactive pursuit of a strategic goal, countering competitive moves and adapting to their environment whilst not rocking the boat too much. Incremental change may be seen as an adaptive process in a continually changing environment.

5.7 Crafting strategies

There is a danger of thinking that the process of strategic management can only be a series of orderly steps from the planning process, building on objective setting and analysis, through the evaluation of different options and ending with strategy implementation. Strategic management can also be thought of as a crafting process, where strategies are developed on the basis of managers' experience, current learning about the operations of the market and their sensitivity to changes in their environments.

Mintzberg likens the management of a strategy to a potter crafting clay. The clay is thrown and by shaping the clay on the wheel, the potter gives it shape through a gradual process. More importantly, forming a strategy and implementing it are 'fluid processes of learning through which creative strategies evolve'.

The potter can introduce innovations during the process of shaping. The gap between thinking and doing is short. However, a sales representative who discovers a new way of providing customer satisfaction may have to convince large numbers of people within the organisation of the idea's merits. The gap between insight and execution is a long one.

The trouble with the long feedback link is that there is a separation between thinking and doing when it comes to strategy. This means that:

- A purely deliberate strategy prevents learning eg, it is hard with deliberate strategies to learn from mistakes, or stumble by accident into strategic growth.

- A purely emergent strategy defies control. It may in fact be a bad strategy, dysfunctional for the organisation's future health.

The strategist must be able to recognise patterns and to manage the process by which emergent strategies are created. In other words, the strategist must be able to find strategies as well as invent them.

According to Mintzberg there are five activities involved in strategic management.

(a) **Manage stability**: managers should know when to change and not assume perpetual environmental change. A large proportion of managers' time should be spent effectively implementing the strategies, not planning them.

(b) **Detect discontinuity**: strategic managers must be able to recognise the changes that are significant to their organisation.

(c) **Know the business**: including an awareness and understanding of the operations in the organisation.

(d) **Manage patterns**: managers should have the ability to detect emerging patterns and help them take shape; knowing which emergent strategies to nurture.

(e) **Reconcile change and continuity**: requires a combination or bringing together of the future, present and past; understanding that an obsession with either change or continuity can be counterproductive.

Conclusion

Strategy calls for a mixture of both technical mastery and intuitive insights. Strategists should not reject analysis and techniques; indeed these are essential ingredients, but they should be used only to stimulate the innovative process. Strategic concepts and the techniques, structure and terminology surrounding them should be a means to an end and not an end in themselves. This point is readily conceded by many originators of these analytical techniques. Michael Porter, for example, has often argued that his models help people to focus on the right things, and to be innovative and creative on the right things, but have little value when deployed mechanically to crunch data.

We started by defining strategic management and then considered the need for planning.

The next section covered the ingredients that are essential for strategic planning if it is to be effective, looking at the levels of planning – strategic, tactical and operational.

SELF-TEST QUESTIONS

Strategic management

1   List the three different levels of strategy. (1.2)

The importance of strategic management

2   Give a simple definition of strategy. (3.1)

3   What are the five Ps of strategy according to Mintzberg? (3.1)

Strategic management: process, content and context

4 According to Johnson and Scholes, what are three elements to strategic management? (4.3)

The process of strategy development

5 What are Drucker's three types of opportunity? (5.2)

EXAM-TYPE
QUESTION

Corporate planning

What is corporate planning, and why is it carried out? Describe and show the relationship between corporate, business and functional levels.　　　**(20 marks)**

For the answer to this question, see the 'Answers' section at the end of the book.

FEEDBACK TO
ACTIVITY **1**

Most of the issues require some contribution from all levels. However, the principle decision-making levels are as follows.

(a) **Corporate level**. Movement of resources between businesses can only be decided at the highest level.

(b) **Business level**. Only managers who understand the particular markets concerned can really work out the most effective strategy (technically called positioning). Senior managers will be interested in associated costs and benefits, while functions will need to know how they can produce a superior product that appeals to the new target market if this option is selected.

(c) **Functional level**. Good functional managers, in operations and cost accounting in particular, should be able to produce a range of alternative projects to reduce costs. Business level strategy will be concerned with the effect the changes may have on other functions, for example it is possible to reduce costs by lowering quality, but this may make the product harder to sell at the same price. Thus the functions would have achieved their cost reduction targets, but the strategic objective of improving the margin may fail if this quality-based option is selected.

(d) **Business level**. The publishers are best placed to know whether they have, or could gain, the skills necessary to diversify in this way. Naturally, the senior corporate levels will be concerned about costs and benefits of this move, compared with other possible projects.

(e) **Corporate level**. Acquisitions and disposals to strengthen the group of businesses can only be made at the highest level.

Chapter 2
STRATEGIC DEVELOPMENT

In this chapter we look at the rational model of strategic analysis. However, strategy is not always a deliberate rational process; many writers argue that organisational politics and culture have at least as big an influence. We will contrast the rational model with others that take a less prescriptive view of the way that strategy develops.

Objectives

When you have studied this chapter you should be able to:

- consider the strategic management process as a decision-making model

- outline the case against deliberate, long term strategy

- explain the nature of emergent strategy

- explain the strategy process according to logical incrementalism

- explain the key points of cultural and political views of strategy

1   Strategic planning

1.1   Rationality

A rational process is considered to be one 'based on reasoning', one that is not subjective but objective, and one that is logical and sensible. Using rational behaviour, policy is formed by firstly defining the goal and then selecting the means to achieve the goal by rational analysis.

Cause and effect are seen to be interlinked and an element of predictability is expected. In many problem-solving situations an assumption is made that the goals or objectives can be measured or assessed in quantitative terms. Rationality in this sense is based on the choice the decision maker makes with reference to clear-cut alternatives. The following areas are present:

- complete knowledge of environmental factors

- ability to order the preferences using some yardstick of utility, mainly with money as the common denominator

- ability to choose the alternative that returns the best outcome.

In process terms, rationality assumes that a decision taker confronts an issue with known objectives. They then gather appropriate information, develop a set of options and select the optimum one. Suppose a company requires more production capacity. There may be several options available:

- buy or lease more machines

- subcontract

- build or lease a new factory.

If the decision maker's preference was to spend as little as possible (a preference for cheapness), then the rational approach would be to choose the option that cost the least.

Accountants come naturally to this approach, but it is important to remember that planning is a multidisciplinary approach so the planning team will include marketers, designers and others who may not work in a rational fashion. Because the process involves co-operative effort, it is not likely that each individual can maximise personal

KEY POINT

The characteristics of the rational approach are:

- complete knowledge of environmental factors

- ability to order the preferences

- ability to choose the alternative that returns the best outcome objectives all the time. The rationality of organisational behaviour should be concerned with group objectives, not with what the individual would do in that situation.

1.2 Limited or bounded rationality

Most versions of the rational model, which have been advocated and tried in practice, have placed considerable emphasis on the determination of objectives, or ends. Once the ends are determined, all possible means of securing them are explored, and their consequences analysed. The course of action with the greatest net benefits is then chosen.

Simon was aware that this ideal model could not readily be realised in practice. In practice, people seldom achieve complete rationality, especially in managing. In the first place, decisions must operate in the future and this almost certainly involves uncertainties. Secondly, it is difficult to recognise all the alternatives that might be followed to reach a goal. This is particularly true when decision-making involves opportunities to do something that has not been done before. Also, in most instances, it is difficult to analyse all the alternatives, even with the newest analytical techniques and computers.

A limiting factor is something that stands in the way of accomplishing a desired objective. Recognising the limiting factors in a given situation makes it possible to narrow the search for alternatives to those that will overcome them.

A manager must settle for limited or 'bounded' rationality. Limitations of information, time and certainty limit rationality even though a manager tries to be completely rational. Because managers find it difficult to be completely rational in practice, they sometimes allow their dislike of risk to interfere with their desire to reach the best solution under the circumstances.

Simon evolved a 'best practicable model', which would fit the problems of real life. In this model the manager does not optimise (ie, get the best possible solution). Instead the manager satisfices. In other words, the manager carries on searching until he or she finds an option, which appears tolerably satisfactory, and adopts it, even though it may be less than perfect. This approach Simon characterised as bounded rationality

1.3 The link between planning and decision-making

Planning and decision-making are closely linked. The existence of a plan is the result of certain decisions having been taken, and at the same time the plan provides a framework for other decisions.

If there is an effective plan, each executive knows what is expected and why. If on the other hand an executive does not know what targets have been allocated there will be no criteria against which alternative courses of action can be evaluated. Without planning there is a danger that the various units in the organisation will be run without adequate co-ordination, and may be under-performing, pursuing different objectives, or optimising their own performance at the expense of the organisation as a whole.

Too often, management consists of managing short-term problems, of trying to find ways out of immediate difficulties, of muddling through from one crisis to the next. Planning forces attention on the longer term, gives the company a direction, and should help to avoid some of the difficulties. It should at least help to predict future difficulties before they reach crisis proportions, so that there is more time to consider possible solutions.

To take a very simple analogy, managing a business is like a planned car journey. Before setting out you decide where you are going and what route you will take. You may hear on your car radio about difficulties ahead and change your route to avoid encountering a traffic jam. However, eventually you will probably resume your normal course in order to reach your specified destination, although naturally you are quite free to change your mind halfway there. However, rational decision-making is only one way that researchers have thought about management decision-making.

1.4 Advantages of strategic planning

The advantages of a formal system of strategic planning include the following.

- As companies increase in size, the risks also increase - risks would be defined as the potential losses from the inefficient or ineffective use of resources. Strategic planning helps in managing these risks.

- Strategic planning can give a sense of purpose to the personnel in the company, leading to an improved quality of management, and it can encourage creativity and initiative by tapping the ideas of the management team.

- Companies cannot remain static - they have to cope with changes in the environment. A strategic plan helps to chart the future possible areas where the company may be involved as well as offering a framework for dealing with sudden turmoil.

- Strategic plans are merely stating on paper the departmental objectives that have always existed. They help to make them more effective and workable.

- A well-prepared plan drawn up after analysis of internal and external factors - risks and uncertainties - is in the long-term best interests of the company because better-quality decisions will be made (on the whole) and management control can be better exercised.

- Long-term, medium-term and short-term objectives, plans and controls can be made consistent with one another. It is quite possible, however, that strategic plans can be rendered ineffective by budgeting systems with performance measures that have no strategic content.

- Publicises direction - strategic planning might appear to be the very antithesis of entrepreneurship. However, Drucker has argued that an entrepreneur who builds a long-lasting business has 'a theory of the business' which informs his or her business decisions. In large organisations, that the theory of the business has to become public knowledge, as decisions cannot be taken only by one person

2 The rational model

2.1 The rational model of strategic planning

The rational model requires a logical approach. It involves the careful and deliberate formulation, evaluation and selection of strategies for the purpose of preparing a cohesive long-term course of action to attain objectives. It is a complex process, which starts with an examination of both the organisation and its environment, at present and in the future, and continues with the development of plans for all aspects of operations.

There are three main stages to the rational/planning model - these are strategic analysis, strategic choice and strategic implementation, which are described in the following sections. To make it easier to remember, the process can be imagined as undertaking a journey.

- Strategic analysis - Where are we now (current location)? Where do we want to go (desired location)?

- Strategic choice - Develop a range of methods to travel from current location to desired location. Choose which method of travel to undertake.

- Strategic implementation - Travel to desired location.

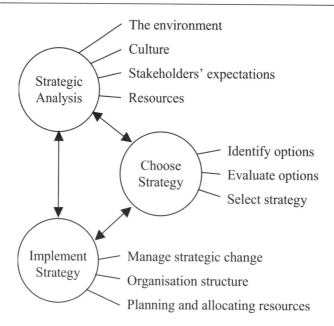

Note that once the strategy is implemented, the new position of the organisation should be analysed; in other words, we return to the strategic analysis stage and the process is continuous. It is quite likely that the elements are interlinked. For example one way of evaluating a strategy might be to begin to implement it and because strategic analysis will be an on-going activity, it will overlap with the implementation of strategy.

This process is not intended as a prescription of what strategic management should be, but as a framework that can be used to structure strategic problems.

2.2　Environmental fit and strategic logic

According to *Hofer and Schendel*, strategic choice follows after the process of strategic analysis, but there are other considerations eg, a strategy might be acceptable in principle, but this does not necessarily make it the right one to choose.

Arguably, the choice of strategy should follow a strategic logic where a proposed sequence of actions is:

- consistently related to the objectives of the organisation; and

- matches the organisation's capability (including its structure, control systems and culture) to its environment.

The idea is that all the pieces of the strategic puzzle should fit together in a predetermined manner and because a strategy must secure a 'fit' with the environment, success flows from this fit. The environment is thus a key factor in the behaviour of any organisation, as organisations derive their inputs from it and distribute their outputs to it. The environment has a variety of influences over the organisation.

Hofer and Schendel also suggest that strategy is a mediating force. The organisation's position can be defined both in relation to competitors and in relation to products, markets and customers.

2.3　Levels of strategy

As we mentioned in the last chapter, the strategic planning process is multi-layered. Corporate strategy is concerned with

- diversifying or limiting the activities of the business;

- investing in existing units, or buying new businesses;

- surviving.

Business strategy identifies how an organisation approaches a particular market, or the activity of a particular business unit and operational and functional strategies involve decisions of strategic importance, but which are made or determined at operational levels. These decisions include such matters as product pricing, investment in plant and personnel policy.

Operational and functional strategies include the following.

- Marketing strategies - creating products and services, pricing, promoting and distributing them, in order to satisfy customer needs at a profit.

- Production strategies - involve issues such as factory location, manufacturing techniques and subcontracting.

- Finance strategies - ensure that the organisation has the financial resources to fund its other strategies. Pricing decisions are both marketing and finance issues.

- Human resources strategies aim to secure personnel in the right quantity, and to ensure that they have the right skills and values to promote the organisation's overall goals.

- Information technology strategies are becoming increasingly important. However, not all information technology applications are strategic, and the strategic value of IT will vary from case to case.

- Change strategies - incorporate many of the above, including changes to organisation structure, an important aspect of strategy.

- Global strategies refer to an organisation's international orientation, and again deal with a variety of issues.

3 Strategic analysis

3.1 The aim of strategic analysis

The aim of strategic analysis is to form a view of the main influences on the present and future well-being of the organisation. This will obviously affect the strategy choice. Strategic analysis would cover the following areas:

- The environmental variables - eg political, economic, social and technological, as well as competitive factors and how they will affect the organisation and its activities.

- The resource availability and its relative strengths and weaknesses.

- The aspirations and expectations of the groups, which have an interest in the organisation eg, shareholders, managers, owners, employees and unions.

- The beliefs and assumptions that make up the culture of the organisation will have an effect because they are the means of interpreting the environment and resource influences.

The environmental variables - as we have already noted in the previous chapter, the organisation exists in the context of a complex commercial, economic, political, technological, cultural and social world. This environment is more complex for some organisations than for others. Since strategy is concerned with the position a business takes in relation to *its* environment, an understanding of the environment's effects on an organisation is of central importance to strategic analysis. The historical and environmental effects on the business must be considered, as well as the present effects and the expected changes in environmental variables. This is a major task because the range of environmental variables is so great. Many of those variables will give rise to *opportunities* of some sort, and many will exert *threats* upon the organisation. The two main problems that have to be faced are, first, to distil out of this complexity a view of the main or overall environmental impacts for the purpose of strategic choice; and second, the fact that the range of variables is likely to be so great that it may not be possible or realistic to identify and analyse each one.

The resources of the organisation - there are internal influences as well as outside influences on the firm and its choice of strategies. One of the ways of thinking about the strategic capability of an organisation is to consider its strengths and weaknesses (what it is good or not so good at doing, or where it is at a competitive advantage or disadvantage, for example). Considering the resource areas of a business such as its physical plant, its management, its financial structure and its products may identify these strengths and weaknesses. Again, the aim is to form a view of the internal influences and constraints on strategic choice. The expectations of different stakeholders are important because they will affect what will be seen as acceptable in terms of the strategies advanced by management. However, the beliefs and assumptions that make up the culture of an organisation, though less explicit, will also have an important influence.

The environmental and resource influences on an organisation will be interpreted through these beliefs and assumptions; so two groups of managers, perhaps working in different divisions of an organisation, may come to different conclusions about strategy, although they are faced with similar environmental and resource implications. Which influence prevails is likely to depend on which group has the greatest power, and understanding this can be of great importance in recognising why an organisation follows or is likely to follow, the strategy it does.

Together, a consideration of the environment, the resources, the expectations and the objectives within the cultural and political framework of the organisation provides the basis of the strategic analysis of an organisation. However, to understand the strategic position an organisation is in, it is also necessary to examine the extent to which the direction and implications of the current strategy and objectives, being followed by the organisation, are in line with and can cope with the implications of the strategic analysis.

3.2   Strategic position of the organisation

Strategic analysis is concerned with understanding the strategic position of the organisation.

The stages of strategic analysis include the following:

- Definition of the mission is of fundamental importance since it answers the question: 'What business are we in?' It might be expressed in a mission statement. It can serve three functions: it can be the fount of the organisation's value system; it can indicate the firm's long-term approach to business and its commercial rationale; and it can be used as the basis of the organisation's public image. A mission rarely changes.

- Goals are not necessarily quantified, but they relate the mission to the needs of different stakeholders such as customers, employees and shareholders. These stakeholders might have conflicting interests. A stakeholder analysis is the technique to use for this part of the analysis.

- Objectives should embody mission. Generally, they are quantitative measures, against which actual performance can be assessed. However, it would be wrong to say that only things that can be measured are important. For example, the ethical dimension of objectives can be very important. Objectives do change. The key tools and techniques include measures such as performance, time scales and deadlines.

- Corporate needs analysis is made up of the environmental analysis (or external appraisal), the position audit (incorporating an internal appraisal), which examines the current state of the organisation, the corporate appraisal and a gap analysis. The corporate appraisal (or SWOT analysis) flows from the first two stages and is a critical assessment of the strengths, weaknesses, opportunities and threats affecting the organisation in order to establish its position prior to the preparation of a long-term plan. The gap analysis is based on a forecast of current activities into the future; the aim is to identify any shortfall in projected results against objectives.

3.3   Expectations and influence of stakeholders

A stakeholder can be defined as someone who has an interest in the well being of the organisation. A typical list of stakeholders for a large company would include shareholders, employees, managers, customers, locality, suppliers, government and society at large.

- **Shareholders** - the owners of the organisation are generally concerned with a steady flow of income (eg dividends), possible capital growth and continuation of the business. For example, if an organisation wishes to follow a strategy that will involve a large capital injection, the shareholders will be unhappy if the injection has an adverse effect on their income stream.

- **Managers** - are generally concerned with pay and status, job security and individual performance measures. If an organisation wishes to follow a strategy that results in a particular department being reduced in size or abolished, the manager of that department is likely to be hostile to the plans.

- **Employees** - are generally concerned with job security, pay and conditions and job satisfaction. For example, if an organisation wishes to follow a strategy that results in workers being given more responsibility for monitoring quality, the employees may be unhappy unless this increased role is supported by an increase in wages.

- **Trade unions** - apart from the problems of the employees noted above, unions within an organisation are generally concerned with taking an active part in the decision-making process. For example, if an organisation wishes to follow a strategy that results in a manufacturing plant being closed, the union will be unhappy if it has not been consulted and if there is no scheme for helping the employees to find alternative employment.

- **Customers** - are generally concerned with receiving goods and services of a reasonable quality and paying a reasonable price for them. For example, if an organisation wishes to follow a strategy that increases the quality of a product at the same time as increasing the price, there may be problems with both existing and potential new customers. Existing customers may not be willing to pay more for the product, while new customers are not attracted to a product that they still view as being of low quality.

- **Suppliers** - are generally concerned with being paid promptly for goods and services delivered and receiving regular repayments of any capital provided (eg banks). For example, if an organisation wishes to follow a strategy that improves working capital management by paying suppliers late, existing suppliers may decide to stop supplying the organisation, leading to the increased cost of finding new suppliers.

- **Government and the general public** - are generally concerned that the organisation is meeting relevant legal requirements and that it does not harm the outside environment. For example, if an organisation wishes to follow a strategy that relies on increased use of shops based in out-of-town retail centres, this will be affected by government attitudes towards increased road building and society's attitude towards this method of shopping.

4 Strategic choice

4.1 Procedure

Strategic choice follows strategic analysis and is based upon the following three elements:

1. Generation of strategic options eg, growth, acquisition, diversification or concentration.

2. Evaluation of the options to assess their relative merits and feasibility.

3. Selection of the strategy or option that the organisation will pursue. There could be more than one strategy chosen but there is a chance of an inherent danger or disadvantage to any choice made. Although there are techniques for evaluating specific options, the selection is often subjective and likely to be influenced by the values of managers and other groups with an interest in the organisation.

4.2 Generation of strategic options

There may be several possible courses of action open to the organisation. For example, an international retailer may need to decide on areas such as:

- which areas of the world are most important to concentrate on

- whether it is possible to maintain a common basis of trading across all the different countries

- whether it is necessary to introduce variations by market focus.

- what strategic directions are necessary for product development and product range

- should the company attempt to follow these strategies by internal development or joint venture activity through franchising

All of these considerations are important and needed careful consideration: indeed, in developing strategies, a potential danger is that managers do not consider any but the most obvious course of action -and the most obvious is not necessarily the best. A helpful step in strategic choice can be to generate strategic options.

Strategic options generation is the process of establishing a choice of possible future strategies. There are three main areas to consider.

1. Porter describes certain competitive strategies which an organisation may pursue for competitive advantage (a condition which is proof against 'erosion by competitor behaviour or industry evolution'). They determine how you compete.

2. Ansoff describes product-market strategies (which markets you should enter or leave). They determine where you compete and the direction of growth.

3. Institutional strategies (ie, relationships with other organisations) determine the method of growth.

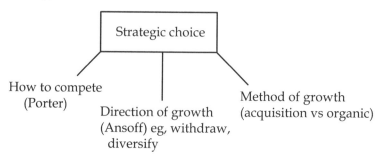

4.3 Evaluation of the options

Strategic options can be examined in the context of the strategic analysis to assess their relative merits. In deciding on any of the options that they face, the organisation might want to know whether they are suitable to the firm's existing position. They need to know which of these options builds upon strengths, overcomes weaknesses and takes advantage of opportunities, while minimising or circumventing the threats the business faces. This is called the search for strategic fit or suitability of the strategy. However, a second set of questions is important.

- To what extent could a chosen strategy be put into effect?
- Could required finance be raised, sufficient stock be made available at the right time and in the right place, staff be recruited and trained to reflect the sort of image the organisation is trying to project? These are questions of feasibility.

Even if these criteria could be met, management would still need to know whether the choice would be acceptable to the stakeholders.

A variety of techniques are used to assess the value of strategies. Some strategies will be assessed on financial criteria (such as net present value). Where this is not possible, or where the uncertainty in the environment is great, more sophisticated models are used.

4.4 Selection of the strategy or option

This is the process of selecting those options, which the organisation will pursue. There could be just one strategy chosen or several. There is unlikely to be a clear-cut 'right' or 'wrong' choice because any strategy must inevitably have some dangers or disadvantages. So in the end, choice is likely to be a matter of management judgement. It is important to understand that the selection process cannot always be viewed or understood as a purely objective, logical act. It is strongly influenced by the values of managers and other groups with interest in the organisation, and ultimately may very much reflect the power structure in the organisation.

5 Strategy implementation

5.1 Implementation process

The implementation of the strategy has to be planned. This is the conversion of the strategy into detailed plans or objectives for operating units.

- Some plans go into detailed specifications as to how the activities should be carried out.
- Others will specify targets which managers are expected to reach on their own initiative.

The implementation process can also be thought of as having several parts.

- Resource planning and the logistics of implementation. The process will address the problems of the tasks that need to be carried out and also the timing of them. There may need to be changes in the mix of resources required to implement the strategy and decisions will need to be taken about who is to be responsible for the changes.
- The organisational structure may need to be changed eg, from hierarchical to matrix or from centralised to decentralised.
- The systems employed to manage the organisation may be improved. These systems provide the information and operational procedures needed in the organisation. It may be that a new information management system is required to monitor the progress of the strategy. Staff may need to be retrained or new staff recruited.

5.2 Resource planning

Resource planning covers finance, human resource management and physical resources such as land and buildings. It involves assessing the key tasks to satisfy the critical success factors, and the resources to be allocated to the key tasks. It is concerned with the following questions:

- What are the key tasks that need to be carried out?

- What changes need to be made in the resource mix of the organisation?

- By when?

- Who is to be responsible for the change?

5.3 Structure

KEY POINT

Organisation structure - lines of authority and communication must be established, which are appropriate to the way the strategy is broken down into detailed targets.

It is likely that changes in organisational structure will be needed to carry through the strategy and there is also likely to be a need to adapt the systems used to manage the organisation.

Organisation structure - lines of authority and communication must be established, which are appropriate to the way the strategy is broken down into detailed targets.

Systems are necessary to provide the necessary strategic information, as well as essential operational procedures. Control systems are used to assess performance. The type of questions that will need answering include:

- What will different departments be held responsible for?

- What sorts of information system are needed to monitor the progress of the strategy?

- Is there a need for retraining of the workforce?

Implementation involves devising sub-strategies for products and markets, human resources and so on.

6 Strategic management in context

6.1 Incrementalism

Between the extremes of an orderly rational corporate planning approach on the one hand and completely ad hoc, reactive decision-making on the other, there is a range of strategic decision-making styles. Incrementalism and rationalism are two models of strategy formulation, which are generally represented as occupying opposite ends of the spectrum of approaches. rational model is associated with Herbert Simon and the leading academic advocate of incrementalism is Charles Lindblom.

Charles Lindblom described incrementalism. He suggested that managing strategies through logical, planning mechanisms was not realistic. Because of the complexity of organisations and the environments in which they operate, it would be difficult for managers to consider all the strategic options and measure them against preset, unambiguous objectives.

KEY POINT

Lindblom argued that strategic choice takes place by comparing possible options against each other and considering which would give the best outcome.

Lindblom argued that strategic choice takes place by comparing possible options against each other and considering which would give the best outcome. He called this strategy building through 'successive limited comparisons'.

For Lindblom, the key constraint on the development of effective strategy (or policy, since he was addressing his remarks to the public sector) was the influence of key stakeholders. For a commercial company, these are no less important.

KEY POINT

The term *incremental strategy* describes the situation where a company plans and implements changes gradually in a piecemeal way by using small fine-tuning strategies.

Incrementalism describes the situation where a company plans and implements changes gradually in a piecemeal way by using small fine-tuning strategies which, although relatively small and incremental in nature, collectively represent a considerable change to the company's strategic position over a long time.

The benefits of developing a strategy incrementally are that it avoids major errors and it is more likely to be acceptable because consultation, compromise and accommodation are built into the process.

Lindblom presents the following comparison of the two approaches.

Rational-comprehensive (Root)	**Successive limited comparisons (Branch)**
Clarification of objectives distinct from and usually prerequisite to empirical analysis of alternative policies	Selection of objectives and empirical analysis of the necessary action are not distinct from one another but are closely intertwined
Policy formulation is therefore approached through means-end analysis: first the ends are isolated, then the means to achieve them are sought.	Since means and ends are not distinct, means-end analysis is often inappropriate or limited
The test of a 'good' policy is that it can be shown to be the most appropriate means to desired ends.	The test of a 'good' policy is typically that various analysts find themselves directly agreeing on a policy (without their agreeing that it is the most appropriate means to an agreed objective).
Analysis is comprehensive; every important factor is taken into account.	Analysis is drastically limited: Important possible outcomes are neglected. Important alternative potential policies are neglected. Important affected values are neglected.
Theory is often heavily relied upon.	A succession of comparisons greatly reduces or eliminates reliance on theory.

Lindblom attempted to discredit rational approaches and suggested that in the real world, the rational model, or even bounded rationality, was not used for the following reasons:

- Managers do not in practice evaluate all the possible options open to them in a given situation, but choose between relatively few alternatives.
- Strategy making tends to involve small-scale extensions of past policy - rather than radical shifts following a comprehensive rational search.
- It is not always possible to distinguish ends from means.
- Strategic policy-making necessitates seeking accommodation or compromises with interested groups - a process Lindblom described as partisan mutual adjustment. Thus policy making was seen as the outcome of political bargaining.
- Strategy making often does not proceed according to any coherent plan but rather proceeds disjointedly. Lindblom used the term disjointed incrementalism.

This might seem a good descriptive model of the way strategy making often proceeds in the real world, especially in the public sector but scarcely something to be recommended. Yet Lindblom thought his incremental model was to be preferred to the rational model.

Lindblom argued that strategy making involving small scale extensions of past practices was more likely to be successful: it would avoid major errors, and was more likely to be acceptable, because consultation, compromise and accommodation were built into the process. Comprehensive rational planning was impossible, and likely to result in disaster if actively pursued.

6.2 Logical incremental view

J B Quinn in his book *Strategies for Change*, wrote that the management process could best be described as logical incrementalism (sometimes called 'adaptive' by other writers). This is the situation where managers have a view of where they want the organisation to be in the years to come but try to move towards that objective in an evolutionary way. They do this by trying to develop a strong, secure but flexible core business, whilst also continually experimenting with 'side bet' ventures. He also recognised that such experiments could not be the sole responsibility of the top managers but they should be encouraged to emerge from lower levels or 'subsystems' in the organisation.

Logical incrementalism is not just muddling through - it is a purposeful, effective, proactive management technique for integrating both the analytical and behavioural aspects of strategy formation.

Effective managers accept the uncertainty of their environment and seek to become highly sensitive to changes through constant environmental scanning and by testing changes in strategy in small-scale steps. Strategy is best described as a learning process in which managers have to deal with major internal or external events. (It is impossible to predict the long-term consequences of decisions made in situations of crisis or change.) For these reasons, managers deliberately keep their decisions small scale, so that they can be tested. However, unlike muddling through which appears simply reactive, the logical incremental model suggests a conscious process of decision-making:

- Managers have an outline notion as to where the organisation should be. Perhaps this relates to 'pursuing a vision'

- Strategies should be tested in small steps, simply because there is too much uncertainty about actual outcomes, although they may be directed in the context of vision

- Precise objectives discourage experimentation by business units.

This process is seen as having benefits to the organisation. Continual testing and gradual strategy implementation provides improved quality of information to help decision-making. There is also a stimulation of managerial flexibility and creativity and, since changes will be gradual, the possibility of creating and developing a commitment to change throughout the organisation is increased.

We can now conclude that the logical incrementalist view does not view strategic management in terms of a neat, sequential model. The idea that the implementation of strategy somehow follows a choice, which in turn has followed analysis, does not hold. Strategy is seen to be worked through in action.

6.3 No strategic planning: 'freewheeling opportunism'

It is possible to do without strategic plans and to operate a system whereby opportunities are exploited as they arise, judged on their individual merits and not within the rigid structure of an overall corporate strategy. This approach is sometimes called *freewheeling opportunism.* The advantages of this approach are as follows.

- Opportunities can be seized when they arise, whereas a rigid planning framework might impose restrictions so that the opportunities are lost.

- It is flexible and adaptable. A formal corporate plan might take a long time to prepare and is fully documented. Any sudden, unexpected change (eg a very steep rise in the price of a key commodity) might cause serious disruption. A freewheeling opportunistic approach would adapt to the change more quickly.

- It might encourage a more flexible, creative attitude among lower-level managers, whereas the procedures of formal planning might not.

There are disadvantages to the freewheeling opportunism approach.

- It fails to provide a co-ordinating framework for the organisation as a whole, so that there would be a tendency for large organisations to break up into many fragments.

- It cannot guarantee that all opportunities are identified and appraised. Strategic planning relies heavily on the creative thinking of its managers to design strategies, and a formal system should be more thorough in exploiting this creativity to the full.

- It emphasises the profit motive to the exclusion of all other considerations.

The way strategic planning is practised will vary with circumstances.

- A large bureaucratic organisation will probably require a formal planning system.

- In circumstances where growth or innovation are required, it will be important to organise for new projects.

- In an uncertain situation with many interest groups involved, it may be advisable to use an incremental or *organisational learning* process - to improve mutual understanding, to explore the problem, and possibly to evolve a consensus.

- If it is necessary to influence decisions in other organisations, there may be a need for special arrangements, such as joint committees and liaison officers, to improve formal and informal contacts.

- Sometimes, an organisation suffers a crisis of identity. This can happen if its social value is questioned or if its future is tied up with new technology with important social implications. If this happens, it may be particularly important to re-examine the future role of the enterprise in society.

6.4 The cultural view

Traditionally, strategy has been viewed as the response of an organisation to its environment. However, faced with similar environments, organisations respond differently; these differences are accounted for by the influence of managerial decision-making on strategy.

Culture is reflected in the way that people in an organisation perform tasks, set objectives and administer resources to achieve them. Culture also influences the selection of people for particular jobs, which in turn affects the way that tasks are carried out and decisions are made.

There are a wide variety of factors that influence the expectations that individuals and groups are likely to have of an organisation. When analysing the significance of these factors in the strategic development of an organisation, it is useful to ask three questions:

- Which factors inside and outside the organisation have most influence on the expectations of people within the organisation?

- To what extent do current strategies reflect the influence of any one factor or combination of factors?

- How far would these factors help or hinder the changes that would be needed to pursue new strategies?

6.5   The political view

Strategy development can also be explained in political terms. Organisations are political entities and powerful internal and external interest groups influence the inputs into their decisions. Different interest groups may be in conflict and there may be differences between groups of managers, between managers and shareholders, or between powerful individuals. These differences are likely to be resolved through processes of bargaining, negotiation or perhaps edict, but they will certainly affect the objectives of the organisation.

Powerful individuals or groups may also influence the sort of information that is seen as being important. Information is not politically neutral, but rather is a source of power for those who control that information which is seen to be important. The withholding of information, or the power of one manager over and another because that manager controls sources of information, can therefore be important. Powerful individuals and groups may also strongly influence the identification of key issues and even the strategies eventually selected. It would be wrong to assume that these emerge in a politically neutral environment. Differing views will be fought for not only on the basis of the extent to which they reflect environmental or competitive pressures, but also because they have implications for the status or influence of different stakeholders.

A political perspective on decision-making would therefore suggest that strategies emerge through processes of bargaining, negotiation and the trading- off of political interests.

Conclusion

In this chapter we looked at different explanations for the development of strategy. The rational (planning) model and its three phases of strategic analysis, strategic choice and strategic implementation were explained. This view argues that the mission is the means by which different stakeholders interests are resolved and the strategy is a rational process of achieving the mission over time. At the other extreme, the incrementalist view holds that strategic choice takes place by comparing possible options against each other and considering which would give the best outcome.

Strategic planning

1   What is the difference between rationality and bounded rationality? (1.1, 1.2)

The rational model

2   What is environmental fit? (2.2)

3   How does corporate strategy differ from operational strategy? (2.3)

Strategic analysis

4   Describe the stages of strategic analysis. (3.2)

Strategy implementation

5   What makes up the organisational structure? (5.3)

Long-term strategic planning

Your managing director has attended a conference at which a speaker said that long-term strategic planning was obsolete. He is naturally concerned about this comment.

You are required to draft a report to your managing director stressing the benefits of long-term strategic planning and examining the case for its abolition. **(20 marks)**

Proactive and reactive styles

McNamee states that 'strategic management is considered to be that type of management through which an organisation tries to obtain a good fit with its environment'. This approach has been characterised as 'proactive'.

There are many successful organisations that do not undertake strategic planning. This approach has been characterised as 'reactive' or sometimes 'freewheeling opportunism'.

You are required:

(a) to explain the essential characteristics of the two approaches (strategic planning and freewheeling opportunism) mentioned above. What are the advantages and disadvantages of the two approaches? **(12 marks)**

(b) to explain in what circumstances you would recommend an organisation to adopt:

(i) strategic planning,

(ii) freewheeling opportunism **(8 marks)**

(Total: 20 marks)

Chapter 3
CULTURE OF THE ORGANISATION

Managers' perceptions of the world, like everyone else's, are coloured by their background and experience, and this can critically affect the decision-making process in the organisation.

Their view of the competition will be influenced by remarks made by customers, by their advertisements, by reported and rumoured performance, as well as by comments made by ex-employees and other managers. This information may then be interpreted by management to fit a stereotype of a particular competitor, based on some past experience where the organisation either 'won' or 'lost' some battle with the competition.

Strong shared values and beliefs can be a tremendous driving force in the organisation. However, these values are deep-rooted and cannot be changed easily. They tend to be a stabilising force keeping the status quo in the organisation and may cause problems if they do not support the preferred organisational strategy.

This chapter considers the main issue of organisational culture. This topic has been paramount in management thinking over the past decade and the business pages of newspapers constantly carry company references to:

- 'going back to care'
- 'promoting a corporate image'
- 'developing a customer based culture', etc.

The existence of culture and the process of changing and developing an organisation's culture affect every aspect of every management position. It therefore touches each chapter in this text.

Objectives

When you have studied this chapter you should be able to:
- define and explain culture
- understand the determinants of culture: Schein
- understand the implications of culture: Pümpin
- describe the cultural web: Johnson and Scholes
- link culture with structure
- discuss models of culture: Handy, Miles and Snow, Peters and Waterman, Mintzberg
- understand changing organisational culture: Kanter, Lewin
- discuss the relationship between strategic leadership and culture
- identify regional and national culture.

1   Culture and organisation

The term culture has its origins in the work of social anthropologists who used the term to refer to 'the complex whole which includes knowledge, belief, art, law, morals, custom and the many other capabilities and habits acquired by a person as a member of a society'. The term was used to refer to total societies, the external environment of the organisation. However, since the mid-1970s the concept of culture has been increasingly applied to organisations. Each organisation is seen as possessing its own distinctive culture, which not only provides a basis for understanding organisational behaviour but also is a key determinant of organisational success.

1.1 The definition of organisational culture

There is no shortage of definitions of organisational culture. It has been described, for example, as 'the dominant values espoused by an organisation' and 'the basic assumptions and beliefs that are shared by members of an organisation'. As it relates to organisations, culture is the general pattern of behaviour, shared beliefs and values that members have in common. Culture can be inferred from what people say, do and think. It reflects the underlying assumptions about the way work is performed and what behaviour and actions are encouraged and discouraged.

It can be defined as 'the collection of traditions, values, policies, beliefs and attitudes that constitute a pervasive context for everything we do and think in an organisation'. Handy describes culture as the 'way things are done around here'.

Despite the variety it is possible to distil the common characteristics and recognise the common features of the definitions.

1.2 The key elements of culture

Schein suggests that there are three elements or levels to culture – artefacts, espoused values and underlying assumptions

- **Artefacts** – these are the things that come together to define a culture and reveal what the culture is about to those who pay attention to them. Although the word 'artefact' suggests tangible things such as the product or service provided, it also embraces behaviour patterns. Modern IT companies often have a very casual dress code where people, even senior executives, might be seen in jeans and sweatshirts, rather than the traditional tailored suit that is the feature of many large companies.

- **Espoused values** – these are the reasons given by an organisation for the way things are done. These often go back to the way business was set up originally. An explosives business has to have a very high safety culture, if only to survive. The Body Shop challenges the work ethic of 'work, work, work' with the notion of 'work, live, love and learn'.

- **Underlying or basic assumptions** – these are the beliefs that are taken for granted by members of an organisation. It is an unspoken 'right way of doing things'. Again, taking The Body Shop as an example, it has questioned the traditional view of feminine beauty.

Schein proposes that the basic assumptions are treated as the essence – what culture really is – and the values and behaviours are treated as manifestations of the cultural essence.

Another way of looking at the elements that make up the culture is to say that in every organisation there has evolved, over time, a system of beliefs, values, norms of behaviour, symbols, myths and practices that are shared by members of the organisation. The key elements can be shown in a diagram:

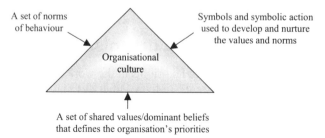

The key elements of organisational culture

Shared values or dominant beliefs - these underlie the culture by specifying what is important and need to be shared by everyone in the organisation so that they are reinforced and widely accepted. Examples of shared values include a belief in the importance of people as individuals and an operational focus, such as guaranteeing delivery on time.

Norms - guide people's behaviour, suggesting what is or is not appropriate. The commitment to shared values must be strong enough to develop norms of behaviour or informal rules, which influence the decisions and actions throughout the organisation. . For example, in a 'quality service' culture, sloppy work affecting the product or service would be informally policed by fellow workers, without reliance on formal systems.

Symbols or symbolic actions there are many examples of persistent, consistent and visible symbols and symbolic actions that make up an organisation's culture. These include the organisation's unique roots established by the personal style and experience of the founder and the original mission, e.g. the concept of entertainment developed by Walt Disney include rituals and other examples such as recruitment techniques, eating lunches and giving impromptu awards and the activities of an executive - visiting the factory floor to speak to employees.

Culture refers to the shared understandings and meanings that members have concerning an organisation. Rather as individuals have distinctive personalities, each organisation is seen as possessing its own distinctive culture, which not only provides a basis for understanding organisational behaviour but also is a key determinant of organisational success.

Two individuals can be doing the same job in different organisations but may go about them in very different ways. For example, consider two accountants, one working in the Civil Service and the other in an advertising agency. It should be apparent that their working methods and the importance, which colleagues put on aspects of their jobs, would be very different. The accountant in the advertising firm may well have to work to a great many short-term deadlines as clients' work is finished. The accountant's colleagues in the agency will probably find his ability to communicate ideas more important than his technical skills.

Why is culture important? Because it affects the whole of an organisation, including

- the values of the organisation, ie the mission
- the expectations of managers, ie the objectives for which they are striving
- the strategy adopted by the organisation
- the attitude of the workforce towards customers, profits, quality etc
- how the employees will react to any changes in plans.

Note that the strength of the culture is as important as its content. A weak culture can more easily be changed than a strong culture. In general, the older an organisation, the stronger its culture will be. It is important to note that culture tends to be self-perpetuating, ie a certain culture attracts people who like working within that culture. This reinforces the culture, which means that in future the organisation will again attract people who like working within that culture.

1.3 Determinants of culture

We can see that the culture of a business is very difficult to define precisely. It is made up of a combination of factors, which influence both the working environment and the way things are done. Some of these factors are:

- the extent of formalisation of the structure;
- whether decisions are made by committees or individuals;
- the degree of freedom allowed to subordinates to show initiative;

- the degree of freedom subordinates expect to be given (again the opportunity to show initiative);
- whether junior employees feel free to talk to senior managers (open door management);
- formalisation of clothing and office layout;
- the kind of people employed (graduates, young, old, etc.).

There are many different models of organisational culture. Schein's ideas are challenging because they focus on certain assumptions and beliefs held by organisations, outlined below.

- *Relationship to environment*. Some organisations believe that they can dominate the business environment and achieve their own ends. Others may assume that they are helpless in the face of swirling currents of change, and have to accept whatever positions and niches they are forced into.
- *Truth and reality*. Organisations have different means of devising and testing what comes to be regarded as truth. In some cases, the experience and wisdom of senior management may lead to a truth by decree. In others, truth might be accorded to whoever can win a political battle. Some firms like to base their truth on information and data, and choose to pay less attention to facets that cannot be easily quantified.
- *Human nature*. Some organisations adopt a 'community' approach, where the approval of peers and support of colleagues are considered motivating factors. In others, financial motivations are considered more important than an intrinsic value in the work or company, whilst in others the culture may be more coercive as the dominant view is that individuals are best motivated by fear.
- *Attitudes to human activity*. While some organisations expect a great deal of commitment from individuals, and expect sacrifices in terms of time spent at leisure with family, some adopt a more balanced approach and do not expect such levels of dedication. There is a contrast of philosophies in many cases, where in some organisations people are valued for what they do, while in others they are appreciated for what they are.
- *Human relationships*. In some organisations the culture is very informal and individuals interact as friends, while in others relationships are expected to be formal and, on the surface at least, professional only. This further extends to the encouragement of individualism, compared to the benefits and tyranny of teamwork at other places.

These things may all change over time, but it is important to see that managers are part of the culture; they do not sit above and do not have a direct means of controlling all its aspects. Further, we are perhaps mistaken to speak of **an** organisational culture. Though it may well be that an organisation possesses a dominant culture it is not always shared by all members. Groups form in organisations e.g. departments and informal work groups who create distinctive shared understandings of their own. This leads to the existence of **sub-cultures** that, though they may share the core features of the whole organisation, are nonetheless distinct. For example a Research and Development department may well have its unique culture as a result of its specialist role, its qualified staff and its geographical separation from other employees. Similar comments could apply to the finance and accounting departments.

At the extreme, organisations may be faced with the existence of **counter cultures** where the aim is to undermine the dominant culture. Examples of this might be in groups that seek to undermine management control, groups who practise vandalism and sabotage, or groups who are simply alienated and apathetic.

In the light of these observations it is important to remember that most writers on organisational culture are referring to the **dominant culture** and tend to ignore or underplay the existence of sub or counter cultures.

1.4 The implications of culture – Pümpin

Professor Pümpin studied a large number of world-class companies in order to understand what made them more dynamic than their rivals. He found that the corporate culture of his dynamic companies included the following four attributes:

(a) *Expansion orientation:* The firms were all ambitious to find success in fast growing markets and would generally choose to accept the consequences of change and diversification.

(b) *Speed orientation:* Dynamic firms pride themselves on doing things quickly. This ranges from opening such activities as shops and airlines in record times, to the swift return of telephone calls and customer despatch.

(c) *Productivity orientation*: World-class firms focus on getting things done, rather than monitoring and controlling activity. Characteristically, they have smaller numbers of corporate staff and few layers of management than average companies.

(d) *Risk orientation*: Generally, world-class companies are willing to act in the face of greater uncertainty than their average competitors. Consequently, they frequently get first move advantage and build upon it. This means that they have to be more tolerant of failure that is not due to incompetence.

Pümpin found that all these traits were strong in the cultures of his world-class companies. This made them weaker in some other behaviours, such as customer service, employee orientation, cost orientation and so on, than less successful rivals. He concludes that firms wishing to change their culture to be more successful may have to give up previously successful behaviours – such as customer orientation – to develop the dynamic corporate behaviours he observed, on the grounds that over specialisation in one particular orientation is an obstacle to world-class performance.

1.5 The cultural web model

This model of cultural behaviour was devised by Gerry Johnson as part of his work to attempt to explain why firms often fail to adjust to environmental change as quickly as they needed to. He concluded that firms developed a way of understanding their organisation – called a paradigm – and found it difficult to think and act outside this paradigm if it were particularly strong.

A paradigm is a shared mindset - formed from the basic or implicit assumptions that members of an organisation unconsciously carry around with them. It can be defined as a constellation of concepts and perceptions shared by a group that determines how the group views the world. There has to have been enough shared experiences to have led to a shared view and this shared view must have worked for long enough so it is taken for granted and dropped out of awareness.

KEY POINT

Pümpin found that the corporate culture of the dynamic organisations he studied included the following features:

- expansion orientation
- speed orientation
- productivity orientation
- risk orientation.

DEFINITION

A paradigm can be defined as a constellation of concepts and perceptions shared by a group that determines how the group views the world.

The cultural web is concerned with the manifestations of culture in the organisation and has six interrelated elements:

(i) *Routines and rituals* – routines are 'the way things are done around here' and may even demonstrate a beneficial competency. Rituals signal that something is especially valued. They include events such as award ceremonies for best-performing salesperson.

(ii) *Stories and myths* – these are told by members of an organisation. They embed the present in its organisational history and demonstrate important events and personalities, as well as mavericks that deviate from the norm.

(iii) *Symbols* – such as logos, offices, cars, titles, type of language and terminology commonly used become a shorthand representation of the nature of the organisation.

(iv) *Power structure* – the dominant coalition is the obvious source of power in an organisation. This may be based on management position and seniority but in some organisations power can be lodged with other levels or functions.

(v) *Organisational structure* – reflects the formal and informal ways in which the organisation works. Structures are likely to reflect power.

(vi) *Control systems* – the measurement and reward systems that emphasise what is important to monitor and to focus attention and activity upon.

The concept of the cultural web is a useful device for mapping out change but its real worth is in the fact that we can identify which elements of culture need to change.

Johnson (1998) has shown that this is a useful management tool. It can allow managers to compare today's organisational culture with one that is more appropriate for the near future.

Put the cultural elements of the NHS into a cultural web.

Feedback to this activity is at the end of the chapter.

2 Culture and structure

2.1 Factors that shape the organisation

The culture and structure of an organisation develop over time and in response to a complex set of factors. The combination of personalities and events - both past and present - will have produced a unique balance of factors that shapes the organisation. The key influences that are likely to contribute to the development of any corporate culture include the following:

Technology - can have a profound effect on work patterns and thus on culture. The more complex the technical system, the more elaborate and professional the support staff. The way in which co-ordination between individuals and groups is exercised determines the appropriate form of organisation and thus significantly affects the culture. The more formalised the work the more bureaucratic the operations and thus the more similar they would be eg, an oil refinery would probably be operated in a very similar way all over the world.

Leadership and the power structure - have a considerable impact and a particularly powerful force is the make-up of the senior management team. The greater the external control exerted on an organisation (e.g. by head office or government), the more centralised and formalised its structure.

Market factors - those most significant to success will tend to be reflected in the make-up of the board of directors of an organisation. For example, a company with an IT director on its board is likely to see information as more important than one that doesn't.

Ownership and history of the organisation - the organisation's founder might have set up a strong set of values and assumptions and even after he or she has retired, these values have their own momentum. Businesses in which the owner is 'hands-on' are likely to have a different culture from those where ownership is divorced from management. An organisation that has only experienced success will have a view of life completely different from a company that has suffered job losses and loss of market share.

Organisational age and size - the older and larger an organisation, the more formalised its behaviour and the more likely it is to be bureaucratic. The larger an organisation, the larger the size of its average unit and the more specialised the jobs and units within it. Each specialisation is likely to be accompanied by an appropriate culture, and thus various cultures will flourish in the organisation.

Environment - the more dynamic an organisation's environment, the more its culture needs to be one that supports flexibility. The more complex an organisation's environment, the more decentralised its structure is likely to be, with a consequent development of cultural diversity.

2.2   The Harrison/Handy classification

Developing the work of Harrison, Charles Handy (in *Gods of Management*) suggests that organisation cultures can be grouped into four basic types. (Most organisations contain more than one of these types)

The four types of organisational culture are differentiated by their structure, processes and management methods.

1. Zeus is the god representing the *power culture* or club culture - (typical of small, entrepreneurial organisations). A power culture has web – like communications structure

2. Apollo is the god of the *role culture* or *bureaucracy* - (larger, more formal organisations). A role culture has a typical pyramid structure

3. Athena is the goddess of the *task culture* - (a matrix or matrix-type organisation looking to achieve integration and synergy)

4. Dionysus is the god of the *existential culture* - the person culture (a structure and a culture built around individuals).

The power culture - this type of culture depends on a central power source with rays of influence from the central figure throughout the organisation. There are few procedures and rules of a formal kind and little bureaucracy. The power culture tends to be found in small organisations where the pattern of communication is simpler than in large ones. The dominant influence of the centre results in a structure that is able to move quickly and respond to change and outside threats. This ability is gained not by formal methods but by the selection of like-minded individuals who in key positions are able to 'guess what the boss would do' without the need for conformist systems. As might be expected attempts to implement a structured system into this culture are likely to be vigorously resisted both on the grounds of constraining flexibility and unnecessary cost. Politics is important here and the ability to anticipate the actions of the boss is essential for survival.

The role culture - is perhaps the most readily recognised and common of all the cultural types. Everything and everybody are in their proper place. There is a presumption of logic and rationality. It is based around the job or role rather than the personalities and is epitomised by what we tend to think of as the traditional hierarchical structure. This culture may be expressed as a Greek temple - a series of job boxes make up the functions (the pillars), which are then co-ordinated through the pediment at the top. Its strengths are in its predictability and stability while its obvious opposites of inflexibility and slowness of reaction are its weakness. People describe their job by its duties, **not** by its purpose.

This kind of culture is best suited to an environment that is relatively stable and a large-sized organisation. Because of the focus on the role this culture tends to be impersonal, and by implication restrictive, suppressing individuals' attempts at any improvements. It doesn't take much thought to work in a role culture. Change is therefore relatively slow and is often only brought about by fear. Although it can adapt, this ability is restricted and a 'role culture' will have problems in surviving a dramatic change. Examples include the civil service, ICI.

Task culture - is best seen in teams established to achieve specific tasks i.e. project teams where the emphasis is on the execution of a particular task. Although a structure exists it is flexible and capable of being formed and reformed depending upon the task in hand. The organisation is therefore a more loosely bound than the role model. Power and respect come from individual knowledge rather than rank or position. People describe their positions in terms of the results they are achieving. An example could be an audit team conducting the annual audit of a particular client or group of clients.

These cultures are suited to organisations that are concerned with problem solving and short-term one-off exercises - often found in rapidly changing organisations, where groups are established on a short-term basis to deal with a particular change Structurally this culture is often associated with the matrix structure, which allows considerable flexibility within the organisation. Examples: market research organisations, entertainment industry, computer software design.

The person culture - less common than any of the other cultures, the person culture is characterised by the fact that it exists to satisfy the requirements of the particular individual(s) involved in the organisation. If there is a small, highly participatory organisation where individuals undertake all the duties themselves, one will find the person culture. More commonly, a key individual heads a support team of different skills. Example: barrister in chambers.

ACTIVITY 2

Which form of culture as described by Harrison/Handy would best characterise a) the army and b) a university?

Feedback to this activity is at the end of the chapter.

2.3 Mintzberg's co-ordinating mechanisms

As we have just noted, Handy observed that organisations could be classified according to four patterns of culture. These descriptions are useful for comparison and analysis purposes. We might compare them also to Mintzberg's ideas on co-ordination mechanisms.

Mintzberg advances the view that:

- All labour in an organisation has to be divided into distinct tasks.
- Co-ordination is needed between the people carrying out the different tasks.

Mintzberg argues that the organisation structure exists to co-ordinate the activities of different individuals and work processes. The nature of co-ordination changes with the increasing size of an organisation. In small organisations, mutual adjustment is sufficient but as organisations increase in size increased reliance is placed upon standardisation as a means of co-ordination. According to Mintzberg, the glue holding organisational structure together involves:

- **Standardised work processes** - exists where the work is specified, and everybody works in the same way. It is usually the work of the technocrats to design and develop these systems of work. Some work or processes cannot be standardised. e.g. in social work or teaching. Control here comes through education and training and the sharing of values and ethical standards, which inspire loyalty. Note that with the introduction of a national curriculum - the discretion of teachers in what they teach becomes regulated (by standardisation of systems and procedures).

- **Standardised outputs** - with outputs defined, the fit between tasks is pre-determined and can be performance monitored. Time, performance dimensions, conversion ratios, and profitability and cost indicators can specify work results. Whilst the results are standardised, the means are not. For example, quality standards will be determined and implemented in a firm that is accredited for ISO 9000. Taxi-drivers are not told how to drive or what route to take - only the address. They can be appraised on the basis that they do not get lost. We arrive at our correct destination on time and the rules on cab charges are applied correctly.

- **Standardised skills and knowledge** - even though each job is performed independently. This is an important co-ordinating mechanism in professional activities and specifies the kind of training needed to perform the work. The rigorous training that a doctor, solicitor or accountant receives provides admission into 'the club of the profession' with its rules of behaviour and ethical values. Workers may appear to be wholly autonomous when working, but the organisation can expect the highest levels of professional conduct and behaviour - externally regulated and espoused by 'chartered members'.

- **Direct supervision** - the organisation outgrows its simplest state. Co-ordination exists by someone taking responsibility for the work of others. One person does the specific planning, scheduling, allocating and instructing ie, has a co-ordinating role. In a rugby team players are distinguished by their work role and even physical requirements; wing-three-quarter, scrum half, stand off half, etc. Mutual adjustment does not quite work in co-ordinating their play so a captain is named to manage tactics on the field.

- **Mutual adjustment** - co-ordination results from internal communication and through informal contact between the people performing their organisational roles. Control of work rests in the hands of the 'doers'. This exists in simple structures where people work closely together. It also works in extremely difficult circumstances and applies to some complex tasks eg, in a research project if the outcome is uncertain, colleagues will adjust their activities in the light of new findings. This is what happened with the space shuttle project: there was an elaborate division of labour and thousands of specialists but at the outset no one was exactly sure what needed to be done.

Mintzberg's elements fall into a rough order. As organisational work becomes more complicated co-ordination seems to shift from mutual adjustment to direct supervision, to standardisation (preferably of work processes, otherwise of outputs or else of skills), finally reverting back to mutual adjustment. Large groups are less able to co-ordinate informally. With further complexity, supervision becomes necessary.

3 Cultural models

3.1 Miles and Snow

Miles and Snow identified four, distinctive cultural types of organisation– *defenders, prospectors, reactors, analysers* – categorised by their approach to innovation and to risk.

Defenders are organisations in which the managers are experts in their organisation's limited area of operation but tend not to search outside their current areas for new opportunities. These organisations have cultures whose stories and rituals reflect historical continuity and consensus. Decision taking is relatively formalised. Their focus is on increasing efficiency.

Prospectors are organisations where the dominant beliefs are more to do with results than with doing the right things. They continually search for market opportunities, regularly experimenting with potential responses to emerging environmental trends.

Analysers are organisations that exhibit both defender and prospector characteristics. They try to balance risk and profits by using a core of stable products and markets as a source of earnings to move into innovative prospector areas. Analysers follow change, but do not initiate it.

Reactors are organisations in which managers are impotent in the face of the change and uncertainty they perceive. They do not have viable strategies and only react when they are forced to do so.

3.2 Deal and Kennedy

Deal and Kennedy argue that two crucial factors shape an organisation's culture. The first is the degree of risk associated with the organisation's activities and the second is the speed of feedback provided to employees concerning the success of their decision strategy. They placed these factors on different axes to produce four distinctive types of organisational culture as shown below:

		Fast	Slow
RISK	High	Tough guy culture	Bet-your-company culture
	Low	Work hard, play hard culture	Process culture

FEEDBACK

Tough guy culture – is made up of individualists who thrive on high risks and fast feedback on their performance. Unfortunately, the short-term need for feedback may divert attention from longer-term efforts. This type of culture is often found in construction, advertising and entertainment organisations.

Bet-your-company culture – is characterised by high stake decisions with a delayed feedback. It is prevalent in oil and aircraft companies where the decisions that risk the company's future are made by technically competent people and necessitate attention to detail.

Work hard, play hard culture – is characterised by low risk taking combined with quick feedback. High activity is the key to survival. This type of culture suits organisations with high volume sales of mass produced goods.

Process culture – has little risk and little feedback. Typical process cultures include government agencies, banks and heavily regulated industries.

3.3 The concept of excellence

A simple distinction can be drawn between strong and weak cultures. A strong culture is marked by the organisation's core values being both intensely held and widely shared. On the other hand, weak cultures show a lack of uniformity and limited commitment. Some writers, noticeably Peters and Waterman, in their *book In Search of Excellence*, have suggested that a strong organisational culture is a key factor in determining organisational effectiveness.

From their study of 62 American companies they recognised that a clear, coherent culture was evident in excellent companies. This culture varies between organisations and is expressed distinctly in different companies:

(a) IBM bases its culture on service

(b) McDonald's is based on consistent quality.

The main aspects of culture in 'excellent' companies are as follows.

(a) **A bias for action** – an urgency to produce and complete results rather than analyse obstacles to action. A positive attitude of 'what can we do now' rather than a negative attitude of 'what is preventing us'.

(b) **Hands-on, value driven** – showing a commitment to the organisational values.

(c) **Close to the customer** – a continuous pursuit to understand the customer's needs and improve the quality offered. Peters and Waterman see improving quality as a motivating force for workers as well as affording opportunities for employees to be innovative. Their concern for quality and customer needs must exist in all functions at all levels.

(d) **Stick to the knitting** – no evidence of conglomerate diversification.

(e) **Autonomy and entrepreneurship** – teams and individuals are encouraged to establish their own targets for improvement. An element of competition is regarded as invigorating. This self-improvement drive encourages innovation and a customer satisfaction based culture.

(f) **Simple form, lean staff** – uncomplicated structures without large numbers of employees at head office.

(g) **Productivity through people** – staff must be treated as intelligent contributors, who are individually valuable and capable of 'extraordinary effort'. Sir John Harvey-Jones in his experience at ICI states that he never ceased to be surprised at the exceptional results that motivated people were capable of achieving.

(h) **Simultaneous tight-loose properties** – tight controls and detailed rules were replaced by common understanding and acceptance of the main guiding values of the organisation. Clearly this philosophy affects a company's recruitment, training and promotion standards and is not attainable overnight. Rather there is a steady change in the balance between control and trust.

(Source: *In Search of Excellence,* Peters and Waterman, 1982)

ACTIVITY 3	Peters and Waterman state that staff are capable of exceptional loyalty and effort if the organisation culture is attuned to this. How could this occur?

Feedback to this activity is at the end of the chapter.

4 Changing culture

4.1 Managing change

Culture develops in the light of a particular set of circumstances, at a certain time and in the light of certain conditions. Times and circumstances change and an old culture may well impede rather than help an organisation cope with change. In such cases management would need to intervene to modify the culture by altering those factors that sustain the present culture.

The argument is that if culture can be learned, it can also be unlearned and replaced by a new, more appropriate culture. Thus, management might seek to change culture by appointing people who are sympathetic to the new culture, introducing new training and socialisation devices, and changing the stories, myths, rituals, language and material symbols that are part of the traditional culture.

Cultures take a long time to develop and, once socialised, people are likely to be very resistant to changes in their culture. Some critics have said that the timescale of managing cultural change makes it an impractical proposition.

4.2 Robbins

Employees may well have chosen to work in an organisation because they find it compatible with their own norms and values and any attempts to change culture will lead to aggression, apathy, absenteeism or a high labour turnover.

Robbins suggests the following list of activities that can be undertaken to accomplish cultural change.

(a) Ensure top management become positive role models, setting the tone through their behaviour.

(b) Create new stories, symbols and rituals to replace those currently in vogue.

(c) Select, promote and support employees who espouse the new values that are sought.

(d) Redesign socialisation processes to align with new values.

(e) Change the reward system to encourage the acceptance of a new set of values.

(f) Replace unwritten norms with formal rules and regulations that are tightly enforced.

(g) Shake up current sub-cultures through extensive use of job rotation.

(h) Work to get peer group consensus through utilisation of employee participation and the creation of a climate with a high level of trust.

4.3 Rosabeth Moss Kanter

Kanter's work on change is contained mainly in her 1984 book *The Change Masters – Corporate Entrepreneurs at Work*. She performed an in-depth case study on 10 major US companies, and drew on research into a further 100 enterprises.

She identified two main approaches to change and innovation – the integrative approach and the segmentalist approach.

- The **integrative approach** describes the methods of firms that see change as an opportunity rather than a threat. These firms take an integrated, holistic view of problems and are ready to re-shape the organisation in search of a response.

- The **segmentalist approach** sees problems as being compartmentalised. The organisation is not a unified whole, but a collection of segments. Managers wish to confine each problem to a particular segment of the organisation and resist any alteration in the balance of the overall structure.

Not surprisingly Kanter's findings suggest that innovation is handled much better by integrative organisations than by segmentalist organisations.

To achieve an integrative approach, organisations must develop three new sets of skills:

- power skills, to persuade others to invest time and resources in new (risky) initiatives

- skills in managing problems arising from team working and employee participation

- an understanding of how change is designed and constructed in an organisation.

Kanter also suggests a number of actions to overcome resistance to change:

- Top management must be committed and must learn to think integratively.

- Management should encourage a culture of pride by highlighting achievements.

- Innovation should be supported by extending access to power sources, such as management committees.

- Cross-functional links should be improved by means of enhanced lateral communication.

- Staff should be 'empowered' in an organisation structure based on devolving authority as low down the hierarchy as possible.

- The plans of the organisation should be communicated widely so as to encourage input from as many people as possible.

4.4 Lewin's model of change

Lewin argued that cultures need to be 'unfrozen' before changes can be made and 'refrozen' after. This is discussed in more detail in Chapter 18.

5 Culture and leadership

The link between leadership and culture is very strong -several researchers have shown the personality of the leader is at least as strong an influence on strategy and structure decisions as the environment, technology or any other of the factors are commonly associated with strategic decisions.

In his book "Organisational Culture and Leadership", Edgar Schein (1992) writes that culture and leadership are two sides of the same coin. He argues that leaders first create cultures when they create groups and organisations. Once the cultures exist, the cultures then determine the criteria for leadership and thus determine who will or will not be a leader. Finally, he cautions that leaders must become conscious of the cultures in which they are embedded, or else those same cultures will manage the leaders. Schein points out that organisations do not come together, or stay together spontaneously, rather a guiding hand in the form of founder or leader is always present. Where the leadership is weak, or dysfunctional, the corporation invariably runs into trouble and cannot act appropriately.

5.1 The influence of the leader

Managers (especially top managers) create the climate for the enterprise. Schein points out that organisations do not come together or stay together spontaneously, rather a guiding hand in the form of founder or leader is always present. Where the leadership is weak, or dysfunctional, the corporation invariably runs into trouble and cannot act appropriately.

The culture of the organisation takes much of its nature from leadership, but leaders cannot change a culture by decree. Much of a leader's style is communicated through symbols and rituals, which become part of the cultural web. Peters listed several symbol acts of a leader that can communicate and energise culture change more effectively than any statement of intent, mission statement or other managerial devices.

- *Use of time:* The leader's stated aims will be contrasted with what he or she spends time on. For example, an attempt to energise and empower lower levels of the organisation will fail if the leader spends no time actively encouraging and supporting activities with those levels. Time spent solely telling middle managers what to do communicates all the wrong signals to both middle and junior levels.

- *Use of language:* An idea can be expressed in many different ways, and the leader can do much to influence the way that people interpret and react to events. On a mundane level, the word challenge seems different from the word problem, yet both can refer to the same thing. On a grander scale, language can be used to highlight issues by making them more emotional in some way.

- *Meetings, agenda and minutes:* There are generally too many things to talk about at any meeting, so the leader must assert priorities. Where the leader is attempting a culture change, it is necessary to ensure that the new behaviours are highest on the agenda. For example, having a new policy of customer service means nothing if key meetings never reach the topic in the agenda.

- *Settings:* The leader can do much to influence activity by manipulating the physical spaces and symbols. When Japanese managers take over a British plant, they usually close down the directors' car park and canteen immediately. They arrive at work early, and park their cars next to the gate so that workers will see that their seniors are working longer hours. They take their lunch in canteens with everyone else, and attempt to mix. The symbols are clear to everyone; hard work and teamwork are considered more important than status.

In addition to the above, it is also worth noting that many leaders communicate their purpose to the organisation by a variety of actions, such as posting themselves to minor jobs for a short period. This has the secondary effect of improving the quality of management information, as they experience things rather than read performance indicators.

5.2   Schein on leadership

Culture is deep seated and difficult to change, but leaders can influence or manage an organisation's culture. It isn't easy, and it cannot be done rapidly, but leaders can have an effect on culture. Schein outlines some specific steps leaders can employ:

What leaders pay attention to, measure and control - something as simple as what is emphasised or measured, over time, can have an effect on an organisation's culture. One example of this is an emphasis on form over substance. If leaders pay more attention to form, an organisational culture can develop where people start to believe that the substance of a recommendation is less important than the way it is presented. Where do you think people will focus their effort once it becomes accepted that a slick presentation is what the leaders are looking for? How could you go about changing that aspect of the organisation's culture?

Leader reactions to critical incidents and organisational crises - the way leaders react to crises says a lot about the organisation's values, norms and culture. Crises, by their nature, bring out the organisation's underlying core values. Often, this is where rhetoric becomes apparent. Reactions to crises are normally highly visible, because everyone's attention is focused on the incident or situation. Disconnects between actions and words will usually be apparent, and actions always speak louder than words. Additionally, a crisis not only brings a great deal of attention, it also generates a great deal of emotional involvement on the part of those associated with the organisation, particularly if the crisis threatens the organisation's survival. This increases the potential for either reinforcing the existing culture, or leading to a change in the culture. Such a crisis can provide an opportunity for a leader to influence the organisation's culture in either a positive or a negative way.

Deliberate role modelling, teaching, and coaching - nothing can take the place of leaders 'walking their talk'. The personal example of a strategic leader can send a powerful message to the members of an organisation, particularly if it is ethical and consistent. Reinforcing that example with teaching and coaching will help others to internalise the desired values.

Criteria for allocation of rewards and status - the consequences of behaviour, and what behaviour is rewarded and what is punished, can significantly influence culture. If the organisation reacts to new ideas by ridiculing the ideas and those who propose them, it won't take long before people believe that new ideas are not welcomed or desired. One belief of perceived organisational culture is reflected in the statement: 'Don't raise questions or suggest improvements, because nothing will come of it and you will just get in trouble'. If you were in an organisation's strategic leader, what steps could you take to alter the reward system to change this aspect of the culture?

Criteria for recruitment, selection, promotion, retirement and excommunication - one of the powerful ways of changing an organisation's culture is through the type of people brought into, retained, and advanced in the organisation. You should be able to establish a desired culture base in an organisation by bringing in and advancing individuals with the values you want, and eliminating those with undesired value bases. That is what organisations are attempting when they propose tightening up admissions standards to screen out undesirables. This strategy is consistent with the belief that the problems experienced by the organisation result from a few 'bad apples' and do not reflect systemic problems. However, if a strong culture bias exists, it may be too strong to be changed by selection alone.

Organisational design and structure - as we mentioned earlier, modifying the organisation's basic structure may be a way of changing the existing norms, and hence the culture. For example, a culture of mistrust between the leaders and the members of an organisation may be exacerbated by a 'line' structure that discourages vertical communication.

Organisational systems and procedures - the simplest definition of culture is 'that's the way we do things around here.' Routines or procedures can become so embedded that they become part of the culture, and changing the culture necessitates changing those routines. We can all think of organisations where a weekly or monthly meeting takes on a life of its own, becomes more formalised, lengthy, and elaborate, and becomes the only way information moves within the organisation. Changing the culture to improve communication may only be possible by changing the meeting procedures or eliminating the meetings altogether.

Design of physical space, facades, and buildings - the impact of the design of buildings on culture can easily be illustrated by considering the executive perks in an organisation. Which organisation do you think will have a more open and participative culture, one where top executives have reserved parking spaces, top floor offices, a special elevator and an executive dining room, or one where the executive offices are not separated from the rest of the company and executives park and eat in the same place as their employees?

Stories about important events and people - this is a way that culture is perpetuated in an organisation, in that it helps define and solidify the organisation's identity. By what events and stories they emphasise, leaders influence that identity.

Formal statements of organisational philosophy, creeds, and charts - this is the way leaders most often try and influence their organisations, and encompasses the vision or mission statement and statements of the organisation's (or the leader's) values and philosophy. By themselves, however, formal statements will have little effect on the organisation's culture. They must be linked to actions to affect culture.

5.3 Schein's guidelines

Schein has five guidelines for the leader:

1   Do not oversimplify culture or confuse it with climate, values, or corporate philosophy. Culture *underlies* and largely *determines* these other variables. Trying to change values or climate without getting at the underlying culture will be a futile effort.

2   Do not label culture as solely a human resources (touchy-feely') aspect of an organisation, affecting only its human side. The impact of culture goes far beyond the human side of the organisation to affect and influence its basic mission and goals.

3   Do not assume that the leader can manipulate culture as he or she can control many other aspects of the organisation. Culture, because it is largely determined and controlled by the members of the organisation, not the leaders, is different. Culture may end up controlling the leader rather than being controlled by him or her.

4   Do not assume that there is a 'correct' culture, or that a strong culture is better than a weak one. It should be apparent that different cultures may fit different organisations and their environments, and that the desirability of a strong culture depends on how well it supports the organisation's strategic goals and objectives.

5   Do not assume that all the aspects of an organisation's culture are important, or will have a major impact on the functioning of the organisation. Some elements of an organisation's culture may have little impact on its functioning, and the leader must distinguish which elements are important, and focus on those.

An understanding of culture, and how to transform it, is a crucial skill for leaders trying to achieve strategic outcomes. Strategic leaders have the best perspective, because of their position in the organisation, to see the dynamics of the culture, what should remain, and what needs transformation. This is the essence of strategic success.

6   Regional and national cultures

6.1   Differences in culture

We can probably identify how differences in the culture of organisations derive from the cultures of the wider community in which they operate. The difference between nations and ethnic groups is obvious when we think about *Vorsprung durch Technik* and its association with German engineering, family values in Italy, the importance of business cards in Japan and the logic in French education.

It is also clear that national culture influences the way that people behave at work, and the expectations that they have of their colleagues, careers and organisation. Pümpin, for example, noticed that his four characteristics of dynamic cultures are quite close to Swedish culture. Perhaps the contrasts are most noticeable when Europeans and East Asian cultures are contrasted.

The economies of East Asia and South East Asia – Japan, China, Taiwan, South Korea, and Hong Kong – have recently been among the most dynamic in the world. Although this is partly attributable to their general political and economic policies, these countries have also benefited from the competitive activity of their business organisations. Japanese, Chinese and Korean management systems have all proved to be highly competitive in their different ways.

A common feature of these management approaches has been their tradition of holding together an organisation as a dynamic group. This suits the norms of Asian cultures.

The traditional model of management and competitiveness in the West has been based on Max Weber's study of the Protestant ethic in the rise of capitalism. Weber argued that a connection exists between the religious and cultural beliefs by which an individual is surrounded and the attitude to economic activity held by that individual. His analysis led to a view of strategic management activity based on individualism, mastery over the world, *laissez faire* economic principles, and the supremacy of market mechanisms.

Analysts studying comparative management have seized on Weber's ideas by trying to show how the different religious and cultural values held in Asian countries have been translated into different styles of management. These commentators have emphasised certain aspects of a 'Confucian' ethic that are believed to underlie much management theory and practice in Japan and other Eastern nations.

- While the Protestant ethic is highly conscious of rights, the Confucian ethic instead emphasises obligation. Individuals should be conscious of their group responsibilities.

- Western approaches to management emphasise adversarial relations, while Eastern approaches are based instead on a fiduciary community. This emphasis on trust implies that laissez faire principles are unwelcome; leadership and intervention by the government are the norm.

6.2 Sub-cultures

Culture in a society can be divided into sub-cultures reflecting social differences. Most people participate in several subcultures.

- Class - people from different social classes might have different values reflecting their position of society.

- Ethnic background - some ethnic groups can still be considered to have a distinct culture.

- Religion - and ethnicity are related.

- Geography or region - distinct regional differences might be brought about by the past effects of physical geography eg, poor communication between communities separated by rivers or mountains. Speech accents most noticeably differ.

- Age - these subcultures exist because of the great shifts in social values and customs in this century.

- Sex - some products are targeted directly to women or to men. Homosexuals might be considered to form a subculture.

- Work - different organisations have different corporate cultures.

The exclusivity of subcultures should not be exaggerated, since each consumer is simultaneously a member of many sub-cultural segments.

6.3 Hofstede

There have been several important attempts to codify cultural differences. The most important of these was carried out by Hofstede who looked for national differences between over 100,000 of IBM's employees in different parts of the world. It is important to see that he was attempting to model aspects of culture that might influence business behaviour, rather than produce national stereotypes or explain the differences he found in historical or socio geographic terms. He mapped each nationality as a mixture of several traits. In general, these traits were positions on a continuum rather than absolute.

Individualism versus collectivism – some cultures are more cohesive than others, with Anglo Saxon cultures more individualistic than the collectivist cultures of South America.

Uncertainty avoidance – some cultures, such as France and Japan, dislike uncertainty and use planning and bureaucracy to reduce it. Other cultures, such as Jamaica and Denmark, tend to be less uncomfortable with uncertainty and ambiguity.

Power distance – the degree to which cultures are willing to accept inferior positions in society. In some cultures, particularly South American ones, disparities of power were tolerated more than in North European cultures.

Masculinity versus femininity – a masculine culture is one where distinctive roles between genders are large, with the male focus on work, power and success. Such cultures include Japan and Italy. Feminine cultures, such as Finland, have smaller differences in gender roles and success is likely to be regarded as a social rather than personal activity.

KEY POINT

Hofstede's work remains controversial, but is used here to illustrate some fundamental differences in national cultures that influence the way that people are likely to behave at work, and think about the future of their business.

Confuscianism versus dynamism – a rather confusing category that tries to capture attitudes to change over the longer term. For example, some cultures might regard globalisation as a threat to culture and wish to delay change to preserve what is good about society, while other cultures might regard cultural obstacles to globalisation as anachronistic and wish to discard them as quickly as possible.

Hofstede's work remains controversial, but is used here to illustrate some fundamental differences in national cultures that influence the way that people are likely to behave at work, and think about the future of their business.

Conclusion

Culture is an important influence on every aspect of a company's operations. Despite this, many practising managers are unable to define and explain the concept. This is because they are not attuned to looking at the organisation as being in a state of constant flux; instead they see change as a temporary occurrence between periods of stability. We have looked at two studies that examined the nature of successful cultures – Pümpin's work on dynamism and Peters and Waterman's work on excellence, and one model that seeks to explain why cultures do not change very quickly, the cultural web model.

SELF-TEST
QUESTIONS

Culture and organisation

1   Define culture. (1.1)

Cultural models

2   What are the common values of excellence according to Peters and Waterman? (3.3)

EXAM-TYPE
QUESTIONS 1

J & T

J & T is a partnership. It is a successful merchanting business which has been selling packaging materials to industry since the 1950s. The senior partners, Jones and Thompson, were joined in the early years by other merchants with detailed commercial knowledge relating to particular areas of the United Kingdom. As a result a network of eight offices was established in major towns in the UK. Each was managed by one of these merchants, who became junior partners in J & T. These new junior partners had been chosen partly because of their knowledge of local conditions, partly because of their contacts in their area, and partly because they shared the same values as their seniors. They were all family men, active, well known, and respected for their community voluntary work. Their business life was conducted to the highest ethical standards, which took precedence over opportunities to make easy money.

The overall aim of the business was to establish itself with its customers as the customer's main supplier. With many major firms it became the sole supplier, because it was known that it would always choose the best source of supply, even if it were not profitable for J & T.

Although supplies were sourced from all over the world, the business had a special relationship with a few UK suppliers to whose products it gave preference, effectively becoming their sole agents. J & T's suppliers were all private limited companies. They produced paper, cartonboard, plastic sheets, bags and bottles – all using continuous processes with a relatively small number of production workers, most of whom were unskilled. Maintenance, purchasing, quality control, and research and development were important functions with skilled and professional staff. These functions were managed by directors who were not themselves shareholders. The main raw materials were wood pulp, raw chemicals, water and electric power.

Each branch of J & T is run as an investment centre. Thirty-five per cent of the profits are shared among the local partner and staff in proportion to their salaries, the rest among the partners as a whole. The branches each employ between 25 and 40 people, including salesmen. The latter are paid a good basic salary, but they also earn commission on their own sales.

During the takeover boom in the 1970s and 1980s, many of the local customers were absorbed by national and multinational organisations. There were also amalgamations among the UK suppliers. Other trends during the last ten years have been the increased number of overseas sources of supply, the much wider choice of packaging materials, and the increased sophistication of their specifications. Following the recent death of Jones, Thompson has decided to retire. A further merger between the suppliers means that all the former UK suppliers of J & T have become a horizontally integrated group of companies employing nearly 2,000 people. Because the group has relied for all its UK sales on J & T, it has proposed a takeover of the business and buying out the partners. The funds for the takeover would be raised by 'going public'. The public flotation would be arranged by placing the shares with a small number of large investing institutions. This would leave the remaining partners and the former owners of the supplier companies as major shareholders, with about half the shares between them, although none of them would hold more than 5 per cent of the shares. The new company would be called IC plc.

Required

(a) Describe the organisational culture at J & T.   **(10 marks)**

(b) Identify the likely cultural changes necessitated by the proposals to merge the businesses and to become a public company.   **(10 marks)**

(Total: 20 marks)

E X A M - T Y P E
Q U E S T I O N **2**

Cultures in 'excellent' organisations

What, according to Peters and Waterman, are the characteristics of the culture of the 'excellent' organisation? Comment on the possible drawbacks of a strong organisational culture.   **(20 marks)**

For the answer to this question, see the 'Answers' section at the end of the book.

FEEDBACK TO ACTIVITY **1**	**Stories** – in the NHS stories and myths cover the following: cures, villains (politicians), heroes and heroism, change agents are fools, abuse of managers and the golden age.

Symbols – include terminology, white coats/uniforms, retinues, bleepers, doctors' dining rooms and big institutions.

Routines and rituals include clinical rituals, consultation ceremonies, blaming the next tier and treating patients like children – waiting rooms, putting to bed, waking up and ward rounds.

Structure – is seen as hierarchical, mechanistic, tribal/functional and with a pecking order of services.

Political systems – include professional bodies, the 'old boy' network, and politicians.

Control – is through waiting lists, financial reporting and responsibility.

The paradigm – covers issues such as:

- the NHS is a public service – it is 'ours' and a 'good thing'
- it is free at the point of delivery
- providers know best
- it has superior acute sector
- clinicians' values.

FEEDBACK TO ACTIVITY **2**	The best classification for:

(a)   the army is a role culture

(b)   a university is a person (or personal) culture

FEEDBACK TO ACTIVITY **3**	Peters and Waterman list three basic requirements:

(a)   The tasks must be obviously worthwhile, e.g. creating satisfied customers, so engendering pride in staff.

(b)   Staff individuals are treated as winners. Positive attitudes and contributions are highlighted.

(c)   The organisation of work allows staff to satisfy the two desires of being highly regarded in their own right and also as a welcomed member of a successful group.

Chapter 4
SCANNING THE EXTERNAL ENVIRONMENT

In an earlier chapter we argued that an important aspect of strategy was the way the organisation adapted to its environment. In this chapter we examine the first stage of the adaptation process, by looking at how strategists might understand the nature of their environment, and decide which elements are important, and how things may change. Writers on strategy differ over how effective these techniques can be, and what the limitations on environmental scanning might be.

Objectives

When you have studied this chapter you should be able to do the following:

- analyse the organisation as an open system

- use a SLEPT analysis to identify the key environmental issues that an organisation might face

- use Porter's diamond to describe the factors that influence the competitive pressures on any particular industry

- describe a range of forecasting and scenario building techniques

- outline the limitations to what can be achieved by such scanning.

1   SLEPT analysis

1.1   Introduction

Today's organisations must respond to a variety of internal and external pressures. This can be termed the organisation's total environment.

It is useful to consider as a starting point what environmental influences have been particularly important in the past and the extent to which there are changes occurring that may make any of these more or less significant in the future for the enterprise and its competitors. However, forecasting is notoriously difficult and the general environmental factors affecting an organisation are extremely numerous.

One way of tackling the problem is to look at environmental trends. For forecasting purposes, the wider environment in which the enterprise and its industry are located can be subdivided into five sectors.

KEY POINT

The wider environment in which the enterprise and its industry are located can be subdivided into five sectors - the social, legal, economic, political and technological environments

1.   Social

2.   Legal

3.   Economic

4.   Political

5.   Technological

1.2   Dimensions of environmental analysis

When analysing the social, legal, economic, political and technological dimensions that have the potential to impact strategies, it is commonly known as a SLEPT analysis.

The examiner may use a number of phrases when asking you to undertake a SLEPT analysis. This same categorisation of environmental factors is sometimes referred to as

- PEST analysis - where legal is subsumed into political
- STEP analysis
- PESTLE analysis (political, economic, social, technical, legal and ecological/environmental)

All of these factors will not necessarily apply but provide a useful checklist against which you can compare in an exam situation. They are explained more fully below.

- The social/cultural environment includes population demographics, social mobility, income distribution, lifestyle changes, attitudes to work and leisure, levels of education and consumerism.
- The legal environment covers influences such as taxation, employment law, monopolies legislation and environmental protection laws.
- The economic environment includes interest rates, inflation, business cycles, unemployment, disposable income and energy availability and cost.
- The political environment includes taxation policy, government stability and foreign trade regulations
- The technological environment is influenced by government spending on research, new discoveries and development, government and industry focus of technological effort, speed of technological transfer and rates of obsolescence.
- The ecological environment, sometimes just referred to as the environment considers ways in which the organisation can produce its goods or services with the minimum environmental damage.

Each of these areas has several types of questions that need addressing:

Social/cultural factors - include changes in tastes and lifestyles. They may also include changes in the demographic make-up of a population. For example in Western Europe people are living longer and in most countries the birth rate is falling, leading to an ageing population. This has obvious implications for the types of products and services, which businesses and other organisations may plan to offer. Typical questions that need to be answered include:

- What are the current and emerging trends in lifestyles and fashion?
- What demographic trends will affect the size of the market or its sub-markets?
- Does the trend represent opportunities or threats?

Legal/political factors - the addition or removal of legislative or regulatory constraints can pose major strategic threats and opportunities. The organisation needs to know:

- What changes in regulations are possible and what will their impact be?
- What tax or other incentives are being developed that might affect strategy?

Economic factors - include interest rates and exchange rates, as well as the general state of the economy (eg, entering or emerging from a recession). The organisation needs to know what the economic prospects and inflation outlets are for the countries that it operates in and how will they affect strategy.

Technological factors - may include changes in retailing methods (such as direct selling via the Internet), changes in production methods (greater use of automation), and greater integration between buyers and suppliers via computer link-ups. The managers would need to know to what extent the existing technologies are maturing and what technological developments or trends are affecting or could affect the industry.

Environmental factors - includes product stewardship, which considers all raw materials, components and energy sources used in the product and how more environmentally friendly substitutes could be used. It also includes ways in which the disposal of the product and product waste could be more effectively recycled. Typical questions that need to be answered include:

- Are we adhering to the existing environmental legislation?
- Are there any new product opportunities that could be exploited that would have a favourable environmental impact on the market?
- What impact will future environmental legislation have?

1.3   Contribution to strategic analysis

There are three main ways that investigating the SLEPT environments can contribute to strategic analysis.

1   The headings can be used as a checklist when analysing the different influences. The organisation can use the checklist to identify which are the most important at the present time and over the next few years.

2   The analysis may help to identify long-term drivers of change. For example, given the increasing globalisation of some markets, it is important to identify forces that lead to this development. These include rapid changes in technology, leading to shorter life spans of these technologies and therefore to the need for greater scale economies in their use.

3   The analysis may be used to examine the differential impact of external influences on organisations, either historically or in terms of likely future impact. This approach builds on the identification of key trends or influences and asks to what extent they will affect different organisations differently.

1.4   International influences - PEST analysis

International businesses engage in transactions across national boundaries. These transactions include the transfer of goods, services, technology, managerial knowledge and capital to other countries. The barrier between the domestic and the international environment is relatively permeable, depending on the product and the relative openness of the market for the product or of the economy as a whole. This influences the seriousness of threats from incoming competition and the opportunities for international activity.

Managers involved in international business are faced with many factors that are different from those of domestically oriented firms. They have to interact with employees who have different educational and cultural backgrounds and value systems. They must also cope with different legal, political and economic factors.

Political issues include the conditions in individual overseas markets or sources of supply, eg people being taken as hostages in certain countries does nothing for travel companies visiting those countries. Relationship between governments is another factor, as is the activities of supra-national institutions, eg EU regulations on product standards.

KEY POINT

Economic factors include the overall level of economic activity, the relative levels of inflation at home and abroad, the exchange rate and the relative prosperity and growth in overseas markets.

Economic factors include the overall level of economic activity, the relative levels of inflation at home and abroad, the exchange rate and the relative prosperity and growth in overseas markets.

Social and cultural aspects include the different ways of doing business in overseas markets, the cultures and practices of overseas customers and the media and distribution systems.

Technological factors relate to an organisation's access to domestic and overseas patents and intellectual property protection. It has a bearing on the degree to which an organisation can imitate the technology of its competitors and on the technology transfer requirements.

The consequences of globalisation and international organisations could include:

- increasing opportunities to export;
- consideration of international strategies and partnerships and the necessity to plan activities on a global scale;
- increasing competition in the domestic (home) market.

A PEST analysis is a very popular examination area. It can also be incorporated into an information-needs question. Make sure that you can apply the technique - an impact analysis can be used to explain both of these topics.

1.5   Impact analysis

Each of the PEST factors can be classified in terms of an impact analysis. The vertical axis on the matrix illustrated below lists potential factors, which affect the business. Information can be gathered and organised from the environmental analysis, including the customer, competitor and market analysis. For example a travel company might want to assess different places to include in their brochure for the next planning period and could be concerned with the areas chosen by main competitors and also new entrants to the market. Other concerns might include the stability of foreign governments, the exchange rate, the communication and distribution systems and the cultural and demographic trends. The entries in the matrix evaluate the effect that the factors will have on the business.

To provide a means of scoring, each factor can be given an 'impact' value ranging from -5 to +5. This relates to the consideration of each factor as either an opportunity (+) or a threat (-). The factor would also be given an 'importance' value ranging from 0 to 10.

For the travel firm, a political factor such as conflict or war may be thought to have an impact of either -4 or -5. The importance of the factor might be high and given around 8. Importance and impact are then multiplied to give a possible negative score of -32 or -40.

Factors	Impact	Importance	Potential (opportunity or threat)
Conflict of war	−4	8	−32
Economic trend			
Cultural trend			
Technology			
Customer segment			
Competitor			
Potential competitor			
			Total

The full assessment would be done after all the important factors within the matrix are taken into account. The organisation would decide at what level the combined score would indicate a negative environmental assessment or a favourable set of environmental conditions.

2   Social/cultural impact on the organisation

2.1   Introduction

The social/cultural environment includes:

- Population demographics
- Social mobility

- Income distribution
- Lifestyle changes - the current and emerging trends in lifestyles and fashion.
- Attitudes to work and leisure
- Levels of education and consumerism.

Business operates within a social framework. Four aspects of this are relevant.

- *Power* – who has it, how effective is it, and how is it used?

- *Leadership* – who are the leaders, what are their qualities and weaknesses?

- *Culture* – the values and traditions within which the business must operate. One problem facing multinationals has often been a failure to cope with the different cultural values of the countries within which they operate.

- *Risk* – the attitudes towards risk and risk taking.

2.2 Demographic trends

Population demographics covers changes in tastes and lifestyles. It may also include changes in the demographic make-up of a population.

Demographic trends are a powerful force in a market. The strategic planner will make use of population trends to determine:

- the size ie, expected growth or decline in national and international population,
- type ie, changes in the age distribution, and
- location of the market place products or services. For example, in Western Europe people are living longer and in most countries the birth rate is falling, leading to an ageing population. This has obvious implications for the types of products and services those businesses and other organisations may plan to offer.

The demographic characteristics include geographical distribution and population density, age and educational levels, nationality and social class as well as the norms, customs and values of the population within which the organisation functions. Many companies use demographic data for consumer targeting and there are market research services offered which map geographically the concentrations of particular types of people. Other services have developed a segmentation of the population based on a combination of life cycle, income and occupation.

Demographic changes can have an adverse impact on demand. Falling birth rates could indicate problems ahead for producers and sellers of baby products and, later, toys. Emigrating populations can reduce demand on a local basis. Culturally, changes in tastes and fashions can have a damaging effect on organisations that fail to anticipate the changes. Clothing is an excellent case in point, and Marks & Spencer is currently experiencing decline for this very reason. Even cars and furniture are susceptible to changes in trends and tastes. Health scares such as the BSE crisis can affect sales (in the case of beef). A change in attitudes is taking place in the United Kingdom at present in relation to willingness to seek compensation from organisations for alleged wrongs. The potential costs of this 'compensation culture' could be huge and may lead to some corporate casualties. The culture has, to a certain extent, been imported from the United States. An increasing concern about greenhouse gases and the ozone layer, testing of products on animals and generally greater social awareness could spell disaster in the future for those firms unwilling to embrace this cultural shift. Indirectly, cultural changes often lead to changes in legislation, such as the banning of CFCs.

2.3 Changing culture

Cultural trends can present both threats and opportunities for a wide variety of firms. Culture used to change slowly, but now every few years brings into focus a new set of attitudes, values and behaviours. Even some of the most fundamental values in a society undergo noticeable variations through time.

Consider some of the major recent changes in our society, and think about how they have changed, or are changing, our culture.

- Family size and characteristics (eg rate of divorce and single parent families).
- The level and nature of education.
- Domestic and geographical mobility, eg the extent of international travel.
- Health and fitness, eg the growing pressure for limitations on genetically modified foods and the trend towards organic food production.
- Ethnic and racial integration.
- General values and expectations - materialism, beauty, youthfulness, success, etc.

2.4 Lifestyles

Lifestyles are the outward manifestations of people's attitudes and values. In recent years, change rather than stability has become the norm for lifestyle in the UK. For example, families account for a shrinking proportion of UK households and fewer of these families include married couples; households consisting of single adults and one-parent families are becoming more numerous.

Other lifestyle changes include a trend towards better education.

Smaller cars, eating out, diet and paid household help are only a few examples of new consumption patterns. Physical fitness has experienced a recent surge in popularity, and other home-centred activities are becoming more prevalent as households distribute their leisure time.

The organisation is influenced by changes in the nature, habits and attitudes of society:

changing values and lifestyles – a widespread change in lifestyle has been the shift away from the historic 9 to 5 working day to a more flexible form. Supermarkets are now open throughout the night and the Internet and other forms of IT allow people to shop or bank in the middle of the night

3 Legal environment

3.1 Introduction

The law constitutes a set of environmental factors that are increasingly affecting strategic decisions. Most of the nations of the world are, or are becoming, regulated economies. Government, or self, regulation of business has four principal aims.

- To protect business entities - eg, laws putting limits on market dominance by acting against monopolies and restrictive practices and providing financial assistance to selected ailing industries and companies.
- To protect consumers - with many detailed consumer protection regulations covering packaging, labelling, food hygiene and advertising, and much more.
- To protect employees - with laws governing the recruitment of staff and health and safety legislation that regulates conditions of work.
- To protect the interests of society at large against excessive business behaviour, eg by acting to protect the environment.

Also at the most basic level, perhaps, laws are passed that enable Government to levy taxes, whereas company law affects the corporate structure of the business and prescribes the duties of company directors.

Managers cannot plan intelligently without a good working knowledge of the laws and regulations that affect their own companies and the businesses they operate in. In addition to those laws, which apply generally to all companies, such as laws regulating Corporation Tax or Value Added Tax, there are laws specifically used to deal with individual industries, eg Petroleum Revenue Tax in the offshore oil and gas industry.

3.2 Legislation and regulations

The legal environment is concerned with how an organisation does business and covers:

- law of contract, law on unfair selling practices, health and safety legislation
- how an organisation treats its employees, employment laws
- how an organisation gives information about its performance
- legislation on competitive behaviour
- environmental legislation.

Regulations governing business are widespread; they include those on health and safety, information disclosure, the dismissal of employees, vehicle emissions, use of pesticides and many more.

Changes in the law can affect organisations in many ways. A tightening of health and safety legislation may increase costs. Premises failing to meet the higher standards could be closed down. Particularly damaging might be the imposition of a complete ban on the organisation's product, clearly made worse should they have failed to develop a product portfolio sufficiently broad to absorb such a loss. Tobacco companies are at present faced with the prospect of a ban on advertising, if not on their products.

3.3 Effect on strategy

The main feature of the legal environment is its increasing complexity. This is typified by company legislation; since 1967 there have been four major Acts. This pattern is repeated in almost all areas. Employee legislation, consumer protection, planning and building regulations are all areas directly affecting business activities in which the legislation has become much more complex.

Organisations can anticipate changes in the law by examining the governing party's election manifesto and the EU's single market programme, which indicates changes in the law. The government often publishes preparatory information (green paper or white paper) for consultation and this may give an indication of future changes in the environment.

4 Economic environment

4.1 Introduction

The current state of the economy can affect how a company performs. The rate of growth in the economy is a measure of the overall change in demand for goods and services. Other economic influences include:

- Taxation levels.
- Inflation rate.
- The balance of trade and exchange rates.

- The level of unemployment
- Interest rates and availability of credit.
- Government subsidies.

General economic conditions and trends are critical to the success of an organisation. Wages, price changes by suppliers and competitors, and government policies affect both the costs of producing products or offering services and the market conditions under which they are sold. The economic factors can either induce competition into an industry, or force companies out. They can prolong or shorten a product's life, encourage companies to substitute automation for people, promote foreign investment or conversely investment by foreigners, advance the substitution of people for automation, make a very strong market relatively weak and turn a safe market risky.

4.2 Economic indicators

KEY POINT

Common economic indicators measure national income and savings, investment, prices, wages, productivity, employment, government activities, and international transactions.

Common economic indicators measure national income and savings, investment, prices, wages, productivity, employment, government activities, and international transactions. All these factors vary over time, and managers devote much of their organisation's time and resources to forecasting the economy and anticipating changes. Most countries now use overall growth as an internal measure of the success or failure of their economic system, but even where there is a high rate of growth there are likely to be areas of high unemployment and poverty. After growth, stability is generally rated as the most desirable attribute of an economy, provided that stability does not bring with it stagnation.

Instability is a socially unsettling phenomenon, because it tends to create unemployment, booms and slumps, price and wage fluctuations and provides the opportunity for certain key groups of workers in the economy to gain a greater share of the national income at the expense of the remainder of the population.

One should also look at international economic issues, which could include:

- the extent of protectionist measures
- comparative rates of growth, inflation, wages and taxation
- the freedom of capital movement
- economic agreements
- relative exchange rates.

A downturn in the economy can lead to corporate failures across a number of industry sectors. Those worst affected will be suppliers of goods with a high income-elasticity of demand. House-builders and related industries (such as home furnishings) are good examples. Suppliers of basic necessities will be less badly hit. Deflationary government fiscal policy (low government spending, high taxation and a planned budget surplus) and central bank monetary policy (high interest rates, restriction of money supply expansion and revaluation of the currency) can have a highly damaging impact on business. They can adversely affect levels of demand both domestically and overseas, and impact on financial strategy through increasing the cost of capital and reducing after-tax profits available for distribution or retention.

Economics is concerned with structural shifts in the economy, e.g. from manufacturing into services. It is also about the comparative advantage of nations and the costs of operating in different countries. IT has made the financial markets into global markets, with money capable of being transferred from one financial centre to another.

The curbs on greenhouse gases agreed at Kyoto will have an impact on the world's energy producers that will take years or even decades to emerge fully. Some expect a general rise in energy prices as governments resort to higher taxes to cut fossil fuel demand.

4.3 Strategy evaluation

The evaluation of most strategies will be affected by judgements made about the local, national and international economies.

The economic future of the local economy will affect wage rates, availability of labour and the provision of roads and other services.

National economic trends, particularly inflation and the general economic health of the country (measured by growth and unemployment), will be important in developing and evaluating strategic plans. Other factors include population growth and changing demographic trends.

An analysis of the balance of payments and other factors affecting the relative valuations of currencies can be relevant for industries with multinational competitors. Heavy investment in a capital-intensive industry might be timed to coincide with a strong economy to avoid a damaging period of losses. The business planner needs to know the essential economic and technological characteristics of the industry and the possible consequences for the company of fluctuations in business activity, government fiscal policy, and/or international events on cost/profit/volume, return on capital employed on new investments or replacements of redundant or obsolete equipment, availability and utilisation of labour resources, cash flow and organisational structure such as its flexibility and adaptability to swift or gradual changes in product service output levels.

4.4 Lobbying parliament

The UK business lobby comprises individual large companies and the representative voice of groups of related organisations. At least the top 50 companies operating in the UK will be in frequent contact with Whitehall and Westminster for other than routine business matters. Some large companies will have senior staff, whose responsibility is to monitor and advise on political and governmental developments, make regular contacts with politicians and officials, organise representation in Brussels, and undertake lobbying operations in London and Brussels. This does not mean, however, that they do not make errors of political judgement or that Whitehall will always accommodate their views.

The organised business lobby consists of four main players:

- The Confederation of British Industry (CBI) - which represents the private business sector as a whole.

- The chambers of commerce - which speak for small businesses.

- The Institute of Directors (IOD) - which represents individual company directors.

- Some 3,500 trade associations and around 300 employers' organisations, which represent companies in particular industries and sectors..

These bodies carry out a vigorous agenda of representation, supported with solid investigation. Whitehall will discuss policy initiatives with the main business representatives, and it is therefore in a company's interest to support, and get involved in the activities of, its relevant trade association, or other representative body.

4.5 Department of Trade and Industry (DTI)

The DTI is of importance when formulating business strategy because of what it does for UK business. It offers an extensive range of services, provides funds for a variety of programmes that are designed to improve business performance, and publishes a huge amount of valuable information and statistics.

Its aim is to foster a competitive market environment in which the interests of consumers are served and producers achieve their objectives. In pursuit of these aims the DTI will:

- promote exports of UK goods and services;

- cultivate an effective regulatory framework that protects customers, creditors and investors;

- stimulate innovation in industry by promoting research, the development of technical skills, the transfer of technologies and closer bonding between industry and the science fraternity.

- respond to the needs of different regions and areas with special problems.

4.6 Competition policy

When a large company dominates an industry, it has substantial control over other industries, which rely on its products (eg, confectionery relies on sugar and flour - both very concentrated industries). Some large manufacturing firms have also spread into distribution and finance, meaning that considerable power now lies in the hands of a relatively small number of very big organisations.

The Secretary of State for Trade and Industry has overall responsibility for UK competition policy. The two main official bodies, which deal with competition and complementary consumer protection responsibilities, are the Office of Fair Trading (OFT) and the Monopolies and Mergers Commission (MMC). In theory both organisations are separate and independent of government. In general terms, the OFT is the central pivot of the system. It monitors the whole business panorama from a competitor and consumer standpoint, carries out initial studies, 'commissions' detailed investigations by the MMC, advises the government on problems and polices relevant regulations.

5 Technological environment

5.1 The technological influences

This is an area in which change takes place very rapidly and the organisations need to be constantly aware of what is going on. Technological change can influence the following:

- changes in production techniques

- the type of products that are made and sold

- how services are provided

- how we identify markets.

Much has been made of the application of new technologies to communications and business, particularly the Internet and, although IT is perhaps the main technological driver for change in business practice, other major changes appear to be widespread.

The impact of information as the raw material in a knowledge-based economy is huge. There are many sources of information external to organisations that can be accessed, e.g. Experian offers a database of about 100 million records in the UK associated with credit worthiness of individuals. Bad medical risks will be identified by genetic testing and houses liable to subsidence will be identified from geological survey.

Within any industry, failure to exploit information technology and new production technology can lead to an organisation falling behind its rivals and losing its competitive edge.

Traditional methods of delivering services have been turned upside down by rapid developments in information technology. This erosion of entry barriers to industries such as banking and insurance through easier access to distribution channels (the Internet rather than a High Street presence) and much lower start-up costs has created threats to the established players which, if they do not respond to them, could lead to decline.

New technology can lead to the emergence of substitutes. The cinema industry went into decline in the early 1980s as a result of video. Examples of recently developed products can be found in biotechnology and pharmaceuticals and data storage devices. The rate of change in these industries, and the high costs of research and development have profound effects on the structure of the industry and the way that the industry competes.

Examples of changes in the way in which products are made include the use of robotics and computers. Their introduction either results in lower costs of production or better quality products or both, although the benefits of the application of computers is often over rated. Advances in material science sees the use of ceramics and carbon-based material where only metal would once have been found.

5.2   Technological development

Government institutions, independent research establishments, universities, and large corporations all carry out basic research. Independent entrepreneurs, business firms, and some government agencies carry the developments out of the laboratory and into the marketplace.

The effect of technological development and change includes the following:

- markets and customers analysed more effectively (using sophisticated databases)

- new products and services being developed;

- changes in work methods leading to a reduction in production, and other, costs;

- better quality products and services at no increased cost;

- products and services available and delivered quicker or more effectively than previously;

- employees freed from repetitive work and able to demonstrate more creativity.

- short product life cycles – an organisation needs to be innovative.

ACTIVITY 1 | Leppards of Dibden is a manufacturer of medical supports for older people. One of its key overseas markets has imposed a tariff on goods imported into the country. How does classifying this in the SLEPT analysis help us think the issue through?

Feedback to this activity is at the end of the chapter.

6   External environmental scanning

6.1   Complexity, dynamism and uncertainty

Unless managers are able to identify the actual and potential forces of change on their organisations, they will have no means of knowing what steps to take to minimise the danger or to cash in on the opportunities which the changes present. It is important for strategic planners to take the steps necessary to collect, analyse and interpret relevant information on the key factors, or segments. It may be a case of closing the stable door after the horse has bolted if only historic information is produced, that is after the changes have taken, or are taking, place. Information must be made available which shows the magnitude and rates of change of significant events and activities.

The main problem for most organisations is that the environment is a source of uncertainty. Decision-makers do not have sufficient information and many factors are out of their control because, unlike risk, probabilities cannot be assigned to the different factors.

An important issue is the degree of uncertainty in the environment in which the organisation operates.

KEY POINT

Four types of business environment have been recognised. They are:

- simple
- complex
- static
- dynamic.

Four types of business environment that have been recognised are simple, complex, static and dynamic.

Simple environment – some organisations are fortunate to operate in business environments in which they only have to cope with relatively few uncertainties or change agents. It could be said that these organisations are in simple environments.

Complex environment – the more complex an organisation's environment is, in other words the more variables there are that can change, the more uncertainty it faces. Complexity usually relates to the **diversity** of the environmental segments, and the extent to which they are interrelated. The environment in which organisations such as the dot.com companies operate, are almost impossible to predict with any accuracy.

It will be necessary for an organisation operating in a complex environment to try to reduce the environmental complexity, perhaps by structuring the management tasks round specialist operating areas. This would probably involve segmenting the environment into discrete sectors on a basis that reflects the significance of the different environmental influences on the organisation.

Static environment – an organisation operating in a static environment faces no change of significance or relatively little change in the variables that give rise to uncertainty. The organisation is thus able to place confidence in its forecasts and assumptions. The business managers will be guided by their experience of the business environment in which they operate. They will be influenced by past events and the impact they had on organisational performance. The forecasting methods will, in the main, be **statistical** by nature based on projecting from past trends. There is, however, still a danger of unanticipated or unpredicted change, which should not be ignored.

For example, the baby-food producers in Europe, companies such as Gerber, and Cow & Gate, failed to anticipate the full impact that the declining birth rates and changing positive attitude of women to breast-feeding babies would have on their market. The European market for baby-foods fell by about 5% in real terms over the five-year period 1976–1980. Exports to the developing countries had also grown very slowly. By failing to spot and act on these trends the industry was plunged into disorder.

Dynamic environment – the degree of environmental dynamism relates to the rate and frequency of change of the factors that give rise to uncertainty. An organisation that operates in an extremely dynamic environment is faced by rapid and probably novel change, and thus plans its future facing uncertainty.

The business planners operating in this type of environment will need to consider the novelty of future events and not be influenced solely by past events and results. They will need to be very sensitive to change, and forecasting will be based on a mix of statistical and intuitive techniques. There is a danger that the organisational structure and culture will be unable to cope with the change required. A dynamic environment is far more risky than a static environment.

We can see from this that different types of environment can be classified into two major groups:

- by speed and nature of change (static or dynamic), and
- by convolution (simple or complex).

A C T I V I T Y **2**	Describe two situations, the first where the environment is simple and dynamic and the second where the environment is complex and stable.

Feedback to this activity is at the end of the chapter.

6.2 Systems thinking

Systems thinking involves 'seeing' inter-connections and relationships, the whole picture as well as the component parts. It is this understanding of the system with its emergent properties and characteristics that facilitates insights when managing change or problem solving in organisations. Systems thinking approaches provide key insights for the management of complexity.

It often involves building models to facilitate understanding and communication at the level of both the individual and the larger group or team. As individuals we all view the world differently. This is to be expected since we are conditioned over time by our cultural traditions, personal experiences and education.

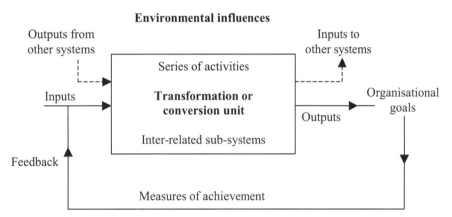

The structure, management and functioning of an organisation is not only determined by internal considerations and choices, but it is also strongly influenced by a range of volatile, external environmental factors. As an open system, the business is in continual interaction with the external environment and to remain effective and maintain survival and growth, the organisation must respond to the opportunities and challenges, and the risks and limitations, presented by it. Changes in the environment will affect inputs and changes to the inputs will affect the transformation or conversion process and hence the outputs.

The increasing rate of change in major environmental factors has highlighted the need to study the total organisation and to adopt a systems approach. To understand the operations of organisations and to improve performance, it is necessary to achieve an internal and external balance and adapt to the changes in the environment and the demands placed upon them.

Feedback control is an important concept in Systems thinking. For closed systems to preserve their status quo, feedback must be negative and continuous. However, in order that an open system can survive in a changing environment, it must utilise positive feedback to eventually change its goals and direction and reduce its entropy.

6.3 The organisation as an open system

Organisations can be viewed as social, informational, financial or economic systems and any one firm is in effect a subsystem of a larger suprasystem. The firm itself is composed of many subsystems with their own goals and objectives.

Although organisations differ in many important respects, they also share some common features. **Open** systems have a dynamic relationship with their environment. They can be viewed as systems that take in resources such as people, finance, raw materials and information from the environment and through a series of activities transform or convert these and return them to the environment in various forms of outputs such as goods produced, services provided, completed processes and procedures in order to achieve certain goals such as profit, market standing, level of sales or consumer satisfaction.

This means that the organisation is open to and in continual communication with the external environment of which it is a part. It must respond to the opportunities and challenges and the risks and limitations presented to it. Changes in the environment, e.g. advances in IT or pressure group campaigners, will affect inputs and changes in inputs will affect the transformation or conversion process and hence the outputs.

The model below shows how the organisation, as an open system, receives inputs, transforms them and exports the outputs to the environment.

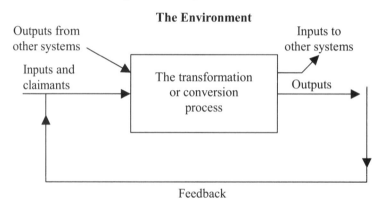

Inputs and claimants – may include capital, raw materials, people, information, managerial and technical skills and knowledge. In addition, various groups of people – stakeholders – will make demands on the organisation. For example, employees push for higher wages, better working conditions and job security; consumers want safe and reliable products or services at reasonable prices; shareholders want high returns on their investment and security for their money; governments expect taxes and compliance of the law; and the local community wants the maximum number of jobs with a minimum of pollution.

The transformation process – Charles Handy considers these processes as sub systems:

- **Production** – in a manufacturing organisation, the transformation of inputs into outputs would be the production department, in an insurance company it would be the underwriting department. The production sub system is the heart of the organisation and all sub systems are usually oriented towards it.

- **Maintenance** – keeps the organisation functioning. It may repair and service the building. Alternatively, the human resource department can be seen as a maintenance sub system, recruiting, retiring, counselling, etc employees.

- **Boundary spanning** – organisations must acquire inputs, raw materials, data, etc, and distribute output – the finished product or service. This sub system can cover a variety of activities, such as purchasing and marketing.

- **Adaptation** – an organisation needs to adapt in order to survive. This sub system can cover such activities as research, engineering, planning and development.

- **Management** – is the sub system which co-ordinates all of the other sub systems, by means of policies, plans, resolving conflict, etc. It is the task of managers to transform the inputs, in an efficient and effective way, into outputs using the managerial functions of planning, organising, staffing, leading and controlling.

Outputs – the type of outputs will vary with the organisation. They generally include products, services, profits and rewards (the satisfaction of the goals of various claimants). For example, employees need not only their basic needs (money for food and shelter) satisfying but also their needs for affiliation, acceptance, esteem and self-actualisation.

Feedback – it is important to note that, in the systems model shown above, some of the outputs become inputs again. For example, the satisfaction of employees becomes an important human input, and parts of the profits are reinvested in machinery, equipment, buildings and stock.

The systems approach expresses a manager's role as being a co-ordinator of the elements of a system, of which people are only one part. A manager is encouraged to spend greater time and effort in improving, planning, controlling and operating systems than motivating staff, since this will lead to greater efficiency.

6.4   The communication system

Communication is essential to the managerial process - it makes managing possible. Firstly, the communication system integrates the managerial functions of planning, organising, staffing, leading and controlling. It is a means of communicating the objectives of the organisation so that the appropriate structure can be organised. To fill the roles of this structure, it is essential in the selection, appraisal and training of managers. Similarly, effective leadership and the creation of an environment conducive to motivation depend on the communication system. Lastly, it is through communication that a manager determines whether events and performance conforms to plans.

Another purpose of the communication system is to link the organisation with its environment. For example, it is used to identify the needs of customers. This knowledge enables the company to provide its goods or services at a profit. Similarly, it is through an effective communications system that the organisation becomes aware of competition and other potential threats and constraining factors.

6.5   Focal zone analysis

For most organisations today commercial survival and success requires a keen strategic understanding of external influences in order to respond in ways that will ensure the organisation's survival and success.

Environmental scanning is one tool in an organisation's arsenal that can be used to gain this understanding. It is the internal communication of external information about issues that may potentially influence an organisation's decision-making process. It focuses on the identification of emerging issues, situations, and potential pitfalls that may affect an organisation's future. The information gathered, including the events, trends, and relationships that are external to an organisation, is provided to key managers and used to guide future plans. It is also used to evaluate an organisation's strengths and weaknesses in response to external threats and opportunities. In essence, environmental scanning is a method for identifying, collecting, and translating information about external influences into useful plans and decisions.

Barriers to Effective Scanning

There are several reasons why environmental scanning may not be effective in an Organisation. The sheer volume of information may be overwhelming, resulting in an information overload in which important pieces of information may be overlooked or missed. There are also many sources of information that scanners may not be aware of, and so they may miss potentially important information. Navigating the ocean of existing information is also difficult due to poor organisation and completeness of the material presented. Even in the best of circumstances, information may no longer be timely by the time scanners are able to locate it. This is particularly true of rapidly changing markets that are influenced by technology or regulatory changes.

There are also problems with environmental scanning related to interpretation of the information that has been gathered. Determination of relevance, familiarity with the topic and information sources, language usage, time limitations, and accuracy of information all play a role in the analysis process. In addition, an overemphasis on scanning could have negative effects on an organisation. This could be due to the focus on a defensive strategy to external forces rather than a continuation of process improvement and growth within the organisation.

Managers need guidelines for a scanning strategy to overcome the barriers to effective scanning. By implementing a scanning process and identifying the focal zones of the information requirements, management can make informed decisions. Organisational leadership can take appropriate steps to position the organisation in the manner that will be most responsive to the opportunities or threats that have been identified.

A formal environmental scanning process has steps that are integrally linked and may overlap with others:

1 **Identify the environmental scanning needs of the organisation**. The overall purpose of the scanning, participants in the process, and allocation of time and resources must be determined prior to beginning the scanning process. This means that senior management has to recognise the need for scanning in order for it to be successful. It is useful to have participants meet to initially discuss potential changes that may influence the organisation based upon their tacit knowledge and experiences.

2 **Gather the information**. The organisation's needs must then be translated into specific elements of information that will be required. A list of questions and selected sources should be prepared in advance in order to make scanning activities more targeted and effective.

3 **Analyse the information**. Once information has been collected, it should be analysed for issues and trends that may influence the organisation. This step may need to be repeated if there are gaps in the information or if new questions arise from the compiled information.

4 **Communicate the results**. Information that has been analysed and translated into potential effects on the organisation can next be reported to the appropriate decision-makers within the firm. Because managers prefer to minimise the amount of time necessary to study information and make decisions, reports should be presented in concise format and customised to meet individual managers' preferences.

Environmental focal zones will be set and may include the following:

- governments; economies and environmental focal zone;
- critical success factors and environmental focal zone;
- market strategy and environmental focal zone;

- market dominance and environmental focal zone;

- innovators and environmental focal zone;

- turbulence and environmental focal zone;

- stakeholder interdependence and environmental focal zone;

A C T I V I T Y **3**	A manufacturer of a traditional fizzy drink was replacing bottles of the product with metal cans of the same drink. A sharp eyed marketer noticed that in some West African and Middle Eastern countries, export sales of the product were rising very quickly, while in others they were falling. Since only the containers had changed (in some cases), the firm wondered what was going on. How would you go about finding out?

Feedback to this activity is at the end of the chapter.

6.6 Porter's diamond

Michael Porter, in his book *The Competitive Advantage of Nations*, tries to isolate the national attributes that further competitive advantage in an industry. He argues that a firm's strategy is closely linked to developments, opportunities and constraints in the domestic market. Only if domestic conditions are appropriate will the firm be able to act globally.

His study argues that, for a country's industry to be successful, it needs to have the attributes and relationships shown in the diagram below. He calls this the 'diamond'.

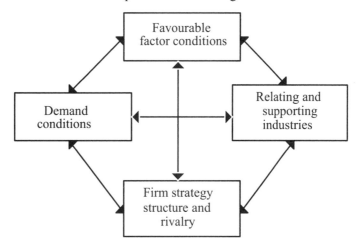

(a) **Favourable factor conditions** – factors include:

    (i) physical resources such as land, minerals and weather

    (ii) capital

    (iii) human resources such as skills, motivation, price and industrial relations

    (iv) knowledge that can be used effectively

    (v) infrastructure.

Porter also found that countries that had factor disadvantages were forced to innovate to overcome these problems. This innovation has been the basis of competitive advantage, e.g. where nations experienced high-energy costs they were forced to develop energy-efficient products and processes that were subsequently demanded worldwide.

(b) **Demand conditions** – there must be a strong home market demand for the product or service. This determines how industries perceive and respond to buyer needs and creates the pressure to innovate. A compliant domestic market is a disadvantage because it does not force the industry to become innovative and excellent.

(c) **Relating and supporting industries** – the success of an industry can be due to its suppliers and related industries. Sweden's global superiority in its pulp and paper industries is supported by a network of related industries including packaging, chemicals, wood-processing, conveyor systems and truck manufacture. Many of these supporting industries have also achieved leading global positions.

(d) **Firm strategy, structure and rivalry** – organisational goals can be determined by ownership structure. Smaller companies may have slightly longer time horizons to operate in because their shares are not traded as much as larger organisations. They might also have different return on capital requirements.

Porter found that domestic competition was vital as a spur to innovation and also enhanced global competitive advantage. Conversely, where governments have encouraged mergers to get the critical mass required to be a global player, these national monopolies have not, on the whole, been successful in establishing a global position.

The implications of company strategy and national economics

There are a vast number of environmental factors that shape business strategy, but these can mainly be grouped into four major forces.

(a) **Competition**

One of the most important characteristics of competition is that it is global. Practically all advanced countries are experiencing competition from abroad. There are few protected industries or regulated monopolies left in the world and even organisations such as telecommunications, airlines, and stock market exchanges are becoming privately owned.

Global competition is often based on strategic considerations. Competitors from abroad are often willing to sacrifice some profit in order to gain a foothold in a large domestic market and are also willing to engage in cross subsidisation.

These facts, therefore, suggest that managing competition in domestic markets is a greater challenge today than it used to be. Organisations, therefore, need a global strategy with emphasis on obtaining and keeping their share of the global market.

(b) **Markets**

One of the characteristics of markets is that customers are becoming global in their orientation. It is not only the industrial and business customers who procure their products or services from global sources, so do the ordinary consumers. Examples of this are consumer electronics, garments, cars, appliances, and even foods and beverages, all of which carry a mixture of domestic and foreign brand names in most countries of the world. The customer, therefore, has expectations of quality, service, and affordability based on world standards. Domestic products such as cars and television sets may not be considered reliable or user friendly once the customer has experienced products from abroad.

In many business markets it is not unusual to find that customers are becoming competitors and are deciding to make the product themselves rather than buy it.

Markets are becoming more and more fragmented, especially consumer markets. This is due to diversity in demographics, such as age and income distribution.

(c) **Government regulations**

There has been a big change over the years in the formation of regional economic alliances such as the European Union (EU) and the freedom of world trade through GATT/ WTO (General Agreement on Trade and Tariffs/World Trade Organisation) negotiations. Such changes have softened national geographic boundaries for products and services.

(d) **Technology**

Technology is available worldwide, especially in areas such as electronics and mechanics. Technical barriers across national borders are easily overcome and it is as easy for a less developed country to produce high quality electronic products such as personal computers and television sets as it is for an advanced country.

Life spans of technologies are also getting shorter and shorter. It is, therefore, becoming necessary to recover capital as soon as capacity is installed. It is less and less desirable to think local first and global second when a business is about to invest in technology, as that technology will rapidly become obsolete. Instead, businesses must think globally in relation to product design, manufacturing capacity, and marketing issues.

6.7 Forecasting and scenarios

Statistical models

The statistical approach to forecasting is concerned with the projection of **time series**. Time series analysis involves the identification of short and long-term patterns in previous data and the application of these patterns for projections.

A variety of methods are available including:

- moving averages
- exponential smoothing
- correlation analysis
- sensitivity and key factor analysis
- risk analysis
- multiple regression analysis.

Where there are numerous short and long term factors at work, forecasting becomes very difficult. If the series of data being analysed is very regular, some simple procedure such as **exponential smoothing** may be sufficient. On the other hand, more complex patterns may require techniques of **regression analysis**, **risk analysis** and **multiple regression**. By using relatively simple mathematics, it may be possible to calculate to a 'level of confidence' the volume of demand, etc. Trend analysis would seem to be a particularly useful tool for companies who have to forecast demand that is influenced by seasonal fluctuations, or where demand is strongly influenced by the business cycle, but in reality many of the techniques are very crude, and cannot predict with adequate certainty.

Intuitive forecasting methods

All forecasting techniques involve judgement. For example, statistical techniques require judgements about the amount of past data that is relevant, and how this data should be weighted, while casual models involve judgements about what are the critical variables in the situation. In both cases, judgements have to be made regarding the reliability of the data, the stability of the relationships between the variables over time, and the accuracy of the predictions. Therefore what distinguishes intuitive techniques is the relative emphasis they place on judgement. Intuitive forecasting techniques include the use of think tanks, Delphi methods and brainstorming.

(a) A **think tank** comprises a group of experts who are encouraged, in a relatively unstructured atmosphere, to speculate about future developments in particular areas and to identify possible courses of action. The essential features of a think tank are: the independence of its members – enabling unpopular, unacceptable or novel ideas to be broached; the absence of positional authority in the group, which enables free discussion and argument to take place; and the group nature of the activity which not only makes possible the sharing of knowledge and views, but also encourages a consensus view or preferred '**scenario**'. Think tanks are used by large organisations, including government, and may cross the line between forecasting and planning. However, the organisations that directly employ, or fund them, are careful to emphasise that their think-tank proposals do not necessarily constitute company or government policy.

Think tanks are useful in generating ideas and assessing their feasibility, as well as providing an opportunity to test out reaction to ideas prior to organisational commitment.

(b) The **Delphi technique** is named after the *Oracle of Apollo at Delphi*, renowned for somewhat ambiguous predictions. The method was pioneered at the Rand Corporation in 1950 to assess the timing and likelihood of new technology, and it since has gained considerable recognition as a valuable planning tool with a great variety of applications. Delphi seeks to avoid the group pressures to conformity that are inherent in the think tank method. It does this by **individually**, systematically and sequentially interrogating a panel of experts. Members do not meet, and questioning is conducted by formal questionnaires. Where the experts are speculating about the future, they are asked for subjective probabilities about their predictions. A central authority evaluates the responses and feeds these back to the experts who are then interrogated in a new round of questions. The subjective probabilities will be used to examine the range of opinion in more detail, with outliers examined in particular detail. After several such rounds, the result, generally, is that widely differing opinions increasingly adapt themselves to one another. The system is based on the premise that knowledge and ideas possessed by some but not all of the experts can be identified and **shared** and this forms the basis for subsequent interrogations. Sometimes, users of this technique are frustrated that experts do not necessarily agree after several iterations, but perhaps users should be more concerned about agreement, as Duncan Reekie points out, this is frequently no more than a consensus of ignorance.

(c) **Brainstorming** is a method of generating ideas. There are different approaches but a popular one is for a number of people (no fewer than six, no more than fifteen) drawn from all levels of management and expertise to meet and propose answers to an initial **single** question posed by the session leader. For instance, they may be asked 'How can we improve product A?' Each person proposes something, no matter how absurd. No one is allowed to criticise or ridicule another person's idea. One idea provokes another, and so on. All ideas are listed and none rejected at this initial stage. Rationality is not particularly important; only after the session are ideas evaluated and screened against rational criteria for practicability. An enlargement on this is for an idea proposed and seen to be promising when matched against criteria to be subjected to a brainstorming session in which the question 'How might the idea fail?' is asked.

6.8 Scenario building

Every leader/manager needs to 'picture the future' – to take a view of the state in which the organisation may be operating when the decisions they are taking today will come into effect. Forecasting has a role in strategic management but, for anything other than the near future, scenarios are needed to provide appropriate views.

Forecasts are made assuming the future can be predicted, scenarios are generated on the assumption that it cannot.

Scenario building is an attempt to construct views of possible future situations.

It is used in strategic planning to allow a number of deductions to be made about future developments of markets, products and technology. The aim is to draw up a limited number of logically consistent, but different scenarios so that managers can examine strategic options against the scenarios and ask such questions as 'what should we do if?', or 'what would be the effect of?'.

For example, Shell have frequently used scenarios to see how current strategies would cope with a drastic rise, or fall, in the price of oil, even though there was no immediate reason to suppose such fluctuations could occur. Once they had begun to think about it, they realised that the prices were potentially much more volatile than they had supposed, and adjusted their strategies and operations to be more flexible (leasing capital equipment instead of borrowing to buy, for example). Consequently, they have been less badly hurt by oil price changes than some of their competitors, who had optimised operations taking the current price levels as stable.

Examples of scenarios that are drawn up so that the strategies can be tested against a range include:

(a) an optimistic scenario, where everything turns out favourably in the future

(b) a pessimistic scenario, which describes the worst possible scenario

(c) a 'most likely' scenario, which is likely to be between the other two.

Strategies will need to be developed which help the organisation either to gain a competitive advantage or to minimise the potential damage deriving from the environment.

The issues facing the industry may be influenced by such things as:

- the entry or exit of firms

- the rate of demand

- changing buyer needs

- innovations in products or production processes

- how easily innovations can be imitated

- stage in the life cycle.

Another benefit of scenario building is that managers can examine the implications of scenarios so as to challenge the assumptions that are taken for granted in the environment in which they operate. This may be important where there are long-term horizons because operating managers may be so concerned with the short term that they ignore the long-term changes.

The main steps in drawing up scenarios are as follows.

(i) The first step is to identify the key assumptions, or forces, that are to be worked on. This may build on a SLEPT (social, legal, economic, political and technical) analysis. It is best to restrict these assumptions to environmental forces, and not include the strategic action of the organisation or of competitors. It is also important that the number of assumptions is kept relatively low, since the complexity in drawing up scenarios will rise dramatically with the number of assumptions that are included.

(ii) Another step is to understand historically the trend with regard to assumptions being considered, their impact on market conditions and organisational strategies, and what these assumptions themselves depend upon. For example, if fuel is being considered, understanding what affects such things as oil or gas prices.

(iii) As explained in the previous section, scenarios are built by considering possible futures, usually based on an optimistic future, a pessimistic future and a 'dominant theme' or mainline future. Two to four scenarios are appropriate to aim for.

Conclusion

In this chapter, we have reviewed a range of ways used to understand the business environment. The first example, SLEPT, is a widely used technique for thinking about events, trends and patterns that will require the business to change its strategy and operations. Porter's Diamond is a model that is used to capture the influence of the home environment on the future of an industry in a global economy.

In the final section, we looked at a range of techniques that are less widely used, but have achieved some spectacular results in the past.

SELF-TEST
QUESTIONS

SLEPT analysis

1   Give two examples of problems with SLEPT that might cause difficulties for someone analysing a case in an examination. (1.2)

Types of business environment

2   Explain how environments can be classified according to rate of change and predictability. (6.1)

The competitive advantage of nations

3   What is the purpose of Porter's Diamond? What factors does it consider? (6.6)

Further techniques for environmental analysis

4   Contrast statistical modelling with Delphi as means of understanding the future. (6.7)

Scenarios

5   Explain the purpose and process of Scenario Building. (6.8)

EXAM-TYPE
QUESTION

Organisations as open systems

Management writers have found it useful to conceptualise organisations as open systems.

CA is a company engaged in the assembly and sale of computers. Components are purchased from around the world, briefly sorted using a just-in-time (JIT) system and assembled in a factory employing the latest technology. The assembly of a computer begins after receipt of a customer order. Post, fax or telephone is normally used to place a customer's order because the company sells direct from the factory. Payment is normally in advance by cheque or credit card and the computer is delivered to the customer by a courier service. CA advertises in national newspapers, and targets the home and small business market. CA is organised on functional lines and includes departments concerned with customer services, technical support, research and development, storage, assembly, packaging, marketing and sales, accounting, personnel and administration.

Required:

(a)   Describe the CA organisation using concepts from open systems theory.

(10 marks)

(b)   In what ways can open systems theory assist in our understanding of the operation of organisations like CA?   **(10 marks)**

(Total: 20 marks)

For the answer to this question, see the 'Answers' section at the end of the book.

FEEDBACK TO
ACTIVITY **1**

In the first instance it is difficult to classify into a particular environment, and there is not any great point in favouring one over another. However, we might think of possible solutions in the following way.

Political – Is it possible to lobby the overseas Government directly or indirectly through UK Government and trade bodies. Industrialists and farmers in USA have been very effective at challenging EU trade protection in this way.

Economic – Is it possible to reduce the price of the products without wrecking profits (a hard look at costs may be required here) or locate some part of the value added process in the foreign country? Japanese companies have successfully built market share in spite of tariffs by both these techniques.

Legal – Are the tariffs legal, in themselves and in the process used to set them up? The UK has lost many of its fishing rights, in particular, as the legal justification for them has been successfully challenged by EU partners.

Note that the consideration of which environment an opportunity or threat comes from is only useful in so far as the discussion might help to generate some possible solutions. It does not matter in any other respect.

FEEDBACK TO
ACTIVITY **2**

(i)   An example of a simple and dynamic environment is one where the product is only being sold in one market (simple) and where the product is still in the introduction stage and demand might be predicted to increase dramatically (dynamic). Virtual reality games in leisure arcades could fit this description.

(ii)   The environment of a group of research scientists working for a pharmaceutical company, funded by an international grant to investigate genetic disorders, might be classified as stable and complex. The stability arises because of the grant which means that they will not be exposed to cuts in funding. The complexity is in the amount of knowledge required which is drawn from different disciplines and is uncertain in its future discoveries.

The company checked to see if sales had fallen in countries where cans had replaced bottles. This was so in some cases, but not others, so the firm investigated environmental conditions more carefully. This involved talking to distributors and agents, who were quickly able to suggest an explanation.

The answer was in a cluster of social, legal and political factors. Islamic restrictions on alcoholic drinks had been increasing at the same time that larger numbers of people were getting married (because of a population bulge) and growing affluence meant that more parties and celebrations were taking place. The drink in bottles was being used instead of sparkling wine. In some places where cans had replaced bottles, wily entrepreneurs were importing the bottles from other local states, exaggerating the rise in sales of some areas.

The manufacturer responded by retaining the bottles, and changing the design to give more of a 'party' look to the product.

Do not be concerned if you did not work this out from the question, as long as the answer makes sense to you. Remember that the manufacturer did not work it out either, and had to investigate to derive this answer.

Chapter 5
CUSTOMERS AND MARKETS

In the previous chapter we looked at the various environmental influences that will influence the development of an organisation's strategy.

In this chapter we sharpen the focus somewhat, and argue that the underlying purpose of strategy is to develop and sell a product to a customer more effectively than competitors. In this chapter, we focus on this aspect by looking at techniques for analysing customers, markets and industry structure.

Objectives

When you have studied this chapter you should be able to:

- describe the various techniques that can be used to analyse customers, markets and market research

- outline the techniques that can be used to describe customers, and customer behaviour

- explain market research as a component of marketing research

- describe and identify the attractiveness and competitive dynamics of an industry using Porter's five forces

- explain the effect of industry structure, competition and collaboration on an industry.

1   Market analysis

1.1   Marketing strategy formulation

A marketing strategy is designed to guide management towards getting products or services to the customers and encouraging them to buy. To arrive at a coherent set of goals and an overall strategy, the main questions that the company may ask itself are:

- What business are we in?

- What broad markets does the company wish to serve?

- What specific market segments does the company wish to concentrate on?

As a result of asking these questions and analysing the market it will be possible to plan and determine a marketing strategy.

An organisation often has to select a strategy from among two or more alternatives. For example, a company that has the objective of achieving a market share of 45% may accomplish this in several ways. It can improve the product or service image through extensive advertising, add salespeople, introduce a new model, lower prices or sell through more/different outlets. Each alternative strategy has different ramifications for the marketing managers. A price strategy may be very flexible, because the price can be raised or lowered more frequently than product modifications can be introduced. However, a strategy based on price is the easiest to copy and may lead to a price war.

Attempting to gain market dominance by being first to launch a new product is known as an offensive strategy. This strategy is the high-risk strategy and careful market analysis is important in order to reduce the risk of launching a product that is not currently wanted.

The defensive strategy involves a more cautious approach to the market, often allowing competitors to test the demand and build up a consumer response before launching their own product. The approach is to ensure that the company adopts a strategy, which makes use of developments. The exploitation of developments may make use of product innovations of competitors, seeking to improve on them or at least differentiate from the original merchandise.

There are many examples of approaches that might be used to halt a product's declining profitability. They include cost reduction and price modification, conversion of non-users or winning competitors' customers, entering new market segments, increasing the frequency of use or developing new and more varied uses, re-launching the product or many types of improvements and modifications to features, style, communication mix and distribution.

1.2 Market structure and concentration

Concentration refers to the extent to which a small number of firms or enterprises account for a large proportion of economic activity such as total sales, assets or employment. Concentration is said to be high, for example, if three organisations account for 90 per cent of industry sales or employment - this is the three-firm concentration ratio. Market share is typically measured by reference to data on sales or net output. High market concentration does not necessarily imply market power.

The two most popular measures of concentration are the concentration ratio and the Herfdindahl-Hirschman index (HHI). The former cumulates the market shares of the four or five largest firms in the market, while the HHI is defined as the sum of the squares of the market shares of all firms in the market.

When we measure market concentration, a more crucial issue is how to define a relevant market. Suppose you want to research on soft drink. Does it include only juices and fizzy drinks? How about spring water, tea, or coffee? Do you include only the market in London, or the UK? A properly defined market includes all firms that compete with each other but excludes all non-competitors. To identify competitors, substitutability on the part of both consumers and producers should be considered

There are at least four distinct concepts embodied within the term concentration:

Aggregate concentration - which measures the relative position of large enterprises in the economy. This measure has interested economists, sociologists and political scientists mainly in the context of theories relating to actual (and potential) economic-political power which big business may be able to exercise because of their economic importance in a country/industrial sector/geographic region.

Sectoral or industry concentration - (also often referred to as seller concentration), which measures the relative position of sectors and geographic areas in the provision of specific goods or services such as automobiles or transport.

Industry concentration is the key element in market structure and an important determinant of conduct and performance and hence of the nature of competition. The two extremes are:

- perfect competition - in which products are homogeneous and firms small in relation to the size of the total market so that they cannot individually influence price (concentration is low), and

- monopoly - in which there is a single seller (concentration is absolute). Most markets in advanced countries have high to intermediate levels of concentration and operate under conditions of monopolistic competition in which prices tend to exceed marginal cost in theory and, even if there is no collusion, barriers to entry may keep concentration high.

Market concentration in this context is used as one possible indicator of market power.

Buyer concentration - which measures the extent to which a large percentage of a given product is purchased by relatively few buyers. At the extreme, a single purchaser of all the production of a good or service would give rise to a situation of monopsony. Buyer concentration may result in countervailing power that offsets the market power that may otherwise arise from high levels of market or seller concentration. See also discussion under bilateral monopoly/oligopoly.

Ownership concentration - which measures the extent to which shares of stock exchange listed companies are widely or narrowly (closely) held. This last concept is often extended to describe the wealth or control of corporate assets among individual families or business entities.

1.3 Analysing the market

Marketing is the management process that identifies, anticipates and satisfies customer requirements efficiently and profitably. Customers' needs are anticipated and identified by marketing research and segmentation and then a marketing mix is employed to satisfy customers.

Market analysis, which also helps identify the appropriate marketing strategy, will include the following:

- Appraisal and understanding of the present situation - this would include an analysis for each product showing its stage in the product life cycle, strength of competition, market segmentation, anticipated threats and opportunities, customer profile. Customer groups or segments can be identified and each targeted with marketing activity that specifically addresses their particular needs

- Definition of objectives of profit, turnover, product image, market share and market position by segment.

- Evaluation of the marketing strategies available to meet these objectives.

There are two purposes of the analysis. The first is to identify gaps in the market where consumer needs are not being satisfied. The second is to look for opportunities that the organisation can benefit from, in terms of sales or development of new products or services.

1.4 Marketing plan/marketing mix

Whatever marketing strategy is chosen, it is necessary to plan the changes necessary to the marketing mix so that buyers will actually want the product.

The marketing mix describes the specific combination of marketing elements used to achieve the marketing objectives and satisfy the target market.

One of the most common ways of presenting the marketing mix is by Jerome McCarthy's Four Ps: *Product; Promotion; Price; and Place.*

Product: Quality of the product as perceived by the potential customer. This involves an assessment of the product's suitability for its stated purpose, its aesthetic factors, its durability, brand factors, packaging, associated services, such as installation, delivery, after sales service and credit facilities.

Promotion: This involves the use of appropriate 'communication' tools to inform target customers of the features of the products. Such tools may involve advertising sales promotions, the company's public relations effort, personal selling.

Price: This involves the process of establishing a price for each set of customers that will be attractive to the buyer and meet the strategic objectives of the seller. Factors to consider will include: customers' incomes, how sensitive demand is to a change in price (price elasticity of demand), the degree of competition in the market, the overall objective of the seller – penetration of the market, premium pricing policy, 'positioning', stage of the life cycle.

Place: This involves decisions on the physical distribution of the product (logistics) and the choice of distribution channel (retail, mail order, internet selling).

One way of viewing the marketing mix model is to see it as a set of four ' weapons' available to the organisation to 'attack' its chosen or target market. The mix between the proportions in which each of the four Ps used in a given market will depend on the key characteristics of that market. The model should be viewed as dynamic rather than static – the mix should be kept under review and changed as the characteristics of the target market change.

Whilst the Four P's are easy to remember, it can confuse some students because of the inclusion of some sales factors in promotion and some in place.

The following 5- part model is sometimes preferred:

- **Product** - same as before

- **Price** - same as before

- **Promotion** - is similar, but excludes sales factors.

- **Sales** - The new 'sales' category includes the size and organisation of the sales force, its management, training, job definitions and objectives and methods of payment.

- Distribution is the Four P's 'place' without sales factors.

Market research is not mentioned in the above market mixes. This does not imply that market research is unnecessary. On the contrary, market research can be regarded as *the source of information* that is used in setting all the variables in the marketing mix.

1.5 Service marketing

Much marketing theory was originally devised for the marketing of tangible goods and was primarily geared towards selling household commodities, clothing, and industrial goods and equipment. As economies become richer, individuals spend a greater part of their income on services of one kind and another. In particular, healthcare, education and leisure activities consist of a larger part of consumption, together with services aimed at managing finances such as banking, investment and insurance spending. The not for profit sector with its many charitable organisations is also included in this section.

The usefulness of the four P's framework for the construction of the marketing mix is acknowledged, however Levitt suggests that marketing to the service sector should be based on four P's, namely, people, people, people and people. One might be forgiven for concluding that this view is somewhat glib but undeniably expresses the right sentiment.

The characteristics that impact upon the design of a marketing plan when considering the service sector include:

- **Intangibility** - in general there can be no results prior to purchase, you cannot use your perceptual senses and therefore the customer will seek 'assurance' of quality to predict outcomes and reduce uncertainty.

- **Inseparability** - whilst physical goods are frequently sold through sophisticated outlets and often after storage, this is not the case with regard to services which are often produced and consumed simultaneously. The existence of such chains of marketing outlets adds to the feeling of comfort or 'quality' for the consumer of products. However the chain is absent for the service client.

- **Variability** - services vary greatly and such variations can precipitate confusion and, in the worst-case scenario distrust in the purchaser of services.

- **Perishability** - unlike many physical products, services cannot be stored. This removes the buffer frequently employed by manufacturing businesses to cope with fluctuations in demand. Controlling quality and matching supply to demand are therefore significant management problems within service-oriented organisations. Such problems are often exacerbated by the presence of the customer during the service delivery process.

1.6 The marketing process

One of the most important decisions an organisation must take is to define its market and then subsequently to choose the customer group(s) or segment(s) upon which to focus their activities. The process of market definition, segmentation and targeting is an overt recognition by marketers that customers are not all the same and as such will be driven and respond to value very differently. It may also be recognition that the organisation has insufficient resources to service every customer in the market with individual offers, or that competitors already have a strong foothold in that market and that the organisation must find a niche or gap in the market that is not being serviced with an appropriate offer.

The marketing process is divided into a strategic and a tactical phase.

The strategic phase has four components: scope, segmentation, targeting, and positioning.

1. **Define market**	Determine an appropriate market boundary
2. **Segment the market**	Identify similar groups of customers which comprise segments
3. **Target the market**	Select target segments which are meaningful and viable
4. **Position offer in market**	Create or design the appropriate value for each segment targeted

The tactical phase includes designing and implementing various procedures to achieve its intended strategies. These are commonly referred to as the 'marketing mix'.

This positioning decision is crucial to strategic decision-making. Several studies have shown that good position strategies can lead to highest profits, even when the industry attractiveness is very low. It is important to avoid the following positioning errors:

- taking a position in which you have inadequate skills and competences

- taking a position that does not correspond to customer's preferences.

2 Customer behaviour

2.1 Buyer, customer and user

A customer may be an institution, such as a hospital or government agency; it may be another firm, such as a distributor or manufacturer - sometimes referred to as a buyer-to-buyer (B2B) relationship; or it may be an individual consumer - - sometimes referred to as a buyer-to-customer (B2C) relationship.

KEY POINT

This positioning decision is crucial to strategic decision-making. Good position strategies can lead to highest profits, even when the industry attractiveness is very low.

The customer market may be highly competitive, with large numbers of potential buyers and sellers seeking the most congenial arrangements. In such markets, managers must be especially concerned about price, quality, and service and product availability if they want to keep old customers and attract new ones.

For many products and services on many occasions, the buyer, customer and user are the same person. Where this is the case, marketing effectiveness depends upon the accurate determination and satisfaction of that person's needs.

Business-to-business marketing differs from consumer product marketing:

- The buying centre, which may include three distinct groups of people (economic buyers, technical buyers and users), is responsible for making purchasing decisions.

- *Soft costs*, such as downtime, opportunity costs, and human resource costs are associated with the compatibility of systems in the buying decision.

- Business-to-business marketing is often a two-way street with each firm marketing products that the other firm buys.

- In business-to-business marketing, the buyer and seller are more likely to be dependent on one another, particularly in client relationships.

In most industrial marketing, and in a significant part of consumer marketing, the buyer is not the user. For salespeople of grinding wheels, their customer is a company. The buyer is a member of the purchasing department, and the user is a grinding machine operator.

The marketing of the product is affected by all three; by the company, its overall purchasing policy and the latitude it allows its buyers; by the purchaser himself or herself, his or her level of skill in negotiation, his or her attitude towards the supplying company and its salesperson; and by the user, who will soon have clear ideas about the product in use. The manufacturer's product and marketing have to satisfy the company, the buyer and the user.

Similarly, consider a male perfume - perhaps an after-shave lotion. The manufacturers would probably describe their customer as male, but the retailer might find that the majority of its customers are female. In the former case, the term customer refers to the user, in the latter to the buyer. The after-shave must be marketed in such in a way as to satisfy both the user who must associate the product with positive attributes such as enhanced sexual attractiveness and freshness and the buyer, who must be persuaded that the product is desirable to the user and who must be encouraged to make a purchase at the point of sale.

Whenever the buyer, customer and user are not the same, the process of need satisfaction is made more complex by the existence of several sets of needs.

2.2 Market segmentation

The recognition of differences in the market implies the division of the total market into a series of sub groups on the basis of some common characteristic or criteria. These sub groups are called segments - which can be very large or very small. They may also be very loosely defined for example as 'business users' or very tightly defined as 'people who travel internationally more than three times a year with private medical insurance' By further and further refinement through the application of statistical analysis, segments can be reduced to a series of 'niches', which are small and precise customer groups.

Market segmentation is the subdividing of a market into distinct subsets of customers, where any subset may conceivably be selected as a market target to be reached with a distinct marketing mix.

Within the defined segments, the role of the marketer is to facilitate the desired exchange by targeting marketing activities precisely suited to the subgroup either with different forms of an offer (features, attributes and benefits), different ways of accessing the same offering (physical or electronic delivery) or by using direct communications or representations (different brand or offer images).

Scope

The first task in undertaking market segmentation is to define the scope of the market in which the organisation wishes to operate. A market is a group of customers who exhibit broadly similar needs. For instance, the travel market is a generic or total market. Within this market we can determine different forms of travel eg, airline, bus, train and cruise ship and for each segment we can determine budget or economy travellers versus first class travellers. Often marketers will refer to the total market in 'industry' terms and the words are often used synonymously eg, the travel industry (market). Generic or total markets are useful to organisations because they summarise the market and often define it in terms of a benefit sought by the customer, not in terms of particular products or technical specifications eg, 'We operate in the entertainment market'

The next level of analysis is where you can start to think carefully about the ways in which the market subdivision is handled.

- It may be organisationally defined in terms of the product or service provided. For example, Easyjet's total market is air travel but they concentrate on budget travellers. Alternatively, it may be through the provision of a physical product to satisfy a particular need such as toothpaste, shelving or shoes.

- Another way of looking at the market is to describe the different customers or consumers who will buy or use the product. The most usual definitional terms here would focus on whether they are business or household buyers, whether they are resellers or manufacturers or where they reside. These are broad customer characteristics, which could at any time be more closely defined.

- Finally, you can describe a market in terms of the alternative ways in which the exchange of value is performed. You can include the technology through which the delivery takes place, such as the Internet, phone or face-to-face through retail outlets. You might include aspects associated with channel partners eg, delivery through agents, recognised distributors or value aggregators.

In each case the organisation is attempting to delimit or define a broad market boundary. Particular organisations may be happy with broad definition such as 'healthcare market' as market boundary. Others will require a more specific definition to focus their activities or reflect the specialist nature of their business or the intensity of the competition.

Segmenting the market

Having defined the broad market boundary the next phase in the market segmentation process is to actually segment the market by dividing the market into segments in order to create an offer that best fits the desires of the groups found to exist in the market.

2.3 Business to customer (B2C) segmentation variables

The value of segmentation is that it identifies segments that are sufficiently large to be profitable and have definable characteristics. Market segmentation allows organisations to treat similar customers in similar ways, whilst distinguishing between dissimilar customer groups.

The essential qualities for effective segments are as follows:

- Measurable - the segments must be able to be measured / assessed for market potential

- Substantial - in order to warrant marketing activity, the identified segment must be large enough to be viable

- Accessible - must be able to action a marketing programme with a finely developed marketing mix to targeted consumers.

- Stable - an assessment of the short, medium and long term viability

There are different bases used to segment a market. The traditional method was segmentation on demographic grounds. This is still the starting point for many segmentation exercises, though further investigation often finds that demographic influences are not the prime determining factors of purchase.

- **Demographic segmentation** – market research studies are frequently broken down by age, income, social class, sex, geographical area, occupation, family unit, etc. This can be highly relevant with some products. For example, certain brands of breakfast cereals have regular sales only in families where there are children aged under eight, whereas other brands (e.g. Bran Flakes and Shredded Wheat) sell almost entirely to adults. In other areas, demographic influences appear to have no effect – for instance, own label products are believed to sell equally to high and low incomes, to families and single people, and across age groups.

  The most widely used form of demographic segmentation in the UK is the socio-economic classification shown in the table below:

Class	Social status	Job descriptions
A	Upper middle class	Higher managerial, administrative and professional
B	Middle class	Middle management, administrative and professional
C_1	Lower middle class	Supervisory, clerical, junior management, administrative staff
C_2	Working class	Semi and unskilled manual jobs
D	Subsistence	Pensioners, widows, lowest grade workers

  This form of segmentation is particularly useful in advertising. Socio-economic class is closely correlated with press readership and viewing habits, and media planners use this fact to advertise in the most effective way to communicate with their target audience.

- **Geographic segmentation** – markets are frequently split into regions for sales and distribution purposes. Many consumer goods manufacturers break down sales by television advertising regions.

- **Application segmentation** - the athletic shoe industry segments into the serious athletes (small in number but influential), the weekend warriors and the casual wearers who wear athletic shoes as normal footwear. Because the casual wearer represents 80% of the market and does not really need performance, Reebok and LA Gear employ a style-focused strategy.

- **Value segmentation** – is present in most markets. Value can be defined as the customer's view of the balance between satisfaction from the product and its price. Thus, many products have a premium-priced, high quality segment, a mid-priced segment and a low-price segment, e.g. shoes. In such a market, fashion and quality differences can outweigh price variations. In other markets, e.g. petrol and cigarettes, small differences in price can outweigh the small differences in satisfaction perceived by the purchaser.

- **Psychological** – consumers can be divided into groups sharing common psychological characteristics. One group may be described as security-oriented, another as ego-centred and so on. These categories are useful in the creation of advertising messages.

- **Life style segmentation** – a recent trend is to combine psychological and socio-demographic characteristics to give a more complete profile of customer groups. This kind of segmentation uses individuals to represent groups which form a significant proportion of the consumer market. It defines these individuals in terms of sex, age, income, job, product preferences, social attitudes, and political views.

- **Purchasing characteristics** – customers may be segmented by the volume they buy (heavy user, medium user, light user, non user), by the outlet type they use, or by the pack size bought. These variables, and many others, are useful in planning production and distribution and in developing promotion policy. A food manufacturer will approach supermarket chains very differently from the small independent retailer, probably offering better prices and delivery terms, using different sales techniques and delivering direct to the supermarket chain. They might also supply own label products to the large chain but they are unlikely to be able to offer the same terms to the corner shop.

- **Brand loyalty** - the way in which the product or service brand affects the buying decisions is important. Most consumers prefer to buy branded products because the brand provides them with information about the product. For example, if a person goes to a shop to buy a TV, they are likely to be faced with a number of brands eg, Sony, Philips, Panasonic, Toshiba and Bush. They will make an assumption about the probable quality, reliability and comparative price level base on the name. Brand awareness makes the shopper more efficient because the onus for maintaining good quality rests with the supplier of the brand. The shopper knows which brand fits the family tastes and budgets and is prepared to try new products from the same brand family.

KEY POINT

There are many different bases used to segment a market, e.g. demographic, socio-economic, geographic, value, psychological, life style, purchasing characteristics, benefit and family life cycle.

- **Benefit** – customers have different expectations of a product. Some people buy detergents for whiteness, and are catered for by Daz or Persil. Others want economy, for which Surf may fit the bill. Some customers may demand stain removal; one of the biological products is appropriate. An understanding of customers' benefits sought enables the manufacturer to create a range of products each aimed precisely at a particular benefit.

- **Family life cycle segmentation** – a form of demographic segmentation dividing customers by their position in the family life cycle.

The benefits of segmentation to the company adopting this policy is that it enables them to get close to their intended customer and really find out what that customer wants (and is willing to pay for). This should make the customer happier with the product offered and hence lead to repeat sales and endorsements.

ACTIVITY 1

Give reasons why demographic segmentation, by itself, is not a successful basis for car manufacturers targeting their customers.

Feedback to this activity is at the end of the chapter.

2.4   Industrial segmentation

According to Mitchell and Wilson, business-to-business (B2B) segmentation is an ongoing iterative process of examining and grouping industrial buyers into subgroups with similar characteristics. Many of the segmentation variables employed in consumer-based segmentation are also applicable to B2B markets. For instance, business buyers can be segmented by location, size, income (turnover) or benefits.

Industrial and commercial buyers are generally more rational in their buying decisions; they have different benefit expectations than consumers. They may be oriented towards quality, performance requirements, desired features, reliability, durability, versatility, safety, serviceability, assistance from suppliers or ease of operation. They are always concerned with value for money.

The purchasing characteristics are a way of classifying customer companies by their average order size, application, the importance and frequency of purchase, the choice criteria, purchasing procedure and distribution channel etc or according to the type of business they are ie, what they offer for sale. The range of products and services used in an industry will not vary too much from one company to another.

It is frequently useful to analyse marketing opportunities in terms of company size. A company supplying canteen foods would investigate size in terms of numbers of employees. Processed parts suppliers are interested in production rate, and lubricants suppliers would segment by numbers of machine tools.

A market could also be segmented by the size of the buyer. A food manufacturer will approach supermarket chains very differently to the small independent retailer, probably offering better prices, delivery terms, use different sales techniques and deliver direct to the supermarket chain. They might also supply own label product to the large chain but they are unlikely to be able to offer the same terms to the corner shop. The benefit of segmentation to the company adopting this policy is that it enables them to get close to their intended customer and really find out what that customer wants (and is willing to pay for). This should make the customer happier with the product offered and hence lead to repeat sales and endorsements.

2.5   Customer motivation

Once the customer segments have been identified, the next step is to consider what motivates them. For example, the business traveller is interested in easy to use airports or stations, convenient schedules and reliable and comfortable service, whereas the general holiday or recreational traveller may be much more concerned with the price. The small business owner will have different objectives and requirements for PCs than someone in a large company.

Knowledge of motivations can indicate relevant assets and skills, which can provide the basis for a sustainable competitive advantage (SCA). It can highlight the potential for new strategic thrusts for the organisation or of new channels of distribution that could be developed. In terms of airlines, we have already noted that the business sector values convenience, schedule flexibility and service that is relatively insensitive to price. Easy and quick check in procedures can provide an SCA; flights that arrive at inconvenient times can be a substantial weakness. A viable organisation must have the key relevant assets and skills to be able to offer at least the basic requirement of the target customer to gain a competitive advantage.

2.6 Unmet needs

Unmet needs of customers are strategically important because they represent opportunities for organisations that want to break into a market or increase their market share. They can also represent threats to established organisations because they identify areas for competitors to disrupt an established position. Customers may not always be aware of their unmet needs either because they are used to the limitations of existing equipment or the unmet needs are not obvious.

A reaction to the recognition of an unmet need is for an organisation to develop a product or product modification that will be responsive. Sometimes customers will not only have identified problems but will have developed solutions.

In the 1970s in southern California, bicycle sales people and shop owners noticed that youngsters were fixing up their bikes to look like motorbikes with chopper style handlebars and different wheels. The manufacturers came up with a new line of 'motocross' models, which were developed further to produce the mountain bike. This is an example of a user-developed product that grew from an unmet need.

2.7 Targeting approaches

Having identified relevant and viable market segments an organisation is faced with a decision about which segment or segments to serve. There are numerous approaches to this decision and many of the criteria will be specific to the organisation or the market being served. However, the three different targeting approaches are

* *Niche or target marketing* (sometimes referred to as concentrated marketing) – specialising in one or two of the identified markets only, where a company knows it can compete successfully. It acquires a great deal of expertise in its market segment, which must be large enough to sustain profitability. For example, Saga holidays offer a variety of holidays for the older market niche only. Ramblers concentrate on walking holidays.

* *Differentiated marketing* – offers a variety of products to suit all of the needs. Companies like Thompson Holidays offer a variety of holiday types to appeal to most markets. These holidays may be at different prices, in different resorts, at different times of the year and advertised in different brochures.

* *Mass or undifferentiated marketing* – is the opposite of differentiated marketing, in that it treats all customers and potential customers as identical. In the holiday sector, if a company offers just one type of holiday hoping that it would appeal to the majority of people, it would be competing against all of its rivals, who have become specialists in their own areas. Interestingly, Internet marketing can be seen as a form of mass marketing, enabling any size of business, including small businesses, to reach worldwide markets merely by having a website. This is how Amazon, the online shop, which claims to be 'Earth's most customer-centric company ', started trading in 1994. The US division recently set a record of 2.8 million orders taken in one day.

Some companies, and some products, do not require the use of segmentation techniques. Two alternatives are undifferentiated marketing and concentrated marketing.

* *Undifferentiated marketing* – segmented marketing is sometimes referred to as differentiated marketing because it differentiates between customer groups. Undifferentiated marketing is the opposite, in that it treats all customers and potential customers as identical.

* *Concentrated marketing* – some businesses have become specialised in single segments of the market, and do not attempt to market in others. They acquire a great deal of expertise in their market segment, which must be large enough to sustain profitability.

Examples of companies with a clear segmentation policy are Procter & Gamble and Lever in the household detergents market. Sugar is a product that is sold in a relatively undifferentiated way. Morgan cars are a good example of concentrated marketing.

2.8 Positioning

The third step in the process once segments have been selected and target strategies considered is creating an offer of value to be made to the segment. This process is one of market positioning which requires the marketer to design, communicate and deliver value. It creates a particular image, reputation or perception of the company, its brands, its messages or its offer. It helps to identify unique characteristics and unique value propositions. Positioning will often be based around a set of attributes and features, benefits and image factors. The positioning takes into account how other offers are positioned in the market and seeks to differentiate along these important dimensions.

3 Marketing research

3.1 Introduction

Organisations exist in a constantly changing environment. To be able to respond to these changes, they must collect information on which to base decisions. Decisions based on inadequate information are no more than hopeful guesses. Marketing research has seen major growth in recent years in the United Kingdom for three reasons.

- The environment in which organisations operate is changing fast.

- Technological changes coupled with economies of scale have meant that the risk of substantial loss is much greater, so the producer has to be even more certain that the product will meet market needs.

- The boundaries of markets are expanding, so the cost of failure is becoming much larger.

3.2 Marketing and market research

Many people use the terms *marketing research* and *market research* in the same way; in fact they refer to different things. Market research, which focuses on the size and nature of markets, asks, 'is there a market?' whereas marketing research, which is wider to include all the aspects of the company's marketing effort, asks 'is there a market and, if so, how should it be entered and developed?'

DEFINITION

Marketing research is the systematic and objective search for, and analysis of, information relevant to the identification and solution of any problem in the field of marketing.

Marketing research is the systematic and objective search for, and analysis of, information relevant to the identification and solution of any problem in the field of marketing.

Marketing research is not just obtaining information, but it also *involves:*

- framing questions whose answers will provide data to help solve problems

- asking questions to those best qualified to answer them

- recording answers correctly

- interpreting answers

- translating interpretations and making recommendations for marketing action.

Market research is the means used by those who provide goods and services to keep themselves in touch with the needs and wants of those who buy and use those goods and services. It consists of:

KEY POINT

Market research consists of:

- market research
- distribution research
- economic research
- evaluation of product(s)
- communication analysis.

- *market research* (analysis of the market size, trends, market shares, etc)
- *distribution research* (analysis of present channels of distribution, warehouse and other storage locations, discount policy, transport needs, etc)
- *economic research* (analysis of trends including social and forecasting)
- *evaluation of product(s)* (customer requirements analysis, product life cycles, quality measurements, reliability)
- *communication analysis* (of the media usage, suggested media combinations, e.g. T.V. and newspaper advertising, etc).

The firm's marketing research needs will first be determined by which elements of the marketing environment are critical to success. Marketing research can be divided into two broad categories: desk research and field research.

Desk research involves the analysis of data that already exists in one form or another. It can be anything from a company's own sales statistics to Department of Trade and Industry reports. Other secondary sources of information include journals, company reports, government statistics, surveys published by research organisations and electoral registers.

The main reason for undertaking desk research is to gain additional information and intelligence on the following:

Competitors – Who, where and how many are there?

Businesses – How many of a particular type are there and where are they located?

Economic trends – Are people spending more or less on particular products/services?

Householders – How many of a particular type in an area?

Market trends – For which particular business sectors?

Desk research has the advantages of being cheaper and quicker than field research. The disadvantages of this method of research lie in the fact that you do not know if the findings are accurate, or how relevant they will be to your product or service.

Field research is research by direct contact with an identified (or targeted) group of potential clients. The principal reason for undertaking this type of research is to acquire information such as:

- How often do customers purchase?
- How likely are they to purchase from you?
- What is the expected market price?
- How do they select a vendor?
- Are there enough customers to build a viable business?
- What are the main factors considered by customers in a purchase decision?

3.3 Methods of market research

Market research falls into two chief types: motivational research and measurement research.

- **Motivational research** – the objective is to unearth factors that may be important to the product concerned. It does not discover how important they are, nor does it give particulars of the extent to which the factors exist. Some of the more common techniques in motivational research are:

- *Depth interviewing* – undertaken at length by a trained person who is able to appreciate conscious and unconscious associations and motivations and their significance.

- *Group interviewing* – where between six and ten persons are asked to consider the relevant subject (object) under trained supervision.

- *Word association testing* – on being given a word by the interviewer, the first word that comes into the mind of the person being tested is noted.

- *Triad testing* – where people are asked which out of a given three items is least like the remaining two, and why. If the three are brands of a given type of product (or three similar types) replies may show a great deal about attitudes.

In these and other techniques, the basic idea is always to find out what people in general (and the potential customer in particular) believe is relevant to the product.

- **Measurement research** – where the importance of the factors is measured. This type of research uses samples, which should be representative of the population or some known subsection of it. By finding out how often some features occur in the sample, it can give a reasonable expectation that the same proportions will occur in the whole population. Sample surveys are used to find out how many people buy the product(s), what quantity each type of buyer purchases, and where and when the product is bought.

It is also possible (less accurately) to assess roughly the importance of some reasons for buying or not buying. The main types of measurement are:

- random sampling

- quota surveying

- panelling

- surveying by post – the mail shot method

- observation.

3.4 Identifying unmet needs

Several structured market research approaches exist that can help identify opportunities or threats.

- Semi structured interviews with product/service users, in which their experience with the product/service is discussed.

- Problem research develops a list of potential problems with the product/service. The problems are then prioritised by asking a group of 100 to 200 respondents to rate each problem as to whether the problem is important, whether it occurs frequently and whether a solution exists. A problem score is obtained by combining these ratings.

- Benefit structure analysis – has product users identify the benefits desired and the extent to which the product delivers those benefits. The result is an identification of benefits sought that current products are not delivering.

- Customer satisfaction studies are repeated at regular intervals to identify events leading to dissatisfaction that can lead to unmet needs.

3.5 Marketing audit

KEY POINT

A marketing audit examines the organisation's marketing objectives, marketing activities and marketing environment with the aim of assessing its present effectiveness and recommending future action.

Part of marketing research is concerned with the way an organisation responds to the demands of the market place. The best way to evaluate its marketing effort is to carry out a marketing audit, which examines the organisation's marketing objectives, marketing activities and marketing environment with the aim of assessing its present effectiveness and recommending future action. A comprehensive audit would cover the following aspects of the organisation's marketing system.

- **The marketing environment** will provide information on economic and demographic trends, technological change, legal developments, social change, markets, customers, competitors (relevant market shares, product developments and promotional plans) and suppliers.

- **The marketing strategy** consists of corporate objectives, marketing objectives, the marketing plan, marketing resources and the strengths and weaknesses of the organisation.

- **The marketing plans and control** incorporate sales forecasting, product development, control procedures and market research.

- **The marketing mix** includes product evaluation (price acceptability, suitability for customer requirements, quality and reliability), advertising and sales promotion, sales force, pricing policies and distribution activities (analysis of current channels of distribution, discount policies, warehousing and transportation).

- **Profitability and cost effectiveness** includes the profitability of products and markets and marketing costs.

4 Demographic and economic issues

4.1 Social change and social trends

Demographic trends can be a powerful underlying force in a market. Demographic variables include age, income, education, ethnic mix and geographic location. These factors are the determinants of many of the long-term changes in society.

One major statistic is the estimate that there are more people alive today than ever have lived, which is a very sobering thought. In developed countries a significant concern is the size of the ageing population. One study has pointed out the strong and continuing trend toward the population growth of women between the ages of 50 and 70. This group has a higher per capita income, more free time and fewer home responsibilities than younger women. Ethnic populations are rising rapidly and support whole firms and industries, as well as affecting the strategies of main line companies. In the USA Hispanic populations are growing about five times faster than non-Hispanic populations and are gaining in income as well.

Throughout their lifetime, individuals' patterns of consumption depend on their personal desires. The following factors lead to these patterns:

- the average standard of living of the individual's society

- the pattern and level of consumption of the person's social class (and in childhood the class of the parents)

- the age of the person.

There is clearly a lifetime pattern to the changes in a person's consumption of goods and services. This arises from an individual's social, physical and economic development overlaid by changes such as economic growth.

4.2   Influences on the size and structure of the population

Many developed countries face an increasingly serious problem. Developments in medicine and the ensuing improvement in the general health of populations, with changes such as the reduction in tobacco smoking, mean that in a number of countries there is a steadily increasing proportion of old people. Supporting more dependants puts increasing demands on a nation's finite economic resources. A proportionately smaller workforce must meet the rising costs of pensions and medical care. This group has in many countries been reduced by unemployment and an increase in the numbers remaining in full-time education or undertaking training.

Governments are increasingly having to question whether their current commitments, methods, and targets for provision for the elderly can be kept up. When we look at developing countries we find that there may be a mismatch between the growth of the economy and the growth of the population. One measure of the standard of living is the per capita national income. If the population is growing faster than the growth in national income then inevitably there will be a fall in the average person's standard of living. The expansion of the population may be taking resources away from investment that could increase the productive capital of the country.

Total population figures for a country may be of no use for purposes of analysis, but they are a starting point and give a broad measure of the size of an economy. China has a population of over 1,200 million today while the population of the United Kingdom is 57 million: a massive difference that gives no indication of the lack of parallels in the two economies and their relative productivity.

The size of the population is affected by three main influences: the birth rate, the death rate and net effect of migration. Birth and death rates are normally expressed as the number of births or deaths in a year per 1,000 people. For the United Kingdom both rates have fallen dramatically over the last two centuries. Taking both birth and death rates together we arrive at the net reproductive rate of natural increase or decrease in population, excluding migration effects.

Today the population of the United Kingdom is virtually static but that is not true for all countries. Some such as China and India have a rapidly increasing population.

Migration flows have been very important in the development of some countries. Both North America and Australia have benefited from massive net inflows of migrants while Ireland, for example, has suffered a net outflow. A further important factor to consider is the flow of temporary migrants, especially those seeking employment. In Europe many countries have had significant inflows of temporary migrant workers, many of whom may send back to their country of origin some of their earnings.

4.3   The implications of demographic change for staff planning

Company staff planning is the management technique of assessing the future supply and demand for labour in the organisation and deciding how the two can be reconciled. The future supply of labour can come from existing employees who will be with the company within the planning horizon and also from potential sources outside the company such as new entrants to the labour market.

KEY POINT

The planning horizon for staff numbers may be just one or two years ahead but given the years it may take to train and develop employees it is often essential to look five or more years ahead.

The planning horizon for staff numbers may be just one or two years ahead but given the years it may take to train and develop employees it is often essential to look five or more years ahead.

Demographic change can affect the company in two main ways.

- It can alter the internal supply of labour by affecting an organisations policies and practices.

- Depending on the availability of state and occupational pensions and the customary retiring age, the company will probably determine its policy for retirement and therefore the length of the working life with the company. In the United Kingdom it has been the practice for women to retire at 60 and men at 65. Many organisations are revising their policies because of changes in state pension provisions, economic pressures arising from the increase in the life expectancy of retirees, and in the light of European and national legal decisions. In 1991 the life expectancy for British males at 60 was 17.8 years while for females at 60 it was 21.8 years

4.4 Economic forecasting

Given the seriousness and the suddenness of economic changes, an organisation should carry on a programme of continuous economic analysis, consisting of identifying and appraising opportunities and threats. The major economic indicators that are central to the exercise include:

- the rate of inflation
- the level of business activity (GNP growth rates, recession, etc.)
- interest rates
- unemployment level, and the effect of labour supply, and cultural change, on trade union power
- wage rates
- the levels of corporate and personal taxation
- the nature and extent of government imposed credit controls
- the levels of excise and value-added taxes
- the scarcity and price of inputs
- the balance of trade, and foreign exchange rate(s).

Individual enterprises are affected differently by these economic factors. All organisations though must watch what is happening within their own industry and particular areas of activity, and some will also need to consider them in terms of an international dimension.

Among sources of information for assessing likely economic change influencing an industry or industries will be:

- government publications such as the *Monthly Digest of Statistics* and *Trade and Industry* (with which the student should make himself familiar);
- government reports on particular industries;
- reports prepared by international bodies such as UNO, OECD, and EEC;
- commercial publications dealing with economic matters of particular industries;
- publications by trade and professional organisations;
- bank reviews.

5 Competitive analysis

5.1 The build up of a detailed picture

The competitive analysis portion of the 'environmental analysis' for a company will need to focus on four areas of concern:

- identifying the company's major competitors
- establishing on what basis competitive strengths are to be assessed
- comparing the company with its major competitors
- identifying potential new competitors.

5.2 The five forces model

Michael Porter's approach to estimate the profitability of a market is called industry structure analysis, but it can be applied to a market or sub-market within an industry.

Porter explains that there are five competitive forces inherent in a market, which jointly determine the intensity of competition and profitability of an organisation. These five forces reflect the underlying structure of the market and are distinct from the short run fluctuations that can affect market behaviour, such as supply shortages, tax changes, strikes, etc.

The diagram below depicts the five forces that determine the extent of competition in an industry.

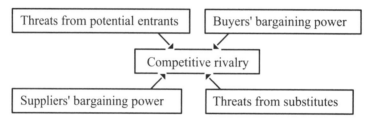

The problem for the strategist is to determine which of these forces are relevant, and to what extent.

It is important to realise in an examination context that the model is concerned with the 'inherent profitability' of an industry (as measured by, say, long term return on investment) and that four of the forces have their effect through *intensifying* competitive rivalry which in turn impacts on rates of return.

5.3 Threats from new entrants

New entrants into a market will bring extra capacity and intensify competition. This will affect the organisation in the following ways.

- An increase in supply usually leads to lower prices.

- The new entrant threatens the market share of existing companies.

- Existing companies will often face increased costs either through competition for supplies or by increased spending on items such as marketing in order to protect market share.

Below we briefly discuss barriers to entry. These can be regarded as an element of 'analysis' but also may come across as choices (ie strategic options) to reduce the threat of entry. Be careful in the exam!

The threat from new entrants will depend on the strength of the barriers to entry and the likely response of existing competitors to a new entrant. Barriers to entry are factors that make it difficult for a new entrant to gain an initial foothold in a market. There are many sources of barriers to entry.

- **Economies of scale** - in the type of industry where unit costs or technical cost factors that decrease cost with size decline significantly as volume increases, a new entrant will be unable to start on a comparable cost basis. This is also true where high levels of fixed costs raise barriers to entry. For example many industries, such as cement and chemicals, offer increasing returns to scale, and companies benefit by being able to lower unit costs by increasing output volume. Thus potential entrants would be at a considerable cost disadvantage, unless they can immediately set up their operations on a scale large enough to reap similar economies.

  The patterns of distribution or access to distribution channels may be restricted - if there are only certain outlets for a product it is harder to break in to the market.

For example items such as televisions tend to be sold through a small number of high street retailers. Two companies dominate the soft drinks industry in the UK because brewers such as Bass and Whitbread own the soft drinks companies and the distribution outlets (ie the public houses). This pattern of distribution, however, has been forced to change with recent government legislation restricting the number of public houses that can be owned by brewers.

- **Capital requirements** – how much capital will be required to start up in the industry? In some industries the initial capital requirements are prohibitive. This would apply, for example, in the supermarket sector or rail transport. However, the *amount* of capital required may not be the major barrier to entry but rather the *availability* and *cost* of raising finance.

- **Brand (or product) differentiation** - some brands generate a greater consumer loyalty than others and consumers will not be easily lured away by competing products even though they are similar or close substitutes. The cost for a new entrant attempting to penetrate the market in such a situation is likely to be high. Products can be differentiated in terms of: price, quality, brand image, features, distribution, exclusivity, packaging or value and can be reinforced through advertising or marketing, patent control of superior design/product, control of distribution or licensed brand dealers

- **Switching costs** - these are one-off costs facing a company that switches from one supplier's product to another's. Switching costs may include costs of certification, product redesign, costs and time in assessing a new source, or even the cultural problems of severing a relationship.

- **Cost disadvantages independent of scale** - established companies may have cost advantages not available to potential entrants, no matter what their size and cost levels. Critical factors include: proprietary product technology, favourable locations, learning or experience curve, favourable access to sources of raw materials and government subsidies. Cost advantage as a barrier to entry is one of the main causes of concentration in a market. This can be due to patents, secrecy, imperfections in factor markets making factors cheaper to some firms than others (e.g. union vs. non union), new firms having to bid up factors for use and capital scarcity

- **Access to distribution channels** -one of the biggest dilemmas facing the producer is obtaining shelf or floor space in retail outlets. In order to sell brands the producer must not only persuade the retailer to stock them, but to give them a fair share of shelf/floor space and to feature them periodically. Shelf and floor space is limited (consider here how much high street space an electric dish-washing machine takes to display), and already faced with a bewildering array and assortment of similar products (for example a large Sainsbury store carries some 7,000 products) retail management are not anxious to accept new products, particularly from new entrants lacking a proven track record in the market

- **Likely retaliation** from existing producers - is it likely that the existing operators in an industry will try to force the new entrant out of the market?

- **Government legislation** - still prevents companies from entering into direct competition with some industries although deregulation and privatisation have meant that extensive barriers to entry have now been lowered in an attempt to make markets contestable. Patents and copyright offer inventors some protection against new entrants. Governments also license the right to produce certain categories of products. Japanese companies use the complexity of the distribution and legal system in Japan to deter potential entrants in the domestic market.

- **The 'learning curve'** phenomenon could put new entrants at a cost disadvantage. Initially, in the early stages of entry, new firms would probably be operating at higher average costs than existing organisations until they have 'learnt' from experiences to operate in a more efficient manner.

There are other barriers to entry such as advertising, patents and trade secrets, but it is not possible to state which are the most important. What is important is the recognition that barriers to entry have a major impact on the threat of potential entry.

The following two items can *lower* barriers to entry if they are present in an industry.

- Cost advantages independent of size – for example a hotel may be successful simply because of its location.

- Product differentiation – where established organisations have a good brand image and customer loyalty, the costs of overcoming this can be prohibitive. However, if a company can persuade customers that its product is 'different' it can overcome barriers to entry by creating its own market.

What is the effect on strategy of potential new entrants to a market?

- If a company is inside the industry it will try to raise barriers to entry and stop rivals entering the market. Examples include airlines trying to protect favourable slots (take-off times) so that new entrants are left with unattractive slots.

- If a company is outside an industry it will try to lower barriers to entry in order to enter the market. Examples include the personal computer industry. Computers were originally sold through chains of high street electrical retailers. In order to set up their own distribution chains, personal computer manufacturers set up their own shops or sold their computers via mail order and over the Internet.

5.4 Threats from substitutes

The threat of substitute products is across industries, eg rail travel v bus travel v private car, or within an industry, e.g. long-life milk as a substitute for delivered fresh milk. Porter explains that 'substitutes limit the potential returns.... by placing a ceiling on the price firms in the industry can profitably charge'. The better the price/performance alternative offered by substitutes, the easier the customer will switch. An organisation may find its products under threat from any of the following factors.

- Alternative product. Customers can easily switch to a rival product (direct substitution), for example buying one brand of washing machine rather than another. The point here is that there are many brands available, often with little to distinguish one from another.

- Different industry. Customers may switch to a product in a different market that has similar qualities. For example customers may switch from buying butter to buying margarine (indirect substitution).

- Going without the product. Customers may decide they do not want to buy the product from anyone. For example they may decide to give up smoking cigarettes.

What is the effect on strategy of the threat from substitutes?

- If there are a large number of substitutes a company will try to prevent customers switching to alternative products. One common method of doing this is to promote brand images, which set the product apart from its rivals.

- A company may find that to prevent customers switching to a different product it is necessary to reduce the price of their own product. A good example is the methods of travelling from London to Edinburgh where the substitutes are: air, rail, coach and private car.

5.5   Threats from the bargaining power of buyers

Buyers can reduce profits in an industry by exerting their market power. For example, the concentration of the UK grocery business into a small number of large firms has allowed those powerful retailers to set high quality targets and low costs. This has dramatically reduced profitability in agricultural markets.

The power used by buyers can have the secondary effect of increasing competitiveness by:

(a) forcing down prices

(b) bargaining for higher quality or improved services

(c) playing competitors against each other.

Porter purports that the power of the industry's buyer groups depends on the characteristics of its market situation and of the relative importance of its purchases from the industry compared with its overall business. He suggests that buyers are particularly powerful in seven situations, when:

* purchases are large relative to sellers

* purchases represent a significant proportion of the buyers' costs

* purchases are undifferentiated

* buyers earn low profits

* buyers have the potential for backward integration

* the buyer's product is not strongly affected by the quality of the suppliers' product

* the buyer has full information.

What is the effect on strategy of buyers' bargaining power? If buyers are powerful then a supplier cannot pass on any cost inefficiencies in the form of higher prices. Because of this more attention will be directed at cost reduction within the supplier company.

5.6   Threats from the power of suppliers

Suppliers can exert bargaining power over companies within an industry in two main ways.

(a) threatening to raise their prices

(b) threatening to reduce the quality of their goods and services.

The effect of this power will be to squeeze profitability out of an industry unable to recover cost increases by raising its own prices. This can be seen in the PC business, where software and processor suppliers make great profits, but PC manufacture remains relatively less attractive.

Porter suggests that suppliers are particularly powerful in six situations, where:

* there are few suppliers - buyers have few alternatives to choose from.

* there are few substitutes for their products

* the industry supplied is not an important customer

* the supplier's product is an important component to the buyer's business

* the supplier's product is differentiated

* suppliers can threaten forward integration (ie suppliers can purchase or establish their own customer and direct all supplies there)

Good examples of suppliers with strong bargaining power are airports and the pharmaceutical industries. It is worth pointing out that highly skilled labour also meets the criteria above. Suppliers of such labour, ie skilled personnel are in demand and can command very favourable terms for supplying their skills.

In not-for-profit organisations, there may be only a limited number of suppliers of funding. This enables such suppliers to command favourable terms when offering to supply funding.

What is the effect on strategy of the bargaining power of suppliers? If suppliers are powerful then buyers will find it difficult to squeeze costs by reducing the cost of inputs. The organisation is also more susceptible to increases in the cost of supplies.

5.7 Rivalry and competition among competitors

This is the most obvious form of competition: the head-to-head rivalry between organisations making similar products and selling them in the same market. Rivalry can be intense and cut-throat, or it may be governed by unwritten 'rules' - agreements that help the industry avoid the damaging effects of offensive strategies. Tactics commonly used to implement these strategies include product innovations and improvements, price competitions, advertising battles and increased customer services. Rivalry occurs because one or more companies feels threatened or sees a market opportunity to improve its position, although competitive moves by the initiator company usually results in counter-defensive strategies from its competitors. This interactive pattern of offensive and defensive strategies may not leave the initiating company and the industry better off, and on the contrary may leave all the companies in the industry worse off than before.

Porter suggests that there are seven main determinants relating to the strength of internal competition and rivalry within an industry. There are:

- many equally balanced competitors

- slow rate of industrial growth

- lack of differentiation

- capacity can only be increased by large amounts

- high fixed costs in the industry

- there are many diverse competitors

- there are high exit barriers.

What is the effect on strategy of the degree of competitive rivalry?

- If there is a high degree of competitive rivalry then organisations must consider rivals' responses to their strategy. This may mean that the organisation develops an initial strategy followed by two or three follow-up plans, depending on the response from rivals to the initial strategy.

- If there is little competitive rivalry then the organisation need only develop its initial strategy.

ACTIVITY **2**

Pains Fireworks is one of the UK oldest companies. These days, most of its revenue comes from Firework displays, rather than the manufacturing of fireworks themselves. When asked about the marketing issues he faces, M.D. Bill Deeker said

"You know how to buy a pair of shoes because you know what leather looks like, you know what good stitching looks like and you can pull the sole and the top and the upper apart to see if it's glued or stitched. You can't do that with firework displays because you're not buying the products when you're buying the display. You don't see it"

What are the additional factors to be taken into account when marketing services, rather than products?

Feedback to this activity is at the end of the chapter.

5.8 The purpose and weaknesses of the model

The main purpose of the model is to provide a structure for discussion and debate around the theme of strategy. Some particular ways in which it can be used are:

- Competitive rivalry, look for niches where there are few firms as rivals and then benchmark against them. Or else look for growing markets in which more firms can still hold on and grow shares. Use it to focus on the competitor nature and number questions.

- Bargaining power of suppliers, use this to explore issues of balance and how to develop advantageous relationships. For example, if the supplier is exploiting its strong bargaining position (like the steel maker) then a strategic response on the customer firm's part might be to explore alternative sources of supply or even alternative materials or processes so as to reduce this dependence. Equally if the supplier power is weak one strategy might be to exploit this weakness by tying the supplier into price reduction or other contract requirements, which provide strategically advantageous inputs to the customer firm.

The danger in this is that it often becomes a see saw of power relations. For example, in the car industry the historical pattern was one of adversarial relations, with an overall 'lose-lose' outcome. New thinking on supplier (and downstream relations towards customers) is concerned with developing co-operative relationships along the whole 'value stream'. Instead of optimising one part of the chain at the expense of another this approach seeks to develop 'win-win' strategies. For example, in the car case discussed above firms are now trying to develop suppliers (even to the extent of providing cash, equipment, and engineering support) in order that those suppliers can provide them with uninterrupted supplies of the right quality, quantity and just in time. In the new VW plant in Brazil suppliers are actually based within the assembler's factory, which carries the partnership model to new levels.

It is important to be aware that this model, though a powerful structure for discussion, has its limitations. For example:

- It provides a good framework for analysis but does not really consider issues around implementing changes to reposition for strategic advantage.

- It is also, because of its simplification of complex relationships, apparently linear in structure whereas much competition is more in the form of networks and clusters. A comprehensive description and analysis of all five forces gets very difficult in complex industries with multiple interrelations, product groups, by-products and segments. A too narrow focus on particular segments of such industries, however, bears the risk of missing important elements.

- The model assumes relatively static market structures. This is hardly the case in today's dynamic markets.

ACTIVITY 3	Do the five forces help us to understand why European steel companies generally perform poorly?

Feedback to this activity is at the end of the chapter.

5.9 The role of government and regulation

This is a complicated area covering the Companies Acts, employment legislation (determining the basic employment rights), health and safety regulations, consumer legislation (credit regulations, etc) and so on. There is an almost endless list of laws, or categories of legislation that affect business enterprises, in domestic, national or international dimensions.

The main categories are listed below:

- Local by-laws (planning permission, construction of roads, licenses etc)

- Labour legislation (safety at work, employee protection, redundancy payments etc).

- Trade union legislation.

- Consumer protection legislation.

- Company legislation

- Taxation legislation

- Anti-trust (monopolies) legislation and rulings.

- Trade legislation (countries restricted for export, etc.

- Business legislation (contract and agency law, etc).

- Social legislation (welfare benefits, etc.

The law constitutes a set of environmental factors that are increasingly affecting strategic decisions. Most of the nations of the world are, or are becoming, regulated economies. Government, or self, regulation of business has four principal aims.

1   **To protect business entities** - eg, laws putting limits on market dominance by acting against monopolies and restrictive practices and providing financial assistance to selected ailing industries and companies.

2   **To protect consumers** - with many detailed consumer protection regulations covering packaging, labelling, food hygiene and advertising, and much more.

3   **To protect employees** - with laws governing the recruitment of staff and health and safety legislation that regulates conditions of work.

4   **To protect the interests of society at large** against excessive business behaviour eg, by acting to protect the environment.

Also at the most basic level, perhaps, laws are passed that enable Government to levy taxes whereas company law affects the corporate structure of the business, and prescribes the duties of company directors.

Managers cannot plan intelligently without a good working knowledge of the laws and regulations that affect their own companies and the businesses they operate in. In addition to those laws which apply generally to all companies, such as laws regulating Corporation Tax or Value added Tax, there are laws specifically used to deal with individual industries eg, Petroleum Revenue Tax in the offshore oil and gas industry.

6 Competition and collaboration

6.1 Types of collaboration

Economists argue that strong competition between many firms usually creates the best outcomes for consumers. From the seller's point of view, competition may be viewed as a destructive force that reduces profits in both the long and short run. It is not surprising, therefore, that firms frequently collaborate with each other, rather than try to put their competitors out of business.

The nature of the collaboration can be wide ranging, and new variations are continually devised by the more adventurous businesses. Some common examples of collaboration are given below:

(a) **Collaborations of buyers**: Smaller firms are often able to improve the power of buyers by joining consortia that buy in bulk thereby negotiating lower prices. Sometimes, these consortia become so successful that they are able to trade effectively on the open market. An example in the UK is Spar/Costcutter, as buying associations of small retailers formed in an attempt to compete against the major supermarkets.

(b) **Collaborations of suppliers**: Firms are able to reduce competitive rivalry and limit new entrants by agreements concerning safety, standards, service and so on. Industries as diverse as furniture removal and accountancy protect themselves from outbreaks of low price and low quality based competition that damage profits, and may be against the buyer's best interests.

(c) **Collaborations to reduce competitive pressure**: In industries where there is an over supply, such as cars, there are a large number of collaborative arrangements that prevent prices falling as far as they might otherwise do. Weaker players are often kept in business by ensuring that ownership and risk are dispersed throughout the industry.

(d) **Collaborations to reduce risk**: Firms in particularly risky environments frequently collaborate to prevent over exposure to a particular project. The European Aircraft industries have collaborated in the development of large airliners, and pharmaceutical companies frequently create joint ventures to collaborate with their rivals in the development of new drugs. This reduces the financial risk if the drug does not work, and the marketing risks associated with having two similar drugs produced by competing companies at the same time.

(e) **Collaboration to enter new markets**: Firms may enter a new market with some, but not all, of the skills and competencies necessary to compete effectively. Often, existing competitors with excess capacity are willing to provide such services as distribution, maintenance and retailing. When establishing a presence overseas, it is commonly necessary to collaborate with a domestic firm – and a legal requirement in some countries.

(f) **Collaboration for leverage**: Some firms have become greatly skilled at borrowing the skills and knowledge of others for particular projects. Chaparral Steel in the USA do not have a dedicated research and development function, but are highly skilled at getting possible customers to carry out the research and development for a specified new project.

6.2 Government regulation

The examples given in the discussion above do not appear to make consumers worse off, but this may not be the case with many such collaborations. Most countries have a variety of laws and statutory instruments in place to prevent misuse of such agreements to the detriment of buyers. Naturally, the details of such regulation will vary from country to country, but in the UK collaborative agreements between firms are regulated by five pieces of legislation:

- The Fair Trading Act (1973) dealing with monopolies and mergers

- Restrictive Practices Act (1976) dealing with agreements between individuals and companies that limit free trade

- The Competition Act (1988) dealing with anti competitive practices

- The Resale Price Act 1(976)) dealing with attempts to impose minimum prices

- Articles 85 and 86 of the Treaty of Rome, where restrictive practices and mergers have an effect on interstate trade.

Competition policy in the UK seeks to protect two groups:

- buyers and consumers who may have insufficient power to enforce change or buy from other sources

- companies that are disadvantaged by trying to compete fairly against those using unfair tactics.

When investigating collaborative agreements, the term 'monopoly' is used, which can be confusing since the term is usually applied to a single supplier in economics. In the UK, the 1973 Fair Trading Act allows for firms to be referred to the Competition Commission on the basis of the 'existence, or possible existence, of a monopoly situation'. This can be an investigation based on a scale monopoly (usually involving an appraisal of one firm) or a complex monopoly (where the behaviour of a number of firms comes under scrutiny). A complex monopoly situation exists when, in relation to the supply of goods of any description, at least 25% of suppliers conduct their business in a way that prevents, restricts or distorts competition.

Inquiries can focus narrowly on a particular industry practice but most complex or scale monopoly investigations involve a wider appraisal of whether competition is functioning effectively.

The OFT can require firms to stop practices that are against consumers' interests, e.g. firms' attempts to restrict competition. Firms often have an incentive to restrict competition because reduced competition will lead to higher profits and an easier existence. The ways in which firms may seek to restrict competition are many and various. For example, a firm may try to:

- reach agreement with other firms about the prices each will charge

- arrange with other firms the territories for which each will be the sole or main supplier

- reduce the supply to the market with a view to forcing up prices

- devise ways of preventing other firms from entering its market, e.g. by tying retailers into exclusive deals

- take over its competitors to reduce the degree of competition it faces.

In countries, including the UK, with strong competition laws, all of these practices are likely to be subject to legal scrutiny. With the power of the law to support it, the OFT enforces competition and consumer protection laws in several ways, including:

- uncovering and deterring anti-competitive behaviour

- putting an end to any abuse of market power, e.g. charging excessive prices to a captive market or forcing out competitors through predatory pricing

- identifying mergers (two firms joining together) that might be against the public interest so that these can be further investigated by the Competition Commission

- applying robustly the rules that protect consumers.

6.3 The Competition Commission

The Competition Commission is an independent public body established by the Competition Act 1998. It replaced the Monopolies and Mergers Commission on 1 April 1999.

The Commission conducts in-depth inquiries into mergers, markets and the regulation of the major regulated industries. Every inquiry is undertaken in response to a reference made to it by another authority: usually by the Office of Fair Trading (OFT) but in certain circumstances the Secretary of State, or by the regulators under sector-specific legislative provisions relating to regulated industries. The Commission has no power to conduct inquiries on its own initiative.

The Enterprise Act 2002 introduces a new regime for the assessment of mergers and markets in the UK. In most merger and market references the Commission is responsible for making decisions on the competition questions and for making and implementing decisions on appropriate remedies. Under the legislation that the Act replaces, the Commission had to determine whether matters were against the public interest. The public interest test is replaced by tests focused specifically on competition issues. The new regime also differs from the previous regime where the Commission's power in relation to remedies was only to make recommendations to the Secretary of State.

6.4 Office of Fair Trading (OFT)

The Enterprise Act 2002 establishes the Office of Fair Trading (OFT) as an independent statutory body with a Board, giving them a greater role in ensuring that markets work well to the benefit of all. The OFT board consists of a chairman (John Vickers) and six other members, appointed by the Secretary of State. The tenure of OFT members (including the Chairman) is determined by the Secretary of State although terms of office may not exceed five years.

The OFT's job is to make markets work well for consumers. Markets work well when businesses are in open, fair and vigorous competition with each other for the consumer's custom. They ensure that consumers have as much choice as possible across all the different sectors of the marketplace.

As an independent professional organisation, the OFT plays a leading role in promoting and protecting consumer interests throughout the UK, while ensuring that businesses are fair and competitive. To carry out this work they are granted powers under consumer and competition legislation.

They have three main operational areas:

1   **The Competition Enforcement** (CE) - The CE division plays a key role:

    - enforcing current legislation including The Competition Act 1998

    - stopping cartels and other damaging anti-competitive agreements

    - stopping any abuse of a dominant market position

    - promoting a strong competitive culture across a wide range of markets

    - informing business, through a widespread education programme, about changes in legislation

    - working with the European Commission on EC cases

2 **Consumer Regulation Enforcement** (CRE) - The CRE team:

- ensures that consumer legislation and regulations are properly enforced

- takes action against unfair traders

- encourages codes of practice and standards

- offers a range of information to help consumers understand their rights and make good choices

- liaises closely with other regulatory bodies that also have enforcement powers.

3 **Markets and Policies Initiatives** (MPI) - there are three main areas of activity within MPI.

- economic and statistical advice and financial analysis

- market investigations and competition

- relations with stakeholders, including government departments and public enquiries.

Each branch works closely with the other two, and often in project teams involving colleagues across the OFT.

6.5 Different market environments

The scope for competitive and collaborative behaviour varies depending upon the different types of market.

	Typical competitive activity	**Typical collaborative activity**
Competitive market: Many buyers and sellers Little difference between products (i.e. PC industry)	Intense price competition Competitive advantages short lived	Co-operative buying
Monopolistic market (i.e. automobiles) Several sellers, many buyers Clear differences between products	Firms can charge high prices, but normally have excess capacity Occasional outbreaks of price competition	Collaboration to restrict competition, power of suppliers and buyers Collaboration to develop new products and services Frequently buy and sell products from each other
Oligopolistic market (i.e. petrol market) Small number of sellers Little difference between products	Intensive non-price competition Occasional price competition	Price agreements – cartels Quality and service agreements Frequently buy and sell products from each other
Monopolist or monopsonist Only one buyer or seller	Price is set to maximise profits without attracting new entry	International collaboration for new market entry – i.e. telecommunications industry

6.6 Cartels and oligopolies

A cartel is a formal agreement among firms in an oligopolistic industry. Cartel members may agree on such matters as prices, total industry output, market shares, allocation of customers, allocation of territories, establishment of common sales agencies, and the division of profits or combination of these. Cartel in this broad sense is synonymous with 'explicit' forms of collusion. Cartels are formed for the mutual benefit of member organisations.

The theory of 'co-operative' oligopoly provides the basis for analysing the formation and the economic effects of cartels. Generally speaking, cartels or cartel behaviour attempts to emulate that of a monopoly by restricting industry output, raising or fixing prices in order to earn higher profits.

A distinction needs to be drawn between public and private cartels. In the case of public cartels, the government may establish and enforce the rules relating to prices, output and other such matters. Export cartels and shipping conferences are examples of public cartels. In many countries depression cartels have been permitted in industries deemed to be requiring price and production stability and/or to permit rationalisation of industry structure and excess capacity. In Japan for example, such arrangements have been permitted in the steel, aluminum smelting, shipbuilding and various chemical industries. Public cartels were also permitted in the United States during the depression in the 1930s and continued to exist for some time after World War II in industries such as coal mining and oil production. Cartels have also played an extensive role in the German economy during the inter-war period. International commodity agreements covering products such as coffee, sugar, tin and more recently oil (OPEC: Organisation of Petroleum Exporting Countries) are examples of international cartels, which have publicly entailed agreements between different national governments.

Crisis cartels have also been organised by governments for various industries or products in different countries in order to fix prices and ration production and distribution in periods of acute shortages. In contrast, private cartels entail an agreement on terms and conditions from which the members derive mutual advantage but which are not known or likely to be detected by outside parties. Private cartels in most jurisdictions are viewed as being illegal and in violation of antitrust laws. Successful cartels, be they public or private, require 'concurrence', 'coordination' and 'compliance' among members. This means that cartel members need to be able to detect when violations of an agreement take place and be able to enforce the agreement with sanctions against the violators. These conditions are not easily met and this often explains why cartels tend to break down over time.

Conclusion

In this chapter we have considered a range of techniques for developing a better understanding of the competitive environment in terms of analysing the behaviour of customers and competitors. The important role of marketing was identified, and the various techniques and models open to understanding how buyers act were considered.

We further examined the role of competition in developing profits within an industry. The five forces model helps an analyst to understand how profits may be divided up between competitors, suppliers and buyers according to the strength of their bargaining position.

Finally, we looked at the scope for collaboration between competitors, and the means by which such activity is regulated.

Customer analysis

1 How might a market be segmented? (2.2)

Marketing research

2 What are the distinctions between market research and marketing research? (3.2)

Competitive analysis

3 Explain the purpose and process of Porter's five forces. (5.2)

Competition and collaboration

4 Outline the different features of competitive, monopolistic, monopsonist, and oligopolistic markets. (6.5)

Market segmentation

In the last few decades, companies have moved increasingly towards the targeting of particular customer segments rather than seeking to sell a single product range to all customers.

Required:

(a) Explain the advantages that a company might hope to gain by targeting particular segments of the market. **(10 marks)**

(b) Describe three variables you think would be useful as a basis for segmenting the market for clothing sold by a large retail chain, and two variables for segmenting the market in paint sold to other businesses by a paint manufacturer.

Explain your reasons for the choice of all five variables. **(10 marks)**

(Total: 20 marks)

For the answer to this question, see the 'Answers' section at the end of the book.

Reasons include the following:

(a) A car manufacturer may use buyers' age in developing its target market and then discover that the target should be the psychologically young and not the chronologically young. (The Ford Motor Company used buyers' age in targeting its Mustang car in America, designing it to appeal to young people who wanted an inexpensive sporty car. Ford found to its surprise that the car was being purchased by all age groups.)

(b) Income is another variable that can be deceptive. One would imagine that working class families would buy Ford Escorts and the managerial class would buy BMWs. However, many Escorts are bought by middle-income people (often as the family's second car) and expensive cars are often bought by working class families (plumbers, carpenters, etc).

(c) Personal priorities also upset the demographic balance. Middle-income people often feel the need to spend more on clothes, furniture and housing which they could not afford if they purchased a more expensive car.

(d) The upgrading urge for people trying to relate to a higher social order often leads them to buy expensive cars.

(e) Some parents although 'well off' pay large fees for the private education of their children and must either make do with a small car, or perhaps no car at all.

There are many differences. You may have observed the following:

- The producer / provider of the service is present at the point of consumption

- The users of the service interact with the providers of the service rather more than they do with a manufacturer

- There is greater variation in the delivery, quality and experience of the service than with product quality

- The benefits of a service are frequently intangible

- There is little that can be done to experience service quality in advance of a purchase – how could a customer try out an insurance policy or a film first?

In order to incorporate these kinds of considerations, marketers have extended the elements of the marketing mix for services with three items, *People, Physical Evidence and Process.*

People

Since the customer and the service provider often meet, it is important that those involved in the service are sensitive to customer needs. Perversely, in many countries and occupations, there is almost a pride in treating the customer poorly. For example, many medical receptionists in the UK public sector still see their job as protecting the doctor from bothersome patients, rather than helping them get the service they need. The attitude is less common in the private sector, although far from unknown. In the private sector, many services are traditionally handled very poorly, including almost all of those involved with conveying property. As Tom Peters famously remarked, 'any company that treats its customers with common decency is likely to get the lion's share of any market it wants, because it's alone.'

Much can be done to improve the customer interface, including training and appropriate recruitment. The service can often be outsourced – BA use external companies to deal with some important aspects of the customer interface although this is not obvious from the way the service is delivered.

Physical Evidence

Since the user cannot trial the service directly, other clues will be used to infer service quality. This can be somewhat unreasonable. The head of an American airline once remarked that coffee stains on cabin trays imply that engine maintenance might be equally sloppy.

- Service providers can do much to indicate the experience of the service in advance:

- *Users' charters and performance indicators.* Indicators of what might be expected by users might be used in publicity material. In the UK, the authorities impose this on some sectors – particularly in education – by compiling performance indicators, and publishing them in the form of a league table. A parent can thereby see which of the local schools perform particularly well. Similarly, an insurance company might use information about the average time taken to process a claim

- *External validation* of quality by the national quality. Such awards as ISO 9000 can be used to imply service quality. Membership of appropriate trade bodies will usually imply some standards of performance.

- *Ambience* at first point of contact and the point of service delivery can convey much about how the service operates. In such businesses as catering and beauty treatment, a great deal turns on first impressions.

- *Corporate Image.* Where the firm is big enough, it is possible to set standards that will be recognised. For example, the experience of eating in at McDonalds or Burger King can be predicted in advance anywhere in the world.

- In cases where service quality cannot be regulated so effectively, it is possible to create a corporate image through other elements of the communications mix, described below.

Process

Quality can be instilled into the process whereby the service is produced. Much of this will result from the people in the organisation who provide the service to customers . In this context 'non-technical' (receptionists, telephonists etc) members of staff may be just as important as those actually producing the service. Training, supervision, quality controls and complaints procedures may all have a major part to play here.

FEEDBACK TO ACTIVITY 3

The five forces for steel are adverse, often severely so. There are many companies, often subsidised by national governments, and threat of entry is always high, through subsidised exports or acquisition of foreign steel merchants. The fixed costs in the industry are very high, which puts pressure on prices because individual firms are always tempted to discount to increase contribution, lowering industry prices generally.

The number of substitutes is growing for an ever-wider number of applications. Users of steel are generally large companies – auto manufacturers and so on, who have a wide choice and can switch suppliers easily. The merchants themselves are often very large. Consequently, in most years the steel sector performs poorly, doing well only when the world economy is expanding.

Chapter 6
COMPETITION AND COMPETITIVE ADVANTAGE

There are a number of planning tools, or methods, which might help the company to examine the competitiveness and attractiveness of its products and Strategic Business Units. This enables better strategies to be set at both business and corporate levels, and the correct level of capital support to be set.

Objectives

When you have studied this chapter you should be able to:

- understand the portfolio analysis approach

- explain and demonstrate the purpose of competitive intelligence and the tools to analyse competitor intelligence

- explain competitor benchmarking

- define sustainable competitive advantage and contrast the different means of achieving it

- discuss generic strategies

- outline the nature and purpose of critical success factors

- compare efficiency and effectiveness

- discuss quality issues.

1 Portfolio analysis

1.1 Introduction

Most of us associate a portfolio with a mix of shares in the stock market, each of which promising different characteristics of risk and reward. The same argument could be put forward for companies that have a portfolio of products or services with different characteristics such as market growth, investment requirements, projected profitability and the volume of the product's sales. It is all a question of balance. With the range of products or services, the balance question is designed to reveal whether the organisation has:

- too many declining products or services

- too few products or services with growth potential

- insufficient product/service profit generators to maintain present organisation performance and to provide investment funds for the nurturing of tomorrow's successful ventures.

1.2 Techniques

There are a number of techniques to help organisations to analyse the effectiveness of their business. One method, the product life cycle, looks at the lifecycle stages of their products/services, to ensure that the firm has the required mix ie, some aiming for long-term growth, some for an increase in cash flow where high initial sales are expected but the life is short. This theory holds that a product or service has a life cycle and that each different phase of the cycle requires different financing requirements.

The Boston Consultancy Group (BCG) provides another useful model, which relates products to market share.

1.3 Contribution to strategic capability

Portfolio analysis can be very valuable in assessing how the balance of activities contributes to the strategic capability of the organisation. However, there are some points to note:

- The analysis should be applied to SBUs ie, units dealing with particular market segments not whole markets.

- The management must develop the capability to review to role of each SBU in the overall mix of the organisation's activities, and devote time to it.

- The outcome will be different targets and expectations for different parts of the organisation, which will extend to the resource allocation processes - both capital and revenue budgets.

2 The Boston Consulting Group model

2.1 Product Market Portfolio

Whilst there are companies that produce a single product or service, most organisations are multi-product or consider diversification into other products. Within a multi-divisional company, there may be some products at maturity, some at the design stage, and others in decline. Each of these may be in different markets, and different countries. This is a complex planning process, and the Product Market Portfolio (PMP), developed by the Boston Consulting Group (1972), is a technique developed to try to handle it.

Similarly, as companies grow, their portfolio of products becomes wider. Consequently, strategists in those businesses need to divide the business up into a portfolio of strategic business units.

KEY POINT

The product market portfolio is a tool for strategic planning that allows the planners to select the optimal strategy for individual units whilst aiming for overall corporate objectives.

The product market portfolio is a useful tool for strategic planning, in that it allows the planners to select the optimal strategy for individual units whilst aiming for overall corporate objectives. It extends strengths assessment in three directions:

- Portfolio analysis combines the assessment of business position with a market attractiveness evaluation.

- It includes multiple SBUs in the same analysis and addresses investment issues such as which units should receive resources, which should have resources withheld and which should be resource generators.

- It offers baseline recommendations concerning the investment strategies for each SBU based on the assessment of business position and market attractiveness.

Portfolio planning is a phrase used to describe methods of expressing a product/market relationship in a manner meaningful for management decision-making. There are two main aims; the first one is to ascertain the current strengths or weaknesses of a company's products, their position in the markets and the state of attractiveness of each of those markets. The second is to indicate a strategy that would emphasise the strong positions and remedy the weak ones. One of the techniques used for this planning is the Boston Consulting Group matrix.

2.2   The Boston Consulting Group (BCG) growth share matrix

The BCG growth share matrix suggests that an analysis of the market can best be summarised by knowing its growth rate and that the best indication of an organisation's strength in a market is its relative market share.

- Growth is the best measure of the product life cycle.

- Market share is assumed to be gained more easily in a growth context when new users with no developed loyalties are attracted to the product/service.

This two by two matrix classifies businesses, divisions or products according to the present market share and the future growth of that market.

Assessing the rate of market growth as high or low is tricky because it depends on the market. New markets may grow explosively while mature markets grow hardly at all. The midpoint of the growth dimension - although arbitrary - is usually set at 10% annual growth rate; markets growing in excess of 10% are considered to be high growth markets and those growing at less are low growth markets

Relative market share is defined by the ratio of market share to the market of the largest competitor. The log scale is used so that the midpoint of the axis is 1.0, the point at which an organisation's market share is exactly equal to that of its largest competitor. Anything to the left of the midpoint indicates that the organisation has the leading market share position. The money value of product sales is plotted in the display by the relative size of the circle.

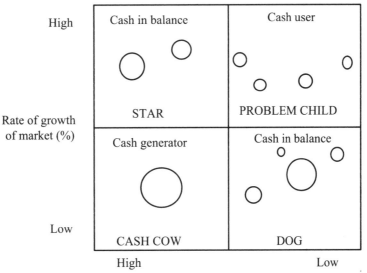

Relative market share (ratios of share to share
of largest competitor)

2.3   Interpretation of matrix

Given the high degree of subjectivity, the four divisions are described below:

A dog is a low market share product in a low growth industry. A dog usually has cost disadvantages and few growth opportunities. An organisation with such a product can attempt to appeal to a specialised market, delete the product or harvest profits by cutting back support services to a minimum.

The primary assumption of the BCG matrix is that the higher an organisation's market share, the lower its costs and the higher its profitability. This is the result of economies of scale (firms can mechanise and automate production and distribution) the experience curve (as projects and operations are repeated, time requirements are reduced) and improved bargaining power.

A Cash cow has a high relative market share in a low growth market and should be generating substantial cash inflows. The period of high growth in the market has ended, (the product life cycle is in the maturity or decline stage), and consequently the market is less attractive to new entrants and existing competitors. Cash cow products tend to generate cash in excess of what is needed to sustain their market positions. Profits support the growth of other company products. The firm's strategy is oriented towards maintaining the product's strong position in the market. A **Star** product has a high relative market share in a high growth market. This type of product may be in a later stage of its product life cycle.

A star may be only cash neutral despite its strong position, as large amounts of cash may need to be spent to defend an organisation's position against competitors. Competitors will be attracted to the market by the high growth rates. Failure to support a star sufficiently strongly may lead to the product losing its leading market share position, slipping eastwards in the matrix and becoming a problem child. A star, however, represents the best future prospects for an organisation. . Market share can be maintained or increased through price reductions, product modifications, and/or greater distribution. As industry growth slows, stars become cash cows.

A **Problem child (sometimes called question mark)** is characterised by a low market share in a high growth market. Substantial net cash input is required to maintain or increase market share. The company must decide whether to do nothing – but cash continues to be absorbed or market more intensively or get out of this market. The questions are whether this product can compete successfully with adequate support and what that support will cost.

The Dog product has a low relative market share in a low growth market. Such a product tends to have a negative cash flow, which is likely to continue. It is unlikely that a dog can wrest market share from competitors. Competitors, which have the advantage of having larger market shares, are likely to fiercely resist any attempts to reduce their share of a low growth or static market. An organisation with such a product can attempt to appeal to a specialised market, delete the product or harvest profits by cutting back support services to a minimum.

2.4 Strategic movements

The general strategy is to take cash from the cash cows to fund R&D, the source of future SBUs, and those question marks that have the potential to gain share to achieve star status. The cash cows should receive a maintenance investment level, but any tendency to automatically reinvest the cash they are generating should be avoided.

Stars, on the other hand, should be managed to maintain share; current profitability is of lesser concern. Given that the stars are adequately financed, a limited number of the most promising question marks are selected for investment to try to improve their shares. The other problem children should not receive investment. They should be sold, abandoned or milked for whatever cash they can produce. Dogs present a challenge because several alternatives are available. First, a dog can become very profitable through the pursuit of a focus segmentation strategy, in which the business specialises in a small niche where it can dominate. In effect, it would be the star or cash cow of the redefined market. An example of this could be chimneys used as garden planters. Second, investment can be withheld and the business milked or harvested of whatever cash is forthcoming until the business dies. Lastly, the business could be divested from the portfolio.

Stars tend to move vertically downwards as the market growth rate slows, to become cash cows. The cash that they generate can be used to turn problem children into stars, and eventually cash cows.

The ideal progression is illustrated below:

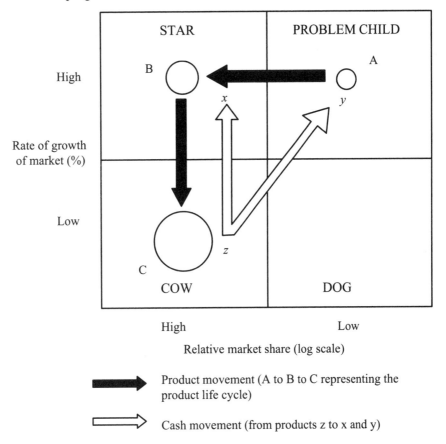

Product movement (A to B to C representing the product life cycle)

Cash movement (from products z to x and y)

2.5 The importance of portfolio analysis

The strategies for the **overall** portfolio are concerned with balance. The organisation would want to have:

(a) cash cows of sufficient size and/or number that can support other products in the portfolio

(b) stars of sufficient size and/or number which will provide sufficient cash generation when the current cash cows can no longer do so

(c) problem children that have reasonable prospects of becoming future stars

(d) no dogs, and if there are any, there would need to be good reasons for retaining them.

In deciding which strategy to adopt, numerous factors other than those in the matrix display need to be considered, e.g:

(a) risk attached to the strategy

(b) nature of the products/markets.

Nevertheless, the matrix position provides a good and objective indication of the competitive position of the products.

ACTIVITY 1

The marketing manager of Fruity Drinks Ltd has invited you in for a chat. Fruity Drinks Ltd provides fruit juices to a number of supermarket chains, which sell them under their own label. 'We've got a large number of products, of course. Our freshly squeezed orange juice is doing fine - it sells in huge quantities. Although margins are low, we have sufficient economies of scale to do very nicely in this market. We've got advanced production and bottling equipment and long-term contracts with some major growers. No problems there. We also sell freshly squeezed pomegranate juice: customers loved it in the tests, but producing the stuff at the right price is a major hassle: all the seeds get in the way. We hope it will be a winner, once we get the production right and start converting customers to it. After all the market for exotic fruit juices generally is expanding fast.'

What sort of products, according to the Boston classification, are described here?

Feedback to this activity is at the end of the chapter.

3 Shell directional policy matrix

The Directional Policy Matrix (DPM) is a method of business portfolio analysis formulated by Shell International Chemical Company. It has nine cells in which businesses are located depending upon their scores on each of the two axes, expected market profitability and competitive positions. The axes are labelled 'business sector prospects' or 'prospects for market sector profitability', and 'company's competitive capabilities'.

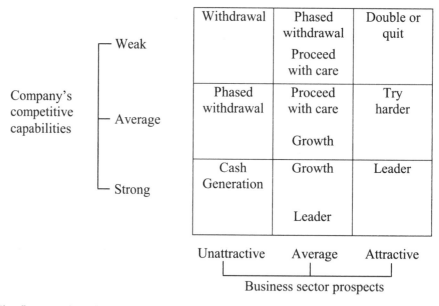

The first step is to identify the main criteria by which the prospects of a business sector may be considered favourable or unfavourable. Depending on the context, these might include:

- **market** – demographic factors, growth, seasonality, maturity
- **competition** – number and size of competitors, price competition, barriers to entry, substitutes
- **technology** – sophistication, rate of change, lead time, patents
- **economic** – leverage, capital intensity, margins
- **government** – subsidies/grants, purchases, protection, regulation, taxation
- **geography** – location, markets, communications, environment
- **social** – pressure groups, trade unions, availability of labour.

This will result in a rating on a scale from 'unattractive', through 'average', to 'attractive' depending upon an evaluation of its industry's market growth, market quality, etc.

The quantification of the competitive capabilities should proceed in a similar fashion. Criteria are identified by which the organisation's capability in a business sector can be judged on a scale that runs from 'weak' through 'average' to 'strong' competitive position. Examples of criteria include:

- **market** – share, growth, product maturity, product quality, product mix, marketing ability, price strategy, customer loyalty

- **technological** – skills, patent protection, R&D, manufacturing technology

- **production** – costs, capacity utilisation, inventory control, maintenance, extent of vertical integration

- **personnel** – employee quality, top management quality, industrial relations, trade union strength, training, labour costs

- **financial** – resources, capital structure, margins, tax position, financial control, investment intensity.

3.1   Possible strategic choices

The cell labels shown above represent possible strategic choices or types of resource deployments most appropriate for the firm, given its score on each of the two axes. More specifically these cell labels have the following implications:

- Withdrawal – likely already losing money; net cash flow negative over time. Losses may be minimised by divesting or even liquidation.

- Phased withdrawal – probably not generating sufficient cash to justify continuation; assets can be redeployed.

- Cash generation – equivalent to a 'cash cow' in the BCG grid. This cell would be occupied by a firm or product in later stages of the life cycle that does not warrant heavy investment, but can be 'milked' of cash due to its strong competitive position.

- Proceed with care – similar to a 'problem child'; firms falling in this sector may require some investment support but heavy investment would be extremely risky.

- Growth – a firm, product, or SBU in these sectors would call for investment support to allow growth with the market. It should generate sufficient cash on its own.

- Double or quit – units in this sector should become 'high fliers' in the not too distant future. Consequently those in the upper rightmost corner of this cell should be singled out for full support. Others should be abandoned.

- Try harder – external financing may be justified to push a unit in this sector to a leadership position. However, such a move will require judicious application of funds.

- Leader – the strategy for this segment is to protect this position by external investment (funds beyond those generated by the unit itself - occasionally); earnings should be quite strong and a major focus may be maintaining sufficient capacity to capitalise on strong demand.

3.2   Strategic movements

In addition to considering the position on the directional policy matrix in static terms, changes over time need also to be considered.

Ideally, products in the cash generating sectors should be able to finance expenditure on products in the attractive business/weak position sectors, so as to move them to the attractive business/strong position sectors. Later these products move down to become cash generators themselves and the cycle is completed:

3.3 Understanding portfolio analysis

Portfolio models can help organisations that are operating in diverse businesses to understand their group of businesses and to allocate resources among them. Options for the future can be plotted onto a matrix and it can highlight the long-term rationale of business development. For example, using the BCG matrix, the following questions could be asked:

- Which strategies are most likely to ensure a move from question marks through to stars and eventually to cash cows - ie, will the strategy move the company to a dominant position in its markets?

- Since stars generally require an investment of funds, will there be sufficient cash cows to provide the necessary investment?

- Will there be a balance of activities that matches the range of skills within the organisation - question marks and stars can be very demanding on management time.

The matrix can also help in thinking about acquisition strategy. Organisations that embark on acquisition programmes often forget that the most likely targets for acquisition are not the stars and cash cows of the business world but the question marks or dogs - providing the resources are available to move them towards stardom.

The directional policy matrix can be used for assigning development priorities among the various SBUs eg, by requiring managers to match competitive strategy to key forces in the environment and perhaps concentrating resources on the SBUs that enjoy a relatively high attractiveness and that can achieve a strong competitive position.

4 The product life cycle

4.1 Introduction

The Product Life Cycle concept commonly known as the S-curve, is valid for most

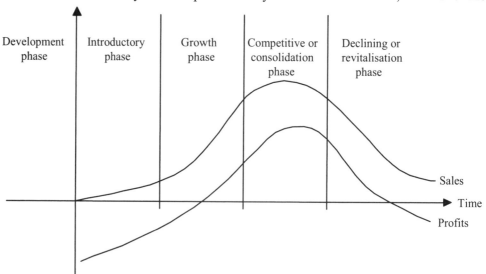

products, markets, economies, industries, technologies, fashions and companies, which pass through a number of stages in their history until they eventually decline in the face of outside competition or a change in consumer tastes. A standard life cycle could be drawn as::

4.2 Life cycle phases

The length of the cycle will vary with the type of product and technology, e.g. long for aircraft, short for fashion garments.

The characteristics of the various **phases** are as follows:

Development - the product is being designed and developed; market research may be undertaken to determine the potential market.

Introductory - the product is launched; losses are made; few companies are in the field; design changes are being made. (For this last reason it does not always pay to be an innovator: it may be better to wait until someone else has ironed out all the snags.)

Growth - the product becomes more widely known and sales begin to take off, prompted by active marketing. Good profits can be made and more companies enter the industry. The rate of growth and length of the growth phase depends on factors such as novelty value of the product; usefulness of the product; availability of substitutes; rate of growth of consumer incomes and proportion spent on luxuries/necessities; expenditure on advertising, etc.

It's worth pointing out that much of the growth phase is caused by stocking in the distribution system, rather than end user demand. When the distribution chain is full, growth will begin to slow down, even if retail demand continues to grow. This causes weaker firms to struggle, even if growth is still significant. Thus, even in growth markets, a shakeout of weaker firms can occur.

Competitive or consolidation - sales have reached saturation point. There is no room for new companies in the industry and there is stiff competition among the existing ones. This is a time for looking at cost reduction: profit margins are falling. There is a tendency for companies to merge, which achieves cost reduction and puts up further barriers to the entry of new companies because they would be too small to compete. Some companies will drop out of the market altogether.

Decline or revitalisation - sales of the product fall off and the decline will continue unless the product can be revitalised by new technology, advertising (likely to be of limited use only) or finding a new use for the product. For instance, the introduction of colour television revitalised the television market

A company is in a weak position if all its products are at the same phase of the life cycle. If they are all in the growth phase there are problems ahead: if they are all in one of the other phases there are immediate difficulties.

Companies try to overcome this problem by introducing new products that are growing as the old products are declining and by having products with life cycles of different lengths.

Ideally, a company needs a balanced range of products in its portfolio passing through different stages of the life cycle. There should be a mix of:

- today's breadwinner;
- tomorrow's breadwinner;
- yesterday's breadwinner;
- productive specials;
- development products;
- Cinderellas and maybe even some failures, as evidence of the search for new products.

The lifecycle will vary significantly between industries, for example, an industry subject to rapid fashion or technological change will not follow a smooth curve. Also, some products and markets enter the decline phase but refuse to die (eg. Brasso (a brass cleaner) was launched in the late 1920's and has had a limited market for many years). The life cycle of a product can be distorted by finding new uses for old products, by finding new markets and new user groups, or by creating a new brand image for an existing product.

The duration of the stages also varies with different types of products (the periods are only shown in the diagram as being of equal size for convenience). For example, product development may take three years but the product may be in decline for four years after market introduction. This shows how important it is to consider when to start developing new products so that a steady rate of growth in both turnover and profits for the whole company can be achieved.

A product life is influenced by many factors, such as, technological innovation, customer behaviour, government fiscal policies (ie, the incidence and rates of Value Added Tax), the activities of competitors and much more. It is these factors, which need to be forecast in order for the lifecycle curve to be projected with any confidence of accuracy.

4.3 Lifecycle theory

Lifecycle theory allied to portfolio analysis forms the main basis of position analysis. We can trace the strategic implications of the product lifecycle stages.

	Introduction	Growth	Maturity	Decline
Buyers	Need educating Early adopters	Wider acceptance Copycat buyers	Mass market Repeat buying Brand choice	Knowledgeable Choosy
Products	Experimental quality No standards or design stability Design and development offer best success	Reliability Quality Technical and design differences established	Standardised products across segments	Product range shrinks Quality variable
Risk	High	Growth covers wrong decisions	Measurable	Fluctuating widely
Manufacture and distribution	Over-capacity High production costs Short runs Specialised distribution	Under-capacity Some standardisation Batching Mass distribution	Some over-capacity Mass production Mass distribution	Overhang of excess capacity Mass production Selective distribution
Profit margins	High prices High margins High investment Low profits	Highest profit Fairly high prices and margins	Falling prices Lower profits and margins	Low prices and margins Selected high prices possible

Johnson and Scholes use the illustrative example of the calculator industry tracing the move from:

- **Introduction**: large, unsophisticated machine for office use to;
- **Early growth**: micro circuitry smaller, more versatile machine for office use to;
- **Massive growth**: improved micro circuitry, portable and more expensive calculators for personal and office use, to;
- **Shake out**: low cost circuitry, deeply discounted prices for mass market, high cost/low volume manufacturers forced out, to;
- **Maturity**: chip based calculators with additional features (watches, music) serving specific segments.

5 Benchmarking

5.1 Definition

Benchmarking is a process that allows a company to measure its operation profile against other companies that are considered 'best-in-class'. According to Michael Spendolini, an authority on the subject and the author of *The Benchmarking Book*, benchmarking is defined as: 'a continuous, systematic process for evaluating the products, services, and work processes of organisations that are recognised as representing best practices for the purpose of organisational improvement'.

5.2 Benchmarking activities

Any activity that can be measured can be benchmarked. However, it is impracticable to benchmark every process and organisations should concentrate on areas that:

- tie up most cash;
- significantly improve the relationship with customers; and
- impact on the final results of the business.

The choice of the activity to be benchmarked will determine the approach that needs to be taken. Types of benchmarks that can be used include:

Internal benchmarking assumes there are differences in the work processes of an organisation as a result of geographical differences, local organisational history, customs, differences among business units, and relationships among managers and employees.

Competitive benchmarking concerns the identification of specific information about a competitor's products, processes, and business results to make comparisons with those of its own organisation.

Process or activity benchmarking involves the identification of state-of-the-art products, services, or processes of an organisation that may or may not be a company's direct competitor. The objective of this type of benchmarking is to identify best practices in any type of organisation that has established a reputation for excellence in specific business activities such as manufacturing, marketing, engineering, warehousing, fleet management, or human resources.

5.3 Embarking on benchmarking

When doing a benchmark study success will hinge on the level of commitment from top managers, who must take their blindfolds off and realise that dramatic change needs to be made in certain areas. The process may go through the following stages:

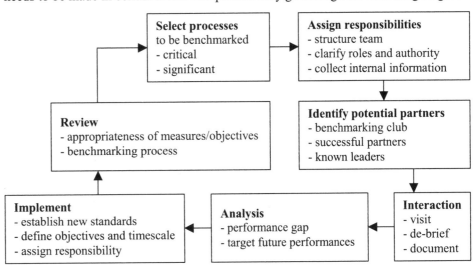

Companies need to be as specific as possible when identifying areas to benchmark. For example, if a company is interested in studying customer service, it needs to determine what specific area or activity within customer service needs to be examined. Customer service encompasses a broad base of activities, such as order taking, answering inquiries, handling irate customers, issuing credits, or invoicing. They are all different - having their own thought processes, techniques, and management controls.

The next step is to establish a work team comprised of strategic, functional, and tactical representatives from all affected areas. For example, if a company needs to reduce the amount of returns coming back to the warehouse, its benchmarking team would likely consist of a customer service representative, a receiving clerk, a loading clerk, and a quality control manager.

The team will determine the issues to be benchmarked, and then determine what company to study.

Once the best practices have been identified, the benchmarking team collects the data, analyses it and then plots its company's performance against the best practices to help them identify improvement opportunities.

The team then determines the level of effort required to re-engineer the best practices to suit its company's unique circumstances. The benefits versus the costs involved with eliminating the gaps between current processes and the best practices are evaluated, and then implementation priorities are established.

5.4 Competitive positioning grid

The positioning of a product refers to both the place a product or brand occupies in customers' minds relative to their needs and competing products and to the marketer's decision making intended to create such a position.

The first step in creating a competitive positioning grid is to identify the current and potential competition. Once these have been identified and have been described in the marketing plan in full detail, an analysis of their strengths and weaknesses is given.

The grid is basically a scale that lists all major competitors based upon their applicable skills and assets. Once the relevant assets and skills are identified, the next step is to position them alongside your own on a scale, showing their relative strength or weakness. A sustainable competitive advantage is generally based on having a better rating on the scale, compared to that of the target competitors, on one or more assets or skill areas that are relevant to the industry and the strategy employed.

If a superior position is not highlighted, it will probably have to be created or the strategy will have to be modified. A skill that all competitors possess will not be the basis for competitive advantage. In the example shown below, flight safety is important among all airline passengers, but if airlines are perceived to be equal on pilot quality, plane maintenance, new product capability and customer orientation, it cannot be the basis for a competitive advantage. However, if one or two airlines are able to convince passengers that they are strong on anti terrorist security, then an advantage could emerge.

Assets and skills	Weakness									Strength		
Pilot quality								C	D	A	B	
Plane maintenance									A	D	C	B
New product capability									B	A	C	D
Customer orientation								A	B	C	D	
Anti terrorist security			A	B	C	D						

The grid will have identified a series of dimensions that are critical to customers in this market. Once the organisation has these critical dimensions, they can be represented pictorially as the basis of a perceptual map.

5.5 Perceptual mapping

Perceptual mapping is a visual way of representing a market and the way in which different clusters of customers or users perceive the importance of different product attributes. Maps are used to chart consumers' perceptions of brands currently on offer and to identify opportunities for launching new brands or to reposition an existing brand. A company considering introducing a new product will look for areas with a high density of ideal points. They will also look for areas without competitive rivals. The position of a product, product line, brand, or company is generally displayed relative to their competition.

The map can be used to plot the interrelationships of consumer products, industrial goods, institutions, as well as populations. Virtually any subjects that can be rated on a range of attributes can be mapped to show their relative positions in relation both to other subjects as well as to the evaluative attributes.

For example, the illustrative perceptual map below plots brands (the letters in squares) along two dimensions: price and quality.

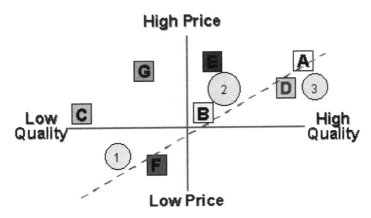

Brand A is perceived to be relatively high priced with high quality; brand F is low quality and low price (perhaps an economy brand); and brand G is in the unstable position of being perceived to be low quality, but high price. The circled numbers indicate the **ideal points** - combinations of price and quality - that are desired by each of 3 illustrative segments (good, better, best).

Proximity rules on perceptual maps. In general, a brand will accrue most of its sales from the market segments with ideal points closest to where the brand is positioned (e.g. brand A is likely to draw most from segment 3) and brands positioned closer to ideal points will capture a disproportionate share of that market segment's sales (e.g. F should outperform C in segment 1).

ACTIVITY **2** | Why do marketers use perceptual maps in product positioning decisions?

Feedback to this activity is at the end of the chapter.

6 Sustainable competitive advantage

A sustainable competitive advantage (SCA) can be described as the competitive edge sought by a firm that will allow it to satisfy customer needs while maintaining an advantage over its rivals because of the uniqueness of its products or its lower production or marketing costs.

6.1 The external analysis

The external analysis should be motivated throughout by a desire to generate or evaluate strategic options. It should contribute to the investment decision, the selection of functional area strategies and the development of sustainable competitive advantage, as shown in the diagram below.

When an organisation is making an investment decision on where to compete, the types of questions asked include the following:

- Should existing enterprise areas be invested in for growth, maintained, milked or liquidated?

- Should new enterprise areas be entered?

- Should there be market penetration, product expansion or market expansion?

The development of a sustainable competitive advantage ie, how to compete, addresses the identification of key (or critical) success factors and the skills and assets that should be created, enhanced or maintained.

Decisions on the functional area strategies include the positioning strategy, segmentation strategy, distribution strategy and manufacturing strategy etc.

An external analysis can also help to identify significant trends and future events, such as concern with GM foods or the emergence of a new competitor. Threats and opportunities can be highlighted; a new technology can represent both an opportunity for a new entrant and a threat for an established organisation. Strategic questions are different from strategic decisions in that they focus on uncertainties that will affect the outcome of a strategic decision. A strategic question might ask how sensitive the market is to price, whereas a strategic decision might be 'A strategy on maintaining price parity'. Strategic questions often lead to useful sub-questions eg, one common strategic question is whether a technology will be replaced. One sub-question might address uncertainty about technological improvements, whereas another might look at the cost/benefit levels achieved by competitive technologies.

Once the identification of significant trends and future events, threats and opportunities and significant questions has been identified, there may be information need areas and scenario analysis potential. An information need area is an area of uncertainty that should be monitored and analysed continuously. A scenario is an alternative view of the future environment that is prompted by a prospective future event or trend or by an alternative answer to a strategic question.

6.2　Competitive advantage - the definition and meaning

Competitive advantage can be defined as 'a condition which enables a company to operate in a more efficient or otherwise higher-quality manner than the companies it competes with, and which results in benefits accruing to that company'

A competitive advantage exists when the firm is able to deliver the same benefits as competitors but at a lower cost (cost advantage), or deliver benefits that exceed those of competing products (differentiation advantage). Thus, a competitive advantage enables the firm to create superior value for its customers and superior profits for itself.

Examples of competitive advantage include:

- industries where the cost of entry is high, thus restricting the number of newcomers to the market place. These barriers to entry may be in the form of high advertising expenditure in order to capture a part of the market, or high levels of skill and technological knowledge required in production, etc.

- industries where the demand to capacity ratio is out of balance. In industries where demand outweighs capacity, pricing can give high profit margins and the ability to expand capacity rapidly.

- market dominance - achieving market dominance allows price determination, but also allows the organisation to have a more direct control of several of the elements in its environment. Achieving market dominance is naturally difficult, although it is possible to arrive at this situation through innovative products, efficient production, marketing strategy or a mixture of the three.

Cost and differentiation advantages are known as *positional advantages* since they describe the firm's position in the industry as a leader in either cost or differentiation.

A *resource-based* view emphasises that a firm uses its resources and capabilities to create a competitive advantage that ultimately results in superior value creation. The following diagram combines the resource-based and positioning views to illustrate the concept of competitive advantage:

A MODEL OF COMPETITIVE ADVANTAGE

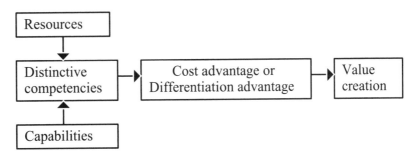

According to the resource-based view, in order to develop a competitive advantage the firm must have resources and capabilities that are superior to those of its competitors. Without this superiority, the competitors simply could replicate what the firm was doing and any advantage quickly would disappear.

- **Resources** are the firm-specific assets useful for creating a cost or differentiation advantage and that few competitors can acquire easily eg, patents and trademarks, proprietary know-how and reputation of the firm

- **Capabilities** refer to the firm's ability to use its resources effectively. An example of a capability is the ability to bring a product to market faster than competitors. Such capabilities are embedded in the routines of the organisation and are not easily documented as procedures and thus are difficult for competitors to replicate.

- The firm's resources and capabilities together form its **distinctive competencies.**

- These competencies enable innovation, efficiency, quality, and customer responsiveness, all of which can be used to create a cost advantage or a differentiation advantage. A firm positions itself in its industry through its choice of low cost or differentiation. This decision is a central component of the firm's competitive strategy.

The firm creates value by performing a series of activities that Porter identified as the value chain. In addition to the firm's own value-creating activities, the firm operates in a *value system* of vertical activities including those of upstream suppliers and downstream channel members.

To achieve a competitive advantage, the firm must perform one or more value creating activities in a way that creates more overall value than do competitors. Superior value is created through lower costs or superior benefits to the consumer (differentiation).

Another important decision is how broad or narrow a market segment to target. Porter formed a matrix using cost advantage, differentiation advantage, and a broad or narrow focus to identify a set of generic strategies that the firm can pursue to create and sustain a competitive advantage.

6.3　Generic strategies

Porter explains that competitive strategy is formed to cope with competitive forces, reflect the environmental influences and provide a superior return on investment. His main contribution was to point out that there are only two routes to superior performance.

- You either become the lowest-cost producer in your industry or

- You differentiate your product/service in ways that are valued by the buyer to the extent that he or she will pay a premium price to get those benefits.

By applying these strengths in either a broad or narrow scope, three generic strategies result: cost leadership, differentiation, and focus. These strategies are applied at the strategic business unit (SBU) level. They are called generic strategies because they are not firm or industry dependent. The following diagram illustrates Porter's generic strategies

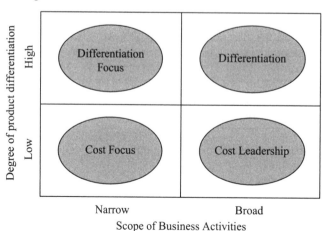

Cost leadership

For companies competing in a 'price sensitive' market, this generic strategy calls for being the low cost producer in an industry for a given level of quality. The firm sells its products either at average industry prices to earn a profit higher than that of rivals, or below the average industry prices to gain market share. In the event of a price war, the firm can maintain some profitability while the competition suffers losses. Even without a price war, as the industry matures and prices decline, the firms that can produce more cheaply will remain profitable for a longer period of time. The cost leadership strategy usually targets a broad market.

Some of the ways that firms acquire cost advantages are by improving process efficiencies, gaining unique access to a large source of lower cost materials, making optimal outsourcing and vertical integration decisions, or avoiding some costs altogether. If competing firms are unable to lower their costs by a similar amount, the firm may be able to sustain a competitive advantage based on cost leadership.

Cost leadership must be a goal of every organisation, regardless of their specific market orientation. It enables companies to:

- **Defend market share -** enabling the company to defend itself against powerful buyers, because buyers only have power to drive the price down to the level of the next most efficient competitor.

- **Defend supply -** in the same way a low-cost position enables the company to cope with any price increases imposed by powerful suppliers.

- **Build entry barriers -** the factors that lead to a low-cost position, such as scale of economies, the use of advanced manufacturing technologies, quality systems and synergies, provide the company with substantial entry barriers.

- **Weaken threat of substitutes -** the dangers of substitutes are reduced in a low-price market.

- **Defend market share against rivals -** having a low-cost position yields the company above-average profits in its industry despite strong competitive pressures. Its cost-leadership position also provides the company with a strong defensive position against rivalry from existing or potential competitors.

- **Increase market share -** cost leadership allows the company to provide its targeted customer group with the best price to quality relationship, by having (i) the resources to vigorously innovate and continuously improve the quality of its products and services, and (ii) the ability to price its products more aggressively than its competitors.

- **Enter new markets -** a cost leadership position enables the company to successfully penetrate new domestic and foreign markets often by brand extension or 'brand stretch' strategy. Its low cost and high quality position permits it to be selective when targeting markets.

- **Reduce the cost of capital -** the benefits described above allow the company to maintain a strong financial position and to generate superior returns to its shareholders. These in turn reduce the company's costs of capital of both borrowed funds and the cost of raising funds from the equity market.

Achieving a low-cost position thus protects the company against all five of the competitive forces highlighted by Porter. However, attaining a low overall cost position requires sustained commitment throughout the organisation, from senior executives to line employees.

Each generic strategy has its risks, including the low-cost strategy. For example, other firms may be able to lower their costs as well. As technology improves, the competition may be able to leapfrog the production capabilities, thus eliminating the competitive advantage. Examples of companies employing cost leadership strategies are Nissan, Tesco and Dell Computers.

Differentiation

A differentiation strategy calls for the development of a product or service that offers unique attributes that are valued by customers and that customers perceive to be better than or different from the products of the competition. In the differentiation focus strategy, a business aims to differentiate within just one or a small number of target market segments. The special customer needs of the segment mean that there are opportunities to provide products that are clearly different from competitors who may be targeting a broader group of customers. The important issue for any business adopting this strategy is to ensure that customers really do have different needs and wants - in other words that there is a valid basis for differentiation - and that existing competitor products are not meeting those needs and wants.

- Differentiation strategies may be successful if a company can:

- Reduce the ongoing cost to the customer of using the product (eg manufacture a better quality product, easier to use, cheaper to run etc).

- Increase the customer satisfaction with the product (eg manufacture a product that performs better than its rivals).

- Modify the customer's perception of value (this is very common in industries such as clothes manufacturing where brand names are marketed).

For similar reasons discussed for cost-leadership, a highly differentiated market position will protect the company against the five competitive forces in its industry. Its 'uniqueness', brand loyalty and resulting lower sensitivity to price, will protect it against new entrants, the power of buyers, the power of suppliers, the effects of new entrants to the market and rivalry within its markets. However differentiation does have its downside. The customer's perception of 'exclusivity' is often incompatible with high market share. Also a lowering of price sensitivity will only be achieved within a price range. Although customers perceive the superiority of the offerings they might not be willing to pay prices significantly higher than the industrial average.

The risks associated with a differentiation strategy include imitation by competitors and changes in customer tastes. Additionally, various firms pursuing focus strategies may be able to achieve even greater differentiation in their market segments.

Focus

A focus strategy concentrates on a narrow segment (a particular buyer group, market segment, geographical region, service need, product feature or section of the product range) and within that segment attempts to achieve either a cost advantage or differentiation. The premise is that the needs of the group can be better serviced by focusing entirely on it. A firm using a focus strategy often enjoys a high degree of customer loyalty, and this entrenched loyalty discourages other firms from competing directly. An example of a company adopting a low-cost focus is EasyJet - a low-cost airline. It competes on price by offering a no-frills service and by not operating through travel agents. Customers book directly with the airline.

Because of their narrow market focus, firms pursuing a focus strategy have lower volumes and therefore less bargaining power with their suppliers. However, firms pursuing a differentiation-focused strategy may be able to pass higher costs on to customers since close substitute products do not exist.

An important advantage of focus strategies is that they may be the only way into a market for a small company competing against larger companies.

Some risks of focus strategies include imitation and changes in the target segments. Furthermore, it may be fairly easy for a broad-market cost leader to adapt its product in order to compete directly.

Combination of generic strategies - stuck in the middle

These generic strategies are not necessarily compatible with one another. If a firm attempts to achieve an advantage on all fronts, it may achieve no advantage at all. For example, if a firm differentiates itself by supplying very high quality products, it risks undermining that quality if it seeks to become a cost leader. Even if the quality did not suffer, the firm would risk projecting a confusing image. For this reason, Porter argued that to be successful over the long-term, a firm must pursue only one of these three generic strategies.

Where a firm fails to adhere clearly to one of these three generic strategies then it is termed 'stuck in the middle'. Porter states 'the firm stuck in the middle is almost guaranteed low profitability. It either loses the high volume customers who demand low prices or must bid away its profits to get business away from low cost firms. Yet it also loses high-margin business ie, the cream, to firms who are focused on high-margin targets or have achieved differentiation overall'.

7 Preventing replication

A sustainable advantage depends upon preventing imitation and replication by rivals. In particular, innovative differentiators have to be aware that cost leaders can often copy the product or service, market it at similar or lower prices, and achieve a greater margin. Techniques to defend a competitive advantage include branding, patents, copyrights and trademarks.

7.1 Branding

Branding is a means of identifying a product or group of products. It provides a means of distinguishing the product clearly from competitive items and frequently, in the mind of the consumer, symbolises the particular qualities, which apply to the branded manufacturer. It tells the customer roughly what to expect of the product, and is of great value in promotion of the company's goods.

> **KEY POINT**
>
> Branding is used by cost leaders and differentiators. Branding adds to differentiation, if the values of the brand support it.

Branding is used by cost leaders and differentiators. It adds to differentiation, if the values of the brand support it. For example, the Sony brand conveys both innovation and product quality. Consequently, customers are prepared to try a Sony product more willingly than other brands and this allows them to recoup research and development costs before imitators have appeared. Cost leaders also use branding to support and build the volumes upon which their cost leadership depends, although naturally it has to be based on different values, such as consistency or appeal to a particular client group. Breweries, for example, launch a range of similar products that cannot usually be told apart, but build volume by branding for particular age and social groups.

> **KEY POINT**
>
> Patents, copyrights and trademarks prevent direct copying by legal means.

7.2 Patents, copyrights and trademarks

Patents, copyrights and trademarks prevent direct copying by legal means. A patent is an exclusive right granted for an invention, which is a product or a process that provides a new way of doing something, or offers a new technical solution to a problem. A well conceived patent on a technological innovation can provide the most assurance that a resulting advantage will be sustainable and offering inventors some protection against new entrants. Patent protection means that the invention cannot be commercially made, used, distributed or sold without the patent owner's consent. These patent rights are usually enforced in a court, which, in most systems, holds the authority to stop patent infringement. Conversely, a court can also declare a patent invalid upon a successful challenge by a third party.

Copyright is a legal term describing rights given to creators for their literary and artistic works. The kinds of works covered by copyright include: literary works such as novels, poems, plays, reference works, newspapers and computer programs; databases; films, musical compositions, and choreography; artistic works such as paintings, drawings, photographs and sculpture; architecture; and advertisements, maps and technical drawings.

Royalties - many creative works protected by copyright require mass distribution, communication and financial investment for their dissemination (for example, publications, sound recordings and films); hence, creators often sell the rights to their works to individuals or companies best able to market the works in return for payment. These payments are often made dependent on the actual use of the work, and are then referred to as royalties.

A **trademark** is any sign, which can distinguish the goods and services of one trader from those of another. A sign includes, for example, words, logos, pictures, or a combination of these. It is used as a marketing tool so that customers can recognise the product of a particular organisation.

Cost leaders will protect industrial processes – such as Pilkington's extended monopoly of the float glass process it had invented. Differentiators, such as pharmaceutical companies, will use patents to protect innovative products. Innovative marketers, such as Body Shop, find it more difficult to legally protect what they do, although they can use laws that prevent imitations that get too close.

It is worth mentioning that firms can rely too much on these legal protections. A small company holding an innovative patent might lack the resources to defend it against encroachment from a larger one. Similarly, many companies have grown rather sloppy behind a legal protect, and are unable to respond when a rival finds a way of creating similar value for the customer using a different process.

7.3   National advantage

National advantage can confer an advantage on firms that can be exploited in foreign markets. This issue was discussed in relation to Porter's Diamond in an earlier chapter. For example, a large, but competitive home market allows the development of several large, competitive firms. Some governments are willing to protect and subsidise particular firms and industries, for example Harley Davidson's revival in the global motorcycle industry followed a protective strategy carried out by the USA Government.

In the Competitive Advantage of Nations, Porter identified ten of the most important preconditions to improving competitiveness in a country (or geographic areas). They are most directly applicable to the case where a country is working systematically — such as through a formal project — to enhance competitiveness.

First, there must be a sense of urgency about improving competitiveness that is broadly shared. The task for national leaders is to create a clear and compelling argument for why change is really necessary. If they can put the country on a path from which business leaders perceive no turning back, that may stimulate the urgency required.

Second, a shared paradigm of what competitiveness is must be created. Until there is a common definition of competitiveness and an understanding of how to improve it, it is hard to get people to work together. Competitiveness is a lot about attitudes; it is a matter of getting people to think the right way about the problem. The diamond theory that we discussed in an earlier chapter, provides a holistic, useful concept, which helps individuals from business, government, labour and other institutions talk constructively about improving the environment for productivity.

Third, the cluster-based approach has become a very powerful tool for making rapid progress. Why are clusters the focal point rather than sectors or industries? The latter tends to evoke industrial policies — targeting, interventions and subsidies — which can reduce rivalry, distort competition through subsidies, or create cartels. The cluster-based approach recognises the reality of what determines productivity — that is, the interdependence and the joint activity among related fields.

Fourth, social and economic policies must be integrated rather than being seen as separate, different or conflicting. Educated, safe, healthy citizens are required for a productive economy. Reducing industrial pollution eliminates waste and improves productivity in the use of resources. Leaders must communicate that these areas — which need to be in alignment — are complimentary and interdependent.

Fifth, business and government must play different and more appropriate roles than in the past. Traditionally, business goes to government with a tin cup asking for subsidies, protective tariffs or special financing schemes. The typical government role is attempting to "direct" the economy and getting involved in allocating capital. These traditional roles need to change.

Sixth, the traditional business-government dialogue must be transformed. Typically, business and government interaction occurs around episodic lobbying on specific issues; it is adversarial and, in developing countries, often paternalistic. The character of this dialogue must shift, and an ongoing consultative dialogue on competitiveness and the constraints to productivity is needed. To achieve these goals, effective business-government collaborative mechanisms — such as cluster groups and public-private competitive institutions — must be created.

The seventh and eighth preconditions relate to cross-fertilisation through parallel efforts on the state and city levels, and through complimentary reinforcement between national and regional initiatives. Experience shows that productivity is not only affected within, but across borders.

The ninth precondition for economic progress is that the whole effort must have an action — not analytical — orientation.

Tenth and finally, there is need for leadership in both the public and private sectors. This is a cliché, but as a result of the tremendous inertia built into economies and their institutions, it is really true

7.4 Strategic role of marketing mix

The marketing mix summarises the factors which must be managed to satisfy customers needs at a profit. It has four elements - product, place, price and promotion (the four Ps).

Product - the product has two roles in the mix. First, it plays a key role in satisfying the customer's needs. Second, product differentiation is also an important part of the firm's competitive strategy. The core product consists of the product's essential features; augmentations are additional features, which can be used to differentiate it. A standardised product with no frills but not lacking in quality could be developed for a cost leadership strategy or alternatively the product could be differentiated, even customised for niche market strategies. This dual role is most important in new product development. 'New product' is a broad term covering:

- products that open up an entirely new market;
- products that replace existing products;
- alterations to existing products.

New product development is a complex function involving the R&D function, but probably led by the marketing department since potential customer needs must be identified and new ideas tested in the market. To minimise the chance of failure, new product ideas are put through a *screening process*. This includes business analysis, development, test launch and commercialisation. It aims to answer the following questions.

- Is the product compatible with company objectives, strategies, resources and competences?

- Do potential customers like the product? If so, will they actually buy it?

- Can the product be marketed profitably?

- Is the product sound, technically and commercially, to justify the investment?

- Do market tests meet expectations? How have customers, distributors and competitors reacted?

Only if the answers are positive should the product be launched.

Place - is the name given for mnemonic purposes to *distribution*: how the product finally reaches the customer. Some firms deliver to wholesalers, who then deliver to retailers. Direct marketing avoids intermediaries. This includes mail order, telephone ordering and the use of the Internet for e-business. The distribution strategy being developed could be aimed at a wide distribution or it could be focused on the target market depending on whether a cost leadership or differentiation strategy is used.

Price - this element of the marketing mix brings in revenue. Whilst marketers do not have complete freedom to determine price as there are cost and market considerations, different pricing strategies can be adopted in different conditions. For instance, there are two common price strategies for product launch.

- Penetration prices are low. They build sales volume and to erect barriers to entry to competitors.

- Skimming prices are high. They aim to maximise cash flow to finance the build up of production

A higher-priced product may be regarded as being of premium quality. Price could be set below industry average where a cost leadership strategy is being developed and higher than industry average where a differentiation strategy is being used.

Promotion - in practice, this is the element of the marketing mix over which the marketing department has most control. Its purpose is to gain the potential customer's attention, generate interest, arouse desire and stimulate action to purchase. Promotion can be widespread, emphasising the common customer requirements or it can cover specialist media, emphasising point of differentiation.

8   Critical success factors

8.1   Introduction

Critical success factors (CSFs), sometimes called key results areas (KRAs), are the limited number of areas in which results, if they are satisfactory, will ensure successful competitive performance for the business. They are the vital areas where 'things must go right' for the business to flourish. These areas include core activities, new markets and new products. For example, one of the critical success factors to run a mail order service is speedy delivery.

An organisation will identify its CSFs when it determines its goals and objectives. The factors that are critical to accomplishing the objective are given performance measures. The next phase is to identify the key tasks, which must be undertaken to underpin the critical success factors and then the priorities, which need to be actioned to get the plan under way. The identification of priorities and key tasks also provides a basis for the allocation of responsibilities. The plan needs to be explicit about:

- who is responsible for each of the key areas;
- where the key areas interlink;
- who is responsible for co-ordination;
- what things can or should be left until later; and
- which of the priorities need to be followed up.

The plan sets out what resources need to be obtained or disposed of. This may take the form of a budget, but might also be expressed as a timetable of priorities, a sequence of actions or a written plan.

Knowing the units of measurement for each objective makes it easy to identify the information required. It is this measure, which is used to monitor the actual success of each factor, and information will need to be supplied to managers in a form that they can use.

Rockart claims that there are four sources for the CSFs:

1 **the industry that the business is in** - each has CSFs that are relevant to any company within it.

2 **the company itself and its situation within the industry** - actions taken by a few large dominant companies in an industry will provide one or more CSFs for small companies in that industry.

3 **the environment** eg, the economy, the political factors and consumer trends in the country or countries that the organisation operates in. An example use by Rockart is that, before 1973, virtually no chief executive in the USA would have stated 'energy supply availability' as a critical success factor. However, following the oil embargo many executives monitored this factor closely.

4 **progressive organisational factors**, which are areas of company activity that are unusually causing concern because they are unacceptable and need attention. Cases of too little or too much inventory might classify as a CSF for a short time.

Examples of CSFs will include 'develop new products', 'market success' and 'support field sales representatives'.

Some CSFs are industry-specific, as we noted above. For example, one of the car industries' is 'Compliance with the Department of Transport's pollution requirements with respect to car exhaust gases'.

8.2 Johnson and Scholes

Johnson and Scholes used a six-step approach to achieving competitiveness by use of critical success factors.

1 *Identify the success factors that are critical to profitability.* Naturally, these are specific to particular target customers. A car parts manufacturer might identify just three: zero defects, speed of delivery and cost.

2 *Identify the behaviours, or critical competencies, that allow superior performance in the critical success factors.* An office supply company with a critical success factor of customer care would underpin the CSF through the three key tasks of responding to enquiries, supplying accurate information and an efficient and quick breakdown and maintenance service. These tasks are dependent on the office supply company's infrastructure, particularly the database of customer installations

This would require the development of an appropriate culture, as well as systems that can consistently achieve the required behaviours.

3   *Develop the levels of competence so that a competitive advantage is achieved in the critical success factors*. Superior performance depends upon advantage in the critical success factors; a threshold level will ensure industry average profits at best. Since such technologies as statistical process control can usually be copied, the firm has to look at its own development policies to see that it is learning faster than the competition.

In our example of the office supply company mentioned above, the CSFs were identified as responding to enquiries, providing information and efficient maintenance. It would therefore be necessary to profile the company's performance in these measures, benchmarked against rivals.

Usually, several important competitors would be investigated to build up a wider profile of competition characteristics.

4   *Identify appropriate performance indicators to stretch competencies and achieve an advantage.* These are measurable performance indicators that can be used to assess the firm's performance against competitors.

5   *Emphasise the development of competencies in areas that rivals will find difficult to match.* Clearly, this is the basis of sustainable competitive advantage.

6   *Monitor competitor's performance* and the critical performance indicators and projected targets.

8.3   Measuring success

After the critical success factors have been outlined, milestones of performance are drawn up. These will be of a quantitative and qualitative nature including:

- Market share
- quality measures
- innovation
- customer satisfaction

Milestones - are short-term steps towards long term goals. They guide the organisation towards its objectives. Milestones must monitor actions and results eg, whether a new product has been launched and the success of the launch.

Organisations need to be efficient in doing the right things, in the optimum use of their resources and in the ratio of outputs to inputs. But organisations must also be effective in doing the right things and in their outputs related to some specific purpose, objective or task.

Efficiency and Effectiveness

- Effectiveness is a measure of the match or mismatch between what an organisation produces and what it should be producing.
- Efficiency is a measure of the resources used in producing the organisation's actual outputs.

The effectiveness of an organisation might be assessed against Drucker's eight key areas in which objectives need to be set in terms of business performance and results:

- market standing
- innovation
- productivity

- physical and financial resources
- profitability
- manager performance and development
- worker performance and attitude
- public responsibility

When setting target achievement levels:

- Targets must be reasonably precise
- Targets should suggest strategies and tactics

Competitive benchmarks are targets set relative to the competition. It is difficult to obtain competitor data, but a relative advantage ie, performance in relation to competitors, rather than absolute terms, is important to maintain.

Many organisations do not define explicit strategic objectives or milestones that are regularly and formally monitored as part of the ongoing management control process because:

- a narrow focus on individual strategic objectives can blind managers to wider issues
- informality promotes flexibility
- formal systems can be over-bureaucratic - the system will develop but it may decline in relevance
- open communication is necessary
- any chosen objective might unbalance the business eg, choosing market share as an objective implies that profitability is less important
- predetermined objectives overlook nuances especially in human resource management. For example, an objective like 'employee commitment' is necessary for success, but hard to measure quantitatively.

8.4 Relative cost

Where strategies are dependent on achieving a cost advantage or cost parity, a cost analysis of a product or service and its components can be critical.

Value analysis, otherwise known as 'cost engineering' and 'value engineering' is a technique in which a firm's products, and maybe those of its competitors, are subjected to a critical and systematic examination by a small group of specialists. They can be representing various functions such as design, production, sales and finance. Value analysis asks of a product the following questions:

- Does the use of the product contribute value?
- Is its cost proportionate to its usefulness?
- Does it need all of its features?
- Is there anything better for the intended use?
- Can a usable part be made better at lower cost?
- Can a standard product be found which will be as usable?
- Is it made on appropriate tooling, considering the quantities used?
- Do material, labour, overheads and profit constitute total cost?
- Will another dependable supplier provide it for less cost?
- Is anyone buying it for less than its stated price?

The strategic implications can be measured in terms of a components relative cost versus its relative performance. There are four different situations:

(i)   If a component is both more expensive and inferior to that of a competitor, a strategic problem requiring change might be necessary. It could be, however, that the component is such a small item both in term of cost and impact on the customer that it should be ignored.

(ii)   If the component is competitively superior, a value analysis, where a component's value to the customer is quantified, may suggest a price increase or promotion campaign.

(iii)   If a component is less expensive but inferior to that of a competitor, a value analysis might suggest either de-emphasising that part or upgrading the relative rating.

(iv)   If a component is less expensive and superior to that of a competitor, a value analysis might suggest that component is emphasised, perhaps playing a key role in promotion and positioning strategies.

A cost advantage may be obtained in many ways eg, economies of scale, the experience curve, product design innovations and the use of no-frills product offering. Each provides a different way of competing on the basis of cost advantage.

8.5   Quality issues

Quality management suggests a concern that the organisation's products or services meet their planned level of quality and perform to specifications. Management has a duty to ensure that all tasks are completed consistently to a standard, which meets the needs of the organisation. To achieve this they need to:

- set clear standards;

- plan how to meet those standards

- track the quality achieved;

- take action to improve quality where necessary.   .

Setting standards- to manage quality everyone in the organisation needs to have a clear and shared understanding of the standards required. These standards will be set after taking account of:

- the quality expected by the customers;

- the costs and benefits of delivering different degrees of quality;

- the impact of different degrees of quality on the customers and their needs, its contribution to departmental objectives and employee attitude and motivation.

Having decided on the standards these must be communicated to everyone concerned to ensure that the right standards are achieved. Documentation of the standards must be clear, specific, measurable and comprehensive.

8.6   Businesses and not-for-profit organisations

Many of the techniques of strategic management can be usefully applied to not-for-profit organisations and firms. However, there are differences between the two that are particularly relevant to strategic management. These differences flow from the fundamental purpose or purposes for which the two types of organisation were established, in other words, from their objectives and the expectations of stockholders and shareholders.

If we assume that firms need to make profits and that all other objectives (eg. sales growth, market share, social responsibility, caring for employees) take a lower priority. That is not to say that these (and other) objectives are not important or relevant to many firms, merely that, when it comes to the crunch the firm that does not make a profit does not survive. We can view some of these other objectives more as ways of making profits rather than as objectives in their own right (eg. trying to increase market share because it is linked to profitability). We could also take a rather jaundiced view of various social objectives that are promoted by firms for public relations reasons. For example, 'this firm cares about the environment' (as long as it does not cost anything).

In some firms other objectives not directly related to profits can, from time to time, predominate. For instance, survival may be of paramount importance to a firm in dire straits, but this must be a temporary objective. In other circumstances, notably where the shareholders are not in a position to influence directly the management of the firm, 'managerial' objectives may come to the fore (like empire building, enhancing status through company cars and other perks). These managerial objectives can persist, although there may come a point where profits fall so low that shareholders eventually reassert their power. Up until this point, of course, the firm must still be making some level of profit.

If you accept the notion that firms exist to make money, then managing the firm's strategy becomes a much clearer task. Other ideas can be evaluated against the profit objective and performance can be measured and compared with that of other firms. Above all, the basic need to make profits can underpin the entire management process, enhancing the authority and the decision-making abilities of management. This clear goal can help guide decision-making at all levels of the firm, not just at the top.

Now consider the situation of the not-for-profit organisation. If we take a school as an example, education must be its objective. But how is performance measured? Pass rates in examinations could be a straightforward interpretation of the purpose of the school and may suit some of those associated with the school, but others may see different aims as being important. For example, developing all the different talents of children (which would include music, dance, art, sport, drama, hobbies, etc). There is a strong lobby for religious education, while others complain about political indoctrination (there is either too much, or not enough).

Most people would acknowledge the school's role in preparing children to take a useful role in society. This can extend to having a strong vocational orientation in the way that subjects are selected and taught. Others see this preparation for life to be more to do with developing the children's personality and social skills.

To complicate matters, who controls the school? We know that in the last resort shareholders have the power over the firm, but which group of 'stakeholders' prevails if there are conflicting objectives in the school? Is it the teachers, the parents, the local authority, the Department of Education, or the pupils? The confusion about who controls the school, coupled with the lack of clarity (and measurability) of objectives, makes the strategic management task extremely difficult. The absence of a 'bottom line' (like profits) means that the management of the school cannot act with clarity and certainty in making decisions. Good strategic managers in these circumstances tend to be able to combine acute political and interpersonal skills (to manage the disparate interest groups) with a clear set of values, or a 'vision'. Armed with this clarity of purpose they are then able to set direction and make judgements between conflicting requirements. So in this sense, the strategic managers of not-for-profit organisations are more in need of well-developed 'strategies' or 'missions' (if they are going to inspire others, give them a sense of direction and a feeling of confidence) than managers in firms.

Efficiency, effectiveness and economy, known collectively as the 'three Es', are used to assess the performance of public sector organisations and other bodies, which do not have profit or the maximisation of shareholder wealth as a primary objective.

Economy means obtaining the appropriate quantity and quality of physical, human and financial resources (inputs) at the lowest cost. An activity would not be economic, if, for example, there was over-staffing or failure to purchase materials of requisite quality at the lowest available price.

Efficiency is the relationship between goods or services produced (outputs) and the resources used to produce them. An efficient operation produces the maximum output for any given set of resource inputs; or it has minimum inputs for any given quantity and quality of product or service provided.

- **Effectiveness** is the measure of achievement and the extent to which policy objectives have been attained.

Conclusion

This chapter has examined models and evidence related to the creation of competitive advantage. You will have seen that none of the routes suggested offer any easy answers, but all agree that success at creating competitive advantage is prerequisite to satisfying the wants of stakeholders.

The BCG matrix is a portfolio approach that privileges relative market share above other factors as the main source of competitive advantage. The Shell matrix does not have a generic theory of competitiveness, and allows each analyst to identify the critical success factors for each industry and the objectives for each business. The life cycle model is one of the strategy's building blocks, it is assumed by nearly all the other models. However, its use as a generator of strategy solutions is limited by the difficulties associated with predicting transition from one stage to another.

Porter's generic strategy model is the most sophisticated general theory of competitiveness, and can be used to think through strategy issues with great effect, particularly when used in conjunction with the five forces model. However, the belief in the mutual exclusivity of the cost leadership and differentiation may mislead managers into focusing on one element to the detriment of the other.

You should also note that all the models suggest strategic directions, and emphasise that superior operation is paramount. For example, if all the businesses in an industry try for cost leadership, the winner will be the firm that harmonises its operations most effectively to achieve it. That is to say that the strategy guides, but does not replace, operations management. There is no such thing as a strategy that compensates for sloppy operations management. This point also explains why firms are able to gain advantages using a strategy model, even if the same model is known and used by their rivals. Competitive advantage is not achieved by knowing strategy models that others do not. Rather, it is a question of applying the models more creatively, and developing superior competencies so that the critical success factors are carried out more effectively.

SELF-TEST
QUESTIONS

The product market portfolio

1   What is the relationship between cash generation and each of the four quadrants in the BCG matrix? (2.3)

The product life cycle

2   What are the stages of the product life cycle? (4.1)

Generic strategies

3   Why are cost and differentiation advantages are known as *positional advantages*? (6.2)

Preventing replication

4   Give four ways of resisting competitor replication. (7.1, 7.2)

Critical success factors

5   What are the stages of Johnson and Scholes' application of critical success factors? (8.2)

E X A M - T Y P E
Q U E S T I O N **1**

The product life cycle

Explain the product life cycle concept and why it is important to a company planning for the development of new products. Illustrate your answer using examples with which you are familiar.   **(20 marks)**

E X A M - T Y P E
Q U E S T I O N **2**

Porter's strategies

Michael Porter suggests that there are three generic strategies for creating and sustaining superior performance. These strategies are:

(a)   overall cost leadership

(b)   differentiation

(c)   focus.

Required:

(a)   Describe each of these strategies and indicate how each strategy will result in competitive advantage.   **(6 marks)**

(b)   What factors are important in achieving 'overall cost leadership'?   **(7 marks)**

(c)   Discuss the risks faced by an organisation that adopts the strategy of 'overall cost leadership'.   **(7 marks)**

(Total: 20 marks)

For the answer to these questions, see the 'Answers' section at the end of the book.

F E E D B A C K   T O
A C T I V I T Y **1**

(a)   Orange juice is a cash cow.

(b)   Pomegranate juice is a question mark, which the company wants to turn into a star.

F E E D B A C K   T O
A C T I V I T Y **2**

Marketers use perceptual maps to obtain a graphic presentation of how their product is perceived by consumers relative to competitors' products.

Chapter 7

INTERNAL ASSESSMENT AND SWOT ANALYSIS

This chapter is devoted to understanding the internal strengths and weaknesses of an organisation. Recent developments in the literature suggest that this area is crucially important in developing and sustaining a competitive advantage, and finding appropriate uses for this in the market place.

The initial stage is the **resource audit**. Companies find that a useful procedure is to start with an understanding of the company's present position, and then to extrapolate this into the future while adjusting it for factors that are expected to produce deviations from trends.

Corporate analysis or SWOT analysis can be a very useful way of summarising many of the previous analyses and combining them with the key issues of environmental analysis. SWOT stands for strengths, weaknesses, opportunities and threats. The aim is to identify the extent to which the current strategy of an organisation and its more specific strengths and weaknesses are relevant to and capable of dealing with the changes taking place in the business environment.

Objectives

When you have studied this chapter you should be able to:

- explain and carry out a resource audit

- explain and identify capabilities and competencies

- use the resource audit to identify strategic priorities.

1   Internal appraisal

1.1   Introduction

An organisation needs to understand its present position before strategy can be planned. Although managers maintain awareness of their individual positions on an informal and intuitive basis, the position of the overall organisation is more complex. Many organisations therefore conduct a periodic, formal, systematic and comprehensive analytical audit, which is focused on current operational aspects, and which is sometimes called a Position Audit. The data obtained from this audit can be used to assess the company's strengths, highlighting the areas in which it has exclusive skills or does well as compared with competitive standards, and weaknesses, to show areas where significant improvements are needed. It can also be used to extrapolate the company's position forward in time, and to evaluate the feasibility of intended strategic changes.

1.2   Position audit

A Position Audit is an important (some would say essential) part of the strategic planning process. The carrying out of a Position Audit focuses the attention of those responsible for the formulation of strategic plans upon the question of 'where are we now?' In other words it is an examination of the organisation's current situation.

A position audit can be described as part of the planning process, which examines the current state of the entity in respect of:

- resources of tangible and intangible assets and finance;
- products, brands and markets;
- operating systems such as production and distribution;
- internal organisation;
- current results;
- returns to stockholders.

An organisation's operational environment is composed of those dimensions, which directly or indirectly influence corporate success or failure. Most external factors are beyond the control of the company, whereas internal dimensions are generally within its management ambit. The essential purpose of a strategic Position Audit is to collect and analyse all the relevant and available information about the company and its current operations, which will provide strategic planners with information on:

- The competitive strengths and weaknesses of the company's current strategic position;
- The consequences of the company continuing its present strategy;
- The internal resources that are available for implementing any strategic change, which may be required.

The audit would cover all aspects of the company; it would not just concentrate on one or two activities that seem to be problematic and it is often most relevant if it contains a comparison with noted good performers or competitors. Activities are interrelated and a problem in one may be caused by troubles in another.

The data obtained from the Position Audit will be input into the corporate appraisal stage, (the SWOT analysis), which we examine later.

1.3 Performance analysis

Performance analysis can be used to identify strengths and weaknesses and influence strategy choice. Profitability and sales provide an evaluation of past strategies and an indication of the current market viability of a product line. A target rate of return can be applied that takes into account the fact that not all strategies have the same degree of risk. Shareholder value analysis is based on generating a discounted present value of the cash flow associated with a strategy. It is theoretically sound and appropriately forward-looking, as opposed to current financials that measure the results of past strategies. Unfortunately, it focuses attention on financial measures, rather than other indicators of strategic performance.

Other non-financial performance measures are available that offer better measures of long-term organisation health. These include:

- Customer satisfaction/brand loyalty - how is the organisation doing relative to its competitors at attracting customers and building loyalty?
- Product/service quality - is the product delivering value to the customer and is it performing as expected?
- New product activity - has the organisation got a stream of new products or product improvements that have made an impact?
- Relative cost - is the organisation at a cost disadvantage with respect to materials, assembly, product design or wages?

- Associations - how do the customers associate with organisation in terms of perceived quality, innovation and customer orientation etc?

- Manager/employer capability and performance - has the organisation created the type, quantity and depth of management required to support projected strategies?

2 Resource audit

2.1 Resources and their implications for strategy development

The resource audit can be a starting point in understanding strategic capability. It is a review of all aspects of the resources - assets, capabilities, organisational processes, information, knowledge, etc - the organisation uses. It should indicate:

- the capability (or otherwise) of the organisation to exploit present and future environmental opportunities

- the ways in which resources might be changed to create competitive advantage and to improve the organisation's wealth-producing capacity.

The audit should include all the resources *available* to the organisation ie, that it can access to support its strategies.

The type of information to be surveyed in making the appraisal may be classified under the following headings:

Human resources – the analysis will include an assessment of the number and types of different skills within the organisation and the availability of labour of all categories both in the short- and long-term. It will also consider:

- the size of the labour force

- the adaptability of these resources

- the efficiency of the workforce

- the state of labour relations in the company

- the rate of labour turnover

- the facilities for all training and education

- the salary and wages structure

- the proportion of the organisation's added value or sales revenue that is accounted for by labour costs.

Ratios for capital employed, turnover and overhead per employee should be evaluated and compared with historical data and other firms' figures.

Management – although part of the human resources audit, management can be assessed separately by asking the following questions:

- What is the size of the management team?

- What are its specialist skills?

- What management development and career progression exists?

- How well has management performed in achieving targets in the past?

- How hierarchical is the management structure?

Financial – this should include the sources and uses of money, such as obtaining capital, managing cash, the control of debtors and creditors and the management of relationships with suppliers of money (shareholders, banks etc). Information over a period of say five years, plus forward projections if available, should be produced, covering balance sheet positions, profit and loss accounts analysed by product groups or activities, an analysis of long-term and short-term sources of funds, and financial ratios interpreting the significance of the trends revealed by these reports.

Cash balance questions should seek to establish whether the organisation has too much or too little cash or near cash and to identify what a more attractive balanced situation would look like. Organisations with excessive reserves of cash (near cash) resources such as debtors and stock will miss out on the additional wealth that would accrue if excess reserves were to be invested in profit-making projects. Highly liquid companies can be in danger of takeover.

Physical – all plant and property should be analysed considering the location with reference to the convenience of customers, suppliers, employees and administration. The age, suitability and condition, the valuation of these assets and the possibility of realising them should be calculated. The takeover possibilities and leasehold/freehold status of property should also be considered.

The following types of questions could be used in an audit:

- What fixed assets does the organisation use?

- What is their current value (on a going concern basis and on a break-up value basis)?

- What is the amount of revenue and profit per £1 invested in fixed assets?

- How old are the assets?

- Are they technologically advanced or out of date?

- What are the organisation's repairs and replacement policies?

- What percentage of the organisation's capacity is in use? This is particularly important for service industries, such as cinemas, football grounds and trains, where fixed costs are high and resources need to be utilised as much as possible to earn good profits.

Intangible resources – must not be overlooked as there should be no doubt that they have a value. They include such resources as patents, trademarks and corporate image. In some service-based businesses such as professional services or the catering industry, goodwill could represent the major asset of the company and may result from brand names, good contacts, company image and many other sources. Other intangible resources to assess include:

- Human resources – the skills and motivation of the employees. Knowledge includes the ability to generate and disseminate ideas and innovation.

- Technological resources – the knowledge of process and product that the organisation has control of. These are capable of sustaining a competitive advantage if the knowledge is difficult to discover, or protected by patents and so on.

- Reputation – the values and trust that stakeholders, particularly customers, build up about a company and its brands.

- Organisational resources – some firms manage innovative project management teams very well, others are very good at controlling costs, and some manage information particularly well.

Products and markets – a detailed examination should be made of the markets in which the company has been selling in recent years, and of the products it has sold. The sales should be analysed by products, product groups, areas, customers and outlets; in volume and value, and in relation to their profit margins.

Marketing performance could be measured in terms of sales achieved to advertising expenditure incurred. Sales outlet performance can be ascertained in terms of branch sales to square feet of selling space and one of the measures of the production department's performance might be the total output to rejects and returned goods.

The market size and rate of growth forecast and the company's own share of that market should be reviewed. Details should be obtained of competitors' performance, including the number of new products or services, and of major improvements to existing products, that they have introduced with reports on their success or failure. It is often useful to delineate the life cycle of various products and to decide what stage each product has reached in the cycle.

Organisation – The suitability of the organisation for the work to be done should be assessed and any future developments that will be needed must be planned. Organisational structure is the sum total of the ways in which the organisation divides its labour into distinct tasks and then achieves co-ordination between them. Future management needs must be evaluated and the quality, availability and use of management information should be considered.

Internal controls - every business, from the largest to the smallest, needs to organise its affairs efficiently, run itself in an orderly fashion and safeguard its assets. Administrative controls consist of the plan of organisation and all methods and procedures that are concerned with operational efficiency and adherence to managerial policies. Accounting controls are all the methods and procedures concerned with the safeguarding of assets and the reliability of the financial records.

Distribution – the standards of delivery service compared with those of competitors should be assessed, as well as the effects on profit and sales of investment in distribution outlets in different areas, having different types of organisation or using different transport facilities. Consideration must be given as to how changes in population and developments in transport facilities available may affect future distribution patterns.

Research and development – current R&D projects should be reviewed and their relevance to the marketing programme, their possibility of success from production, technical and marketing aspects and the probable development and productions costs should be assessed. The present R&D load and schedule for project completion should be considered.

Production and supply – points to consider include:

- trends in output in relation to capacity
- trends in demand in relation to capacity
- the pattern of order intake
- delivery performance compared with due dates
- changes in manufacturing processes and their effect on costs of production
- price trends of supplies; changes in material specifications; material yields and scrap.

Corporate vulnerability – The susceptibility of the company to adverse conditions must be considered:

- Technically it may be susceptible resulting from products becoming obsolete; products may be vulnerable because their range is either too broad or too narrow.
- A company must be certain that it will have liquid resources available at all points in the future.
- Markets, particularly overseas, may dry up very quickly unless a constant check is kept on them.
- Competitors may change their nature and strength very quickly following a takeover; this possibility must always be considered.
- If the prices being charged for products are too high – inviting undercutting, or too low – making the profit too small, there is vulnerability.

Once there is an analysis of resources the methods by which the activities of the organisation underpin its competitive advantage can be identified.

ACTIVITY 1

Briefly describe four key areas that might be assessed in the resource audit.

Feedback to this activity is at the end of the chapter.

2.2 Unique resources and competencies

According to Johnson & Scholes, strategic capabilities can be related to three main factors:

- Resources available to an organisation

- The competencies with which the activities of an organisation are undertaken

- The balance of resources, activities and business units in the organisation.

DEFINITION

A unique resource is one that is better than its equivalent employed by competitors and difficult to imitate.

They classify resources into four groups- physical, human, financial and intangible resources, arguing that all of them are necessary to support the strategy chosen by an organisation.

Unique resources - are particularly valuable and an important source of competitive advantage because they are better than their equivalent employed by competitors and difficult to imitate.

Industry norms will offer hints about competitors' competence level and also benchmarking helps to assess competencies.

Competencies - an organisation needs to reach a threshold level of competence in all activities it undertakes, however only some of these activities are core or distinctive competencies. Core competencies underpin the organisation's ability to outperform competition (or demonstrably provide better value for money). They must be *rare* and *costly to imitate* for competitors, provide *value to customers* and have to be *integrated* within the organisation. Core competencies can be used to exploit more than one market. This ability requires a capacity for innovation and a willingness to change e.g. by adding valuable services to core products or by spreading geographically when traditional markets reach maturity and/or saturation.

The figure below summarises the relationship between necessary and unique resources as well as threshold and distinctive/core competencies.

	Same as competitors' or easy to imitate	Better than competitors' or difficult to imitate
Resources	Necessary resources	Unique resources
Competencies	Threshold competence	Distinctive/Core competence

We might find that threshold competencies include the following.

- Keeping prices below a certain level, eg supermarkets

- Having staff of a required calibre, eg accountancy firms

- Having a reasonable network of outlets for customers to purchase products, eg car dealers

- Maintaining good relations with customers (particularly if the organisation sells to another firm rather than direct to the public), eg companies supplying materials to just–in–time producers.

Similarly, we might find the following distinctive competencies.

- Efficient manufacture leading to economies of scale and low prices, eg McDonald's

- Manufacturing high-quality products for which customers will pay a premium, eg Mercedes Benz

- Efficient distribution systems allowing goods to reach customers quickly, eg mail order firms

- Specialised knowledge of dealing in certain areas, eg long-haul holiday companies

An important issue faced by some organisations is that certain departments may be undermining the organisation's competencies. For example a manufacturing company might seek to gain an advantage through a high degree of after-sales service. This might be undermined by any or all of the following shortcomings.

- Poor quality of training for service staff so that they are unable to deal with various types of problem

- Recruitment of poor quality staff who do not have the right type of skills to operate effectively

- Poor location of service centres leading to long journeys for customers

- Out-of-date telephone systems making it difficult for customers to contact the company

- Poor purchasing systems or poor manufacturing leading to delays in obtaining spare parts to use in servicing

Note that the last two items affect the service department even though they are outside the control of the service department manager.

2.3 Resource use

Investigating organisational productivity performance is important in an internal analysis. Johnson and Scholes define efficiency as 'how well the resources have been utilised irrespective of the purpose for which they have been employed'. They define effectiveness as' whether the resources have been deployed in the best possible way'. It is possible to be efficient doing things that have little or no value and it is possible to be effective in getting a job done, but use resources inefficiently in doing so.

A first step in evaluating resource use performance is to decide which ratios are to be measured. The most widely used financial ratios measure profitability, liquidity and efficiency. These are usually derived from an analysis of the organisation's financial accounts. These measurements can be supplemented by more in-depth analysis, which measures the ratios of outputs to inputs for different functions in the enterprise eg, marketing performance could be measured in terms of sales achieved to advertising expenditure.

The next step in the process of resource use measurement is to compare the performance ratios against such criteria as:

- performance trends - is it part of an improving or worsening trend?

- performance against industry norms - provides a useful indication of the performance;

- comparison with specific competitors - in competitive markets this is an important measurement. If an enterprise's major rivals are outperforming it in terms of wealth, growth and liquidity generation, then something needs to be done.

- comparison with market conditions - a trend of improving performances in mature or declining market situations suggests a healthy productivity capability. Declining performances where the industry is growing suggests poor competitive performance.

- comparison against targets

- comparisons using opinions from industry - will usually have a good idea of what constitutes acceptable performance.

2.4 Resource flexibility

This refers to the effectiveness of the organisation in rearranging and re-deploying resources to meet new situations. In a dynamic environment, organisations make frequent changes in direction and a new organisational approach or resource use needs to be implemented quickly. Questions to be asked include:

- Is management too set in its ways and too prone to follow older, out of date success procedures?

- Is the workforce sufficiently motivated and multi-skilled to handle change effectively?

- Is the organisation locked into a particular industry, product or method because of heavy investment in specialist plant and machinery and a shortage of finance?

The analysis should highlight areas where a lack of flexibility might lead to a loss of competitive position.

2.5 Availability of resources

The formulation of strategies for the acquisition of adequate resources is an essential part of management planning.

Finance and supplies are key operating resources and management must ensure that the right amount is available at the right time. Financial resources mean long-term finance to finance growth and capital investment more particularly than short-term finance, the need for which is highlighted by the annual cash budget and which can probably be covered by a bank overdraft.

KEY POINT

Capital investment may be described as any expenditure designed to yield returns over a (relatively long) period

---

Capital investment may be described as any expenditure designed to yield returns over a (relatively long) period e.g., the purchase of productive equipment. The need for capital investment should become apparent from the company's corporate planning process.

Projects may be categorised as follows:

- Cost reduction – investment programmes that will result in cost savings as a result of more efficient or reliable machinery.

- Expansion – projects that expand existing capacity by new equipment and/or facilities.

- New products – introduction of new product lines.

- Plant renewal and replacement

- Welfare projects – e.g., new canteens, which yield no immediate tangible benefits.

- Statutory projects – e.g., safety equipment to comply with legislation.

Supplies i.e., the availability of raw materials, bought-in components, etc. is of considerable importance to a manufacturing company because adequate material supplies are crucial to the company's operations and because materials typically form a high proportion of the total cost. An organisation's access to raw materials can provide a sustainable competitive advantage. Supplies strategies have three components:

- acquisition of resources of the right quality in the right quantity at the right time and place at the right cost

- control of the efficient utilisation of resources (this is essentially an operating problem)

- conservation of resources - consideration must be given to re-cycling, substitution of less scarce materials, etc.

A company used to be able to decide on its product-market strategy and assume that adequate resources would be forthcoming. Now it must consider available raw materials as an essential part of strategy formulation. Its audit of strengths, weaknesses, opportunities and threats must highlight any 'resources gap'.

An analysis must be made of the number of sources, price, delivery times and possible threats, such as a supplier with a poor industrial relations record. If there is a gap in quantity or quality of resources, or the price or time at which they can be obtained it will be necessary to:

- revise objectives or devise a new strategy to meet the objectives, diversifying if necessary

- improve efficiency in the utilisation of resources - reduce wastage, use recycled material, etc.

- investigate the prospects of making the product from a new material (long lead times can be involved here)

- find new suppliers

- integrate backwards to become one's own supplier.

It is essential to retain flexibility in supplies strategies to be able to avoid delay in obtaining supplies, high prices, and poor quality and drying up of supplies.

Specific supplies strategies that might be adopted include the following:

- Avoiding over-dependence on one supplier.

- Promoting competition among suppliers by wide tendering and by 'shopping around' for the best prices. However, it might not always pay to take the lowest price or to drive too hard a bargain - if suppliers have under-estimated their costs they might go out of business. In such circumstances, companies that have not retained flexibility often have to 'prop up' their suppliers in order to maintain key supplies.

- Promoting closer co-operation with one's suppliers, eg, by paying premium prices in return for specific assurances.

- Taking advantage of quantity discounts while at the same time retaining flexibility. This would involve placing large orders with one supplier to obtain the discounts, but at the same time placing smaller orders with other suppliers to retain flexibility.

- Obtaining supplies from different parts of the world so that political instability or government regulations in one area will not affect the entire supply.

- Carrying large stocks - but not so large that there is a danger of obsolescence.

- Having contingency plans.

2.6   Material culture

As we have already noted, advantages arise out of the organisation's environment. The organisation's resources have a major impact on its ability to exploit these opportunities. It is no good having a wonderful strategy if you don't have the resources necessary to carry it out. Even 'possessing' the physical resources is insufficient; it is knowing how to use them and having the ability to implement them at the right time.

Tangible resources, such as machines and buildings, as well as less intangible resources, such as scientific know-how and budgetary systems, interact with members of an organisation to produce what anthropologists call 'material culture'. This emerges when goods reflect, directly or indirectly, the beliefs of the individuals who made or used them.

For example, the car was invented and developed in Europe as a luxury machine built by skilled craftsmen for the affluent. The Americans reinvented the car as a standardised, low-cost machine built by unskilled labour for the multitudes. This reflects deep differences in culture: the Europeans had a long tradition of craftsmanship, while the Americans compensated for their shortage of skilled workers by learning to standardise products and master the art of mass manufacturing. The competition that eventually arose between American and European car manufacturers turned out to be a competition between two different cultures. The idea that it is not products that compete in the marketplace but systems of production is not new. Economists have long held that the efficiency of a production system plays a central role in competition.

3   Analysis of capabilities and core competencies

3.1   Formulate a SWOT analysis

To assist in closing the gap between its predicted and desired performance, the organisation's strengths, weaknesses, opportunities and threats need to be ascertained. The work involved draws on the data obtained about objectives, current position, extrapolated position, gaps and environmental forecasts, and is sometimes called **corporate appraisal**.

A SWOT analysis is a critical assessment of the internal appraisal of the organisation's strengths and weaknesses, and an external appraisal of the opportunities and threats open to organisations in competition within the industry. Therefore, strengths and weaknesses are peculiar to an individual organisation but opportunities and threats are open to all organisations within the market place. The factors involved in SWOT analysis are wide ranging and include decision variables which strengthen or constrain the operational powers of the company, such as the size of its markets, the competitive forces in the markets, opportunities for new products, availability of skilled labour, control of vital raw materials and access to additional capital.

The purpose of SWOT analysis is to provide a summarised analysis of the company's present position in the market place.

Strengths are those positive factors or distinctive attributes or competencies that provide a significant competitive advantage that the organisation can build on. These are characteristics of the organisation eg, present market position, size, structure, managerial expertise, physical or financial resources, staffing, image or reputation. Searching out opportunities that match its strengths helps the organisation to optimise the effects of synergy.

Weaknesses are negative aspects in the organisation eg, deficiencies in the present competencies or resources, or its image or reputation, which limit its effectiveness and which need to be corrected. Examples of weaknesses include limited accommodation, high fixed costs, a bureaucratic structure, a high level of customer complaints or a shortage of key managerial staff.

Opportunities are favourable conditions that usually arise from the nature of changes in the external environment eg, new markets, improved economic factors or a failure of competitors. Opportunities provide the organisation with the potential to offer new or to develop existing products, facilities or services.

Threats are the opposite of opportunities and also arise from external developments. Examples include unfavourable changes in legislation, the introduction of a radically new product by a competitor, political or economic unrest, changing social conditions or the actions of a pressure group.

The main areas considered in the internal appraisal would include:

- *products* eg, age, life span, life cycle stage, quality comparisons

- *marketing* eg, market share, presence in target segments, identifiable and non identifiable benefits, success of promotions, advertising

- *distribution* eg, delivery promise performance, depot location

- *production* eg, age/obsolescence, valuation, capacity

- *research and development* eg, number of commercially viable products, costs/benefits, relevance of projects

- *human resources* eg, manpower plan, management in depth, training levels, morale

- *finance* eg, cash availability, risk exposure, short and long-term funding, contribution levels.

The external appraisal is the opportunities and threats analysis part of SWOT analysis. For *opportunities* it is necessary to decide:

- what opportunities exist in the business environment

- what is their inherent profit-making potential

- whether the organisation can exploit the worthwhile opportunities

- what is the comparative capability profile of competitors

- what is the company's comparative performance potential in this field of opportunity.

For *threats* it is necessary to decide:

- what threats might arise, to the company or its business environment

- how competitors will be affected

- how the company will be affected.

It may be a little simplistic to assume that blame can be apportioned exclusively to the organisation's environment when, in fact, weaknesses in, say, the management team or the organisational structure may have led to a compounding of the problems arising externally. Indeed, throughout our analysis we must bear in mind the linkages between issues and the possibility that it may have been a combination of various issues that led to the problems being experienced.

There are four components of external appraisal:

- Customer analysis - identifies the organisation's customer segments and each segment's motivations and unmet needs.

- Competitive analysis - covers the identification of current and potential competitors. Some competitors will compete more intensely than others and, although they should be examined in more detail, all competitors are usually relevant to the strategy development.

- Market or industry analysis - has two main objectives. The first is to measure the attractiveness of the market and of the individual sub-markets to find out whether competitors will earn attractive profits or lose money. The market will be no place to invest if it is so difficult that everyone is losing money. The second objective is to understand the dynamics of the market so that threats and opportunities can be detected and strategies formed.

- Environmental analysis - will attempt to identify and understand emerging opportunities and threats created by these forces. Opportunities and threats might relate to economic factors, government legislation, social and cultural factors and/or technology.

An outline of a SWOT analysis process is shown below.

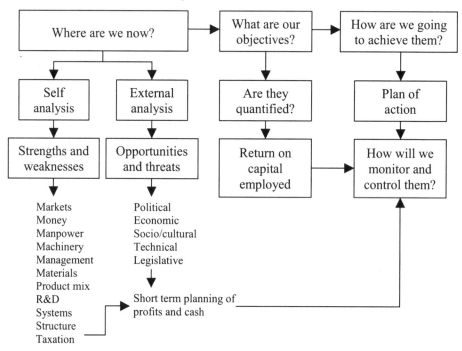

A SWOT analysis can be used to assess:

- a company (its position in the market, commercial viability, etc)

- a method of sales distribution

- a product or brand

- a business idea

- an accounts department

- a strategic option, such as entering a new market or launching a new product

- an opportunity to make an acquisition

- a potential partnership

- changing a supplier

- outsourcing a service, activity or resource

- an investment opportunity

The internal and external appraisals will be brought together, and perhaps shown on a cruciform chart, so that potential strategies can be identified. A cruciform chart is simply a table listing the significant strengths and weaknesses, and opportunities and threats.

The SWOT analysis example shown below is based on an imaginary business-to-business manufacturing company that historically relies on distributors to take its products to the end user market. The opportunity, and therefore the subject for the SWOT analysis, is for the manufacturer to create a new company of its own to distribute its products direct to certain end-user sectors, which are not being covered or developed by its normal distributors.

STRENGTHS	WEAKNESSES
• End-user sales control and direction.	• Customer lists not tested.
• Right products, quality and reliability.	• Some gaps in range for certain sectors.
• Superior product performance versus competitors.	• We would be a small player.
• Better product life and durability.	• No direct marketing experience.
• Spare manufacturing capacity.	• We cannot supply end-users abroad.
• Some staff have experience of end-user sector.	• Need more sales people.
• Have customer lists.	• Limited budget.
• Direct delivery capability.	• No pilot or trial done yet.
• Product innovations ongoing.	• Don't have a detailed plan yet.
• Can serve from existing sites.	• Delivery-staff need training.
• Products have required accreditations.	• Customer service staff need training.
• Processes and IT should cope.	• Processes and systems, etc
• Management is committed and confident.	• Management cover insufficient.

OPPORTUNITIES	THREATS
• Could develop new products.	• Legislation could impact.
• Local competitors have poor products.	• Environmental effects would favour larger competitors.
• Profit margins will be good.	• Existing core business distribution risk.
• End-users respond to new ideas.	• Market demand very seasonal.
• Could extend to overseas.	• Retention of key staff critical.
• New specialist applications.	• Could distract from core business.
• Can surprise competitors.	• Possible negative publicity.
• Support core business economies.	• Vulnerable to reactive attack by major competitors.
• Could seek better supplier deals.	

Feedback to this activity is at the end of the chapter.

ACTIVITY 2	Opportunities and threats might relate to PEST factors. What does this mean?

3.2 Interpret a SWOT analysis

Having gained information about its environment, market structure and product/market mix, the next task is to develop strategies. SWOT analysis is a way of identifying the extent to which an organisation has managed to obtain a fit with the environment: it identifies internal strengths and weaknesses, and external opportunities and threats.

The purpose of the SWOT analysis is twofold. It helps to generate strategic alternatives and to provide criteria to select among them.

The first step is to rank in order of importance the findings of the SWOT analysis.

- Strengths that match no opportunity are of little use without an opportunity
- A distinctive competence is a strength that can be exploited.

Strategies can be developed which:

- Neutralise weaknesses or convert them into strengths
- Convert threats into opportunities
- Match strengths with opportunities

The internal appraisal highlights areas within the company which are strong and which might therefore be exploited more fully, and weaknesses where some defensive planning might be required to protect the company from poor results. Strengths and weaknesses show up inherent potential and the analysis is intended to shape the organisation's approach to the external world. For instance, the identification of shortcomings in skills or resources could lead to a planned acquisition programme or staff recruitment and training.

The external appraisal should identify opportunities that can be exploited by the organisation (such as growth in market demand, or new technological possibilities) and should help managers anticipate environmental threats eg, competitors' actions, declining economy, legislation etc.

We can show how to develop strategies that take into account the SWOT profile in the matrix below:

	Strengths	**Weaknesses**
Opportunities	S-O strategies	W-O strategies
Threats	S-T strategies	W-T strategies

S-O strategies pursue opportunities that are a good fir to the organisation's strengths.

W-O strategies overcome weaknesses to pursue opportunities

S-T strategies identify ways that the organisation can use its strengths to reduce its vulnerability to external threats

W-T strategies establish a defensive plan to prevent the organisation's weaknesses from making it highly susceptible to external threats.

Example

We can use the example below to illustrate that the SWOT analysis yields a much clearer view of the extent to which the environmental changes and influences provide opportunities or threats, given current strategies and organisational capabilities.

STRENGTHS	WEAKNESSES
• £8.5 million of capital available • Production expertise • Willing and experienced workforce • Appropriate marketing skills	• Heavy reliance on a small number of customers • Limited product range, with no new products • Expected market decline. • Small marketing organisation
OPPORTUNITIES	THREATS
• Government tax incentives for new investment • Growing demand in a new market, although customers so far relatively small in number	• A major competitor has already entered the new market

In this example, we might note that the company is having problems and might be in imminent danger of losing its existing markets and must diversify its products, or its products and markets. The new market opportunity exists to be exploited, and since the number of customers is currently small, the relatively small size of the existing marketing force would not be an immediate barrier. A strategic plan could be developed to buy new equipment and use existing production and marketing to enter the new market, with a view to rapid expansion. Careful planning of manpower, equipment, facilities, research and development and so on would be required and it would be necessary to meet the threat of competition so as to obtain a substantial share of a growing market. The cost of entry at this early stage of market development should not be unacceptably high.

ACTIVITY 3

What types of strengths, weaknesses, opportunities and threats would a 'no frills' airline have?

Feedback to this activity is at the end of the chapter.

4 Product life cycle issues

4.1 Competencies and the product life cycle

Markets can change unpredictably, and this shifts the critical success factors as seen in the last activity (no frills airline). However, some changes are more predictable, and should be part of the organisation's long term thinking. In general, the profile of required competences is a function of the product life cycle.

Introduction stage	Innovation, flexible manufacturing, marketing
Growth stage	Logistics, marketing, product development, flexible manufacturing
Maturity	Brand management, low cost manufacturing,
Decline	Cost control, logistics

This list is not exhaustive, but gives the idea of the changing balance of resources and competencies. Some writers argue that this implies that the firm must continually change its skills to be able to compete. Others, such as Miles and Snow discussed earlier, argue that this is not feasible in most cases, and firms should look to switch products and markets when the cycle moves away from their skills, and network with larger firms who have the new competences. For example, few modern car assemblers do much designing, as their competencies are in supply chain management and assembling. However, there are a large number of specialist designers who have retained the innovative capabilities more commonly found in the early stages of the cycle.

4.2   Resource balance - product life cycle

Balance questions can be applied across the whole range of organisational resources. For example, when considering 'balance' in the context of the product/service portfolio, the question would be designed to reveal whether the organisation has:

- too many declining products/services

- too few products or services with growth potential

- insufficient product/service profit generators to maintain at least the present performance and to provide funds for the nurturing of tomorrow's successful ventures

The product life cycle analysis and the BCG matrix can be used to aid this analysis. With the BCG matrix, underlying assumptions equate high market share with higher profitability/competitive advantage and prescribe that growing markets are more commercially attractive than static or declining markets.

Balance can also be applied to the organisation's cash situation. Those with excessive reserves of cash or 'near cash' (debtors and stocks) will miss out on the additional wealth that would accrue if excess reserves were to be invested in profit-making projects. Highly liquid companies are also in danger of takeover from bigger, less liquid predators. Alternatively, organisations with a tight liquidity situation will have to forego investment opportunities because of a shortage of finance. An over-tight liquidity position also increases the risk of insolvency, bankruptcy or liquidation.

4.3   Detecting maturity and decline

One important set of turning points in market sales is when the growth phase of the product life cycle changes to a flat maturity phase, and when the maturity phase changes into a decline phase. These transitions are important to the health and nature of the market. Often they are accompanied by changes in key success factors. Historical sales and profit patterns of a market can help to identify the onset of maturity or decline, but the following often are more sensitive indicators:

- Price pressure caused by overcapacity and the lack of product differentiation. When growth slows or even reverses, capacity developed under a more optimistic scenario becomes excessive. Furthermore, the product evolution process often results in most competitors matching product improvements. Thus, it becomes more difficult to maintain meaningful differentiation.

- Buyer sophistication and knowledge - buyers tend to become more familiar and knowledgeable as the product matures and thus become less willing to apply a premium price to obtain the security of an established name. Computer buyers over the years have gained confidence in their ability to select computers and as a result, the value of big names like IBM recedes.

- Substitute products or technologies - the sales of CD players provide an indicator of the decline in tape players.

- Saturation - when the number of potential first-time buyers declines, market sales should mature or decline.

- No growth sources - the market is fully penetrated and there are no visible sources of growth from new uses or users.

Customer disinterest - a reduction in the interest of customers in applications, new product announcements, and so on.

5 Strategic options

5.1 The seven S model

The 7-S-Model is better known as McKinsey 7-S. This is because the two persons who developed this model, Tom Peters and Robert Waterman, were consultants at McKinsey & Co at that time.

The model is a tool for managerial analysis and action that provides a structure with which to consider a company as a whole, so that the organisation's problems may be diagnosed and a strategy may be developed and implemented.

The 7-S diagram below illustrates the interconnections of the elements that define an organisation's ability to change. The theory helped to change manager's thinking about how companies could be improved. It says that it is not just a matter of devising a new strategy and following it through. Nor is it a matter of setting up new systems and letting them generate improvements. To be effective, the organisation must have a high degree of fit, or internal alignment among all the seven Ss. Each S must be consistent with and reinforce the other Ss. All Ss are interrelated, so a change in one has a ripple effect on all the others. It is impossible to make progress on one without making progress on all.

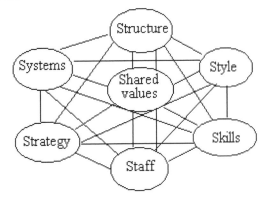

Strategy, structure and systems can be considered the 'hardware' of success whilst style, staff, skills and shared values can be seen as the 'software'.

The seven 'S' characteristics - divided into hard and soft - are as follows.

Hard S

Strategy (objectives and resource allocation) – the formally declared goals of the organisation. In this context it refers to the organisation's business and competitive strategies and the plan to allocate resources to achieve organisational objectives. It also incorporates the integrated vision and direction of the company, as well as the manner in which it derives, articulates, communicates and implements that vision and direction. ***Structure*** – the way the organisation is arranged to implement that strategy. This refers to the formal organisation structure (eg, the division of tasks, responsibility and authority)***Systems*** – (processes and procedures) - describe the accounting system, which processes financial data and produces information, the reward systems and information systems that ensure that the strategy is actually carried out. Also the policies and procedures that govern the way in which the organisation acts within itself and within its environment. The decision-making systems within the organisation can range from management intuition, to structured computer systems to complex expert systems and artificial intelligence. It includes computer systems, operational systems and HR systems.

Soft S

Staff (motivation, loyalty, groups, abilities) – the people and their attitudes. Staff means that the organisation has hired able people, trained them well and assigned them to the right jobs. Selection, training, reward and recognition, retention, motivation and assignment to appropriate work are all key issues.

Skills (capabilities of organisation as a whole) – this is what the organisation does well. This is more than just the aggregate of individual skills, because it results from the ways in which these are deployed in pursuit of organisational objective. Skills refer to the fact that employees have the skills needed to carry out the company's strategy. Training and Development - ensuring people know how to do their jobs and stay up to date with the latest techniques.

Style (image, management behaviour) – this refers to the various options from a great deal of supervision to almost none, or even the informal organisation as well as the cultural attributes that make the organisation actually work. Style refers to the employees shared and common way of thinking and behaving - unwritten norms of behaviour and thought.

Shared Values (super-ordinate goals, common purpose) – the beliefs and goals of the employees and their culture. Shared values means that the employees share the same guiding values. Values are things that you would strive for even if they were demonstrably not profitable. Values act as an organisation's conscience, providing guidance in times of crisis. Identifying corporate values is also the first essential step in defining the organisation's role in the larger community in which it functions.

The hard elements are feasible and easy to identify. They can be found in strategy statements, corporate plans, organisational charts and other documentations. The four soft S's however, are hardly feasible. They are difficult to describe since capabilities, values and elements of corporate culture are continuously developing and changing. They are highly determined by the people at work in the organisation. Therefore it is much more difficult to plan or to influence the characteristics of the soft elements. Although the soft factors are below the surface, they can have a great impact of the hard Structures, Strategies and Systems of the organisation. Organisations in which these soft elements are present are usually more successful at the implementation of strategy. This system can be used to evaluate the strategic options of an organisation in that the 7 S's give us a checklist of areas to address. Effective organisations achieve a fit between these seven elements. This criterion is the origin of the other name of the model: Diagnostic Model for Organisational Effectiveness.

If one element changes then this will affect all the others. For example, a firm is doing poorly and so it decides to improve the quality of its products and to introduce a greater degree of customer service (Strategy).

- It will need to set up a customer service department and organise the staff into teams (Structure).

- The staff may need to be trained in customer service skills (Skills).

- The company may recruit staff who are innovative to improve the level of quality (Staff).

- The culture of the company will need to be changed to ensure that everyone focuses on quality (Shared values).

- Management will probably become more hands-off to allow employees to be more innovative (Management style).

- Procedures may be changed to encourage more standardisation but with the flexibility to do whatever is necessary to solve problems (Systems).

In change processes, many organisations focus their efforts on the hard S's, Strategy, Structure and Systems. They care less for the soft S's, Skills, Staff, Style and Shared Values. Peters and Waterman commented however, that most successful companies work hard at these soft S's. The soft factors can make or break a successful change process, since new structures and strategies are difficult to build upon inappropriate cultures and values. These problems often come up in the dissatisfying results of spectacular mega-mergers. The lack of success and synergies in such mergers is often based in a clash of completely different cultures, values, and styles, which make it difficult to establish effective common systems and structures.

In the examination be prepared to think big and note how changes affect the entire organisation.

Successful organisations take an active role in managing all seven aspects in order to be successful. This active management will require constantly looking at changes in the outside world, the market place, the product mix, competitors, strengths and weaknesses of the organisation.

5.2   Determinants of strategic options

Self-analysis should also review characteristics of the organisation that will influence the choice of strategy. Have the target segments changed? What is the sustainable differential advantage? The past and current strategy provides an important reference point. Has it involved milking, maintenance or growth? Has it been one of differentiation or low cost?

If there is a strategic problem, it could be that, if uncorrected, it could have damaging implications. For example, an instrument firm could have a quality problem that must be corrected. A weakness is more of an inherent characteristic that the organisation can live with eg, poor location in terms of access for a garden centre. In general, problems are corrected and weaknesses are neutralised by a strategy or compensated by strengths.

An analysis of the financial resources available for investment either from planned cash flow or from debt financing could identify a financial constraint on the strategic choice. Other constraints may be identified when the internal organisation ie, its structure, systems, employees and culture, is analysed. For example, the culture in some organisations can be so strong and positive that it provides the basis for a sustainable competitive advantage. Other strengths may be based on assets, such as a brand name or skills eg, marketing.

5.3   Core competences and threshold competences

Up until this point, we have argued that competences need to be identified in relation to critical success factors and industry attractiveness. However, writers have begun to challenge the product market orientated way that strategists have frequently thought about this, by arguing that the strategy should be about developing and extending competencies across markets, rather than focusing on one industry and trying to guess what resources and capabilities will be needed some years hence. Such thoughts have come from the study of companies such as Marriot, that one normally associates with hotels. However, most of the company's profits come from activities that they learned in the hotels business, but have managed to transfer across the organisation – facilities management, hospitality, conference organisation and very many others. The point is that their experience of competing in hotels has helped them develop a range of competences in which they are world class – known as core competences.

These core competences are complex harmonisations of knowledge, organisational routines and the integration of production, design and marketing skills. This is a wider use of the term than simply the competences one needs to be effective in a particular market (the tasks that lie behind the critical success factors discussed earlier). The term threshold competence is reserved for these skills that the firm must have to put a saleable product in front of a customer.

Hamel and Prahalad have argued that thinking of businesses as a portfolio of products and markets, rather than a bundle of competences, is a critical mistake. In their view, strategic management is about identifying, developing and harmonising the core competences across the organisation. They use the term strategic architecture to discuss the way that information and skills are moved around the organisation. Sony and Honda, in particular, have a routine of moving experts away from their expertise into different projects and technologies. Consequently they have a large number of expert generalists working on projects, and can bring technologies together in unexpected ways and find innovative applications for even relatively straightforward ideas.

In this approach, finding new and appropriate markets is often less problematic than for the SBU type organisation. Although firms can use all the market research techniques available to any firms, they can also rely rather more on the strategic architecture to bring them into contact with customers and partners. Resource based firms can then diversify on the basis of superior competences and may shatter the existing patterns of competitive behaviour. For example, Canon entered the photocopier business against Xerox, a company many times their size. However, they had had superior skills in optics from their experience in cameras and had developed technologies that did not infringe Xerox's patents. Marriot moved into many of its new areas by simply noting what went on in its hotels, and thinking about the value added of the various activities.

6 Product attributes

6.1 Product elements

It is important to learn to see how a product appears to the target market in terms of what is offered in the wider package. The product attribute model suggests that there are three layers to product attributes, as shown below:

Stage	Example
Core Product	The basic functions required of any effective product in the market
Secondary Product	Additional features, brand image
Augmented Product	Warranty, after sales service, reputation

This model has helped strategists to understand that competition increasingly takes place at the secondary and augmented levels. However, developing skills here is not straightforward. For example, the extra features have to be ones that the buyer is prepared to pay for, not ones that the engineer is capable of building in at extra cost. Brand values do not come through increased advertising expenditure, but through a genuine commitment to make the brand represent quality, reliability and service.

ACTIVITY 4

†

Think of a recent routine consumer purchase you have made. How relevant is the product attribute model to your behaviour?

Feedback to this activity is at the end of the chapter.

6.2 Product and service quality and reliability

A product (or service) and its components should be critically and objectively compared both with competition and with customer expectation and needs. How good a value is it? Can it really deliver superior performance? How does it compare with competitor offerings? How will it compare with competitor offerings in the future given competitive innovations? One common failing is to avoid tough comparisons with a realistic assessment of competitors' offerings now and those that will likely be soon announced.

Product and service quality usually are based on several critical dimensions that should be identified and measured over time. For example, a car manufacturer can have measures concerning defects, ability to perform to specifications, durability, reliability, and features. A bank might be concerned with waiting time, accuracy of transactions, and making the customer experience friendly and positive. A computer manufacturer can examine relative performance specifications, and product reliability as reflected by repair data. A business that requires better marketing of a good product line is very different from one that has basic product deficiencies.

An often-overlooked asset of a product or service is what customers think of it - what are its associations? What is its perceived quality? Perceived quality, of course, can be very different from actual quality .It can be based on past experience with prior products or services and quality cues such as retailer types, pricing strategies, packaging, advertising, and a profile of the typical customer.

A detailed examination by Jacobson and Aaker of the relationship of perceived quality and other key strategic variables in addition to ROI provides insights into how perceived quality creates profitability:

- Perceived quality affects market share - after controlling for other factors, products of higher quality are favoured and will receive a higher share of the market.

- Perceived quality affects price - higher perceived quality allows a business to charge a higher price. The higher price can directly improve profitability or allow the business to improve quality further to create even higher competitive barriers. Furthermore, a higher price tends to enhance perceived quality by acting as a quality cue.

- Perceived quality has a direct impact on profitability in addition to its effect on market share and price. Improved perceived quality will, on the average, increase profitability even when price and market share are not affected. Perhaps the cost of retaining existing customers becomes less with higher quality or competitive pressures are reduced when quality is improved. In any case, there is a direct link between quality and ROI.

- Perceived quality does not affect cost negatively. In fact, it does not affect costs at all. The conventional wisdom that there is a natural association between a quality/prestige niche strategy and high cost is not reflected in data. The concept that 'quality is free' may be, in part, the reason that enhanced quality leads to reduced defects and lowered manufacturing costs. John Young of Hewlett-Packard noted that a focus on quality is one of the best ways to control costs and mentioned one study that demonstrated that 25% of its manufacturing costs were involved in responding to bad quality.

Conclusion

In this chapter we have examined the issues relating to internal assessment, taking a resource and position audit that can be used to develop some strategic priorities. We have also considered how to go about identifying and using core competencies. Finally, we looked at quality and product issues that help a customer remain loyal to a particular producer.

Resource audit

1   Explain the purpose of the resource audit. (2.1)

2   Illustrate, with examples, the differences between tangible and intangible resources. (2.1)

Analysis of capabilities and core competencies

3   What is the purpose of the SWOT analysis? (3.2)

Strategic options

4   How does Hamel and Prahalad's competence approach to strategy differ from traditional views of portfolio and product market strategy? (5.3)

Product attributes

5   Why does perceived quality have a direct impact on profitability? (6.2)

Strengths and Weaknesses

In ascertaining an organisation's strengths and weaknesses, management often concentrate on certain key areas.

Required:

Specify and describe five key areas and explain the way that an assessment of this type may be conducted.   **(20 marks)**

For the answer to this question, see the 'Answers' section at the end of the book

Cuddles Limited

Cuddles Limited is a garment manufacturer based in Nottingham in the United Kingdom, producing clothing for babies and infants. The company is owned and managed by Richard, and his wife, daughter and two sons are all working in different capacities within the firm.

The company's small range of garments is being sold successfully to retail clothing outlets specialising in baby and infant wear. Richard has ambitions of growing his company substantially over the next few years.

Required:

(a)   What general environmental factors are likely to influence Cuddles Limited?
                                                                      (6 marks)

(b)   What are the competitive forces that the company is going to face as Richard attempts to achieve his ambitions?   **(8 marks)**

(c)   What competitive strategies can Cuddles Limited adopt to achieve and sustain its need for growth?   **(6 marks)**

                                                                 (Total: 20 marks)

For the answer to this question, see the 'Answers' section at the end of the book.

Financial resources – this consists of constructing a series of accounting ratios to measure profitability, growth and liquidity, and then comparing them with earlier results and also with results of other firms in similar circumstances.

Profitability – might include an analysis of sales and profit involving sales mix, pricing strategy, discount facilities, and an assessment of the returns on total assets employed. Costs obviously have important implications for profitability and, therefore, determination of operational costs and internal efficiency is also required.

Product range – involves the determination of the profit contribution of each product in relationship to the resources it utilises. It is also necessary to pay particular attention to market trends to ascertain whether, in the product mix, certain products need upgrading whilst others require phasing out.

Human resources of the organisation – an analysis will ensure that personnel are suitably motivated and that adequate facilities are available for appropriate staff development.

PEST factors are:

Political - legislation may affect a company's prospects through the threats/opportunities of pollution control or a ban on certain products, for example.

Economic - a recession might imply poor sales

Social attitudes

Technology - new products or means of distribution may be developed

Strengths:	Weaknesses:
• Airports used are better than those used by competitors • Management skills • Lower costs than established airlines • Ease of booking flights • Recognised logo • IT facilities • Good employee relations	• Airports used are worse than those used by the big carriers • Punctuality • Cash flows • No established safety record • Poorer than average customer service
Opportunities:	Threats:
• Strong business demand for cheap air fares • Strong leisure demand for cheap air fares • The Internet • Many secondary airports underused	• Higher airport charges • Stringent security checks • Entry of subsidiaries of big carriers

The point of picking a routine purchase is that you may well have long ceased to think about making a choice, and simply follow a habit. Coffee, tea, and tobacco products, for example, are rarely thought through each time a purchase is made. Providing the core product is sound, and the secondary attributes are in place, a consumer is likely to feel confident in their purchases and not think too much about alternatives. Only when a customer is disappointed, or their needs change, will they make a review of the product offerings available.

Chapter 8
ADDING COMPETITIVE VALUE

The first step in moving from a resource audit to an understanding of strategic capability is to find a way of relating the organisation's resource profile to the strategic performance ie, to identify how the activities of the organisation underpin its competitive advantage. Value chain analysis has been widely adopted as a method of achieving such an understanding.

Objectives

When you have studied this chapter you should be able to:

- explain the value chain and its link with organisational structure and strategy
- explain the value system and strategic architecture
- discuss differentiation strategies
- outline the effect of value systems on marketing behaviour.

1   Value chain

1.1   Definition

One way of gaining a deeper insight into buyer needs is through value chain analysis. It breaks down the firm into its strategically relevant activities in order to understand the behaviour of costs and the existing or potential sources of differentiation. A firm gains competitive advantage by performing these strategically important activities more cheaply or better than its rivals. A value chain can be defined as a strategic collaboration of organisations for the purpose of meeting specific market objectives over the long term and for the mutual benefit of all 'links' of the chain. Chain formation may be motivated by a number of different drivers; the three most common chain drivers include:

- **Market differentiation** - typically involves the development of niche markets and is most appropriate for smaller organisations working to develop speciality markets.

- **Quality assurance** - the development of detailed quality assurance systems from primary production to retail.

- **Chain optimisation** - a focus on reducing logistics costs, which include transaction, delivery, warehousing and delivery costs. Typically these chains require a strong operations research focus to identify system bottlenecks and to seek out inefficiencies best suited for improvement.

Porter's definition of value is 'the amount buyers are willing to pay for what a firm provides them. Value is measured by total revenue, a reflection of the price a firm's product commands and the units it can sell. A firm is profitable if the value it commands exceeds the costs involved in creating the product. Creating value for buyers that exceeds the cost of doing so is the goal of any generic strategy. Value, instead of cost, must be used in analysing competitive position since firms often deliberately raise their cost in order to command a premium price via differentiation'.

The concept of value should be continually assessed from the point of view of the final consumer or user of the product or service. This is especially important for organisations that are distanced from their final users by intermediaries such as distributors. The consumers' idea of value may change over time eg, by competitive offerings that give better value for money

1.2 Porter's value chain

Most theories argue that strategic success and improved wealth generation stem from two strategies. The first is to reduce the 'bottom line' costs of operation and the second is to increase the value of the organisation and its offerings in the eyes of the customers, so they will buy more or pay more for what they receive.

In the analysis so far, we have provided a basis for a more systematic search for wealth-generating changes. Michael Porter suggests that resources should be arranged to enhance least-cost production or differentiation strategies. These are Porter's generic strategies for achieving competitive advantage and above average profits. Creating value for buyers that exceeds the costs of doing so is the goal of any generic strategy. Value, instead of cost, must be used in analysing competitive position since firms often deliberately raise their cost in order to command a premium price via differentiation.

All organisations in a particular industry will have a similar value chain, which will include activities such as obtaining raw materials, designing products, and building manufacturing facilities, developing co-operative agreements, and providing customer service. It is therefore necessary that organisations should strive to understand their value chain and also that of their competitors, suppliers, distributors, etc.

The value chain, shown in the diagram below, looks at the total value added by the industry and by the particular organisation within that industry, and then the contribution of each primary and support activity carried out by the organisation is separated. The objective of this analysis is to highlight the activities, which contribute most significantly to the total value added, and to develop strategies to improve on or defend the current share of that value-added, which is gained by the organisation.

Value activities are the physically and technologically distinct activities of a firm, which represent the building blocks by which value is created for the buyers of the product or service. The margin is the difference between the total value and the collective cost of performing the value activities. Value chain analysis looks at where the organisation can add value or cut costs.

We should stress at this point that in Porter's analysis, business *activities* are not the same as business *functions*.

Functions are the familiar departments of a business such as the production function, or the finance function, and reflect the formal organisation structure.

Activities are the actual work that is done. A single activity can involve work by a number of functions in sequence or concurrently. Activities procure inputs and process them, adding value to them in some way, to generate outputs for customers. Activities incur costs, and, in combination with other activities, provide a product or service, which earns revenue.

Porter's value chain

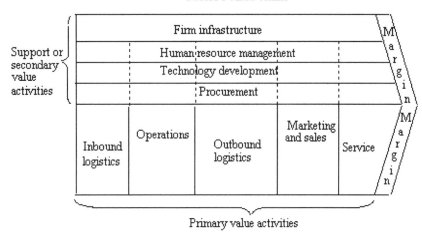

1.3 Value chain analysis

Porter analysed the organisation by distinguishing five primary activities and four support activities, shown in the diagram. The five primary activities are at the bottom of the figure, while the four support activities are at the top

- **Inbound logistics** - are the activities concerned with receiving, storing, and distributing the inputs to the organisation system (materials handling, stock control, transport etc)

- **Operations** - transforming inputs into final products/services (machining, packing, assembly, testing and equipment maintenance)

- **Outbound logistics** - collecting, storing and distributing final products (for tangible products this includes order processing, warehousing, stock control, distribution and vehicle scheduling. In the case of services it may be more concerned with arrangements for bringing customers to the service if it is in a fixed location eg, theatre, sports event)

- **Marketing and sales** - activities that attract customers to purchase (includes sales administration, advertising, selling, channel selection, pricing and promotion)

- **Service** - activities that ensure that customers enjoy their purchases by providing installation, training, maintenance, repair and breakdown assistance etc.

All of these primary activities are linked to the secondary, or support activities: which Porter classifies under four headings:

- **Firm infrastructure** - includes the systems of planning, finance, quality control and estate management. Infrastructure also consists of the structures and routines of the organisation, which sustain its culture. It supports the entire value chain and can help or hinder the achievement of competitive advantage

- **Human resource management** - how people within the firm are managed. It is concerned with those activities involved in recruiting, training, developing and remuneration of people within the organisation. Some companies recognise the potential advantage that can be gained through co-ordinating these activities across the organisation and through investing heavily in them. The recruitment and retention of good staff has emerged as a major strategic issue for firms like chartered accountants and software consultancies.

- **Technology development** - covers know-how as well as machines and processes. The key technologies may be concerned directly with the product or with processes, such as oil refinery, or with a particular resource such as the use of information technology

- **Procurement** - how the resources for the above are purchased. It includes all the procedures for dealing with suppliers. Procurement activity goes on across the whole organisation; it is not just limited to the purchasing department. Although the costs of procurement form only a small proportion of overhead costs, the impact of poor procurement can be dramatic, leading to higher costs and/or poor quality.

1.4 Examples illustrating the use of Porter's value chain

The analysis helps managers to decide how individual activities might be changed to reduce costs of operation or to improve the value of the organisation's offerings. Such changes will increase 'margin' - the residual value created by what customers pay minus the organising costs. For example, a clothes manufacturer may spend large amounts on:

- buying good quality raw materials (inbound logistics)

- hand-finishing garments (operations)

- building a successful brand image (marketing)

- running its own fleet of delivery trucks in order to deliver finished clothes quickly to customers (outbound logistics).

All of these should add value to the product, allowing the company to charge a premium for its clothes. Another clothes manufacturer may:

- reduce the cost of its raw materials by buying in cheaper supplies from abroad (inbound logistics)

- making all its clothes by machinery running 24 hours a day (operations)

- delaying distribution until delivery trucks can be filled with garments for a particular request (outbound logistics).

All of these should allow the company to be able to gain economies of scale and be able to sell clothes at a cheaper price than its rivals.

ACTIVITY 1	A washing machine manufacturer has introduced some technologically advanced methods to its production but still needs to make improvements.
	Use Porter's value chain analysis to decide how individual activities might be changed to reduce costs of operation or to improve the value of the organisation's offerings.

Feedback to this activity is at the end of the chapter

1.5 Managing linkages

Because core competencies on their own are likely to be eroded over time by competitors, Porter stresses the importance of linkages between activities. For example, good communication between sales, operations and procurement can help cut stocks (of inputs and finished goods); the purchase of more expensive (but more reliable) equipment can lead to cost savings and quality improvements in manufacturing operations. Therefore, it is important that these activities are not dealt with in isolation. If each activity is assessed independently, important benefits like these might not be realised.

External linkages also exist eg, between the company and its suppliers. An important part of resource analysis is to identify how resource activities and linkages can be rearranged to create greater value for the customer. For example:

Type of linkage	Example
Primary-primary	A just-in-time manufacturing process where goods are only produced when customers order them shows inter-departmental co-operation between outbound logistics and marketing
Support-primary	Computer-based operations, involving co-operation between IT and operations departments eg, automated paint spraying to paint each product a different colour eg, in car manufacture.
Support-support	Computer-based systems that automatically monitor suppliers' prices and recommends which supplier to purchase from

Primary activities should be examined together. For example if operations are geared towards low-cost high-volume output (ie, standardised goods are being produced) whereas marketing is geared towards flexibility (ie, producing non-standardised goods) then the firm may end up not satisfying any of its customers.

One of the notable features of value analysis is that it recognises that an organisation is much more than a random collection of machinery, money and people. These resources are of no value unless they are organised into structures, routines and systems, which ensure that the products or services that are valued by the final consumer are the ones which are produced. The organisation must assess how the resources are utilised and linked to competitive advantage

1.6 Value chain and organisational structure

Value Chains are intuitively simple and they respond to the demands of the customer more effectively and efficiently. They do so by building collaborative management structures as well as information systems that enable each 'link' in the chain to work together. Hence the value chain in its entirety is better able to respond to customer demands and market changes.

Though conceptually simple, value chains represent a marked change in management behaviour and organisational strategies. Traditionally, profit came from:

- profit potential of the industry structure and the position within it

- intensity of rivalry of competitors

- control of precious resources

Prosperity came from the ability to compete against competitors, suppliers and customers

Within this context, the further removed a chain link is from the final customer, the less knowledge it has of customer preferences. Further, traditional relationships are often characterised by a measure of mistrust. Consequently, this system is not well positioned to respond to market change. Necessary change is either slow or perhaps missed altogether. This phenomenon is referred to in some sectors as a 'series of disconnects' - the fractured or inefficient flow of information from the customer back to each link of the chain.

In contrast, value chains provide a process and a structure to respond to specific markets and customers more effectively. To this end, the value chain is defined by collaboration across the links and is rooted in the development of 'trust' relationships and the sharing of information, costs and benefits. The chain structure is linked by means of interactive information systems and data sharing that are vital to each chain link in responding to customer preferences in the immediate term and more importantly, market change over the long term.

Flexibility seems to be vital if the organisation is going to be able to respond to changing client needs. Decentralised decision-making would seem to be an important feature, permitting the experts closest to the clients' problems the freedom to make decisions.

These two features will lead to a structure very different from the stable bureaucracy found in the production firm pursuing a cost leadership strategy. Opportunities for standardising work are unlikely to present themselves, as each client's problem will be in many respects unique. Clear reporting relationships (hierarchies) with well-defined job descriptions would also seem to be out of tune with the need for flexibility. And in an organisation of highly skilled, independent-minded individuals often working autonomously we would not expect to find a strong management hierarchy with 'top-down' decision making. It would be quite difficult to draw up an organisation chart for this type of firm because of overlapping project team membership, no clear line/staff distinctions and a limited management structure.

If team-working is necessary to carry out the clients' assignments, then this suggests a limit to the size of units. Project teams co-ordinate through face-to-face communication and this gets tricky when teams get to be large. So, even if the form as a whole employs hundreds of staff, to deliver results they must be formed into many smaller units.

1.7 Forming an alliance

Value chains are often comprised of horizontal and vertical alliances. Horizontal alliances are formed via the integration of companies at the same level in the chain (eg, grower co-operatives or groups) in order to achieve:

- greater critical mass
- continuity and consistency of supply
- quality
- efficient response to consumer requirements.

Vertical alliances are between parties at different levels of the chain (eg, producers and processors/manufacturers).

Alliances can take many forms from formal to informal networks to joint ventures and acquisition. International and domestic retailers and food service companies prefer to source a large range of products with a large supply capacity and guaranteed quality assurance from a single, or small number of, preferred suppliers.

Alliances allow large numbers of smaller producers to enjoy the benefits usually enjoyed by larger organisations and to facilitate the development of effective value chain linkages.

Benefits include:

- achieving critical mass, and the ability to meet buyer specifications and requirements via increased supply capacity
- increased efficiencies (input and expenditure)
- greater access to capital and equipment
- ability to service larger clients.

2 Value systems

2.1 Organisational boundaries

An organisation is a complex system with a particular identity and must therefore have some frontiers separating it from its environment. All organisations fall somewhere on a continuum between a totally open system where the environment is so important that the organisation merges into it and has no real identity of its own and a totally closed system which is self-contained and has no environment at all.

However, the concept of organisational boundaries is not as clear-cut and as well-defined as one would imagine. Take a public limited company. This could be viewed as being a collection of shareholders, personnel, directors and physical assets with an environment containing customers, suppliers, competitors and other elements in the 'outside world'. Yet its shareholders probably own shares in other companies too, and, of course, institutional investors such as pension funds or investment trusts will be organisations in themselves. Employees may also be members of trade unions and other external bodies (political parties, for instance, or local government) and could also purchase the products/services of the company - making them its customers, or consumers.

The company's value chain does not exist in isolation. There will be direct links between the inbound logistics of the firm and the outbound logistics of its suppliers, for example. For example, a manufacturer of motor cars might purchase many components, such as tyres, brakes and engines from suppliers, and assemble these components into a finished product. The finished product is then transferred to car distributors, who sell them to customers. The suppliers of the component parts to the car manufacturer will obtain parts and materials from other suppliers. The supply chain stretches from the producers of the basic raw materials (rubber, metal, plastic and so on) to the end-consumer. Each organisation has a position in the supply chain. An understanding of the value system, and how the organisation's value chain fits in to it will therefore aid in the strategic planning process.

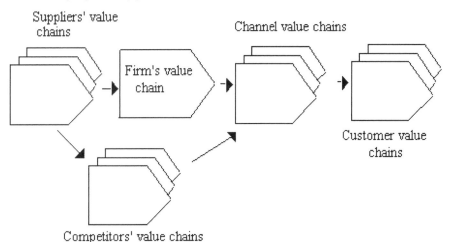

Some companies operate in ignorance of the wider value chain – even if they have a successful strategy of being close to the customer. This is a dangerous policy however, because value creation depends upon being part of a successful value creation system, and not merely the prowess of individual performers. There is no point in being an outstanding firm that is locked into an inferior system.

Other firms make a point of active involvement in the wider value creation system. Toyota, for example, actually creates about 15% of the value added on their vehicles, but they are actively involved in the management of all their component suppliers and similar operations. Consequently, they are able to gain a cost advantage over most of their rivals. If they had chosen to work in a more isolated way, their best efforts would only apply to 15% of costs, and this would not be enough to deliver a resounding cost advantage no matter how effective they were.

2.2 Resources in the value chain

One of the notable features of value analysis is that it recognises that an organisation is much more than a random collection of machinery, money and people. These resources are of no value unless they are organised into structures, routines and systems that ensure that the products or services, which are valued by the final consumer, are the ones that are produced. The organisation must assess how the resources are utilised and linked to competitive advantage. An analysis of resource utilisation can be undertaken, comprising the following steps:

- Identify the value activities - this stage should include an assignment of costs and added value and an identification of the critical activities. These are the various value activities that underpin the production and delivery of its products or services, including the supply and distribution chains. It is important for the organisation to identify the value activities that are critical in terms of its competitive advantage. For example, for one organisation the low price of its product to the consumer may be underpinned by a low cost supply of parts and a low mark-up by the distributor. By strengthening and building on the key activities the organisation is likely to achieve success.

- Identify the cost or value drivers - the factors that sustain the competitive position are called the cost drivers or value drivers. In the example of a low cost supply, the factors may be related to physical proximity of the suppliers and could disappear with geographical expansion.

- Identify the linkages - an organisation's value activities and the linkages between them are the source of competitive advantage. There may be important links between the primary activities. For example, good communications between sales, operations and purchasing can help cut stocks; the purchase of more expensive or more reliable machinery and equipment may lead to cost savings and quality improvements in the manufacturing process.

Choices will have to be made about the relationships and how they influence value creation and strategic capability. Holding high levels of finished goods might ease production scheduling problems and give a faster customer response time but will probably add to the overall cost of operations. An assessment as to whether the added value of high stocks is greater than the added cost needs to be made.

Linkages between the organisation's support activities may also create value. The extent to which human resource management has been involved in new technologies has brought about successful implementation of new production and office systems.

Because of the linkages it is important that the organisation's activities are not dealt with in isolation. Competitors can often imitate the separate activities of an organisation but it is more difficult to copy the linkages within and between value chains.

3 Differentiation

Differentiation means the provision of a product or service regarded by the user as meaningfully different from the competition.

3.1 Sources of differentiation

A successful differentiation strategy requires that the product should be made special – almost to the point of uniqueness – in ways that the buyer is prepared to pay a premium for. It is worth mentioning that marketers tend to use the term more widely, so that it covers any means to make a product recognisably different from another. Both uses of the term are legitimate, but in this unit we take the strategist's meaning of the term.

A product can be differentiated in an almost unlimited number of ways. Mintzberg has made life simpler by providing a series of categories, within which firms can differentiate. The categories are:

Design differentiation – where the product is designed so fundamentally differently that it is almost a separate product category. Sony, for example, has been particularly good at producing products of this kind. Of course, they are frequently easy to copy, and the firm must be ready to follow each success with others.

Image differentiation – where marketing, brand management and the more superficial elements of design make one product stand out. It is worth noting that this is difficult to achieve – and often expensive – but is open to both differentiators and cost leaders.

Quality differentiation – where buyers believe that a product is more reliable, durable or has superior performance. This form of differentiation is difficult to achieve, but is commonly associated with high profits in an industry.

Price differentiation – where a lower price makes the products different from others in the industry. To be successful, this strategy requires that the market is price sensitive and the firm has, or is capable of getting, a cost advantage. Sadly, many firms in the UK opt for this approach without the slightest hope of gaining a cost advantage, and are found to be performing very poorly.

3.2 Product differentiation

Product differentiation means having unique products or varying them in such a way that they appear to be different from those offered by competitors. Information technology can help in the design of products eg, computer-aided design. Information systems can enhance an organisation's ability to compete by providing it with up-to-the-minute information as to customer needs and in tailoring their products or services to a customer's specific requirements. Information systems can also be used to compare customer purchases of the organisation's goods with those of other suppliers, allowing an organisation to differentiate its products on factors other than price.

3.3 Market differentiation

Market differentiation can be achieved by the organisation that can create significant switching costs. By switching costs is meant the actual or perceived costs for a buyer of changing the source of supply of a product or service. This might be because the buyer is dependent on the supplier for particular components, services or skills. For example, it could be that a manufacturing company is following a strategy where low stock levels are of significant strategic importance. A supplier might therefore choose to work closely with the manufacturer to ensure speed of delivery and information on availability of components. The supplier is seeking to build linkages between different parts of the value chain and build switching costs into the service provided.

3.4 Marketing and innovative differentiation

According to Danny Miller, differentiation can be divided into two types:

1   **Innovative differentiation** - to stay ahead of its rivals the firm has continually to develop new products, approaches, packages, systems, etc. As a consequence the organisation must be flexible, and may need a healthy turnover of staff to ensure the latest ideas are being brought into the firm.

2   **Marketing differentiation** - achieves higher prices largely through marketing efforts such as heavy advertising, promotion, a large and vigorous sales force.

There is no great requirement for product innovation: all the creativity goes into the marketing of the product. Many successful producers of branded consumer products would fall into this category (e.g. Unilever, Reckitt and Colman, Nestle).

There are interesting organisational implications associated with this strategy .The firm can adopt the dual structure - pursuing cost leadership and differentiation simultaneously - the product (which is essentially standardised) can be produced in the most cost-efficient way, because this differentiator may well have the large market share that will enable it to exploit all the available economies of scale and experience. This part of the organisation would resemble the successful cost leader.

On the other hand, the marketing part of the structure needs to be creative and innovative, encouraging, rewarding and retaining people with flair and imagination. It might make sense, therefore, to locate these characters somewhere else. The culture of the efficiency- orientated part may well spill over into this smaller, creative section with adverse consequences.

3.5   Innovation

A successful company is one that is outward looking, has accepted the reality of constant change and the necessity to review its product-market policy continuously. It places emphasis on vigorous initiative, always looking to the future towards new markets, innovative products, better designs, new processes, improved quality, increased productivity. It has a structure designed for innovation in which management and staff are stimulated to think and act innovatively, which recognises potential 'intrapreneurs' and ensures that everyone (particularly senior people) welcome changes for the better. Innovation demands a culture, which focuses on the task, stimulates creativity, and rewards ideas and supports individual and team abilities.

Within the value chain of all functions that serve to produce goods and services, achieving superior innovativeness, relative to that of competitors, can help the firm to acquire new customers. Innovation can be achieved through either producing a new or novel product, or operating the firm in a new or novel way. Some examples of how a firm can build a competency in innovation include achieving close integration between operations and marketing, an ability to minimise the time a product reaches the market, and good project management.

Superior innovation gives a company something unique, something that its competitors lack until they are able to imitate the innovation. By the time competitors succeed in imitating the innovator, the innovating company has already built up such brand loyalty that its imitating competitors will find it difficult to attack their position

3.6   Technical development

Another competitive approach is to maintain technical superiority, especially for high-tech firms. The question that is often raised is whether the superiority is sustainable in the face of rapid technological innovation. Some businesses manage to stay consistently ahead of the competition because they have developed skills in R&D, manufacturing and new product introduction that have provided the basis of their success.

There is also the concept of intangible associations. Some firms have the image of being technologically advanced because their products over the years have been up-to-date. When this intangible association is established it is often hard to dislodge and competitors are at a disadvantage.

Technological advances have been a critical source of productivity and efficiency gains in many organisations and those that are earlier adopters of the right technology have typically been financially successful. Technological progress implies change, and continuous change can be characterised as the' technology treadmill'.

This notion of the technology treadmill actually accelerates the adoption of technology. As a new technology is introduced, the first few organisations to adopt the practice gain doubly. They increase the volume of their product and, in addition, gain revenue at market prices largely dependent upon the volume of production from the old technology. Thus, there is tremendous incentive to be the early adopter. Subsequently, as more and more organisations adopt the practice, the supply of commodities increases and this drives down the price. This forces the remaining organisations to adopt the new technology to increase their production to compensate for the lower prices. The key to success in technology adoption in this treadmill environment is to continually scan for new technology options, to be early in the adoption process and to be right! You probably do not want to be first in technology adoption, but a close second - maybe an optimal adopter.

3.7 Distribution channels

Access and/or control of distribution can be a key asset. For example, access to supermarket shelves can be a sustainable competitive advantage for some companies. The access can be due to a track record of new product success, the ability to support the product with promotion and advertising, and an effective sales force. In contrast, a competitor that is not in the top five brands will constantly have difficulty gaining shelf space and might have to look for new channels to bring its goods to the market.

Channel institutions do not stand still, like most other things they exhibit a life cycle. A particular channel organisation or system may emerge (suddenly perhaps), grow, reach a level of relative stability, and eventually move into a period of decline. Some companies create their own channels and outlets - a strategy that is particularly relevant for a company entering a new market and finds itself locked out from existing channels, or which considers existing channels inadequate for the needs of its products.

For example, Mullard Furniture Industries (now MFI) built up a market base in furniture by direct mail. To reduce breakage in transit, MFI innovated with flat-packed furniture, but damages on road and rail persisted. As a result MFI invested by opening its own retail warehouses on edge-of-town sites. Low rental, plus the ability to offer manufacturers long production runs, enabled MFI to set low selling prices, often half the high-street price for the equivalent product. Customers were prepared to accept the inconvenience of going a distance to shop.

The revolution caused by information technologies has permanently changed distribution channels. Customers and suppliers can be tied into the supply chain or the distribution chain using electronic data interchange (EDI). Automated teller machines (ATMs) created new distribution channels enabling 'bank branches' to be set up in airports, by out-of-town supermarkets and other areas where there are many potential customers. These machines provided not only expansion of the total market, but also a low-cost method of overcoming the barriers to entry in the areas where the cost of entry was high and space was at a premium. The Internet and e-commerce means that a lot of companies have the opportunity to reach new markets and potentially develop a new distribution channel.

3.8 Identifying new target markets

The value system may develop skills in primary and secondary activities that can be transferred to completely different markets. For example, Lex developed a great reputation for servicing automobiles, but found diversification into related markets difficult. However, they realised that their great success in their main business was largely due to their logistical skills in the movement of spare parts. Consequently, they deployed these skills by diversifying into the distribution of electronic components. Similarly, many manufacturing companies also develop merchandising and distribution skills, and discover that these are both cost drivers and significant sources of differentiation. Consequently, they can factor a whole range of products that can be sold under the brand name competitively. Virgin's skills in marketing and customer service, learned in retail and the airline business, have successfully transferred into the selling of financial services, even though the firm has little expertise in the underlying products.

3.9　New distribution channels and market segments

The value system can also be developed to create opportunities for detecting new market segments within the existing market, and new means of reaching them. In particular, the internet shows great potential in both these respects, although returns so far have been disappointing.

A typical example is the growth of businesses selling wine directly to the consumer. The crucial cost drivers are procurement and outbound logistics in most cases. A large segment of the market enjoys, but does not particularly understand, wine and its peculiar language. Consequently, firms have been able to reduce costs in the value system by omitting established retail outlets, and providing 'tutorial' style clubs and articles to sell their products directly to consumers.

3.10　Sudden environmental shocks

The value chain is set up to optimise the value system given the present environment. As such it is at great risk when the environment changes rapidly. Much can be done by environmental scanning to reduce these risks, but it is important to see that the whole value system must be aware of the changes that are taking place. Firms locked into a good strategic architecture may fare rather better than remote ones.

ACTIVITY 2	A firm makes automatic filling machines, which are used in the catering industry, It has a large customer base, who are loyal because of good customer service and a differentiated product based on a patented metal coating process. A foreign company has attacked the market with lower prices, and ceramic components that equal the performance of the domestic company's machines. What are the implications for the value system?

Feedback to this activity is at the end of the chapter.

Conclusion

In this chapter we looked at the importance of creating value for customers, shareholders and the future. We then looked at the role of the value chain and the value system in creating superior value for buyers and above average profits for the business. The links between value and generic strategy were explored in some detail. The role of strategic architecture as an alternative to a market based value system was considered. Finally, the wider uses of the value chain in finding new business opportunities and identifying appropriate responses to environmental shocks were examined.

Value chain

1   What are primary and support chain activities? (1.3)

2   Why are linkages between activities important? (1.5)

Value systems

3   What steps are required to undertake an analysis of resource utilisation? (2.2)

Differentiation

4   Give four ways to differentiate. (3.1)

Firebridge Tyres Ltd

Firebridge Tyres Ltd (FTL) is a wholly owned UK subsidiary of Gonzales Tyre Corporation (GTC) of the USA. FTL manufactures and sells tyres under a number of different brand names.

Firespeed, offering high product quality, at a price which offers good value for money.

Freeway, a cheap brand, effectively a standard tyre.

Tufload, for lorries and commercial vehicles.

FTL has good relationships with car firms and distributors.

GTC is rather less focused; not only does it make tyres and some other components, but it also owns a chain of car service centres specialising in minor maintenance matters such as tyre replacement, exhaust fitting, and wheel balancing.

FTL has experienced a fall in sales revenue, partly as a result of competition from overseas producers, in what is effectively a mature market. Moreover, sales of new cars have not been as high as had been hoped, and consumers are more reluctant than before to part with their money.

FTL's managers have had meetings with GTC's managers as to how to revive the fortunes of the company. FTL would like to export to the US and to Asia. GTC has vetoed this suggestion, as FTL's tyres would compete with GTC's. Instead, GTC suggests that FTL imitate GTC's strategy by running a chain of service stations similar to GTC's service stations in the US. GTC feels that vertical integration would offer profits in its own right and provide a distribution network which would reduce the impact of competition from other tyre manufacturers. GTC has no shortage of cash.

You are a strategic consultant to FTL.

Required:

(a)   What are the principal factors in the external environment that would influence FTL's strategic choice?   **(6 marks)**

(b)   Describe the barriers to entry that FTL might face if it decided to enter the service centre business.   **(6 marks)**

(c)   Can FTL's distinctive competences satisfy the critical success factors of the service business?   **(8 marks)**

(Total: 20 marks)

For the answer to this question, see the 'Answers' section at the end of the book.

A University which derives most of its funds from the government provides undergraduate courses (leading to bachelors degrees) and post-graduate courses (leading to masters degrees). Some of its funds come from contributions from student fees, consultancy work and research. In recent years, the University has placed emphasis on recruiting lecturers who have achieved success in delivering good academic research. This has led to the University improving its reputation within its national academic community, and applications from prospective students for its courses have increased.

The University has good student support facilities in respect of a library, which is well stocked with books and journals and up-to-date IT equipment. It also has a gymnasium and comprehensive sports facilities. Courses at the University are administered by well-qualified and trained non-teaching staff that provide non-academic (that is, not learning-related) support to the lecturers and students.

The University has had no difficulty in filling its courses to the level permitted by the government, but has experienced an increase in the numbers of students who have withdrawn from the first year of their courses after only a few months. An increasing number of students are also transferring from their three-year undergraduate courses to other courses within the University but many have left and gone to different universities. This increasing trend of student withdrawal is having a detrimental effect on the University's income as the government pays only for students who complete a full year of their study.

You are the University's Management Accountant and have been asked by the Vice Chancellor (who is the Chief Executive of the University) to review the withdrawal rate of students from the University's courses.

(You do not require any knowledge of University admission and withdrawal processes to answer this question.)

Required:

Apply Value Chain Analysis to the University's activities

(20 marks)

For the answer to this question, see the 'Answers' section at the end of the book.

The first step is to outline the primary activities that may be a source of advantage. Then link these to the support activities, showing how each of them cuts across all of the primary activities.

HR management	Training	Stable workforce Quality of work		Retention of best salespeople	Training service staff
Procurement		Highest quality components	Best located warehouse		Quality parts replacement
Technology development	Material handling and sorting	Unique product features	Special purpose vehicles	Engineering support	Advanced servicing techniques
Firm infrastructure	Reduced damage	Low defect rates	Quick order processing	Extensive credit to buyers	Rapid installation Service quality
	Inbound logistics	Operations	Outbound logistics	Marketing and sales	Service

Primary activities

The technology development activity, shown in the diagram, indicates material handling and sorting adding value at the inbound logistics stage. Other sources of potential advantage are sought with the unique product features at the operations stage, special purpose delivery vehicles at the outbound logistics stage and engineering support and servicing techniques in the marketing, sales and service stages.

The company faces some problems, but the problem is not yet critical. It has advantages in service, and a good market position. There are two attacks on the value chain:

Lower prices – is this an entry tactic, or does the foreign firm have lower cost drivers? Are the ceramic parts giving the rival a cost advantage?

Loss of differentiation – the ceramic parts produce equal performance. Can ceramics be developed faster than metal coatings to raise the specifications? Will higher specifications actually add to value?

Depending upon the answers to the questions above, the firm can adjust its value chain, by switching to ceramics, developing metal coatings, reducing costs and so on.

Chapter 9

HUMAN AND OPERATIONAL RESOURCES

In this chapter we continue to investigate the resources as a means of assessing the organisation's strategic capability. The concern about the organisation's resource profile is not confined to strategic analysis. It should be a key determinant during strategic choice, helping to identify directions that best match the organisation's strategic capabilities. Detailed resource planning and deployment are also important ingredients in the successful implementation of strategies.

Objectives

When you have studied this chapter you should be able to:

- understand skills and competencies
- discuss workforce adaptability and innovative capability
- understand management information and control systems
- understand production and process control systems
- understand financial control systems
- understand capital structure
- define the 'balanced scorecard': Kaplan and Norton.

1   Analysis of human resources

1.1   Introduction

It is widely recognised that skilled employees create a sustainable competitive advantage for an organisation. The advantage comes from organisation-specific, valuable resources that are difficult to imitate

When analysing the human resources of the firm it is not just a matter of numbers on the payroll; the analysis may need to establish:

- the proportion of women employed in the organisation
- the proportion of part-time staff - employment rights are weaker for this category of employee
- the number of graduates - they may be the organisation's future managers and technicians; changes in education may affect the number and quality
- the age profile of employees - an ageing workforce may possess greater skill, experience and loyalty than a younger workforce, but may also be less flexible, less motivated, and less creative
- the numbers involved in training - the training should be developing the right skills and the cost should be appropriate
- the status/level of seniority of employees - career paths should be clear and promotion should be for the right reasons

1.2 Skills and competences

A strategy is generally based on an organisational skill that, in turn, is based on the skills of the workforce. Depending on the strategy, it is important to know the number and quality of the people required with respect to their experience, depth, skills and competencies.

A skill is the ability to apply knowledge and do something. . It varies in its complexity from walking or riding a bicycle to managing an organisation. Managerial skills are slightly different from those required to operate machines and deal with customers on the telephone. They include the ability to:

- observe
- communicate
- motivate
- select relevant data
- diagnose problems
- formulate solutions
- make decisions.

The rate of skill development depends on the nature of the skill itself, the individual, their age, level of motivation and state of fatigue. Most skills require regular repetition if they are to be maintained at their optimal level, although few skills, once acquired, are ever completely lost.

Competencies are the critical skills, knowledge and attitude that a job-holder must have to perform effectively. They are expressed in visible, behavioural terms and reflect the skills, knowledge and attitude (the main components of any job), which must be demonstrated to an agreed standard and must contribute to the overall aims of the organisation.

As a general definition, a competent individual can perform a work role in a wide range of settings over an extended period of time.

Competences associated with work quality include:

- technical and task knowledge
- accuracy and consistency
- exercise of judgement and discretion
- communication skills
- cost consciousness.

Competences associated with work quantity include:

- personal planning and time management
- capacity to meet deadlines or work under pressure
- capacity to cope with upward variations in work volume.

Supervisory and managerial skills and competences include:

- planning and organising
- communication and interpersonal skills
- directing, guiding and motivating
- leadership and delegation
- co-ordination and control

- developing and retaining staff

- developing teamwork.

KEY POINT

There are three different types of competence: behavioural, occupational and generic.

There are three different types of competence:

- behavioural competences include the ability to relate well to others

- occupational competences cover what people have to do to achieve the results in the job

- generic competences that apply to anyone, e.g. adaptability, initiative.

The assessment of the effectiveness of the skills and competencies will be related to how well they match the needs of the client group and will apply to issues such as delivery, technical back up, credit and design. For example, are the systems for communicating with clients before, during and after purchase adding value to the relationship? This would apply to marketing literature, technical information and corporate image.

Control is another criterion for assessing the organisation's strategic capability. There could be situations where good quality resources have been deployed efficiently and in the right way, but where performance is still poor because the resources are badly controlled. For example, costing systems are often criticised because they provide information long after the event. Managers need to be informed in time to affect their judgements and decisions.

1.3   NVQs (National Vocational Qualifications)

NVQs are a qualification framework based on standards of competence. They were devised because it was felt (by many employers) that qualifications were not closely related to the needs of employment. The previous system was over complicated and too few people had vocational qualifications.

Qualifications in vocational subjects are now firmly rooted in standards of competence required by employers. There is one single employment-led standard in each occupational area and the NVQs are offered at levels to indicate the extent of a person's competence in that occupational area.

1.4   Workforce adaptability

KEY POINT

Workforce adaptability refers to the range of skills and competencies available to the organisation allowing management to rearrange and re-deploy resources to meet new situations.

Workforce adaptability refers to the range of skills and competencies available to the organisation allowing management to rearrange and re-deploy resources to meet new situations. It is an indication of the organisation's ability to react to changing customer demands and environmental conditions. Adaptability within the workforce allows the deployment of resources to cope with the changes.

Flexibility has been mentioned as a desirable attribute of an organisation. Faced with a changing, uncertain and increasingly competitive environment, human resource managers are being required to develop a workforce, which combines flexibility with quality performance.

What seems to be emerging in the UK is a varied pattern of careers for the foreseeable future, and it is probable that many people will not be able to rely on a linear career path through their working lives. Human resource planning will be increasingly concerned with lifetime learning, continuous professional development and employability through the acquisition and development of key competencies.

If a strategy requires capabilities that are not now available within the organisation, they will have to be obtained. There are three approaches:

- the 'make' approach – developing a broad managerial or technical base by hiring and developing workers ensures that people will fit the organisation, but can take a long time

- the 'convert' approach – converting the existing workforce to the new strategy takes less time, but may fail if employees find it difficult to adapt

- the 'buy' approach – bringing in experienced people from the outside is the immediate solution when a dramatic change in strategy needs to be implemented quickly, but it involves the risk of conflict where people are used to different systems and culture.

DEFINITIONS

Functional flexibility refers to an organisation's ability to adjust and deploy the skills of its workforce to match the tasks required by its changing workload, production methods or technology.

Numerical flexibility describes the organisation's ability to adjust the level of labour inputs to meet fluctuations in output.

Distancing strategies refer to the replacement of internal workers with external subcontractors.

There are several types of flexibility:

- **Functional** – an organisation's ability to adjust and deploy the skills of its workforce to match the tasks required by its changing workload, production methods or technology.

  A multi-skilled workforce, often working in teams, can give rise to new forms of organisation structure and job design.

- **Numerical** – the organisation's ability to adjust the level of labour inputs to meet fluctuations in output.

- **Distancing strategies** – the replacement of internal workers with external subcontractors.

There are indications that flexible working methods have been adopted and are part of the expectations of many workers. There has also been a growth in outsourcing non-core activities.

An important variation in working patterns has been the growth in telework or home working. In some instances they form the competitive advantage of the organisation, especially where they are based round the growth in information technologies e.g. on the Internet.

1.5 Innovative capability

Invention is the act of creating or producing through the use of imagination, while innovation is the commercial exploitation of an invention. An innovation may be a new product or a new way of producing the product. It may be a new service e.g. distance learning, or a new way of organising the delivery of a service. It may be a change in the way the organisation is structured or a change in the way employees are recruited. Innovation is the process of introducing new developments of all kinds into the organisation. The rate of change might be fast or slow, depending on the organisation's circumstances and the environment in which it operates. A rapidly changing or turbulent environment requires a more innovative response than a stable one. The chief purpose of being innovative is to ensure the organisation's survival and success in the changing world.

- An innovation strategy calls for a management policy of encouraging creativity. This means that employees must be given the opportunity to work in an environment where the exchange of ideas for innovation can take place. Appropriate management style and organisation structure are needed. Strategic planning should result in targets being set for innovation and successful achievements by employees should be rewarded. Innovation and entrepreneurial attitudes are best nurtured in a climate that permits and actively encourages new ideas and new ways of doing things.

- People must be trusted and given the control and opportunity to make things happen. Managers must teach members how to perceive, think and feel in relation to problems and how to cope with external adaptation and internal integration.

- Participation in development decisions might encourage employees to become more involved with development projects and committed to their success.

- Development teams can be set up and an organisation built up on project teamwork. The creation of a more permissive climate encourages ideas and information to flow and new perspectives on problems and opportunities to be developed.

- Recruitment policy can be directed towards appointing people with the necessary skills for doing innovative work. Employees should be trained and kept up to date.

- Certain managers can be made responsible for obtaining information about innovative ideas from the environment and for communicating it throughout the organisation.

- Conflict must be contained and channelled constructively to find new and better ways of achieving results. This process helps managers anticipate change and plan for it.

ACTIVITY 1

How can managers encourage innovation and entrepreneurial attitudes within their workforce?

Feedback to this activity is at the end of the chapter.

1.6   Skills and personality types

Organisations must possess the balance of skills needed to run a business successfully. They need the capability to manage their production and marketing systems as well as controlling the financial and personnel aspects properly. Indeed the way these different skills are linked together in the value chain is likely to be a source of competitive advantage and they have been referred to as the non-tradable assets of the organisation.

This is especially important for professional service organisations where a variety of different skills have to be blended together in circumstances where each professional group can be fiercely independent.

According to R W Belbin the success of a team, in terms of group morale, behaviour and performance, can depend significantly upon the balance of individual skills and personality types within the group. He originally suggested that there were eight main character types that a well-balanced group would contain, but extended this to nine quite recently. These types are:

- **Leader** – co-ordinating (not imposing) and operating through others

- **Shaper** – committed to the task, may be aggressive and challenging, will also always promote activity

- **Plant** – thoughtful and thought-provoking

- **Monitor-evaluator** – analytically criticises others' ideas, brings group down to earth

- **Resource-investigator** – not a new ideas person but tends to pick up others' ideas and adds to them; is usually a social type of person who often acts as a bridge to the outside world

- **Company worker** – turns general ideas into specifics; practical and efficient, tends to be an administrator handling the scheduling aspects

- **Team worker** – concerned with the relationships within the group, is supportive and tends to defuse potential conflict situations

- **Finisher** – unpopular, but a necessary individual; he is the progress chaser ensuring that timetables are met

- **Expert** – has technical information.

2 Analysis of operations resources

2.1 Resource use

One of the features of value chain analysis is the recognition that organisations are much more than a random collection of machines, money and people. These resources are of no value unless organised into routines and systems that ensure that products or services are produced which are valued by the final consumer or user.

According to Porter, it is the value activities and linkages between them, which are the source of competitive advantage for organisations. An analysis of resource use can be undertaken and linked to competitive advantage. The procedure is shown below.

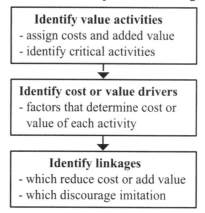

- **Identify the value activities -** this stage should include an assignment of costs and added value and an identification of the critical activities. These are the various value activities, which underpin the production and delivery of its products or services, including the supply and distribution chains. It is important for the organisation to identify the value activities that are critical in terms of its competitive advantage. For example, for one organisation the low price of its product to the consumer may be underpinned by a low cost supply of parts and a low mark-up by the distributor. By strengthening and building on the key activities the organisation is likely to achieve success.

- **Identify the cost or value drivers -** the factors, which sustain the competitive position, are called the cost drivers or value drivers. For example, in a manufacturing organisation raw materials depend upon two cost drivers - price, which in turn is a function of location and volume purchased; and the yield of finished product per unit of input of raw material. Direct production labour depends upon four cost drivers - the number of direct operatives in each plant, hourly wage rates; benefit rates (pensions, national insurance and similar employment costs) and volume of production per hour. In the example of a low cost supply, the factors may be related to physical proximity of the suppliers and could disappear with geographical expansion.

- **Identify the linkages -** competitive advantage is likely to be sustained by the linkages, which have been made between value activities and also within the wider value system of suppliers, channels or customers. It is the planning of these linkages, which can either provide distinctive cost advantages or become the basis on which the organisation's product/services are differentiated from other offerings. Whereas competitors can often imitate the separate activities of an organisation, it is more difficult to copy linkages within and between value chains

There may be important links between the primary activities. To recap, these are: inbound logistics, operations, outbound logistics, marketing and sales and services. Choices will have to be made about the relationships between the linkages and how they influence value creation and strategic capability. For example, good communications between sales, operations and purchasing can help cut stocks; the purchase of more expensive or more reliable machinery and equipment may lead to cost savings and quality improvements in the manufacturing process. Holding high levels of finished goods might ease production-scheduling problems and give a faster customer response time but will probably add to the overall cost of operations. An assessment as to whether the added value of high stocks is greater than the added cost needs to be made.

Linkages between the organisation's support activities may also create value. These activities, according to Porter, are the firm's infrastructure, human resource management, technological development and procurement. The extent to which human resource management has been involved in new technologies has brought about successful implementation of new production and office systems.

2.2 The production function

Production is a process whereby resources are profitably converted into saleable goods/services by various technical processes. Production management is generally associated with the manufacture of goods, and operations management covers all of this functional area.

Innovations in the production process can provide the basis of a competitive advantage. The problem often is to make them sustainable. The choices are:

- keep them secret by providing plant security and incentives for employees to stay

- keep improving them so that the competitors must match a moving target

- make capacity expansion decisions visible to discourage competitors.

The prime objective is to ensure that resources are utilised in the most effective way to meet customers' product quality and delivery requirements at an acceptable cost.

However, the new focus of operations management appears to be: resource utilisation to yield low costs of production, acceptable quality standards and a high level of customer satisfaction. To achieve this, companies need to use modern plant and equipment (probably including advanced manufacturing technologies), effective computerised production and cost-control systems (probably based on just-in-time (JIT), or manufacturing resource planning (MRP) or optimised production technology (OPT) systems), supported with detailed information systems based on budgetary control principles and a good industrial culture.

2.3 Availability of resources

The formulation of strategies for the acquisition of adequate resources is an essential part of management planning.

Finance and supplies are key operating resources and management must ensure that the right amount is available at the right time.

Financial resources mean long-term finance to finance growth and capital investment more particularly than short-term finance, the need for which is highlighted by the annual cash budget and which can probably be covered by a bank overdraft.

Capital investment may be described as any expenditure designed to yield returns over a (relatively long) period, e.g. the purchase of productive equipment.

The need for capital investment should become apparent from the company's corporate planning process.

Projects may be categorised as follows:

- Cost reduction – investment programmes that will result in cost savings as a result of more efficient or reliable machinery.

- Expansion – projects that expand existing capacity by new equipment and/or facilities.

- New products – introduction of new product lines.

- Plant renewal and replacement

- Welfare projects – e.g. new canteens, which yield no immediate tangible benefits.

- Statutory projects – e.g. safety equipment to comply with legislation.

Supplies, i.e. the availability of raw materials, bought-in components, etc, are of considerable importance to a manufacturing company because adequate material supplies are crucial to the company's operations and because materials typically form a high proportion of the total cost. An organisation's access to raw materials can provide a sustainable competitive advantage.

Supplies strategies have three components:

- acquisition of resources of the right quality in the right quantity at the right time and place at the right cost

- control of the efficient utilisation of resources (this is essentially an operating problem)

- conservation of resources – consideration must be given to re-cycling, substitution of less scarce materials, etc.

A company used to be able to decide on its product-market strategy and assume that adequate resources would be forthcoming. Now it must consider available raw materials as an essential part of strategy formulation. Its audit of strengths, weaknesses, opportunities and threats must highlight any 'resources gap'.

An analysis must be made of the number of sources, price, delivery times and possible threats, such as a supplier with a poor industrial relations record. If there is a gap in quantity or quality of resources, or the price or time at which they can be obtained, it will be necessary to:

- revise objectives or devise a new strategy to meet the objectives, diversifying if necessary

- improve efficiency in the utilisation of resources - reduce wastage, use recycled material, etc

- investigate the prospects of making the product from a new material (long lead times can be involved here)

- find new suppliers

- integrate backwards to become one's own supplier.

It is essential to retain flexibility in supplies strategies to be able to avoid delay in obtaining supplies, high prices, poor quality and drying up of supplies.

Specific supplies strategies that might be adopted include the following:

- Avoiding over-dependence on one supplier.

- Promoting competition among suppliers by wide tendering and by 'shopping around' for the best prices. However, it might not always pay to take the lowest price or to drive too hard a bargain - if suppliers have under-estimated their costs they might go out of business. In such circumstances, companies that have not retained flexibility often have to 'prop up' their suppliers in order to maintain key supplies.

- Promoting closer co-operation with one's suppliers, e.g. by paying premium prices in return for specific assurances.

- Taking advantage of quantity discounts while at the same time retaining flexibility. This would involve placing large orders with one supplier to obtain the discounts, but at the same time placing smaller orders with other suppliers to retain flexibility.

- Obtaining supplies from different parts of the world so that political instability or government regulations in one area will not affect the entire supply.

- Carrying large stocks – but not so large that there is a danger of obsolescence.

- Having contingency plans.

2.4   Management information and control systems

In general, information systems exist to support decision-making. A person must be aware of a problem, or a range of alternatives, before a decision can be taken. In finding and solving a problem the decision maker must gather information about it. The need for more and more information has led to the evolution of systems to process data quickly and efficiently.

DEFINITION

An **MIS** is a set of procedures designed to provide managers with appropriate information, from all relevant sources, to enable them to make decisions for planning and controlling the activities they are responsible for.

A management information system (MIS) has been defined as a set of formalised procedures designed to provide managers at all levels with appropriate information, from all relevant sources (internal and external), to enable them to make timely and effective decisions for planning and controlling the activities for which they are responsible.

Its scope is to provide good information to those who need it, but will depend on the nature and type of information required.

There are four categories of information that managers need:

1. Foundation information eg, cash flow and profitability, provides information for exception accounting.

2. Productivity information eg, benchmarking and measures of productivity being developed for knowledge and service based management.

3. Competence information eg, unexpected uses for products or services - giving the ability to do something that others cannot do or cannot do well.

4. Resource allocation information.

Most MIS will happily provide regular formal information eg, sales information about:

- success in certain markets

- payments information

- gross profit margins by product or service.

This means that they can be used at the operational and tactical level of management to process transactions, perform bank reconciliations, update files, produce exception reports, investigate and analyse data acquired at the operational level and produce a cash flow.

Unfortunately, they might be less efficient at presenting information that is relatively unpredictable, informal or unstructured eg, a new competitor in the market. This type of information is required at the strategic level. The issues at this level of management will be integrated with the organisation's commercial strategy, the market and the availability of long-term debt or equity funding. The inputs to this system would include plans, competitor information, general market information and other economic and political information. The outputs from it could include summaries of strategic plans, key ratios and ad hoc market analysis.

Strategic information is mainly used by directors and senior managers to plan the organisation's overall objectives and strategy and to measure whether these are being achieved. Examples of this information include:

- profitability of main business segments
- prospects for present and potential markets
- investment appraisal studies
- cash requirements
- availability and prospects for raising long term funds, etc.

Tactical information is used by managers at all levels, but mainly at the middle level for tactical planning and management control activities, such as pricing, purchasing, distribution and stocking. Examples include:

- sales analysis
- stock levels
- productivity measures
- current purchasing requirements
- budgetary control and variance reports
- labour turnover statistics, etc.

Operational information is used mainly by managers at the operational level who have to ensure that routine tasks are properly planned and controlled. Examples of this information include:

- listings of debtors and creditors
- payroll details
- raw materials requirements and usage
- listings of customer complaints
- machine output statistics
- delivery schedules, etc.

A management information system can provide the information to support all of these types of decision. A model is shown below:

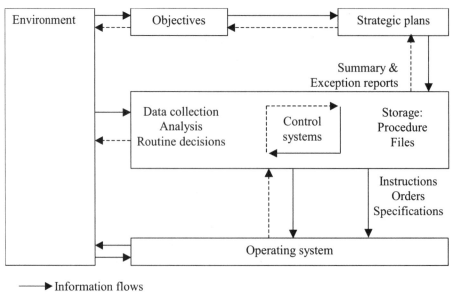

2.5 Control systems

Management considers both internal and environmental information in the process of establishing objectives at strategic level. Assumptions with regard to political conditions, competitors, customer needs and desires, internal capabilities and other factors form a frame of reference for strategic and comprehensive planning. Plans for the organisational activities are transmitted to the operating system and to storage in the control and co-ordination systems for later comparison with operating results. Detailed orders, instructions and specifications flow to the operating system.

Feedback is obtained on the output of the system in terms of quality, quantity and cost. The operating system is monitored to maintain process control, and input inspection provides feedback at the earliest stage in the operating system. Information flow is an integral part of the control system because it provides a means of comparing results with plans. Feedback data from various phases of the operating system are collected and analysed.

The analysis involves processing data, developing information and comparing the results with plans. Decisions are also made within the control system itself because routine adjustments can be pre-programmed in the set of procedures or instructions.

Within the control system there is a flow of information to implement changes to the program based on feedback from the operating system.

> **KEY POINT**
>
> Summary and exception reports are generated by the control system and become part of a process of review and evaluation.

Summary and exception reports are generated by the control system and become part of a higher level process of review and evaluation that may lead to an adjustment of goals. Subsequent planning activity reflects such feedback and the entire process is repeated.

2.6 Production planning and control

The production planning and control department is directly responsible for progress planning and control, the objectives of which are to minimise:

- excessive work in progress
- idle time
- broken delivery promises.

Production planning and control can pursue two alternative strategies. The first is to maximise the use of capacity, the second is to operate a 'just in time' system of customer flexibility.

> **KEY POINT**
>
> The objective of production planning and control is to produce plans and controls that will satisfy marketing demands as to quality, quantity and delivery as well as utilise resources available) in an economical manner.

The objective is to produce plans and controls that will satisfy marketing demands as to quality (quality control), quantity (stock control) and delivery (progress control) as well as utilise resources available (materials control) in an economical manner (cost control).

The effectiveness of this operation is constrained by the following:

- conflicting objectives within the organisation, e.g:
  - maximise use of capacity versus maintain reserve capacity
  - maintain constant output level versus being flexible
  - minimise finished stock levels versus minimise delivery time
- reliability of sales forecasts and other information
- efficiency of production departments
- availability of raw materials – depends on the reliability of suppliers as to quality and delivery and also on the existence of storage space within the organisation.

3 Analysis of financial resources

3.1 Financial control systems

An understanding of financial performance measures and ratios is essential for strategic management. It is a pre-requisite to:

- identify and state the current position of the entity.

- assessing the likely impact of proposed strategies and planned objectives upon entity survival and profitability

Almost every decision taken by management has a financial or accounting aspect. Accounting is a major information system and should provide information for three broad purposes:

- external reporting to investors, bankers, the government for taxation purposes and other interested outside parties

- internal reporting to managers for use in making non-routine decisions such as investment, product pricing, formulating overall policies and drawing up plans for the short and long term

- internal reporting to managers for use in the controlling and planning of routine operations.

The external parties and their interests include the following:

- shareholders – profitability; use of assets; capital structure; and investment

- potential shareholders – profitability; use of assets; and investment

- creditors – liquidity; and capital structure

- lenders – liquidity; capital structure; and profitability

- government (for taxation and statistical purposes) – profitability

- potential buyers of the business – use of assets; capital structure; and investment

- competitive firms – profitability; and use of assets.

Besides being a useful tool for assessing company performance, ratios and other financial indicators can be used: to summarise data; to show interrelationships between variables; to identify business problems before they become too serious; as the basis for decision making, and as the data upon which forecasting and planning are based. Ratios can indicate where things may be going well or badly and suggest where action needs to be taken by the company to improve performance. They can usefully indicate trends in a company's performance, but they do not in themselves tell the whole story about a company's activities.

Financial ratios are also used to compare and contrast the performance of one entity within an industry with that of another within the same industry. It is also possible to compare and contrast the performance of one firm with that of the whole industry, or a large sample or particular segment of that industry. However, these comparisons may suffer from one or more of the following limitations:

- Different accounting methods may be used by individual firms making up the industry sample, or by the firm being compared.

- The industry figures may be biased by one or a few very large firms within the sample.

- Conversely, an industry mean may be misleading for a small or large firm being compared with the mean. Ratios may vary for different sizes of firms.

- The companies within the industry sample may span across more than one industry classification.

- The industry figures may be relevant for a different financial period, and could possibly be out-of-date.

There is no exclusive or standard set of ratios and performance measures. A number of different relationships can be developed and measured, depending upon the information needs of management. For instance, personnel management measures are usually not included within the commonly recognised financial ratios (e.g. the percentage of lost time through industrial accidents and sick leave, etc. compared with total paid hours).

Other measures may include the percentage of export sales to total sales, or the percentage of reject parts to total parts produced, or the percentage of late deliveries to total deliveries. There is no constraint on the types of ratios that management may require for planning and control purposes.

The more common financial ratios may be grouped or categorised into liquidity, activity, debt/equity, coverage, profitability and other ratios. The relevance or significance of each ratio within each category will vary depending upon the financial structure of the firm and the nature of the industry. In particular, relevance will depend upon whether the entity:

- Produces and sell products.
- Purchases finished products for resale.
- Provides personal or professional services.
- Provides other services or infrastructure, such as a building or civil engineering project.

3.2 Investment-based analysis

All companies, public and private, have to decide (if they are profitable) whether to 'plough back' their profits into the business, or whether to distribute profits as dividends to ordinary shareholders.

'Earnings per share' is the amount of profit (or 'earnings') on a company's ordinary activities, after tax and all other charges, earned for each ordinary share.

$$EPS = \frac{\text{Net profit for shareholders}}{\text{number of shares issued}}$$

When a company declares the dividend it is paying to shareholders, the dividend is expressed as a percentage of the 'nominal' share value e.g. per £1 share. However, in the case of a public company whose current share price is quoted on the Stock Exchange, the 'nominal' value of a share is much less meaningful than the 'market price', i.e. the price at which the company's ordinary shares are traded 'second hand' on the stock market.

The dividend calculated as a percentage of the current share price is the 'dividend yield'.

$$\text{Dividend yield} = \frac{\text{Declared dividend per share} \times 100}{\text{Market price per share}}$$

By contrast with dividend yield, 'dividend cover' is a measure of a company's ability to maintain the level of dividend paid to shareholders. It is the number of times the available earnings (net profits) could pay the current dividend. The lower the dividend cover, the less likely it is that the company will be able to maintain the level of the dividend, so the less attractive it is to shareholders.

$$\text{Dividend cover} = \frac{\text{Post - tax profit available for distribution}}{\text{Dividend to be paid}}$$

These three financial indicators are all examples of 'shareholders' ratios'. These ratios enable a shareholder or financial analyst to make an assessment of the return on an

KEY POINT

'Earnings per share' is the amount of profit (or 'earnings') on a company's ordinary activities, after tax and all other charges, earned for each ordinary share.

investment. Another 'shareholders ratio' is the 'price/earnings ratio' (P/E ratio), for which the formula is:

$$\text{Price/Earnings Ratio} = \frac{\text{Market Price Per Share}}{\text{Earnings Per Share (post tax)}}$$

The P/E ratio provides a measure of the profitability of the share in terms of both earnings and capital value.

3.3 Capital structure

Bankers and other providers of interest-bearing loans need information on the risk attached to the loan. They will analyse the capital structure of the company:

- the amount of share capital

- its division into shares and the amount of each share

- the amount deemed to have been paid up for each share.

Liquidity ratios are designed to measure or predict the ability of an entity to meet its maturing financial obligations (liabilities due for payment) out of its 'current' or most liquid assets.

It is important to note that businesses do not fail in the short-term because they are unprofitable; they fail because they run out of cash (i.e. cash outflow commitments exceed cash inflows). Thus profitable businesses and growing businesses in particular, may fail through a liquidity crisis or poor cash management.

$$\text{Current ratio} = \frac{\text{Current assets}}{\text{Current liabilities}}$$

$$\text{Liquid ratio} = \frac{(\text{Current assets - Inventory})}{\text{Current liabilities}}$$

$$\text{Cash position ratio} = \frac{(\text{Cash + short - term investments})}{\text{Current liabilities}}$$

Although the above ratio measures are helpful and meaningful to prospective lenders and investors, they should also be supported by a detailed cash flow budget.

Lenders will also be looking at the gearing ratio and interest cover – relating interest payments to profit.

Gearing occurs when a business is financed, at least in part, by contributions from outside parties. The extent to which this happens (the level of gearing) is often an important factor in assessing risk. When a business borrows heavily it takes on a commitment to pay interest charges and make capital repayments. This can be a heavy financial burden and can increase the risk of the business becoming insolvent.

A highly geared company has greater risk of financial failure than a low geared company, because interest payable on loan funds must be met from the cashflows as and when the debt falls due. The firm has a legal obligation to meet interest payments and eventual payment of loan funds when they become due for payment, whereas a firm financed by equity capital is under no obligation to pay a dividend or to return capital to the equity holder.

Thus a highly geared company is more vulnerable in times of an economic or industry downturn affecting cashflows.

It follows that entities within declining or volatile industries, where cashflows are uneven or irregular, should gear conservatively.

- **Gearing ratio** – measures the contribution of long-term lenders to the long-term capital structure of a business:

$$\frac{\text{Long-term liabilities (creditors due beyond one year)}}{\text{Share capital} + \text{Reserves} + \text{Long term liabilities}}$$

- **Interest cover ratio** – measures the amount of profit available to cover interest payable:

$$\frac{\text{Profit before interest and taxation}}{\text{Interest payable}}$$

Because companies have only an incomplete knowledge of the future it is important that they retain flexibility, enabling them to react to any given situation. They should be in a position to benefit from any new breakthroughs and must insure against catastrophes. Internal flexibility is achieved by having sufficient liquid funds and reserve borrowing power in order to be able to react quickly in a new situation. It is measured by ratios such as the current ratio, acid test ratio, and debt to equity ratio (gearing). You will notice that there is a conflict between high flexibility requiring liquidity and reserve borrowing power (low gearing), and return to the shareholders, which is boosted by high gearing and which implies making use of all available funds (not having surplus liquid funds). Circumstances will dictate which is the most important consideration. The flexibility 'cushion' obviously has a cost in ROI terms.

Questions asked of the company regarding its capital structure might include the following.

- Is its capital structure appropriate or perhaps relevant to what it aspires to achieve?
- Has it sufficient funds?
- Is the gearing appropriate?
- Is it over dependent on leasing or fixed interest finance?
- Is leasing its only option if it wishes to move forward?

A family business may be growing very effectively, but relying on loans and fixed interest finance rather than going to the market. As a result, it becomes vulnerable to a predator. Equally, many of the recently privatised UK transport undertakings are relying heavily on debt and lease finance. Is that appropriate for long-term financial health and success?

3.4 Operational performance

Most businesses have two main objectives:

- to achieve, maintain and increase profits
- to generate sufficient funds to achieve profits, i.e. to maintain both liquidity and solvency.

Managers within the company will be using financial analyses to identify the organisation's operational position, which is a prerequisite to achieving the aspirations of other stakeholders over a period of time.

This might include an analysis of sales and profit involving sales mix, pricing strategy, discount facilities, and an assessment of the returns on total assets employed. Costs obviously have important implications for profitability and, therefore, determination of operational costs and internal efficiency is also required.

These ratios also enable a shareholder or financial analyst to make inter-firm comparisons of business performance and to evaluate a particular company's performance over a number of years. For example, a financial comparison between rival public limited companies would try to establish the following:

- which company has the better profits record (ROI, growth in profits and EPS)
- which company has the better financial structure (financial gearing, debt ratio, interest cover)
- which company has 'better quality' profits or better growth prospects (P/E ratio comparison)
- which company has a better cash flow position (judged perhaps by cash in the balance sheet and the cash flow statements of each).

However, there are three reasons why the comparison of profit earned by different businesses should be approached with great care:

- different status of owners and managers of the business
- different cost structures arising from owning different assets, e.g. one business may own its premises whilst another may rent
- different capital structures where a business financed by loans will incur a charge against profit for the interest.

4 The balanced scorecard

4.1 Financial and non-financial performance indicators

In recent years, the trend in performance measurement has been towards a broader view of performance, covering both financial and non-financial indicators. The term 'balanced scorecard' (BSC) is credited to Kaplan and Norton. It has become a tool for performance measurement in a number of significant businesses in the UK and North America.

The concept is based on the idea that no single measure can be used to control performance. Measures such as return on investment (ROI), net profit and earnings per share (EPS) are often criticised as being short-termist and ignoring vital factors that are significant in the long term purely because they cannot be measured by some objective basis such as money value. The balanced scorecard still includes the financial indicators, but it balances those with 'soft' measures such as customer acquisition, retention, profitability and satisfaction; product development cycle times; employee satisfaction; intellectual assets and organisational learning.

The measures should:

- cover all areas
- include all stakeholders
- be long term as well as short term
- be linked to strategy.

The rationale of the approach uses the analogy of flying an aircraft. In order to keep an aircraft safely airborne, the pilot uses a number of control devices such as rudder, airspeed measurement, visual checks and radar in order to avoid hazards such as mid-air collisions or losing ability to fly at all.

The balanced scorecard is an attempt to align behaviour in the business to actions that create shareholder value. It considers four main areas of concern to organisations - two external and two internal:

- financial perspectives
- customer perspectives
- internal processes
- learning/growth.

The two external perspectives focus on how well the organisation is doing when looked at from the financial – mainly shareholder – perspective and the customer point of view. The internal perspectives are concerned with current business processes and with how the organisation is developing itself for the future. The term 'balanced' is used because managerial performance is assessed under all four headings. Each organisation has to decide which performance measures to use under each heading.

The concept of the BSC can be illustrated in a diagram.

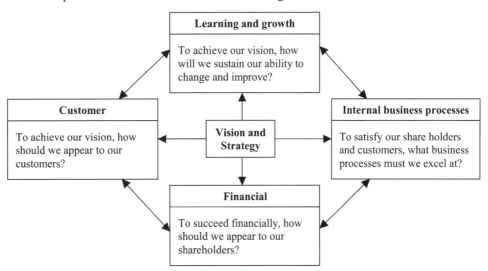

Each quadrant represents a feature of business performance.

The corporate vision of a business looks at features of performance dispassionately in order to establish indicators of performance that show that managers are meeting the expectations of shareholders, customers, employees and trading partners.

The financial perspective

The financial perspective concentrates on how the firm appears to its shareholders and considers what the firm's financial objectives are. The measures used to assess whether these objectives are being achieved highlight the observable financial results of past management actions and typically include, profit, sales, ROI, cash flow or economic value added (EVA).

The customer perspective

The customer perspective focuses on the question, what must the firm do to satisfy its customers so as to achieve its financial objectives? To answer this question, managers must initially identify the firm's target market and clarify its marketing objectives. The measures chosen for the customer perspective focus on the achievements of the firm in reaching and satisfying its target market.

The five elements of the customer perspective are:

1   **Market share** – this reflects the proportion of the business in a given market expressed in terms of customer, pounds spent or volume sold. The size of the market can easily be obtained from trade associations, government statistics or even something like Yellow Pages.

2   **Customer acquisition** – this measures, in either absolute or relative terms, the rate at which a business unit attracts or wins new customers or business. Ratios can be monitored, e.g. the ratio of conversion to initial solicitation. How many cold calls? How many interested responses? How many follow ups needed? Literature requests? Existing customers can also be targets for developing related business.

3   **Customer retention** – this measures in either absolute or relative terms the rate at which a business retains its customers. Where customers can be easily identified, customer retention can be measured both by the duration of their stay, and the growth of that business with individual customers.

4   **Customer satisfaction** – this purports to measure the satisfaction level of customers along specific performance criteria. Large businesses have difficulty with this particular measure. The difficulty lies in obtaining sufficient valid responses. The traditional methods of mail surveys, telephone interviews, and even personal interviews are expensive and have become a very lucrative and rapidly growing part of the market research industry. One simple measure for the small business might be recommendation. Where the business has a record of the client, the source of the client can be included. Thus a measure is achieved by identifying clients acquired by the recommendation of other clients. Repeat business is another simple measure of satisfaction. If the customer was satisfied once, he/she will frequently return.

5   **Customer profitability** – this measures the net contribution from a customer or a segment.

The internal business perspective

The internal business perspective considers the question, what must the firm do well internally in order to support the product/market strategy and to achieve its financial objectives? Typical outcome measures include those relating to innovation (product and process) and operations (cycle times, defect rates). As for the customer perspective, the outcome measures for the internal business perspective will require sub-division into driver measures which flow from the specific strategies the firm is adopting to achieve its internal business objectives. Measures will include cycle time, yield, efficiency, new product introduction scheduling and comparisons of manufacturing configuration with the competition. Other performance measurement will need an information system such as an executive information system that allows the manager to drill down into lower level information.

Learning and growth perspective

In the learning and growth (innovation) perspective, the measures focus on the question what infrastructure must the firm build to create long-term growth and improvement? In other words, what capabilities must be improved or acquired to achieve the long-term targets for the customer and internal business process perspectives?

Outcome measures may include metrics on employee satisfaction, training and retention. Typical measures of performance are:

- new money saving ideas

- registration of trade marks and/or patents

- reduction in waste or scrap by new processes

- reducing machine down time by re-engineering.

4.2   Linkages

All the measures are linked and must be viewed as a whole. For example, excess capacity can be a by-product of quality improvements. Increasing productivity may mean that fewer employees are required for a given level of output. Increasing sales may result in these improvements being exploited. The financial measurements remind management that improved quality, productivity and response time only benefits the organisation when it create a sustainable competitive advantage or is translated into improved financial results.

Customers are concerned with four main issues:

- Lead time - the time it takes from receipt of the order to delivery

- Performance of the product

- Quality - defect levels

- Service - what is the average time taken before the maintenance person comes?

To measure performance in these areas, the organisation will use market research methodologies to ascertain customer acquisition, retention, profitability and satisfaction.

Internal business - is linked to the customer perspective and identifies the processes that they must excel at ie, the ones that have the most impact on customer satisfaction eg, quality. To ensure continued success and competitive leadership, the organisation should attempt to identify and measure their distinctive competencies and the technologies required.

Measures will include cycle time, yield, efficiency, new product introduction scheduling and comparisons of manufacturing configuration with the competition. Other performance measurement will need an information system such as an executive information system that allows the manager to drill down into lower level information.

Innovation and learning - the organisation needs to learn and innovate to satisfy future needs. Measures of likely future success include:

- length of time to develop new products (compared to competition)
- percentage of revenue from new products
- investment in innovative products/materials and processes
- intellectual assets and organisational learning;
- employee satisfaction.
- process time to maturity

Financial - performance indicators show whether the organisation's strategies are effective. Cash flow indicates the likelihood of survival. Measures of monthly sales growth, market share and ROI give an indication of success.

4.3 How does the BSC work?

The idea behind the BSC is to arrive at a single score or number that is made up of a number of individual scores for each measure or key performance indicator. In order to smooth out or 'normalise' the process, each score is multiplied by a weight or constant in order to assign a degree of importance to the measure. This is not a novel concept and is used by people like internal auditors who try to measure relative risk. Like all such measures experience of the users and a consensus view on the relative importance of the various measures is critical to the process. It is unlikely that any organisation applying the BSC will get it right first time. It will be an adaptive process of learning before the technique is fully fledged. The most obvious problem is the difficulty of measuring qualitative criteria. A measure like ROI may be flawed but it can be measured from historic money value data. It is a 'hard' measure because it is measurable in quantitative terms. A measure like improving customer care is a 'soft measure' in that there is no objective formula that you can apply (unlike ROI). Consequently there must be a consensus view among the users on which measurers when taken together indicate that customer care has improved in the year 2005 over the year 2004.

4.4 Advantages of the balanced scorecard approach

The balanced scorecard approach to performance measurement offers several advantages:

- performance is measured in a variety of ways, rather than relying on one figure
- managers are unlikely to be able to distort the performance measure - bad performance is difficult to hide if multiple performance measures are used
- it takes a long-term perspective of business performance

- success in the four key areas should lead to the long-term success of the organisation

- it is flexible - what is measured can be changed over time to reflect changing priorities

- because managers know they are being appraised on various aspects of performance they will pay attention to these areas, rather than simply paying 'lip service' to them.

ACTIVITY 2

Many supporting quantitative measures of key aspects of organisation performance will be non-financial. Identify measures to assess the following:

- customer service

- customer satisfaction

- competitiveness

- product quality

- delivery/lead time

- resource utilisation

- employee satisfaction

- innovation.

Feedback to this activity is at the end of the chapter.

Conclusion

Resource analysis is an important means of assessing an organisation's strategic capability. It is a basis for making sensible choices of future strategy. The concept of the value chain is useful in understanding what the organisation is capable of since it concentrates on value activities and the linkages between activities – rather than resources in isolation. This underlines the fact that capability is strongly related to the way in which resources are used and controlled.

SELF-TEST QUESTIONS

Analysis of human resources

1   Name three competences associated with work quality. (1.2)

2   What are the three types of competence? (1.2)

3   What choices does the organisation have of obtaining capabilities that it does not currently possess? (1.5)

Analysis of operations resources

5   Give examples of strategic information. (2.4)

Analysis of financial resources

5   What is a P/E ratio? (3.2)

6   How is liquidity measured? (3.3)

The balanced scorecard

7   Identify the four perspectives outlined in the balanced scorecard. (4)

EXAM-TYPE QUESTION	**Balanced Scorecard** The Balanced Scorecard is organised into four perspectives - financial, customer, internal business process and finally learning and growth. Kaplan and Norton develop the Balanced Scorecard as means of combining financial control measures with non-financial measures. **Required:** Critically evaluate the usefulness of the Balanced Scorecard in assisting organisations, both profit-motivated and not-for-profit, to achieve improvements in their operational performance　　　　　　**(20 marks)** *For the answer to this question, see the 'Answers' section at the end of the book.*

To create the climate that will encourage and reward innovation, managers must do the following things.

- Set clear objectives and spell out the freedom to achieve them. Guiding beliefs will focus strategy and give creativity purpose and direction. Managers must be dynamic but also tolerant and must encourage commitment.

- Offer recognition and reward for creative behaviour and for tasks well done. For creative individuals the scope to think creatively and to achieve results may, to some extent, be its own reward.

- Encourage new ideas and be willing to listen to subordinates' suggestions. Managers must make it clear that they welcome ideas for improving things and making changes. Employees must be allowed to participate in making decisions to change things that will affect them.

- Permit more interaction between employees within their own work group and between work groups. The creation of a more permissive climate encourages ideas and information to flow and new perspectives on problems and opportunities to be developed.

- Accept and allow for failure. Some ideas may prove impracticable and lead to lost time and resources but this must not be allowed to stifle creativity.

To be entrepreneurial is to take risks and show initiative in an attempt to make profits. Managers must encourage certain attitudes and build up certain abilities. The main drive that motivates the entrepreneurial person is a high need for achievement. The manager must therefore promote and encourage the following attitudes and motivations:

- the desire for responsibility and accountability for results

- the willingness to take moderate risks in an attempt to achieve high performance

- self confidence and the willingness to make judgements

- future orientation to search for and anticipate future opportunities and plan for their successful exploitation

- the willingness to organise work and obtain resources to achieve goals. Entrepreneurs want to get the job done efficiently.

FEEDBACK TO
ACTIVITY **2**

Measures for assessment include the following:

- customer service (e.g. complaint response time)

- customer satisfaction (e.g. number of customer complaints; complaints per customer; complaints per £ of sales)

- competitiveness (e.g. market share; customer base; % sales growth)

- product quality (e.g. number of customer complaints; number of product rejects; % rejects; customer returns as % of total sales)

- delivery/lead time (e.g. number of deliveries on time; % of deliveries on time) – applied to purchases as well as to sales

- resource utilisation (e.g. m/c hours worked as % of capacity; m/c downtime as % of m/c hours worked)

- employee satisfaction (e.g. labour turnover)

- innovation (e.g. length of product development cycle; % of total sales from new products).

Chapter 10

DETERMINANTS OF STRATEGIC DIRECTION

This chapter looks at the how the cultural and political situation of an organisation can be analysed and understood as part of the strategic analysis. All enterprises must consider carefully the elements that comprise their environment. Another method or model for understanding the relationship between an organisation and its environment is to consider the various groups, both internal and external, that can affect or be affected by the accomplishment of its objectives. Each of these groups has a 'stake' in the survival of an enterprise. Assessing the expectations of stakeholders enables an organisation to gauge whether its objectives will provide the means to satisfy the demands of its various stakeholders.

In theory, an organisation's mission - why it exists in society at all - is the guiding idea behind the organisation's activities. Goals and objectives are devised to fulfil the mission. The terms are often used interchangeably: if there is a difference, objectives are more likely to be quantified, and so progress towards them is more measurable. Goals and objectives can also be said to interpret the organisation's mission to a number of different client groups or stakeholders, who all have an interest in what the organisation does.

Objectives

When you have studied this chapter you should be able to:

- identify national and local culture
- understand organisational culture and objectives
- understand stakeholder power and influence
- carry out stakeholder mapping: Mendelow

1   The cultural context

1.1   Strategic analysis

A strategic analysis can help provide an understanding of the factors and processes that drive the strategy of an organisation. This can be achieved by firstly analysing the way in which culture drives organisational strategies. Secondly by systematically analysing the political processes that shape strategy.

The diagram below outlines the framework for strategic analysis:

- The cultural context reflects the beliefs of people both inside and around the organisation that are taken for granted.

- The stakeholder expectations can be assessed to show how they can influence the purposes of the organisation.

- The purpose of the organisation is often expressed through the mission statement or the objectives. Objectives tend to emerge as the wishes of the most dominant stakeholder. However, in pursuing these objectives the members of the dominant group are influenced by the political situation and are likely to set aside some of their expectations to improve the chance of achieving others.

1.2   National and local culture

In management literature definitions of culture refer to:

- national or ethnic grouping, including summations of characteristics with reference to distinctive (culture-specific) management style or negotiating style

- the special qualities of an organisation (corporate culture)

- mental attributes (as in Hofstede's, 1980 definition): Culture is the collective programming of the mind which distinguishes the members of one human group from another

Attitudes to work, authority, equality and a number of other important issues are constantly shaped and changed by society. From the point of view of organisational strategy, it is important to appreciate this process for two reasons:

- values of society change and adjust over time so that policies that were acceptable twenty years ago may not be so today. There has been an increasing trend within many countries for the activities of companies to be constrained by legislation, public opinion and the media.

- companies that operate internationally have the added problem of coping with the very different standards and expectations of the various countries in which they operate.

There have been a number of research studies into how national culture influences employee motivation, management styles and organisational structures. The conclusions are that individual countries are markedly different from each other. For example, British culture appears to be far more tolerant of uncertainty than many other societies - notable European examples being France, Spain and Germany.

This research is as a reminder that the way in which organisations analyse and respond to their environment is strongly tied up with national culture, which is a key frame of reference for managers.

Schneider drew up a checklist, shown below, to assess the influence of national culture on the strategic management process.

Strategic issues	Alternative approaches to management issues
Relationships with environment Coping with uncertainty	• avoid or tolerate? • reduce or accept?
Influencing the environment	• manage or adapt? • behave proactively or reactively? • prefer action or fatalism?
Assessing truth/reality	• analyse facts or theoretical logic? • assess inductively or deductively?
Attitude to time/change	• relate to past or future? • prefer continuous or step change?
Internal relationships Power and status	• use hierarchy or networks?
Individualism	• respect individuals or groups?
Social orientation	• emphasise tasks or social needs

Although it is difficult and perhaps dangerous to stereotype nations against the checklist, two extreme stereotypes can be identified:

- A culture where uncertainty is managed by attempting to reduce it; when organisations are seen as having control and being proactive; and where the hierarchy, the individual and the work tasks are stressed. Here strategies are likely to be *planned*. US culture comes close to this stereotype.

- In contrast, the *adaptive* model of strategic management is more likely to be found in cultures where uncertainty is accepted as given; where the organisation has less control and is reactive; and where the orientation is towards the group and social concerns. Japanese culture is close to this stereotype.

1.3   Organisational culture

Deshpandé and Webster (1989) defined organisational culture as a 'pattern of shared values and beliefs that help individuals understand organisational functioning and thus provide them with the norms for behaviour in the organisation'. The elements of organisational culture range from fundamental assumptions through values and behavioural norms to actual patterns of behaviour. Values typically act as the defining elements of a culture, and norms, symbols, rituals, and other cultural activities revolve around them. When the members of a social unit share values, an organisational culture or value system can be said to exist.

Characterising an organisation's culture in terms of its central values means identifying the range of relevant values and then assessing how strongly held and widely shared they are. The Organisational Culture Profile (OCP) identifies seven dimensions of organisational culture:

- innovation
- stability
- respect for people
- outcome orientation
- detail orientation
- team orientation
- aggressiveness

Although several studies have focused on identifying the value dimensions that characterise an organisation's culture, only a few have investigated the extent to which an organisation's values affect actual outcomes. Concentrating on only Japanese firms, Deshpandé and colleagues (1993) found that higher levels of business performance were most closely associated with a market culture ie, one that emphasises the values of competitive aggressiveness and outcome orientation, and an adhocracy culture (one that emphasises the values of flexibility and innovation).

1.4 National culture

The fact that the West and East - and more specifically, the United States and Japan - have vastly different cultural values is well acknowledged.

- The U.S. is characterised by such values as assertiveness, decisiveness, innovativeness, and risk-taking, which stem from its frontier-conquering history (Hall and Hall, 1990).

  The U.S. culture is also characterised by individualism - the belief in the power and autonomy of the individual, emphasis on results and lack of flexibility. For instance, Easterners, particularly the Japanese, complain that Americans are too legalistic and less willing to be flexible.

- Alternatively, Shinto, Buddhism, and Confucianism have heavily influenced the cultural value system in Japan. As a result, the Japanese tend to emphasise the virtues of hard work and attention to detail. Indeed, a detail orientation is a major factor that has attributed to the successes of prominent Japanese firms.

  Further, Japan has a consensus-bonded, group-oriented culture that emphasises conflict avoidance, respect and concern for people, and the importance of close, long-lasting relationships with others. The culture focuses individual and corporate success criteria on harmony, uniformity, and subordination to the group (Hall and Hall, 1990). Thus, it is particularly important for Japanese employees to feel that they 'fit in'. Employees tend to identify with their firms, resulting in a relatively high level of company loyalty.

It is known that cultures provide consumers with an understanding of acceptable behaviour within their respective societies. Further, culture influences work practices and has a profound impact on the way consumers perceive the organisations from which they purchase. Past research shows that national culture is not something apart from business, but determines its very essence. A study that surveyed over a thousand managers from U.S. and Japanese firms showed that corporate values reflect those of the national culture and these cultural differences lead to specific behaviour within organisations, which is different for Japan and U.S. firms. For instance, as compared to Japan, the U.S. culture, which is high on individualism, predisposed the U.S. companies to use more communication and co-ordination and resort to short-term performance evaluations. While in Japan, a people orientation and an emphasis on harmony and tolerance have led to humanistic management practices, worker loyalty, a non-competitive workforce, lifetime employment, and slow evaluation and promotion.

The pervasive effects of national culture have important implications. For instance, the values that characterise organisations are likely to parallel those of the national culture in which the organisation operates. Hence, Japanese firms, as compared to U.S. firms, are more likely to have cultures characterised by flexibility and people and detail orientation. Possibly, these cultural factors are the driving force behind the success of Japanese firms. That is, Japanese firms may rely heavily on the virtues of flexibility, people orientation, detail orientation, and team orientation to achieve greater business performance and customer satisfaction. And relative to Japanese firms, U.S. firms are more likely to have cultures characterised by innovation, outcome orientation, and aggressiveness.

- The relationships between the cultural values of flexibility, people orientation, detail orientation, and team orientation and outcomes (customer satisfaction and business performance) will be greater for Japanese than for U.S. firms.

- The relationships between the cultural values of innovation, outcome orientation, and aggressiveness and outcomes (customer satisfaction and business performance) will be greater for U.S. than for Japanese firms.

It is expected that organisations whose cultures match those of their home country will experience lower outcome levels when they operate in other countries with vastly different cultural orientations. This is because the consumers in other countries with cultural orientations different from those of the organisation may not completely understand and assimilate the operational procedures of the foreign subsidiaries, creating somewhat weaker impression about the firms from other countries. Thus, the cultural mismatch may lead to lower customer satisfaction and business performance. For instance, U.S. subsidiaries whose cultures reflect those of the U.S. will experience lower outcome levels when they operate in Japan than when they operate in the U.S.

Organisations whose cultures match those of their home country will exhibit lower levels of outcomes (customer satisfaction and business performance) when they operate in other countries with different cultural orientations.

1.5 Industry characteristics and organisational culture

Past research has shown that technology relates to organisational types and outcomes and that growth rate partially determines business strategy.

Technology - since culture defines how things are done within organisations, technology restricts the variation in how things are done by defining what is being done. Therefore, greater similarities in technology across firms in the same industry should be associated with less variation in their cultures.

The values that characterise firms are likely to vary across industries. Organisations in industries characterised by intensive technologies should have cultures depicted by high levels of innovation, since projects require non-routine problem solving. Because of an intense, hard-driving work pace and a lack of predictability, these organisations tend to place a greater emphasis on human resource issues. Intensive technology firms are likely to have a strong team orientation, since ill-structured tasks are more likely to require that members collaborate to solve problems.

On the other hand, firms with long-linked technologies are likely to have high levels of stability, because tasks are repetitive and predictable. These firms have a strong detail orientation, since only refinements to processes are needed. They tend to rely on formal control mechanisms, such as policies and procedures, to direct members' efforts. A relatively high level of job structure also characterises these organisations.

Therefore, we can expect that firms in industries with intensive technologies will have cultures that more strongly emphasise innovation, flexibility, people orientation, team orientation, and aggressiveness than firms in industries with long-linked technologies.

Similarly, firms in industries with long-linked technologies are likely to have cultures that more strongly emphasise outcome and detail orientations than firms in industries with intensive technologies.

Growth - past research has shown that technology and growth rate move together and that growth in industries is linked to technological development. Indeed, technological progress driven by a desire to reduce uncertainty often fosters growth. New technologies and improved methods are commonly incorporated because they are related to an industry's type of work, and adoption of these advances often increases production capacity. Hence, industry growth is likely to relate to organisational culture.

It seems reasonable to expect that the relationship between organisational culture and outcomes will depend on the type of technology governing and the level of growth experienced by the firm in question. That is, business outcomes are likely to be higher in those firms whose cultural values are consistent with those of particular industry technology-type and growth-level characteristics. Specifically,

- The relationships between the cultural dimensions of innovation, flexibility, people orientation, team orientation, and aggressiveness and outcomes (customer satisfaction and business performance) will be greater in firms characterised by intensive technologies and high growth.

- The relationships between the cultural dimensions of outcome orientation and detail orientation and outcomes (customer satisfaction and business performance) will be greater in firms characterised by long-linked technologies and low growth.

It is convincingly argued that, even within a framework of global strategy, there is a need for multinational organisations to attempt to understand the culture of the host country and to localise their competitive strategies on the basis of national characteristics. There is a significant relationship between cultural awareness, strategic planning and performance among organisations operating within three different national cultures. Given the multi-level approach of competitive strategic analysis, perhaps the ideal solution is to develop a theoretical perspective, which synthesises organisational, global and national views.

2 Stakeholder expectations

2.1 Introduction

Each stakeholder will have a link of dependency to the organisation. Each will make demands on, and have expectations of, the organisation. These expectations may clash and conflict with the interest of other stakeholder groups. For instance, the rate of growth expectations of the managers of a family owned company might conflict with those of the family shareholders whose main interest may be in maintaining family control.

There will be occasions where the objective specified by the organisation is a formal statement of stakeholder expectations, for example:

- Return on capital employed expressing shareholders' expectations;

- Pledges on non-pollution of environment expressing society's expectations.

Clearly, some stakeholder groups wield greater power than others. The government's legislative power is comprehensive, and rulings of the Competition Commission have a direct effect upon the objectives and strategies of companies affected. Examples are:

- breweries, where Bass was required to sell off a major part of its tied public houses;

- newspaper publishing, where Rupert Murdoch was blocked from taking over other newspapers on the grounds of safeguarding freedom of opinion across a range of views.

Stakeholder analysis involves 'identifying and prioritising key stakeholders, assessing their needs, collecting ideas from them, and integrating this knowledge into strategic management processes'.

2.2 Identifying stakeholders

Cyert and March suggest that the goals of an organisation are a compromise between the members of the coalition comprising the parties affected. If the strategy is not acceptable to powerful groups from any of the stakeholder categories, it may fail. Managers have to balance a number of values, beliefs and assumptions in attempting to navigate a strategy to a successful conclusion. The ability to be able to identify stakeholders and discern stakeholder values, beliefs, assumptions and expectations is a positive tool in the managers 'competence toolbox', not least because they often conflict and may not always be benevolent to the strategy.

Stakeholders exist at the level of the individual, groups and organisations and can be internal or external to the strategic process Stakeholders might exist in the form of sponsors, banks providing capital, suppliers and contract organisations, the client organisation, analysis and design groups and the individuals involved. All are embedded in some form of organisational culture that will fuel and/or influence the individual.

One of the problems in analysing stakeholders is that they tend to belong to more than one group and will line up in different groupings depending on the issue in hand eg, marketing and production departments could be united in the face of dropping certain products while being in fierce opposition regarding plans to buy in new items to the product range.

It is often specific events that will trigger off the formation of stakeholder groups. Management should speculate on the degree of unity or diversity between the different groups if faced with a number of possible future events. This will help uncover potential alliances or rifts that may be significant when thinking about future strategic choices.

2.3 Stakeholder power

Power is the mechanism by which expectations are able to influence strategies. In most organisations, power will be unequally shared between the various stakeholders. Stakeholder power is more elusive than stakeholder interest because it is exercised in subtle, invisible ways.

Sources of power include the following:

- **Hierarchy** - provides people or groups with formal power over others and is one method by which senior managers influence strategy. Central and local government agencies and regulators enjoy statutory authority.
- **Influence** - may arise from personal qualities (leadership) or because a high level of consensus exists within the organisation ie, people are willing to support the prevailing viewpoint. An important task of management is to shape the culture of the organisation to suit its strategy because those individuals most closely associated with the core beliefs are likely to accrue power eg, doctors in the health service have considerable power through their influence on others.
- **Control of strategic resources** - the relative importance of different resources will change over time eg, the power of organised labour is most potent when demand for output is high and labour supply short. R&D departments may be powerful in organisations developing new products or processes and the marketing department may dominate an organisation, which is primarily concerned with developing new markets. Stakeholders that can withdraw their resources have an advantage eg, suppliers, financiers and bankers.

- **Knowledge and skills** - is an extension of the previous point. Certain people may be viewed as irreplaceable by the organisation and some will jealously guard this privilege by creating a mystique around their positions.

- **Control of the environment** - knowledge, contact and influence where the environment is concerned can be a source of power for some groups since they are able to reduce the uncertainty experienced by others. It is probably for this reason that financial and marketing managers have traditionally been seen as dominant in strategy determination.

- **Ability to exercise discretion** - many people in an organisation will need to interpret and execute particular parts of the strategy and in doing so will use their own personal discretion in the successful adoption and implementation of the strategy.

2.4 Assessing power

There are four indicators of power that can be used when analysing and assessing the internal sources of power:

- Status - the position in the hierarchy, the individual's job grade or salary or the reputation that a group or individual holds with others will be relevant in the assessment.

- The claim on resources - can be measured by the size of the department's budget or the number of people involved in that group. Assessments can be made with comparable groups in similar organisations.

- Representation in powerful positions - in hierarchical organisations representation on the board of directors can indicate the relative importance eg, the weakness of the production function may result from the lack of representation either at board level or in important committees.

- Symbols of power - may be indicated by the size and location of people's offices and whether they have newspapers delivered daily. In more bureaucratic organisations the existence of distribution lists for internal memos and other information may also provide pointers as to who is viewed as important within the organisation.

No single indicator is going to uncover the structure of power but by looking at all four indicators shown, it may be possible to identify which people or groups appear to have power.

There are also four indicators of power that can be used when analysing the external stakeholders

- Status - the power of an external stakeholder such as a supplier can be indicated by the way they are discussed among employees and whether members of the organisation respond quickly to the supplier's demands

- Resource dependence - can be measured directly eg, by the proportion of an organisation's business tied up with any one customer or supplier. A key indicator is the ease with which the supplier, customer or financier could be switched at short notice.

- Negotiating arrangements - are another indicator eg, whether external parties are kept at arm's length or are actively involved in negotiations with the company. A customer that is invited to negotiate over the price of a contract is in a more powerful position than one that is given a fixed price on a take it or leave it basis.

- Symbols - may be indicated by the actions of the management team in wining and dining some customers or suppliers and not others. The care and attention paid to correspondence with outsiders will tend to differ from one party to another depending on the power held.

Again no single measure will give a full understanding but a combined analysis will be useful to gain a full understanding of the extent of the power held by external groups.

2.5   Stakeholder influence

Once stakeholders are identified they can be mapped in relation to:

- The likelihood of each stakeholder group attempting to impress their expectations on others

- The power and means available for them to do so

- The impact of stakeholder expectations on the strategy

Mapping out the various expectations within an organisation and where they conflict contributes significantly to an understanding of the core beliefs in the organisation and its strategic position. Together with an assessment of power structure, management can assess future strategies in relation to their cultural fit and how easy or difficult change is likely to be.

Two matrices can be developed from this analysis that aid the manager in understanding the threat and management approach to key stakeholders (following Mendelow, 1991). These are shown below. The first one maps stakeholder power against predictability and shows where political efforts are best channelled during the strategy development. The second one maps stakeholder power against interest in the strategy to understand the best way to manage expectations.

	Predictability			**Level of interest**	
	High	Low		High	Low
Low	Few problems	Unpredictable but manageable	**Low**	Minimal effort	Keep informed
Power			**Power**		
High	Powerful but predictable	Greatest danger or opportunity	**High**	Keep satisfied	Key players
	(a) Power/Dynamism			(b) Power/Interest	

Power/dynamism matrix - this is a useful way of assessing where the political efforts should be channelled during the development of new strategies. The most difficult group to manage are those with high power and low predictability since they are in a position to block or support new strategies but it is difficult to predict where they stand. New strategies must be tested on these stakeholders before an irrevocable position has been established. In contrast, the powerful but predictable stakeholders are likely to influence strategy through the process of managers anticipating their stand and building strategies that will address their expectations. Stakeholders in the other two segments cannot be ignored because their active support may, in itself, have an influence on the attitude of the more powerful stakeholders.

Power/interest matrix - this classifies stakeholders in relation to the power they hold and the extent to which they are likely to show an interest in the organisation's strategies. The key players must be considered during the formulation and evaluation of new strategies. Although the other stakeholders might be relatively passive, managers must be aware that stakeholder groups tend to emerge and influence strategy as a result of specific events. It is very important that the likely reaction of stakeholders towards future strategies is given full consideration. A disastrous situation could occur if their level of interest is underrated and they suddenly become key players and frustrate the adoption of an intended strategy. Where stakeholders have low power and interest, they need to be kept informed because they can be important allies in influencing the attitudes of more powerful stakeholders.

2.6 Strategies and mapping

Using the power/interest matrix, Scholes suggests the following strategies to deal with the four quadrants:

- Low interest/low stakeholder power - **Direction** - their lack of interest and power makes them malleable. They are most likely to accept what they are told and follow instructions.

- High interest/low stakeholder power - **Education/Communication** - this stakeholder group may lobby others to support the strategy. If the strategy is presented in a logical way and shown to be rational, this may stop them joining forces with more powerful dissenters.

- Low interest/high stakeholder power - **Intervention** - the key is to keep these stakeholders satisfied to avoid them gaining interest. Reassuring them of the likely outcomes of the strategy well in advance usually does this.

- High interest/high stakeholder power - **Participation** - these stakeholders can be major drivers of change and also major opponents of the strategy. Initially there should be communication to assure them that the change is necessary followed by discussions on the implementation of the strategy and how it affects them.

For example, consider three different types of organisation that are investigating the same strategy of bringing down costs by reducing wages and making employees work more flexible shifts.

- *Contract cleaning company* - the main employees affected will be the cleaners themselves. Since unskilled workers are relatively easy to replace, they have high interest in this decision but low power. The organisation will therefore keep the cleaners informed of the decision but will probably impose the decision on the workforce. This imposition is likely to be enacted quickly, ie the strategy will take place almost immediately.

- *Accountancy training company* - the main employees affected will be the lecturers. Since these lecturers are very difficult to replace, they have high interest in the decision and high power. The organisation will need to bear in mind the feelings of the lecturers and may decide that this strategy will not succeed.

- *Local public library service* - the main employees affected will be the library staff. Although these employees may be easy to replace, they are likely to be heavily unionised. The power of the union will affect the decision-making process. The organisation may decide to consult with the union before any final decisions are made. Owing to the lengthy procedures that often exist within the public sector, it is likely that any change in working conditions will be subject to a number of reviews, and implementation will not be rapid.

In the private sector the shareholders are usually the key stakeholders. In the public sector the different groups of stakeholders should be mapped to identify who are likely to be the key stakeholders and what outcomes they want from any particular strategy. Any strategy chosen will need to be accepted by these key stakeholder groups.

Abrams emphasises the importance to an organisation of maintaining 'an equitable and working balance among the claims of the various directly interested groups'. Senior management may seek to achieve a balance. However, a dominant stakeholder group can impose its demands at the expense of others. A typical example would occur when an organisation over-expands and its gearing ratio dictates that capital restructuring is necessary for survival. In these circumstances, the company's bankers will assume a dominant role and dictate the terms of the company's future with token regard to the interest of shareholders and employees.

Bryson suggests that in formulating strategy it is important to consider how stakeholder groups might react in the implementation stage. He constructs the following 'Mendelow' matrix to interpret stakeholder positioning.

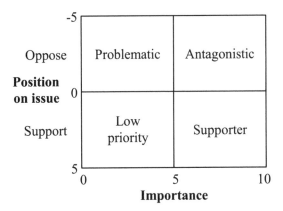

Those responsible for the 'drawing up' of strategy must consider how to encourage coalitions of the most important and supportive stakeholder groups and develop mechanisms to encourage 'low priority groups' to be more involved. For those more problematic and antagonistic groups, the priority is to defend the strategy, possibly by redefining it, and communicate the purpose of the strategy.

Senior managers are the servants of stakeholders. They must identify the most important groups and create strategies that meet their ends. They must establish the purpose of the organisation by reflecting principal stakeholder needs and desires. They can do this through mission. But mission also requires the support of employees, for they have to implement strategy. Thus, their importance must not be overlooked.

2.7 Completing the matrix

The matrix is normally completed with regard to the stakeholder impact of a particular strategy. The purpose is to assess:

1   whether stakeholder resistance is likely to inhibit the success of the strategy

2   what policies may ease the acceptance of the strategy.

Completing the matrix is a two-step process:

1   Place the stakeholder in the appropriate quadrant of the matrix

Some stakeholders may contain sub groups with different degrees of interest or power. For example in a branch closure the skilled and unionised workers will have greater power and interest than the casual or temporary staff, who may not be unionised

2   Assess their attitude to the strategy

a + is used to indicate that the group will support the strategy

a – is used to indicate that the group will oppose the strategy

Consider the example of the branch closure mentioned earlier:

Level of interest

	Low	High
Low	**A** Casual unskilled (–) General public (–) Small shareholders (+)	**B** Small local suppliers (–) Local council (–) Non unionised labour (–) Local press and media (–/+)
High	**C** Central government (–) National media (–) Customers (–/+) Minor fund managers (–/+)	**D** Skilled unionised labour (–) Key managers (–) National suppliers (–) Major fund managers (–/+)

Power is indicated along the left (Low at top, High at bottom).

Strategies to deal with stakeholders

Having established the make up of the matrix relating to a given decision as it is at present, the next stage is to establish what the matrix will need to show if the decision is going to be successful.

In the example above the key concerns where alignment is poor are:

- the negative attitudes of skilled labour, key managers and national suppliers
- the ambivalent attitude of shareholders and customers
- the potentially negative interventions of national media and central government
- the possible search for power from local council and media.

Scholes (1998) suggests the following *strategies* to deal with each quadrant:

Box A *Direction* - Their lack of interest and power makes them open to influence. They are more likely than others to accept what they are told and follow instructions.

Management should not reappoint the casual staff but rather provide limited redundancy support. There is no need to tell the small shareholders or customers.

Box B *Education/Communication* - The positively disposed groups from this quadrant may lobby others to support the strategy. Also if the strategy is presented as rational or inevitable to the dissenters, or a show of consultation gone through, this may stop them joining forces with more powerful dissenters in C and D.

Management should brief all groups here on the reasonableness of the case for closure and of the provisions being made for the redundant staff. Advance notice will give each more time for adjustment.

Box C *Intervention* - The key here is to keep the occupants satisfied to avoid them gaining interest and shifting into D. Usually this is done by reassuring them of the likely outcomes of the strategy well in advance.

Managers should assure the government and suppliers that the closure will result in a more competitive firm that is able to compete worldwide. A similar message may reassure investors if it is backed up with a reassuring short-term dividend forecast.

Box D *Participation* - These stakeholders can be major drivers of the change and major opponents of the strategy. Initially there should be education/communication to assure them that the change is necessary followed by discussion of how to implement it.

Managers should involve the unions in determining the redundancy package or redundancy policy. Key managers should be involved in deciding the basis on which early retirements should be handled and how redeployment or outplacement should be managed. Key shareholders will be consulted throughout to reassure them that costs will not be excessive.

2.8 Stakeholder management

The concept of *stakeholder management* refers to a method for systematically taking stakeholder interests into account. It is defined as 'communicating, negotiating, contracting and managing relationships with stakeholders and motivating them to behave in ways that are beneficial to the organisation and its other stakeholders'. Not all organisations manage their stakeholders to the same extent -- stakeholder management capability may reside at one of three levels, indicating increased sophistication:

- Level 1 - the *rational* level - entails identifying the stakeholders and their stakes. This is the level of stakeholder maps where management seeks to become familiar with their stakeholders.

- At Level 2 - the *process* level - organisations actually develop and implement processes to scan the environment and receive information about stakeholders to be used for decision-making. Typical approaches might include strategic review, environmental scanning and issues management. At this level a consideration for stakeholders is integrated into decision making.

- Level 3 - the *transactional* level - is the bottom line for stakeholder management – the extent to which managers actually engage in transactions (relationships) with stakeholders, take the initiative to meet them face to face and attempt to be responsive to their needs. This *communication* level is characterised by communication pro-activeness, interactiveness, genuineness, satisfaction and resource adequacy (i.e. management spending resources on stakeholder transactions).

3 Organisational purpose

3.1 Introduction

The discussion so far has been concerned with understanding how the cultural context of an organisation influences the expectations of individuals and stakeholders. In turn, these expectations influence the purposes of the organisation, as a result of the power that the group possesses. The purposes tend to be formulated by those that have the most power.

An essential requirement for a meaningful strategic plan is the establishment of a set of goals and objectives for the organisation. The process of developing these can be shown as a progression or hierarchy of aims or purposes.

- A strategic vision is based on a forward-looking, long-term perspective. A strategic vision can take many forms. Mercedes were guided by a vision of being the best in their field in terms of delivering quality products and services. Weight Watchers had a vision of building and exploiting its unique associations of dietary weight control and nutrition to gain a presence throughout the supermarket.

- Mission statements - should outline the specific role that the organisation plans to fulfil within society over the long term and therefore limits the scope of its operations by implicitly excluding areas outside its stated mission. An example is the mission statement of Federal Express 'Absolutely, Positively, Overnight'. This sets out to the customer how importantly it takes the business of delivering packages. It also focuses staff on making the delivery of packages their top priority.

- Goals - generally apply to shorter time frames than the more general mission statement but they are still non-specific and not quantified. They should interpret the mission statement into more understandable statements for the different groups of stakeholders, so that internal conflicts between stakeholders are minimised. Separate goals may be developed for customers, suppliers, employees and shareholders.

- Long-term objectives - might be exemplified by such aims as 'to remain a biscuit manufacturer' or 'to provide a productive and satisfying work environment for employees'. These are very often objectives without a time limit ('open' objectives) and expressed in qualitative rather than quantitative terms. Statements of this nature are also frequently designated strategies rather than objectives. But a basic objective may be quantitative, for example 'to increase shareholders' earnings by 5% per annum'.

- Detailed objectives - convert the basic objectives into general action plans capable of being interpreted in quantitative terms and given a limited time scale. These are the key result areas in which performance is essential for the success of the enterprise. Examples might be 'to increase our market share for product A to 20% within three years' or 'to market our new executive car during year 2'. Objectives of this nature may emerge either from fundamental analysis of the company's problems or at the time of selecting strategies for achieving the basic policies.

- Budget objectives - set targets for achievement in a budget period within the framework of the basic and detailed long-term objectives

- Departmental action plans - include objectives for short-term achievement by various functional managers.

- Individual objectives - include performance and personal development objectives.

3.2 Strategic vision

Vision Statements are seen as documents that set out the strategic intentions of the organisation. They are about 'animating the dream'. These statements offer aspirations about the future strategic direction of the organisation and are often incorporated in Mission Statements. A vision is more a goal than a way of thinking or behaving. At this stage the organisation is developing a view of what it should look like once its strategies are achieved and developed to their full potential. It is the organisation's 'Vision of Success'.

This vision may begin at the very earliest stage of the planning process - the initial agreement - but it can develop at this later stage. Indeed, many organisations may not need a vision of success, particularly if they only need to identify and resolve a few strategic issues.

The vision statement is general and the time scale unclear and it can be unachievable in practical terms. However, it can still provide a target for the organisation to keep heading towards. The questions that need to be posed before developing the vision include:

- What trends will mature or emerge during that time?

- What will be the driving forces of the market be?

- What will be the key success factors in the market?

- Who will be a competitor?

- What strategies will be viable?

- What assets and skills will be required to underpin those strategies?

The end result will be a vision of what strategy should be in place in the future - what product markets to serve and what synergies, assets and skills will be necessary to win - and a commitment to pursue that strategy.

3.3 Mission statements

After deciding who the strategy is for, the overriding purpose or intent of the organisation must be established. This is usually formalised in a Mission Statement. Many organisations find the vision statement too vague and prefer to use the mission statement as their most general expression of purpose. It should outline the specific role that the organisation plans to fulfil within society over the long term and therefore limits the scope of its operations by implicitly excluding areas outside its stated mission. Drucker states that three questions underline the definition of a mission statement, namely:

- What is our business?
- What should it be?
- What will it have to be?

The purpose of the mission statement is to communicate to those making the strategic decisions the broad ground rules that the organisation has set for itself in conducting its business. A good mission statement will include:

- a statement of beliefs and values
- the needs that the organisation will satisfy
- the markets where the organisation will trade
- how those markets will be reached
- the technologies the organisation will use
- the organisation's attitude to growth and financing.

Good mission statements or visions are exciting and inspiring. A well-crafted statement that is understood and believed can be a powerful force for change. As a vision it can provide the framework for exercising initiative, influencing attitudes from the top to the bottom of the organisation.

The mission of an organisation is generally influenced by five key elements:

- the history of the organisation
- the current preferences of the organisation's management and owners
- the environmental factors influencing the organisation
- the organisation's resources
- the organisation's distinctive competence.

Producing a formal mission is not an easy task. It will relate to a lot of factors and people, including in many cases, shareholders, customers, employees and the public. The organisation's mission acts as an 'invisible hand' that guides widely dispersed management to work independently, and yet collectively towards the achievement of the organisational goal.

The differences between mission and vision are as follows.

- Mission is about the here and now, whereas vision refers to the future.
- A vision may be too vague to motivate, whereas a mission is designed to motivate.
- A vision, when achieved, might lose motivating power, unless it can be reinvented.

A mission statement has many consequences leading from it. It may aim to provide employees, customers and other organisational stakeholders with a business definition that captures the essence of the strategic vision of the business, in order to establish a sense of purpose, identity and commitment. This is particularly true in a service industry where customers are more likely to come into contact with employees.

The development of the mission statement can also provide a vehicle for generating and screening a wide variety of strategic options, as long as it considers generic customer needs rather than having a myopic product focus. For example, if organisations regard themselves as being in the transportation business rather than the coach business, the energy rather than the petrol business, or the communications rather than the telephone business, they are more likely to exploit opportunities.

ACTIVITY 1	Draft a mission statement for a firm that you have some knowledge of.

Feedback to this activity is at the end of the chapter.

3.4 Characteristics of a good mission statement

Mission statements are formal documents, which might be displayed in a number of places eg, at the front of an organisation's annual report, on publicity material and in communal work areas. There is no standard format, but they should have the following characteristics.

- *Brevity* - they should be easy to understand and remember.

- *Flexibility* - they must accommodate change.

- *Distinctiveness* - they should make the firm seem different from the rest.

If the examiner requires a mission statement to be drafted for an organisation, the following characteristics should be borne in mind. The mission statement should be:

- a brief statement – often a single paragraph. A short credo that says it all belongs to PepsiCo. PepsiCo's mission has long been simply to *'Beat Coke'*, a mission it has yet to achieve. If an organisation cannot sum up why it exists in one paragraph then it is unclear why it exists. This will make it difficult for it to state what makes it distinct from its competitors

- a general statement about what the organisation believes in. This may be something specific such as the Body Shop's distinctive attitudes towards the environment.

- a statement of the aims of the organisation. For a profit-making organisation this may be to produce profit for the shareholders. A non-profit organisation may aim to provide a particular level of service.

- a statement of the areas in which the organisation will operate. This may be important if a company is involved in a number of different areas. This should provide some focus for divisional managers as to whether a particular opportunity is consistent with what the organisation is trying to achieve.

- a basis for communicating with people inside the organisation. For example, if the organisation's main focus is on quality, then it is important that all the members of the organisation are aware of this in order to ensure that quality standards are met.

- long-lasting (sometimes the phrase 'not time-assigned' is used to describe this aspect of a mission statement).

- a starting point for formulating objectives and short-term targets.

More importantly, from an examination point of view, is to show that, by defining the business in terms of the basic customer need involved, rather than the product, it can foster creativity in generating strategic options and can avoid an internally oriented, product/production focus. Xerox attempted to change its focus from copiers to the 'document' company. Visa has defined itself as being in the business of enabling a customer to exchange value for virtually anything, anywhere in the world. As the business is redefined, both the set of competitors and the range of opportunities are often radically expanded.

Consider the usefulness, or otherwise, of the following mission statements:

1   Courses for careers, research for results

2   To be a pioneer in graphite communications

3   To be excellent in our chosen field, and provide the best in customer service and quality that resources permit

4   Kill Caterpillar

Feedback to this activity is at the end of the chapter.

3.5   Strategic intent

Hamel and Prahalad argue that the most successful firms in the world rarely tie the organisation down to a series of mission statements, goals and objectives in the way described above. Rather, their notion of strategic intent is based upon the belief that good firms should set goals that are so far in excess of the company's current capabilities that it is impossible to articulate a series of steps that would ensure their achievement. Strategic intent works by reinforcing clear long-term goals, which are achieved by a series of incremental steps that cannot be foreseen at the outset.

It encompasses an active management process that includes: focussing the organisation's attention on winning; motivating people by communicating the value of the target; leaving room for individual and team contributions; sustaining enthusiasm; and using intent consistently to guide resource allocations.

The characteristics of strategic intent include the following:

*   Strategic intent captures the essence of winning

*   Strategic intent is stable over time - consistency for short term action while leaving room for reinterpretation as new opportunities emerge

*   Strategic intent sets a target that deserves personal effort and commitment ('unseat the best' is more motivational than 'increase shareholder value') Planners ask 'How will next year be different?' Winners ask 'What must we do differently?' It is difficult to 'plan' for global leadership with a detailed strategy.

*   Strategic intent stretches the organisation. It creates an extreme misfit between resources and ambitions. Challenges also stretch the organisation. Corporate challenges come from analysing competitors as well as from the foreseeable pattern of industry evolution. For a corporate challenge to be affective and engage the entire organisation, top management needs to:

    -   create a sense of urgency, or quasi crisis (Komatsu budgeted on basis of worst case exchange rates)

    -   develop a competitor focus at every level through widespread use of competitive intelligence (Ford showed video tapes of more efficient Mazda plant)

    -   provide employees with skills they need to work effectively

    -   give the organisation time to digest one challenge before launching another

    -   establish clear milestones and review mechanisms to track progress

This approach is seen as more effective for several reasons. Firstly, strategies will be evolving and dynamic, rather than preordained. Secondly, it is possible for individuals to express themselves, rather than conform (or appear to conform) to a plan that they might not have cared for in the first place. Thirdly, it allows senior management to guide behaviour toward it in the way they allocate resources behind the activities they support, not to stoke them up in advance by rhetoric. Fourthly, it means that failure of a small part of the strategy does not result in widespread dismay and abandonment as other parts of the incremental processes will be experiencing some successes.

Strategic intent is a means of strategy that depends upon motivation and energy, rather than control, and is attractive for those reasons.

3.6 Strategic scope

Hofer and Schendel defined an organisation's strategy as the 'fundamental pattern of present and planned resource deployments and environmental interactions that indicates how the organisation will achieve its objectives'. They noted four components of organisational strategy:

- Strategic scope - deals with the organisation's environment, and the extent to which it currently interacts and plans to interact with that environment. It deals with factors outside the organisation's control

- Resource deployment - deals with the internal environment of the organisation; its strengths and weaknesses

- Competitive advantage - can be developed by meeting specific needs of the external environment through a strategic deployment of resources that maximises the organisation's strengths

- Synergy - results from the favourable joint effects of strategic decisions based on scope

By defining its strategic scope (either explicitly or implicitly), the organisation selects a 'niche' or position for itself in the general environment as well as its industry. To promote success and survival, the organisation must conform to or fit its niche by devising operations to produce, promote and distribute products to serve the needs of its customers.

- a 'prospector' organisation - being constantly on the lookout for new products, technologies and segments - has a high need for longer-range information. The longer-term time horizon is needed to anticipate and organise offerings to meet the ever-changing needs of these changing markets in which prospectors compete. As the prospector plans to embark on new product and target market segments it needs to have anticipated the future demand potential in these segments.

- a 'defender' strategy - one that concentrates on serving a stable target population better and more efficiently - has a high need for control over its internal processes. This control helps the defender to keep inventories and costs down, schedule personnel, and monitor operations. Longer range planning processes, while they may be of some benefit, add significantly to the costs of planning and are thus difficult to justify for this strategy that depends on efficient use of resources. Year-to-year budgeting processes - typical short-term plans - meet these needs.

This 'fitting process' (between the organisation and its selected environment) will largely determine the structure of the organisation, and both the set and nature of the activities that the organisation's personnel must deal with and/or perform from day to day (eg, warehousing, personal selling). Because many of an organisation's operational characteristics (eg, gross margin, selling expenses), strategic variables (eg, product development) and performance criteria (eg, sales per salesperson) are so closely tied to its purchasing, production and marketing activities, the decision as to which customers and needs to serve with a given technology (and the degree of scope and differentiation on these dimensions) should effectively structure and constrain the organisation's business operations so as to influence their mean level.

An organisation can expand its scope along three dimensions:

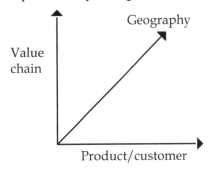

Geography and product/customer are intuitively easy to understand. Value chain follows the material flow - procurement, processing, distribution etc but is not simply about resource or activity sharing but also about governance ie, the institutional arrangements for co-ordinating a set of transactions through markets or hierarchies. For example can a manufacturer of juice concentrate earn more by owning or subcontracting bottling facilities in soft drinks?

Governance issues also arise in horizontal expansion. For example, should an organisation own the expanded activities within an industry or seek ways to appropriate profit through alliances, contracts or franchises?

4   Objectives

4.1   Mission, goals and objectives

The mission statement is often highly abstract in its expression. In its 'raw' state it is not a useful guide, except in a very general sense, to managers taking day-to-day decisions. Strategic goals and objectives are developed to bridge the gap between current capability and the mission. They are aligned with the mission and form the basis for the action plans. Objectives are sometimes referred to as performance goals.

Objectives are normally quantified statements of what the organisation actually intends to achieve. They are expressed in a manner that allows a future assessment of whether an objective has been achieved. Whereas mission statements describe a value system for the organisation and some indication of the business it is in, objectives are well defined, as the following example demonstrates.

- Mission: deliver a quality service
- Goal: enhance manufacturing quality
- Objectives: over the next twelve months, reduce the number of defects to 1 part per million

All of the organisation's objectives should be directed towards achieving the organisation's mission.

Corporate objectives are concerned with the firm as a whole. The corporate objectives outline the expectations of the firm and the strategic planning process is concerned with the means of achieving the objectives. Objectives should relate to the key factors for business success, which are typically the following.

- Profitability (return on investment)
- Market share
- Growth
- Cash flow
- Customer satisfaction
- The quality of the firm's products
- Industrial relations
- Added value

Examples of long-term objectives for an organisation could be to double sales volume over five years, to increase dividends by 10 per cent over three years, or to build up public awareness of a particular brand. These long-term objectives can then be broken down further into short-term targets setting out what the organisation hopes to achieve over a relatively short-term period such as a year.

Similar objectives can be developed for each strategic business unit (SBU) which is a part of the company that for all intents and purposes has its own distinct products, markets and assets.

Unit objectives are objectives that are specific to individual units of an organisation. Examples are as follows.

Commercial

- Increasing the number of customers by x% (an objective of a sales department).

- Reducing the number of rejects by 50% (an objective of a production department).

- Producing monthly reports more quickly, within 5 working days of the end of each month (an objective of the management accounting department).

Public sector:

- Introduce x% more places at nursery schools (an objective of a borough education department).

- Respond more quickly to calls (an objective of one of the emergency services).

In addition to overall performance, we can list the following types of objective.

- Resources (eg finding cheaper sources of raw materials, reducing borrowing costs, 'hiring top-quality college graduates').

- Market (eg market share, market standing).

- Employee development (eg training, promotion, safety).

- Innovation (in products, processes, eg 3M's policy is that a set percentage of revenue each year should derive from new products).

- Productivity - (the amount of output from resource inputs)

4.2 Characteristics of objectives

Objectives are time-assigned targets derived from the goals, and are set in advance of strategy.

Dr Ted Johns has suggested that objectives can be assessed against the following criteria (For which the mnemonic is TRAMPS or SMART if you rearrange the criteria and leave the P out).

- *Time-bounded*: there should be a deadline.

- *Result-oriented*: objectives should be concentrated within the organisation's (or the individual's) key tasks or performance areas, ie those responsibilities which genuinely make an added-value difference; objectives are far less productive if they deal with *inputs* (like personal efficiency).

- *Achievable*: an objective should not appear impossible: many people are discouraged by apparently unattainable goals.

- *Measurable*: there must be some quantifiable yardstick of attainment (though one aspect of this yardstick may well be the delivery deadline, ie the time boundary).

- *Precise*: all objectives should deal with some manageable feature of the organisation or the individual.

- *Stretching*: achieving objectives should require positive effort and willpower, so that the result evokes a conscious sense of triumph and accomplishment.

One thing that is clear is that objectives must be capable of being quantified otherwise progress towards them cannot be measured. For a local authority, for instance, to state a goal as 'to improve the welfare of old age pensioners in the Borough' is not precise enough. The goal needs to be translated into objectives which state how it is going to measure the achievement - in terms perhaps of the number of places made available in old people's homes by x date, the number of meals-on-wheels served in x period, the number of patients treated in geriatric wards - so that several targets may make up its overall objective.

In other words, for objectives to be of use in practice, they must have three components:

- attribute chosen to be measured, e.g. profit, return on capital, output
- scale by which it is to be measured, e.g. £, %, tonnes
- target, i.e. the level on the scale which it is hoped to achieve, e.g. £1m, 12%, 350,000 tonnes.

4.3   Explicit and implicit objectives

This is to do with what the company is actually setting out to do and what will also happen as a result of their action. 'Explicit' means something that is directly stated or referred to, without any room for doubt. 'Implicit' means something that is implied or referred to in a less obvious fashion. The objectives will be understood but not expressed.

In our example of improving the welfare of old age pensioners, the authority might have a stated (explicit) objective of improving access and service with an implicit objective of cutting costs.

Generally, organisations have long-term objectives for such factors as return on investment, earnings per share, or size. Furthermore, they set minimum acceptable standards or common-sense minimums. In addition, certain limitations, either explicit or implicit, such as 'must provide jobs for existing employees' may exist.

4.4   The primary objective

Some objectives are more important than others in the hierarchy of objectives, there may be a *primary corporate objective* (restricted by certain constraints on corporate activity) and other *secondary objectives* whose attainment should ensure the achievement of the primary corporate objective.

- For example, if a company sets itself an objective of growth in profits, as its *primary objective* it will then have to develop strategies by which this primary objective can be achieved. An objective must then be set for each individual strategy; many secondary objectives may simply be targets by which the success of a strategy can be measured.
- *Secondary objectives* might be concerned with sales growth, technological innovation, customer service, product quality, efficient resource management (eg labour productivity) or reducing the company's reliance on debt capital.

To achieve success, the primary objectives of a business organisation are generally:

- to continue in existence
- to maintain growth and development; and
- to make a profit

All three objectives are linked because it is a matter of debate whether the organisation survives and develops in order to make a profit or makes a profit so that it can survive and develop. Survival is an implicit, overriding objective in every organisation and if we consider it as the ultimate objective, then this involves the need for a steady and continuous profit. A reduction in short term profitability is required to provide for future investments and maintain growth and development.

Although there have been suggestions that the main objective of a company is simply survival, we can surely agree with Argenti that this is inadequate. Survival is not an end in itself; most organisations would want to reach a certain minimum performance level better than just 'hanging on', and if this was not attainable the shareholders might not wish for the survival of the company. Shareholders are obviously a major group to be taken into account when setting objectives. If we ask 'why does the company want to survive?' the answer must be to make a profit or to maximise the wealth of investors in the company, ie, the shareholders.

| ACTIVITY 3 | The primary objective for a company must be a financial objective based on earning profits, but there are different ways of expressing such an objective in quantitative terms. Outline the various financial objectives that could be used. |

Feedback to this activity is at the end of the chapter

4.5 Policies

Policies provide the parameters within which the decisions are made. Conceptually, it is useful to think of policies at three levels:

- Organisational policies - reflect the mission of the organisation and the means of evaluating the actions. These might include the target rate of return, the geographic area to be served, the product mix and product quality.

- Functional policies - might specify advertising media, sales policy, product design and research and discounts.

- Operational policies - are concerned with day-to-day matters such as staffing, customer refunds or complaints

Policies are guidelines for organisational action and the implementation of goals and objectives. They are translated into rules, plans and procedures; and relate to all activities of the organisation, and to all levels of the organisation. Clearly stated policies can help reinforce the main functions of the organisation, make for consistency and reduce dependency on the actions of individual managers. Policies clarify the roles and responsibilities of managers and other members of staff and provide guidelines for managerial behaviour. Securing agreement to a new or revised policy can help overcome reliance on outdated practices and aid the introduction of organisational change.

Policy provides guiding principles for areas of decision-making and delegation. For example, specific decisions relating to personnel policy could include:

- giving priority to promotion from within the organisation;

- enforcing retirement at government pensionable age;

- whenever possible, employing only graduate or professionally qualified accountants;

- permitting line managers, in consultation with the personnel manager, to appoint staff up to a given salary/wage level.

Objectives and policy together provide corporate guidelines for the operations and management of the organisation. Their formulation, and the allocation of resources, provide the basis for strategic planning which is the first stage in the planning and control processes of business organisations

4.6   Economic versus accounting concept of profit

The economist's concept of profit may differ quite sharply from the accountant's.

To an economist profits can be regarded as the reward to the owners of a business for their 'enterprise' or for putting their financial capital at risk. Normal profits are treated as a necessary opportunity cost for a business and it is only supernormal profit which constitutes *pure* profit.

Economic profit consists of sales revenue minus the explicit (clearly stated and recorded) costs of the business and the implicit costs. The implicit costs are benefits foregone by not using the factors of production in their next most profitable way.

An accounting profit is conventionally defined in terms of the increase in an organisation's net assets resulting from its ordinary business activities. Thus items such as profits from the sale of assets other than the output of products and capital contributions from investors are excluded from the calculation of the change in the value of net assets. An alternative but equivalent definition is in terms of the difference between the total amount of revenue from sales of products (or services) for that time period and the amount of assets and resources consumed in earning those revenues.

The principal defects of this method are the accounting conventions relating to the valuation of assets. The use of historical cost as the valuation base may result in estimates of profit, which do not accurately reflect 'reality' - particularly in periods of inflation. The adoption of alternative concepts of capital valuation would in turn result in different profit measurement.

4.7   Behaviourist theories of organisational objectives

Herbert Simon argues that objectives may be seen as the set of constraints that the organisation must satisfy ie, profit for the shareholders, satisfaction of employees, meeting government demands, pacifying environmentalists and meeting customer requirements. In a practical context, other factors are important because they pull against profit maximisation. These are:

Separation of management and ownership - in large companies there are many shareholders, each with a relatively small share of the company and directors, who may not have a large shareholding, manage the company. Provided that they can earn enough to satisfy the shareholders, such directors might be more interested in factors such as geographical market spread, prestigious buildings, the company's public image, and so on, rather than obtaining the maximum return. This ties in with Cyert and March's Behavioural Theory of the Firm.

In the classical economic model the shareholders determine the firms objective (profit) and the other groups (eg, employees) accept wages (or some other 'side payment') as their reward for striving for this objective. In the Cyert & March model these rewards or 'side payments' may be non-monetary and may involve commitments to some way of working, or type of action or policy, thus influencing the firm's objectives.

So the outcome for the firm is the pursuit of objectives, which enable a minimum level of resources to be generated in order to satisfy the various demands of the various sub-groups. If resources exceed the demands of the various groups then the organisation builds up 'slack'.

Cyert and March have proposed a consensus theory of company objectives. They suggest that 'organisations do not have objectives, only people have objectives' and therefore the objectives that are pursued by an organisation represent a compromise between objectives of various groups within the organisation, shareholders and directors among them. They believe that personal objectives tend to emerge as corporate objectives. Certainly, a company can reflect the personal ambitions of a dominant chairman or chief executive.

In recent years, with improvements in financial communication and greater safeguards for employee and investor, there has developed a consensus view of objectives. This consensus view takes account of the interests of all important stakeholder groups and seeks to set objectives that will satisfy several groups rather than a single primary stakeholder group.

One of the implications of the 'coalition theory' is that decisions are made within a business to try to 'satisfy' the aspirations of the different groups that make up the coalition. The business is seen as a 'satisficer' rather than as a 'maximiser' ie, objectives are formed and decisions are made so as to attain a satisfactory outcome, which won't upset the coalition, rather than the largest possible profits ('profit maximisation') for the shareholders or owners of the business.

Responsibilities and constraints - companies have obligations to groups other than shareholders, employees, customers and the public at large. Although the economic objective may remain the primary one, because it is fundamental to the company's survival, the company may set itself other objectives. These could be concerned with improving the welfare of, (or its relations with) other groups; objectives, which may well reduce the amount of profit which could otherwise have been earned. These are internal constraints. There may also be external constraints, for instance in the form of legislation. In formal terms, constraints are decision rules that preclude certain courses of action.

Conflict between long and short-term - a company might be able to improve its profit in the long run by sacrificing some profit in the short-term, for instance by spending money on product development. Conversely, if the company concentrated on short-term profitability it would be likely to find itself in an unhealthy position in the long-term.

For all the above reasons, a company should think of profit optimisation, ie, maximisation subject to constraints, rather than of profit maximisation.

Cyert and March also believed that organisations make decisions based on very small proportions of the total available information. They believe the decision process concerns three basic characteristics of organisations - organisational goals, organisational expectations and organisational choice. In addition there are four features of the decision-making process, which explain how decisions are arrived at. They are:

- Quasi-revolution of conflict - an organisation is a coalition of conflicting interests.
- Uncertainty - is something with which all organisations must live.
- Problemistic search - is the means used by organisations to determine what choices are thought to be available.
- Organisational learning - takes place through individuals in the decision-making process.

They believe that individuals fight for the right to participate in decision-making, and then do not exercise that right with any vigour, that information is ignored, more is requested, and then that is ignored.

4.8   The stakeholder approach

The 'stakeholder' approach suggests that the objectives of an organisation should be derived by balancing the often conflicting claims of the various stakeholders (or coalitions) in the organisation. These stakeholders consist of coalitions of people within the organisation, and external groups. The organisation has responsibilities to all these groups, and it should formulate its strategic goals to give each a measure of satisfaction. The difficulty is balancing the conflicting interests and differing degrees of power. For example, there might be conflicts of interest between a company's shareholders and its employees. If the strategy of the organisation is to reflect the interests of its stakeholders, the strategic planner will need to consider, and be influenced by, factors relating to them. These are:

- Composition and significance of each group.

- Power that each group can exert.

- Legitimate claims that each group may have on the organisation.

- Degree to which these claims conflict and significant areas of concern.

- Extent to which the organisation is satisfying claims.

- Overall mission of the organisation.

In practice, the assessment of the *political risk* inherent in various strategies can be an important deciding factor between strategies. For example, a strategy of market development might require the cutting out of wholesalers, hence running the risk of backlash, which could jeopardise the success of the strategy.

Management normally undertakes the responsibility of maintaining an equitable and working balance among the claims of the various directly interested groups, but usually the most powerful group of stakeholders, termed the *dominant coalition*, will determine the organisation's *prime* objectives.

Bowen proposed the idea of a *social audit,* to establish the needs and expectations of the various stakeholder groups that had been satisfied. Similar ideas were expressed by Humble with his *social responsibility audit* and since the publication of the 'Corporate Report' many company annual reports carry sections devoted to this idea. However, in normal circumstances all stakeholders would support Peter Drucker's view that survival is the central purpose, which involves maintaining or increasing the net worth of the organisation.

Conclusion

Goals are determined within the overall sense of purpose. The organisation's mission can be formal (say, in writing) or informal, and represents its basic purpose or *raison d'être*. That is what the organisation wants to be, or to accomplish. Defining the mission of the organisation is important because it affects everything else, including the strategic choices taken by the organisation. The *'mission statement'*, if produced, is part of the management information system.

Having established the organisation's mission and its goals within the mission (relating these to the expectations of the various coalitions), the strategist can then set about translating them into objectives and strategic imperatives. Objectives need to be attainable, explicit, and measurable. Once the set of objectives are decided management is ready to move on to the detailed work of strategy formulation and budgeting.

Strategic intent is a more recent way of developing the organisation's sense of purpose. It projects long-term goals, but relies upon incremental and emergent processes to achieve it. Thus, it does not break down into the hierarchy of goals and objectives that the tradition and somewhat discredited system tends to derive.

.

SELF-TEST
QUESTIONS

The cultural context

1 What are the seven dimensions of culture according to the Organisation Culture Profile (OCP)? (1.3)

Stakeholder expectations

2 List three sources of stakeholder power (2.3)

Organisational purpose

3 List at least eight characteristics of a *'Mission Statement'*. (3.4)

Objectives

4 What does the mnemonic TRAMPS stand for? (4.2)

EXAM-TYPE
QUESTION

TDM plc

The managing director of TDM plc has recently returned from a conference entitled 'Strategic planning beyond the 90s'. Whilst at the conference, she attended a session on 'corporate mission statements'. She found the session very interesting but it was rather short and she has asked the following questions:

(a) 'What does corporate mission mean? I don't see how it fits in with our strategic planning process.'

(b) 'Where does our mission come from and what areas of corporate life should it cover?'

(c) 'Even if we were to develop one of these mission statements, what benefits would the company get from it?'

Prepare a report that answers the managing director's questions. **(20 marks)**

For the answer to this question, see the 'Answers' section at the end of the book.

FEEDBACK TO
ACTIVITY **1**

A good mission statement captures the sense of purpose of the organisation in as few words as possible. If your statement captured the idea of the target customer, product/service offering and distinctive competence you are on the right lines. However, it's important to remember that the important issue is whether or not management are able to turn a mission statement into a sense of purpose that is accepted by movers and shakers in the organisation, including those who drafted the statement. This is several orders of magnitude more difficult than writing a few sentences.

FEEDBACK TO
ACTIVITY **2**

1 This is the mission statement of a British University. It identifies that the range of courses offered will be restricted to those that lead to an obvious career path, and research will be developed in partnership with those who have a commercial interest in discovery, rather than simply a sense of curiosity. As you might expect, this is a University with great ambition but relative few resources, which therefore focuses its activity into areas where it may compete effectively against its more august rivals. Note that the mission statement here implicitly describes both the customers it seeks and the services it wishes to offer.

2 This is the mission statement of a manufacturer of lead pencils. This is not a silly joke, something very much like it can be found. The important point is that it suggests innovation in a field more usually noted for cost based competition. Part of the company's business is providing jokey, amusing slogans on its pencils, and the mission statement was chosen to reflect this. Note that this

mission is directed at the customers, any message for employees is rather too subtle to operate effectively.

3   Nigel Piercy has argued that any mission statement containing the word 'excellent' (such as the third example in the activity) should not be taken seriously. Excellence subject to resource constraints also appears rather qualified. However, this particular firm embarked on a rapacious programme of take-overs in a field where this was comparatively unknown. The resource base expanded, but very little of these extra resources found their way into product quality and customer service, leading to great cynicism from staff.

4   The final statement is a translation of the mission of Komatsu, who set their sight on taking Caterpillar's domination of the tracked vehicle market. They picked out the weaker points of their rival's operation, its softest markets and poorest products, and spent two decades building up the competences and driving them out.

FEEDBACK TO ACTIVITY 3	

Various financial objectives would include the following:

-   Profitability (and value added)

-   Return on capital employed (ROCE) or return on investment (ROI)

-   Survival

-   Growth in earnings per share and a target PE ratio (ie, share price/earnings)

-   Growth in dividends to shareholders

-   Various management ratios

-   Return on shareholders capital with an allowance for the element of risk.

Chapter 11
DEVELOPING THE STRATEGY

The overall process of corporate planning will generate a number of alternative strategies to meet the formulated objectives. The components of these strategies will be in terms of particular products for various markets and will involve resource requirements in order to achieve implementation. The strategy will involve areas such as image as well as products and markets, although these latter factors often dominate. The product/market mix that is the most appropriate strategy may be obvious, but in many cases a selection procedure must be embarked upon. The end product of the efforts of management must be decisions and action

Objectives

When you have studied this chapter you should be able to:

- show the approach of PIMS analysis

- contrast market based and resource based approaches

- show the difference between withdrawal, consolidation and market based strategies

- explain Ansoff's growth vector analysis

- describe and discuss internal methods of development

- describe and discuss growth by acquisition

- describe and discuss growth by joint development.

1   Developing strategies

1.1   Strategy direction

There are three parts to a strategy - generic strategy, direction and method. For example, an organisation pursuing a generic strategy of differentiation may also pursue a strategic direction of product or service development. However, this leaves a further choice as to the method by which the new developments are best achieved eg, through the organisation's own efforts, jointly with others or by acquisition.

We have already discussed the generic strategies in a previous chapter

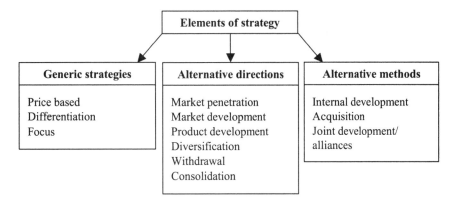

Elements of strategy		
Generic strategies	**Alternative directions**	**Alternative methods**
Price based	Market penetration	Internal development
Differentiation	Market development	Acquisition
Focus	Product development	Joint development/
	Diversification	alliances
	Withdrawal	
	Consolidation	

1.2 Components of strategy

The level of risk that a company undertakes, the incidence and rate of change, and the way in which resources are distributed can all be governed through analysis of the product/market mix. In short, the product/market mix analysis can shape the strategies that dictate a company's future. Ansoff suggests a number of links, or strands in a common thread between existing and possible new strategies, which help to give such specific guidance.

Four strands in the thread, sometimes referred to as the 'components of strategy' are:

- The product market scope - the scope within which the business currently operates. It is the definition of the types of activity currently undertaken by the firm and of the markets to which its products are applied.

- Growth vector components - the possible directions of growth starting from the current product market position. A vector is a line for which both length and direction are defined.

- Competitive advantage - the special characteristics looked for in growth opportunities in order to achieve a strong competitive position. Possible limiting factors on growth decisions might be, for example, the desire for strongly innovative products, for the protection of patent rights against short-term competition, or for a quasi-monopoly status.

- Synergy - the firm must have the capabilities for success in any new venture undertaken, and this may limit the acceptance of growth opportunities. The possibility of synergy is obviously greatest in the case of simple expansion opportunities, but subject to relatively high risk when undertaking diversification.

1.3 Strategic or planning gap analysis

If strategies are assessed only in absolute terms or against industry norms, it does not address the need to identify the incentive to change from the present strategy to a new one. It is often useful to use the do nothing situation to assess the organisation's incentive to change. The do nothing situation represents the likely outcome if the organisation were to continue with current strategies. The purpose of gap analysis is to identify the extent to which existing strategies will fail to meet the organisation's targets for achievement over the planning period.

DEFINITION

A **strategic gap** is the shortfall between the targeted performance and the projected momentum line at a specific point of time ahead.

A **strategic gap** is the difference between the present position of an organisation and its desired future position. Strategic planning gap analysis involves establishing performance projections based on existing strategy, in a forecasted environment, to determine the projected deficiency in performance at the strategic level.

In this approach attention is first focused on the gaps between the actual or anticipated values that certain variables take on and the values that are most desirable. Once the gaps are identified, attention shifts to devising ways to close them.

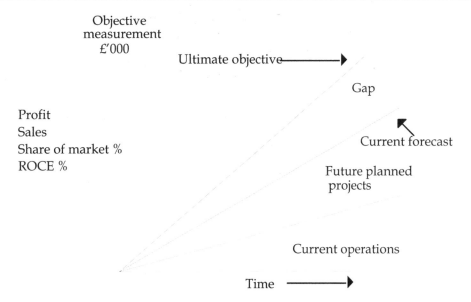

An analysis of the difference between forecast results and stated objectives should provide an idea of the dimension of strategy required and may also suggest possible alternative approaches to formulating it. Careful analysis of gaps can help the corporate planning process in two ways. It can assist the identification and evaluation of possible strategies, and the selection of strategies.

Assuming that the current forecast and the target profit figures can be defined, it is possible to present the results of different combinations of strategy in the form of a profit chart as illustrated in the figure below. The profit from the existing business currently carried on is first charted, and then augmented by the estimated profits obtained from the evaluated opportunities. Estimated profits can be divided up between main headings such as improved efficiency, product modification, the introduction of new products, and the opening up of new markets.

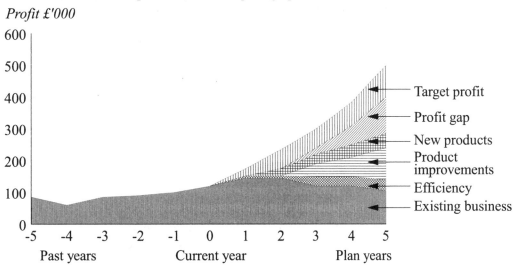

The object of the chart is to show the extent to which the evaluated profits fall short of, or exceed, the target profit; in other words the 'profit gap'. The planners can then modify the assumptions made, or develop further strategies, with the object of filling the gap to the greatest extent possible.

A selection of strategies will then emerge which, combined together and superimposed on the existing business, will yield results over the planning period that are in the closest possible conformity with the long-term objectives, and will be within the forecast financial capabilities of the business.

A point that should not be overlooked is that the planning gap is calculated for specific periods eg, each year, over the whole planning period. Therefore objectives have to be quantified into targets or goals to be attained in each time period up to the planning horizon, and less precisely into the future beyond.

1.4 Types of gap analysis

Gap analysis has been advocated for strategic choice decisions within the following four primary contexts: Environmental analysis, functional-level policy analysis, business-level strategy analysis, and corporate-level strategy analysis.

Environmental gap analysis - for purposes of environmental analysis, gap analysis is a way of focusing on differences between the firm's strategy set and resources and the threats and opportunities that make up its environment. More specifically it is used to identify gaps between where a firm would be if it continued with its present strategy and was subjected to expected environmental developments, and where the strategist would like the firm to be in terms of strategic goals. Thus this 'planning gap' can be filled by implementing new action plans, or strategic goals can be altered.

Gap analysis at the function level - a popular use for gap analysis is to compare actual and potential market variables for marketing strategy purposes. Webber proposes a form of gap analysis for analysing the differences between industry market potential and the firm's own sales by product line. This overall gap is made up of four segments as follows:

- Product-line gap: the portion due to each product in the full product line.

- Distribution gap: the portion caused by an inadequate distribution system.

- Usage gap: the part caused by less than full usage.

- Competitive gap: the segment caused by sales that are lost to direct competitors.

Each type of gap may be closed through its own set of strategic or tactical moves. Accurately determining the type and magnitude of each kind of gap is the difficult part of market gap analysis. However, this technique focuses attention on defining the various elements of a firm's sales shortfall.

Gap Analysis at the business level - there are profound similarities between gap analysis at the business level and gap analysis for environmental audit and functional-level analysis purposes. At the business level, however, the gaps of interest are those related to the performance of the business unit as a whole. The focus is on gaps between actual and planned-for results according to such criteria as various profit measures, cash flow generation, management expertise, company image, and relative product quality. Consequently gap analysis at the business level is very much like analysis of budget variances.

Gap Analysis at the Corporate Level - when applied to the corporate level, gap analysis focuses on the consolidated performance of the portfolio of business units. Differences between desired values of performance variables (gross, operating, or net profit on total assets or equity; growth rate of sales; geographical coverage; and so on) and actual values can trigger corporate-level strategic decisions.

1.5 The analysis aspect

Companies are faced with a chicken and egg situation. Which comes first – targets or strategy? A strong body of opinion favours the approach we have just discussed, that is it inclines towards a company developing an aspirational set of targets and then attempting to generate strategies capable of reaching them. There is another school of thought, which concludes that targets and ratios ought not to dictate the structure of the strategic plan: their function is to assist in direction and control. Alternative strategies should be formulated against the background of available corporate expertise, available and potential resources and the envisaged operating environment. Targets should emerge logically from the selected strategy.

1.6 Appropriate strategy development

A sound strategy is based on the priorities identified in the internal and external audits. A strategy is appropriate if it offers the means to develop a competitive advantage in key areas, and minimise the risks and resource deployment in weak ones. In some cases, this might mean withdrawal from the market altogether.

Some examples are given below, but it must be remembered that context is important, and these are not hard and fast rules.

Position audit	Appropriate strategy
Weak competitive strength, growing market	Competence based strategy
Competitive strengths and growing market	Growth strategy
Competitive strengths, stable, competitive market	Consolidation and diversification
Competitive weakness, poor market	Withdrawal strategy

A C T I V I T Y 1

Suggest an appropriate strategy for each of the following:

1   A weak software company

2   A strong specialist steel company

3   An average motor insurance company

4   A small niche brewery that finds difficulty in competing at the market price

5   A strong, multi-product international conglomerate with strengths in fruit farming and soap powder but weaker performance in cosmetics

Feedback to this activity is at the end of the chapter.

2 Profit impact of marketing strategies (PIMS analysis)

2.1 Introduction

Strategic marketing has three interrelated elements.

- The first is to determine areas in which to invest or disinvest. Investment could go to growth areas such as new product markets or programmes designed to create new strength areas or to support existing ones.

- The second is the specification and implementation of functional area strategies involving product policy, manufacturing strategy, distribution choices, and so on.

- The third element of strategic market management is to develop bases of sustainable competitive advantages in the product markets where a firm competes.

In making strategic decisions, inputs from a variety of types are relevant. However, the core of any strategic decision should be based on three types of assessments.

- The first concerns organisational strengths and weaknesses,

- The second evaluates competitor strengths, weaknesses, and strategies, because an organisation's strength is of less value if it is neutralised by a competitor's strength or strategy.

- The third assesses the competitive context, the customers and their needs, the market and the market environment. These assessments focus on determining how attractive the selected market will be, given the strategy selected.

The goal is to develop a strategy that exploits business strengths and competitor weaknesses and neutralises business weaknesses and competitor strengths, The ideal is to compete in a healthy growing industry with a strategy based on strengths that are unlikely to be acquired or neutralised by competitors.

2.2 Strategic options

The vision and other business goals and the organisation's position encapsulated in a SWOT table will provide the focus to search for a set of strategic choices.

The organisation must decide on the number and range of its options and on the possibilities of augmenting its present portfolio or reducing it. The possible changes to the portfolio that an organisation can make are indicated below.

Changes in the organisation's portfolio

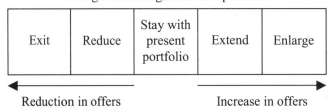

| Exit | Reduce | Stay with present portfolio | Extend | Enlarge |

Reduction in offers · Increase in offers

2.3 Profit and market share approaches

Profits and market share are the two main goals for many organisations. The differences in a market share approach and one focussed on profits and profitability are:

- Market share measures what has been put into a relationship, profits measures what has been taken out

- Market share faces outwards to the community, profitability faces inwards

- With the market share approach, customers are ends in themselves. In profit calculations, customers are a means to the end

- A focus on market share provides a quicker signalling system to the organisation - changes show up sooner in shifting customer needs than is the case with a profit-oriented approach

- The greater the market share, the more customers and possibly suppliers there are to learn from.

2.4 Relative market share

In an earlier chapter we discussed the growth share matrix and identified an organisation's relative market share. This is used as an indicator for several reasons:

- The largest share organisation will very likely enjoy advantages of size such as economies of scale, high brand recognition, channel dominance and the strongest bargaining position with customers and suppliers.

- The market leader is in the best position to exploit the experience curve because it will accumulate experience faster than competitors.

- Studies show that market share is related to profitability

2.5 The PIMS approach

The PIMS approach was initiated by General Electric (GE), as an attempt to identify the factors that affect ROI, the relationship between market share and operating economies, and how to manage GE's diversified activities. When information is collected from PIMS members (or subscribers) it is added to the database for analysis and interpretation by PIMS researchers in an endeavour to identify the most important variables associated with profitability, and to establish any relevant correlation between market shares, strategies, product quality, environmental conditions and profits.

The underlying belief of PIMS is that there is a pronounced relationship between market share and financial return and that the higher the market-share, the better the chances of earning a higher-than-average return-on-investment (ROI) - for the reasons outlined above and because high share companies have to offer a better product and better service to maintain their market share.

Companies must not think, however, that gaining increased market share will automatically improve their profitability. Much also depends on their strategy for gaining increased market share. For example, the investment involved may far exceed its revenue value.

2.6 How PIMS operates

The objectives of PIMS programmes are as follows:

- to develop an up-to-date database which truly reflects the business experience of the participating businesses;
- to develop a research programme, using the database to discover the 'laws of the market place' that govern business strategy;
- to develop an applications programme, to make the findings available to the participating businesses.

From the research and applications programmes, several reports on the individual businesses are produced. These are further explained below:

- The Par report - gives the ROI that is normal for the business sector, and identifies major strengths or weaknesses in the individual business.
- Strategy analysis report - simulation of the consequences of alternative strategies.
- Optimum strategy report - the combination of strategic decisions that promises the best results.
- ROLA - Report on Look-Alikes - a report on other businesses that are similar.

2.7 The influences on profitability and cash flow

Investment intensity - two indices are used to measure this - investment ÷ sales and investment ÷ value added. It has been found that the higher the level of investment intensity, the lower the level of ROI.

Productivity - this is the value added per employee. Generally the higher the productivity, the higher is the ROI.

A high relative market share is correlated with a high ROI and positive cash flow. The reasons are economies of scale, experience effects, and bargaining power.

Where a business has a weak market position, the suggested strategy is to minimise R&D, avoid expensive marketing, keep capacity loaded and be wary of investing in vertical integration. In general, there is evidence that striving for market share is not always worthwhile.

Market growth has a positive effect on total profit, a neutral effect on percentage profit and a negative effect on cash flows.

Quality of product/services, profitability and market share are strongly linked. Improving quality is important in all situations and generally improves market position. However, in the short-term it has a negative effect on profit.

The effect of cost-push - wages and raw material price rises - can be complex depending on the ability of the business to pass on higher costs.

2.8 The market share options

There are three basic options when offer positioning is considered in terms of market share:

- **To maintain market share** - to consolidate. But a firm is unlikely to maintain market share if it does nothing - to stay exactly the same is not a viable option in the longer term, as competitors will enhance their own offers and leave them behind. Firms have to run fast to stand still; they have to enhance their capabilities or lose market share and/or they will lose margin.

- **To increase it** - market penetration. A firm can increase market share either by reducing prices or by increasing perceived value or by doing both of these together or sequentially.

- To let it fall - harvest. This way means not enhancing the offer features and accepting that the value for money in the offer will decline as competitors upgrade and the offer will lose market share. The attraction of this is that money will be saved through not upgrading. This harvesting strategy is not necessarily a bad idea if the offer faces insurmountable long-term competitive disadvantages.

What the organisation sees as appropriate revolves around how it views both its future and the importance of market share.

2.9 A resource based (competence) view

The resource-based view argues that strategy should be focused upon generating superior competencies that can be deployed in the market place.

Frequently, resource based companies develop competencies in advance of product market strategies, and find places to deploy them. In an earlier chapter, we saw how Marriott had used the competencies developed in the hotel business to enter a range of industries that required similar competencies. By working in this way, resource based firms are frequently able to upset competitive pressures in an industry to their own advantage.

The resource based theory or resource-based view (RBV) of firms - emphasises economic rent creation through distinctive capabilities. Economic rent, or Economic Value Added (EVA), is what companies earn over and above the cost of the capital employed in their business. It is the measure of the competitive advantage, and competitive advantage is the only means by which companies in competitive markets can earn economic rent.

According to this view, a company's competitive advantage derives from its ability to assemble and exploit an appropriate combination of resources. Sustainable competitive advantage is achieved by continuously developing existing and creating new resources and capabilities in response to rapidly changing market conditions.

Traditional strategy models such as Michael Porter's five forces model focus on the company's external competitive environment. Most of them do not attempt to look inside the company. In contrast, the resource-based perspective highlights the need for a fit between the external market context in which a company operates and its internal capabilities.

In contrast to the Input / Output Model (I/O model), the resource-based view is grounded in the perspective that a firm's internal environment, in terms of its resources and capabilities, is more critical to the determination of strategic action than is the external environment. Instead of focusing on the accumulation of resources necessary to implement the strategy dictated by conditions and constraints in the external environment (I/O model), the resource-based view suggests that a firm's unique resources and capabilities provide the basis for a strategy. The strategy chosen should allow the firm to best exploit its core competencies relative to opportunities in the external environment.

Resources are inputs into a firm's production process, such as capital, equipment, and the skills of individual employees, patents, finance, and talented managers. Resources are either tangible or intangible in nature. With increasing effectiveness, the set of resources available to the firm tends to become larger. Individual resources may not yield to a competitive advantage. It is through the synergistic combination and integration of sets of resources that competitive advantages are formed.

A **capability** is the capacity for a set of resources to perform a stretch task or an activity. Through continued use, capabilities become stronger and more difficult for competitors to understand and imitate. As a source of competitive advantage, a capability should be neither so simple that it is highly imitable, nor so complex that it defies internal steering and control

Resource and competence-based approaches are particularly valuable when an organisation is considering changing the boundaries of its business, for example:

- By acquisition or divestment
- By entering joint ventures or other partnership arrangements
- When considering Make versus Buy alternatives
- When entering new markets
- Taking on new technologies

When disaster is at hand.

3 Alternative strategy directions

3.1 Ansoff's product-market matrix

There are a number of strategic directions that an organisation can pursue. Ansoff modelled potential growth strategies based on the extent to which new products and/or new markets are sought. Ansoff's analysis is summarised in a 2-by-2 matrix, with 'market' on one axis and 'product' or 'service' on the other.

		Product	
		Existing product	New product
Market	Present market	– Market penetration	– Product development or innovation
	New market	– Market development (sometimes called 'exploration')	– Diversification

To illustrate how this works, consider the following possibilities:

- A business seeks growth while offering its **present** products to its **present** market; this is a strategy of market penetration, i.e. achieving wider adoption of an existing product by the existing target customers.

- A business seeks growth by offering **new** products to its **present** market; in other words, a strategy of new product development.

- A business seeks growth by offering its **present** products in **new** markets; this is a strategy of market development, i.e. finding new customers who may wish to acquire the products already on hand.

- A business seeks growth by offering **new** products in **new** markets; this is a strategy of diversification. In effect, managers conclude that existing products and markets do not offer the most attractive option, and they look for something better.

The balance of risk changes between markets; in some the cost of new product development is extremely high and therefore risky. In other markets, there may be high entry barriers or branding difficulties that make market development the great risk. The rule is to try the least risky first (market penetration), but it may be that using both will still not close the strategic gap, and diversification – the most risky of all – must be attempted.

Improvements in internal efficiency are not something about which strategic decisions are taken. They should be constantly sought as part of the day-to-day running of the firm and so are covered in the operations plan (which is one of the sub-plans which elaborate the strategy).

3.2   Market penetration - existing markets and products

This is a strategy by which a company seeks to increase the sales of its present products in its existing markets It is aimed at increase usage by methods such as recipes on tins and packets, attracting customers by offers and price reductions and by attracting new users. The advertising for Guinness has been trying to attract younger, rather than their traditional older drinkers. Note the link here with a problem child/star product.

Methods of growth might include the following.

- Build market share - particularly suitable if the overall market is growing. The business might use discounting, increased advertising etc.

- Develop niches - target growth in a range of targeted niches within the industry, building up overall market share. This may be particularly suitable if the organisation is small compared to competitors.

- Hold market share - particularly if the market is reducing.

- Withdrawal - seek withdrawal of other companies, through, for example, using economies of scale to lower costs and make other firms uncompetitive.

The ease with which a business can pursue a policy of market penetration will depend on the nature of the market and the position of competitors. When the overall market is growing it may be easier for companies with a small market share to improve quality or productivity and increase market activity rather than in static markets, where it can be much more difficult to achieve. The lessons of the experience curve stress the difficulty of market penetration in mature markets where the cost structure of the market leaders should prevent the entry of competitors with lower market share.

Market penetration strategy would be contemplated for the following reasons:

- When the overall market is growing, or can be induced to grow it may be relatively easy for companies entering the market, or those wishing to gain market share, to do so relatively quickly. (Some companies established in the market may be unable or unwilling to invest resources in an attempt to grow to meet the new demand). In contrast, market penetration in static, or declining, markets can be much more difficult to achieve.

- Market penetration strategy would be forced on a company that is determined to confine its interests to its existing product/market area but is unwilling to permit a decline in sales even though the overall market is declining.

- If other companies are leaving the market for whatever reasons, penetration could prove easy - although the good sense of the strategy may be in doubt.

- An organisation that holds a strong market position, and is able to use its experience and competence to obtain strong distinctive competitive advantages, may find it relatively easy to penetrate the market.

- A market penetration strategy requires a relatively lower level of investment with a corresponding reduction in risk and senior management involvement.

Opportunities for improving business performance within the existing pattern of trading will generally fall under the following headings:

- Advertising and promotion to increase the volume of sales into existing markets.

- Improved selling and distribution methods to improve the service offered and possibly to rationalise the market coverage.

- Modifications to products or to packaging in order to improve and broaden their appeal, and ideally to reduce costs. Some rationalisation of products may be involved.

- Improvements in productivity to make a greater volume of products available without a disproportionate increase in costs. This may involve the modification or rationalisation of production methods.

- Changes in selling price, which can be increased if the market is relatively inflexible, or reduced in order to achieve a proportionately higher volume of sales.

Even though market penetration is seen as the least risky of Ansoff's options, it should not be assumed that risk is always low. When Yamaha attempted to gain share over Honda, it provoked a retaliation that left Yamaha in a worse position than before. The example should serve to remind us that Ansoff's strategies still require a competitive advantage to be effective (a point Ansoff made many times, but which is frequently forgotten).

3.3   Product development - existing markets and new product

This strategy has the aim of increasing sales by developing products for a company's existing market. For our purposes new-product development is a generic term that encompasses the development of innovative new products and the modification and improvement of existing products. By adopting this strategy the company could:

- develop new product features through attempting to adapt, modify, magnify, substitute, rearrange, reverse or combine existing features

- create different quality versions of the product

- develop additional models and sizes.

A company might show a preference for product development strategy for the following reasons:

(a) It holds a high relative share of the market, has a strong brand presence and enjoys distinctive competitive advantages in the market.

(b) There is growth potential in the market. (You may remember that the Boston Consulting Group, for instance, recommend companies to invest in growth markets.)

(c) The changing needs of its customers demand new products. Continuous product innovation is often the only way to prevent product obsolescence.

(d) It needs to react to technological developments.

(e) The company is particularly strong in R&D.

(f) The company has a strong organisation structure based on product divisions.

(g) For offensive or defensive motives, for example responding to competitive innovations in the market.

However, product development strategy does have its downside and there are strong reasons why it might not be appropriate for a company. For example, the process of creating a broad product line is expensive and potentially unprofitable, and it carries considerable investment risk. Empirical research reveals that companies enjoying high market share may benefit in profit terms from relatively high levels of R&D expenditure, while companies in weak market positions with high R&D expenditure fare badly.

There are reasons why new-product development is becoming increasingly difficult to achieve:

(a) In some industries there is a shortage of new product ideas.

(b) Increasing market differentiation causes market segments to narrow with the effect that low volumes reduce profit potential which in turn increases the risk of the investment involved.

(c) A company typically has to develop many product ideas in order to produce one good one. This makes new-product development very costly.

(d) Even when a product is successful it might still suffer a short life cycle with rivals quick to 'copycat' in the market but with their own innovations and improvements.

(e) There is a high chance of product failure.

Success frequently depends upon stretching a brand further than the market is willing to take it.

ACTIVITY 2

Levi's once attempted to move away from casual clothing into suits. Market research showed that there was nothing wrong with the clothing, yet the project failed. What might have gone wrong?

Feedback to this activity is at the end of the chapter.

3.4 Market development - existing products and new markets

Market development strategy has the aim of increasing sales by repositioning present products to new markets. (Note: this strategy is also referred to as **'market creation'**.)

Kotler suggests that there are two possibilities:

(a) The company can open additional geographical markets through regional, national or international expansion.

(b) The company can try to attract other market segments through developing product versions that appeal to these segments, entering new channels of distribution, or advertising in other media.

For example, during 1992 Kellogg undertook a major television and promotion campaign to reposition Kellogg Cornflakes (traditionally regarded as a breakfast cereal) to provide afternoon and evening meals. In the same way, the malt drink Horlicks had previously repositioned from a once-a-day product ('a night meal') to become a through-the-day 'relaxing drink' for young professionals. This was not successful. On the other hand, Lucozade have successfully moved their brand from a product associated with infirmity to a sports related product.

Market development strategy would be contemplated for the following reasons:

(a) The company identifies potential opportunities for market development including the possibilities of repositioning, exploiting new uses for the product or spreading into new geographical areas.

(b) The company's resources are structured to produce a particular product or product line and it would be very costly to switch technologies.

(c) The company's distinctive competence lies with the product and it also has strong marketing competence. (Coca-Cola provides a good example of a company that pursues market development strategies, as does the fast-food restaurant chain of McDonalds.)

3.5 Extensions and reductions

The Japanese call offer extensions 'food chains' or 'offer generations'. Offer extensions may be differentiated by whether they are predominantly extensions to the core product or service, generally simply called product extensions, or whether the emphasis is on market extensions.

Product extension would particularly suit a firm that had a strong brand and is prepared to undertake what is known as *brand extension* or *brand stretching* - using a well-respected brand name with the new offers.

Brand extension refers to the use of a successful brand name to launch a new or modified product in a same broad market. A successful brand helps a company enter new product categories more easily. For example, Fairy (owned by Unilever) was extended from a washing up liquid brand to become a washing powder brand too.

Brand stretching refers to the use of an established brand name for products in unrelated markets. For example the move by Yamaha (originally a Japanese manufacturer of motorbikes) into branded hi-fi equipment, pianos and sports equipment.

When done successfully, brand extension can have several advantages:

- Distributors may perceive there is less risk with a new product if it carries a familiar brand name. If a new food product carries the Heinz brand, it is likely that customers will buy it

- Customers will associate the quality of the established brand name with the new product. They will be more likely to trust the new product.

- The new product will attract quicker customer awareness and willingness to trial or sample the product

- Promotional launch costs (particularly advertising) are likely to be substantially lower.

However, brand stretching can be dangerous. Mercedes is in danger of destroying the value of its brand name by using its name on the smaller cars that it has introduced. In Volkswagen has retained the brand names on its Audi, Seat, Skoda and VW ranges.

Market extension occurs when an offer is introduced into a market segment other than the one where it's currently positioned. The UK supermarkets are engaging in market extensions because they are seeing their 'traditional' areas becoming saturated. For example, Esso and Tesco are combining to provide local stores on garage forecourts.

3.6 Market positioning strategy

We are going to outline the steps to take when drawing up a market positioning strategy for positioning services in competitive markets eg, a new hotel.

1   **The search for competitive advantage** in services requires differentiation and focus:

- Intensifying competition in service sector threatens firms with no distinctive competence and undifferentiated offerings

- Slowing market growth in mature service industries means that only way for a firm to grow is to take share from competitors

- Rather than attempting to compete in an entire market, firm must *focus* efforts on those customers it can serve best

- Must decide how many service offerings with what distinctive (and desired) characteristics

2   **Standing apart from the competition -** a business must set itself apart from its competition. To be successful it must identify and promote itself as the best provider of attributes that are important to target customers.

3   **Basic focus strategies for services**

Breadth of service offerings

	Narrow	Wide
Many	Service focused	Unfocused (everything for everyone)
Few	Fully focused (service and market focused)	Market focused

(Number of markets served)

4   **Four principles of positioning strategy**

1 Must establish position for firm or product in minds of customers

2 Position should be distinctive, providing one simple, consistent message

3 Position must set firm/product apart from competitors

4 Firm cannot be all things to all people--must focus

5   **Uses of positioning in marketing management**

- Understand relationships between products and markets
  - compare to competition on specific attributes
  - evaluate product's ability to meet consumer needs/expectations
  - predict demand at specific prices/performance levels
- Identify market opportunities
  - introduce new products
  - redesign existing products
  - eliminate non-performing products
- Make marketing mix decisions, respond to competition
  - distribution/service delivery
  - pricing
  - communication

6   **Possible dimensions for developing positioning strategies**

- Product attributes
- Price/quality relationships
- Reference to competitors (usually shortcomings)
- Usage occasions
- User characteristics
- Product class

7   **Developing a market positioning strategy**

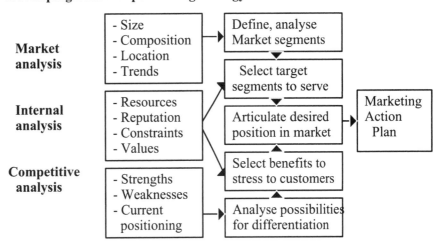

8   **Positioning of Hotels in Midville - price versus service level**

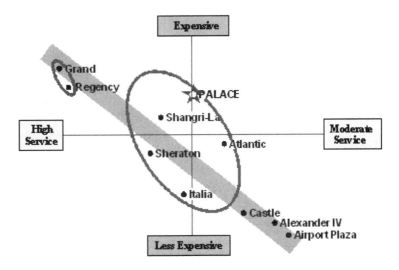

9   **Positioning of Hotels in Midville - location versus physical luxury**

10   **Positioning maps help managers to visualise strategy**

- Positioning maps display relative performance of competing firms on key attributes
- Research provides inputs to development of positioning maps
- Challenge is to ensure that
  - attributes employed in maps are important to target segments
  - performance of individual firms on each attribute accurately reflects perceptions of customers in target segments
- Predictions can be made of how positions may change in the light of new developments in the future

- Simple graphic representations are often easier for managers to grasp than tables of data or paragraphs of prose

- Charts and maps can facilitate a 'visual awakening' to threats and opportunities and suggest alternative strategic directions

3.7 Growth by diversification - new products and new markets

Diversification is the deployment of a company's resources into new products and new markets. The company thus becomes involved in activities that differ from those in which it is currently involved. Diversification strategy means the company selectively changes the product lines, customer targets and perhaps its manufacturing and distribution arrangements.

The term diversification actually covers a range of different techniques:

- *Concentric diversification* – the firm moves into new markets based upon technological know how. Firms following a resource-based approach usually take this route, since it enables them to develop and extend their existing core competencies. This form is also known as related diversification.

- *Conglomerate diversification* – a firm moves into markets that are unrelated to its existing technologies and products to build up a portfolio of businesses. Sometimes this is because the company has developed skills in turnaround or brand management, and can buy an ailing company very cheaply and quickly create value. Hanson have achieved great things in this way, based upon a nucleus of around 500 people. On other occasions, a company might use conglomerate diversification if it believes it has no real future in its existing product market domain. Finally, many entrepreneurial leaders move in and out of markets simply because of opportunities – Virgin being a good example.

- *Horizontal diversification* - synergy is highest in the case of horizontal diversification, especially if the technology is related eg, Cadbury/Fry but the disadvantage is that little additional flexibility is provided. This type of strategy affects all parts of the value chain since fixed costs can be spread over an increased number of units. Most diversification strategies are of this type. The strategy is undertaken when a company extends its activities into products and markets in which it already possesses necessary expertise, for example a manufacturer of televisions branching into the manufacture of video recorders, camcorders and hi-fi equipment.

- *Vertical integration* – a firm buys up different parts of the wider value system.

  Forward integration - moving towards the consumer - control of distribution eg, tied public houses

  Backward integration - moving away from the consumer - control of supplier eg, Whitbread buying hops growers

  Many manufacturers find particular specialist component suppliers are achieving higher returns than they are, and buy into the market. In difficult markets it might be necessary to own distributors or retail outlets to place the product before a customer.

  Suppose that a company currently manufactures cars - if the company were to buy a chain of car dealers, this would represent forward integration since it is moving towards the final consumer or if the company were to buy a manufacturer of car components (headlights, windscreens etc) this would represent backward integration. A good way to understand when a vertical integration strategy should be considered and how it should be evaluated is to consider its possible benefits and costs:

Benefits	Costs
Operating economies	Operating costs
Access to supply or demand	Management of a different business
Control of the product system	Increase in risk
Entry into a profitable business	Reduced flexibility
Enhancing technical innovation	Costs of being 'in-grown'

Example

Discuss the advantages and disadvantages for the M Company, a clothes manufacturer, in integrating forward by buying up a chain of retail outlets and integrating backwards by buying a company, which manufactures cloth.

Solution

There are several reasons why M might pursue forward integration. It will be easier for a chain of retail outlets to differentiate its clothes from those of its competitors through branding. This gives an opportunity for higher margins to be earned. The M Company can produce clothes as the shops demand them (JIT), leading to reductions in inventory levels. They will also have a guaranteed customer for its output.

There are also reasons against this course of action. The reaction of the customers that the M Company presently supplies may be hostile. If they stop stocking M Company's products, will the chain of retail outlets be able to sell enough to cover this fall in demand? What is the likely effect of the increased costs of distributing clothes to the shops, rather than to the depots of current customers?

A strategy of backward integration into the supply chain would give the M Company a dedicated supplier with both guaranteed quality and price. The material could be manufactured when required by M Company, leading to lower inventory levels.

The down side to this course of action is that, if alternative cheaper suppliers become available, the M Company will not be able to use them, since it will be committed.

There are also arguments against integration generally, whether forwards or backwards.

To be successful may require different skills from those presently possessed by the company. For example, M Company may know little about retailing or material manufacturing. To be successful it will have to stretch its current competencies to cover these areas.

In addition, there may be a very different focus for each of the businesses. For example, the chain of retail outlets may well be successful if it can differentiate its products from those of its competitors using innovative colours and material, while the cloth manufacturer is likely to be successful by keeping its costs low by using basic materials and standardised colours. It will be difficult for the M Company to maintain both of these at the same time.

In the exam the relevant theory here is likely to be Porter's generic strategies, not Ansoff. The reason is that each type of integration has an effect on the value chain.

Because of the extent of the change there is clearly more risk involved than in a strategy of product-market expansion (i.e. remaining within the existing product-market scope), so we must consider the reasons why companies nevertheless diversify. Ansoff suggests three main reasons.

(a) Objectives can no longer be met without diversification. This would be identified by the momentum line (status-quo) forecast and gap analysis. The reason for the dissatisfaction with the present industry might be either due to poor return caused by product decline, with little opportunity for technological innovation in the same field, or due to lack of flexibility, e.g. unavoidable dependence on a single customer or a single product line.

(b) The company has more cash than it needs for expansion. Whether it prefers to invest this outside the business or to seek opportunities for diversification will depend on the relative rates of return obtainable (in general the return from operations exceeds the return from outside investments, but of course more risk is involved) and management preference (management have to balance the internal flexibility achieved by keeping reserves in liquid form with external flexibility offered by diversification).

(c) Companies may diversify even if their objectives are being or could be met within their industry, if diversification promises to be more profitable than expansion.

3.8 Withdrawal (Liquidation or divestment) strategies

These strategies are used whenever the organisation believes that it can no longer compete effectively, or would prefer to use the shareholders' funds in another sphere of activity.

(a) **Deliberate curtailment**

A reduction strategy involves the curtailment of some activities.

A company could therefore be said to be adopting a reduction strategy when there is a planned cutback or retrenchment in the overall level of its business activities, and thus when one or more of the following policies ensues:

1 reduction in the range of markets served

2 cutback in the range of products offered

3 decline in the volume or absolute value of sales

4 reduction in geographical scope

5 decrease in the total assets of the company.

(b) **The circumstances that favour a reduction strategy**

Companies have frequently been forced to make strategic withdrawals from products and markets in the face of untenable product, social, political or technological conditions. Causes for reduction strategy include the following:

1 **The environment**

– There are reductions in the market.

– The effects of general economic recession.

– The company is forced to withdraw from a market as a direct or indirect result of political pressures.

– The company is forced by social pressures to withdraw from the market place.

2 **The competition**

– The company can no longer compete effectively with its products or services in terms of cost, price, quality and delivery against its opponents' product and service offerings.

– The company is forced to retreat from the market due to the superiority of competitive technology and the lack of internal technological resources.

3   **The company's resources and competence**

- It experiences poor operating results.

- It has inadequate resources to sustain its current strategic structure.

- It has an incompatible or ineffective product/market portfolio.

Often perceived as a somewhat negative strategy, withdrawal can be appropriate in certain circumstances where opportunities for synergistic gains represent an increase in value. For example large, diverse companies may view their subsidiary companies as assets to be bought and sold as part of an overall corporate strategy, particularly with which it has a clear strategic fit but with activities peripheral to those of the divesting organisation.

Sometimes organisations will partially withdraw from a market by licensing the rights to other organisations. This became common in the public sector where particular services have been privatised (eg, laundry services in hospitals).

The most extreme form of withdrawal is when an organisation's position becomes so untenable that voluntary or forced liquidation may be the only possible course of action.

The benefits of divestment include providing the company with additional cash resources that could be used for reinvestment in successful areas of the organisation, identifying and undertaking potentially successful projects, which would be of more benefit to the firm, or increasing dividends to shareholders.

3.9   Consolidation strategies

Consolidation focuses on the maintenance of market share. It implies changes in the way the company operates, making better use of fixed assets and reducing manufacturing expenses, although the range of products the company produces and promotes may remain unchanged.

Consolidation is equally relevant to growing, static or declining markets and may take several forms; maintaining share in growing markets, consolidation of position in mature markets, and consolidation of position in declining markets. Consolidation can also mean strengthening and reinforcing the position of the organisation as a market leader.

PIMS analysis indicates that high product quality is important is a consolidation strategy is to succeed.

Consolidation in mature or declining markets is clearly the most difficult to attempt. Failure to grow at least in line with the competition can lead the organisation into an uncompetitive cost situation and a vicious circle of low share-cost disadvantages - reduced cash flow - inadequate resources to invest - poor products and marketing - low share and so on cycle.

It is possible that non-growth strategies are adopted because of the prevailing socio-political economic climate. Some large companies are confronted by anti-monopoly legislation or are constrained by public opinion. They might have too large an effect on a particular local population: for instance, a company might face pressure to abandon plans to modernise a certain factory with the consequent reduction in the labour force, since that would cause too serious an increase in the unemployment rate in the locality where that factory is the main employer. In addition, there is a debate about the quality of life, as opposed to continued economic growth, which calls into question some of the fundamental philosophies of large companies. Thus the company cannot always be guided by purely economic motives.

Apart from the external pressures, there may be internal reasons for deciding on a non-growth strategy. It might be that once the company gets above a certain size, management problems rise out of proportion to the growth in size. Owner-managers might prefer to keep their firms at a size that they personally could control comfortably, rather than have to appoint other managers or raise outside capital with perhaps the eventual risk of losing control of their organisations. Also, some managers with a loyal, dedicated and high calibre work force would be reluctant to grow if that meant that the quality of the new employees would not match the old, or if the door might be opened to disruptive elements. Furthermore, the production system might be such that growth led to diseconomies of scale.

A company might pursue a non-growth strategy if it saw its non-economic objectives as more important than its economic objectives (given a certain minimum level of profit), although a non-growth strategy does not imply a lack of attention to economic objectives. Strictly speaking, a non-growth strategy means no growth in **earnings**. This does not necessarily mean no growth in **turnover** – if margins are falling, turnover will need to increase to maintain the same level of earnings. Capital equipment will have to be kept up-to-date, but there will be no net increase in investment – all the earnings can therefore be paid out as dividends to the shareholders.

Or there could even be negative growth, by paying out dividends larger than current earnings, so that shareholders are effectively receiving a refund of their capital investment, and there is a net fall in assets employed. A negative growth strategy can be employed in pursuit of an objective to increase the percentage return to the shareholders – if the company pulls out of the least profitable areas of its operations first, it will increase its overall return on investment, although the total investment will be less.

KEY POINT

It is emphasised that pursuing a negative growth strategy is not the same as simply allowing the company to run down. The negative growth strategy consists of an orderly, planned withdrawal from less profitable areas, and while the shareholders' dividend may eventually decline their return can rise since the capital invested also falls. If the company simply runs down, their return will also fall.

It is emphasised that pursuing a negative growth strategy is not the same as simply allowing the company to run down. The negative growth strategy consists of an orderly, planned withdrawal from less profitable areas, and while the shareholders' dividend may eventually decline their return can rise since the capital invested also falls. If the company simply runs down, their return will also fall.

3.10 Neutral strategy

Circumstances that might favour a neutral strategy are:

(a) **The environment**

This could be where the environment does not encourage change or where no change is anticipated and the company's current and future environments are considered to be fairly stable.

(b) **The competition**

The company has a good competitive position and any attempt to **'rock the boat'** may bring more dangers than advantages.

(c) **The company's resources and competence**

The company may have little choice because it only has the resources required for the same strategies as it pursued in the past.

(d) **The goals of the company**

Where past goals, and the achievement of them, are satisfactory, and it is thought that similar performance will be obtained from the same strategy.

(e) **The culture of the organisation**

This is the easiest strategy to implement. It is doubtful that it will be resisted.

The points made above seem to suggest that if a strategic formula appears successful the best way forward is not to 'tinker' and to limit the number of changes. However many would say that this is a dangerous supposition. The rate of change occurring today in some respects is accelerating exponentially; shifting so fast it is difficult to make even short-term predictions accurately

4 Internal or external growth

4.1 Internal growth

Internal growth has a number of particular advantages over acquisition or joint development.

- The company will develop and retain the core competencies upon which the growth is based.

- The rate of change can be controlled.

- Development costs are spread over time and can be budgeted more accurately.

- Value creating activities can be brought in when the firm does not have competencies; there is no need to buy another company.

Consideration of internal growth usually commences with an estimate of the best growth rate that the company can achieve. Since actual growth is usually somewhat less, the firm then uses a range of options associated with its products and markets.

4.2 Greiner's growth model - organic growth

Internal growth may be seen as a relatively secure option, even if a little slower than the potential gains in growth from buying a whole company. However, the work of Greiner reminds us that even organic (internal) growth is not without disruptions. He argued that growth brings with it some predictable crisis that only major organisational change can resolve.

Greiner identifies five phases of growth. Each evolutionary period is characterised by the dominant management style used to achieve growth, while each revolutionary period is characterised by the dominant management problem that must be solved before growth can continue.

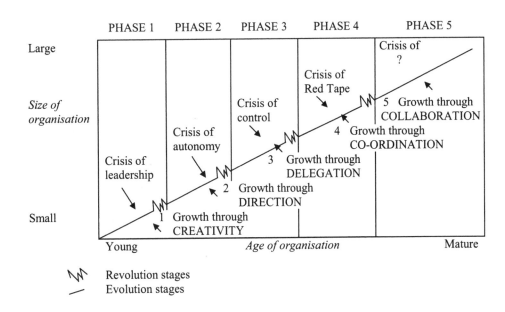

Growth through Creativity

A small firm working informally – making and selling. This is the creative stage where control comes from the feedback gained from customers/clients. However, as the firm grows, the management cannot manage the complexity in this way, and a **crisis of leadership** emerges.

Growth through Direction

Leadership, professional management and formal systems drive the firm forward. Continued growth makes leadership more remote, and those employees at lower levels feel constrained by top management, leading to a **crisis of autonomy**.

Growth through Delegation

The successful firm learns to delegate important activities to middle managers rather than keep top management involved in day-to-day activities. With this delegation of authority comes departmentalisation, in-fighting and increasing remoteness of top management, leading to a **crisis of control**.

Growth through Co-ordination

Growth continues with co-ordinating and control mechanisms to keep delegated managers to the organisational purpose. Over time, these systems become more complex, and it gets harder to achieve change, or even create value, without creating a **crisis of red tape**.

Growth through Collaboration

Co-ordination mechanisms are replaced by shared values and meanings, and action through teamwork. Greiner does not say that there are no crises that follow this, but they are less well articulated. Teamwork in particular may place limits on growth by reducing individual reflection and initiative.

In summary, organic growth is a relatively safe means of developing the organisation. Its great strength is the ability to develop competencies in prime areas as the firm develops. However, it may be rather slower than other methods available, and is not without the need for disruptive organisational change as the firm gains in size, scope and complexity.

4.3   Growth by merger or acquisition

A merger is the coming together of two organisations, often of a broadly similar size. Negotiations are usually friendly because the merger is deemed to be mutually beneficial.

In contrast, an acquisition is the purchase of one company by another and a takeover is a hostile acquisition – where the directors of the target company do not wish their organisation to be acquired.

Advantages of mergers and acquisitions

Acquisition has some significant advantages over internal growth:

KEY POINT

The advantages of mergers
and acquisitions include:

- access to resources

- avoids barriers to entry

- less likelihood of
  retaliation

- can block a competitor

- helps to restructure

- boosts earnings per share

- asset valuation.

- High speed access to resources – this is particularly true of brands; an acquisition can provide a powerful brand name that could take years to establish through internal growth

- Avoids barriers to entry – acquisition may be the only way to enter a market where the competitive structure would not admit a new member or the barriers to entry were too high

- Less reaction from competitors – there is less likelihood of retaliation because an acquisition does not alter the capacity of the competitive arena

- It can block a competitor – if Kingfisher's bid for Asda had been successful it would have denied Walmart its easy access to the UK

- It can help restructure the operating environment – some mergers of car companies were used to reduce overcapacity

- Relative price/earnings ratio – if the P/E ratio is significantly higher in the new industry than the present one, acquisition may not be possible because it would cause a dilution in earnings per share to the existing shareholders. But if the present company has a high P/E ratio it can boost earnings per share by issuing its own equity in settlement of the purchase price

- Asset valuation – if the acquiring company believes the potential acquisition's assets are undervalued it might undertake an asset stripping operation.

Disadvantages of mergers and acquisitions

There are some disadvantages associated with this method of growth:

KEY POINT

The disadvantages of mergers
and acquisitions include:

- more costly then internal
  growth

- cultural mismatch

- salary mismatch

- disposal of assets

- risk

- reduction in return on
  capital employed.

- Acquisition may be more costly than internal growth because the owners of the acquired company will have to be paid for the risk already taken. On the other hand, if the company decides on internal growth it will have to bear the costs of the risk itself.

- There is bound to be a cultural mismatch between the organisations – a lack of 'fit' can be significant in knowledge-based companies, where the value of the business resides in individuals.

- Differences in managers' salaries – another example of cultural mismatch which illustrates how managers are valued in different countries.

- Disposal of assets – companies may be forced to dispose of assets they had before the acquisition. The alliance between British Airways and American Airlines was called off because the pair would have had to free up around 224 take-off and landing slots to other operators.

- Risk – of not knowing all there is to know about the business it seeks to buy.

- Reduction in return on capital employed – quite often an acquisition adds to sales and profit volume without adding to value creation.

ACTIVITY 3

List all the possible motives you can think of for a company attempting to acquire the ownership of more, or all, of another company.

Feedback to this activity is at the end of the chapter.

At the end of the 1990s (and still continuing) there has been a renewed growth in merger and acquisition activity. However, currently the focus is on related industries. There is an awareness that different industries may need different skills and resources. Concentration is now on building relationships with firms operating in similar or related technologies. Acquisition for the sake of diversification is not a major factor in these moves. These linkages vary from strategic alliances and joint ventures to full-scale integration with mergers or acquisitions.

4.4 Growth by joint development

Joint development is seen as an attractive way forward for companies that do not have the resources or capabilities needed for future expansion. This does not mean that the firms involved will be small. It is common to find large companies undertaking joint development where the costs and risks of a project are high, such as for construction and pharmaceuticals.

KEY POINT

The term 'joint development' covers a range of possible arrangements including networks, licences and franchises, and joint ventures.

The term 'joint development' covers a range of possible arrangements including:

- **Networks** – loose associations of companies that co-operate for mutual advantage. Many biotechnology companies share resources through such arrangements. Of paramount importance is the ability of the network to learn together.
- **Licences and Franchises** – where other firms undertake part of the value creation process under contractual arrangements.
- **Joint ventures** – where assets are formally integrated and jointly owned.

ACTIVITY **4**

Indicate the appropriate form for each of the following:

1 Two young entrepreneurs develop a successful format for theme bars, but cannot raise the capital for organic growth.

2 A maritime firm specialising in hull cleaning needs the services of a scaffolding firm.

3 Two pharmaceutical companies are both working on similar drugs, and see the wisdom in co-operating.

Feedback to this activity is at the end of the chapter.

4.5 Strategic alliances

A strategic alliance can be defined as a co-operative business activity, formed by two or more separate organisations for strategic purposes, that allocates ownership, operational responsibilities, financial risks, and rewards to each member, while preserving their separate identity/autonomy. The technical difference between a strategic alliance and a joint venture is whether or not a new, independent business entity is formed. A strategic alliance is often a preliminary step to a joint venture or an acquisition. A strategic alliance can take many forms, from a loose informal agreement to a formal joint venture. Alliances include partnerships, joint ventures and contracting out services to outside suppliers. The types and motives for strategic alliances are outlined in the diagram below.

	Loose (market) relationships	Contractual relationships	Formalised ownership/ relationships	Formal integration
Forms of alliance	Networks Opportunistic alliances	Subcontracting Licences and franchises	Consortia Joint ventures	Acquisitions and mergers
Influences	Assets do not need joint management	Asset management can be isolated	Assets need to be jointly managed	
Asset separability	Assets cannot be separated	Assets/skills can be separated	Assets cannot be separated	
Asset appropriability	High risk of assets being appropriated	Low risk of assets being appropriated	High risk of assets being appropriated	

Seven characteristics of a well-structured alliance have been identified:

- **Strategic Synergy** – more strength when combined then they have independently.

- **Positioning Opportunity** – at least one of the companies should be able to gain a leadership position (i.e. to sell a new product or service; to secure access to raw material or technology).

- **Limited Resource Availability** – a potentially good partner will have strengths that complement weaknesses of the other partner. One of the partners could not do this alone.

- **Less Risk** – forming the alliance reduces the risk of the venture.

- **Cooperative Spirit** – both companies must want to do this and be willing to fully cooperate.

- **Clarity of Purpose** – results, milestones, methods, and resource commitments must be clearly understood.

- **Win-Win** – the structure, risks, operations, and rewards must be fairly apportioned among members.

Some organisations are trying to retain some of the innovation and flexibility that is characteristic of small companies by forming strategic alliances (closer working relationships) with other organisations. They also play an important role in global strategies, where the organisation lacks a key success factor for some market. This may be distribution, a brand name, a selling organisation, technology, R&D or manufacturing capability. To remedy this deficiency internally would often require excessive time and money.

A strategic alliance is a long-term collaboration bringing together the strengths of two or more organisations to achieve strategic goals. For example, IBM formed links with Ricoh for distribution of low-end computers. This allowed them to move into the Japanese market quickly, inexpensively and with a relatively high prospect for success. It can also help result in improved access to information and technology.

Some organisations are using strategic alliances to extend their reach without increasing their size. Others are motivated by the benefits associated with a global strategy. A strategic alliance can take many forms, from a loose informal agreement to a formal joint venture. They include partnerships, joint ventures and contracting out services to outside suppliers.

4.6 The role of the budgetary process

Financial planning is concerned with translating the resource implications of decisions into financial statements of one sort or another. This is generally done through the various types of budget that managers use. Budgets have many uses and perform different roles in organisations. The concern here is with budgets as plans and as models.

A budget may take the form of a *consolidated* statement of the resource position required to achieve a set of objectives or put into effect a strategy. To achieve such a statement it is necessary to identify and think through the required resource position of the organisation. A budget expresses these in a monthly or yearly form, perhaps divided into departments in the organisation. At both an organisational and a departmental level, a budget is in effect a model of required resources. A model can be examined, tested and adjusted to see the implications of changing assumptions about the future, or about the progress that might be achieved in a project. This can be achieved easily if the budget is set up on a computer spreadsheet package.

The following types of budget or financial plan might typically be used in resource **planning of strategy implementation:**

Capital budgeting is concerned with generating a statement of the flow of funds related to a particular project or decision. In particular, capital budgeting often relates to specific strategies but neglects the impact on overall organisational performance.

Annual revenue budgets are commonly used to express the detailed resource plan in financial terms. They are also used as a means of measuring and controlling performance against the plan.

Financial plans and projected profit and loss accounts may well be useful in projecting, perhaps over a period of years, implications of decisions on an organisation's overall performance. They are usually less detailed than annual budgets.

One of the very real difficulties experienced in budgeting is the extent to which the process actually helps the reallocation of resources to fit future strategies. This is because the budgeting process is usually tied into the power structure in the organisation.

Conclusion

In this chapter we have examined the process of thinking through strategic options to develop the strategy. We have contrasted the PIMS based, product market approach with Hamel and Prahalad's stretch strategy. The important role of strategic objectives in terms of withdrawal, consolidation and growth were considered. The links between aspirations expressed by the strategic gap, and meeting those aspirations in terms of Ansoff's mix, were examined.

We contrasted these internal means of developing strategy with external techniques, involving acquisitions, joint ventures and other alliances with other firms.

SELF-TEST QUESTIONS

Developing strategies

1   What is a strategic gap? (1.3)

Market based and competence based strategies

2   What is the underlying belief of PIMS? (2.5)

Ansoff's product-market growth vector

3   What is the name of the strategy by which a company seeks to increase the sales of its present products in its existing markets? (3.2)

Internal or external growth

4   Why might a firm chose external, rather than internal growth? (4.2)

5   What are the key problems with strategic development by acquisition? (4.3)

EXAM-TYPE
QUESTION

Strategic objectives

Until quite recently, many firms pursued a policy of conglomerate diversification. This was usually linked with the strategic objective of growth and often effected by mergers.

Required:

(a) Assess the appropriateness of growth as a strategic objective.   **(8 marks)**

(b) Explain why a company might follow a policy of conglomerate diversification.

(12 marks)

(Total: 20 marks)

For the answer to this question, see the 'Answers' section at the end of the book.

FEEDBACK TO
ACTIVITY 1

1   The market for software products continues to be promising. It is only necessary to be competent to do well. Thus a competence based strategy would be appropriate, followed by a growth strategy.

2   The market for specialist steel is good, and the company should pursue growth. However, it would be dangerous to diversify into the wider steel market, as this is unattractive. If there is little room for growth in the niche, the firm needs to develop other competencies to try related niche areas.

3   The motor insurance business runs on relatively small margins. An average competitor may struggle to generate a good return on investment. Clearly attempting to grow in such a difficult market would be risky, so the firm should try to consolidate its position and improve operational competencies.

4   The whole point of competing in a niche is that specialist competencies create differentiation or cost leadership. In this case, no such competencies can be necessary – cost leadership would enable the market price to be reached, while differentiation would mean that the products could compete above the market price. If the firm cannot restore its advantages, it should withdraw.

5   The firm should try to leverage abilities in logistics and merchandising across the product lines. Individually:

Fruit farming: The market for foodstuffs is not growing, but there may be opportunities to diversify – particularly at the quality and organic niches.

Soap Powder: Consolidation is important. Loss of share will quickly lead to rising costs if there are strong economies of scale involved. Since it is very difficult to differentiate the product directly, high levels of marketing expenditure will be required to create and maintain brand loyalty.

Cosmetics: The market remains attractive and fast moving, but the firm's performance is weak. A competence based strategy is implied. It may be that the merchandising and branding skills the company has developed in food and soap are less appropriate in this sector, and appropriate learning needs to take place.

FEEDBACK TO ACTIVITY 2	Market research suggested that there were two market groups – Levi customers that might buy suits and those who did not ordinarily buy Levi but did buy suits. In practice, the former group did not associate the values of the Levi brand with smart apparel and did not stretch their loyalty to the new market. The latter group were actually put off by the brand.

FEEDBACK TO ACTIVITY 3	Possible aims are:

(a) **General**:

- obtain joint synergy
- buy management talent
- buy time while the strategy of the acquiring company develops.

(b) **Marketing**:

- preserve the balance of market power
- control spheres of influence of potential competitors
- break into a new market (perhaps export or beachhead)
- take advantage of joint marketing synergies (for example by way of rationalisation of distribution, advertising, sales organisation and sales costs in general)
- reposition markets and products
- obtain the reputation or prestige of the acquired company
- take over 'problem child' products
- obtain a critical mass position.

(c) **Manufacturing**:

- acquire technical know-how
- amalgamate manufacturing facilities to obtain synergies (economies of scale, group technology, shared research, rationalisation of facilities and working capital, and so on)
- extend manufacturing involvement (for example the provision of field maintenance services).

(d) **Procurement of supplies:**

- control spheres of supply influence
- safeguard a source of supply for materials
- obtain operating cost synergies
- share the benefits of the suppliers' profitability.

(e) **Financial:**

- acquire property
- acquire 'cash cow' organisations
- obtain direct access to cash resources
- acquire assets surplus to the needs of the combined businesses and dispose of them for cash
- obtain a bigger asset backing
- improve financial standing (market price and earnings per share)
- speculative gain purposes.

1   Franchising should be undertaken quickly. Formats can usually be copied, and the firm is unlikely to have the resources to enforce its distinctiveness legally. With a franchise, the owners of each bar will pay a fee to the entrepreneurs in exchange for fittings, items, training and corporate level advertising.

2   The firm could hire scaffolding firms on an opportunistic basis. However, the specialist nature of the business might mean that there are particular skills that need to be developed, and a simple network arrangement might serve. Indeed, labour in the scaffold company might be trained to carry out some of the low skilled activities in hull cleaning once confidence has been established.

3   The two companies would probably create a joint venture as joint shareholders of a new company. Any discoveries made would be owned by both parties, but losses would not create liability for the parent companies.

Studies tend to suggest that joint development activities are closely connected with resource and skills development. Some organisations have the specific intent of learning skills from a partner, so that they can later operate independently. This process is called hollowing out, and is a good way for a firm to develop new skills. Obviously it is necessary for firms to safeguard their own particular competences in the venture.

Writers taking the resource based view make much of abilities to act in networks as this gives firms access to resources and knowledge beyond those that they own. It is a prime element of Hamel and Prahalad's notion of leverage, and Kay's notion of strategic architecture.

Chapter 12
STRATEGIC EVALUATION

In the last chapter we examined how options might be developed from a range of strategic models. A good test of a creative manager is his or her ability to devise a range of options that seem appropriate to a given set of problems, as several studies have shown that insufficient effort is usually made in this area. Once a range of options have been devised it is necessary to evaluate and select the option that is most likely to succeed.

Johnson and Scholes have outlined a set of evaluation criteria based on three categories: suitability, feasibility and acceptability. These categories emphasise how an organisation's circumstances might influence the broad types of strategy they should follow.

Objectives

When you have studied this chapter you should be able to:

- use appropriate techniques to evaluate the suitability of a range of options

- use appropriate techniques to evaluate the acceptability of a range of options

- use appropriate techniques to evaluate the feasibility of a range of options

- discuss the different ways that strategists use these evaluation techniques to make a decision.

1   Corporate strategy

1.1   A framework for evaluating strategies

Johnson and Scholes, in their book *Exploring Corporate Strategy*, have outlined a set of evaluation criteria based on three categories: suitability, feasibility and acceptability.

These categories emphasise how an organisation's circumstances might influence the broad types of strategy they should follow. Here we introduce them all briefly, before expanding each one to show the range of techniques that can be applied to assist the strategic evaluation.

(i)   **Suitability**

Suitability is an evaluation criterion for assessing the extent to which a proposed strategy actually fits the situation identified in the strategic analysis, and how it would sustain or improve the competitive position of the organisation. The strategic analysis would include the major opportunities and threats that face the organisation, its particular strengths and weaknesses, and any expectations that are an important influence on strategic choice.

Suitability is a useful criterion for screening strategies, asking the following questions about strategic options:

- Does the strategy exploit the company strengths, such as providing work for skilled craftsmen or environmental opportunities, e.g. helping to establish the organisation in new growth sectors of the market?

- How far does the strategy overcome the difficulties identified in the analysis? For example, is the strategy likely to improve the organisation's competitive standing, solve the company's liquidity problems or decrease dependence on a particular supplier?

KEY POINT

Johnson and Scholes have outlined a set of evaluation criteria based on three categories: suitability, feasibility and acceptability.

KEY POINT

Suitability is an evaluation criterion for assessing the extent to which a proposed strategy actually fits the situation identified in the strategic analysis, and how it would sustain or improve the competitive position of the organisation.

- Does the option fit in with the organisation's purposes? For example, would the strategy achieve profit targets or growth expectations, or would it retain control for an owner-manager?

(ii) Feasibility

An assessment of the feasibility of any strategy is concerned with whether it can be implemented **successfully**. The scale of the proposed changes needs to be achievable in resource terms. At the evaluation stage there are a number of questions that need to be asked when assessing feasibility. These include:

- Can the strategy be funded?
- Is the organisation capable of performing to the required level, e.g. quality or service?
- Can the necessary market position be achieved, and will the necessary marketing skills be available?
- Can the organisation cope with competitive reactions?
- How will the organisation ensure that the required skills at both managerial and operative level are available?
- Will the technology (both product and process) be available to compete effectively?
- Can the necessary materials and services be obtained?

(iii) Acceptability

Acceptability is strongly related to people's expectations, and therefore the issue of 'acceptable to whom?' requires the analysis to be thought through carefully. Some of the questions that will help identify the likely consequences of any strategy are as follows:

- How will the organisation perform in profitability terms? The parallel in the public sector would be cost/benefit assessment.
- How will the financial risk (e.g. liquidity) change?
- What effect will it have on capital structure (gearing or share ownership)?
- Will the function of any department, group or individual change significantly?
- Will the organisation's relationship with outside stakeholders, e.g. suppliers, government, unions, customers need to change?
- Will the strategy be acceptable in the organisation's environment, e.g. higher levels of noise?

A wide range of tools, some of which have been introduced, is available to assist managers in the strategy evaluation process. These tools are discussed below.

The framework below shows how the criterion of suitability can be used as a means of screening options. Suitability is assessed for strategic logic, cultural logic and research evidence. The workable shortlist is then assessed in much more detail using the criteria of feasibility and acceptability.

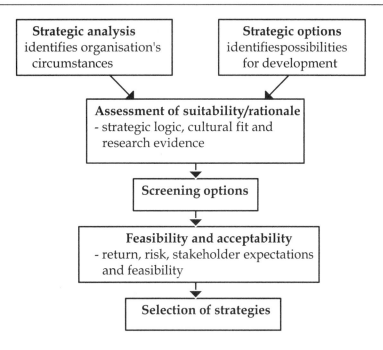

2 Assessment of suitability

2.1 Audit of strategic fit

The audit of strategic fit is concerned with the suitability of the proposed strategy ie, the fit between what is proposed and the organisation's aspirations and capabilities and whether the proposed strategy is a suitable response to environmental events and trends.

Examples of strategic fit revolve around the choices of

- market share - eg, consolidation would appear to fit strategically eg, when an owner-manager wishes the organisation to remain the same size as it is now, because they are near to retirement.

- market extensions - market penetration occurs when market share is increased in one of the organisation's segments. It would appear to fit strategically eg, where present customers can be induced to buy more or where the organisation has spare production or distribution capacity

- market reductions - harvesting occurs when the market share is allowed to decline and this would appear to fit strategically when eg, there is no money available for the enhancements needed to retain market share or where the firm's markets are being hit by cheap imports.

Suitability is a useful criterion for screening strategies, asking the following questions about strategic options:

- Does the strategy exploit the company strengths, such as providing work for skilled craftsmen or environmental opportunities eg, helping to establish the organisation in new growth sectors of the market?

- How far does the strategy overcome the difficulties identified in the analysis eg, improve the organisation's competitive standing, solve the company's liquidity problems or decrease dependence on a particular supplier?

- Does the option fit in with the organisation's purposes eg, achieve profit targets or growth expectations, or would it retain control for an owner-manager?

The techniques used to assess suitability include the following:

- life cycle/portfolio matrix
- resources and competences analysis
- profile analysis
- screening techniques
- decision trees.

2.2 Life cycle analyses

Life cycle analysis relies on the belief that there are predictable relationships among the stages in product or business unit life cycles on one hand, and certain elements of strategy on the other. The typical product life cycle curve is shown below. Note the relationship between unit profit margin and sales revenues at the different stages.

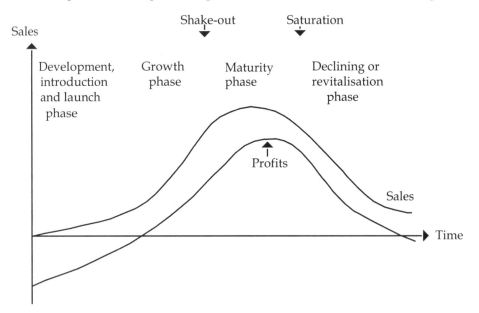

Life cycle curves can be useful devices for explaining the relationships among sales and profit attributes of separate products, collections of products in a business, and collections of businesses in a conglomerate or holding company. Life cycle analysis has been suggested by some of its advocates as a basis for selecting appropriate strategy characteristics at all levels. It also may be viewed as a guide for business-level strategy implementation since it helps in selection of functional-level strategies.

- Introduction Strategic Implications - during the early stages of the life cycle, marketing strategy should focus on correcting product problems in design, features, and positioning so as to establish a competitive advantage and develop product awareness through advertising, promotion, and personal sales techniques. At the same time, personnel strategy could focus on planning and recruiting for new product human resource needs and dealing with union requirements. Also, one would expect the nature of research and development strategy to shift from a technical research orientation during the phase prior to introduction to more of a development orientation during actual introduction.

  Financial strategy would be likely to address primarily sources of funds needed to fuel R&D and marketing efforts as well as the capital requirements of later production facilities. Capital budgeting decisions would be outlined during these early stages so that capacity would be adequate to serve growth needs when sales volume began to accelerate.

- Growth Stage Strategy Implications - during the growth stage, strategic emphases change relative to introduction. Marketing strategy is concerned with quickly carving out a niche for the product or firm and for its distribution capabilities, even when doing so might involve taking risks with overcapacity. Too often, firms have unadvisedly accepted quality shortfalls as a necessary cost of rapid growth. Widening profit margins during growth may even permit certain functional inefficiencies and risk taking. Communication strategy is directed toward establishing brand preference through heavy media use, sampling programs, and promotion programs, and strategy should emphasise resource acquisition to maintain strength and development of ways to continue growth when it begins to slow.

  Personnel strategy may focus on developing loyalty, commitment, and expertise. Training and development programs and various communication systems are established to build management and employee teams that can deal successfully with the demands of impending tight competition among firms during the maturity phase.

- Maturity-Stage Strategy Implications - efficiency and profit-generating ability become major concerns as products enter the maturity stage. Competition grows as more firms enter the market and the implication is that only the most productive firms with established niches and competent people will survive. Marketing efforts concentrate on maintaining customer loyalty and in strengthening this with distributors personally selling to dealers, sales promotions, and publicity.

  Production strategy concentrates on efficiency and, at the same time, sharpens the ability to meet delivery schedules and minimise defective products. Cost control systems are often put in place.

  Personnel strategy may focus on various incentive systems to produce manufacturing efficiency. Advancements and transfers are used and some firms try to fit management positions to managers who have personalities more attuned to the belt-tightening needs of products and SBUs at the maturity stage.

- Decline-Stage Strategy Implications - when a product reaches the point where its markets are saturated, an effort is often made to modify it so that its life cycle is either started anew or its maturity stage extended. When falling sales of a product cannot be reversed and it enters the decline stage, management's emphasis may switch to milking it dry of all profit. Advertising and promotion expenditures are reduced to a minimum. People are transferred to new positions where their experience can be brought to bear on products in earlier growth stages (if management was skilful enough to have created such products).

  Various strategies have been suggested for products that have entered the decline stage. Hofer and Schendel suggest four choices when sales are less than 5 percent of those of the industry leaders:

  - concentration on a small market segment and reduction of the firm's asset base to the minimum levels needed for survival

  - acquisition of several similar firms so as to raise sales to 15 percent of the leaders' sales

  - selling out to a buyer with sufficient cash resources and the willingness to use them to effect a turnaround liquidation.

2.3   Life cycle/portfolio matrix

This is a very broad based technique, in which the strategist checks that the product market strategies of the options are consistent with the product life cycle analysis. For example, it would not usually be wise to enter a market and invest in building a competitive advantage if the industry were well into its decline phase. There are several formulations of the matrix; the one that is shown here is the simplest, and relates competitive strengths to the life cycle stage:

	Early	**Mature**	**Late**
Strong competitor	Build dominant position	Defend position Defend margin	Control costs, harvest profits
Average competitor	Develop competences Find niches	Niche markets Turnaround strategies	Divest
Weak competitor	Develop competences or harvest profits	Withdraw/divest	Withdraw

Many writers are very critical of models like this. For example, Hampden-Turner argues that many innovative companies have rejuvenated markets and built a strong competitive position by refusing to accept the industry logic and thinking about the business in a new way.

2.4   Resources and competences

This part of the suitability test examines the capabilities of the firm in relation to the demands that will be made by the new strategy. It attempts to answer the following questions:

- What capabilities will be necessary?
- Will these capabilities lead to competitive advantage?
- How sustainable is this advantage?

2.5   Example

Lathams is a traditional firm that makes silver teapots. Much of the work is hand crafted, and the pots sell at a premium price in a market segment that is prepared to pay for individually crafted products. However, profits have been low because of quality problems in the manufacturing process. Poor quality teapots rarely leave the plant because inspection is very good, but scrap and reworking costs are high.

A suggestion has been made to solve these quality issues with use of modern techniques, such as statistical process control and design for manufacture, against the firm's traditional response of improving the quality of craftsmanship.

	Capabilities needed	**Competitive advantage**	**Sustainability**
Statistical process control	Investment in tools and plant redesign.	Unlikely, SPC identifies problems after they have occurred. Might reduce costs, as inspectors would not be needed.	Competitors could use the same technology.

Design for manufacture	Modern design techniques, probable part mechanisation of process.	Should reduce costs, enabling higher margins. Mechanisation of some parts of the process may be invisible to buyers.	Hybrid of craftsmanship and mechanisation may be hard to replicate.
Craftsmanship	Develop craft processes to reduce waste. Training and development of craftsmen.	The product already sells on the quality of craftsmanship. Could reduce wastage, but this may be offset by increased time in manufacturing.	Craft skills already developed beyond those of rivals in this market segment.

Using this model, we see that SPC solutions are less suitable that the other two proposed. On balance, the hybrid solution looks most suitable, but the traditional craft solution may also work.

2.6 Business profile analysis

This technique compares the options against the PIMS (Profit Impact of Marketing Strategy) prescriptions for higher profitability. A variety of scoring methods are possible – here we show the simplest.

An option is assessed by showing whether or not it brings the firm closer to the PIMS ideal. The model is demonstrated with reference to the activity above in which the firm part mechanises its production line to reduce the costs of poor conformance quality.

Profitable PIMS	+	0	-
High relative perceived quality		Quality problems have not reached the market. Improvements in conformance quality will not be obvious to the buyer	
High relative market share		Strategy is not based on expansion	
Capital Intensity			Mechanisation
Capacity		Unchanged	
Productivity	Should be a major improvement		
Marketing expenditure		Unchanged	
Bargaining power		Unchanged	
Logistics		Unchanged	

In this example, the benefits of productivity should offset the problems of increasing mechanisation. However, the technique also suggests that the strategy will not build upon the firm's advantage, and the strategists should consider the scope for a more aggressive strategic posture.

2.7 Screening options

In this section we look at techniques that try to match the strategic option against its effect on the issues raised by the resource audit.

The options available include:

- **scoring** methods that rank options against a set of predetermined factors concerning the organisation's strategic situation

- **decision trees**, that also assess specific options against a list of key strategic factors.

Scoring methods are a systematic way of analysing specific options for their suitability or fit with the picture gained from the strategic analysis.

Ranking is a simple scoring method where each option is assessed against a number of key factors. The illustration below is an example of how such a ranking might be performed. More sophisticated approaches to ranking assign weightings to each factor in recognition that some will be of more importance in the evaluation than others. The method can also be combined with sensitivity analysis to test out the likely impact on the company if the assumptions about each factor should change.

	Options	Desire for small company	Need to control quality	Need for high margins	Threat of competition	Dependent on supplier	Rank
1	Do nothing (i.e. current strategy)	✓	✓	✓	X	X	C
2	Seek new suppliers	✓	✓	?	X	X	C
3	More customers of same type	X	✓	✓	X	✓	A
4	Expand nationally	X	X	✓	✓	✓	A
5	Expand product range	✓	X	✓	X	✓	B
6	Seek new outlets	X	X	X	X	✓	A
7	Diversify	?	X	?	X	X	B

✓ = Favourable influence   X = Unfavourable influence   ? = Uncertain or irrelevant

A = Appear most suitable   B = Moderately suitable   C = Appear least suitable

The ranking process shown in the chart is used to group the various options into three categories (A, B and C) in relation to their suitability. It should be noted that each strategic factor might not carry the same weight or importance. The need for growth to counter competition was in fact of overriding importance, so options 4 and 6 were identified as most suitable despite their lack of fit with other factors.

Decision trees – this approach ranks options by the process of progressively eliminating others. This elimination process is achieved by identifying a few key elements which future developments are intended to incorporate such as growth, investment and diversification.

The greatest limitation of decision tree analysis is that the choice at each branch on the tree can tend to be simplistic. Nevertheless, as a starting point for evaluation, decision trees can often provide a useful framework.

3 Feasibility

Feasibility assesses whether or not the organisation is actually capable of carrying out the most suitable strategy. When the strategist has identified several suitable strategies, they are all assessed for feasibility. It is often the case that the second or third most suitable strategy is more feasible than the most suitable. The techniques used for assessing feasibility are:

- funds flow – an assessment of financial resources

- break even analysis – an assessment of market conditions

- resource deployment – an assessment of the firm's competences.

3.1 Funds flow analysis

Funds flow analysis estimates whether or not the firm can obtain the financial resources to carry out the strategy. The first stage is to estimate the costs of the strategic option. The following stages estimate the funds available from particular sources. The order of assessment given is general, but in practice there is likely to be some variation between 4 and 5.

1 Estimate the financial costs of the strategy

2 Estimate strategic funds

3 Estimate augmented strategic funds

4 Estimate leveraged strategic funds

5 Shareholder funds

Strategic funds are profits net of interest, dividends and taxes, plus non cash expenses (such as depreciation), plus receipts from asset sales (including divestment of SBUs) less financial commitments already made.

Over a business year, shareholder's funds should have been increased by retained profits and repayments of principal. This will have reduced the gearing. *Augmented strategic funds* are strategy funds plus increased borrowings to restore the previous gearing ratio.

In many cases, lenders will be willing to allow the company to increase its gearing. *Leveraged strategic funds* are augmented strategic funds plus additional debt.

If the sum that could be raised by leveraged strategic funds is still insufficient, the firm must consider raising equity by rights issues, placement or some other technique to raise *shareholder funds*.

3.2 Break even analysis

This is a conventional management accounting technique that you will have met elsewhere in the programme. It is used in project appraisal to estimate the contribution to fixed costs of a margin project. In this context, it is used to assess the market feasibility of the project in terms of the volumes and prices that might be achieved.

3.3 Resource deployment analysis

This test shows the growing influence of the resource based view on strategic thinking. It tries to estimate the firm's competences against those necessary for crucial parts of the strategy, by identifying weaknesses that must be eradicated and opportunities for learning and developing. *Threshold competences* are the minimum standards of capability necessary to compete. In some industries, this is very high. For example, zero defects is a threshold in many electronic industries.

Core competences are the basis of competitive advantage. The firm has very strong capabilities in an area that is of direct relevance to profitability. There is no point in developing a core competence in an area that buyers are not willing to pay for. Neither is there any long-term advantage in developing only threshold competences in the critical success factors.

Learning/resource growth refers to creating strategic stretch by continually finding opportunities to develop and applying core competences to new areas. A feasible strategy should always look for opportunities to extend the firm's knowledge by improving threshold competences and finding new applications for core competences. It is in this section that issues such as culture change should be evaluated.

Major changes in corporate behaviour are among the most difficult things that a management team can attempt to do. The enormous difficulties involved can be weighed against the potential benefit in value creation and resource development by considerations of the relevant competences.

4   Acceptability

Tests of acceptability identify and justify the expected performance outcomes of the strategic options. These can be stated in three questions:

- Are the outcomes (financial returns) of the strategy acceptable to all-important stakeholders?
- Are the risks acceptable to all-important stakeholders?
- Is the strategy ethical?

Ethics are considered in a separate chapter. In this section we examine the following techniques:

- profitability analysis
- cost/benefit analysis
- risk analysis
- shareholder value.

4.1   Profitability assessment

There are different ways in which the returns can be reviewed.

Profitability is a useful evaluation measure in the anticipated return on capital employed x years after a new strategy is implemented. Care must be taken to establish whether this measure is to be applied to the whole company or simply to the extra profit related to the extra capital required for a particular strategy.

When new strategies involve significant sums of capital investment, there are better measures of the relationship between capital expenditure and earnings. One such measure is that of payback, which assesses the period of time required to pay back the invested capital.

The payback period is calculated by finding the time at which the cumulative net cash flow becomes zero. **Discounted cash flow** (DCF) analysis is the most widely used investment appraisal technique and is essentially an extension of the payback period type. Once the net cash flows have been assessed for each of the preceding years they are discounted progressively to reflect the fact that the funds generated early are of more real value than those in later periods.

Cost/benefit analysis attempts to put a money value on all the costs and benefits of a strategic option – including intangibles. One of the difficulties of cost/benefit analysis is deciding on the boundaries of the analysis.

Despite the difficulties with cost/benefit analysis, it is a valuable approach if its limitations are understood. Its major benefit is in forcing people to be explicit about the variety of factors that should influence strategic choice.

4.2 Risk and uncertainty

Strategies, by definition, deal with future events: the future cannot be predicted, and there is always the possibility that events will not turn out as anticipated. We can make a distinction between risk and uncertainty, but often the terms are used interchangeably.

- *Risk* applies to situations where outcomes are not known, but their probabilities can be estimated. This is the underlying principle behind insurance.

- *Uncertainty* is present when the probability of any given outcome cannot be predicted. Uncertainty is the reason why insurance policies exclude war damage, riots and civil commotion from cover.

Risk can occur from many sources, and it is not always possible to estimate it properly. Here are some examples.

- Physical risk - recent earthquakes in Japan and Peru have highlighted this. Other physical risks include fire, flooding, and equipment breakdown.

- Economic risk - strategy is based on assumptions about the economic environment, which might be wrong.

- Financial risk - a strategy might be regarded risky if:

    - it results in increased borrowings and therefore increased gearing;

    - the cash flows from the business are volatile;

    - there is a requirement for significant capital expenditure with uncertain or volatile future returns

A financial risk profile of various strategic options should make it much easier to select appropriate combinations and to highlight unacceptably high or low total risk combinations. An organisation will normally reject a high product risk project with a high financial risk as being an unacceptable combination and only suitable for organisations with a strong appetite for risk. Financial risk can be analysed by the source of funding used by the organisation. Equity can be regarded as the lowest possible risk type of financing; borrowed money (debt) represents much higher risk. Thus for an organisation to decide to finance with debt the development and launch of a completely new product would represent a high total risk combination.

- Business risk - this includes various factors such as:

    - lowering of entry barriers caused by, for instance, the introduction of new technology;

    - changes in the relative power of customers and suppliers;

    - new competitors;

    - factors internal to the firm such as its culture and technical systems, or management misunderstanding of core competences.

- Currency risk - changes in the relative value of different currencies bring risks to the value of an international investment or transaction.

- Political risk - includes nationalisation, sanctions, civil war and political instability, if these have an impact on the business.

- Relationship risk - includes various factors such as:
  1. contractual relationships - could delays in the supply of stock cause damage?
  2. outsourcing - is a recognised way of maintaining business growth but securing long term partnering relationships can be a problem
  3. disputes - the risk and magnitude of claims is escalating
  4. insolvency - many successful businesses fail because of the insolvency of trading partners. How do you minimise your risk when a key customer or supplier runs into financial difficulties?

How can risk be incorporated into strategic decision-making?

- A firm might require that all investments make a minimum return. This hurdle rate could be raised to compensate for extra risk.

- As risk increases the further one attempts to look into the future, it might be made a condition of all new investment projects that they should pay back within a certain period of time, say three to four years. The payback period would depend on the characteristics of the capital investment and the industry: big capital projects tend to need a longer payback period.

- It might be determined that the investment should be financed under strict conditions eg, only from profits.

4.3 Risk appraisal

Some strategies will be more risky than others. One of the problems arising when evaluating alternative strategies is the reliability of the data used. Since the figures are compiled on estimates of the future, there must be considerable uncertainty about the final accuracy of the figures.

Business planners frequently use various operational research techniques to measure the degree of doubt involved. These include the simple 'rule of thumb' methods of expressing a range of values from worst possible result to best possible result with a best estimate lying between these two extremes.

Also, there is the use of basic probability theory to express the likelihood of a forecast result occurring. This would evaluate the data given by informing the decision-maker that there is, for example, a 50% probability that the best estimate will be achieved, a 25% chance that the worst result will occur and a 25% chance that the best possible result will occur. This evaluation of risk might help the executive to decide between alternative strategies, each with its own risk profile.

Risk can be quantified in statistical terms. In decision trees, a variety of possible outcomes are developed. Each is given an expected value (EV), based on probabilities. One way of assessing the risk associated with a decision is to calculate a standard deviation of the EV of profit. The higher the standard deviation, the more volatile the possible outcomes and hence the higher the risk.

4.4 Stakeholders and risk

The evaluation techniques discussed assume that managers are:

- free to choose organisational objectives;
- able to implement them autonomously.

Sometimes stakeholders, have sufficient power to influence management's choice of strategy. There are two aspects of stakeholder risk:

- the risk the strategic option *poses to the interests* of the different stakeholders;
- the risk *stakeholders will respond* in such a way as to reduce the attractiveness of a strategy.

4.5   Shareholder value

Shareholder value is an attempt to integrate the value analysis work that we considered earlier into the evaluation of strategy. Rather than evaluate individual options and their effects on different perceived problems, there is a greater attempt to integrate the influences throughout the organisation and its value system.

It operates by relating all strategic options to the value drivers identified at the strategic audit stage. It is then possible to estimate the effects in terms of reducing costs in the creation of existing value, creating greater (differentiated) value at the same cost, and both simultaneously where possible.

It must be said that this model frequently gives different answers to the more traditional profit/returns based models. Whether that means that this way of thinking is superior or inferior to traditional methods remains strongly contested.

5   Strategic selection

After reviewing tests of suitability, acceptability and feasibility, it remains to make a decision and then implement it. In many companies there is a lack of strategic confidence, and the firm does not actually take decisions in spite of carrying out a great deal of analysis. Indeed, there is a condition known as 'Paralysis by analysis' caused by continual reassessment of the data, models and prescriptions that prevents senior managers developing a sense of purpose and taking appropriate actions. Several approaches to overcoming this have been observed, and they are described below as:

- strategic planning/formal evaluation
- enforced choice
- learning/experience
- dominant stakeholder.

One particularly effective method is to identify several strategies that score most effectively in the suitability models (there is unlikely to be one outstanding option). These are evaluated for acceptability – particularly those that do not attract stakeholder resistance. Some suitable strategies will be eliminated by this process. Finally, feasibility is used to eliminate some options that are suitable and acceptable. At this point, any of the remaining options is likely to be effective, and selecting the 'correct' one is much less problematic.

5.1   Strategic planning and formal evaluation

Many senior managers would like to have formal processes that select the best strategy in an objective fashion. This usually requires quantitative objective setting and formal evaluation of options against these criteria. However, such techniques must, by definition, exclude many important things, or make unrealistic (but objective) proxies.

5.2   Enforced choice

Frequently, firms have, or believe they have, no choice in the matter of their strategy. A particularly strong stakeholder, or the pressure of the market, enforces choice in a particular direction.

In many senses, this is a symptom of poor strategy. The defining characteristic of good management is the choices and decisions it makes. To allow itself to reach a position where is has no choice implies poor managerial thinking in the past.

There are always exceptions. The dominant stakeholder may keep a very tight rein on expenditure and strategic direction, or may even impose a strategy from outside. In such cases, management's goal must be to create more strategic space to make decisions in the organisation.

The enforced choice rhetoric is often used by weak managers in change management issues. By doing so, they can say that the unpleasant consequences of change are outside their control. They throw away much of their own credibility and make it difficult for supporters of change to generate the enthusiasm necessary to bring about change effectively.

5.3   Learning and experience

The logical incremental model suggests that strategic options arise from small-scale experiments at the margins of the organisation. As the firm learns to do new things, opportunities will develop and the organisation will gain experience. For example, the international division will present a strategy based upon an observed opportunity overseas, while those involved in diversification will learn about different opportunities and situations. Senior management will have to choose their strategic options from the opportunities presented.

In strategic management, a distinction is sometimes made between learning and experience. Learning involves new ideas and changes in behaviour, while experiences lead to refinements and efficiencies. Clearly both are very important for the development of long-term competitiveness.

5.4   Dominant stakeholder

Organisations are political entities and powerful internal and external interest groups influence the inputs into decisions. A particularly strong stakeholder, or the pressure of the market, can enforce choice in a particular direction.

The dominant stakeholder may keep a very tight reign on expenditure strategic direction, or may even impose a strategy from outside. In such cases, management's goal should be to create more strategic space to make decisions in the organisation' s, rather than stakeholders' interest.

Conclusion

In this chapter we have examined the tools and techniques of strategic evaluation. Johnson and Scholes' tests of Suitability, Feasibility and Acceptability were discussed in some detail. The chapter concluded with a discussion of how these techniques might be brought together and a decision made. We observed that the deliberate strategies tended to look for integrative, objective processes, while emergent, incremental strategies were likely to take an opportunistic stance. However, both would find that the three tests greatly simplify the task of choosing a strategy by reducing the range of possible options to those that would be successful. Management taking an enforced choice approach need to create strategic space to make decisions in the firm's best interests before they can devise, choose and implement strategy effectively.

Corporate strategy

1   Why is it important to assess all options formally? (1.1)

2   Outline the broad differences between suitability, feasibility and acceptability. (1.1)

Assessment of suitability

3   What techniques are used to assess suitability? (2.1)

4   Explain how PIMS and similar ideas can be used in a business profile analysis. (2.6)

Feasibility

5   How does feasibility relate to the audit of resources? (3)

Acceptability

6   Describe three sources where risks can occur(4.2)

Strategic selection

7   How do formal evaluation techniques differ from what might be found in a firm using logical incrementalism? (5)

Business environment

P McNamee wrote - 'Strategic management is considered to be that type of management through which an organisation tries to obtain a good fit with its environment.'

Required:

(a)   Explain briefly how forecasting can assist an organisation to obtain 'a good fit' with its environment.   **(8 marks)**

(b)   Explain briefly the relationship between a gap analysis and forecasting.
                                                                             (12 marks)

                                                                      (Total: 20 marks)

For the answer to this question, see the 'Answers' section at the end of the book.

Chapter 13

MARKETING ISSUES

This chapter begins our look at strategic implementation. We begin with marketing, as this is the crucial link in the value-added chain. If customers are not engaged by the product offering, the rest of the strategy means nothing. The chapter begins by examining some ideas of industry level positions, and then develops some basic strategic marketing issues, such as segmentation, targeting and positioning. Bowman's model of strategic clock is used to make the important links between what a company offers its customers in the market place, and the strategic basis of competitive advantage.

The final section explores the issues that most matter to consumers; the marketing mix.

Objectives

When you have studied this chapter you should be able to:

*   explain positioning, targeting and segmentation

*   examine the range of strategies open to leaders, followers and niche marketers

*   demonstrate the development of the marketing mix.

1   Segmentation, targeting and positioning

1.1   Introduction

Segmentation, targeting, and positioning are marketing tools used by a company to gain competitive advantage in the market. They help the company to differentiate its product offering from that of its competitors and ensure that the same reaches the exact market profile for which it is intended. Market segmentation is the process of dividing the market into similar groups according to the characteristics intended for the product at hand. Targeting is the process of selecting the most lucrative market segments for marketing the product. Positioning involves the formulation of a definitive marketing strategy around which the product at hand would be finally marketed amongst the target audience.

Rolls Royce and Skoda are in the same industry, yet they do not compete. This is because the two companies have developed different positioning strategies. This implies at least some of the following:

*   The companies do not compete with each other.

*   Their customers are different.

*   The basis of competition is different.

*   The core competences required to compete effectively are different.

*   The products are promoted and distributed differently.

1.2   Strategic group analysis

Strategic group analysis is an approach toward understanding the competitive structure of an industry. It identifies which firms are directly competing. A strategic group could have similar characteristics eg, size, could pursue similar competitive strategies over time eg, heavy advertising and the use of the same distribution channel or could have similar assets and skills eg, quality image.

A set of strategic groups generally includes a set of mobility barriers that inhibit or prevent organisations from moving to another group. For example an industry like sausages has national brands, price leaders, own label suppliers and local butchers' products. Entry barriers, such as low cost production, brand names, low overheads or a local customer base, protect each of these groups. A member of a strategic group can also face exit barriers. For example plant investment or a specialised labour force can represent a significant exit barrier.

This concept is important because one way to develop a sustainable competitive advantage is to pursue a strategy that is protected from competition by assets and skills that represent barriers to competitors. It also helps to gain a better understanding of the bases of rivalry within strategic groups and how it differs from that within other groups. For example the multinationals compete in terms of branding and the control of manufacturing resources across countries. The own label suppliers are especially concerned with keeping costs down.

Steps in strategic group analysis -

- Select appropriate axes - different for each industry, should not be related to one another and they should distinguish between companies in the industry

- Plot companies

- Interpret

- Identify groups and spaces

- Explain why companies seem to form groups

The analysis below illustrates the local grocery market.

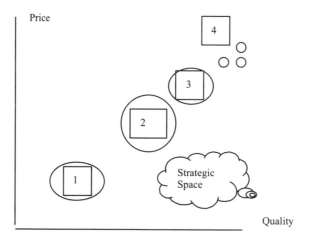

The two critical success factors here are price and quality. Of course, others, such as location, opening hours, marketing expenditure and so on, might be important too under some circumstances.

Group 1 are the price discounters. The business cuts cost wherever it can. Product ranges are restricted and there are few attempts to make the store decorative or service friendly.

Group 2 are the main market retailers. They compete on price, but offer more and better ranges, better customer service and so on.

Group 3 offer a higher quality range, and do not attempt to compete on price at all.

Group 4 are delicatessens. They offer a great deal of service and specialist items. Prices are very high.

It is a great strategic mistake to try to position oneself where there are no customer groups. For example, several companies have tried to cross between groups 1 and 2, usually without success.

Wakefields had struggled to maintain its position in strategic group 1 because it could not keep its costs down. A new MD decided to go upmarket by renaming the chain, updating the shop dress and a national advertising campaign showing higher quality products than the store had previously stocked. It was a spectacular failure, as most attempts to move up market tend to be. What might have gone wrong?

Feedback to this activity is at the end of the chapter.

1.3 Strategic groups and strategic space

Using the local grocery market example, *Strategic Space* is the term given to gaps that do not appear to be covered in the map. One is shown to the right of strategic group 1, beneath strategic group 2. This implies the existence of a group of customers that appreciate low prices, but also wish the benefits associated with higher quality – including choice, service, and a more pleasant shopping environment. Group 2 has been quicker to move into this, by simply adding a budget range to their own branded goods.

An understanding of strategic groups can make the process of competitor analysis more manageable. Numerous industries contain many more competitors than can be analysed individually. Often it is simply not feasible to consider 30 competitors, to say nothing of hundreds. Reducing this set to a small number of strategic groups makes the analysis compact, feasible, and more usable; little strategic content and insight will be lost in most cases, because firms in a strategic group will be affected by and react to industry developments in similar ways. Thus, in projecting future strategies of competitors, the concept of strategic groups can be helpful.

Strategic groupings can refine the strategic investment decision. Instead of determining in which industries to invest, the decision can focus on what strategic group a firm should invest in. Thus, it will be necessary to determine the current profitability and future potential profitability of the strategic group. One strategic objective is to invest in those strategic groups that will tend to be profitable over time and to disinvest or avoid strategic groups that will not be profitable.

Ultimately the selection of a strategy and its supporting assets and skills will often mean selecting or creating a strategic group.

The concept of strategic groups can also be helpful in projecting competitive strategies into the future. One of the transformations that will influence the business models and the work of strategists in the decades ahead is that the strategic space available to companies will expand.

Consider for example, the highly regulated power industry. All utilities once looked alike and their scope of operations were constrained by public utility commissions and government regulators. Due to deregulation, utilities can now determine their own strategic space. Today utilities have a choice regarding the level of vertical integration - 'do I need to be in power generation? Do I need to be in power transmission?' Companies can unbundle assets and can also segment their businesses. 'Should we focus more on industrial or domestic consumers'? They can decide their geographical scope. 'Should I become global, regional, national or just remain local'? And finally, they can change their business portfolio. 'Should I invest in water, telecommunications, gas lines, services'?

The forces of change - deregulation, the emergence of large developing countries such as India, China and Brazil as major business opportunities provide a new playing field. Simultaneously, forces of digital technologies, the emergence of the Internet and the convergence of technologies, provide untold new opportunities for strategists. The canvas available to the strategist is large and new.

One of the problems with the strategic group model is that it implies each group competes on the same critical success factors. Further, it does not adequately capture strategies that attempt to place an SBU in each strategic group while drawing out whatever synergies are possible. However, it is very useful for matching up groups of customers to groups of competing companies.

There is clearly a close relationship between strategic groups and market segmentation (which was discussed earlier). Moving between segments, or breaking into a new segment is clearly a major strategic initiative, and not undertaken lightly. A few pointers to improve the chances of success are given below:

- Ensure that the objective conditions (income, lifestyle, habits, etc) of the new segment actually exist.

- Investigate how the people in the segment see themselves and their distinctiveness (i.e. young, attractive, ethnic, cosmopolitan, etc).

- Identify where leaders of the segment are open to information and influence.

- Identify the product attributes that appeal to this segment (economy, style, fashion etc).

- Find where, and in what circumstances, consumers make their choice and purchase (mail order, telesales, department stores, etc).

- Discover the price range that is consistent with their aspirations and incomes, and identify what they are prepared to pay extra for.

Once these factors are known, it is possible to put together a marketing mix that would be attractive to the new segment. However, there is only a strategic value in doing so if the company can offer this product mix based upon a competitive advantage. Bowman's strategic clock model has been helpful to marketers in analysing this particular point.

1.4 Market segmentation analysis

DEFINITION

Market segmentation is used as a strategic marketing tool for defining markets and thereby allocating resources.

Market segmentation is used as a strategic marketing tool for defining markets and thereby allocating resources. Segmentation studies use statistical techniques called factor analysis and cluster analysis to combine attitudinal and demographic data to develop segments that are easier to target. In many situations it is better to identify your target groups and aggressively market to smaller, more defined segments.

To avoid missing a useful way of defining segments, a wide range of variables must be evaluated to identify segments where different strategies are, or should be, pursued. A segment that justifies a unique strategy needs to be a worthwhile size and the strategy chosen for the business segment needs to be cost effective. However, the selection of the most useful segment-defining variables is rarely obvious. Among the variables commonly used are segments based on customer characteristics that are unrelated to the product or service involved, eg type, location and size of organisation or group. The second category includes those that are related to the product or service, eg user type and brand loyalty.

In addition to superior satisfaction of customer needs, segmentation encourages better analysis of opportunities and often leads to higher sales. An example could be the Ford Focus car, one of the best selling cars in the UK in recent years. The basic car has been differentiated to appeal to different segments of the market. The lowest priced model in the range appeals to the budget motorist or first-time new car buyer. This is clearly a very different segment of the market from the racy saloon. Both these segments are different from the fleet car buyer whose purchases tend to be mid-range models.

1.5 Recognising the segment

In any strategy of segmentation, markets not only need to be identified, but should also be responsive, ie demonstrate effective demand. This means the presence of money (income, assets, credit worthiness), authority to buy and a desire to buy.

When segmenting the market it is important to consider the following.

- Measurability - is there sufficient published data to enable the group to identify and select accurately the companies to include within the segment?

- Accessibility - how can a sales force or promotional media reach the segments effectively?

- Appropriateness - is the segment compatible with the objectives and resources of the group?

- Stability - is the segment sufficiently constant so that it can be predicted in the future?

- Substantiality - is the segment of sufficient size to be financially viable and attractive?

If a segment fails on a number of these tests then it will be difficult to develop and maintain a successful segmentation strategy.

1.6 Segmentation by factor, market or organisation

The first task in undertaking **market segmentation** is to define the scope of the market in which the organisation wishes to operate. Is your product international or national in scope? Or will you sell it primarily in your own region or community?

Let's say that your primary market is local or regional, and that you live in a community with a population of about 25,000 people. The first thing you'll need to do is research the 'demographics' of your community, and divide it into market segments.

- It may be **organisationally defined** in terms of the product or service provided. Another way of looking at the market is to describe the different customers or consumers who will buy or use the product. The most usual definitional terms here would focus on whether they are business or household buyers, whether they are resellers or manufacturers or where they reside.

Next, you need to segment the market as much as possible using 'psychographics' as your guide:

- Lifestyle: conservative, exciting, trendy, economical

- Social class: lower, middle, upper

- Opinion: easily led or opinionated

- Activities and interests: sports, physical fitness, shopping, books

- Attitudes and beliefs: environmentalist, security conscious.

Finally, you can describe a market in terms of the alternative ways in which the exchange of value is performed. You can include the technology through which the delivery takes place, such as the Internet, phone or face-to-face through retail outlets. You might include aspects associated with channel partners eg, delivery through agents, recognised distributors or value aggregators.

Note: if you are a B2B company, you'll also need to consider the types of industries available to you, and their number of employees, annual sales volume, location, and company stability. In addition, you might want to find out how they purchase: seasonally, locally, only in volume, who makes the decisions? It is important to note that businesses, unlike individuals, buy products or services for three reasons only: to increase revenue, to maintain the status quo, or to decrease expenses.

1.7 Targeting

It is important here to have an overview of what is meant by segmentation and targeting and how it fits with identifying strategic decisions. Without targeting a specific customer segment, it is impossible to develop effective products or services that meet specific customer needs and requirements. Each segment, by definition, has a different set of requirements. While differences may be minor at time, they affect the decision of the customer to purchase the product or service.

Target marketing is choosing the segment or segments that will allow the organisation to most effectively and efficiently achieve its marketing goals. When evaluating potential target markets, care should be taken to ensure that the markets are the right size (neither too large nor too small), reachable (accessible), measurable (i.e. size, purchasing power and characteristics of the segments can be measures), and demonstrate behavioural variation (i.e., consumers share common characteristics within the target market).

1.8 Market and product positioning

After the target market has been chosen, marketers want to position their products or fix them in the minds of the target markets. **Positioning** is based on the perception or image that marketers want to develop or maintain for the product.

- **Market positioning** refers to the user's perceptions of the place a product or brand occupies in a market segment. First, you have to determine a **broad positioning**. This means determining if your product should fall into a niche, be a low-cost leader, or a product differentiator. These are each very different strategy highways, and will take you in different directions when fine-tuning your message. Think of the qualities of your product, its strengths and weaknesses, the opportunities you've uncovered, the pricing you've considered, and your target market to determine which broad position you will take.

- **Product positioning** refers to the way users/consumers view competitive brands or types of products. It is the art of tailoring the image and presentation of a product or service to appeal to a selected market segment. At its best, product positioning enables marketers to draw a direct link between an existing product attribute and a specific customer need. Product positioning is not new. An advertisement for the Holeproof Hosiery Company in 1910 contained the following headline:

  'To the 5,196,267 unmarried men of America'

  The appeal was a long-lasting pair of socks. Unmarried men were assumed to be either not capable of, or not interested in, darning socks. Product positioning is closely related to market segmentation. This is a process in which potential customers are divided into smaller groups based on demographic and psychographic characteristics. The 1910 hosiery advertisement grew out of a specific marketing niche.

Perceptual mapping is used to chart consumers' perceptions of brands currently on offer and to identify opportunities for launching new brands or to reposition an existing brand.

2 Marketing strategies

2.1 The market options matrix

The Market Options Matrix (shown below) differs slightly from Ansoff's Growth vector analysis but still takes the form of a set of product/market strategic choices.

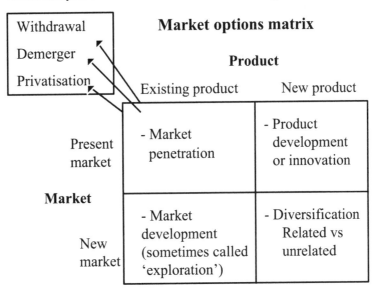

This model differs in that it acknowledges that managers might not be able to take advantage of environmental opportunities for growth. Organisations in stable environments or declining market situations may be mainly concerned with the development of particular core competencies of a specialist nature or with the development of greater efficiency of resource use, or even with the prospect of planning withdrawal from a market. Alternative directions suggested by this model are demerger and privatisation.

Divestment or demerger (often referred to as 'unbundling') is the process of disposing of part of an organisation's activities, and usually the assets and personnel that relate to it. One motive for doing so might be simply an opportunistic attempt to make a swift profit. Another reason might be a strategic decision to focus management effort on core activities while disposing of areas that distract from them. There are several options for a failing company under pressure to boost its flagging share price. They can split in half, focus, spin off hidden jewels, sell assets, break up; or introduce new faces. An example of a demerger is the split of British Gas into BG and Centrica in the late 1990s.

2.2 Strategic clock

Assuming that the products or services of different organisations are more or less equally available, customers may choose to purchase from one source rather than another because:

- the price of the product or service is lower than that of the other firm
- the product or service is more highly valued by the customer from one firm than another - here the term 'perceived added value' is used.

Although these are broad generalisations, they lead to decisions being taken on the type of strategy that the organisation will implement. The strategy clock, shown below, is another suitable way to analyse a company's competitive position in comparison to the offerings of competitors.

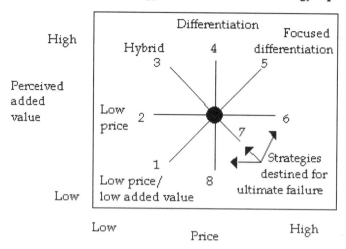

The Strategy Clock: Bowman's Strategy Options

As with Porter's Generic Strategies, Bowman considers competitive advantage in relation to cost advantage or differentiation advantage. There are six core strategic options:

Option 1	Low price/low added value	Likely to be segment specific
Option 2	Low price	Risk of price war and low margins/need to be a 'cost leader'
Option 3	Hybrid	Low cost base and reinvestment in low price and differentiation
Option 4	Differentiation *Without a price premium*	Perceived added value by user, yielding market share benefits
	With a price premium	Perceived added value sufficient to bear price premium
Option 5	Focused differentiation	Perceived added value to a 'particular segment' warranting a premium price
Option 6	Increased price/standard	Higher margins if competitors do not value follow/risk of losing market share
Option 7	Increased price/flow values	Only feasible in a monopoly situation
Option 8	Low value/standard price	Loss of market share

2.3 Price based strategies

Strategies 1 and 2 compete on the basis of price. With strategy 1, all unnecessary attributes are removed from the product, leading to lower costs and the opportunity to lower price. It is the 'cheap and cheerful' option, which entails reducing price and perceived value-added and focusing on a price-sensitive segment. It might be viable because there could exist a segment of the market, which, while recognising that the quality of the product or service might be low, cannot afford or chooses not to buy better-quality goods. Strategy 2 offers an average product but charges a lower price for it. Porter describes this as proximity of differentiation. Option two entails reducing price, while trying to maintain the quality of the product or service. The problem here is that this is likely to be imitated by competitors who can also reduce price. Therefore, the only way competitive advantage can be achieved is if lower prices can be sustained while others are unable to do so. This does get back to the notion of cost leadership. In the end, an organisation can sustain reduced prices only if it has *the lowest* cost base among competitors and is prepared to sustain a price-based battle; but it has been seen that this is very difficult to achieve. For an organisation that does not have such leadership, but chooses to compete on price, the danger is that the result is a reduction in margins in the industry as a whole, and an inability to reinvest to develop the product or service.

Two conditions are necessary for this strategy to work:

- Significant numbers of buyers must be price sensitive – the market must be price elastic.
- The firm must have a substantial cost advantage over its competitors.

ACTIVITY 2

Predict the outcome of the following strategies:

1 A new entrant tries to overcome strong brand loyalty by offering low prices

2 A firm drops prices in the expectation that increased volumes will lead to economies of scale and a cost advantage

3 A firm with a significant cost advantage realises that the market is not price sensitive, and keeps prices at the industry average.

Feedback to this activity is at the end of this chapter.

2.4 Added value and differentiation strategies

These are shown on the strategic clock as *Strategy 4*. It is, in effect, a broad differentiation strategy: offering perceived added value over competitors at a similar, or somewhat higher, price. The aim is to achieve higher market share, and therefore higher volume, than competitors by offering 'better' products or services at the same price; or enhanced margins by pricing slightly higher. The product must be differentiated from its rivals in a significant way that buyers are prepared to pay extra for. For this strategy to succeed, the following are necessary:

- The product must be differentiated in a way that is important for buyers.
- The buyers must be prepared to pay extra for the features.
- Costs must be well controlled.
- The source of the differentiation must be sustainable.

ACTIVITY 3

1 During the 1980s, IBM built a dominant position in the PC market based upon conformance quality, reputation and customer service. The only way for rivals to compete was to differentiate the product on features, but charge less. What happened to IBM?

2 Churchill Potteries purchased a superior design for a new product range in an attempt to move upmarket, as their budget range was becoming uncompetitive. What else must they do to achieve a competitive advantage?

Feedback to this activity is at the end of the chapter.

Differentiation is an effective strategy, and most industry leaders tend to differentiate their products in some way. It must be remembered that differentiation is not easy to *sustain*:

- Costs of replication are much lower than innovation. The advantage tends to lie with a firm that can replicate at lower costs
- The basis of competition may change. In the example above, IBM found that advanced product features became more important than service and reputation, and high conformance quality became the industry standard
- New entrants from abroad may enter the market with superior product features or quality
- Features of differentiation may become industry standard over time.

These points should serve to remind us that differentiation is not a static attribute. It is most sustainable when it is firmly based in a superior core competence that can be extended and recycled as the industry evolves.

2.5 Hybrid strategies

The important addition in this model is the 'hybrid' strategy (shown as *Strategy 3* of the strategic clock) that is an optimal balance between price and the added value perceived by the customer. This coincides with experience when purchasing household goods. The offerings may often fall into three broad categories. There are 'cheap' offerings which have minimal facilities and appeal to customers to whom price is the most important issue. At the other end of the scale are the 'luxury' offerings that have demonstrably high quality or numerous features and appeal to customers who want the best and the most differentiated. In the middle are the 'good-value' offerings that compromise between the two extremes by offering a good trade-off between price and value. This category often accounts for a sizeable percentage of the total market. The Sainsbury's slogan 'Good food costs less at Sainsbury's' can be seen as an attempt to capture this middle segment. Sainsbury's was the leading food retailer in southern England for many years. If it has lost this position this would seem to be because its original strategy has been successfully imitated rather than because it was a poor strategy. Hybrid strategies are perhaps the most difficult strategy to sustain, as ordinarily differentiation adds to cost. There may be a few exceptions, however:

- internationalisation may reduce costs but leave the differentiation unchanged

- superior cost advantage can generate profits that are invested in differentiation without destroying the cost advantage if this results in economies of scale

- differentiation may lead to high sales volumes, economies of scale, and lower costs

Such writers as Danny Miller have shown that the successful use of price or differentiation strategy can lead to opportunities to develop the other strategy as well. However, it is often found that when a firm attempts both simultaneously, the company does not develop a competitive profile and remains stuck in the middle.

Many Japanese organisations choose hybrid strategies. They have been simultaneously providing added value in customer terms while keeping prices down consistently. It is also the strategy pursued by IKEA, where the success of the strategy depends on the ability to understand and deliver against customer needs, while also having a cost base that permits low prices, which are difficult to imitate.

It is a strategic approach to new market development that Japanese organisations sometimes use on a global basis. They search for a weakness in a competitor's portfolio of SBUs e.g. a poorly run operation in a particular geographical area of the world. They will enter that market with a superior product, and if necessary a lower price. The aim is to take share, divert the attention of the competitor and establish a foothold from which they can move further. However, in following such a strategy it is important to ensure that the overall cost base is low enough to sustain margins, and a clear follow-through strategy has been considered for when entry has been achieved.

2.6 Focused differentiation

Strategy 5 picks out a particular market segment and builds differentiation into its products. As more markets globalise, this strategy is likely to become more widespread as companies target similar segments across national borders.

Some organisations can compete by offering higher value to the customer at a significantly higher price. However, the choice may have to be made between broad differentiation across a market or a more focused strategy. Indeed, this may take on global proportions, as managers have to decide between a broad approach in increasingly global markets, or much more selective focus strategies. In the market for saloon cars Ford, Peugeot, Renault, Volkswagen and Japanese competitors are all competing within the one market - trying to convince customers that their product is differentiated from those of their competitors. BMW is not seeking to compete directly with them because it is trying to attract a different market segment by offering a product with higher perceived value often at a substantially higher price. However, a focused differentiation strategy means that it is important to be clear as to which market segment the organisation is competing in, defined in terms of a coherent set of customer values and needs; and this must be translated into action, which consistently satisfies those customer values and needs. This may be difficult to do, particularly if the organisation is attempting to compete in different market segments, with different needs. For example, department stores attempt to sell wide ranges of products in one shop. They also may attempt to appeal to different customer types. They can run into difficulties because the store itself, the fixtures and fittings, the decor and store ambience, and the staff may not be differentiated according to the different market segment needs. Moreover, the buying may be done centrally and fail to provide product ranges sufficiently focused on the market segments.

A firm that succeeds in developing competences to build a focused differentiated strategy is often hard to defeat in the market place. However, the strategy has several limitations. The competences may be specific to that sector, and not easily transferable. Once the firm has grown to dominate its niche, it may struggle to find further growth opportunities. Further, if the basis for differentiation changes, the firm may find itself without threshold competences in important areas.

2.7 Failure conditions

Strategies 6, 7 and 8 in the strategy clock are failure conditions, i.e. they involve reducing the value added while retaining price, raising price without improving value added or reducing value while increasing price. Unless the whole industry follows suit, or the firm has a monopoly, these moves will result in failure.

Quite often, the firm ends up in these positions because it has attempted, but failed, to implement one of strategies 1 to 5, or has not developed a strategy to achieve competitive advantage in the first place.

3 Niche marketers, leaders and followers

The marketing strategy is devised by considering the basis of competition, as discussed using the strategic clock, and the range of strategic marketing options open to a company seeking growth.

Given the wide variety of strategic options, establishing the suitability of particular strategies in relation to the stage of industry maturity and the organisation's competitive position is not a simplistic affair.

3.1 Strategies based on market share

Kotler has identified various strategies to adopt based on market share. He suggests that market leaders (those with highest market share) should:

* expand total market by finding new users (market development)

* protect current market share by improving products (product development).

Market challengers, wishing to challenge the market leader, should

* attempt to exploit opportunities overlooked by the leader (market penetration)

* attempt to buy market share by acquiring small companies within the market

* attack the leader through tactics such as price wars (if their financial resources allow).

Market followers (those companies not seeking to challenge for leadership) should attempt to shadow the market leader. This often calls for high levels of production efficiency to avoid being driven out of the market.

3.2 Niche marketers

Niche marketers – weak organisations are not likely to survive through the life cycle unless they identify and exploit a market niche and become a strong provider within that niche. As growth declines, organisations will need to be more selective in their choice of strategy. Market-niche strategies are those that are intended to avoid competition, as the market pursued is either too small or too specialised for the market leaders to be interested. These market segments may be based on customer type, a price segment or a geographic area.

A niche strategy is an extreme example of focus and needs the organisation to make judgements on the products/services/markets that will be pursued and the ones to be discontinued. A strategy of retrenchment might be the first step, followed by attempts at turnaround of the organisation's performance. Divesting parts of the organisation or withdrawing from particular markets/products will also be considered.

3.3 Market leader

There are five competitive strategy options for a market leader to consider:

- Market expansion is where the market leader attempts to expand demand for the product category. Apart from stimulating primary demand for the product category a market leader could attempt to broaden the market by expanding into related product or categories or related market segments.

- Market share protection is where the market leader attempts to protect its share of the market with strategies such as outspending its competitors in advertising, using consumer and trade sales promotions to maintain customer loyalty, extending the product line to cover all market segments, lowering prices and increasing distribution.

- Pre-emptive strike is an offensive strategy, which anticipates or discourages competitive entry; for example, tying up the distribution channels by providing attractive trade incentives or by launching a fighting brand designed to offset any competitive product.

- Counterattack is attacking a competitor either by taking an individual competitor head on or by mounting a flanking strategy such as by moving into to an emerging market segment that the competitor has not entered.

3.4 Market challenger/follower

A market challenger is basically a strong no. 2 or no. 3 in the mainstream market in which it is perceived as an alternative to the leader. Generally these organisations are innovative and aggressive and quite often seek market leadership. Their marketing objective would therefore be to increase their market share. Market followers are smaller and are usually around the midpoint of the market structure. Quite often they compete with value-for-money alternative products (based on being adequate in quality but at a lower price). They may not compete in all of the mainstream markets but would cover the largest segments. In most cases their marketing objective would be to maintain or increase market share. Market challengers and market followers can choose between three proactive strategies of head-to-head competition, flanking strategies and encirclement and one reactive strategy of following the leader.

- Head-to-head competition is a dangerous strategy to pursue and the market challenger should be confident that it has a competitive advantage based on product superiority and/or cost. This competitive advantage must not only be real but also be capable of being perceived by the customer to exist and to be significant.

- Because head-to-head competition is so risky, the alternative strategy of *flanking* is often considered to be a preferred option. This strategy involves determining a need that the market leader (or leaders) has overlooked and in response to offer a product that satisfies those needs. That is, a flanking strategy seeks to compete in an uncontested area.

- A third alternative for a proactive strike is *encirclement*. This involves an aggressive move against the market leader on several fronts. This may involve introducing a product range that surrounds the market leader or switching the customer's attention to benefits or attributes that the leader currently does not offer.

- The final strategic alternative for the market challenger/follower is the reactive strategy of *follow the leader*. This minimises the risk of retaliation and is essentially a 'me-too' approach.

4 Marketing mix strategies

4.1 Introduction

The marketing mix is the set of controllable variables that a firm blends to produce desired results from its chosen target market.

There are four basic elements (the 'four Ps'), which must be managed to satisfy customers' needs at a profit.

- Product
- Promotion
- Place
- Price

The marketing mix is essentially the working out of the tactical details of the positioning strategy. An organisation should ensure that all of the above elements are consistent with each other. This is the primary way to project a consistent and believable image. Thus a firm that seizes upon the 'high quality position' knows that it must produce high quality products, charge a relatively high price, distribute through high-class dealers and advertise in high quality magazines. A high-cost product with a wide range of features and advertised in up-market magazines would not sell if sold in newsagents.

Having decided on the 'positioning' of the product (or product range) and on the 'unique selling propositions', that is going to be used in marketing the product(s), the organisation can set some operational objectives and agree the strategies to implement.

4.2 Product strategies

A product mix (or product range) includes all the products (or product lines) that a particular strategic business unit (SBU) offers for sale to buyers. In rapidly changing product markets, companies are constantly planning product improvements in order to encourage customer migration to higher-valued, higher priced items.

The product has two roles in the marketing mix. First, it plays a key role in satisfying the customer's needs. Second, product differentiation is also an important part of the firm's competitive strategy. The core product consists of the product's essential features; augmentations are additional features, which can be used to differentiate it.

Most important is how the customer perceives the product. They are looking at the following factors - any of which might be enough to set the product apart from its competitors.

- Aesthetics and styling
- Durability
- Brand image
- Packaging
- Service

The product policies that the organisation can choose from include:

- Developing a standardised product with no frills but not lacking in quality for a cost leadership strategy or alternatively the product could be differentiated, even customised for niche market strategies.

- Line featuring - this means that one or two items in the product line are selected to play a special role eg, low-end models at modest prices to act as 'traffic builders', or high-end models at high prices with heavy promotion to create a high class image

- Line pruning - many product lines include 'deadwood' that is taking much time from sales personnel and management but do not sell well. Sales and cost analysis will help to identify these products so that they can be removed

- Strategic alliances and/or joint ventures may be a solution.

As part of the strategy you also need to think about elements of the product that can be strategic to its success, such as its packaging and warranty. These elements help create the value the customer sees in the product.

The main thing to remember about packaging is that it communicates to the person buying it right up until they make the decision to place down their money and take it home. If it's sitting on a shelf with eight similar products, it can't just look nice, it has to stand out in order to get noticed. The packaging should be noticeable within three seconds in a store-shelf situation.

The same goes for warranties. Make sure you give buyers some level of comfort that if the product doesn't do what they thought, they can easily get their money back.

Another aspect of product is branding. Brand names should be:

- unique
- easy to remember
- easy to say.

Possible branding policies, with examples of advantages and disadvantages, are summarised in the table below

Company name	Company and product name	Product name	Own-label branding
Baxter's soups	Coke	Procter and Gamble	Marks and Spencer
Power of family name	Two are synonymous	Random purchases across brands	Supply under own name
Introduce new products easily	Automatic purchasing	Widen portfolio – more sales gained	Concentrate on production
Problems damage whole range	Difficult to enter market place	Wasteful in terms of advertising	Expectation of lower selling price

Developing and maintaining a brand is a rather expensive affair. However there are other possibilities such as 'distributor's brands' or 'licensed brand names'.

NIKE is a powerful brand, but the company that owns the brand does not own a single shoe production facility. They contract other shoe producers to make the shoes to their specifications. In this situation it is better to have a market than to own a factory.

Some soft drink producers have already started to produce Coca Cola, Fanta, etc -as licensed brand names under contract.

In Europe many of the big supermarkets sell their own 'distributor's brands'.

Other independent companies (beer brewers, sausage makers, detergent manufacturers etc.) produce these to the supermarket's specifications.

This dual role of satisfying customer needs and differentiation is most important in new product development. 'New product' is a broad term covering:

- products that open up an entirely new market;
- products that replace existing products;
- alterations to existing products.

New product development is a complex function involving the R&D function, but probably led by the marketing department since potential customer needs must be identified and new ideas tested in the market. To minimise the chance of failure, new product ideas are put through a screening process. This includes business analysis, development, test launch and commercialisation. It aims to answer the following questions.

- Is the product compatible with company objectives, strategies, resources and competences?
- Do potential customers like the product? If so, will they actually buy it?
- Can the product be marketed profitably?
- Is the product sound, technically and commercially, to justify the investment?
- Do market tests meet expectations? How have customers, distributors and competitors reacted?

Only if the answers are positive should the product be launched.

4.3 Price strategies

Pricing is considered by many to be the most powerful marketing instrument. Pricing strategies are concerned with the price at which the product is sold. Amongst the factors the company will need to consider are the following.

- The overall objectives of the firm
- Is it trying to make short-term profits (perhaps before competitors enter the market)?
- Is it trying to build up its market share through low prices?
- Is it trying to complement a high quality and brand image through higher prices?
- Is it trying to exclude competitors by setting low prices?

The price element of the marketing mix brings in revenue. Whilst marketers do not have complete freedom to determine price as there are cost and market considerations, different pricing strategies can be adopted in different conditions.

- as low as possible, aimed at maximum sales growth or aimed at maximisation of sales revenue ($Q \times P = max$)
- premium price based on premium quality

- follow the leader / follow the market / going rate pricing
- discriminatory pricing (here companies ask different prices for more or less the same product from different groups of customers).
- product-line pricing (here companies producing a whole line of products may set different prices for different products in the line more with an eye to distinguish the products from each other, than that it is based on real cost price differences).

There are two common price strategies for product launch.

- Penetration prices start straight at introduction with a very low price in order to occupy space both in the distribution channel and in the customer's minds to make it difficult for competitors with 'me too' products. They aim to build sales volume and to erect barriers to entry to competitors.
- Skimming prices - starting with a high price and lowering it gradually while building up production capacity. They aim to maximise cash flow to finance the build up of production

A higher-priced product may be regarded as being of premium quality. Price could be set below industry average where a cost leadership strategy is being developed and higher than industry average where a differentiation strategy is being used.

Please note that the price interacts strongly with the other marketing mix elements. The price must take into account the product's quality and promotional expenditures relative to the competition. In almost every market the following observations can be made:

Brands with average quality but high relative advertising budgets are able to charge premium prices. Consumers are apparently willing to pay higher prices for known products than for unknown products.

Brands with high relative quality and high relative advertising obtain the highest prices. Conversely, brands with low quality and low advertising budgets sell cheap.

The positive relationship between high prices and high advertising holds strongly in the later stages of the product life cycle, for market leaders and for low cost products.

Discounts on the listed prices are also frequently used as a deliberate pricing strategy. The following discount strategies can be distinguished:

- **Cash discounts** - for prompt payment
- **Quantity discounts** - price reductions given to customers buying large quantities
- **Functional discounts** - offered to traders if they perform certain specific functions, such as promoting the product
- **Promotional pricing** - these are temporary discounts with a special promotional objective eg, to attract first-time buyers during introduction.

4.4 Place strategies

Place is the name given - for mnemonic purposes - to distribution: how the product finally reaches the customer. A marketing channel (or a distribution channel) performs the task of moving goods from the producers to the consumers. It overcomes / bridges differences in place, time, quantity and ownership. It is concerned with how goods are distributed and where the outlets will be located. Possible methods of distribution include the following.

- Direct to customer (eg phone banking)
- Through agents (eg holiday companies selling through travel agents)
- Through wholesalers (eg, to corner shops)
- Through retailers such as supermarkets

Some firms deliver to wholesalers, who then deliver to retailers. Direct marketing avoids intermediaries. This includes mail order, telephone ordering and the use of the Internet for e-business. The distribution strategy being developed could be aimed at a wide distribution or it could be focused on the target market depending on whether a cost leadership or differentiation strategy is used.

Traditional distribution methods such as franchising, licensing and distributors are good choices, but businesses must also explore newer options such as strategic partnering and the Internet. The Internet has provided a distribution channel for information-based products and consumer goods. Strategic partnering can increase revenues and provide fast access to new customers and new markets.

Why would a producer delegate some of its marketing activities to intermediaries?

Using trade intermediaries, producers do gain several advantages:

- if you are a really big producer (e.g. Heineken beer) with a world wide distribution it is physically impossible to own all your selling points

- producers may earn a higher return on investment by enlarging their core business instead of investing money in a distribution channel. After all their core business is what they know best. There is the differential advantage.

The two best-known distribution strategies are called 'pull' and 'push'.

A 'pull' strategy means massive advertising to create consumer demand and this demand more or less forces the retailers to include this product in their assortment (not having this product in stock means disgruntled consumers that may go elsewhere to shop).

A 'push' strategy means that the producer does not try to create consumer demand through heavy advertising, but instead offers high margins to the trade channel members (retailers and wholesalers) and expects that in return they will actively promote and market the product.

Also companies may adopt strategies such as:

- exclusive distribution - using just one retailer in each geographical market

- selective distribution - using more than just one, but less than all distributors that are willing to retail your product. Good working relations (loyal resellers) may develop if indeed the company succeeds in making the product attractive in the eyes of the final consumer (pull strategy),

- intensive distribution - placing the product with as many outlets as possible

When assessing/evaluating the distribution structure of a company economists use concepts such as the level of penetration (the numerical distribution, the number of shops your product is actually being sold as a percentage of the total number of shops selling this kind of produce in a given geographical area) and 'weighted' or real distribution (the proportion of the total market covered by those shops that are also selling your product).

The same as with pricing, the places where your product is available say a lot about its quality and 'status'. The channels of distribution must match the image goals of the product and with your customers' perception of the product. Stay on top of changes in the market that should also make you change your distribution strategy. Make sure your product can get the attention it needs in your chosen channel -- both from the sales staff (are they knowledgeable?) and from a shelf-space standpoint (how many competing products does the distributor also carry?).

4.5   Promotion strategies

A successful marketer has to develop an effective way to communicate with his or her customers. The 'unique selling proposition' has to be brought to the attention of the target customer. If he does not know that the product is for sale he will definitely not buy it.

In practice, promotion is the element of the marketing mix over which the marketing department has most control. Its purpose is to gain the potential customer's attention, generate interest, arouse desire and stimulate action to purchase. Promotion can be widespread, emphasising the common customer requirements or it can cover specialist media, emphasising point of differentiation.

Do not confuse the term marketing mix with promotional mix.

The means by which a firm informs prospective customers about the attributes and nature of its products (or services) is known as the promotional mix.

The promotional mix is made up of four main elements.

- *Advertising* – involves the placement of an advertisement in the media. The place, time frequency and form of advert needs to be carefully considered, eg, should the firm use informative or persuasive advertising?

- *Sales promotion* – involves the use of any incentive designed to 'encourage' the customer to buy the product (service). For example, discounts, trial samples, competitions, gifts etc have all been used by many firms. Again they need to be considered carefully – remember the Hoover experience!

    Hoover offered free flights to customers in an attempt to increase sales. Unfortunately the sales promotion was far too 'costly' for Hoover to offer and they attracted a lot of negative public relations.

- *Public relations (PR)* – involves promoting the company's image in general to establish a favourable public attitude towards the firm and its products.

- *Personal selling* – involves direct contact between the firms' sales representatives and prospective customers. Unlike advertising and PR, face–to–face meetings with customers facilitate a more proactive approach, with sales representatives being able to explain fully the details of a product, advise and answer customers' queries about it and, where appropriate, demonstrate the 'use' of the product.

The promotional mix shows various ways how to reach the target customer. Which technique is fitting for what product at what time is a matter for the general management to decide. There are many solutions to this problem. It depends on the kind of product, the target customers, the communication channels available, etc.

As we have already noted, the four elements of promotion can be 'aimed' at the customer to increase sales, in which case it is referred to as *pull promotion*. They can also be 'aimed' at the trade, in which case it is referred to as *push promotion*. Alternatively (and the most likely) a mix of *pull* and *push* would be considered when promoting the product.

4.6   Defending a competitive advantage

A sustainable competitive advantage depends upon preventing imitation by rivals. Managers must be aware that cost leaders can copy the product or service, market it at a similar or lower price and achieve a greater margin. Techniques to defend a competitive advantage include branding, patents, copyrights and trademarks.

Branding - is a means of identifying a product or group of products. It provides a means of distinguishing the product clearly from competitive items and frequently, in the mind of the consumer, symbolises the particular qualities, which apply to the branded manufacturer. It tells the customer roughly what to expect of the product, and is of great value in promotion of the company's goods.

Patents - A patent is an exclusive right granted for an **invention**, which is a **product** or a **process** that provides a new way of doing something, or offers a new technical solution to a problem. A well conceived patent on a technological innovation can provide the most assurance that a resulting advantage will be sustainable and offering inventors some protection against new entrants. Patent protection means that the invention cannot be commercially made, used, distributed or sold without the patent **owner's consent.** These patent rights are usually enforced in a court, which, in most systems, holds the authority to stop patent infringement. Conversely, a court can also declare a patent invalid upon a successful challenge by a third party

Copyright is a legal term describing rights given to creators for their literary and artistic works. The kinds of works covered by copyright include: literary works such as novels, poems, plays, reference works, newspapers and computer programs; databases; films, musical compositions, and choreography; artistic works such as paintings, drawings, photographs and sculpture; architecture; and advertisements, maps and technical drawings.

Royalties - many creative works protected by copyright require mass distribution, communication and financial investment for their dissemination (for example, publications, sound recordings and films); hence, creators often sell the rights to their works to individuals or companies best able to market the works in return for payment. These payments are often made dependent on the actual use of the work, and are then referred to as royalties.

A **trademark** is any sign, which can distinguish the goods and services of one trader from those of another. A sign includes, for example, words, logos, pictures, or a combination of these. It is used as a marketing tool so that customers can recognise the product of a particular

Conclusion

To gain an understanding of competitors, we have analysed them on the basis of several dimensions. Their size, growth and profitability provide a measure of their relative importance. An analysis of objectives and of past and current strategies can provide insights into intentions. Cost structures and exit barriers can give clues to likely pricing strategies and staying power. Market analysis is intended to help determine the attractiveness of a market to current and potential participants and to understand the market's structure and dynamics.

SELF-TEST QUESTIONS

Segmentation, targeting and positioning

1   How does product positioning differ from market positioning? (2)

2   Which of Bowman's strategies are destined for failure? (2.2)

Market based

3   What are the 4 Ps?(4.1)

4   How would a manager defend a competitive advantage? (4.6)

EXAM-TYPE QUESTION	**Market segmentation**

Required:

(a) Discuss the four principal factors that affect the feasibility of market segmentation. **(10 marks)**

(b) Discuss the idea that 'people don't actually buy what they may appear to be buying – there are deeper reasons involved'. **(10 marks)**

(Total: 20 marks)

For the answer to this question, see the 'Answers' section at the end of the book.

FEEDBACK TO ACTIVITY **1**	Going upmarket does not mean selling nicer things. The higher prices charged in strategic group 2 partly reflect the extra costs involved. Moving upmarket without a cost advantage meant that Wakefields could not make the market prices in their new group. Further, they had difficulty in recruiting and training more and better staff. Some of their stores were too small to display the new product ranges attractively. Their logistical and merchandising systems were not able to cope with the extended product ranges. In short, Wakefields did not have the threshold competences in activities that created customer value.

All of these things could have been put right, but shareholders did not give the new MD long enough. The group was sold to a rival, who closed down most of the stores.

FEEDBACK TO ACTIVITY **2**	1 High brand loyalty will reduce the price sensitivity of the market. The new entrant may have to drop prices and incur heavy marketing expenditure to make this known to buyers. It will also create customer expectations of low price from the new brand. This is clearly a very expensive strategy, but one that is commonly employed by an international entrant to break the patterns of domestic competition.

2   If competitors follow suit, the market will become less attractive and all competitors will lose out. Even if the market does not follow the price reduction, it could easily be the case that potential gains from economies of scale do not compensate for the reduction in price. Wong and Saunders note that there is a tendency for British firms to try to compete in this way, and it frequently results in poor profitability.

3   This can occur when economies of scale are not particularly important in the industry's cost structure. The firm's difficulty will be in achieving growth, rather than profit, as there is no obvious means of attracting more customers. In general, firms will try to invest their superior profits in some form of differentiation that does not erode their cost advantage.

Cost advantages can arise in several ways:

- design of product and manufacturing process (strategy 1)
- superior operations management
- economies of scale
- cheap supply of factors – labour, raw material, etc. This is often significant in the internationalisation of commercial activity.
- advantages from within the wider value system – corporate synergies within a group, for example.

FEEDBACK TO
ACTIVITY **3**

1   IBM believed that they were secure in their differentiation. However, many firms matched them in service and conformance quality, achieving parity of differentiation with IBM's strengths, with additional superiority of features. IBM crashed to the greatest loss in corporate history as a result.

2   The firm eventually realised that investment in plant was necessary to bring costs down to achieve the higher margins possible upmarket. Further, it was necessary to invest in design to ensure that the product range could be enhanced further to sustain the advantage they had gained.

FEEDBACK TO
ACTIVITY **3**

Chapter 14

STRATEGIC IMPLEMENTATION ISSUES

In the last chapter, we saw the links between the strategic options and the activities that the marketers will carry out to ensure that the plan is actually implemented. In this chapter we examine the role of finance, research and development and quality in contributing to the implementation of an effective strategy.

Objectives

When you have studied this chapter you should be able to:

- describe the financial contribution to the implementation of strategy

- outline the strategic role of innovation and the research and development function

- describe the importance of techniques of quality management.

1 Finance issues in strategic management

The accounting function has two key roles in implementing a strategy:

- evaluating the performance

- finding suitable funding.

The previous sections have been concerned with the acceptability of strategic options, but the management need to look at ways of assessing the feasibility ie, whether strategies are achievable in resource terms. An assessment of the returns likely to accrue from specific options is a key measure of the acceptability of an option. The analysis should embrace two principal areas:

- the ongoing evaluation of marketing decisions; and

- the evaluation of strategic investment decisions.

1.1 Performance evaluation

Traditional ratio analysis is used to monitor the effectiveness of many parts of the strategic implementation process. In adopting these measures, it is important that they reflect the degree of decision-making responsibility held by the unit whose performance is being evaluated – i.e. use controllable data. As an example, if cash balances are managed centrally by the parent company, it would not be appropriate to evaluate performance of a group company using figures that include the cash which happens to appear on its balance sheet at a given point in time.

In addition, performance measures used are often linked into motivation and reward systems. In this context, 'goal congruence' becomes an important criterion – managers and decision-making units should be motivated to take decisions, which are in the best interest of the organisation as a whole, not simply in the best interest of the managers of their business unit. Evaluating performance of a salesman based on sales generated will not enhance the profit of the organisation if it encourages sales to be made on credit to customers who are not able to pay.

Current thinking on performance evaluation would adopt a broad approach focusing on a wide range of perspectives, not just the financial perspective, as depicted, for example in the 'balanced scorecard'.

Three of the commonly used traditional investment appraisal techniques to evaluate the acceptability of strategies are ROCE, payback period and discounted cash flow.

- **ROCE** - forecasting the return on capital employed (ROCE) a specific time after the new strategy has been implemented eg, the new strategy will result in a return on capital of 20% in three years' time

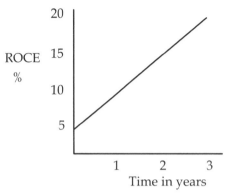

- **Payback period** - can be used where a significant capital injection is needed to support a new venture. The payback period is calculated by finding the time at which the cumulative net cash flow becomes zero -in the example illustrated it is three and a half years. The judgement is then whether this is regarded as an adequate outcome and if the company is prepared to wait that long for a return. This will vary from one industry to another, and also between companies within the same industry. In capital-intensive industries, major investments normally have to be justified over a minimum of five years. In contrast, in fast-moving consumer goods and services, payback is usually required more quickly.

  Although this may imply that managers seek very different rates of return depending on the industry (which is divergent with corporate finance theory), such behaviour is better understood if payback is being used as a targeting device.

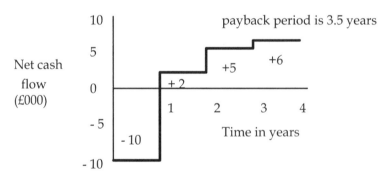

- Discounted cash flow (DCF) - any long-term investment eg, over a product life cycle, is likely to produce a variable stream of future cash flows over the life of the asset. When evaluating such investments, it requires the estimation of these future cash flows and the valid comparison of them against the required investment, which can only be done if all the cash flows are directly equivalent. This requires converting all the future cash flows to their equivalent present values by using an appropriate exchange rate - this is the discount rate or the negative interest rate. This discounted cash flow technique (DCF) is therefore converting cash flows of different time-based currencies into money of a single time period, where relative values can be directly compared. Control at the strategic level should be based on measurements of the actual cash flows for the period just ended and the revised forecasts of future cash flows.

  Once the net cash flows have been assessed for each of the preceding years they are discounted progressively to reflect the fact that funds generated early are of more real value than those in later periods. In the example shown below, the discounting rate of 10 per cent reflects the value placed on money tied up in the venture. So the projected net cash flow of £2,000 in year 2 is discounted to £1,820 and so on. The net present value (NPV) of the venture is then calculated by adding all the discounted annual cash flows over the anticipated life of the project. DCF analysis is particularly useful for comparing the financial merits of strategies that have very different patterns of expenditure and return.

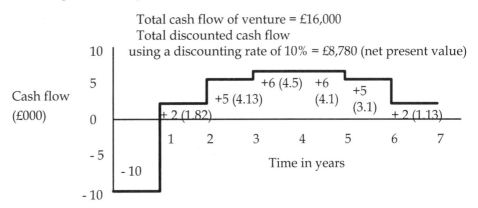

1.2 Evaluation of marketing decisions

Traditionally, accountants have provided the inputs to strategy development and appraisal approaches, normally under the control of strategy and marketing executives. The modern team approach is to encourage the accountant to work with marketing executives to evaluate price review decisions and also the management of the marketing and sales budgets.

Decisions in both of these areas will need information to be extracted from a database, which allows revenue and cost information to be retrieved and analysed by product and customer. In the past there has been a tendency for accountants, utilising absorption costing systems to focus on product profitability without giving due regard to the variability of profit between different customers and market segments.

Similarly, in pursuing a policy of product differentiation, the balance between additional revenue arising from unique product attributes will have to be assessed against the additional costs associated with the provision of the product features. Marketing and sales budgets, which involve significant levels of expenditure, also need to be evaluated and new approaches are needed to assess the effectiveness of expenditures in these 'discretionary' areas. For example, some marketing costs (such as advertising) involve a significant time lag between increase in marketing costs and the resulting increase in sales revenue, which makes it difficult to evaluate this kind of expenditure. At a broader level, the linkage between general marketing expenditure and the creation of intangible assets (such as brand image, customer base) is even more problematic given the number of factors that can influence the creation of such assets.

1.3 Evaluation of strategic investment decisions

The evaluation of strategic investment decisions will require the accountant to widen the scope of analysis beyond investments, which fit with the accountant's convention of distinguishing capital and revenue expenditures. Capital investment decisions to enter new markets or to build share in existing markets based on investment in new or updated production facilities are important but do not represent the full range of strategic decisions made by an organisation.

The development of intangible assets of the kind discussed within the area of marketing above, also applies to other functional areas within the organisation (eg, development of a corporate culture change programme) and these need be evaluated even though there is no capital expenditure involved. Decisions to invest in tangible or intangible assets will require the accountant to set their well understood financial appraisal techniques (such as discounted cash flow analysis) within a wider strategic context.

Bromwich and Bhimani (1991), in reviewing the difficulties of appraising investment in advanced manufacturing technology (ATM) argue that it is inappropriate to restrict the analysis to the quantifiable costs and benefits. They point to three categories of benefit, which need to be taken into account:

- those which can be stated in direct monetary terms;

- those which can be 'converted' into monetary terms; and

- those which cannot be expressed in monetary terms.

They suggest that:

- ATM investments impact organisational performance in a wide range of areas eg, product enhancement, risk reduction, organisational structure and that the three kinds of benefit can arise in all of these areas.

- the different kinds of benefit can be systematically appraised within a strategic planning matrix that summarises the impact of an investment in different areas without attempting to merge the three kinds of benefits into a composite measure.

- impacts which cannot be expressed in monetary terms are assigned scores on a rating scale of -10 to +10 to indicate negative and positive consequences respectively. The approach allows a wide range of impacts to be appraised and emphasises that the investment decision must be a question of management judgement as opposed to a decision based on strict financial criteria.

1.4 Finance issues

The major issues to be aware of are:

- These techniques were developed for capital investment appraisal and therefore focus on discrete projects where the incremental costs and cash flows are easily predicted. The assumptions may not be valid in many strategic, corporate image or brand image developments. The precise way in which a strategy might develop, and the costs and income flows, tend to become clearer as the implementation proceeds. There are often significant time lags between revenue expenditures and income benefits, so confining financial analysis to capital items is inappropriate. Nor are strategic developments easy to isolate from the ongoing business activities in accurately assessing costs and projected income.

- Financial appraisals tend to focus on the tangible costs and benefits rather than on the strategy in its wider context eg, a new product launch may look unprofitable as an isolated project, but make real strategic sense through the market acceptability of other products in the organisation's portfolio. Or, in reverse, the intangible cost of losing strategic focus through new ventures is readily overlooked.

- Because return on capital is backward rather than forward looking, it does not concentrate on assessing the business's capability of generating future cash flows or value.

- A crucial element of all these analyses is the position taken on the cost of capital, since this affects the hurdle that a strategy must clear to be regarded as acceptable. For strategic investments where there are long time frames, cost of capital is very important. In shorter-range investments, cost of capital may be much less important than other assumptions in the analysis. However, setting 'tough' hurdles during analysis could tie the company to apparently low-risk strategies and miss some developments of major potential. In many cases the overemphasis on hurdles merely encourages analysts to re-do the analysis until it just satisfies the hurdle criterion -in other words, the analysis degenerates into a 'game' within the organisation.

A C T I V I T Y 1

A firm intends to expand its operations in a market penetration strategy. What use can the accountant make of ratio analysis to assist the process?

Feedback to this activity is at the end of the chapter.

1.5 Strategic development through acquisition

Up to now we have assumed that evaluation is concerned with strategic options pursued through internal development and not considered the effects of strategic development through acquisition. Here an important additional factor is the need to assess the value of the company being acquired:

- cost savings which can be accomplished post acquisition

- likely proceeds from divestments or sale of assets

- the anticipated impact on the value of the merged companies.

There are three main ways in which a company can be valued:

- The balance sheet value of the net assets. There are dangers with this approach since some key assets may not appear eg, goodwill and others maybe undervalued eg, property.

- Earnings potential is probably the key strategic issue if the intention is to continue the business as a going concern or to merge the organisation's activities into the acquiring company. The methods used to make an assessment of this type are those outlined above - where the cost of acquisition is simply regarded as the 'investment' from which returns flow.

- Unfortunately, the reason an acquisition is attractive is that the costs of the business are currently too high and the post-acquisition benefit is derived from a rationalisation of these costs (particularly overheads) and/or synergy gained from the merger of activities and forecasting these savings and benefits can be difficult, since the analyst is unlikely to have access to 'inside' information to make such assessments.

- Market valuation will usually represent the minimum cost to acquire a publicly quoted company. During the bidding period the cost is likely to rise beyond the starting share price.

2 Funding the implementation

2.1 Funds flow analysis

The assessment of financial feasibility would normally be an important part of any strategy evaluation. A valuable piece of analysis is a funds flow forecast, which seeks to identify the funds, which would be required for any strategy and the likely sources of those funds. For example, in the diagram below the evaluation of a proposed strategy might proceed by the following steps:

- An assessment of the capital investment required eg, new buildings, machinery and vehicles.

- A forecast of the cumulative profits earned over the period. 'Funds from operations' of £15m are calculated from an estimate of future profits plus the adding back of any non-fund items such as depreciation, and represents the real flow of funds into the company forecasted for that period.

- An estimate of the necessary increases in working capital required by the strategy can be made by the separate consideration of each element of working capital (stock increases, increased creditors, etc.), or by using a simple pro rata adjustment related to the forecasted level of increase in sales revenue.

- Tax liability and expected dividend payments can be estimated (in relation to the anticipated profitability).

- The calculation may leave a shortfall in funds. The forecast is then finalised by looking at alternative ways of funding the shortfall and this is where the critical appraisal of financial feasibility occurs

Funds flow forecast for strategy ABC (2004-2005) (£000)

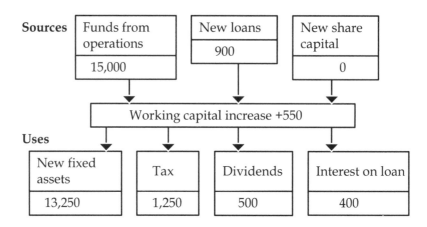

2.2 Funding

Conventionally, funding is considered to be short, medium or long term - although the definitions are not clear-cut.

Short-term funds are those to cover normal operations and can be taken to mean finance available for up to one year. Examples include overdrafts, factoring and bills of exchange. They include bank term loans, hire purchase, leasing, mortgaging property and corporate venturing.

Long term is greater than five years. A major form of long-term funding is internal - from retained profits. The other main forms are external: equity (the sale of shares in the company) and debt (the sale of bonds by a company or a term loan). Hybrid forms of funding that combine characteristics of both equity and debt are also available.

Most strategic decisions will involve investment of funds (new products, new markets, etc). The investment required is likely to comprise both short-term and long-term elements.

- Short-term investment will often be needed to finance additional working capital – e.g. a higher level of stocks and debtors may result for a new product development strategy. A general principle of finance would suggest that short-term assets should be financed by short-term sources of funds, such as bank borrowings and trade credit, but the company should be careful to avoid the problem of 'over trading' – expanding its activities beyond the level which can be sustained by available sources of finance. Over trading can result in severe liquidity problems.

- Long-term investment (fixed assets, acquisitions) would typically be financed from long-term sources, usually equity or long-term debt. Here, financial management theory indicates that the company should choose that mix of finance that minimises its cost of capital. This in turn will maximise the net present value of future cash flow generated by the project, which will, according to the theory, maximise the wealth of the shareholders. As you may be aware from your finance studies, not all writers believe that such an optimum capital structure exists.

Students should be aware that it is essential that they possess the skills and ability to appraise a given scenario and undertake relevant financial analysis. The Paper 3.5 examiner has recently commented, 'There is increasing evidence that the quantitative data is being better used but there continues to be a significant number of candidates who still use the data descriptively and fail to analyse or apply the information appropriately. A calculation of financial ratios alone is no substitute for incisive analysis. Many answers also still do not reflect the questions asked'

2.3   Capital and capital allocation

Capital is one of the most fundamental concepts in finance. It is also one of the most elusive. Capital is the value of a firm or other investment - it is the value of assets less the value of liabilities. As such, it represents financial resources that are available to absorb unforeseen losses. Investors and regulators are interested in capital because a firm without capital is insolvent. The more capital a firm has relative to its assets, the more confident stakeholders are that it will meet its obligations to them. Of course, capital alone is no guarantee of solvency. A well-capitalised firm can fail due to a lack of liquidity.

We may sometimes think of capital as the liquidation value of a firm. If all the assets and liabilities of a firm were liquidated, how much money would be left over for equity investors? Of course, liquidating a firm can be a costly undertaking, so most firms are worth more to equity investors as a going concern than they are liquidated. It is complications like this that make capital an elusive notion. The challenge is to measure capital in a way that is both precise and relevant.

According to accountants, capital is book-value assets less book-value liabilities, perhaps with adjustments for off-balance-sheet items. This accounting definition is precise, but it is not always relevant. A firm's assets may comprise un-depreciated investments in obsolete technology or 'goodwill.'

A different measure of capital is the market value of the firm's equity. For a firm with a single class of stock, this equals the number of shares outstanding multiplied by the current stock price. Unencumbered by accounting formalism, market value of equity reflects the market's assessment of the firm's value. Of course, stock prices are subject to human emotions and crowd mentality. A firm's stock price may fluctuate widely without any fundamental change in its business' prospects. If the stock market soars with a speculative bubble or crashes amidst a panic, this says little about the fundamental value of the firm.

Regulators and risk managers think of capital as financial resources available to, in some sense, absorb unanticipated losses. From this perspective, capital is those sources of funding that protect parties with claims on the firm's assets from such losses. It can be controversial deciding which items to include in this definition. These might include owners' equity, retained earnings and long-term subordinated debt.

Once we settle on a definition of capital, a next step is to determine how much capital a firm should have. Traditionally, this question was answered for financial institutions in terms of their **capital ratio**, which is defined in terms of the book value of capital and assets as

$$\text{Capital ratio} = \frac{\text{capital}}{\text{assets}}$$

Deregulation during the 1970s and 1980s exposed financial institutions to increased risk. In this environment, capital became more important as a buffer against losses. The more risk a firm took, the more capital it needed. Because assets are a poor indicator of risk, regulators and practitioners started modifying the traditional capital ratio or abandoning it completely.

Modifications took the form of **risk-adjusted capital ratios**:

$$\text{Risk-adjusted capital ratio} = \frac{\text{capital}}{\text{risk - adjusted assets}}$$

- where risk-adjusted assets are calculated by applying risk-based weights to specific assets and summing the results.

In other cases, regulators and practitioners abandoned the capital ratio concept completely and focused instead on directly quantifying a firm's risks and specifying capital requirements in terms of the results. During the 1980s and 1990s, this work contributed to the development of concepts such as value at risk and portfolio credit risk modelling, which make it possible to assign incremental capital charges to individual transactions or business lines.

Once they are calculated, individual capital charges are summed, perhaps with an adjustment to reflect hedging or diversification effects. A firm needs to have capital in excess of its sum capital charges. This is called a **risk-based capital** requirement to distinguish it from the assets-based requirements obtained with capital ratios

Practitioners have used risk-based capital calculations to support performance assessment and decision-making within financial firms. The idea is to assign capital charges to individual business lines or transactions based on their risk. Performance is assessed by comparing the profitability of a business line or transaction to its capital charge. Some metric of the return on capital for a business line or transaction can then be calculated. With this model, a financial institution will pursue those businesses or transactions that offer the highest return on capital. In a sense, senior management becomes like venture capitalists, deciding in what ventures to invest their limited capital. The process is called **capital allocation**.

Conceivably, firms might perform such capital allocation based on the formulas for capital and capital charges specified by applicable regulations. While some firms have done this, most have not. The problem is that regulatory capital and regulatory capital charges are designed for more modest goals than analysing specific business lines or transactions. They generally do not make fine distinctions between the riskiness of similar but modestly different transactions. For example, the 1988 Basel Accord assigned a uniform 8% capital charge for all corporate debt -so banks would have to hold as much capital for debt issues to an AA-rated borrower as a BB-rated borrower. For this reason, financial institutions have developed their own proprietary formulas for capital and capital charges. To distinguish these from regulatory capital calculations - and to emphasise their purpose of more accurately capturing the economic impact of specific business lines or transactions - these are referred to as economic capital calculations.

While economic and regulatory capital calculations are defined differently and serve largely different purposes, the two are philosophically similar. They have evolved together over the years. Regulators have borrowed concepts from the economic capital calculations performed by banks. Economic capital calculations have similarly benefited from the innovations of regulators.

2.4   Shareholders' funds

Shareholders' funds consist of the following items from each reported balance sheet:

Ordinary capital

+ Reserves

+ Preference capital

= Shareholders' funds

It is a commonly used ratio in financial analysis giving some indication of the relative profitability of a business from the shareholders' point of view. Usually calculated as Profit after tax/Shareholders funds (or Net Assets).

3 Research and development activities

3.1 Invention and innovation

It is difficult to distinguish between the two processes because they tend to be closely associated with each other. Both processes begin with the creativity and the generation of novel ideas. Invention is the creation of new and useful products and processes from a basic concept whereas innovation is the commercially successful application of an invention. The process of innovation includes the phases and stages that an idea needs to go through before it is commercially exploited and becomes an innovation. Product innovation applies to the products or services that the organisation produces or provides, whereas process innovation applies to the various business processes carried out in the organisation.

Alvin Toffler argues that technical innovation has three main phases.

- The first phase is invention; someone has a creative idea.

- The second phase is exploitation; practical applications are developed.

- The third phase is diffusion; more people see the advantages of the new idea and apply it. This third phase then triggers more creative ideas.

Invention is largely associated with research and development (R&D) departments but innovation involves people in every department. The job of the R&D department might involve:

- monitoring the scientific journals and new patent applications;

- developing new products or prolonging the lifespan of old products; as well as

- getting ahead of or catching up with the technology of the organisation's competitors

There are different types of innovation.

- Incremental innovation involves small changes built incrementally over time into a competitive advantage eg, the various types of washing powder/liquids that include biological, colour-safe and concentrated.

- Radical innovation is a step change, which represents a major departure from the established method. Examples of products in this category are Rolls Royce turbo fan engines and vertical take-off engines. Manufacturing techniques include the assembly line that was introduced by Ford to mass-produce motor cars. By contrast, the introduction of robots into areas of car manufacture and steel works are a means of upgrading existing manufacturing techniques.

3.2 The role of innovation in strategy

KEY POINT

Research and development (R&D) can be defined as 'the organisation of innovation at the level of the firm'

Research and development (R&D) can be defined as 'the organisation of innovation at the level of the firm'. R & D aims to satisfy a market need by developing new products and by improved methods of production. It must also find applications for scientific and technical developments. However, an R&D (innovation) strategy cannot sensibly be pursued in isolation from the rest of the organisation. The business strategy will concentrate on the broad range of products that the organisation wishes to have and the broad markets in which it wishes to compete. This strategy will be supported by the organisation's competence strategy, focused on the technologies the organisation needs if it is to pursue its business strategy successfully.

The R & D function should have a major innovative role in all organisations. The pressures to introduce new ways of doing things may be 'demand pulled', that is the innovation filling a market need, or it may be 'technology pushed', the innovation coming from the application of discoveries. In many organisations, there is a group of people, not necessarily called R & D, whose responsibilities include the creation of new business ideas and techniques.

An innovation strategy calls for a management policy of giving encouragement to innovative ideas. This has a number of aspects.

- Financial backing must be given to innovation, by spending on R & D and market research and risking capital on new ideas.

- Employees must be given the opportunity to work in an environment where the exchange of ideas for innovation can take place. Appropriate management style and organisation structure are needed.

- Management can actively encourage employees and customers to put forward new ideas. Participation by subordinates in development decisions might encourage them to become more involved with development projects and committed to their success.

- Development teams can be set up and an organisation built up on project teamwork.

- Where appropriate, recruitment policy should be directed towards appointing employees with the necessary skills for doing innovative work. Employees should be trained and kept up to date.

- Certain managers should be made responsible for obtaining information about innovative ideas from the environment, and for communicating it throughout the organisation.

The importance of innovation in strategy is one of the most hotly disputed questions in the subject. In many cases, the most innovative companies in an industry consistently fail to be among the most profitable. This creates a divergence of opinion over the role of innovation-based strategy.

A company that chooses not to be innovative is still influenced by the effect of innovation. It is innovation that frequently undermines the basis of competition in existing markets, and creates new markets that may supersede old ones. Firms must learn to innovate with greater commercial effectiveness than is the case at present, or learn to replicate innovations more quickly than they would choose to as the rate of innovation is often too quick for a balanced assessment of it to be carried out in a sensible time period.

Richard Lynch identifies three distinctive roles for innovation within a business level strategy:

- achieving new growth through entry into new products and markets

- retaining competitive advantage by strengthening the product offering

- achieving competitive advantage through jumping ahead of existing rivals.

The indications are that organisations with high market share develop strategies of higher price and/or higher quality than low share competition. These organisations tend to be more profitable, thus providing the cash to invest in R&D to improve and differentiate products, enhancing their market position and also justifying higher prices.

In this section of the chapter, we will examine the role of innovation in different parts of the marketing strategy.

	Existing customers	**New customers**
Existing product	• Innovation of existing products	• Development of existing technology to new markets
New products	• Leapfrogging technologies • Customer driven strategies	• New technologies

3.3 Acquiring new technologies

New technologies often emerge in one of two ways. *Technology push* is based upon an understanding of the technology, but a less well-developed idea of *market pull* has important applications. A technology push based innovator always has difficulty in finding product/market applications for the discoveries he or she makes. Consequently, a firm using technology push may frequently develop strategies by emergent processes to exploit the latest discoveries. The danger is that the new innovation might be ahead of complementary applications, and the advantage lost by the time other technologies catch up. It is possible to see this in the information technology business where hardware runs in excess of the specifications for existing software, and sellers find it increasingly difficult to justify margins at the high performance end of the market. On the other hand, breakthrough technologies are almost invariably of the technology push kind.

New ideas frequently emerge through *market pull*. In this case, new technologies are developed based upon a good understanding of customer requirements, or close collaboration with a customer. In such cases, finding a product market is less problematic, but may still be fraught with difficulty.

Naturally, these two approaches are not mutually exclusive, and frequently support each other. For example, an attempt to store films on a compact disc was an example of market led innovation, but the technology was more effectively applied to data storage for computers after the failure of the original product. It is far better to think of these as the two fundamental drivers to innovative activity.

3.4 Exploitation of existing technologies

An organisation that develops an advantage in a particular technology should consider a strategy of market development. That is, that the knowledge and competencies can be applied to new markets. An illustration of switching from entertainment to data storage based upon knowledge of a particular technology is one such example. Where the company has a diversified product range, discoveries in one area can be readily applied to another.

3.5 Innovation and existing products

In certain stages of the product lifecycle, innovation may be a threshold competence. For example, in mobile telephones and software it is vitally important to maintain product features at least as good as those of competing products. Technology driven strategies tend to be more effective than market ones because many users will be unaware of the possibilities of the technology or the uses to which it might be put. Innovation plus good sales skills are threshold competencies.

3.6 Innovation and intrepreneurship

According to Buchanan and Huczynski, an entrepreneur is more than one who founds businesses, he or she is: 'someone who introduces new technical and organisational solutions to old problems, an innovator who introduces new products processes, new organisational arrangements. ...A person with the entrepreneurial spirit has what is called 'executive drive', a need to do a good job and a need for recognition.'

They claim there is a link between the entrepreneurial spirit and self actualising man's need for achievement - in fact they are singling out the opportunistic entrepreneurs who seek out and thrive on uncertainty, believing that such actions can lead to large rewards.

The motivations of small businessmen vary tremendously although Golby and Johns feel that:

'The need for independence sums up a wide range of highly personal gratification provided by working for oneself and not for anybody else - psychological satisfactions which appear to be much more powerful motivators than money or the possibility of large financial gains.'

Gifford Pinchot makes the distinction between the intrepreneur and the entrepreneur. Specifically, an intrepreneur is a person who focuses on innovation and creativity and who transforms a dream or an idea into a profitable venture by operating within the organisational environment. In contrast, the entrepreneur is a person who does the same, but outside the organisational setting. Most people use the term 'entrepreneur' to mean a person working within or outside the organisation.

Innovation is the life-blood of a successful organisation and the management of innovation is central to this success. Strategic planning in some organisations results in targets being set for innovation, with successful achievements being rewarded through bonuses. New products and services can be developed following a major technical breakthrough in the field, or changes in society, or simply to copy existing products or services. None of this can happen without financial backing. Innovation means spending on R&D and market research and risking capital on new ideas. Certain managers can be made responsible for obtaining information about innovative ideas from outside and disseminating it throughout the organisation.

A successful company is one that is outward looking, has accepted the reality of constant change and the necessity to review its product-market policy continuously. It places emphasis on vigorous initiative, always looking to the future towards new markets, innovative products, better designs, new processes, improved quality and increased productivity. It has a management style and structure designed for innovation in which employees are stimulated to think and act innovatively, which recognises potential 'intrapreneurs' and ensures that everyone welcomes changes for the better. Management can encourage customers and employees to put forward ideas. The company might require people to work in cross-disciplinary teams with employees becoming more involved in the development of new products or processes, to move around and experiment with fresh ideas or to brainstorm various issues. It might adopt a 'suggestions box' for all interested parties to contribute to, with a reward scheme based on the best ideas per month/year. There is obviously a link between the creative and the entrepreneurial organisation and much depends on the structure adopted to encourage innovation and creativity.

Burgelman feels that this structure should be based on the strategic importance of new business to the organisation and how related that business is to the organisation's current activities. This premise leads to nine organisational designs for **intrapreneurship**.

Strategic importance — Operational relatedness	Very important	Uncertain	Not important
Unrelated	Special business unit	Independent business unit	Complete spin off
Partly related	New products department	New venture division	Contracting
Strongly related	Direct integration	Micro new venture department	Nurturing and contracting

In some cases, the innovative activity relates to a particular strategy put forward by senior management. In this case, getting the new idea accepted and market tested is relatively straightforward. However, in the majority of cases, innovation will disrupt existing activities and must be justified to senior managers and operational management. Often, the accountant is cast as the demon of this process.

Some managers and writers argue that truly innovative behaviours can only be delivered by a strong planning approach. The large expenditures and volumes of information and functional skills need to be co-ordinated and kept to its product market focus. This is contrasted with the logical incremental approach suggested by Quinn, that sees innovation arriving in a fairly chaotic way that is frequently disruptive to established thinking and business processes. Many studies have shown that these obstacles are most successfully overcome by a change champion, or product champion, who becomes somewhat obsessed by the importance of the project and takes steps to bring about mutual adjustments to existing processes.

The evidence suggests that neither answer is entirely convincing and good examples can be found of both. However, it is worth noting that consistently innovative companies tend to allow strategy to emerge, rather than adopt a planning approach.

Lynch identifies several characteristics that are associated with the effective management of innovative activity.

- Managers question strategies and market definitions as routine, and think widely about their customers, potential customers, technologies and innovations.

- The purposes of products are continually questioned to find more appropriate technologies and processes.

- Explore markets for innovation and technology gaps – where there is a clearly articulated market need that existing technologies do not satisfy adequately.

- Innovate into areas of competitive weakness – a market leader might not notice the emergence of a new technology or changing market need. This is a cheaper approach than innovating against competitors' strengths, where customer loyalty may be strong.

- Managers think about innovation in terms of value added to the customer. This enables the innovations to be better focused, and priced more effectively.

- Managers welcome critical thinking about critical success factors and performance indicators.

4 Management and control of quality

The role of quality management has been shown to be one of the most important characteristics of successful companies. In this section, we examine the ways that management can gain a clear quality advantage that can lead to a sustainable competitive advantage. This concept is often referred to under the heading of 'quality as a strategic variable'.

4.1 Role of quality in strategy

In recent years quality has become the key in determining many organisations' position in respect of their competitive advantage. The PIMS database has been analysed in hundreds of studies, most trying to find clues to strategic success. Perhaps the most definitive finding from this research is the role of product quality. It showed that the perceived quality of its products and services, relative to those of competitors, was the most important single factor affecting a business unit's performance.

In earlier chapters we looked at Porter's generic strategies and how an organisation can seek to gain competitive advantage over its rivals. An organisation may try to differentiate its product from others by improving its quality and hoping that the increased costs of making the product are at least matched by the increased prices customers are prepared to pay.

Alternatively a company may *reduce* the quality of its product to allow the product to be made and sold more cheaply. This process has limits: there will always be a minimum level of quality, which is expected by the customer.

Quality is also important if the organisation sells its products to other manufacturers rather than to a final consumer (for example a supplier of a car manufacturer). Porter's value system (which was studied in an earlier chapter) shows that the company should look at what its customers want and produce goods of an appropriate quality.

4.2 Quality procedures

Deming, in his book *Quality, Productivity and Competitive Position*, suggests that improving quality leads to improved productivity, reduced costs, more satisfied customers and increased profitability. His system for management to improve quality and competitiveness covers the following main areas.

- The organisation should have a constant purpose of improving their product or service.

- Quality objectives should be agreed and action taken to accomplish them.

- Systems for production and service delivery should be improved, eliminating all waste.

- Consideration of quality and reliability should be just as important as price when choosing a supplier.

- Attention must be paid to training people so they are better at their jobs and understand how to optimise production.

- Mass inspection of goods ties up resources and does not improve quality.

- Education and self-improvement should be encouraged in all members of the organisation. Management should enable staff to take a pride in their work.

- Barriers between staff areas should be broken down.

Unfortunately, quality is difficult to define because it has a wide range of meanings, covering a wide range of businesses and processes.

By developing the right approach to quality, organisations can benefit by 'getting it right first time' and avoiding the problems those faulty goods and dissatisfied customers can bring.

Management has a duty to ensure that all tasks are completed consistently to a standard that meets the needs of the business. To achieve this they need to:

- set clear standards
- plan how to meet those standards
- track the quality achieved
- take action to improve quality where necessary

Quality control is concerned with maintaining quality standards. There are usually procedures to check quality of bought-in materials, work-in-progress and finished goods. Sometimes one or all of these functions is the responsibility of the research and development department on the premise that production should not self-regulate its own quality.

Statistical quality control through sampling techniques is commonly used to reduce costs and production interruptions. On some occasions, where quality assurance has been given, customers have the contractual right to visit a manufacturer unannounced and carry out quality checks. This is normal practice with Sainsbury's and Tesco's contracts with manufacturers producing 'own label' goods (eg, Tesco Baked Beans).

In the past, failure to screen quality successfully has resulted in rejections, re-work and scrap, all of which add to manufacturing costs. Modern trends in industry of competition, mass production and increasing standards of quality requirements have resulted in a thorough reappraisal of the problem and two important points have emerged:

- It is necessary to single out and remove the causes for poor quality goods before production instead of waiting for the end result. Many companies have instigated 'zero defects' programmes following the Japanese practice of eradicating poor quality as early in the chain as possible and insisting on strict quality adherence at every stage – as Crosby points out in his book *Quality is Free*, this is cost effective since customer complaints etc reduce dramatically.

- The co-ordination of all activities from the preparation of the specification, through to the purchasing and inspection functions and right up to the function of delivery of the finished product, is essential.

It is accepted that it is not possible to achieve perfection in products because of the variations in raw material quality, operating skills, different types of machines used, wear and tear, etc. but quality control attempts to ascertain the amount of variation from perfect that can be expected in any operation. If this variation is acceptable according to engineering requirements, then production must be established within controlled limits and if the variation is too great then corrective action must be taken to bring it within acceptable limits.

4.3 Quality assurance

Quality assurance echoes the ideas of the writers Armand Feigenbaum and Phil Crosby. Feigenbaum argues that prevention is better than cure. He emphasises the role of systems design to eliminate errors. Similarly, Crosby argues that companies should operate a *right first time* process ie, that the goal should be zero defects.

Quality assurance is about designing a process of which the end result is guaranteed to be of an acceptable standard, because of the checks that have been made along the way.

When used in the car manufacturing industry, it would mean the workers involved in each process of manufacture checking that their work was up to required standards before passing the car to the next stage in the production process.

Quality assurance often looks at 'internal customers'. Workers are asked to develop internal customers and treat them as they would any external customers. The goods they supply to their internal customers should be of an acceptable standard. In the car manufacturing example, these internal customers would be the workers at the next stage of the production process. The theory is that having internal customers focuses all employees on the importance of their work towards the goal of having a zero defect product.

Quality assurance requires employees to be more responsible for their work, which means that changes in attitude and management style may be required. This, and the length of time it takes to implement, will deter some firms.

5 Total quality management (TQM)

Total quality management (TQM) is the name given to programmes that seek to ensure that goods are produced and services are supplied of the highest quality. Its origin lies primarily in Japanese organisations and it is argued that TQM has been a significant factor in Japanese global business success. The basic principle of TQM is that costs of prevention (getting things right first time) are less than the costs of correction.

This contrasts with the 'traditional' UK approach that less than 100% quality is acceptable as the costs of improvement from, say, 90% to 100% outweigh the benefits. Thus in the analysis of quality related costs there may be a trade-off between a lowering of failure (internal and external) at the expense of increased prevention and appraisal costs.

Which view is correct is a matter of debate but the advocates of TQM would argue that in addition to the cost analysis above, the impact of less than 100% quality in terms of lost potential for future sales also has to be taken into account.

5.1 Features of TQM

The philosophy of TQM is based on the idea of a series of quality chains, which may be broken at any point by one person or service not meeting the requirements of the customer. The key to TQM is for everyone in the organisation to have well-defined customers – an extension of the word, beyond the customers of the company, to anyone to whom an individual provides a service. Thus the 'Paint shop' staff would be customers of the 'Assembly shop' staff who would themselves be the customers of the 'Machine shop' staff. The idea is that the supplier/customer relationships would form a chain extending from the company's original suppliers through to its ultimate consumers. Areas of responsibility would need to be identified and a manager allocated to each, and then the customer/supplier chain established. True to the principle outlined above the quality requirements of each 'customer' within the chain would be assessed, and meeting these would then become the responsibility of the 'suppliers' who form the preceding link in the chain.

Quality has to be managed – it will not just happen. To meet the requirements of TQM a company will probably need to recruit more staff and may also need to change the level of services on offer to its customers, which includes 'internal' customers. This would probably entail costs in terms of the redesign of systems, recruitment and training of staff, and the purchase of appropriate equipment.

Thackray indicated the following features of companies that follow TQM.

(a) There is absolute commitment by the chief executive and all senior managers to doing what is needed to change the culture.

(b) People are not afraid to try new things.

(c) Communication is excellent and multi-way.

(d) There is a real commitment to continuous improvement in all processes.

(e) Attention is focused first on the process and second on the results.

(f) There is an absence of strict control systems.

The last two points appear to go against the central thrust of UK management accounting. The point being made is that concentrating on getting a process right will result in an improved result. A process is a detailed step in the overall system of producing and delivering goods to a customer. Improving a process without worrying about the short-term effects will encourage the search for improvement to take place, the improvement will more likely be permanent, and will lead to further improvements. A concentration on results and control generally means attaching blame to someone if things go wrong. Therefore employees would not have an incentive to pick up and correct errors but rather would be encouraged to try to conceal them.

5.2 Analysis and restructuring of resources

DEFINITION

Discretionary activities are activities such as checking, chasing and other tasks related to product failures.

In many businesses, employees' time is used up in discretionary activities – activities such as checking, chasing and other tasks related to product failures.

Some/most of this time may be capable of being redeployed into the two other categories of work:

(a) Core activities – these add direct value to the business. They use the specific skills of the particular employees being examined and are the reason for their employment.

(b) Support activities – those activities that clearly support core activities and are thus necessary to allow core activities to add value. The importance of this analysis can be seen in a quote from a US Chief Executive some years ago: 'The only things you really need to run a business are materials, machines, workers and salesmen. Nobody else is justified unless he's helping the worker produce more product or the salesman sell more product.'

Analysis of employees' time will provide a clearer view of the costs of poor quality and whether efforts in other departments could reduce the amount of time spent by a department further down the product chain on discretionary activities. For example, suppose there are seven processes from purchasing of raw materials through various stages of production to delivery of the product to the customer. If each process is 90% effective then there will be only a 48% success rate at the end of the seventh stage (90% × 90% × 90%, etc). What happens in practice however may be that personnel employed in stage 4 of the process spend a lot of their time on discretionary activities trying to remedy the effect of defects at earlier stages. It is suggested that it would be more sensible for departments in the earlier stages to get things right the first time.

An example has been quoted of an office equipment supplier that analysed employees' time into core, support and discretionary activities. It was found that half of the salesmen's face-to-face selling time with customers consisted of listening to their complaints about poor customer service.

5.3 Quality circles

Quality circles consist of about ten employees possessing relevant levels of skill, ranging from the shop floor through to management. They meet regularly to discuss the major aspect of quality, but other areas such as safety and productivity will also be dealt with.

The main aim is to be able to offer management:

(a) ideas connected with improvement and recommendation

(b) possible solutions and suggestions

(c) organising the implementation of (a) and (b).

The development of quality circles allows the process of decision making to start at shop floor level, with the ordinary worker encouraged to comment and make suggestions, as well as being allowed to put them into practice. Circle members experience the responsibility for ensuring quality, and have the power to exercise verbal complaint. Quality circles may be applied at any level of organisational activity, being used to cover all aspects, and could conceivably involve all employees.

Conclusion

In this chapter we have examined the contribution of several functions to the overall achievement of the strategy. Firstly, we identified the vital role of the finance function in ensuring that the strategic funds for the strategy are available, and that the financial targets of the strategy are met as implementation proceeds.

Secondly, we appraised the role of the research and development function in producing innovations that supported or extended the firm's competitive advantage, and we contrasted two approaches to integrating research and development into the strategy making process.

Finally we considered the most import single element of the competitiveness profile, the role of quality. Managerial techniques from several key writers were presented, but the overall message is that achieving quality is a cultural behaviour, not a managerial device.

Finance issues in strategic management

1   Give two ways that the accountant supports a new strategy. (1)

Funding the implementation

2   Explain what is meant by strategic funds. (2.2)

Research and development activities

3   Why is innovation important to a strategy? (3.2)

4   How do different research and development strategies influence the organisation and the strategy? (3.2)

Management and control of quality

5   Why is the management of quality important strategically? (4)

Total quality management

6   Outline the difference between quality management as technique, and quality management as philosophy. (5.1)

W Limited

You have recently been appointed to lead the management accounting department of W Ltd, which is a small engineering company engaged in the manufacture of precision parts. The market in which the company sells its products is small, and W Ltd faces severe competition. Owing to the production facilities available, the company is able to undertake only small-scale engineering work. Large-scale engineering jobs are turned away, as the company does not possess the manufacturing facilities to undertake them. At best it can act only as agent for another contractor to do the work.

The board of W Ltd is aware that the volume of work, which is being turned away, is increasing. This is particularly frustrating as the company is unable to utilise its capacity to the fullest extent all the time. W Ltd has achieved a steady increase in profit over the last few years. Nevertheless, the board of the company believes that it could increase profitability still further by expanding and thus being able to carry out the larger-scale work, which is currently being turned away.

Budgetary control and standard costing information has for many years been provided as the sole output of the management accounting department. The previous management accountant prided himself on the punctuality and comprehensiveness of the reports produced. Each job is priced by adding a percentage to its total cost, calculated in accordance with the company's standard costing procedures. The annual cost budget is split into monthly parts and flexed to take account of a particular period's actual production. Monthly cost variances, comprising those for direct materials, direct labour, variable and fixed production overheads, are produced and provided to the relevant manager. In addition, sales price and volume variances are produced each period by the management accounting department.

The company does not have a marketing department, although new customers are obtained from advertising within professional engineering journals and by attendance at trade shows. At one such recent trade show the managing director was introduced to the concept of benchmarking. He believes that there may be advantages in W Ltd undertaking benchmarking.

Required:

(a) In consideration of the need for the board of W Limited to be provided with information, which assists its strategic decision making, comment critically on the management accounting reports currently provided. (In other words are they helpful for strategic decision-making?) **(8 marks)**

(b) State and justify what changes you would make in providing information, which facilitates strategic planning in the company. Within your answer, describe what financial and non-financial information you would supply which is different from that already provided. **(12 marks)**

(Total: 20 marks)

For the answer to these questions, see the 'Answers' section at the end of the book.

FEEDBACK TO
ACTIVITY **1**

Very few ratios will be entirely unhelpful. The following should be monitored as a minimum:

Margin – it is important that the firm does not expand by reducing price or selling unprofitable items unless this was calculated as part of the strategy.

Liquidity – sales expansion creates a need for working capital to finance extra throughput. If extended credit terms are offered for the sale, acid test and current ratios may fall unacceptably low. Good monitoring, and anticipation, is necessary to prevent poor cash management.

Stock ratios – particularly work in progress as a proportion of sales. Expanding the throughput may create bottlenecks and greater work in progress rather than higher outputs of products. This can exacerbate the working capital problem.

Profitability – the accountant is the only person with the information to check that the strategies are actually achieving their performance targets in terms of profitability. On the assumption that the business unit responsible for the decision under review is an investment centre (i.e. with responsibility for management of its balance sheet as well as its profit and loss account), two performance measures are used – return on capital employed (also called return on investment) and residual income.

ROCE is the profit before tax and interest as a proportion of capital employed. It can be considered as a measure of the opportunity cost of the decision to the business.

Residual Income tries to take into account the perceived risks of the business. It is calculated by the following formula:

(earnings before interest and tax) – (capital employed x imputed rate)

where the imputed rate is a measure of the degree of risk.

In a relatively safe market, the prevailing deposit rate might be used as a proxy for opportunity cost, but where the industry is volatile a large rate will be used.

ROCE gives a measure of the efficiency of resource use, and can be compared with similar firms. Residual income gives a measure of improving, or falling, shareholder wealth – it is an absolute rather than percentage measure.

In addition to the above financial analysis, a balanced score card would consider a range of other perspectives, including, for example, the impact of the move on the competitive position of the company – this could perhaps be assessed based on market share statistics.

Chapter 15
IS/IT AS A STRATEGIC RESOURCE

For many businesses, information technology and information systems are critical to their operations. For instance, without computing banking would break down completely. Processing power is needed to handle cheques and account processing, and to control the nation-wide network of automatic teller machines.

It is necessary that management understand whether, why and how IT is crucial to the organisation. In some cases information technology may have little effect on the overall operations, whereas in other companies IT is critical to current operations but not necessary to strategic planning. In companies where IT is necessary to current operations and strategic operations, e.g. a credit card company, then IT can be termed as a truly strategic resource.

IS and IT can be used as strategic weapons in a number of ways. They can pursue competitive advantage; be used to disturb, enhance or limit competitive forces; be used to enhance a product or service; or be used in the distribution and supply in order to change the basis of competition against rivals.

It is possible to create new business through telecommunications, mass storage and software engineering advances. Examples include the information services provided for the financial markets, expert systems for professionals and data analysis services for market research companies.

Objectives

When you have studied this chapter you should be able to:

- define the usefulness and application of information technology
- discuss how IT can be used to gain a strategic advantage
- describe IT as a strategic weapon
- describe how information technology permeates the value chain
- identify other frameworks to help identify options to use IT strategically
- be aware of information as a strategic device
- discuss information and organisational structure
- evaluate the application of IT.

1   Information Technology (IT) and Information Systems (IS)

1.1   IS/IT as a strategic resource

There are many examples where information systems and information technology have given competitive advantage to an organisation. When they are analysed, they can be classified into those instances where IS:

- links the organisation to customers or suppliers;
- creates effective integration of the use of information in a value-adding process;
- enables the organisation to develop, produce, market and deliver new products and/or services based on information;
- gives senior management information to help develop and implement strategy.

However they are categorised, the revolution caused by information technologies has permanently changed:

- distribution channels eg, ATMs have changed the way cash is distributed;

- production economies and product life cycles eg, CAD/CAM and robotics have altered the physical production industries;

- value-added services eg, information handling related to the acquisition, storage and repackaging of information.

To gain a competitive advantage, an organisation must be able to define when the technology is strategic to its business. They must be able to make a distinction between technology hype, technology capability, useful technology and strategic technology.

- Technology hype is the area of the salesperson's pitch.

- Technology capability represents what technologies can actually do today - the organisation can see these demonstrated.

- Useful technology is the small set out of a larger set of actual capabilities that the organisation would find useful.

- Strategic technology is the area of IS that would lead to the organisation being damaged if it is not adopted.

Management need to understand whether, why and how IT is crucial to the organisation. In some cases information technology may have little effect on the overall operations, whereas in other companies IT is critical to current operations but not necessary to strategic planning. In companies where IT is necessary to current operations and strategic operations e.g. a credit card company, then IT can be termed as a truly strategic resource.

IS and IT can be used as strategic weapons in a number of ways. They can pursue competitive advantage; be used to disturb, enhance or limit competitive forces; be used to enhance a product or service; or be used in the distribution and supply, in order to change the basis of competition against rivals.

It is possible to create new business through telecommunications, mass storage and software engineering advances. Examples include the information services provided for the financial markets, expert systems for professionals and data analysis services for market research companies.

1.2   McFarlan's grid – criticality of IT

The McFarlan Strategic Grid was devised as a way of plotting the overall expected contribution of IS/IT to the business success.

Information systems do not have the same level of importance for all organisations. Nevertheless, information processing has become critical to many. Because there is little advantage to some organisations in investing in information technology (IT), the organisation must understand whether IT is critical to them or not. If it is critical then management needs to investigate whether the structure of the organisation is such that it can take advantage of the opportunities that IT can offer.

To assess the criticality of IT to the organisation, McFarlan's strategic grid could be used to identify the current dependence on information systems (IS). It displays an organisation's existing applications against those currently under development.

Strategic impact of future systems

	Low	High
Low	**Support** Applications that improve management and performance but are not critical to the business	**Turnaround** (or high potential) Applications that may be of future strategic importance
High	**Factory** Applications that are critical to sustaining existing business	**Strategic** Applications that are critical for future success

(Left axis label: Strategic impact of current systems)

The meaning of each of these sectors is discussed in turn.

- **Support** - IT is a necessity for day-to-day operations of the organisation but the business is not fundamentally dependent on the smooth running of the systems. Examples are using IT for functions such as preparing payroll etc. There is no apparent way of using IT to gain competitive advantage. An example might be a college, which relies mainly on lectures to deliver courses to students or a landscape business where investment for competitive advantage could rely on having more efficient earth moving equipment rather than additional information systems.

- **Factory** - Information systems are necessary for the smooth running of the organisation. Even one hour of disruption to their booking system or order processing system could severely impair their competitive performance. However, there is little further competitive advantage that can be gained from future IS developments

- **Turnaround** - IT has a high potential to create future competitive advantage. Although the organisation receives considerable IS operational support, it is not dependent on the uninterrupted, cost-effective functioning of this support to achieve either long term or short-term objectives. However, the applications under development have a high potential to contribute to the organisation's strategic objectives. A firm in turnaround needs to plan IT development carefully.

- **Strategic** - IT will be a major element in gaining and sustaining competitive advantage in the future. The organisation relies in IS for the smooth running of the day-to-day activities.

The current and planned systems portfolio represents a collection of IS activities, each of which holds a different value to the organisation and so should be treated differently. As shown in the diagram below, Parson's generic IS strategies have a relationship to the four segments of McFarlan's strategic importance grid.

Parsons' six generic IS strategies are:

- Centrally planned - users control IS department. IS department is a service provider to user departments

- Leading edge - 'entrepreneurial advantage', risky, costly, but gains can be high as well

- Free market - similar to centrally planned. Difference is IS department is set up as a profit centre competing for business of the user departments

- Monopoly - opposite of free market strategy. IS department is set up as a monopoly provider to the user departments and the user department are required to use the services of the monopoly department

- Scarce resource - management see information as a resource with limited value. User departments have to justify any projected IS expenditure that they require and will possibly have to bid against each other to acquire the limited resources

- Necessary evil - extreme version of the scarce resource strategy. Based on the belief that IT has little value for business and that any expenditure should be very strictly controlled

Each segment has a 'best fit' IS strategy (the **bold** text).

Strategic impact of future systems

	Low High	
	SUPPORT	**TURNAROUND**
Strategic impact of current systems	**Scarce resource** Free market Necessary evil	**Leading edge** Free market Centrally planned
	FACTORY	**STRATEGIC**
High	**Monopoly** Scarce resource	**Centrally planned** Leading edge

1.3 Application portfolio

Each application of information technology in the business eg, payroll or sales analysis or capacity planning, etc, can be positioned in one segment of the matrix according to its existing and anticipated contribution to the business. Then each application can be managed in accordance with that contribution.

A possible application portfolio for a manufacturing company is shown below:

Support	**Turnaround**
• Time recording • Budgeting • Expense reporting • Cost accounting • General accounting • Payroll • Word processing	• Electronic data interchange (EDI) with wholesaler • Manpower planning • Electronic mail • Decision support • Expert diagnostic systems • Image processing
Factory	**Strategic**
• Employee database • Maintenance scheduling • Inventory management • Shop floor control • Computer-aided design of products • Product (bill of material) database • Accounts receivable/payable	• Computer-integrated manufacturing • MRP II (manufacturing resource planning) • Links to suppliers • Quality control • Sales forecasting • Product profitability analysis

The position on the grid is highly likely to change over time depending on the industry sector and the need to stay competitive.

Forces that drive an organisation round the strategic grid may be internal or external.

- Internal forces will be concerned with matching the potential of information technology to the organisation's operations and strategy, such as a decision to improve productivity. Porter's value chain is a good model to identify internal forces

- External forces will be associated with changes in the competitive environment, such as actions of competitors, suppliers or customers. Porter's five forces model can be used to provide a framework to discuss areas where information technology and systems can yield competitive advantage. The advantages may be in defending the organisation against the competitive forces or by attacking and influencing them in its favour.

ACTIVITY 1

In the past, ShoeMaker's spending on IT has been strictly controlled and used mainly for accounting, processing sales orders and printing invoices. One of its major customers has sent a letter with the following passages in it: 'We have always valued speed and responsiveness, and this has been the main reason behind our sourcing from domestic suppliers of shoes. However, we have recently had offers from suppliers in the Far East offering a wider ranging flexibility in design with new production technology. Can you offer anything similar?' One of the suggestions from the customer was that ShoeMaker should automate their sales order processing system to become interlinked with their purchasing systems to increase responsiveness.

(i)   Explain which position on the grid ShoeMaker currently occupies.

(ii)   If the managers decide to introduce new ordering systems and production technology, will their position change?

(iii)   Are there any forces driving it round the grid?

Feedback to this activity is at the end of the chapter

1.4   BCG and the strategic importance grid

Since the strategic importance grid is closely related to the Boston Consulting Group (BCG) growth-share matrix, the product portfolio management implications can be lifted into the IS strategy world. The growth-share matrix helps organisations with a portfolio of SBUs decide whether to invest to increase market share, use a business as a source of finance for investment in other businesses or whether to divest. So it contributes to the strategic planning process by supporting strategic option generation.

The diagram below shows the BCG matrix segment name matched onto the strategic importance grid. It also illustrates the viability of the IS strategy, the dominant structural pressure, the strongest influencing factor, the level of justified resource use and behavioural focus of the responsible manager or group.

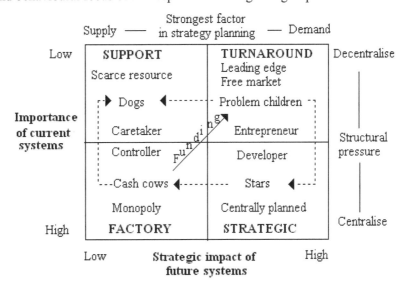

Not all of the organisation's applications will be strategically important and so a scarce resourcing strategy will be relevant for some parts of the portfolio. Similarly, not all of their applications will be valueless and a centrally planned strategy may be appropriate for some parts of the portfolio.

2 The usefulness and application of IT

2.1 Review of strategic frameworks

Decision-makers within the organisation are expected to set successful global company strategic directions and to translate strategies into measurable results. Many strategic frameworks or management models are developed, evaluated and applied in order to generate, select and formulate strategies. The reasons given for using Strategic Frameworks are:

- structure to analyse complex systems
- relation between business strategy and information technolgy becomes clear
- it is a shorthand for complex relationships
- it highlights dimensions of importance

The negative aspects of Strategic Frameworks:

- they are not theories, they cannot be proven
- they are not enough for making decisions, they are descriptions
- they try to categorise, make relationships which are dynamic static
- they do not explain how to use information technology

Frameworks can be used by managers to understand the firms business environment and to seek opportunities for improvement. The types of frameworks include the following.

- **Foundation Frameworks** - Porter's Five Forces Model and Wiseman's Strategic Thrusts help to understand the industry structure.
- **Opportunity Seeking Frameworks** - Value Chain Analysis and Strategic Options Generator examine where the firm fits within the industry and searches for strategic opportunities.
- **Strategic Impact/Value Framework** - Strategic Grid (McFarlan, 1983) assesses the value and cost of adding IT. What will IT do the the firms position in the industry?
- **Contingency Factors Framework** - Critical Success Factors (Rockart, 1979), Sustainability Analysis (Feeny and Ives, 1989). These identify factors which are unique or specifically significant to an individual firm or industry.

2.2 Using the five forces model

Porter's five forces model may be used to help clarify the overall business strategy. The model provides a framework to discuss areas where information technology and systems can yield competitive advantage. The advantages may be in defending the organisation against the forces or by attacking and influencing them in its favour.

Management should use the model to determine which of the forces poses a threat to the future success of the organisation. By ranking these threats in terms of intensity and immediacy, the most critical can then be considered in terms of how information technology or systems can be used to gain advantage or avoid disadvantage.

Threat of entry – new entrants into a market will bring extra capacity and intensify competition. The strength of the threat from new entrants will depend upon the strength of the barriers to entry and the likely response of existing competition to a new entrant.

IT can have two possible roles to counteract the threat:

- **Defensively**, by creating barriers that new entrants to the market find difficult to overcome. IT can increase economies of scale by using computer-controlled production methods, requiring a similar investment in the technology of new entrants. Another defensive move is to colonise the distribution channels by tying customers and suppliers into the supply chain or the distribution chain. The harder the service is to emulate, the higher the barrier is for new entrants.

- **Offensively**, by breaking down the barriers to entry. An example is the use of telephone banking which reduces the need to establish a branch network. Automated teller machines (ATMs) created new distribution channels enabling 'bank branches' to be set up in airports, by out-of-town supermarkets and other areas where there are many potential customers. These machines provided not only expansion of the total market, but also a low-cost method of overcoming the barriers to entry in the areas where the cost of entry was high and space was at a premium.

Intensity of competitive rivalry – this is rivalry between firms making similar products, or offering the same services, and selling them in the same market. The most intense rivalry is where the business is more mature and the growth has slowed down.

IT can be used to compete. Cost leadership can be exploited by IT, for example, where IT is used to support just-in-time (JIT) systems. Alternatively, IT can be used as a collaborative venture, changing the basis of competition by setting up new communications networks and forming alliances with complementary organisations for the purpose of information sharing. When Thomson Holidays introduced their on-line reservation system into travel agents' offices, they changed the basis of competition, allowing customers to ask about holiday availability and special deals and book a holiday in one visit to the travel agent.

Threat of substitute products – this threat applies both between industries (e.g. rail travel with bus travel and private car) and within an industry (e.g. long life milk as substitute for delivered fresh milk). In many cases information systems themselves are the substitute product. Word processing packages are a substitute for typewriters.

IT-based products can be used to imitate existing goods as in electronic keyboards and organs. In the case of computer games, IT has formed the basis of a new leisure industry.

Computer-aided design and computer-assisted manufacture (CAD/CAM) have helped competitors to bring innovative products to the market more quickly than in the past.

Interactive information systems add value by providing an extra service to an existing product. An example of this is provided by ICI's 'Counsellor', an expert system that advises farmers on disease control. It analyses data input by the farmer on areas such as crop varieties grown, soil type and previous history of disease and recommends fungicides or other suitable ICI products to solve the farmer's problems.

The threat from substitutes can be minimised by ensuring that an organisation develops a product before its rivals and then protects that product for a number of years by means of patents. This approach is widely used in the pharmaceutical and biotech industries where specialist software is now widely used in the drug discovery process, enabling drugs to be developed which target specific human and animal diseases.

Bargaining power of customers – the bargaining power of customers can be affected by using IT to create switching costs and 'lock' the buyer in to your products and services. The switching costs may be in both cash terms and operational inconvenience terms. For example, PCs run under Microsoft operating systems are not very efficient when using non-Microsoft application software.

Another form of locking customers in is to develop customer information systems that inform the organisation about the customer's behaviour, purchases and characteristics. This information enables the organisation to target customers in terms of direct marketing and other forms of incentive such as loyalty schemes, where methods of rewarding customer loyalty by giving them 'preferred customer' status are used. If a clothing retailer is launching a new collection it can offer its loyal customers a private viewing. Some airlines have deals such as frequent flyers and air miles as incentives.

The IT techniques at play here include 'data warehousing' – the collection and storage of large volumes of customer information on spending and purchasing patterns, social group, family make up, etc. This then allows for 'data mining' – the extraction of relevant data from the warehouse as the source for target marketing drives. It was reported recently that Tesco, the UK's largest supermarket group, was mining its customer data to identify customers over the age of 60 who regularly purchased children's clothes, food and toys – possibly leading to a marketing push aimed at grandparents.

Bargaining power of suppliers – the bargaining power of suppliers, and hence their ability to charge higher prices, will be influenced by:

- the degree to which switching costs apply and substitutes are available

- the presence of one or two dominant suppliers controlling prices

- the products offered having a uniqueness of brand, technical performance or design, which is not available elsewhere.

Reducing the suppliers' power to control the supply can erode this power. Where an organisation is dependent on components of a certain standard in a certain time, IT can provide a purchases database that enables easy scanning of prices from a number of suppliers. Suppliers' power can be shared so that the supplier and the organisation both benefit from performance improvements. The Ford Motor Company set up CAD links with its suppliers with the intention of reducing the costs of design specification and change. Both the time taken and the error rate were reduced because specifications did not have to be re-keyed into the suppliers' manufacturing tools.

3 Using IS/IT to gain a strategic advantage

3.1 Porter's generic strategies

KEY POINT

Porter identified three generic strategies - cost leadership, differentiation and focus

Porter identified three generic strategies for dealing with the competitive forces. The two basic strategies are overall cost leadership and differentiation. The third strategy - a focus strategy - concentrates on a particular segment of a product line or geographical market - a niche. Porter maintains that organisations wishing to gain competitive advantage must make a choice between these three strategies.

If it is known which strategy an organisation is currently using to promote their products and/or services, it should be possible to define a role for IS to enhance that strategy.

KEY POINT

Overall cost leadership - is about competing by offering products or services at low cost and value for money.

Overall cost leadership - leads to Parson's Scarce Resource and Free market - is about competing by offering products or services at low cost and value for money. The emphasis is on cost reduction, primarily through simplification and automation. For example, driving down inventory levels, with the assistance of IT for supply chain planning and scheduling, can reduce costs. Application packages are available to generate sales forecasts that can be fed into manufacturing resources planning applications. In turn these can be used in shop floor planning and scheduling applications.

Eliminating expensive paper-based ordering by providing on-line ordering for customers may also reduce costs. The use of computer aided design CAD data exchange means that suppliers have accurate details of components. Coupled with on-line purchase schedules, it will ensure that suppliers are able to supply on a just-in-time basis. Robotics can be substituted for labour to reduce costs in the manufacturing process itself and automatic sensing of machine performance can reduce machine down time and schedule maintenance.

Differentiation - leads to Parson's Monopoly and Leading Edge - is about showing that your product or service is different from those of your competitors through eg, brand image, customer service or design. A way of differentiating may be to make the ordering process as easy and flexible as possible. This can be done by providing on-line information services eg, expert systems to identify the most appropriate product or service, followed up by a simple on line ordering process. Where the differentiation is by customisation, CAD can reduce costs effectively. IS can also be used to compare customer purchases of the organisation's goods with those of other suppliers, allowing an organisation to differentiate its products on factors other than price.

Focus - this strategy concentrates on a niche market eg, a particular buyer group, market, geographic area, segment or product line. The opportunities for IS/IT include providing access to customer information, trends and competitors so as to maximise competitive thrust and exclude competitors.

3.2 The strategic options generator

The strategic options generator, developed by Wiseman, is essentially a checklist that guides the executive through all the parameters that must be considered in seeking strategic opportunities. By promoting a series of thoughts and questions that relate to the strategic thrusts identified in the model, it encourages the search for IS opportunities. Wiseman's strategic options generator is outlined in the following diagram:

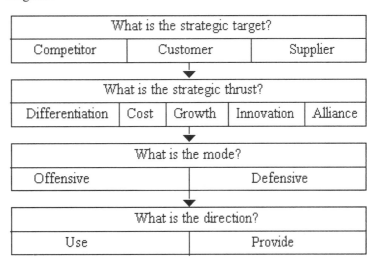

The generator directs its attention towards strategic targets, suppliers, customers and competitors. The strategic thrust is then used to 'hit' them. There are five strategic thrusts that may be used to seek advantage aggressively or defensively to reduce a competitor's advantage. The thrusts are:

- differentiation thrusts - distinguishing a product from others and focus resources on unfilled product or service gaps;

- cost thrusts - lowering the organisation's cost or causing a competitor's cost to be raised;

- innovation thrusts - doing something that might change the way that business within the industry is done; focus on creating new products or new ways to sell, create, produce or deliver products;

- growth thrusts - focus on increasing size of the market size or adding more value adding activities in the value chain;

- alliance thrusts - combine with other groups to create a more competitive position eg, with another organisation through acquisition or merger or for information sharing.

The direction describes whether the organisation is using the strategy for itself or providing it for the target's use.

A firm has two choices for the mode of a strategic thrust:

- it can act offensively to improve its competitive advantage

- it can act defensively to reduce the opportunities available to competitors.

For example, a firm can innovate offensively to gain product leadership in a market, while others use innovation defensively to imitate the product leader.

Wiseman combined the questions of mode, direction and strategic thrust into a strategic options generator.

For example: Dell computer's **initial thrust**:

- Strategic Target: (direct market to) the customer

- Mode: Offensive

- Direction: Use IS to gain advantage

Second thrust: provide customer information to suppliers

Third thrust: let customers auto-configure systems directly via the Internet.

Dell gained a time-based competitive advantage. The Internet is increasing the pace of technological change by refocusing competitive efforts towards creating time-based competitive advantage. Information resources are the key to creating those advantages.

For example, Dell's direct strategy has been to build and deliver computers in as little as 5 days. Thus, the speed at which an organisation adapts its business processes will be the true measure of its ability to maintain competitive advantage.

3.3 IT as a strategic weapon

Information technology can be used as a strategic weapon in a number of ways.

(a) It is a potential supplier of competitive advantage to an organisation.

(b) Information technology and systems can be used as a strategic weapon to improve productivity and performance eg, in manufacturing.

(c) IT can be used in the development of new business. eBay have cornered the on-line auction market and Hotmail were the first to offer e-mail facilities over the Internet.

(d) Information systems can be used to change the management and organisational structure of the organisation to achieve competitive advantage. Computers with modems enable people to work from home, reducing the cost of travel and office space. Telecommuting, video conferencing and electronic mail are available to managers, reducing the necessity for them to travel to meetings and making their time more productive.

4 Advances and changes in information technology

4.1 Competitive advantage and the value chain

Porter and Millar's article on how information gives you competitive advantage outlines three areas where the 'information revolution' affects the rules of competition:

- IT changes industry structure and, in doing, alters the rules of competition.

- IT creates competitive advantage by giving companies new ways to outperform their rivals.

- It spawns new businesses, often from within the organisation's existing operations.

They argue that IT is more than just computers and that the value chain is an important concept linking IT and competitive advantage.

Organisations carry out a range of primary activities and/or support activities, which are concerned with producing the end product or service. All the activities of the value chain have a potential to enhance or impede the organisation's success in adding value to their product or service. The value chain for a company in a particular industry is embedded in a larger stream of activities, that we term the 'value system'.

Every value activity has both a physical and an information-processing component. The physical component includes all the tasks required to perform the activity. The information-processing component encompasses the steps required to capture, manipulate and channel the data necessary to perform the activity.

Porter's value chain model, shown in the diagram below, can be used to analyse these activities for the purpose of identifying IT opportunities. It can be used to suggest areas where IT can interpret activities.

Information technology permeates the value chain

Firm infrastructure	Planning models				
Human resource management	Automated employee scheduling				
Technology dev.	CAD		Electronic market research		
Procurement	On-line purchasing				
	Automated warehouse	Flexible m'facturing	Automated order processing	Remote terminals for sales staff	Remote servicing of equip.
	Inbound logistics	Operations	Outbound logistics	Marketing and sales	Service

Support activities — Primary activities

In the primary activities of inbound and outbound logistics, IT can be used to advantage. Materials planning systems (MRP II) can help capacity and production scheduling. Warehousing can benefit from bar codes to identify information about stock held.

Physical tasks in the operations activities can be automated. Examples are process and machine tool control. Also robots can be used for tasks which are either monotonous or dangerous for people to do eg, paint spraying in the manufacture of cars.

Marketing and services activities can be made more effective by databases such as mailing lists or the information provided by EPOS systems.

In the support activities, IT can be used in procurement activities with electronic data interchange (EDI) to link purchasing with sales order systems. CAD and CAM are an important influence on the technology development activities.

Porter and Millar advocate five steps that senior executives may follow to take advantage of opportunities that the information revolution has created. They are as follows:

- Assess information intensity in the value chain of the entire operations

- Determine the role of IT in industry structure

- Identify and rank the ways in which IT might create competitive advantage.

- Investigate how IT might spawn new businesses

- Develop a plan for taking advantage of IT.

4.2 Intensity matrix

For any organisation it is possible to assess the information content ie, the information intensity, of the value chain activities and linkages. Porter and Millar's information intensity matrix considers the role of IT and suggests how it can be exploited for competitive advantage. The matrix evaluates the information intensity of the value chain (how product value is transformed through activities and linkages in the value chain) against that of the product (what the buyer needs to know to obtain the product and to use it to obtain the desired result).

When assessing the degree of information in the product itself oil, for example, has a low information content and banking has a high information content. The degree of information in the value chain also varies. It is low in the case of a cement manufacturer who makes a simple product in bulk, but high in the case of a complex, sophisticated process such as oil refining

Information content of the product

	Low	High
High	Oil refining Legal services	Newspapers Banking Airlines Education
Low	Cement Bricks	Fashion

Information intensity of the value chain

If the information content of the product is high, information can be used in the product eg, Internet sites for newspapers. When the information in the value chain is high, it implies that sophisticated information systems are required to manage the linkages optimally.

The segment where the information content of the product and the value chain information content are high will be represented by banking and financial services. For example, ATMs, credit cards, debit cards and customer databases have all been integrated to give a much more personalised service as well as lowering service costs. There are banks in the UK eg, First Direct that has no branches and retail solely through ATMs and 24hour telephone phone links.

The segment where the information content of the product and the value chain information content are low contains traditional process-manufactured, widely available commodity products with several potential producers, such as bricks and cement. The fact that information content is low does not mean that there is no scope for exploiting IT to achieve a business advantage. If we assume that most firms in this segment are low-cost producers looking for linkages in the value chain to contribute to overall cost leadership. For example, there could be a niche market for specialist bricks eg, in garden design, where expertise is in short supply. Information about their use could provide added value. The production process offers little scope for IT but, since the process is presumably well known and closely controlled, information could be used to provide a safer operation. For example, airline pilots are encouraged to use autopilot to fly planes because consumption of fuel increases by as much as 30% during a manually controlled flight.

4.3   Linking IT with the value chain

Information systems can provide linkages within and between value chains. The example outlined in the diagram below shows how an information system could provide a competitive advantage. The aim is to:

(a)   identify customer needs and values in the market, defined either broadly or by market segment

(b)   consider and establish which of the generic strategy routes is most appropriate

(c)   meet customer needs through a coherently linked mix of activities that is distinctly different from that of the competitors

(d)   achieve cost stability or reductions through experience in these crucial activities, especially where they give cost advantages over the competition.

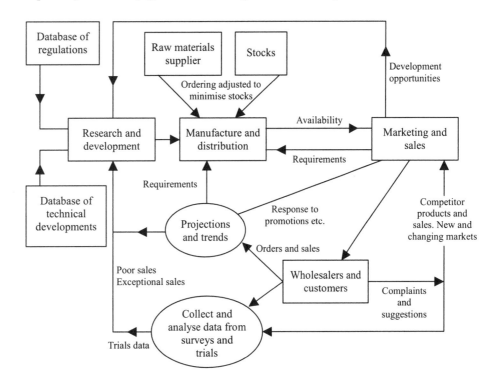

4.4   WWW and value chain

In the near future, it is expected that telecommunications companies will be able to provide a fully integrated service of traditional telephone, digital cable TV, Internet access and home shopping to most households. The system will enable consumers, in both domestic and overseas markets, to order their shopping, browse the Internet, view films on demand and make telephone calls, possibly with integrated video, from their living room. This will have a profound effect on both employment and society.

It will be particularly significant for businesses in the retailing, media and entertainment fields, speeding the development of electronic home shopping and banking, and the 'interactive' communication between a business and its customers. The Internet and electronic commerce technologies will be used to link an enterprise to its customers and to its other external business partners. Many organisations are setting up Web sites with product or service details for people to access from anywhere in the world. Within the banking and financial industries, EDI and related applications are revolutionising the entire system of moving funds. Supermarkets will deliver shopping ordered over the Internet, selected from a list of more than 20,000 different items. International e-mail systems will enable businesses to communicate cheaply and efficiently around the world. E-mail also side-steps busy facsimile machines and increases the ease of communicating across time zones.

Enterprises will not need to be tied to any particular building or country. People will be able to telecommute because communication between computers will enable people to work from remote sites. By combining many different businesses via communication links, a virtual company could be created. This will encourage the development of staff working from home and offer the benefit of flexibility. The organisation will be able to save money on office space and travelling costs might also be reduced if more business can be done with employees using their own telephone connection linked to a computer. It will make part-timers and freelancers easier to use, as they may be happier to work from home. People can work when they want to, rather than during office hours. There will be no routine manual chores of handling and processing data and information. An integrated digital service will mean that a business's human resources can be used more effectively and efficiently for innovation and planning production, decision-making and the servicing of customers' needs.

Developments in 'video conferencing' via personal computers and the telecommunications' system mean that companies can arrange 'electronic meetings' between executives and business partners in different countries. The growing use of video conferencing will reduce dramatically the amount of time and money spent by business executives travelling between subsidiary plants and offices located in different countries and continents.

Never before have there been so many options in terms of how, where, when or with whom to work, learn, buy and sell. Teleworking, telelearning, teleshopping, telebanking and telemedicine are transcending barriers of organisation, distance and time. Because browsing on the Internet knows no boundaries, it is possible for consumers to buy with confidence after comparing specifications of goods available throughout the world. From the comfort of their living room, people will be able to study, work, organise their finances, do their shopping, browse the holiday destinations and book a holiday, chat on the telephone or send an e-mail and choose from many different channels of television. The Internet has been described as a 'network of networks' resembling a computer network co-operative. With a connection to the web, users have access to a huge, up-to-date library of information, which is on line 24 hours a day currently at the cost of a local telephone call. With video on demand, you can pick different films, documentaries, comedy shows, operas, dramas or whatever without having to juggle videocassettes or DVDs.

4.5 Other frameworks to assess the strategical implications of IT

Michael Earl developed a number of frameworks for assessing the strategic implications of IT. These are:

- awareness frameworks
- opportunity frameworks
- positioning frameworks.

(a) **Awareness frameworks** are a series of models that help managers assess the general impact of IT on the organisation.

One of the awareness frameworks – the refocus framework – exists to help change 'mind sets' or to challenge assumptions about the use and value of IT, asking questions such as 'Should the organisation use IT to improve access to the market place or use it to improve the organisation's existing operations?'. A building society might question access into European ATMs against improving its existing operations to reduce the time it takes to clear a cheque.

An example of an awareness framework is the information intensity matrix developed by Porter and Miller. This is based on a 2-by-2 grid, in which the axes represent:

- the degree of information in the product itself (low or high)

- the degree of information in the value chain (low or high)

This leads to four possible classifications; a product's position on the matrix helps to indicate its potential for exploiting information to secure a competitive advantage.

(b) **Opportunity frameworks** are tools designed to analyse whether an organisation has the opportunity of strategic advantage in a particular area. One of these tools – the applications search tool – was used by Ives and Learmouth to develop a customer resource life cycle. This identifies the steps taken by a customer when acquiring a product or service. The phases they identified in the life cycle were:

(i) requirements – covers what and how much of it

(ii) acquisition – includes where it is bought, order and payment methods and acceptability testing

(iii) stewardship – covers how is it cared for, repaired or enhanced

(iv) retirement – incorporates the return or disposal of the product or service.

The life cycle is then used to design applications around actual customer behaviour. After studying a customer resource life cycle for kitchen replacements, a kitchen furniture manufacturer might use a CAD package, installed in a portable computer, to help its field sales staff to 'design to fit' the customer's requirements. The software could be used to simulate the look of a new kitchen and several alternatives can be shown to the customer in the comfort of their home.

(c) **Positioning frameworks** help managers to assess the strategic importance of the current situation of IT for their organisation and their industry. This framework is similar to Nolan's stage hypothesis.

A C T I V I T Y **2**

How can hospitals and doctors use expert systems to gain strategic advantage?

Feedback to this activity is at the end of the chapter.

5 Deploying information systems (IS) resources

5.1 Current good practice

Information is a valuable business asset. In fact it is recognised as the fourth resource of business, next to property, human resources and product. Information is one of the most important assets an organisation has at its disposal. Therefore, information like any other asset needs to be classified, structured, validated, valued, secured, monitored, measured and managed efficiently and effectively.

The British Standards Institution has published BSI-DISC PD 0010, *'Principles of Good Practice for Information Management'*. This provides a practical framework as a guide through the development and operation of new methods and technologies for information management, based upon a set of five Principles. They are intended to act as guidelines for establishing procedures and controls.

The principles state that an organisation should:

1. Recognise and understand all types of information;

2. Understand the legal issues and execute 'duty of care' responsibilities;

3. Identify and specify business processes and procedures;

4. Identify enabling technologies to support business processes and procedures;

5. Monitor and audit business processes and procedures.

There is also a series of ten controls, which help to identify, manage and minimise the range of threats to which information is regularly subjected. These are:

- Information security policy

- Organisation of assets and resources, with relation to managing information security

- Asset classification and control, so that they may be identified and protected

- Personnel security risk management

- Physical and environmental security

- Communications and operations management, ensuring efficiency and security

- Access control to the information

- Systems development and maintenance considerations for built-in security

- Business continuity management

- Compliance with any criminal and civil law, statutory, regulatory or contractual obligations, and any other security requirement

5.2   Costs and benefits

In making investment decisions managers are asking 'is it worth it?' In this context the definition of worth is 'will the benefits be greater than the costs?' To answer this question, in the environment created by modern technology, requires a broader definition of cost and benefit. The concept of cost is expanded to recognise the full range of negative effects that the introduction of an information system could have on an organisation. For example when a new system is planned, the departments affected will operate below their normal levels of productivity because of the concerns that managers and staff will have about how they will be affected.

A cost benefit analysis is an attempt to obtain evidence leading to a decision on the system's acceptance. This is also often called a method for 'system justification' (if the system is justified, then obviously it will be recommended).

This method is fairly straight forward if it is a simple case of replacing a manual system with a computerised one. The benefits can be categorised for convenience into:

- direct benefits - direct savings such as reduction in the expense of carrying out checks because data capture at source is utilised, or staff reductions;

- assessable (measurable) benefits - other financial gains apart from direct cost savings, such as reduction of stock levels;

- intangible benefits - which need a 'notional' or approximate valuation, such as 'improved management decision-making'.

Costs - from the accounting aspect, they may be categorised as:

- revenue costs - running costs (insurance premiums, power, lighting, heating, accommodation, standby facilities, paper, disks, telephone and maintenance,). and development costs - systems analysis, programming, changeover costs, external consultants

- capital costs eg, hardware, software, installation costs (the computer(s), storage media, air-conditioning and dehumidifiers);

There is then the calculation to result in a figure for the return on investment. The major motivation for the acceptance of a new system is to achieve saving, perhaps by raising the profit level through higher turnover and/or reducing costs.

However, systems which are designed to significantly change the way in which an organisation or department operates will, by definition, have no pre-existing manual counterpart upon which they can be based. Therefore the process of development has a greater element of exploration and the unknown, and the cost of developing is less certain than it was with systems installed ten years ago, which typically copied an existing manual system.

From benefits to value -Whilst benefit measurement remains an important concept in assessing the worth of an information system, a larger more encompassing concept is required to fully assess the economic impact of the system on the organisation.

Information economics defines value as' the sum of the discrete benefits and of improvements in business performance factors'. The concept of benefit still remains as an important measure of the various discrete financial gains that the organisation enjoys as a result of implementing the system. In addition, the concept of improved business performance is introduced. In doing this, questions about the strategy of the business are raised. By improving the business and competitive performance of the organisation, substantial economic gains may be made. These gains will often dwarf the kind of savings, which apply to reductions in costs to carry out administrative tasks. This means that the focus of the manager attempting to measure value will be towards business factors and away from technology.

5.3   Information and organisational structure

The positioning and management of the IT function has undergone many changes over the past four decades.

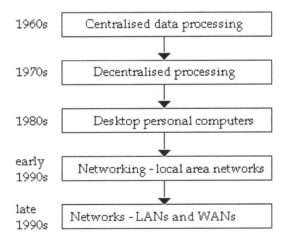

1960s	Centralised data processing
1970s	Decentralised processing
1980s	Desktop personal computers
early 1990s	Networking - local area networks
late 1990s	Networks - LANs and WANs

The arrival of low-cost, user friendly PCs in the early 1980s marked the beginning of a new wave of resource use in which the main types of applications software - spreadsheets, word processors and databases - could be accessed directly at desktops by users with little training or technical knowledge.

The migration of information processing power from the central IT function to departments and desktops undoubtedly gave businesses opportunities to reduce costs and to renew organisational competitiveness, but it also created problems owing to the limited possibilities of integration. By the late 80s a new role for IT specialists evolved - the new focus was on networks, where the principal objective was to ensure connectivity

The current situation is that organisations can use these powerful communications networks to access vast storehouses of information from around the world and they can co-ordinate activities across space and time. The Internet is creating a new 'universal' technology platform on which to build all sorts of new products, services, strategies and organisations. It is reshaping the way information systems are being used in business and daily life because it is eliminating many technical, geographic and cost barriers obstructing the global flow of information.

There is then the calculation to result in a figure for the return on investment. The major motivation for the acceptance of a new system is to achieve saving, perhaps by raising the profit level through higher turnover and/or reducing costs.

However, systems which are designed to significantly change the way in which an organisation or department operates will, by definition, have no pre-existing manual counterpart upon which they can be based. Therefore the process of development has a greater element of exploration and the unknown, and the cost of developing is less certain than it was with systems installed ten years ago, which typically copied an existing manual system.

| ACTIVITY 3 | Where is the IT located in a large retail group of stores such as Sainsbury? |

Feedback to this activity is at the end of the chapter.

Conclusion

This chapter has presented a number of business models that are used to help determine strategy. The strategic role of IT can be assessed by its abilities in dealing with the five competitive forces. These forces represent the bargaining power of existing suppliers and buyers (or customers), the threat of substitutes and new entrants, and the intensity of existing rivalry. Using this model identifies where IT can be used strategically, e.g. to set up barriers, to enhance a generic strategy.

The value chain can also be used to show where an organisation can benefit from the use of information technology and information systems.

Other frameworks for assessing the strategic options include Earl's awareness framework (for assessing the general impact on an organisation), opportunity frameworks and positioning frameworks, such as Nolan's stage hypothesis. Wiseman also developed an options generator model that can be used when assessing the strategic options available.

In this chapter we have discussed the deployment of IS resources in an organisation, looking at the alternatives of centralised, distributed and decentralised processing.

SELF-TEST QUESTIONS

Information Technology (IT) and Information Systems (IS)

1   Describe the 'Factory' sector of McFarland's strategic grid. (1.2)

The usefulness and application of IT

2   Describe the two possible IT roles that can counteract the threat of entry. (2.2)

3   Examine the threat that IT poses on substitute products. (2.2)

Using IS/IT to gain a strategic advantage

4   How can a differentiation strategy be used in IT/IS? (3.1)

5   Describe two of Wiseman's thrusts (3.2)

Advances and changes in information technology

6   Analyse the ways that IT can be used to advantage in three of the primary activities of the value chain. (4.1)

7   List the three frameworks developed by Earl to help identify options to use IT strategically. (4.5)

EXAM-TYPE QUESTION

Competitive edge

Using examples, show how information technology can be used to give an organisation competitive edge.   **(20 marks)**

For the answer to this question, see the 'Answers' section at the end of the book.

FEEDBACK TO ACTIVITY 1

(i)   ShoeMaker are currently in the support sector of the McFarlan grid. The commitment to information systems planning is low and IT seems to have below average investment. IT is perceived as having little relevance to the company's existing or future success.

(ii)   If the new ordering system and production technology is introduced, it will be as a result of the customer's suggestion and the fact that it is critical to ShoeMaker's success. The introduction of the changes would place them in a turnaround role. This is where existing IT is not important but future developments are likely to have a significant impact. The role of IT is being enhanced.

(iii)   The forces driving it round seem to be: the competitive environment shaped by the producer from the Far East and the customer's demands; and the management decision to adopt an IT based strategy in response to the threat.

FEEDBACK TO ACTIVITY 2

Hospitals that can boast a 99% certainty of abdominal pain being treated correctly because of their medical diagnostics expert system have a strategic advantage over those that have to rely on doctors alone.

Expert systems can also be used to identify illnesses and prescribe the correct drug for a patient.

Most large stores like Sainsbury will have both a centralised unit and decentralised units. The local stores have their own system where prices can be adjusted locally to match local competition and analyse shoppers' spending patterns. At least once a day the information will be sent to the Head Office system, which is centralised, where the information is needed for top level decision making.

Chapter 16
HUMAN RESOURCE MANAGEMENT

Human resource (HR) management is a strategy to maintain and improve the ability of the organisation to achieve corporate objectives, through the development of strategies designed to enhance the contribution of HR at all times in the foreseeable future.

Expanding this idea, we see that HR planning deals with human activity directed towards a specific economic aim, and so provides the organisation with the right number of employees who have the skills to achieve the organisation's objectives.

Objectives

When you have studied this chapter you should be able to:

- define the strategic role of human resources

- formulate the human resource plan

- identify recruitment methods

- understand motivational policies

- assess appraisal methods

- understand the importance of the management of change

- describe the management of diversity.

1   The strategic role of human resources

1.1   Overview

Human resource management (HRM) can be viewed as a strategic approach to acquiring, developing, managing and motivating an organisation's key resource.

The people in most organisations are of central importance, and human resource management should be in a position to complement and advance the organisation's objectives.

Most cynics will say it is only a new name or modern approach for personnel management with an involvement in the strategic planning process.

Michael Armstrong describes human resource management as:

'A strategic and coherent approach to the management of an organisation's most valued assets: the people working there who individually and collectively contribute to the achievement of its objectives for sustainable competitive advantage'.

Michael Armstrong's definition sees the role of HRM as:

- suggesting a strategic approach to the personnel function

- serving the interests of management

- dealing with gaining employees' commitment to the values and goals laid down by the strategic management

- aiding the development of the human resources that help the organisation add value to their products or services.

KEY POINT

Human resource management (HRM) can be viewed as a strategic approach to acquiring, developing, managing and motivating an organisation's key resource.

KEY POINT

Michael Armstrong describes human resource management as:

'A strategic and coherent approach to the management of an organisation's most valued assets: the people working there who individually and collectively contribute to the achievement of its objectives for sustainable competitive advantage'.

The strategic element refers to the observation that, in order to make an effective contribution, HRM must complement and advance the organisation's strategic business objectives. It should have clear and consistent policies and encourage all employees to be committed to the organisation's goals. It must be flexible and responsive to internal and external change and work within the framework of constraints and opportunities whilst still contributing to the overall corporate aims.

1.2 The integration of HRM into strategic planning

The activities of the personnel function, culminating in human resource planning, have to be integrated with the corporate planning process. The organisation cannot, in every case, simply adjust the staff to match the needs of the corporate plan; in some instances the current and probable future availability of the human resource (especially in terms of managerial and technical abilities) must be taken into account **before** the plans are outlined.

For this clear reason, there must be direct communication between the corporate planners and the personnel function.

It is often the case that technical change is planned in anticipation of or response to market demand. At the strategic level, the introduction of technical change usually requires major investment decisions. These traditionally concentrate on the technical analysis of competing proposals and on the financial return on them.

The staffing implications of strategic technical change should be part of the corporate planning process, but are often not considered because the managers of personnel functions do not have the information that would be useful in reaching these corporate decisions.

At the management level, the costs of technical change are smaller but are still allocated to 'capital expenditure' or 'wages' budgets. In the minds of most operating managers, these budgets occupy separate pigeonholes. Personnel issues are often not considered until the help of the personnel department is needed to sort out problems that have arisen.

Personnel specialists should seek to increase their involvement at the strategic level by putting themselves in a position where they can make a useful contribution to the corporate planning process.

1.3 Objectives of human resource strategy

An effective human resources strategy must include realistic plans and procedures. The objectives will include the following.

- Identifying, in precise terms, the kinds of talent the organisation will need in order to achieve its strategic goals in the short, medium and long term.
- Recruiting an adequate supply of young entrants with the potential to become outstanding performers, allowing for wastage and for the actions of competing organisations.
- Developing people's potential by training, development and education.
- Retaining as high a proportion as possible of those recruited in this way whose potential is demonstrated in the early years in employment.
- Motivating the talented personnel to achieve high levels of performance and to build ties of loyalty to the organisation.
- Searching for ways of improving the performance and productivity of the most talented.
- Creating an organisational culture in which talent is nurtured and can flourish and in which different streams of talent can be integrated within a framework of shared values so as to form a winning team.

1.4 Human resource plans

Human resource (HR) planning is 'a strategy for the acquisition, utilisation, improvement and preservation of an enterprises' human resources'. It is through planning that a company can determine its recruitment and selection needs, and can assist in the planning of its training needs.

Its purpose is to reduce uncertainty in the environment and assist in shaping a company's personnel policies.

Four main phases are involved in HR planning:

- an analysis of existing staffing resources - its strengths and weaknesses, age spreads, experience and training levels etc;

- an estimation of likely changes in resources - flows into, within, and out of, the organisation - and the ability of relevant labour markets to supply existing or future demands;

- an estimation of the organisation's future HR needs in terms of numbers, type, quality and skill composition; and

- the identification of gaps between supply and demand and the development of policies and plans to close these.

The HR planning process goes beyond this simple quantitative exercise by taking into account the broader environmental factors eg, patterns of employment and developments in automation and uses qualitative techniques, such as scenario planning, for estimating future HR requirements. The process is also linked to the development of the organisation as a whole, and should be related to corporate objectives and to an organisation structure capable of achieving those objectives. It is also concerned with developing people so that they have the skills to meet the future needs of the business and with improving the performance of all employees in the organisation by the use of appropriate motivation techniques.

The stages of human resource planning are outlined in the diagram below:

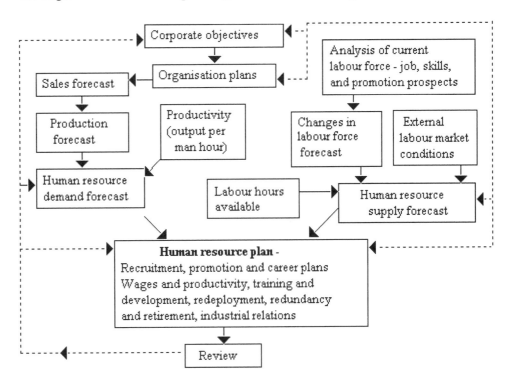

The first step of the plan is to determine the company's long-term objectives so that the human resources can be optimally used. Corporate strategy is a reconciliation process between what an organisation might do (opportunities) and what it can do (resources). This is an impossible process without consideration of human resource requirements.

The planning process serves two functions.

• It fulfils a problem-solving role by identifying human resource requirements, controlling the flow of labour, developing skills and increasing adaptability.

• It also has a strategic role in contributing towards the shape of the organisation as required by external and internal changes.

In both cases, human resource planning represents an important flow of information to aid decision-making and the formulation of policies.

1.5 Predicting human resource requirements

The main problem with human resource planning is that with the speed of change in technology it is difficult to predict not only how many workers will be needed in n years' time, but also what type of skills they will need. Some jobs, which now form a major part of the work content, may be completely automated within a few years. In addition, the rate of growth of the firm's business cannot be accurately predicted. There is thus considerable uncertainty on the demand side.

In addition, people cannot be treated like other resources. They are unpredictable and might leave the company. There is therefore uncertainty on the supply side also.

Nevertheless, an attempt must be made to assess the numbers that will be required in each type of work for some years ahead, even though the estimates will be subject to wide error. Demand and supply must then be reconciled, with decisions being taken as to the level of recruitment required, the extent of internal promotion, the amount of internal training needed, etc. This in turn will lead to decisions about the size of the personnel department needed to handle interviews, training, etc.

2 Recruitment and selection

2.1 Planning the recruitment process

There is no 'ideal plan' for recruitment - no super model to be followed. All organisations have their own way of doing it, with varying degrees of success. Most plans would include:

• a job analysis - a detailed study of the job clarifying the exact nature of the position to be filled - all the tasks performed (or planned to be performed) by the job holder;

• a job analysis - to determining the skills, aptitudes and abilities required for the job;

• a personnel specification - establishing a profile (characteristics and qualities) of the ideal candidate; and

• attracting candidates by advertising or other means.

2.2 Job analysis

Since the procedures of recruitment and selection are expensive and involve substantial use of management time, it is necessary to define, as precisely as possible, the job requirement and the type of person required. The more precise that the organisation can be in defining these aspects, the more effective will be its recruitment procedures.

Remember that the TQM philosophy of 'elimination of non-value added activities' equally applies to HRM. A job is made up of a number of activities, all of which should be 'value added'.

A job analysis requires a detailed activity analysis in terms of the skills and knowledge required of an individual for the efficient and effective completion of tasks. It includes information on the overall purpose, content, accountabilities and standards as well as the skills, knowledge and responsibilities of the jobholder.

Job analysis is important because the outcome is a job description and job specification which are used in:

- selection - to see if candidate's skills match
- promotion - to see if employees can do the new job
- standards - to see how well employees can do their jobs
- appraisal - to see if employees can do their jobs
- training - to see how the job should be done properly
- evaluation - to see how much a job is worth

2.3   Job description

Based on the information from the job analysis, the job description defines the position that needs to be filled. It covers the purpose, duties and relationships of the job and the physical, social and economic factors that affect it.

The drive towards flexibility and changing practices at work has seen new forms of 'work descriptions' being developed. For example, some enterprises have begun to replace or complement job descriptions with performance contracts These contain details of what a job-holder agrees to accomplish over a period of time. A contract will summarise the purpose of a job, how it will be met over the specified time and how the achievement of objectives will be assessed.

2.4   Personnel specification

This is a profile of the kind of person that would be a good match for the job. It is important to distinguish between 'essential' and 'desirable' qualities. Person specifications are used to plan selection interviews and as prompts during them.

Fraser's fivefold framework recommends using the following five headings:

1. impact on others
2. qualifications/acquired knowledge
3. innate abilities
4. motivation
5. adjustment/emotional balance

When drawing up this document, care must be taken not to infringe the provisions of the Sex Discrimination and Race Relations Act.

Organisations are increasingly using competencies to create a specification of the characteristics sought for the position. This is because stereotypes of the 'ideal' person may be contained within personnel specifications. Despite warnings, organisations might be reinforcing the stereotype in the recruitment process.

2.5 Internal and external recruitment

Apart from the preliminary decision as to whether the job needs filling and the determination of the job description and personnel specification, a decision must be reached as to whether the firm is seeking to recruit from within its own organisation or from outside. Each has its own advantages and disadvantages.

Internal recruitment – occurs when an existing employee fills a vacant position. It generally applies to those jobs where there is some kind of career structure, as in the case of management or administrative staff. Most firms invariably recruit supervisors from their own shop floor staff. If a policy of internal recruitment is to be pursued the following points should be noted.

- Recruiting from within by promoting existing employees can act as a source of motivation and may be good for the general morale of the workforce.

- In dealing with existing staff, selection can be made on the basis of known data. The old adage of 'better the devil you know' applies here.

- It can save considerable time and expense in recruitment and selection.

- If training is required this can be costly, but generally no induction is needed, and the firm may be able to train employees to its own specifications.

One of the problems caused by internal recruitment could be the ill feeling it creates among those not selected or the difficulty of promoting someone to supervise ex-workmates.

ACTIVITY 1

Outline some more advantages that arise from recruiting internally.

Feedback to this activity is at the end of this chapter.

External recruitment – occurs when an organisation seeks to bring in someone from outside the organisation to fill a vacancy. In general its advantages and disadvantages are opposite to those of internal recruitment, but the following specific points should be noted.

- External recruitment may be essential if an organisation is seeking specific skills and expertise not available. At some stage external recruitment is necessary to restore manning levels, depleted by employee wastage and internal promotion policies.

- It may be necessary to inject new blood into an enterprise. People from outside the firm often bring with them new ideas and different approaches to the job, gleaned from their experience working in other organisations. With internal promotion policies there is a real danger of producing a succession of employees all with the same ideas; indeed, this may be a prerequisite to progress in the organisation. On the other hand, it should be remembered that newcomers can be equally set in their ways and have difficulties adjusting to new techniques and approaches.

- Although training costs may be reduced since there is the opportunity to recruit personnel with the required expertise, external recruitment does add to replacement and selection costs, and induction is still necessary.

- Bringing in someone from outside may create dissatisfaction among existing employees.

- In order to attract people to change their jobs a firm may have to pay initially higher wages.

There are no hard and fast rules concerning internal and external recruitment. It is largely a policy decision on the part of each individual firm as to which suits it best for different jobs. If internal recruitment is used, then a limited number of methods are available. The most usual is really a form of direct invitation. Assessments are made of employees, and on the basis of these, management decide who will be offered a promotion opportunity. Some firms, however, allow employees to compete for vacancies by advertising internally, either through newsletters or by using notice boards; normal selection procedures then follow. In some concerns it is obligatory that all promotion opportunities be open to competition, although this does not preclude management inviting certain chosen candidates to apply. Even where external recruitment is the main policy it does not prevent an existing employee from applying.

2.6 Attracting suitable candidates

This is the process where the vacancy is brought to the attention of suitably qualified people to stimulate them to apply. This is the sort of process, which, if it goes badly, means the organisation could have too few candidates with no real choice or hundreds of totally unsuitable applicants.

Whatever method chosen, it should deter people who do not meet the requirements without discouraging those who have much to offer but do not quite match the job specification.

There are many ways of encouraging suitable external candidates to come forward for final selection; nomination of existing employees, casual application, agencies (recruitment consultants) and advertising. However, before resorting to external recruitment, it is wise to ensure that all possible internal candidates have been given consideration.

Nomination of existing employees - some companies rely on recommendations from their existing staff and occasionally offer incentive schemes for successful introductions

Casual applications - in periods of high unemployment applicants will write to the company 'out of the blue', saving the time and money involved in a full-scale recruitment campaign.

The government employment services - the unemployed register presents firms with a reservoir of potential employees categorised according to skill and pre-selected according to suitability. The separation of the benefit and employment functions by the creation of Job Centres also provides details of vacancies to people already holding a job.

Recruitment consultants - assist clients in selecting the best staff to fill particular vacancies. They tend to specialise in separate market sectors such as clerical and secretarial, accounting or computing.

Recruitment advertising - before embarking upon an advertising exercise, an organisation must be clear about its objectives in so doing, ie precisely what to say and how to say it and a choice must be made as to the most appropriate media. Plumbley identifies three objectives of recruitment advertising. These are

- To produce a compact field of suitable candidates and deter the unsuitable from applying.
- To achieve a balance between coverage and cost.
- To facilitate future recruitment by presenting an attractive image of the organisation.

The media chosen will depend largely upon the type of vacancy being advertised - there is a wide choice of media, the main ones being press advertising, local radio and television:

2.7   Selection

The objective of the recruitment and selection process is to hire the right person for the right job at minimum cost of the process itself.

To minimise the cost of the process will require the organisation to get it 'right first time'. A standard hiring sequence is given below but in practice (and therefore in the exam) the process will vary with organisations and between levels within the same organisation.

Standard steps in the selection process are as follows.

- Completed job application
- Initial screening interview
- Testing
- Background investigation
- In-depth selection interview
- Physical examination
- Job offer

2.8   Management succession

One of the most important aspects of human resource planning is ensuring the management succession. It is, of course, both possible and desirable to bring in top managers from outside the company, thereby adding a breadth of experience to the top management team, but it is still necessary to have people at the top who have come from within the business. They bring specialist knowledge of different aspects of the firm itself and provide an inspiration for more junior managers who can aspire to the same position. It is thus essential that people with management potential are identified early in their careers.

Good training schemes must be provided for such people to integrate with planned career patterns including a number of development moves to widen experience. However, care must be taken that grooming the chosen few does not take precedence over everyone else's career: if certain people are known to have been singled out, resentment will be caused and the company may miss out on spotting late developers. This points to the need for a thorough appraisal system throughout the organisation. Everyone should be made to feel that his actual and potential contribution is of value.

Management succession planning will probably entail:

(a) for each post, a list of perhaps three potential successors

(b) for each person (at least from a certain level upwards) a list of possible development moves.

These lists then form the basis for long-term plans and development moves and form a contingency plan that will provide a successor for any post which becomes suddenly and unexpectedly vacant (e.g. through death).

The most difficult post to plan for is of course that of Chief Executive: there are plenty of examples of power struggles within organisations. However, the situation where there is more than one potential successor and therefore a power struggle, which can be very disruptive, is not as serious as that where the present Chief Executive is so over-dominant that none of his or her subordinates is able to take over from him, because they are all 'yes men'.

3 Motivation and discipline

3.1 Motivational strategies

Probably the most important aspect of human management is ensuring that employees are motivated to perform their jobs effectively and efficiently in accordance with the organisation's objectives. In addition to the type and quality of the people, the level and nature of their motivation affect strategy implementation.

Motivated people are those who have made a conscious decision to devote considerable effort to achieving something that they value. What they value will differ greatly from one individual to another. There are, of course, a variety of way to motivate people, including the fear of losing a job, financial incentives, self-fulfilment goals and the development of goals for the organisation or groups within the organisation such as teams or quality circles.

The motivational strategy that is decided upon will depend, in no small measure, on the philosophy that is held by the organisation. Different managers may hold very different views on the nature of men and women, why they go to work and what motivates them to work harder and better. Two different models that are worthy of consideration represent radically different views.

The traditional view - finds some of its origins in the work of Taylor and the school of scientific management. At its most extreme, this view postulates the following:

- people dislike work
- people will only work for money
- people are not capable of controlling their work or directing themselves
- simple, repetitive tasks will produce the best results
- workers should be closely supervised and tightly controlled
- extra effort must lead to greater reward
- people will meet standards if they are closely controlled
- firm but fair supervision will be respected

Taylor took the view that there is a right (meaning best) way to perform any task. It is management's job to determine the right way. Workers gain from this approach because the 'right way' is easier and pay is enhanced as a result of increased productivity.

The human relation view - originates in Mayo's research testing various methods of lighting and work organisations. He concluded that the strongest motivational force behind most employees' behaviour at work was the preservation and nurturing of social relationships with their colleagues. The main tenets of this view are as follows:

- people want to be made to feel valued and important
- people want recognition for their work
- people want to be controlled sensibly
- managers must discuss the plans they make for staff
- they must take any objections on board
- they must encourage self-regulation on routine tasks

Mayo's work leads to an approach towards people, which encourages contribution and self-direction, advocating full participation on matters of significance in order to improve the quality of decisions made and the nature of supervision.

3.2 Motivational and supportive policies

Maslow suggested that our needs are organised in a hierarchy, from the most basic life-preserving needs to the ultimate needs of self-fulfilment. He further argued that higher-level needs couldn't be addressed until lower ones have been at least partially satisfied. It follows therefore that the only need that is able to motivate an individual is one that has not been fulfilled. His hierarchy of needs and related aspects at work is shown below:

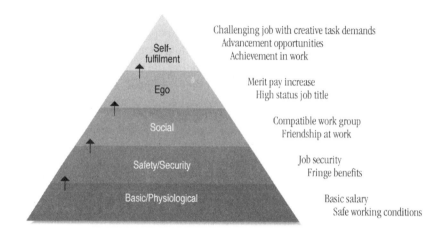

Maslow's theory is useful in that it has a strong element of reality about it and is quite easy to relate to. It tries to explain why people continually strive to achieve more when they already have the basic means of existence. The problem is that it does not address in any detail the reasons why we seek different things when our basic needs are satisfied.

Other theories look at the sources of satisfaction and dissatisfaction at work and recommend ways in which the organisation can increase one and reduce the other. Management plays two key roles here.

- Making the general conditions conducive to motivating staff
- Designing rewarding jobs

Improving general conditions - Frederick Herzberg's theory of hygiene factors and motivators has implications for management trying to ensure that staff are motivated.

Hygiene factors are items that, if absent or unsatisfactory, may lead to *dissatisfaction* among staff.

- There should be sufficient company policies and procedures to act as guidelines for their treatment.
- There should be a suitable level and quality of supervision: too little is as bad as too much.
- The physical and working conditions should be pleasant.
- There should be an appropriate level of salary and status commensurate with the job.
- The organisation should try to foster good relations between colleagues, for example by introducing group bonus schemes if work is carried out by teams. If one member of the team were singled out for a reward then the other members would obviously be resentful.

If all of the above are satisfied, then the staff will be content. However, according to Herzberg, getting the hygiene factors right is not enough in itself to secure positive staff motivation. This merely avoids dissatisfaction. Other factors - motivators - must be in place to induce an individual to perform. While motivations reflect wants, motivators are the identified rewards, or incentives, that sharpen the drive to satisfy these wants.

Five factors stood out as strong determinants of job satisfaction that Hertzberg regarded as motivators:

- achievement
- recognition for work well done
- attraction of the job itself
- responsibility
- advancement.

It follows from this that if an organisation improves its disciplinary and grievance procedures, this on its own will not improve satisfaction among the workforce; it will merely avert the dissatisfaction that would exist if nothing were done. The same applies to working conditions - a brand new, fully equipped, purpose-built office will not satisfy people but simply stem the flow of complaints. Most controversially, pay increases will not, of themselves, satisfy people. They will only serve to reduce feelings of inequality and dissatisfaction. It is only when attention is given to such factors as responsibility, recognition, advancement and autonomy that real job satisfaction will occur.

Designing rewarding jobs - the content of a job can be designed to make it more motivating to an employee. Motivators such as those listed above can be built in to challenge the employee. Additional levels of authority can be included to allow more decisions to be made.

Two specific areas of job design to consider are job enrichment and job rotation.

- *Job enrichment* is a planned process to add challenges and responsibility to a job. For example, an employee may be given responsibility for additional areas outside his usual remit.
- *Job rotation* may occur where there are a number of tasks to be completed by a team of workers. Rotating staff between enjoyable and unpleasant tasks increases motivation.

3.3 Objectives, appraisal, reward and motivation

The work on expectancy models of motivation developed by Victor Vroom and refined by Porter, Lawler and others recognises that people will act only when they have a reasonable expectation that their actions will lead to desired goals. They will perform better if they believe that money will follow effective performance, so if money has a positive value for an individual, higher performance will follow. Briefly, expectancy theorists argue that the strength or 'force' of motivation is a product of how much one wants something, reflecting preference and priority in personal goals (motivation theorists call this the reward value or valence), and expectancy (one's estimate of the probability that a certain action will secure it). The model is summarised in the following diagram:

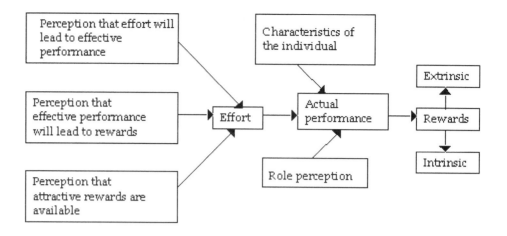

Basically, the model shows that the amount of effort generated depends upon:

- the value of the reward; plus
- the amount of effort seen to be necessary; plus
- the probability of receiving the reward.

An attractive feature of the expectancy theory is that it aims to present a framework for the behaviour of the individual. Rather than making assumptions about what motivates an individual, it suggests that the actual performance is one of the few aspects of motivation that is both observable and measurable. It approaches behaviour as a result of how the situation is perceived and interpreted by individuals themselves.

The heart of the theory is that an individual's performance is the result of a number of factors

- perceptions about the situation,
- the worker's place in the organisation (their role)
- characteristics including skills, personality, training and so on.

The main perceptions that possibly affect effort include the importance and the availability of the attractive rewards, plus thinking that effort will lead to effective performance and that effective performance will lead to the rewards. The nature of the rewards may be intrinsic, such as the feeling of a job well done, or perhaps a feeling of personal growth. Extrinsic rewards are those generally in the control of the organisation rather than the individual, such as promotion and pay

4   Appraisal and performance evaluation

4.1   Introduction

Performance appraisal may be defined as 'the regular and systematic review of performance and the assessment of potential with the aim of producing action programmes to develop both work and individuals'.

Appraisal therefore acts as an information processing system providing vital data for rational, objective and efficient decision making regarding improving performance, identifying training needs, managing careers and setting levels of reward.

At the same time appraisals must assist and encourage open sharing of information regarding employee strengths and weaknesses in order to ensure that the process will aid employee motivation and development.

4.2 The purposes of appraisal

Different organisations will use performance appraisal for different purposes. The most usual rationalisation and justification for appraisal is to improve individual performance.

However there are a number of other reasons, such as:

- help improve current performance

- review past performance

- assess training and development needs and help in the evaluation of training programmes

- assess future potential and promotability

- assist career planning decisions

- set performance objectives

- assess increases or new levels in salary.

4.3 Management by Objectives (MBO)

An additional important motivator is that employees perform better if they can see the relevance that their work has to the overall success of the organisation. This idea has led to the development of a formal scheme called *management by objectives (MBO)*.

Peter Drucker and John Humble are associated with MBO. The ideas of Drucker are based upon McGregor's concept of motivation, in that Theory Y suggests that the individual has untapped reservoirs of intellect, and originality. If an individual receives challenging tasks at work, then the need for self-esteem is satisfied and commitment to the organisation is achieved.

DEFINITION

Management by objectives is a dynamic system that integrates the company's needs to achieve its goals for profit and growth with the individual's need to contribute and to develop himself.

Humble's definition of MBO is that it is a dynamic system which integrates the company's needs to achieve its goals for profit and growth with the individual's need to contribute and to develop himself.

The idea is to start at the top and define objectives for the organisation as a whole.

- The top-level executives define objectives that will lead to meeting the objectives of the organisation.

- Middle-level executives define objectives that will lead to meeting the objectives of the top executives.

- This process is carried out throughout the organisation. Eventually, every employee has objectives, which mesh with those of other employees and are consistent with the overall objectives of the organisation.

Individual managers have to possess sufficient authority and, of course, the opportunity necessary to achieve the job improvement plan, and target periods are set. Performance reviews are established and undertaken systematically, with regard to each manager's results, and there must also be an overall review for the total work unit or department.

You should note the major characteristics of the MBO concept:

- Key results and performance standards are to be achieved by each individual manager.

- The job improvement plan is established for both the individual and the unit and it allows a measurable, quantifiable contribution to be made to the success of the corporate entity;

- performance reviews are disciplined and formal

- assessments of each manager's results, on a regular basis - using key results and performance standards;

- the potential review is held regularly to identify in respect of an individual manager's potential for higher level tasks;

- management training plans emerge to improve skills; and

- there are plans to motivate managers in terms of salary, selection and career development.

4.4　Organisational and individual objectives

With the MBO system subordinates develop their own set of objectives. Concurrently, their boss will have developed a set of objectives for their unit that is consistent with the organisational objectives. In the light of the unit's objectives, the boss and subordinate then reassess and develop the subordinate's objectives until agreement is reached. The subordinate will later be evaluated against each agreed objective.

Basically the approach involves the systematic setting of targets and checking of progress for each management position.

- The first stage is to define the main areas of responsibility and performance for each position. This is usually defined by an analyst completing a questionnaire in discussion with the jobholder.

- The second stage is to agree and define the key result areas (known as KRAs). These are those areas where an individual's failure to perform would damage an important company objective.

- The next step is to develop a means of measuring performance in these KRAs. This resolves itself into two main aspects: firstly, the yardstick to measure performance eg, time, resources, quality and quantity. After deciding the yardstick, the next step is to determine what point of measurement constitutes effective performance. For example, if quality is the yardstick, then what level of quality represents effective performance? So we could define a defective product rate of one per thousand manufactured.

- The next step is to define one or two improvement objectives for each key result area eg, to improve the defective product rate to one per ten thousand manufactured within four months.

- Review periods will be planned where manager and subordinates can discuss progress at regular intervals. The action plan will be itemised which will involve action by the jobholder in the main but often requires supporting action by the boss and other sections. Any obstacles that prevent completion will be separately itemised and an action plan for dealing with each will be given high priority.

- At the final review period, results will be compared to objectives and a factual, constructive discussion will attempt to find the reasons for shortfalls.

- The objectives will be revised and a fresh cycle of review periods will continue the process.

Essentially, the principle of MBO is that measurable objectives are defined and agreed for the key areas of each job and actual performance is measured against these. Middle level managers eg, the production manager or the marketing manager, are involved in setting key-result-area objectives, division objectives and department objectives. The primary objective of lower managers is to set the objectives of departments and units as well as of their subordinates. Individual objectives consist of performance and development goals. Some typical objectives for various managers are now given:

Sales/Marketing manager	Production manager
• Increase the turnover by A% in 6 months at a rate of a% per month.	• Operate plant at maximum practical operating output.
• Increase our share of the market for Widgets from 15% to 20% in the next 18 months.	• Reduce overall costs of manufacturing by 5% over a six-month period using the new equipment.
• Successfully introduce our new baby Widget and obtain sales of £10,000 per week after 3 months.	• Improve the performance of junior managers and supervisors by the use of in-plant training courses.
• Recruit and train effectively six new sales people.	• Contain wage levels to the lowest possible increase but in any case no larger than X% in line with expected domestic inflation.

Appraisal systems can be used to measure attitudes, behaviour and performance. Measurement may be a combination of:

- quantitative measures using some form of rating scale

- qualitative measures involving an unstructured narrative report on specific factors and overall level of behaviour and work performance.

A key issue in performance appraisal is determining what constitute valid criteria or measures of effective performance. The problem is made more difficult because almost all jobs have many dimensions so that performance appraisal must employ multiple criteria or measures of effectiveness in order to accurately reflect the actual job performance of the employee.

A major advantage of appraising in terms of activities is that it helps in generating information that can help in the training and development of poor performers. However, it may only encourage people to concentrate on their activities at the expense of results achieved. This can result in excessive bureaucratic emphasis on the means and procedures employed rather than on the accomplishments and results. There are then problems in incorporating the successful non-conformist into the appraisal system.

4.5 Appraisal process

The appraisal process is illustrated in the model shown below:

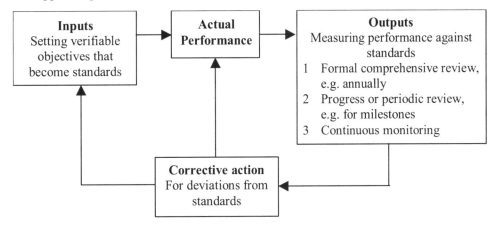

An effective appraisal system needs to have a balance of both measures of results and measures of activities. Establishing organisational and individual objectives is just a start. We also need to measure success in achieving those objectives. However, there are difficulties in measuring the performance of organisations because they tend to have a variety of goals and objectives and use multiple criteria in measuring them.

Performance is measured in terms of effectiveness - the degree to which objectives are accomplished and efficiency - the use of resources in attaining objectives.

Methods of appraising individuals include the following.

- **Employee ranking** - employees are ranked on the basis of their overall performance. This method is particularly prone to bias and its feedback value is practically nil. It does, however, have the advantage that it is simple to use.

- **Rating scales** - under this method the individual's performance is usually broken down into several characteristics or areas of performance, such as

  - quantity of acceptable work;

  - quality of the work;

  - understanding of the work;

  - initiative; and

  - application.

  The individual's performance in each of these areas is then rated. The rating scales used for this exercise vary. The simplest methods used are those where a score (eg, out of 10) or a grade (eg A, B, C, D and E) is awarded. The main problem associated with rating scales is the 'clustering' of results around the 'average' or 'satisfactory' level with little use made of the extreme levels. This negates the whole purpose of an appraisal scheme. To overcome this, some specialists replace terms like 'poor', 'satisfactory' or a numbering system with a series of statements. Each statement is tested for best match with the jobholder's performance.

- **Checklists** - with this method the person rating is provided with a list of statements relating to job performance. He or she must choose the most (and sometimes the least) appropriate statements for each individual.

- **Critical incident method** - this is based on the assumption that focussing on critical incidents is the best way of assessing performance. An incident is considered critical when an employee has done, or failed to do, something that results in unusual success or unusual failure in some part of the job. Such a method involves spotting critical incidents and then recording them on a record sheet for each employee. While the method is useful in highlighting strengths and weaknesses in important areas, it relies upon critical incidents being identified by a superior. It can also be extremely time-consuming.

- **Free reporting** - this method usually involves the completion of a report on each employee. It has the advantage of giving complete freedom in the assessment process. However, it does make comparisons difficult to draw between employees, and to a certain degree depends upon the standard of literacy of the assessor.

- **Achieving objectives** - advocates of methods such as Management by Objectives claim their superiority in assessing performance. The method involves setting individual targets and identifying the actions necessary to achieve them. At the end of a period of time (usually six months), results are reviewed. Studies carried out at the General Electric Company in 1966 revealed that where targets had been jointly agreed between superior and subordinate, there was a distinct improvement in performance

- **Performance 'agreement' or 'contract'** - is based on employees creating a document, agreed with their superior, which sets out the individual's proposed contribution to the business plan of the organisation. The document provides an agenda, which can be referred to during the appraisal period and modified as necessary. Instead of rating performance in terms of a traditional five box scale eg, A, B, C, D or E, the question is simply 'Has the plan been met?' This approach turns the appraisal system into a dialogue. The extent to which the employee has met his or her contract also gives an indication of whether the business plan is realistic.

- **Behaviourally anchored rating scales (BARS)** - are an attempt to provide measurement scales that are directly related to the job being appraised. These differ from the common rating scale in two major respects. First, rather than rate personality, BARS evaluate employees in terms of the extent to which they exhibit effective behaviour relevant to the specific demands of their jobs. Secondly, each item to be assessed is 'anchored' with specific examples of behaviour that correspond to good performance, average performance, poor performance and so on.

- **The appraisal interview** - is a common feature of many appraisal schemes and is normally used in conjunction with one of the rating methods discussed above. It is the vehicle for giving feedback to the employee where they can find out about their strengths and weaknesses and discuss what steps to take to improve future performance. As such it is a crucial part of the appraisal process.

A properly conducted appraisal interview can have a major effect on an individual's self-appraisal and it is this self-appraisal, which will be the main determinant in the continuation of excellent performance and the willingness to improve and develop in those areas where necessary.

4.6 Competence assessment

Competencies are the critical skills, knowledge and attitude that a job holder must have to perform effectively. They are expressed in visible, behavioural terms and reflect the skills, knowledge and attitude (the main components of any job), which must be demonstrated to an agreed standard and must contribute to the overall aims of the organisation. As a general definition, a competent individual can perform a work role in a wide range of settings over an extended period of time.

Some competence-based systems are development-led - they focus on the development of competence and are linked to training and development programmes to develop people to a level of performance expected at work. Other systems are achievement-led - they focus on assessment of competent performance - what people do at work and how well they do it.

This is an important distinction when considering competence-based systems as the system may include many components, each linking to a different aspect of human resource activity within an organisation.

For any competence based system the process is the same:

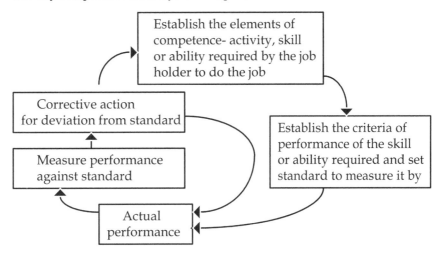

5 Staff training and development

5.1 Introduction

The importance of training as a central role of management has long been recognised by leading writers. According to Drucker, the one contribution a manager is uniquely expected to make is to give others vision and ability to perform. A basic operation in the work of the manager is to develop people and to direct, encourage and train subordinates.

The general movement towards downsizing, flexible structures of organisation and the nature of management moving towards the devolution of power to the workforce give increasing emphasis to an environment of coaching and support. Training is necessary to ensure an adequate supply of staff who are technically and socially competent and capable of career advancement into specialist departments or management positions. There is, therefore, a continual need for the process of staff development - and training fulfils an important part of this process.

5.2 Progression of training

In a survey of nearly a hundred organisations, Fill and Mullins found that training passed through four main stages:

- **Output training** - is centred on the individual, is performed in-house (mainly small organisations) and is only initiated when new equipment, products or persons are introduced to the organisation. The costs must be seen to be absorbed and the transaction completed in the shortest possible time, if only to justify the initial investment risk.

- **Task training** - from the introverted phase of output training, this stage combines the joint needs of the individual and the organisation. It involves selected individuals being sent on short training or college-based courses.

- **Performance training** - plans and budgets are now some of the tools used to manage the training process. Training programmes become the means by which the performance of individuals (and the organisation) can be controlled. Organisations choosing to adjust their quality can only do so by effectively embracing the training function. During this phase appraisal systems become more established to evaluate the training received and to anticipate future requirements.

- **Strategic training** - is achieved when the organisation recognises and practices training as an integral part of the management of human resources, prepares organisational strategies and plans training in the light of both individual and organisational needs. Strategic training is integral to the philosophy and culture of the organisation.

5.3 Training for the management of change

Strategic change will have a significant impact on the people within the organisation. The issues that are important are manpower configuration, recruitment, training and development. Organisations need the capability to manage their systems (production and marketing), as well as controlling the financial and human resources aspects properly. They should possess a balance of skills necessary to implement a strategy successfully and to be able to convince their clients that they can perform better than the competition, not just to get the business but also to justify charging premium prices.

If a strategy requires capabilities not available within the organisation, it will need to obtain them. There are three approaches:

- The 'make' approach, developing personnel by hiring and grooming, ensures that people will fit in, but this approach can be time consuming.

- The 'convert' approach, converting the existing workforce to the new strategy, takes less time.

- The 'buy' approach, bringing in experienced people from outside, is the immediate solution when the strategic changes need to be implemented quickly, but it involves the risk of bringing in people whose experience is with different systems and culture.

Training for change is vital for the long-term survival of the organisation. Increasing emphasis being placed both on the need for continuous training to support change and on training as a vital investment for the future.

5.4 Managing diversity in the workplace

In general, managers expect employees to work with others and be willing to obey, whilst at the same time expecting to see evidence of personality, creativity and independence. Selecting employees that conform to the goals of the enterprise, yet offer valuable individuality is a key to an organisation's health and effectiveness.

As the workforce becomes more diverse in terms of gender, race, culture, age, religion, disability, sexual orientation and ethnicity, organisations need to create cultures in which all employees can develop their potential and flourish. Not only is this the 'right' thing to do, but also how an organisation manages diversity will have a measurable impact on productivity, retention and its profitability.

From the employer's point of view, an organisation's work force is representative when it reflects or exceeds the demographic composition of the external work force. A representative work force reflects or exceeds the current proportions of women, visible minorities and persons with disabilities in each occupation as are known to be available in the external work force and from which the employer may reasonably be expected to draw from.

A representative work force is a good indication that an employer is not limiting access to the skills and talents of workers by discriminating on the basis of sex, race, colour or disability. A non-representative work force signals the need for evaluation and action, so that whatever is blocking or discouraging certain groups from employment and advancement may be corrected.

Some organisations set themselves goals on the representation of certain groups eg, there is an under representation of certain ethnic groups within the police force. To address this type of problem, a diversity assessment will show how an organisation's systems and culture may provide supports or may act as barriers to diversity. The term 'organisational culture' refers to the unwritten rules that impact behaviour, the assumptions, practices, values and myths that shape the experience of employees, and the taken-for-granted ways 'we do things around here'.

A diversity assessment provides information about what helps and hinders:

- Creation of an inclusive work environment where all employees can flourish

- Career advancement

- Teamwork

- High morale, commitment and productivity

- Retention of diverse employees

- Recruitment and hiring of diverse individuals

It is a structured process to gather information about the experience of current employees and, if desired, former employees using focus groups of current employees, personal interviews with senior managers, and telephone interviews of employees who have left the organisation.

5.5   Team working and empowerment

An important development in work redesign and job enrichment is a form of work organisation based on self-managed work groups and team working. This involves a socio-technical approach with technological processes, production methods and the way in which work is carried out integrated with the social system of the organisation, including the informal group structure. Although the effectiveness of self-managed groups does not appear to be all positive, individual members of the group do have higher levels of job satisfaction.

The group assumes greater autonomy and responsibility for the effective performance of the work. Key features of the self-managed work group include the following

- specific goals are set for the group but members decide the best means by which these goals are to be achieved

- group members have greater freedom and choice, and wider discretion over the planning, execution and control of their own work

- collectively members of the group have the necessary variety of expertise and skills to successfully undertake the tasks of the group

- the level of external supervision is reduced and the role of supervisor becomes more one of giving advice and support to the group

- feedback and evaluation is related to the performance of the group as a whole.

Reorganising the workforce into teams is not easy but when successfully developed, team working has been shown to be a way of improving competitiveness and at the same time enhancing the quality of working life doe employees.

DEFINITION

Empowerment is claimed as another way of allowing employees greater freedom, autonomy and self-control over their work, and responsibility for decision-making.

Empowerment is claimed as another way of allowing employees greater freedom, autonomy and self-control over their work, and responsibility for decision-making. However, there are concerns that it does not differ in any meaningful way from other earlier forms of employee involvement. Is empowerment arguably just another somewhat more fanciful term for delegation? Is the primary concern of empowerment getting the most out of the workforce? Does empowerment promote greater motivation and increase job satisfaction?

By employing and adapting terms used in the wider literature on empowerment, *Lashley* suggests it is possible to summarise four managerial initiatives and meanings, which claim to be empowering:

- Empowerment through participation -for example, the delegation of decision-making which in a traditional organisation would be the domain of management;

- Empowerment through involvement -for example, when management's concern is to gain from employees' experiences, ideas and suggestions;

- Empowerment through commitment -for example, through greater commitment to the organisation's goals and through improvement in employees' job satisfaction;

- Empowerment through delayering -for example, through reducing the number of tiers of management in the organisation structure.

Empowerment takes a variety of forms. Managers frequently have different intentions and organisations differ in the degree of discretion with which they can empower employees. *Lashley* concludes therefore that the success of a particular initiative will be judged by the extent to which the empowered employees feel personally effective, are able to determine outcomes and have a degree of control over significant aspects of their working life.

The benefits of empowerment include:

- improved job satisfaction and the changing attitude of staff
- every employee has the power to be innovative and ensure performance is good
- conflict will be abolished as everyone works towards the same goals
- more decision-making closer to the point of impact.
- decision-making process can be speeded up, as can reaction times
- releases the creative innovative capacities.
- provides for greater job satisfaction, motivation and commitment.
- enables employees to gain a greater sense of achievement from their work and reduces operational costs by eliminating unnecessary layers of management and the consequent checking and re-checking operations

Conclusion

HRM is a strategic function within an organisation. It aims to derive the highest possible contribution from employees to the achievement of sustainable competitive advantage. HRM accepts that the organisation's employees are a key resource and this reflects on the strategic business objectives and planning.

Clear and consistent policies should encourage all employees to be committed to the organisation's goals. HRM must be flexible and responsive to internal and external change and work within the framework of constraints and opportunities whilst still contributing to the overall corporate aims. Training and development enhances the knowledge, skills and attitudes of the employees to the benefit of the organisation, the individual, the team and the community.

SELF-TEST QUESTIONS

The strategic role of human resources

1 Define the modern view of HRM. (1.1)

2 Explain why there must be direct communication between the corporate planners and the HRM (personnel) function. (1.2)

3 List and explain the objectives of a human resource strategy. (1.3)

Recruitment and selection

4 What is the purpose of planning human resources? (2.1)

Staff training and development

5 What is the difference between output training and strategic training? (5.2)

EXAM-TYPE QUESTION 1

Installing a training and development system

(a) Describe the steps that should be taken to set up a training system in an organisation. **(5 marks)**

(b) Identify five ways in which such a system would benefit the accounting function. **(5 marks)**

(Total: 10 marks)

EXAM-TYPE
QUESTION **2**

Human resource planning

Required:

(a) Describe the human resource planning process.   **(10 marks)**

(b) Why is human resource planning an important feature of the strategic
management of organisations that employ significant numbers of accountants
and other professionally qualified staff?   **(10 marks)**

(Total: 20 marks)

EXAM-TYPE
QUESTION **3**

Appraisal systems

You have been asked to write a report on performance appraisal systems and in it
you have been asked to describe the following:

Required:

(a) The purpose of an appraisal system.   **(8 marks)**

(b) The objectives of appraisals from the viewpoint of:

   (i)   The individual

   (ii) The organisation

   (iii) The barriers to effective appraisal   **(12 marks)**

(Total: 20 marks)

For the answers to these questions, see the 'Answers' section at the end of the book.

FEEDBACK TO
ACTIVITY **1**

The internal recruit may be fully conversant with the work involved and will
certainly know the people with whom he will be dealing; he may even have been
carrying out the duties either as part of his own job or as the understudy to the
incumbent.

Internal recruitment can also show the organisation's commitment to encouraging
flexibility in the work force.

Chapter 17

MANAGEMENT OF PROJECTS AND OPERATIONS

The difference between project planning and other types of planning is that a project is a 'once-off' activity. On a small scale, it encapsulates many issues of planning and management, including resource allocation. We identify some of the tools and techniques available to the project manager and also explain operational research procedures. This chapter also examines the production function and the strategic significance of operations. The need for quality is emphasised, the efficient control of purchasing and stores and the use of automation in the handling of materials.

Objectives

When you have studied this chapter you should be able to:

- discuss the project life cycle

- explain the objectives of project management

- estimate resource requirements

- understand a variety of project control tools, such as Gantt charts

- assess the strategic significance of operations and operations management

- show the links between operations management and strategic management

- understand the operational significance of purchasing, manufacturing and logistics

- explain the ideas of JIT and BPR.

1 Project management

1.1 Introduction

A project can be defined as an activity that has a start, middle and end, and consumes resources.

Turner defines it as 'an endeavour in which human, material and financial resources are organised in a novel way, to undertake a unique scope of work, of given specifications, within constraints of cost and time, so as to achieve beneficial change defined by quantitative and qualitative objectives. In this way, project management differs from the normal management functions. The project manager acts as a focal point for the concentration of attention on the major problems of the project.

From the definition, the function of project management, irrespective of whether all characteristics are present, is to organise and combine the efforts of specialists in every phase of the progress of a project, giving both inspiration and direction.

1.2 Project life cycle

The life cycle of a project is entirely comparable to the more familiar product life cycle. As for a product, the project goes through initial phases of design, planning, execution, monitoring and completion. We can define the life cycle of a project as the various phases, from inception to completion, which a project must go through to attain its objectives, or goals.

Wysocki *et al.* define the life cycle of a project with five major activities. Namely, these are project scoping, planning, launching, monitoring and closing-out. Each one of these is composed of five sub activities.

Project scope	• State the problem or opportunity • Establish the project goal • Define the project objectives • Identify the success criteria • List assumptions, risks and obstacles
Develop detailed plans	• Identify project activities • Estimate activity duration • Determine resource requirements • Construct and analyse project network • Prepare the project proposal
Launch the plan	• Recruit and organise project team • Establish team operating rules • Level project resources • Schedule work packages • Document work packages
Monitor and control progress	• Establish a progress reporting system • Install change control process and tools • Define problem escalation process • Monitor progress versus plan • revise project plan
Project close-out	• Obtain client acceptance • Install project deliverables • Complete project documentation • Complete post implementation audit • Issue final project report

1.3   The objectives of project management

To achieve the project's purpose it is necessary to manage five project objectives:

A sixth objective, sometimes expressed as a separate item, is risk management. Three of the objectives outlined above – cost, time and quality – are traditional performance measures, which are traded against each other to obtain the best, or optimum, result.

The aim of the **scope** objective is to:

- ensure that the project's purpose is achieved
- specify the work that must be done
- specifically exclude work that is superfluous or otherwise unnecessary.

Developing the scope of the project means planning for **quality**. In project terms this means delivering a project that satisfies the customer and is 'fit for the purpose'.

The aim of project organisation must be to assemble the appropriate resources – human, material, financial and technical – to undertake and complete the project successfully

1.4 Estimating resource requirements

There are different classifications of project cost estimates.

- **Definitive estimates** aim to be accurate to within 5% and are produced after the design stage of the project life cycle.
- **Feasibility estimates** are accurate to within 10%. These are made in the early design stage.
- **Comparative estimates** are made when the project under review is similar to a previous one. The accuracy of this estimate depends on the similarity and the prevailing economic conditions.
- **Ball-park estimates** are a rough guide to the project costs and are often made before a project starts. They may only be accurate to within 25%.

Cost estimation invariably involves some guesswork where the project manager is beginning a new, uncertain project. For projects where there is no margin of safety, it is crucial that the estimates are definitive. The project manager can improve the accuracy by:

- learning from previous mistakes
- having sufficient design information
- obtaining a detailed specification
- breaking the project down into smaller jobs and detailing each constituent part.

The normal approach to project costing is to use the work breakdown structure in order to produce the cost breakdown structure (CBS) at an increasing level of detail. This CBS will be a complete list of every item that can be classed as expenditure.

Work breakdown structure (or WBS) is a hierarchical view of the way a project is structured; in other words, a formal version of a project outline. It is produced by:

- Identifying the key elements
- Breaking each element down into component parts
- Continuing to breakdown until manageable work packages have been identified. These can then be allocated to the appropriate person.

The WBS needs to include all aspects of the project from planning through development to delivery. Identifying the minute stages of a project begins with the whole project, followed by breaking up into smaller parts and then continually breaking down the work until the smallest unit can be identified. This exercise is the best way of discovering the work that must be done, as well as determining the resources required. The sequencing of tasks and the priorities and pitfalls also become more apparent as the project is broken down.

Here is an example of work breakdown structure.

```
                    ┌─────────────────┐
                    │ Total project:  │
                    │  build house    │
                    └─────────────────┘
```

First level

| Foundations | Draining | Brick work |
| Plumbing | Painting | Wiring |

Second level

| Area marking | Digging | Disposal of soil |
| Filling | Damp proofing | |

Second level

| Mains connection | Light sockets |
| Fuse box | Power points |

The process of work breakdown continues until the smallest possible sub-unit is reached. Digging the foundations for example would be analysed so that number of labour hours needed, and hence the cost, could be determined

Project costs can be analysed into:

- direct costs, including labour and materials

- indirect costs, including rent, light, heating and other overheads.

The various costs identified with each part of the work breakdown structure will be collected to provide a useful cost analysis for the various business functions and also to be a mechanism for controlling costs.

Another methodology for cost planning, called the C/SPEC, combines the work breakdown structure, the organisation breakdown structure (labour, sub-contractors, materials, overheads, etc) and the cost breakdown structure. This would have to be done using a computer, because of the three dimensions.

| ACTIVITY 1 | Sketch the outline of a work breakdown structure for recruiting a person to fill a vacancy in the organisation |

Feedback to this activity is at the end of this chapter.

The purpose of planning the time dimension is:

- to plan for a firm delivery date that will make the project viable

- to minimise disruption time

- to co-ordinate the availability of resources

- to optimise cash flow eg, to avoid large cash outflows at an unnecessarily early stage

To estimate the time schedule for the project, the project manager will list the work elements, together with estimates for their key time dimensions. These dimensions are:

- The duration - the time taken to complete the task.

- The early start date - the first date at which the task could commence.

- The late finish date - the last date at which the task could be completed.

- The late start date - the last date at which the task could be commenced and still meet the late finish date.

- The float - the buffer time between the early and the late starts.

For a simple project like the erection of a garden shed, an activity schedule could be prepared:

Activity	Early start day	Duration in days	Late finish day	Float days
Level site	1	3	3	0
Prepare base	4	2	5	0
Prepare timber	1	2	5	3
Assemble shed	6	1	6	0

This type of technique is taken much further with networking techniques, which use critical path analysis or PERT methodology to calculate the schedule. Computer models of these techniques are widely used

1.5 Operational research and quantitative techniques

Operational research is defined by Churchman as 'an application of the scientific method to problems arising in the operations of a system which may be represented by means of a mathematical model; and the solving of these problems by resolving the equations representing the system.'

The distinctive approach is to develop a scientific model of the system, incorporate measurements of factors such as chance and risk, in order to predict and compare the outcomes of alternative decisions, strategies and controls. The purpose is to help management determine its policy and actions scientifically. Information from operational research techniques such as linear programming or critical path analysis is worthwhile if it enables scarce resources to be applied more profitably.

A wide variety of planning and problem-solving techniques can be included under the heading of operational research, including Critical Path Analysis (CPA), Program Evaluation and Review Techniques (PERT), linear programming, queuing theory, game theory and decision trees.

Much of operational research relies on algorithms, which are set procedures for solving problems, often very complex and especially suited to computer processing. Especially important within some techniques are program loops, which will be repeated, 'homing in' on the solution, until it has been obtained with the required degree of accuracy. Such algorithms usually start with a feasible solution to the problem, and this solution is improved each time the program loop is repeated, until no further significant improvement is possible.

Heuristic models rely much more on intuition, discovery and experience in working similar problems. Such guided trial and error approaches can be computerised and according to Burck:

'machines will gradually be able to solve not only well structured but badly structured problems, and so will be able to make many of the decisions now made by middle management.'

Sisk claims that operational research has its limitations - 'Operations research is a direct aid to the decision-making process through its contribution to the steps of analysis and development and, indirectly, OR forces a clearer statement of the problem. It does not, however, make the final choice nor translate the decision into action. The effectiveness of OR is limited to the analysis and comparison of relationships that may be expressed quantitatively and transformed into a mathematical model.'

2 Project management tools and techniques

2.1 Project management tools

Project management is a challenging task, with many complex responsibilities. Fortunately, there are many tools available to assist with accomplishing the tasks and executing the responsibilities. The tools help with all stages of project management: planning, analysing, tracking, monitoring, reviewing, and ensuring delivery of the identified results and benefits.

The following tools are available to support the project management team:

The Analysis Process - provides several documents, which are the foundation for the project. The documented cost benefit analysis for the project provides specific information as to the expected tangible and intangible benefits and results, the alternatives evaluated, and background as to why a specific alternative was viewed as best. The project management team will find a rich source of information for creating the project objectives, risk analysis, and work plan from this document.

Specifications and Standards - provide the detail requirements for the system, expressed in technical terminology. For example, a hardware specification would require that workstations deployed on the project have a 486 processor. Standards provide guidelines, which tell staff members how to complete a portion of the project. For example, programming standards would require all code be commented. Specifications and standards should be established for every aspect of the project.

Work plans - also known as a Work Breakdown Structure, is the path, which charts how the project team will achieve the results and benchmarks. A work breakdown structure is a hierarchical diagram of the project, from the highest level to the most detailed level. Several automated tools are available to assist in construction of the work plan and critical path.

Milestones and deliverables - milestones partition the project into identifiable and manageable phases; deliverables signal and document the accomplishment of the milestone. Each milestone should have an associated deliverable. For example, testing may be identified as a specific milestone. The documenting and reviewing of the test results would be the associated deliverable. Deliverables are an important element to assessing the status of the project and the quality of the work.

Network analysis is a general term, referring to various techniques used for planning projects by breaking them down into their component activities and showing those activities and their interrelationships in the form of a network..

The analysis emphasises the sequence of events and the activities to co-ordinate them.

It has been used very effectively in all types of activities associated with strategy implementation, such as: new product or service launches, acquisitions and mergers, plant construction and relocation.

This type of analysis can help in resource planning by:

- breaking down the programme of implementation into its constituent parts by activity, making it easy to build onto the value chain analysis

- helping to establish priorities by identifying the activities that others depend on

- representing a plan of action, where the implications of changes or deviations in the plan can be examined.

There are two major groups of techniques in network analysis:

- **Critical path analysis** (CPA) – the critical path indicates the most important activities in relation to the time allocated. Used as an integral component of planning and control this provides the basis for allocation of resources to various tasks by dividing the project into specific jobs done, who will undertake them, and the respective target dates.

- **PERT charts** - are flow diagrams, which depict the major phases or partitions in the project, and the phase start and end points. PERT charts are useful to identify the project dependencies, concurrent phases or tasks, the critical path, and the phases or tasks in the project, which are crucial to meeting the completion date.

Network analysis provides these advantages to management:

- identification of both the duration and critical path
- provision of an analytical device for any project which has an introduction (start) time and a finishing point
- progress control is emphasised
- an early indication is given of crises in the project
- the technique stresses and encourages careful appraisal of activities and stages of projects on the part of managers.

GANTT charts - are bar charts, which depict the major phases or partitions in the project - the associated milestones, the chronology of the phases, the elapsed time for each phase, the total elapsed time for the project, and the project completion date. GANTT charts work well to present a high-level view of the project.

The chart shown below shows activities A and B must be completed prior to the commencement of activity

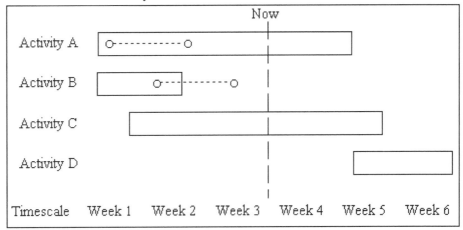

Status Reports - provide a mechanism for all parties to review the current status of the work effort. They will include the following, as appropriate:
- Time budgeted by task.
- Costs budgeted by cost centre.
- Time and costs expended to date.
- Time and costs estimated to complete for the remaining tasks, milestones, and deliverables.
- A comparison of actual project costs to budgeted amounts. These costs will be used to compare the estimated cost of development, versus actual productivity, as a means of measuring program development productivity.
- A list of potential concerns.
- Attainment of benchmarks, benefits, and expected results.

Project Plan - during the project planning process, the agencies will assemble a comprehensive project plan. The completed project plan should include the following individual components, as appropriate:

- Statement of the problem, opportunity, or need;

- The project scope statement;

- The benchmarks, benefits, and expected results;

- The detailed cost estimates;

- The risk analysis;

- A PERT or critical path chart;

- Resource requirements, including staffing, hardware, software, and facilities;

- Security requirements

- The project cost control account, cost and payment schedules, and procedures for reconciliation;

- Project funding; and

- Appropriate approvals

2.2 Statistical approaches

Since future events are always uncertain, all estimates of costs and benefits used in economic evaluation involve a degree of uncertainty. Probabilistic methods are often used in decision analysis to determine expected costs and benefits as well as to assess the degree of risk in particular projects.

In estimating benefits and costs, it is common to attempt to obtain the expected or average values of these quantities depending upon the different events, which might occur. Statistical techniques such as regression models can be used directly in this regard to provide forecasts of average values. Alternatively, the benefits and costs associated with different events can be estimated and the expected benefits and costs calculated as the sum over all possible events of the resulting benefits and costs multiplied by the probability of occurrence of a particular event.

For example, the average cost of a facility in an earthquake prone site might be calculated as the sum of the cost of operation under normal conditions (multiplied by the probability of no earthquake) plus the cost of operation after an earthquake (multiplied by the probability of an earthquake

In formulating objectives, some organisations wish to avoid risk so as to avoid the possibility of losses. In effect, a *risk-avoiding* organisation might select a project with lower expected profit or net social benefit as long as it had a lower risk of losses. This preference results in a *risk premium* or higher desired profit for risky projects. A rough method of representing a risk premium is to make the desired MARR higher for risky projects.

2.3 Statistical process control

Statistical process control (SPC) is a method of monitoring processes and process variation. The purpose is to identify causes for process variations and resolve them. Process variables may include rework, scrap, inconsistent raw materials, and downtime on equipment.

SPC involves using statistical techniques to measure and analyse the variation in processes. Most often used for manufacturing processes, the intent of SPC is to monitor product quality and maintain processes to fixed targets. Statistical quality control refers to using statistical techniques for measuring and improving the *quality* of processes and includes SPC in addition to other techniques, such as sampling plans, experimental design, variation reduction, process capability analysis, and process improvement plans.

SPC is used to monitor the consistency of processes used to manufacture a product as designed. It aims to get and keep processes under control. No matter how good or bad the design, SPC can ensure that the product is being manufactured as designed and intended. Thus, SPC will not improve a poorly designed product's reliability, but can be used to maintain the consistency of how the product is made and, therefore, of the manufactured product itself and its as-designed reliability.

Statistical process control can involve the use of charts to record and monitor the accuracy of the physical dimensions of products.

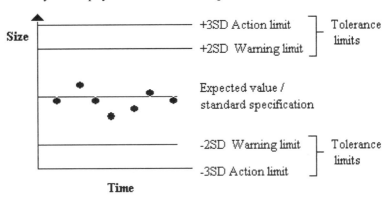

Representational samples of an output manufacturing process may be taken daily or even hourly, and faults in the process which are revealed may be fairly simple to correct by adjusting the appropriate machinery. If output exceeds the control limits consistently, then more urgent management action would be required because this could indicate some inadequacy in production methods or quality of raw materials and components. It could even be due to inefficiency in production or excessively tight tolerances in the first place.

Process charts can be used in hospitals to record patients' temperatures:

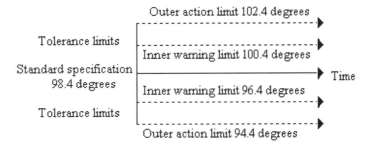

3 Operations management

3.1 The strategic significance of operations

The term 'operations management' refers to the activities required to produce and deliver a service as well as a physical product. Production management used to be associated solely with the manufacture of goods but its expansion to operations management means that it now includes purchasing, warehousing and transportation - dealing with all the operations from the procurement of raw materials through various activities until the product is available to the buyer.

Operations are the link between the strategy and the customer and also between the different functions. In service industries the operational interface with the customer is the crux of the business. Operations management has a bearing on marketing, finance, research and development, administration and job design, which has a knock-on effect on the tasks and the roles that human resources are involved in.

Longer-term decisions, particularly relating to design and the innovation of improved products, cannot be taken by the production department alone; its activities must be integrated with other functions in the firm. Operations plans are made for each department. They are interrelated.

- Product design is co-ordinated with R&D. Production should advise R&D as to the consequences of particular designs for the manufacturing process.

- Job design will involve consultation with human resources specialists.

- The marketing department will detail expected selling quantities, timings, advertising expenditure and sales force activities.

- The human resources department will be involved in managing the work force.

- The finance department might indicate the resources available for new equipment.

The design of an operations system requires decisions on the location of facilities, the process to be used, the quantity to be produced and the quality of the product.

3.2 Operations management and strategy

Corporate strategy is concerned with establishing the overall objectives of the organisation as a whole, in terms of 'What business do we want to be in?' and also 'What are we trying to achieve?' For many organisations, the main strategic objective is a financial one, such as maximising the wealth of the owners of the business.

Business strategy - for each business unit in the organisation, a strategy needs to be developed for how the business unit should compete in its markets, and what products or services it should provide to compete successfully.

Operations strategy is concerned with setting targets for the operations function that will support the overall objectives of the business unit. For example, a business unit might have an overall objective of achieving a 25% growth in its market share within the next three years. The operations strategy might be expressed in terms of an investment strategy for handling the expected increase in volume and a strategy for quality improvements or cost reductions to compete more successfully.

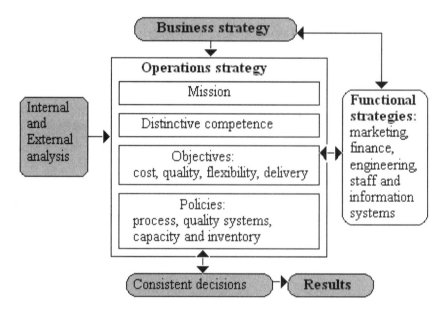

The operational side of a business directly contributes to competitiveness and market leadership. This means that the management of operations needs specified, consistent and achievable objectives and sound implementation strategies. If the organisation knows where it is and where it wants to get to, it has some chance of getting there - otherwise it is lost.

The objectives for operations should be consistent with the perceived requirements of customers. Various 'competitive factors' can be used to express customer requirements in terms of operational performance requirements. An organisation should establish its priorities for operational performance, and set target levels of achievement as a strategic objective.

- When customers want a low-priced product, the performance objectives in operational strategy should focus mainly on reducing costs and producing a low-cost output.

- When customers want a product or service with certain quality characteristics, and are willing to pay more for better quality, the performance objectives in operational strategy should focus on achieving the required quality standards, subject to a constraint that costs should be kept within certain limits.

- If customers want fast delivery of a product or service, the operational performance objective will concentrate on speed of operations or making the product or service more readily available.

- If customers want reliability, the operational objective should be to set targets for reliability and ensure that these are met. For example, a courier service meets customer requirements by ensuring that packages are delivered within a particular time to their destination, and without loss or damage. The operational target should be to meet these requirements on 100% of occasions.

- When customers want products or services to be designed to their own specification, the operational objective must be to achieve sufficient flexibility to handle the variations in customer requirements, and provide differing products or services accordingly.

- When customers want to alter the timing or delivery of services they receive, the main operational objective will also be flexibility. For example, a training company might have to be sufficiently flexible to deal with changes in the location, timing and duration of the training programmes required by their clients, and the number of delegates to be trained.

3.3 Purchasing and inbound logistics

Purchasing - is generally taken to mean the procurement of the supplied for the organisation. The cost of raw materials is a major element in the management of production. Purchasing costs may be incurred directly by the production unit and by other units that aid production. The purchasing department's primary responsibility is to secure sufficient and suitable raw materials, components and the other goods and services needed to ensure that the production is fully supplied in a cost-effective manner.

There is increasing recognition in the manufacturing industry that costs must be minimised. Inventory must be kept low through a very efficient supply of raw materials and components. In some cases this supply involves several deliveries a day. This allows an uninterrupted flow of production without holding expensive buffer stocks.

Typically a purchasing department will have a range of responsibilities:

- the collection of up-to-date market information including potential suppliers, prices, delivery and so on

- the appraisal and selection of suppliers

- negotiating the buying of goods and services which represent the best all-round value in the department's chosen time frame

- maintaining inventories at the most cost-effective levels

- setting up and maintaining effective communications and relationships within the organisation

- developing good, mutually beneficial relationships with current and potential external suppliers.

As we can see from these activities, there is the potential for purchasing to play an important role in the company's strategy. Increasingly, close attention to purchasing is an important characteristic of successful organisations. A central part of this strategy is to develop a mutually beneficial relationship with suppliers. The organisation benefits from the specialist expertise of the supplier, but without the risk and the demands on their limited management resources and capital, which would be needed if they also manufactured the goods they sell.

Inbound logistics – as described in Porter's value chain, are the activities concerned with receiving, storing and handling raw material inputs and assets.

Once the raw materials are purchased, they must be managed like any other resource. This includes stock control and security.

The sub activities within this process for a manufacturer are such things as quality control, materials reception and handling and stock control and the movement of received goods forward to operations. For financial services it would include access to finance and to information.

3.4 The purchasing mix

The purchasing mix includes quantity, quality, price and delivery. The right materials should be in the right place at the right time and at the right price.

Quantity – the size and timing of the purchases will depend on delays in production as a result of stock shortages and the costs of holding the stock in terms of capital tied up, deterioration, pilferage, insurance and obsolescence.

Quality – if this is very important for the manufacturing process, detailed specifications of goods required and tolerances accepted must be prepared. When the goods are received there must be a system to ensure conformity with the specifications. As we have already noted in a previous chapter, some suppliers guarantee the quality of goods supplied and allow the customer access while the goods are being manufactured. This is usually done through supplier quality assurance (SQA) officers, who control the specification of the goods supplied.

Price – should represent the best value considering the quality, delivery and urgency of order.

Delivery – involves the supplier's lead-time and reliability.

Purchasing policy may be concerned with:

- whether to buy when required – limiting the purchases to minimum requirements

- whether to buy on contract on a medium or long-term basis – assuring continuity of supply in very important flow production

- speculative or bargain buying – where material is bought with the hope of future price rises.

Security of supplies is so important to some concerns that they have integrated backwards, e.g. tea producers buying tea plantations.

3.5   Just-in-time supply management

Decisions about the purchasing mix are complex. They require not only extensive internal and external liaison but also a high degree of expertise and experience. For efficient management the **just-in-time** (JIT) approach to activity scheduling has received considerable attention and proved to be of strategic importance to many manufacturing organisations. This technique, where the supplier delivers the components and parts to the production line 'just in time' to be assembled, has revolutionised the acquisition of resources, with a resultant reduction in costs (of stock) or improvement in lead times. Some organisations have gained a competitive advantage on the basis of JIT. However, the following possible disadvantages with JIT should also be recognised.

- JIT systems rely heavily on investment in appropriate information technology systems, including computer links with suppliers and logistics companies. They can therefore be costly to set up and implement.

- Quality assurance schemes are a necessary element of JIT systems – close co-operation with suppliers is therefore essential.

- Any disruption in the supply chain can cause significant problems for manufacturers operating under a JIT regime. The recent disruption to vehicle fuel supplies in the UK caused significant problems for many companies when deliveries from their suppliers suddenly stopped and no ' buffer' stocks were on hand.

3.6   Manufacturing/transformation processes

Manufacturing can be defined as the activity of transforming raw materials or components into finished products. The nature of operations varies enormously between different types of organisation, but all operations can be described in terms of the transformation process model.

External environment

Input	Transformation process	Output
Customers' needs	Organising, staffing, leading	Products
Information	Operating the system	Services
Technology	Organisation structure	Information
Management & labour	Job design	
Plant, machinery, etc	Purchasing/inventory	
Materials and supplies		

Planning
Product/service
decisions and design

Controlling
Information for control
Quality control

Systems improvement

Tools and techniques
Operations research/linear programming
Inventory planning and control
CAD/CAM and MAP
Value engineering – quality circles
Time/event networks – work simplification
Distribution logistics

Inputs may include capital, raw materials, people, information, managerial and technical skills and knowledge.

The transformation process – in a manufacturing organisation, the transformation of inputs into outputs would be the production department; in an insurance company it would be the underwriting department. The maintenance process keeps the organisation functioning. It may repair and service the building. Alternatively, the human resource department can be seen as a maintenance sub-system, recruiting, retiring and counselling etc employees.

Outputs – the type of outputs will vary with the organisation. They generally include products, services, profits and rewards.

Before production commences, production policies must be known and then the processes of manufacture, machine requirements, factory layout, storage and handling systems, skills required in the workforce and the method of training can be determined. These policies are largely determined by the nature of the work. The types of production are:

Job production (or unit production) - output of single product to specific requirements (e.g., suit or ship). Demand is difficult to forecast, and generally production schedules can be prepared only when the customer's order arrives

Batch production - output of a batch or quantity of a product (e.g., furniture). There is repetition, but not continuous production. Production is often for stock.

Mass production - output of products of a uniform and standardised nature - production is continuous and carried out by **specialised units (e.g., cars).**

Process (flow) production - continuous production of products of a more or less identical nature e.g., oil refinery

The production function plans, organises, directs and controls the necessary activities to provide products and services. They procure inputs and process them, adding value to them in some way, to generate outputs for customers. Activities incur costs, and, in combination with other activities, provide a product or service that earns revenue.

ACTIVITY 2

Fill in the three missing sections from the table below:

	Inputs	Transformation	Outputs
1.		Assembling bicycles	Completed bicycles
2.	Students with limited knowledge and skills		Students with enhanced knowledge and skills
3.	Client problem	Consulting: information analysis, evaluation and selection of alternatives, recommendation	

Feedback to this activity is at the end of the chapter.

3.7   Outbound logistics

Outbound logistics are concerned with storing, distributing and delivering the finished goods to the customers – including packaging and warehousing.

Packaging – can be regarded as the vehicle from which a product is to be sold and it must therefore protect and attract. Important issues include:

- special protection in packing, shelf-life, uses of product, conditions of use, type of user, type of market
- predicted volume, special processing needed, e.g. for shipping
- promotional needs
- legal requirements.

Warehousing – despite the efforts of marketing managers to regulate consumer demand, it is very difficult to equate demand to manufacturing programmes, and warehousing is needed to store the finished product. Warehouses are needed to:

- act as a buffer for holding goods between the production process and the user, as many goods are not made against customer orders
- to break bulk and reduce transport costs
- provide a source for quick supply to customers – if located in a suitable position.

Transport is costly so a decision has to be made as to whether warehouses are to be centrally situated or decentralised.

3.8   Distribution channels

The selection of distribution channels is a serious decision for companies because the choice of channels will affect all other marketing activities, e.g. pricing and promotion policies, and the choice of channels will involve the firm in relatively long-term commitments with other firms. The choice of channels is not a static choice. Channels of distribution should be constantly monitored so that their ultimate function – that of making the product available at the time and place of greatest convenience to the user – can be achieved within the general limits established by cost/revenue considerations.

The main distribution channels for manufactured goods are:

- direct sales e.g. sale of a computer to an organisation
- distribution to a retailer direct
- distribution via a wholesaler to a retailer
- via an agent, wholesaler to a retailer
- via an agent to a retailer.

The main factors affecting the choice of distribution channels include:

- Customer characteristics – if customers for a product are geographically distributed, large in number and their frequency of purchase is high (e.g. cigarettes) then there is likely to be indirect distribution with many channels between manufacturer and customer, e.g. from manufacturer to wholesaler to retailer to customer. If, however, the market is small, geographically concentrated, infrequently buying goods of high unit value, e.g. carpet weaving machinery, then there is likely to be as few intermediaries between manufacturer and customer as possible, i.e. direct distribution.
- Product characteristics – if a product is bulky, heavy costs would be incurred in movements through many channels and so there is likely to be a direct distribution channel between manufacturer and customer. Similarly, perishable products, e.g. ice cream, would suggest direct distribution. For goods such as Xmas cards, which

are highly seasonal in nature, indirect distribution with many intermediaries is likely. In this situation, the intermediaries carry the stock.

- The nature of available intermediaries – here the company is concerned with such things as the ability of intermediaries in areas of transportation and storage. Decisions will also be affected by the intermediaries' requirement from manufacturers for such things as credit facilities, training, etc.

- Action of competitors – this has considerable influence on the selection of channels. In extreme cases, competitors may have sewn up all channels, e.g. Avon Cosmetics. Furthermore, if you are in direct competition, it might be necessary to use identical distribution channels to your competitors and if your competitors have granted exclusive franchises you may have to offer similar exclusive franchises in your own distribution channels.

- The manufacturing company's policies and characteristics – the company's size, financial strength and reputation will affect its selection of channels. If it is financially weak, it may employ agents, but if strong it may establish its own outlets. Its past experience with channels will have created preferences and its present marketing policy must affect its choice of channels, e.g. a future planned heavy advertising campaign will mean a choice of channels, who will co-operate in the campaign.

- The environment – if the economy is depressed, producers will try to reduce costs and price by reducing the length of channels. Similarly, legal requirements might reduce possible outlets.

4 Quality

4.1 The concept of quality

The concept of quality was discussed in detail in Chapter 14. Achieving a specified level of quality is often a critical aspect of project management, so issues of error prevention and detection are particularly important.

5 Business process re-engineering (BPR)

Business Process Re-engineering (BPR) was developed because the tendency in the past was to simply automate processes that used to be carried out manually and .it was discovered that in many companies, while the machinery may be changed, the actual processes of the business remain unchanged. This is the reason why, in many offices, the installation of information technology has not resulted in the scale of increases seen in manufacturing productivity in the 1980s. The aim of the process is to reorganise business around processes rather than around functions or departments.

The pioneers of BPR are generally acknowledged as Hammer and Champy. They define it as 'the fundamental re-thinking and rational re-design of the business processes to achieve dramatic improvements in critical contemporary measures of performance such as cost, quality, service and speed.'

The definition contains four key words: fundamental, radical, dramatic, and processes.

- **Fundamental** - BPR is about questioning why the company does what it does, and why it does it the way that it does do it. These are basic fundamental questions, which will force people to re-assess the way that they work. The idea is to question whether all the procedures currently being undertaken are actually relevant to achieving the overall objectives of the company. Very often the rules and procedures that are in place are obsolete or are costing more money to carry out than would be lost if they were eliminated altogether. For instance, many companies regularly perform customer credit checks on new customers, BPR would ask why? And is it really necessary? And does the cost of checking outweigh the bad debts that would be incurred if the checking were not done? Very often BPR will remove processes that have been carried out by companies for many years if those processes have ceased to add value. BPR does not make assumptions that any procedures are necessary. It starts from the beginning and concentrates on what is required in order to achieve the company objectives.

- **Radical redesign** - means going back to the beginning and redesigning each procedure that is required. It is not about changing what already exists or improving the speed and efficiency of current procedures, it means disregarding all existing procedures and regulations and inventing new ways to accomplish the necessary work. BPR is not about improvement, enhancement or modification of existing work methods but reinvention of work methods.

- **Dramatic** - BPR is about making dramatic improvements in business performance. If only marginal improvements are necessary to achieve company objectives then it is unlikely that the company would benefit or have need of BPR. Companies that do undergo re-engineering would expect to achieve quite dramatic changes in their performance and these would be in the areas of cost, quality service and speed.

- **Processes** - the business processes are the various systems within a company that take different types of inputs, and through a series of activities, turn the inputs into an output, which is of value to a customer. This is often the difficult area because most managers focus on tasks, jobs, people and structures but not on the processes.

The technique represents a response to:

- failure of business process to meet customers' needs and deliver customer satisfaction

- the yawning gap between strategic intent in the boardroom and the day-to-day practice of the business

- disappointments following the application of information technology to businesses

This last point is an important one. There is evidence that many companies have failed to benefit as they had expected from their investment in information technology (IT). Often the reason has been that senior managers have failed to align the IT strategy with corporate objectives. Also, organisations tend to use technology to mechanise old methods of doing things. They leave the existing processes intact and use computers to speed them up.

The main aims of BPR are to save time in the operation of processes, and so achieve competitive advantage and to reduce 'time to market', the time taken from inception of a product to its commercial exploitation.

At the heart of BPR is the notion of discontinuous thinking, of recognising and breaking out-of-date rules and assumptions that underlie current business operations.

Quality, innovation and service are now more important for survival than cost, growth and control. Processes that suited command and control organisations no longer suit service and quality driven ones. Earlier assumptions of necessary roles are no longer valid.

When work passes from process to process, delays and errors occur and create further processes to expedite delays and repair the faults. Managers have tried to adapt their processes but usually in ways that just create more problems. For example, if cash flow is poor, debt chasing is stepped up rather than taking steps to avoid marginal accounts. More bureaucracy makes costs rise, which helps give away market share to other, more enterprising, organisations. Dealing with this type of problem is the concern of re-engineering. It is very closely akin to Total Quality Management where management seeks to remove the cause of faults instead of merely detecting them when they occur.

Advantages of BPR include the following.

- BPR revolves around customer needs and helps to give an appropriate focus to the business.

- BPR provides cost advantages that assist the organisation's competitive position.

- BPR encourages a long-term strategic view of operational processes by asking radical questions about how things are done and how processes could be improved.

- BPR helps overcome the short-sighted approaches that sometimes emerge from excessive concentration on functional boundaries. By focusing on entire processes the exercise can streamline activities throughout the organisation.

- BPR can help to reduce organisational complexity by eliminating unnecessary activities.

Criticisms of BPR include the following.

- BPR is sometimes seen (incorrectly) as a means of making small improvements in existing practices. In reality, it is a more radical approach that questions whether existing practices make any sense in their present form.

- BPR is sometimes seen (incorrectly) as a single, once-for-all cost-cutting exercise. In reality, it is not primarily concerned with cost-cutting (though cost reductions often result), and should be regarded as on-going rather than once-for-all. This misconception often creates hostility in the minds of staff who see the exercise as a threat to their security.

- BPR requires a far-reaching and long-term commitment by management and staff. Securing this is not an easy task, and many organisations have rejected the whole idea as not worth the effort.

A widely cited example of business reengineering is Ford Motor Company's invoice-less processing. Ford employed more than 500 people in its North American accounts payable organisation. The accounts payable clerks spent most of their time resolving discrepancies between purchase orders, receiving documents, and invoices. Ford reengineered its accounts payable process, instituting a system wherein the purchasing department enters a purchase order into an on-line database that can be checked by the receiving department when the ordered items arrive. If the received goods match the purchase order, the system automatically generates a cheque for accounts payable to send to the vendor.

Conclusion

Projects are directed towards a specified goal, but while the goal may be specific the means of achieving it may involve dealing with the unexpected. The main objectives of project management are to ensure that the end product or service conforms to its specification and is produced on time and within budget.

In this chapter we looked at the steps in the project life cycle. Part of project management is the estimating of resources and the time needed to complete parts of the project. We outlined some of the techniques used for estimating, e.g. Gantt charts, network analysis and critical path analysis.

It must be possible to measure progress made in acceptable terms, determine and report any deviations, undertake corrective action as necessary and issue specific reports.

Operations management refers to activities necessary to produce and deliver a service as well as a physical product. It also includes purchasing, warehousing and distribution.

The operations management systems model shows inputs, the transformation process, outputs and the feedback system. A variety of tools and techniques make operations more productive.

Project management

1   List the main activities in the life cycle of a large project. (1.2)

2   Why might project cost estimates be inaccurate? (1.4)

Project management tools and techniques

3   How can network analysis help in resource planning? (2.1)

4   What is a GANTT chart? (2.1)

Operations management

5   Identify some inputs to an operations system. (3.6)

6   Describe the different types of production. (3.6)

Business process re-engineering (BPR)

7   What is the key advantage of BPR? (5)

EXAM-TYPE
QUESTION

BPR

The Dose company was established over a century ago and manufactures water pumps of various kinds. Until recently it has been successful, but imports of higher quality pumps at lower prices are now rapidly eroding Dose's market share. The managing director feels helpless in the face of this onslaught from international competitors and is frantically searching for a solution to the problem. In his desperation, he consults a range of management journals and comes across what seems to be a wonder cure by the name of Business Process Re-engineering (BPR).

According to the article, the use of BPR has already transformed the performance of a significant number of companies in the USA which were mentioned in the article, and is now being widely adopted by European companies. Unfortunately, the remainder of the article which purports to explain BPR is full of management jargon and he is left with only a vague idea of how it works.

Required:

Explain the nature of BPR and describe how it might be applied to a manufacturing company like Dose.   **(20 marks)**

For the answer to this question, see the 'Answers' section at the end of the book

---

FEEDBACK TO
ACTIVITY 1

Below is a work breakdown structure for the recruitment of a new person to fill a vacant post.

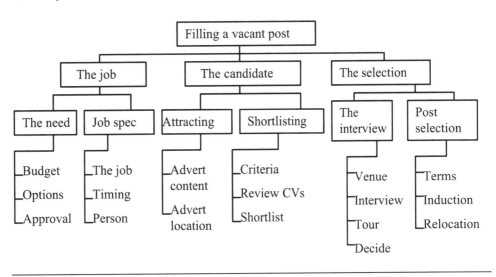

FEEDBACK TO
ACTIVITY **2**

Inputs	Transformation	Outputs
1 Plant, factory, machines, people and materials	Assembling bicycles	Completed bicycles
2 Students with limited knowledge and skills	Lectures, case studies and experiential exercises	Students with enhanced knowledge and skills
3 Client problem	Consulting: information analysis, evaluation and selection of alternatives, recommendation	Consulting report recommending course of action

Chapter 18

ISSUES IN THE MANAGEMENT OF CHANGE

In this chapter we will consider the nature of change and its effects upon organisations. Management has been defined as 'the management of change' and, certainly, change is ever present and occurring at an ever increasing rate.

Organisations inevitably change because they are open systems in constant interaction with their environment. Although the impelling force for change can be attributed to internal or external stimuli (or both), the underlying impetus is the exposure of system boundaries that allow new technologies, skills, values and demands to affect the organisation.

Objectives

When you have studied this chapter you should be able to:

- appreciate the nature of change

- list the reasons for change

- identify and illustrate the different categories of change

- critically examine how change should be introduced

- analyse the relationships between the different levels of change

- discuss Lewin's 3-step model of change

- discuss the views of Kanter and Bennis

- understand change management

- consider the implementation of change through power politics

- define and explain organisational development (OD).

1   Management of change issues

1.1   The motivation to change

Organisations have to respond to change if they wish to survive and prosper. The organisational change has to recognise the changing aspirations and qualities of the workforce - and the changing aspirations of an increasingly educated and discerning customer base

Change can be a gradual evolution or a sudden transformation. This speed of change is often outside the control of the company. The rate may be dictated by technology, the competition or environmental factors. Some companies constantly operate in fast-changing surroundings, eg, companies in the fashion industry.

An important consideration is the cascading effect of change, where a change in one area leads to changes in others. A company may lose an important customer; this does not mean that the company will simply produce less. Instead it is likely that there will be changes in marketing approach, pricing, advertising, packaging, production and purchasing; there may even be changes in management responsibilities. So we should not consider one change in isolation but instead as one stage in a continuing sequence of changes.

The forces for change may come from the environment external to the organisation, from within the enterprise or from the individuals themselves. The factors of change from the external environment will be many and will be different for different companies. Examples include:

- Regulatory changes that organisations must comply with and greater co-operation between government and industry with jointly funded projects.

- Sudden economic shocks can lead to transformational change and gradual change comes about through the spread of multinational companies internationally and other changes in global trade patterns.

- Social changes such as the number of women wanting/needing to combine work with child rearing and a growing recognition that training should continue throughout a life-time's employment, has led to changes in the labour market. There has also been a change in the balance of employment with the shift to knowledge and service workers and away from manufacturing industries

- Technological developments can lead to new products and processes, possibly making the old ones obsolete. The effect of the digital watch on the Swiss watch industry is a classic example. The increasing use of computers, information technology and telecommunications. Now available to even the smallest organisations, the PC with access to the Internet is affecting work patterns and location of businesses;

The internal forces that can bring about change include the following:

- as part of the cascading effect there is a continuous reaction to historical changes, as the initial change works its way through the system

- innovation – the company may develop a new product (eg Philips' development of the compact disc) or a new manufacturing process that alters the economics of the market place (eg Pilkington's development of glass that never needs cleaning

- individual executives' ambition

- the pursuit of growth.

Changes in structure within organisations seem to happen regularly. A frequent change is from a vertical structure to a horizontal structure in order to address a lack of communication between different vertical divisions. This is often followed, after a period of three or four years, by a change back to a vertical structure in order to address a lack of defined responsibility for particular areas of the business.

Several trends, some of them already occurring, will have implications for developing human resources. For example:

- The increasing use of computers, especially microcomputers, requires that teachers as well as students become computer-literate

- Education extends into the adult life. Lifelong learning becomes a necessity and educational institutions and enterprises must recognise the special educational needs of adults.

- The proportion of knowledge workers will increase and the need for skill workers will decrease, which may require more training in knowledge, conceptual, and design skills.

- The shift from manufacturing to service industries requires retraining in preparation for new positions.

- The choice of educational opportunities will increase. For example, many companies already are conducting their own training programmes

- Internationalisation will continue, and managers in different countries must learn to communicate and to adapt to each other. Companies need to train with a global perspective.

There are various ways to respond to these forces. One approach is simply to react to a crisis. Unfortunately, this is usually not the most effective response. Another approach is to deliberately plan the change. This may require new objectives or policies, organisational rearrangements, or a change in leadership style and organisation culture.

1.2   Attitudes to change

The role of management is to anticipate the need for change, create an atmosphere of acceptance of change and manage the stages of introduction and implementation. The manager can expect resistance to change since all major changes threaten somebody's security or somebody's status. There are many spectacular examples of companies and industries, which failed to adapt and change. For example:

- the failure of Volkswagen to introduce a new model to replace the Beetle, which caused severe problems to the group for several years;

- the resistance to change by London Dock workers which encouraged the automation of Rotterdam, now a thriving, international port while London Docks have closed;

- the Swiss watch industry and the German camera industry were world leaders and underestimated the changes necessary to combat Japanese competition. The result, within a few short years, was that Japan dominated these markets worldwide.

Most people attempt to preserve the existing state of affairs against pressure to alter it. However, there are also people who long for change and have many ideas about how it should be achieved. Negative attitudes towards change can be due to the following:

- Lack of understanding of the need for change - what is not known causes fear and induces resistance. People may not trust those initiating the change, or they feel that they have not been told the real reasons for the change.

- Uncertainty of the effect that the change will have on their lives. People may wonder if they are able to cope with the new method. An organisational restructuring can leave a person uncertain about its effect on his or her job. People want to feel secure and have some control over the change.

- Self interest - people may resist change because, in their opinion, it could take away something they value. This could take the form of a loss of prestige, especially if people feel that it may result in reduction of benefits or loss of power.

1.3   Culture and change

Faced with pressures for change, managers will be likely to deal with the situation in ways that protect the paradigm from challenge (look back to Chapter 4 for a reminder of the organisation's paradigm). This raises difficulties when managing strategic change because it may be that the action required is outside the scope of the paradigm and the constraints of the cultural web and that members would be required to change their core beliefs or routines substantially. Managers are much more likely to attempt to deal with the situation by searching for what they can understand and cope with and they will attempt to minimise the extent to which they are faced with ambiguity and uncertainty by looking for a familiar solution.

Changing the culture of an organisation is often the most difficult change to manage. It cannot be done quickly: it is often said that it takes three years to achieve. The dilemma for managers is that they themselves will have to change the beliefs values they have adopted and grown with inside the organisation. They will have ensured that new employees are initiated into the organisation's culture and share the same values and beliefs. The changing of culture may even threaten their own position. On the other hand, if they do not create the conditions for change they find their position threatened by their organisation's poor performance.

1.4 The management of change

The organisation can create a general atmosphere in which employees are willing to consider change. In order to do this the organisation should:

- set simple and clear goals for what the change should achieve (ie demonstrate the current problem or opportunity)

- create an agenda for change (ie, state clearly what is going to be changed and when)

- create a supportive organisational structure (ie, set up help desks to deal with concerns); this includes providing supporting resources and/or reduced performance expectations of employees during the changeover

- select key people to lead change – these should be chosen either because of their position within the organisation or because they are a person by whom other employees will be influenced

1.5 Lewin's model of change

Lewin's 3-step model of change, shown in the diagram below, includes unfreezing habits or standard operating procedures, changing to new patterns and refreezing to ensure lasting effects.

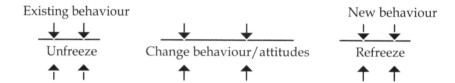

- Unfreezing the present level implies that a change means abandoning existing practice before new practices can be successfully adopted. It creates the initial motivation to change by convincing staff of the undesirability of the present situation. Unfreezing will lead to doubts and to fear of the unknown. This is an opportunity for managers to introduce education and training.

- The change process itself is mainly concerned with identifying what the new behaviour or norm should be. This stage will often involve new information being communicated and new attitudes, culture and concepts being adopted.

- Refreezing or stabilising the change implies reinforcement of the new pattern of work or behaviour by rewards (praise etc). Lewin considered this necessary because success may be short-lived owing to group behaviour reverting to its previous ways Management must develop the belief that the changed situation satisfies organisational and personal values.

The examiner does not want students to simply memorise Lewin's model of change and 'dump it'. In other words, it is not sufficient just to say 'To change culture, management need to unfreeze, change behaviour and attitudes and refreeze'.

1.6 Systems Intervention strategy (SIS)

Systems Intervention strategy (SIS) is a simple methodology applicable to complex uncertain situations in which sufficient time and intention exists to apply the methodology. It is a structured approach that is designed to enable development of a set of intervention strategies for change by a change agent. This development occurs through an iteration process that enables any strategies to be clarified and fully defined. Part of this process can be recursive, which can normally occur in the design of the implementation strategies.

The methodology is not intended as a linear cycle of structured examination, though this may be an attractive way of progressing though an inquiry for a novice inquirer. It is intended that the inquirer (who may be a stakeholder, the problem owner, or a person or group working on behalf of the problem owner) will be able to apply any of the steps of the methodology as necessary in order to satisfy the needs of inquiry.

SIS is essentially a seven-step methodology. In order to deal with complexity, Systems Intervention Strategy conceptualises that three types of change should be addressed:

- technical,

- organisational, and

- personal.

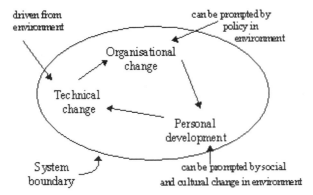

It is a relatively simple but useful methodology that is sensitive to both human needs, and technical (control and prediction) organisation. It has a mission to provide a strategy for intervention intended to balance the environmental forces from the environment.

It does this through three goals: during intervention, to achieve technical development, organisational change, and personal development of the participants within the situation. The aims embedded in the methodology are that an inquirer should attempt to ensure that intervention strategies are robust, and to enhance this a risk and/or decision analysis should be undertaken. SIS is particularly useful for situations in which definable objects of attention can be identified. Unlike some hard methodologies, its practitioners become involved in consulting the participants of a situation, thus attempting to identify their needs.

The methodology seeks to introduce steady state changes that enable new balances with the environment to occur. This in essence derives from the perception that there should be equilibrium between the system and its environment. In many situations that are continually under environmental flux and shifting beyond the threshold of control, balances are continually being disturbed. The problem of seeing the nature of the disturbance in order to reapply the methodology may be problematic.

Systems intervention strategy (SIS) is a systems approach to change.

SIS tries to find the best ways of achieving the ends and is most effective when the ends are already known. Each stage is explicitly stated and highlights the necessary activities to avoid the usual pitfalls of change initiatives. The problem owners, whose support is essential because they are the main stakeholders in the change process, can be thought of as project sponsors or clients.

There are 3 main phases in SIS:

- **Diagnosis/description** - The process of developing a perspective from which to tackle a set of change problems. It includes understanding the problem, developing a perspective and defining the purpose of change. Objectives and measures are defined.

- **Design** - the creation and exploration of options for change. It enables alternative methods or options for achieving change to be identified and explored

- **Implementation** - the process of seeing the change through. This stage represents a commitment to a change, while developing a means for creating and developing a desired change

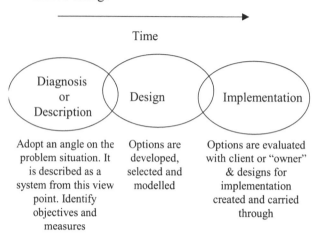

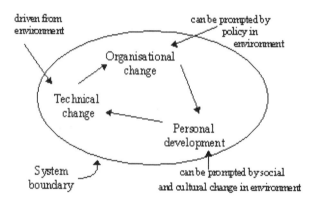

Phase	Steps	Actions	Tools and techniques
Diagnosis *'where are you now?'* *'where do you want to be?'* *'how will you know when you get there?'*	**0** Entry	The entry step 0 provides a pre-evaluation introduction to the situation to enable it to be classified as a mess or a difficulty, and so validates the use of SIS	Start by recognising that change is a complex process
	1 Description	Structure and understand the change in systems terms. Get other points of view on the change problem or opportunity	Use diagrams, conduct meetings and workshops, generate a model of things as they are
	2 Identify objectives and constraints	Set up some objectives for the systems that you are examining. Think of the objectives of the change itself	Prioritise your objectives for change

	3 Formulate measures for your objectives	Decide on ways of measuring whether an objective is achieved	Use '£s' or quantities where possible. Scaling or ranking methods elsewhere
Design *'how can you get there?* 'what will it be like?' 'how will you know when you get there?'	**4** Generate a range of options	Develop any ideas for change as full options. Look at a wide range of possibilities. Your objectives may require new options	Brainstorming, idea writing, interviews and surveys, comparisons with best practice in other organisations
	5 Model option selectively	Describe the most promising options in some detail. Ask of each option What is involved? Who is involved? How will it work?	Diagrams are simple models, cost-benefit analysis, cash-flow models, computer simulations
Implementation 'will you like it?' 'how can you carry to through?'	**6** Evaluate options against measures	Test the performance of your options against an agreed set of criteria	Set up a simple matrix to compare the performance of your options. Score each option against the measures
	7 Design implementation strategies	Select the preferred options and plan a way of putting the changes into place	Look for reliable options. Check back to the 'problem owners'. Plan time and allocate tasks
	8 Carry through the planned changes	Bring together people and resources. Manage the process. Monitor the progress	Sort out who is involved. Allocate responsibility. Review and modify plans if necessary

Step 1: Description

A description of the situation should occur in terms of:

- what people want
- establishing a boundary around the mess
- clarifying the relationships between the major subsystems
- understanding the structure of the mess
- deciding of what objectives will be served by the change

This step therefore involves an examination of the situation in order to understand the behaviour that occurs within it. Clarification of the interests of individuals within the situation should occur.

The problem owner should be clearly identified. This is a term adopted from Checkland who used it in his methodological approach. The problem owner is a plausible role from which the situation can be viewed. The problem owner is chosen by the inquirer who may be a facilitator or a change agent.

The situation should be represented as one of the 'relevant systems' selected. A relevant system is a term employed by Checkland. It is an inquirer's perception of the human activity system that is relevant to a problem situation. Any situation may have as many relevant systems views as perceived by an inquirer.

Simple systems models are used to represent this, like:

- a systems map
- influence diagram
- multiple cause diagram
- input-output model
- flow-block diagram

Step 2: Identify Objectives and Constraints

The problem owner should be consulted about the current evaluation of the situation. The objectives, measures and constraints should also be clearly identified.

In the setting of objectives it may be seen that some are subordinate to others. An objective tree will help identify the list of objectives to be addressed. Some of the objectives can have quantitative measures assigned to them, while others may have to be qualitatively evaluated.

Step 3: Formulate Measures for Objectives

The design of strategies should involve an awareness of the forces at work within the situation that will bias intervention strategies. These should be avoided unless they appear as initial constraints established in Step 2.

Step 4: Generate Options

This is the inventive stage of the inquiry. A wide range of options should be generated without restriction. They will in due course be evaluated both logically and with the problem owner.

Step 5: Modelling Options

Modelling options may sometimes involve physical representations of an idea. More typically in human activity systems they may involve such classes as:

- simulation model (e.g., computer based, stochastic, statistical)
- cashflow models
- cost/benefit analysis
- strategic models

Step 6: Evaluation of Options

The evaluation of options is often best undertaken through the use of a comparative matrix that operates as a decision table.

Step 7: Planning implementation

There are 3 main implementation strategies: Big bang, pilot study and parallel running.

Step 8: Take action

The heart of change is taking action.

Notes:

SIS is a rational, goal-oriented approach and therefore suited for challenges that can be cast in terms of how best to achieve an agreed end.

2 The dynamics of change

2.1 Why change is a challenge to management

For managers the management of change is about maintaining a dynamic equilibrium. By diagnosing events and situations, and making adjustments which are appropriate for coping with current conditions the management would ensure that:

- there is enough stability to achieve current goals

- there is continuity to allow orderly change in either ends or means

- the organisation is adaptable and can react to external opportunities and demands as well as changing internal conditions

- there is enough innovativeness for the organisation to be proactive and initiate change when conditions are right.

The managerial role involves coping with accelerating change in both the external environment and the internal subsystems that affect the managerial process.

Accelerating change can lead to increasing complexity, making the job of the manager increasingly difficult. They need a tolerance for ambiguity and an ability to diagnose situations and identify opportunities and problems.

As decision makers, managers are the ultimate change agents, whether they are centrally involved or merely guiding and co-ordinating activities. Change can stem from adjustments in managerial behaviour, e.g. leadership style, approach to planning and controlling or degree of participation in decision making. When the focus is more technical, structural or psychosocial, managers may respond to suggestions from others or actively instigate changes.

There are external or internal consultants that facilitate organisational change. Specialists in economic and marketing research, industrial relations and organisational development are all examples of change agents.

2.2 Organisational change

For organisations and management, change can take place in many areas including the following:

- The environment, e.g. changes to any of the variables in the SLEPT analysis. Routine economic developments are unlikely to lead to transformational change, but the type of sudden economic shock that occurred on September 11 2001 certainly was disastrous for many organisations.

- The products/services provided by the organisation – customer needs change and regulatory changes that must be complied with will affect certain organisations.

- The way the products are made – technological developments can lead to new products and processes, sometimes making existing ones obsolete.

- Structure and size of the organisation.

- Management and working relationships – an interesting development is the increasing number of women who wish to combine work with child rearing. This has led to major changes in the organisation of jobs including the expansion of part time and job sharing.

The change process is often described as logical and sequential. Unfortunately, neither people nor change is rational or logical; and yet we all pretend we are, and that decisions are based on a well argued, objective and well-informed basis.

In reality the change process means:

- Delay in recognising there is a problem to be addressed/a stimulus to respond to:
    - too much time spent on analysis, strategy and planning
    - distancing of people from the issues that may require them to change
    - resentment from staff at the delay and secrecy; rumour abounds.
- Once the plan is launched, the workload seen to have doubled – keeping the show on the road and making changes.
- Time for implementation now short, so no room for experimentation or involvement in decision making.
- Manipulation, pressure and persuasion to 'make' people change.
- Time drags on, key people leave, energy fades and the change fails.
- Cynicism, apathy, frustration and resentment abound.

2.3 Types of change

As we noted in an earlier chapter, most organisations are inclined to change incrementally with their strategies being formed gradually or through piecemeal change. Mintzberg noticed a tendency towards 'momentum' of strategy where, once an organisation had adopted a particular strategy, it tended to develop from and within that strategy, rather than fundamentally changing direction. There were periods of continuity in which the established strategy remained unchanged and periods of fluctuation where the strategies did change but in no clear direction. Global or transformational change was infrequent, tending to occur at times of crisis in organisations when performance had declined significantly.

Arguably, it is beneficial for an organisation to change incrementally because it will build on the skills, routines and beliefs of those involved. In this way, change can be efficient, smooth and most likely to win the commitment of those in the organisation.

Transformational change involves changing one or more assumptions in the organisational paradigm and with it the values of the organisation. Examples are the changes in the processes associated with doing things very differently, and with undertaking different activities.

3 Developing a strategic change programme

3.1 Gemini 4Rs framework

The transformation process must create a vision, make the company lean and fit, create market opportunities and impart new ways of doing things.

Gouillart and Kelly describe a four-dimensional process for organisational transformation using four Rs – reframe, restructure, revitalise and renew. This is known as the Gemini 4Rs framework.

Reframing – is the process of finding a new strategic understanding about the organisation involving fundamental questioning. The components of this dimension include:

- achieve mobilisation – create the will and desire for change
- create the vision of where the organisation is going
- build a measurement system to set targets and measure performance.

Restructuring – is often the most visible part of a transformation and is seen by employees as a test of the top management's commitment. It involves examining the organisation's structure and is likely to include cultural changes. It covers the following:

- construct an economic model to show in detail how value is created and where resources should be deployed
- align the structure with the strategy
- redesign the processes so they interact to create value.

Revitalising – is a company's commitment to the future. It is the process of finding new products and markets and of securing a good fit with the environment.

- achieve market focus
- invent new businesses
- change the rules of competition by exploiting technology.

Renewal – is the process of development that focuses on the individuals. It is needed to align individual skills with organisational requirements and ensure that the people in the organisation support the change process.

- create a reward system in order to motivate
- build individual learning
- develop the organisation and its adaptive capability.

The role of force field analysis

The force field model suggests two ways of dealing with change. The first is by strengthening your own side and the second is by weakening the opposing forces.

Force field analysis is a general-purpose diagnostic and problem-solving technique, developed by Kurt Lewin. He argued that managers should consider any change situation in terms of:

- the factors encouraging and facilitating the change (the driving forces); as well as
- the factors that hinder change (the restraining forces).

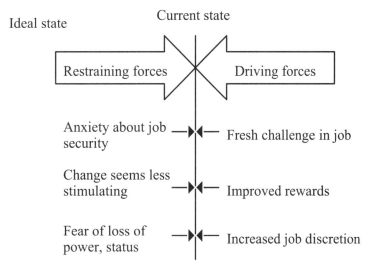

Restraining and driving forces in a change situation

The change process consists of:

(i) identifying the restraining forces and overcoming/removing/getting round them

(ii) carrying out the change

(iii) stabilising the new situation by reinforcing the (now changed) behaviour of individuals and work groups with praise and encouragement.

If the forces offset each other completely, it results in equilibrium and status quo. Change can be brought about by either increasing the driving forces or by reducing the restraining forces. New pushing forces can also be added. Reducing the restraining forces is often easier because to increase driving forces without attention to the restraining forces may increase pressure and tension in the system to the point that creative problem solving becomes impossible.

Using a common individual and organisational problem, that of lack of time, we can illustrate the use of force field analysis. To work on the problem effectively we need to state the situation in terms of current and desired conditions, where we are and where we want to be.

Current condition = no time spent on planned change.

Desired condition = large blocks of time to critically appraise the organisation.

In order to understand the situation we have to identify the forces that are keeping us in equilibrium, which is no change from the current condition.

Driving forces:

- knowledge of theory that says it would be 'better'
- feeling that it would be 'better'
- success stories about increased productivity from current literature
- success stories from acquaintances in similar organisations
- consultants selling the virtues of a new approach.

Restraining forces:

- programmed activity increases to absorb available time
- current deadlines leave no time to analyse the problem of lack of time
- we seem to be doing satisfactory work, there is no sense of urgency
- reluctance of participants to rock the boat by analysing group processes
- assumption that time is not currently wasted.

This list is not exhaustive but it leads to the next step, which is to pick one or more of the forces, starting with restraining forces and generating ideas for increasing them or decreasing them.

After alternatives have been evaluated, action plans can be designed and implemented.

3.2 Factors affecting an individual's responses to change

Whilst there is no doubt that change affects all our lives, considerable debate is currently taking place as to the desirability of some of the changes and the necessity for their rapid introduction.

Tofler argues that change is out of control and that man is suffering from the increased pace of life and its accompanying transient relationships.

Others argue that change is being introduced too slowly and that organisations, particularly within the UK, are left behind by their major competitors.

Much depends on the organisation's relation with its environment. As a consequence of the environment becoming more turbulent and complex, there is a need for organisations to develop more effective adaptive response systems.

Huczynski and Buchanan claim there are four basic features of organisational change.

Triggers

Change is initiated by some kind of disorganising pressure or trigger arising either within or outside the organisation. Changes may thus be triggered by the discovery that one of the company's machines is old or beyond repair, or by changes in legislation that affect the ways in which employees have to be treated.

Interdependencies

The various facets of an organisation are interdependent. Change in one aspect of an organisation creates pressure for adjustments in other aspects. The introduction of word processing in the typing pool may require authors to alter the style in which they write and present reports and letters for typing.

Conflict and frustrations

The technical and economic objectives of managers may often conflict with the needs and aspirations of employees and this leads to conflicts, which in turn create pressures for and resistance to change. The new machine that management want to buy may lead to demands for a new payment system from the people who will have to operate it.

Time lags

Change rarely takes place smoothly. Instead it happens in an untidy way. Some parts of the organisation change more rapidly than others. People and groups may need time to 'catch up' with everyone else. The maintenance staff may still be learning new skills months after that new machine has been installed.

The above characteristics evolve from the open systems perspective and the feedback mechanisms described earlier in the text.

KEY POINT

Positive feedback invokes change whereas negative feedback leads to stable and consistent behaviour.

Whether a change does or does not take place within an organisation is dependent on the relative strength of the various positive and negative feedback loops affecting the situation. Positive feedback invokes change whereas negative feedback leads to stable and consistent behaviour.

If we take the introduction of a new machine as an example, then, in very simple terms, wear and tear would form part of a positive feedback loop whilst maintenance and repair would be contained in a negative feedback loop. As long as the machine could be repaired equilibrium would persist but when this loop became no longer viable then the positive wear and tear loop would take over and the machine would have to be eventually replaced. Obviously, costs of repair and replacement, together with many other factors, would have to be included in the multiple-cause diagram analysing such a situation.

Internal triggers for change are those factors that can cause organisational disequilibrium and include:

(a) questioning authority and intra-organisational conflicts

(b) adverse organisational climate

(c) poor performance – unstable labour relations, low output and high costs

(d) presence of entrepreneurs and other innovators

(e) changes in or reordering of organisational goals

(f) favourable changes experienced in the past.

These internal triggers may, or may not, be related to external forces operating within the organisation's environment which, according to Martino, revolve around:

(a) changes in knowledge both technical and social

(b) economic opportunities

(c) distribution of political power

(d) demographic make-up of the population

(e) ecological considerations

(f) ideological and culture factors.

There are varying attitudes to change, as Robertson's classification shows:

(a) **Inactivists** could be focused on either of the following:

- **Business as usual** – such people seek stability and survival within the organisation and include those conservative satisficers who make up the establishment at large. They work very hard to keep still – a process termed 'dynamic conservatism'.

  Their efforts appeal to placid and pragmatic people including both moderate reformers and those content with the present situation.

  This attitude attracts defeatists, cynics and the worldly wise.

- **Disaster** – appeals to calm and thoughtful people although it can attract pessimists, preachers and doomsters.

(b) **Reactivists** would be interested in **totalitarian conservation** and would include all those reactionaries who prefer a previous state to the one they are in.

Such people:

- feel there is more to lose from disorder than dictatorship

- are of an authoritarian, dominating temperament

- take a low view of other people

- think they belong to a governing class.

(c) **Preactivists** These liberal optimisers are interested in much more than mere survival and they are generally means oriented.

Their approaches appeal to optimistic, energetic, ambitious, competitive people for whom material growth is more important than personal and social growth. Such persons are often male, toy loving and over intellectual.

(d) **Interactivists** must be interested in a **sane, humane, ecological** future and as radical idealisers they want to control their own destiny. Optimistic, participating, reflective people are attracted to such an attitude together with a number of cranks.

3.3 Why people may resist change

The following sources of resistance can be commonly expected.

Sources of resistance:

- fear of the unknown

- need for security

- vested interests threatened

- contrasting interpretations

- poor timing

- lack of resources.

Suggested responses:

- information, encouragement, involvement
- clarification of intentions and methods
- demonstrate problem or opportunity
- enlist key people in change planning
- disseminate valid information and facilitate group sharing
- await better time
- provide supporting resources and/or reduced performance expectations.

Such sources of change should be compared with those identified by Schein who differentiated between:

Economic fears:

- pay reductions
- redundancies.

Social fears:

- impaired status
- reduced satisfaction
- implied criticism of past performances
- break up of working group.

Resistance to change can be directed against the change itself, the change strategy or the change agent, and should be viewed, by those managing the change, as a form of negative feedback which could be constructively employed to modify their approach.

4 Managing change

4.1 Planned change

Earlier, the arguments for strategic choice versus determinism were aired including interactivists' belief that people have the potential to control change.

Predictions are often

- **self-fulfilling** (if something is forecast it can be made to happen); or
- **self-defeating** (undesirable predictions can provoke activities for their avoidance).

Whilst change can never be fully planned due to unexpected problems and follow on effects, many organisations are adopting a positive attitude to the need for change.

Theodore Levitt recognised four variables that can be affected by change and claimed that these 'entry points' can become specific targets for managerial efforts to instigate change.

The variables are:

(a) **technology** – the processes employed by the organisation to carry out its business

(b) **business** or 'task' – the activities an organisation undertakes to achieve its overall goals

(c) **people** – the employees of the organisation whose behaviour has been discussed in detail earlier. Changes in employees' attitudes, beliefs, skills, abilities and behaviour, together with structured changes, have been evaluated

(d) **structure** – the various ways in which organisations can be structured and changes to such structures, together with people changes, have been explored.

The interdependence of these four variables can be illustrated as follows:

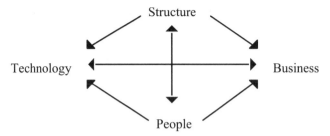

As a result of these interdependencies changes in one variable could lead to unanticipated, and possibly undesirable, changes to other variables. Moreover, it is possible to deliberately change one variable to bring about a desired change in another variable – the increasing adoption of mass production technologies has led to the spread of capitalist structures.

4.2 Key issues in successful change management

The five strategies for managing change are:

- participation
- education – communication
- power/coercion
- manipulation
- negotiation.

(a) Participation

This approach aims to involve employees, usually by allowing some input into decision making. This could easily result in employees enjoying raised levels of autonomy, by allowing them to design their own jobs, pay structures, etc.

Employees are more likely to support changes made and give positive commitment as they 'own' the change. Another advantage of participation is the improved utilisation of employee expertise.

Studies undertaken by Coch and French from America and Pirelli UK demonstrate the effectiveness of this strategy. Coch and French, in their book *Overcoming Resistance to Change*, suggest involving the people affected as early as possible, as deeply as possible.

The possible disadvantages include:

- The time element. The process can be lengthy due to the number of people involved in the decision-making process.
- The loyalty element. There is a need for a strong trusting relationship to exist between management and workforce.
- The resistance element. Management may suffer from restricted movement as the amount and direction of change acceptable to employees will have some influence.

(b) Education and communication

Usually used as a background factor to reinforce another approach. This strategy relies upon the hopeful belief that communication about the benefits of change to employees will result in their acceptance of the need to exercise the changes necessary. The obvious advantage is that any changes could be initiated easily. However, employees may not agree about the benefits of proposed changes as being in their best interests. Also, the process of education and persuasion can be lengthy to initiate and exercise unless there is a firm mutual trust. Without this they are not likely to succeed.

(c) **Power/coercion**

This strategy involves the compulsory approach by management to implement change. This method finds its roots from the formal authority that management possess together with legislative support. When there is a state of high unemployment, management enjoys greater power and is therefore able to use this strategy with more success. The advantages of this method are:

- changes can be made with speed

- adhering to management's requirements is easy when opposition from the workforce is weak.

The disadvantages are:

- the lack of commitment of the workforce and determination to reverse policy when times change

- poor support resulting in weak motivation, low morale and performance.

Future implications also need to be considered. For example, when employees enjoy a stronger position, i.e. union representation, they are less likely to co-operate due to their experiences of past management treatment.

(d) **Manipulation**

A manipulative strategy has many of the advantages and disadvantages of the power strategy. *It can therefore be viewed as part of a power strategy.*

(e) **Negotiation**

This particular strategy is often practised in unionised companies. *Simply, the process of negotiation is exercised, enabling several parties with opposing interests to bargain.* This bargaining leads to a situation of compromise and agreement.

Branching from this are two strategies.

- Each party involved seeks to negotiate for itself, at the cost of the other parties involved.

- Each party aims to find an agreement with aspects advantageous to all concerned.

The advantage of negotiation strategy is that it offers the company the opportunity to note possible conflict and allows it to be dealt with in an orderly fashion. This hopefully prevents such problems as industrial action. Also, when an agreement has been made, the outcome can be to encourage commitment, preserve morale and maintain output.

The main disadvantage is that this approach may be time consuming, and should opposition be strong enough the management might choose to adopt a power strategy instead.

ACTIVITY **1**

Changes in organisations can be seen as threatening. You will possibly know this from your own experience. Think about the possible effects of change and then list the reasons why people might fear or resist organisational change. Think further on the matter and then list where resistance might occur in an organisation, and describe what senior management might be able to do to eliminate resistance or reduce its effects.

Feedback to this activity is at the end of the chapter.

4.3   How organisations can create readiness for change

The senior management group has responsibility for establishing the organisation's vision and objectives and for making sure that the whole organisation pursues the same vision.

The managers are then responsible for creating the conditions that will promote change and innovation. To manage the change process successfully, the culture of the organisation will need to be permissive and flexible. Bureaucracies are very slow to change because they do not have this culture.

Managers need to encourage individuals to use their initiative and must put the emphasis on teamwork. An autocratic management style is not conducive to change because the manager should act as a facilitator of change rather than just telling people what to do.

Ronald Corwin, in his book *Strategies for Organizational Intervention*, argues that an organisation can be changed more easily:

- if it is invaded by creative and unconventional outsiders with fresh ideas

- if those outsiders are exposed to creative, competent and flexible socialisation agents

- if it is staffed by young, flexible, supportive and competent boundary personnel

- if it is structurally complex and decentralised

- if it has outside funds to lessen the cost of innovation

- if its members have positions that are sufficiently secure and protected from status risks involved in change

- if it is located in a changing, modern urbanised setting where it is in close co-operation with a coalition of other organisations that can supplement its skills and resources.

4.4   The role of the leader

There must be a leader of the change process who accepts the responsibility. Such a leader must have certain skills and attributes, such as:

- inspiration

- interpersonal skills

- the ability to resolve a multitude of interdependent problems

- the ability to plan

- opportunistic abilities

- the gift of good timing.

To maximise the advantages and minimise the disadvantages of the change process, the role of the leader should be to:

(i)   Give all staff concerned the maximum possible warning of impeding change to give them time to get accustomed to the idea.

(ii)   Explain as far as possible the reasons for change as the provision of both adequate and accurate information scotches rumours before they can be circulated.

(iii)   Involve individuals and/or work groups in the planning and implementing of change as much as possible. Employees will be more likely to become committed to change if they feel they can have some influence on the change and its outcome. It is also a way of gaining valuable suggestions.

(iv)   Keep lines of communication going, monitor progress, give regular feedback and communicate results.

(v)   Try to introduce changes gradually; phased change stands a better chance of success.

(vi)   Offer and provide appropriate training.

(vii)   Ensure the workforce are aware of the benefits to them of the change, e.g. increased responsibility, job enrichment.

(viii) Consider the effects of change on individuals, giving counselling where necessary.

(ix)   Follow up regularly and be supportive.

(x)   Develop a favourable climate for any subsequent changes envisaged.

5   The change process

5.1   Framework for the management of change

The idea of change that is planned assumes that the management can identify gaps between current conditions and desired conditions on the following dimensions:

(i)   How can this organisation be more effective?

(ii) Can we operate more efficiently?

(iii) How can we make it a more satisfying place to work?

Whenever the organisation can identify differences between where it currently is and where it would like to be on any of the dimensions, it can pursue planned change or improve the organisation.

Systems would be implemented to identify and diagnose particular problems within these general areas, e.g. poor morale, inefficient computer programs, lack of quality control or inadequate downward communication. Depending on the problem, a suitable change effort can be designed.

Leavitt

Leavitt found that approaches to change that succeeded in one organisation were not necessarily successful in another. He suggests that the chosen approach to change in a particular organisation reflects the underlying beliefs within that organisation.

Leavitt viewed any organisation as having four interacting variables, each of them giving rise to different approaches to change.

(a) **Tasks** – approaches to change will be largely technical, that is seeking to improve the quality of decisions. The task approach will be interrelated to the other three approaches.

(b) **Structure** – the traditional performance approach is of ensuring proper division of labour, levels of authority and responsibility, defining chain of command and span of control. Another approach is the creation of project centres and localising of decision making creating a high level of local autonomy. The communication channels and flows may also need to be changed. Repetitious, predictable work may succeed with a highly centralised communication structure, whereas for novel, loosely-structured tasks, a more open multi-channel communication network may seem more appropriate.

(c) **Technology** – An early example of a change approach to this category includes method study approaches where an outsider views the work pattern and suggests changes in a technological approach (Taylor). Updating and replacement of equipment is a natural example of an external approach. The essence is that the approach occurs outside the work group itself.

(d) **People** – Group working, attitude training, and changes in styles of management are examples of the people approach.

Implementing change through power politics

If transformational change is required in an organisation, it is likely that there will be a need for the reconfiguration of power structures.

Any manager of change needs to consider how it might be implemented from a political perspective. For example, a critical report by an outside change agency such as market research findings on customer perceptions of service may be 'rubbished' by the board because it threatens their authority and power.

There is often need to plan changes within this political context. The political mechanisms include:

(i) **the control and manipulation of organisational resources.** Acquiring, withdrawing or allocating additional resources, or being identified with important areas of resource or expertise, can be an important tool in overcoming resistance or persuading others to accept change. Being able to manipulate the information opposing the changes can also be important.

(ii) **association with powerful groups or elites** can help build a power base. This may be useful for the change agent who does not have a strong personal power base to work from. Association with a change agent who is seen as successful or who is respected can also help a manager overcome resistance to change.

(iii) **handling the subsystem effectively** can achieve acceptance of change throughout the organisation. Building up alliances and a network of contacts and sympathisers may help win over powerful groups.

(iv) **symbolic devices** that may take different forms. To build power the manager may become involved in committees that reinforce and preserve the change model. Symbolic activity can be used for consolidating change by positive reinforcement towards those who most accept change. These rewards include new structures, titles and office allocation.

Warren G Bennis

Bennis is an influential American author on leadership and change. He focuses on the need to inspire change rather than merely imposing it.

He identifies five 'avenues of change':

- Dissent and conflict. Top management impose change by mans of their position power, the result being rancour amongst those affected.

- Trust and truth. Management must gain trust, express their vision clearly, and persuade others to follow.

- Cliques and cabals. Cliques have power, money and resources. Cabals have ambition, drive and energy. Unless the cliques can co-opt the cabals, revolution is inevitable.

- External events. Forces of society can impose change, e.g. by new government regulation or through overseas competition.

- Culture or paradigm shift. Changing the corporate culture is the most important avenue of change.

Bennis also provides advice on avoiding disaster during change:

- recruit with scrupulous honesty

- guard against the crazies (Innovation may attract people who will distort its ideas.)

- build support among like-minded people

- plan for change from a solid conceptual base

- don't settle for rhetorical change

- don't allow those who are opposed to change to appropriate basic issues

- know the territory

- appreciate environmental factors

- avoid future shock

- remember that change is most successful when those who are affected are involved in the planning.

6 Strategy review and strategic issue management

6.1 The importance of reviewing progress

The success of any change should be reviewed to make sure that it meets the objectives that it was supposed to achieve.

By building into the change process a means of reviewing its progress, the organisation is making strategic change more coherent, which in itself is a way of making the change a success. Being coherent across all aspects of the organisation means that:

- There is a consistency between the intended strategy, the stated strategic objectives, their expression in operational terms, the behaviour of executives in reinforcing the strategy and a means of assessing performance and progress.

- The direction of strategic change is consistent with what is happening in the environment and with what is understood in the organisation.

- The strategy is feasible in terms of the required resources, the structuring of the organisation and the changes that need to occur in organisational culture and operational routines.

- The strategic direction is clearly related to achieving competitive advantage or excellent performance, and internally it is understood how this is happening.

The key issue is finding an appropriate means of reviewing the progress and success of any strategic change and identifying strategic issues as they arise.

Performance measures for strategic change are not easy and, more often, financial results are relied upon. In their book *Strategic Control: Milestones for Long-Term Performance*, Goold and Quinn suggest that most companies take a pride in fostering a performance-driven culture that emphasises profitability as the key goal for business management, but too much emphasis on budgetary control and short-term profit can disguise strategic problems from senior managers.

6.2 A framework for strategy review

The introduction of a strategic control system to monitor the organisation's strategic position has advantages that include:

- planning realism

- encouraging higher performance standards

- motivation

- ability to intervene when the activity is not going to plan.

Goold and Quinn identify a formal and an informal system of strategic control.

The **formal** process begins with a strategy review where the organisation's key success factors are outlined. A cost leadership strategy would identify cost measures, which are one of the easiest to monitor. Milestones of performance are then identified, both of a quantitative and a qualitative nature. These milestones are short-term steps towards long-term goals and act as a way of pulling the organisation towards its goals. Milestones are the means to monitor both the **actions** such as the launching of a new product and the **results**, e.g. the success of the launch. The areas that milestones cover include:

- market share

- quality measurement

- innovation

- customer satisfaction.

When setting target achievement levels the targets must be reasonably precise, suggesting strategies and tactics. Competitive benchmarks are targets that are set relative to the competition. It may be difficult to obtain data about the competitor, but a relative advantage is important in competitive terms.

Informal systems of strategic control exist where the organisation does not define explicit strategic objectives or milestones that are regularly and formally monitored as part of the management control system. The argument in favour of informality mainly concentrates on aspects such as flexibility and openness of communication. However, these systems do not always work because they enable managers to ignore important strategic issues.

6.3 The importance of strategic issue management

Goold and Quinn suggest the characteristics of strategic control systems can be measured on two axes:

(i) the formality of the process

(ii) the milestones that are identified for performance.

Whilst there may be no optimum degree of formality of the process and no optimum number of milestones identified for performance, the following guidelines are recommended.

- If there are important linkages among businesses, the formality of the process should be low, to avoid co-operation being undermined.

- If there is a lot of diversity, it is doubtful whether any strategic control system is appropriate, especially where the critical success factors for each business are different. Formal processes may not find the right objectives while informal ones may confuse the issue.

- Where an organisation's strategic stance depends on decisions which can, if they go wrong, destroy the company as a whole (e.g. launching a new technology), then there is a need for strategic control systems which have a large number of performance criteria so that emerging problems in any area will be easily detected. Where there is high environmental uncertainty, a strategic control process monitors some of the background assumptions.

- Fashion-goods manufacturers, and other industries which are prone to many changes, must respond to relatively high levels of environmental turbulence and must be able to react quickly. Where changes are rapid, a system of low formality and few measures may be appropriate, merely because the control processes must allow *ad hoc* decisions to be taken.

- For businesses with few sources of competitive advantage, control can easily focus on the key factors, where market share or quality is the source of success. Where there are many sources of advantage and success covers a wide area, e.g. market share, sales, mix, pricing policy and distribution, there is the danger that control can be misdirected because it focuses on inappropriate objectives and carries a high cost because measurement of performance is difficult.

Conclusion

The future is going to bring change and at an accelerated rate; if the organisation is to survive it has no choice but to participate in the development of more humane and democratic systems. Much of this accelerated change will be uncontrollable and managers must practise management with incomplete information and little stability. Peters states that managers must welcome and expect chaos since this will prevail under conditions of rapid change.

**SELF-TEST
QUESTIONS**

Management change issues

1   What are the four basic features of organisation change? (1.2)

2   Describe the factors identified by Lewin in his force field analysis. (1.5)

3   Draw a diagram showing Lewin's 3-step model of change. (1.5)

4   What are the main sources of resistance to change? (3)

Managing change

5   List the five strategies for managing change. (4.2)

The change process

6   Explain the four interacting variables identified by Leavitt that give rise to a different approach to change. (5.1)

Strategy review and strategic issue management

7   In a formal review of strategy, what types of milestone can be measured easily? (6.1)

Managing change

Explain **four** strategies for managing change, giving the advantages and disadvantages of **each**. **(20 marks)**

For the answer to this question, see the 'Answers' section at the end of the book.

People tend to resist change because they fear one or more from the following list:

(a) A loss of job security

(b) A loss of status

(d) The loss of work they enjoy

(c) Possibility of having to work for a different manager

(e) A break up of working relationships

(f) Having to work in a different location (moving home, etc)

(g) Having to work at a different time (shift work, etc)

(h) An inability to cope with new duties/responsibilities

(i) Inconvenience of the change (training, etc)

(j) The closing of potential promotion (career implications)

(k) Economic aspects (loss of overtime, etc).

Cultural resistance tends to occur in different ways and at different levels of an organisation. Often resistance is confined to a particular coalition. The main types of resistance are:

(a) Organisation-wide resistance

(b) Hierarchical resistance – at a particular level of management

(c) Departmental resistance – in a particular department

(d) Individual resistance – by particular individuals

(e) Collection (or coalition) of people – by a particular group or trade union group, etc.

Resistance to cultural change be managed or reduced in the following ways:

(a) Total, genuine and visible support for the change by top management

(b) Positive reinforcement (e.g. by first changing in areas where managers approve)

(c) The use of a rewards system, such as promoting managers willing to change

(d) Good communication/participation systems associated with the change

(e) Recruiting people already experienced in working in the changed system or environment

(f) The use of external organisational development (OD) experts

(g) Redesign of the organisation structure

(h) Negative reinforcement (e.g. punishing managers who refuse to accept change by lack of promotion, etc).

Chapter 19
STRATEGY AND STRUCTURE

For senior managers, the implementation of strategy is always somewhat problematic, as they will generally carry out few of the activities themselves. Consequently, managers make structural changes to focus the organisation on the new work to be done. In this chapter, we examine the role of these structural changes in more detail.

Objectives

When you have studied this chapter you should be able to:

- describe the influence of different structures on strategic management

- outline the relative strengths and weaknesses of centralisation versus decentralisation

- examine Mintzberg's configuration model of organisational design.

1 The determinants of structure

1.1 Meaning and determinants of structure

Organisational structure has been defined in many different ways. For example:

- How job tasks are formally divided, grouped and coordinated.

- The established pattern of relationships between the component parts of an organisation, outlining both communication, control and authority patterns.

- The formal pattern of interactions and coordination designed by management to link the tasks of individuals and groups in achieving organisational goals.

The purpose of structure is the division of work among members of the organisation, and the co-ordination of their activities so they are directed towards the goals and objectives of the organisation.

Structure is the pattern of relationships among positions in the organisation and among members of the organisation. It determines how work is co-ordinated, how decisions are taken and how work and information flow through the organisation.

Structure makes possible the application of the process of management and creates a framework of order and command through which the activities of the organisation can be planned, organised, directed and controlled. The structure defines tasks and responsibilities, work roles and relationships, and channels of communication.

A distinction is sometimes made between formal and informal structures. Informal structures are not explicit and are based on personal relationships and influence, in contrast to formal structures, which are characterised by:

- planned divisions of responsibility;

- power centres which control its efforts;

- substitution of personnel;

- the ability to combine its personnel in different ways.

Structure is clearly important for any organisation, whatever its size. However, in smaller organisations there are likely to be fewer problems of structure. The distribution of tasks, the definition of authority and responsibility, and the relationship between members of the organisation can be established on a personal and informal basis. With increasing size, however, there is greater need for a carefully designed and purposeful form of organisation. There is need for a formal structure. There is also need for a continual review of structure to ensure that it is the most appropriate form for the particular organisation, and in keeping with its growth and development. This is likely to be of particular importance for the very large companies such as, for example, British Gas.

1.2 Principles of structure - Mintzberg

Mintzberg considers that any organisation structure is based on the following principles.

- Job specialisation, which is about the number of tasks in a given job and the division of labour.

- Behaviour formalisation, that is to say, the standardisation of work processes.

- Training, which is needed to enforce work standardisation.

- The indoctrination of employees in the organisation's culture

- Unit grouping such as organisation by function, geographical area, or product.

- Unit size within the organisation

- Planning and control systems

- Liaison and communication devices like networks, committees and matrix structure.

Mintzberg argues that the organisation structure exists to co-ordinate the activities of different individuals and work processes.

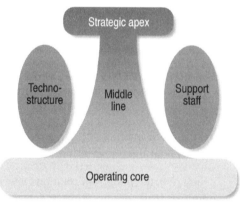

- The *operating core* contains those people directly involved in production (ie in securing inputs and processing them into outputs and distributing those outputs). In other words, they might be directly responsible for the *primary* activities of the value chain.

- The *strategic apex* emerges with the need for supervision and control. It ensures that the organisation follows its mission and serves the needs of its owners. Its job is supervision, boundary management and strategy. The strategic apex in a public limited company would be the board of directors.

- The *middle line* is the hierarchy of authority between the operating core and the strategic apex. People in this area administer the work done. The chain of middle managers with formal authority runs from senior managers to front line supervisors. It converts the wishes of the strategic apex into the work of the operating core.

- The *technostructure* standardises the work. This is a further layer of administration and planning. Work-study engineers standardise production processes by analysing and determining the most efficient method of doing a job. Accountants standardise financial processing and control systems. Quality staff standardise outputs. Personnel analysts standardise skills by arranging for training programmes.

- *Support staff* provide ancillary services such as public relations, legal advice and the cafeteria. Support staff are different from the technostructure, as they do not plan or standardise production. They function independently of the operating core.

These elements are linked in five ways.

- There is an organisation hierarchy of formal authority.

- An organisation is a flow of regulated activity. Inputs are processed into outputs. The activities in the value chain are controlled and linked.

- There is a flow of informal communications. This denotes the real structure of communication, supplementing or bypassing the formal communication system.

- An organisation is a system of work constellations. Groups of people work on distinct tasks. These constellations might be temporary. For example, producing a set of annual financial statements might require involvement from people from the finance department (for the numbers), the sales department (for detailed statistics) and public relations (for presentation).

- An organisation is a system of ad hoc decision processes. A decision process involves recognising a problem, diagnosing its causes, finding a solution and implementing it. For any one decision, these activities occur in a number of different places in the organisation. For example, customer care personnel might first hear of a problem with faulty goods, but the decisions as to how to prevent the problem happening again will be taken in the production department.

1.3 Strategy and structure

Regardless of how well it may have been conceived, a competitive strategy without effective organisation of human resources is doomed to sub-optimise, if not fail completely. Since strategies can only be implemented by and through people, the manner in which human resources are co-ordinated through hierarchical and lateral assignments of responsibility and authority becomes a central management challenge. As Cannon notes, 'Neither strategy nor structure can be determined independently of the other ... If structure cannot stand alone without strategy, it is equally true that strategy can rarely succeed without an appropriate structure'.

Ideally a strategy/structure format would dictate appropriate organisational forms for different strategic postures. But researchers and practitioners have yet to come up with something that works effectively. Indeed the best that can be offered at this point is the familiar 'contingency' approach to the problem. By contingency approach we mean that the choice of an appropriate organisation structure is contingent upon an array of factors, the combination of which is likely to be unique to the firm at hand. These factors can be categorised as

- strategic thrusts,

- environmental circumstances

- complexities introduced by growth

- management culture and style

1.4 Strategic thrusts

As part of its strategic decision-making, an organisation identifies its distinctive competencies (strengths) and then attempts to capitalise on these in identified niches or segments of the marketplace. In doing this, the ideal organisation structure may naturally fall out. For example, a fully integrated firm may find the need to establish separate marketing organisations to handle its different products. If the growth prospects for the company hinge on the success of these efforts, then this organisational differentiation may be exhibited at the highest levels of the structure, as opposed to being subsumed elsewhere.

Similarly the firm relying on new product development as a major component of its strategy may find it advantageous to have authority and responsibility for research and development reflected explicitly at higher organisational levels. On the flip side, a firm going through retrenchment may organisationally de-emphasise those components of the enterprise being retrenched - by collapsing a declining product division into a more prosperous one, for example.

To a large extent, the concept of the strategic business unit (SBU) represents the organisational manifestation of strategic thrust. By grouping 'businesses' according to commonality of mission, related product/market segments, similarity of competition, size, and facilities/technology, adopters of the SBU concept explicitly recognise strategic thrust as an organisational cutting edge. Of course, in the case of SBUs, not only are differences between units magnified, but also the existence of a co-ordinating mechanism becomes both crucial and organisationally distinct.

1.5 Environmental circumstances

Glueck boldly suggests, 'All organisation structures work; the key is to match the organisation structure with the characteristic of the environment. He goes on to conclude:

- In general, functional organisations work best in stable environments, with less need for cross-department co-ordination and communication and less need for innovation

- Divisional organisations work best in changing environments, which require faster adaptation, more co-ordination and communication, and innovation.

Lawrence and Lorsch address the role of environment in organisation design by suggesting that the degree of formality of structure (part of what they refer to as differentiation) is positively related to the degree of environmental uncertainty. Further, the more differentiated, the greater is the need for collaboration and co-ordination (integration). Thus organisations, or sub-units, that face wide, indeterminate fluctuations in product demand would tend to be more highly structured than those facing more stable environments. And this would tend toward a greater need for lateral interaction across organisational units.

Finally, both environmental threats and opportunities can lead to the establishment of 'boundary spanning' units specifically designed to deal with the environmental circumstance at hand. Concern over pollution in the chemical industry has led many member firms to establish corporate-level offices to deal with the matter.

1.6 Complexities introduced by growth

In his classic work *Strategy and Structure*, Alfred Chandler examined the structural evolution of 70 large firms over several decades. He generally concluded that structure follows strategy as a firm expands. Structural changes are necessary so that internal resources can be administered efficiently and effectively in light of changing market conditions brought about by expansion.

Chandler's work set off a string of research dealing with structural correlates of growth, many of which supplemented his model with additional contingency variables. Without going into the refinements of each, they may be summarised through the notion that firms evolve somewhat definable organisational forms as they grow-entrepreneurial, functional, divisional, and, occasionally, matrix.

1.7   Management culture and style

Though it may be argued that strategy should dominate the design of organisation structure, the internal workings and styles of management are going to shape it as well. Mintzberg suggests that 'power' factors play an important role. These include the personal needs of organisation members, organisational 'fashions of the day' (eg, participative versus non participative styles), and the presence of outside control (eg, degree of control by the board of directors). He argues that pressures for centralisation and formality arise from needs for personal power at the strategic level as well as from higher degrees of external control. And the culture surrounding structures 'in fashion' leads to pressures for their adoption.

What this suggests is that the choice of organisation structure is not simply a matter of weighing impersonal strategic, environmental, and technical circumstances. Instead organisation design is going to be tempered by the human factor, including the capabilities of those organising and being organised, and their collective needs, aspirations, and expectations.

2   Different types of organisational structure

2.1   The influence of structure on strategy

The people in an organisation are one of the most important resources and how they are organised is crucial to the effectiveness of strategy.

The tools and techniques of strategic management in implementing plans are theoretically independent of the business organisation. However, the way in which a plan is *implemented* must in practice be influenced by the type of organisation.

The *influences* that have a bearing on organisational structure and design include:

- the types of problems the organisation has when constructing strategies
- a consideration of whether it is operating in a stable environment or in a highly complex or changing environment
- the diversity of the organisation: the needs of a multinational are different from those of a small company
- the technology
- the type of ownership.

Because of all of these different influences, it is not possible to have a simple set of rules that can prescribe organisational structures and systems. The structure of the organisation is only a skeleton on which the flesh of the strategy can be hung and, unfortunately, the structure in itself will not ensure the success of the strategy, although an inappropriate choice of structure could impede success.

Developing the flesh on the structure consists of three elements:

(i)   *organisational configuration* – matching the detailed structure with the context in which the organisation is operating

(ii)   *centralisation/decentralisation* – where the responsibility for operational and strategic decision making should lie

(iii) *management systems* – how the systems relate to the structure and influence the behaviour of people.

2.2 Classification of organisation structures

There are many ways of classifying organisation structure.

A common analysis views organisation structures that develop in response to the size of the organisation. There is thus:

(a) a small business structure

(b) a functional structure (which arises when (a) develops beyond a small business)

(c) a divisional structure (which arises when an organisation grows by diversification into many different products).

2.3 Simple business structure

Also known as the entrepreneurial structure, it has the great advantage of simplicity so that the owner/manager can adjust employee tasks to the latest opportunity. This is illustrated below:

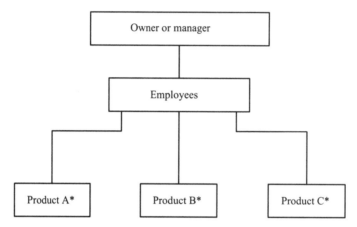

*(Although, throughout, the term 'product' is used to describe the output of a business, this section could apply equally well to companies that produce only 'services'.)

This type of business produces a single product, or a related group of products, and the owner, or manager, is responsible for strategic and operational management. Thus, it is a discrete, self-contained and largely self-controlled business unit. It is equivalent to a strategic business unit in a divisionalised organisation.

2.4 Functional structure

The functional structure is usually chronologically the next stage in the development of a business, and is illustrated below:

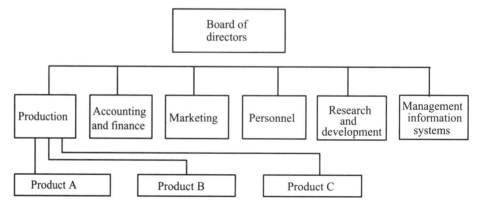

Planning is divided between the corporate and functional levels, with strategic planning being decided at board level and being executed at the functional level.

2.5 Divisional structure

Where the functionally structured business grows by diversification, the above structure will be found to be inappropriate, and the divisional structure illustrated below is likely to be adopted:

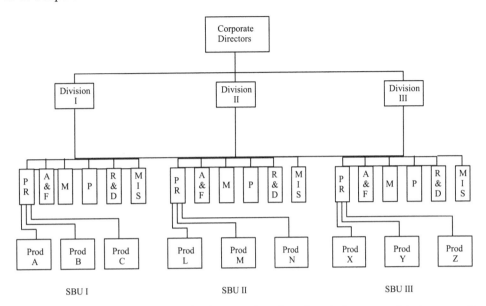

Each division is now responsible for its own functions in relation to a related group of products. Thus, each division may be regarded as a Strategic Business Unit (SBU).

Strategic planning in this environment becomes a complex hierarchical process:

(a) Corporate strategic planning takes place at central board level. This is concerned with guiding the divisions so that the competitive advantages of a diversity of business accrue to the company, and encouraging each division to plan to take maximum advantage of its individual position.

(b) Divisional planning is concerned with developing a portfolio of products.

(c) Operational planning is at the functional level within divisions.

2.6 Holding company structure

The holding company is a radical form of divisionalisation. Subsidiaries are separate legal entities. The holding company can be an organisation with a permanent investment or one, which buys and sells businesses.

- In its most extreme form, a holding company is really an investment company.

- It may simply consist of shareholdings in a variety of individual, unconnected business operations over which it exercises little or no control.

- It may be an enterprise, which operates a portfolio of virtually autonomous business units itself. Although part of a parent company, these business units operate independently and probably retain their original company names. The role that the parent company takes may be limited to decisions about the buying and selling of such companies, with little involvement in their product/market strategy. Arguably, this is the situation as far as Lonrho or BTR is concerned

An example of a holding company structure is shown below. Central corporate staff and services may be very limited. The essential differentiating feature for a holding company is the extent of the autonomy of the business units, particularly over strategic decisions. The advantages that a holding company can offer are based on the idea that the constituent businesses will operate to their best potential if left alone, particularly as business environments become more turbulent.

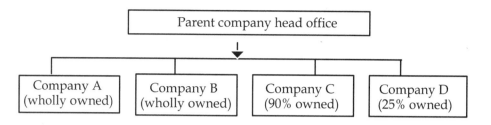

There are other organisational advantages and disadvantages of the holding company structure. For example:

- the organisation does not have to carry the burden of a high central overhead, since the office staff of the parent is likely to be quite small

- the business units can offset profits against others' losses can obtain cheaper finance for investment from the parent company

- the holding company can spread the risk over many business ventures

- divestment of individual companies is easy

2.7   The role of the strategic business unit (SBU)

Corporate Parenting is the search for a fit between the skills of the corporate centre and the strategies of SBUs so as to add value to those SBUs

Goold and Campbell (1991), have identified three broad approaches or 'parenting' styles reflecting the degree to which staff at corporate headquarters become involved in the process of business strategy development (i.e., strategic planning, strategic control and financial control).

Strategic planning companies (e.g., Cadbury Schweppes, B.P) focus on a limited number of businesses where significant synergies exist and corporate management play a major role in setting the strategies for each of the SBU'S. This approach is based on the belief that strategic decisions occur relatively infrequently and when they do, it is important for corporate headquarters to frame and control the strategic planning and decision-making process.

In contrast, **financial control companies** (e.g., Hanson, GEC) take a `hands off' approach but set stringent short term financial targets which have to be met to ensure continued funding of capital investment plans. Failure to meet financial targets will lead to the possibility of divestment. Such companies generally have a wide corporate portfolio with limited links between divisions and acquisition and divestment is a continuing process as opposed to an exceptional event.

Strategic control companies (e.g., ICI, Imperial Group, Plessey) are seen to take a middle course, accepting that subsidiaries must develop and be responsible for their own strategies (whilst being able to draw on headquarters' expertise). Evaluation of performance extends beyond short term financial targets to embrace strategic objectives such as growth in market share and technology development, which are seen to support long-term financial and operational effectiveness.

In light of the above, it will be apparent that the role of the corporate accounting activity will be strongly influenced by the parenting style adopted by the corporate headquarters.

Goold and Campbell considered three styles of managing relationships between a head office and its strategic business units (SBUs). The figure below shows the extent to which the centre gets involved in the strategic planning process.

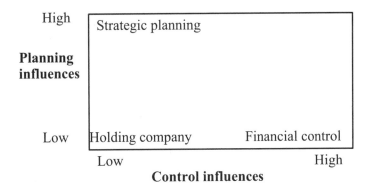

Control influences

In the **'strategic planning' style** the head office sets the broad strategy but accepts input from the subsidiary units. It is felt that the high risks involved cannot be left to subsidiary managers. This helps to provide good integration across the units, particularly useful when resources such as distribution may be shared. Because the decisions are made at senior level there is less likelihood of short-term views predominating. However, the difficulties in communication and co-ordination may slow down development. Furthermore there may be less 'ownership' of the strategies by the operating unit managers. There is strong empirical evidence that there are fewer low-risk strategies pursued, which might otherwise be the case if strategy was centred on the unit managers. However, there is also a likelihood that this strategy formulation from the centre might result in getting 'locked into' failing businesses. There may be a resistance to the closing down of poorly performing units if the strategies have been sanctioned at the centre. This type of strategy style leads to a concentration on a few core areas where it is possible to have a degree of expertise.

The **'financial control' style** is at the opposite end of the spectrum. The business unit managers lead the strategy but within a budgetary control framework. Empirical evidence suggests that lower risk strategies are pursued but with resultant higher profitability ratios. The timescale tends to be shorter. This type of strategy allows for diversity and there is a propensity to be risk averse and possibly to 'milk' the business. Much of the growth in this scenario comes from acquisition as distinct from internal growth.

A critical question here is how can this type of decentralisation exploit any potential synergies? Additionally there is a danger that the control framework set up by the head office might constrain flexibility.

'Strategic control' attempts a balance between the other two styles. Strategy formulation rests with the business units but it has to be tested by the corporate management. As one might expect, this model may be able to cope with diversity more readily than the 'strategic planning' style but there is also a danger of greater ambiguity.

2.8 Matrix structure

(a) The matrix concept

The grid/matrix approach came into being because the US Government decided it did not wish to deal with a number of specialised executives when negotiating defence contracts and insisted that contractors appointed project managers.

The concept has now been extended to whole organisations (Lockheed Aircraft, British Airways) as well as to major divisions as in ICI and in schools of polytechnics/universities, etc, e.g.:

Course Responsibility (Product)	BA Business Studies	BA European Business	MBA	etc
Subject Responsibility (Function)	Mr R White	Miss J Brown	Mrs T Black	
Accounts Miss V Red	Fred	Susan	Simon	
Economics Mr A Green	Ian	Frank	Jill	
Sociology Mr G Blue	Mary	Tony	Alan	

In this approach the course leaders (project/product co-ordinators), responsible for course management, would share their authority with the subject leaders (functional heads), responsible for academic development and research.

The matrix structure may be appropriate where there are at least two significant criteria for success. For example, a multinational company produces three sets of product ranges – Product A, Product B and Product C – and sells the product in three geographical areas Europe, U.S.A. and South America.

The management of each product range is equally important, as is the responsiveness to the needs of the different geographical areas. The product managers and area managers have equal weight. Thus the manager of the U.S. area must liaise with the managers of Products A, B and C but does not have authority over them or vice versa.

This position can be generalised as follows:

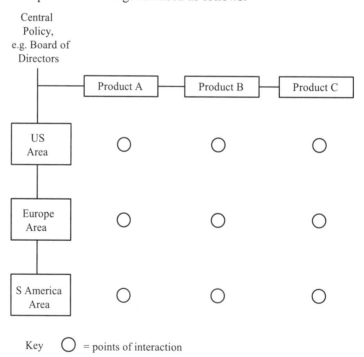

Key ◯ = points of interaction

(b) **Advantages of matrix structures**

- Retains functional economies and product co-ordination.

- It is organic – open communications and flexible goals.

- Improved motivation through:

    - people working participatively in teams

    - specialists broadening their outlook

    - encouraging competition within the organisation.

(c) **Disadvantages of matrix structures**

- Higher administrative costs.

- Conflict between functional and product managers leading to individual stress arising from:

    - threat to *occupational identity*

    - reporting to more than one boss

    - less clear expectations.

3 Transitional and adaptive structures

It is unlikely that organisations conform to these model types completely or retain stable structures over the longer term. Structural adaptations occur as organisations arrange for the co-ordination and control of activities that are brought together in ways that the existing structure does not allow. Over time, as disputes and problems are formally resolved, organisations tend to move between structural forms, so that at any one time the structure is likely to be transitional. It has to be said that, unfortunately, structure is a variable that senior managers seem to like changing, and many structures are simply transitional in the sense that they are lurching from one structure to another without any sense of adding value.

3.1 Virtual organisations (networks)

The virtual organisation is one that has rejected the traditional work patterns of bringing people to one location for a fixed period, and organising them into departments and functions.

This type of organisation is based upon the more flexible notions of networking and collaboration by use of information technology. Activities are managed by self-organising project teams.

This enables flatter structures to be used, and greater spans of responsibilities for individuals. Fewer activities will be attempted in house, allowing the company to specialise in only those activities that add value. For example, the Virgin financial services arm is close to a virtual organisation, in the sense that Virgin's activities are confined to managing the company/client interface, and co-ordinating all the other activities that are carried out by other companies. Many biotech companies operate in a similar way, managing teams of researchers spread between a number of research establishments.

There are seen to be two main principles at play that may lead an organisation to adopt a network structure. These are:

Transaction cost theory – organisations choose between two methods of obtaining control over resources, the ownership of assets (hierarchy solutions) and buying-in the use of assets (the market solution). The decision is based on a comparison of the transaction costs of the two approaches.

Matthews (1986) defines transaction costs as 'the costs of arranging a contract ex-ante and monitoring and enforcing it ex-post'.

'Asset specificity', the extent to which particular assets are only of use in one specific range of operations, tends to increase transaction costs whereas vertical integration will usually reduce transaction costs. In simple terms, network partners 'own' the assets; we obtain the use of those assets.

The resource based view of the firm – a firm's long-term competitive advantage lies in the possession of unique and scarce resources and capabilities that cannot easily be imitated by other firms. Kay (1993) identified a firm's 'network architecture' (its relationship with the group of firms with which it collaborates) as a major source of distinctive capabilities.

3.2 Multinational and global structures

The basic form of structure for the multinational is the retention of the 'home' structure and the management of whatever overseas subsidiaries through direct contact between the manager of the subsidiary and the chief executive of the parent company. This is most common in single-product companies or where the overseas interests are relatively minor. Beyond this simple structure the critical issue is the extent to which local independence or responsiveness should take precedence over global co-ordination. The different types of multinational structure are shown in the diagram below:

Local independence and responsiveness

	Low	High
Global co-ordination Low	International divisions	International subsidiaries
High	Global product companies	Transnational corporations

- International divisions - here the home-based structure may be retained at first, whether functional or divisional, but the overseas interests are managed through a special international division. The international subsidiaries will draw on the products of the home company and gain advantage from this technology transfer. The disadvantage is a lack of local tailoring of products or technology. Such structures tend to work best where there is a wide geographical spread but quite closely related products.

- International subsidiaries - are geographically based and operate independently by country. In these companies virtually all the management functions are nationally based, allowing for higher degrees of local responsiveness. The control of the parent company is likely to be dependent on some form of planning and reporting system and perhaps an ultimate veto over national strategies, but the extent of global co-ordination is likely to be low.

- Global product companies - represent a move away from the international divisional or subsidiary structure to an integrated structure. Here the multinational is split into product divisions, which are then managed on an international basis. The logic of such an approach is that it should promote cost efficiency (particularly of production) on an international basis, and should provide enhanced transfer of resources (particularly technology) between geographical regions. The international development of many Japanese companies in electronics and car manufacture has been managed in this way. Research has shown that the theoretical benefits of the global product structure are not always realised: Although cost efficiency is improved, it does not appear that technology transfer is necessarily enhanced. Also, while the structure is well suited to promoting defensive or consolidation strategies, it does not seem to meet the expected benefits of better strategic planning and is not suited to the promotion of aggressive or expansionist strategies.

- Transnational corporations - are structures that attempt to combine the local responsiveness of the international subsidiary with the advantages of co-ordination found in global product companies. The key lies in creating an integrated network of interdependent resources and capabilities.

- Each national unit operates independently, but is a source of ideas and capabilities for the whole corporation.
- National units achieve global scale through specialisation on behalf of the whole corporation.
- The centre manages a global network firstly by establishing the role of each subsidiary and then by sustaining the culture and systems to make the network operate effectively.

3.3   Intermediate structures and structural variations

Few organisations adopt a pure structural type; the skill is in blending the structure to the organisation's circumstances. There is a whole range of 'shades of grey' between these pure types of structure eg, a company may move from a functional structure to a divisional structure by a series of smaller incremental changes.

Problems first arise within the functional structure as new products/markets compete for resources. Initially these conflicts might be resolved by pushing the decision upwards until a sufficiently senior manager makes the decision. Problems are dealt with by manipulating methods of control and operation rather than by structural changes

As the new products/ markets become more important and create competition for resources, it may be necessary to create interdepartmental liaison roles: for example, a committee or a temporary taskforce may be set up to advise on priorities. This may lead to either permanent teams of co-ordinators or special co-ordinating jobs (the product manager is a good example). Another step, which may prove necessary to maintain the functional structure, is the creation of departments with the sole function of co-ordination. Ultimately, the organisation will divisionalise as the diversity increases and the 'costs' of maintaining the functional structure become unacceptably high.

It is also common to adopt a mixed structure to address such problems as a functional structure with subsidiaries. The main business, which employs the majority of employees, might have a functional structure, with more peripheral business interests organised as divisions or subsidiaries. The converse of this is the company that is divisionalised except for certain key functions which remain at the centre and which have responsibilities across all the divisions.

3.4   Choice of organisation structure

This can be seen as an application of 'contingency theory' (see below) – matching an appropriate structure to the key features of the organisation. Among the factors to be considered when deciding on the organisation structure appropriate to a particular company are:

(a) **Size**

Clearly a business controlled by one entrepreneur has quite a different structure from a multi million pound, multi national giant.

(b) **Chosen strategy**

A company pursuing a growth strategy will probably need a different organisation structure from one pursuing a non-growth, low-risk strategy. It must be able to move quickly, so the organisation structure must allow quick decisions. This means that chains of command should not be too long.

A department specifically concerned with promoting change is needed. The Research and Development manager will have a high status in the company. The organisation must be forward-looking; it cannot afford to dwell on yesterday's mistakes.

(c) **Management style**

An ideal organisation structure cannot be imposed on an organisation regardless of management style. For instance, a programme of decentralisation, however desirable in other circumstances, will be doomed to failure if the chief executive is an autocrat who is reluctant to relinquish control to any appreciable degree.

(d) **Potential synergy**

The greater the potential synergy, the greater the desirability of integrating a new operation or a new acquisition with the existing operations. If integration is not achieved in some degree, the potential synergy cannot be realised. On the other hand, weak synergy might suggest a holding company/subsidiary company relationship.

(e) **Extent of diversification**

With very diverse operations there might even be negative synergy if top management try to interfere in areas they do not understand. This points to decentralisation.

(f) **Extent of geographical separation**

The greater the geographical distance from the centre, the greater the necessity for decentralised control.

Choice of the best structure is not easy. Each has advantages and disadvantages. For instance, the matrix structure overcomes the difficulties of lack of communication and co-ordination inherent in more traditional structures, but has the disadvantage that a person is trying to serve two masters. However, this may only be admitting a conflict that existed anyway, and if this is true, it is better that the conflict should be brought into the open.

Whatever type of structure is adopted it is essential that the form facilitates communication at and between all levels of management. This means that chains of command should not be too long – and that the structure defines clearly the areas of responsibility and authority of different managers. In general, the higher up the organisation tree a decision is taken the longer term its effects will be, the more departments it concerns, and the greater the number of unquantifiable factors which affect the decision.

3.5 Consequences of structural deficiencies

According to Child, the following deficiencies may arise out of weak structure:

(a) *Motivation and morale* may be depressed, because of:

(i) apparent inconsistency

(ii) little responsibility

(iii) lack of clarity as to what is expected

(iv) competing pressures

(v) overloading due to inadequate support systems.

(b) *Decision making* may be delayed and faulty, because:

(i) information may be delayed in the hierarchy

(ii) decision making is too segmented

(iii) decision makers are overloaded – no delegation

(iv) past decisions are not evaluated.

(c) *Conflict* and lack of co-ordination, arising from:

    (i) conflicting goals that have not been structured into a single set

    (ii) no liaison – people working at cross-purposes

    (iii) operators not involved in planning.

(d) *No response to change*, because:

    (i) there is no established specialist in research and development (R&D) or market research (MR)

    (ii) R&D and MR do not talk to each other

    (iii) R&D and MR are not mainstream activities.

(e) *High administrative costs*, associated with:

    (i) 'too many chiefs, too few indians'

    (ii) excess of procedure and paperwork

    (iii) some or all of the other organisational problems being present.

3.6 Effect of structure

(a) *Structure is affected by various contingencies.* **Contingency theory** was a body of knowledge that attempted to identify the right strategies and structures for particular market and technological conditions. A study by Burns and Stalker was one important investigation in this area. The various factors upon which strategy and structure were thought to be contingent included the following:

- size of the organisation
- age of the organisation
- the degree of threat in the environment
- the diversity of the environment
- rate of change in the environment.

It is something of a disappointment to many that the evidence does not allow researchers to elaborate the nature of the contingencies in very much detail. John Child eventually changed his mind about the theory, and pointed out that firms frequently adopt different structure and strategy styles in the same industry. Consequently, much of the debate has moved on to strategic choices about how managers make their decisions, and then make the resulting structure operate effectively.

(b) *The effect of structure is limited* – it is a means to achieve objectives and cannot be successful if the organisation:

- adopts the wrong strategy
- does not possess the requisite skills
- falls foul of over-politicisation
- possesses inherently bad morale.

Moreover, structure by itself cannot resolve *conflict*, although it might bring such conflict out into the open. Several studies have shown the structure rarely has the importance that managers tend to give it.

4 Centralised and decentralised decision making

4.1 Effect on organisation

Another method of analysing structures is by reference to the level at which decisions are made.

Absolute decentralisation of authority is not possible because any delegated authority can derive only from the top, and the activities delegated must conform to the policy decided at a higher level. Also, absolute centralisation of authority is not practical except in very small concerns, because day-to-day decisions must be taken at lower levels.

'**Centralisation** is a condition where the upper levels of an organisation's hierarchy retain the **authority** to take most decisions.' (John Child)

Delegation is a particular meaning of the term 'decentralisation', and describes a condition when the **authority** to make specific decisions is passed down to units and people at lower levels in the organisation's hierarchy.

The choice of organisation will depend to a certain extent on the preferences of the organisation's top management, but equally important are the size of the organisation and the scale of its activities. Thus the small business structure is likely to be centralised, and the divisional structure is likely to be decentralised.

4.2 Advantages of centralisation

Those who support a high degree of centralisation claim advantages such as:

(a) co-ordinated decisions and better management control, therefore less sub-optimising

(b) conformity with overall objectives – goal congruence is more likely to be achieved

(c) standardisation, e.g. variety reduction and rationalisation

(d) balance, between functions, divisions, etc – increased flexibility in use of resources

(e) economies of scale – general management, finance, purchasing, production, etc

(f) top managers become better decision makers, because:

- they have proven ability

- they are more experienced

(g) speedier central decisions may be made in a crisis – delegation can be time-consuming.

Research shows that **centralisation of strategic decisions** and **delegation of tactical and operating decisions** can be very effective.

4.3 Disadvantages of centralisation

(a) Those of lower rank experience reduced job satisfaction.

(b) Frequently, senior management do not possess sufficient knowledge of all organisational activities. Therefore, their ability to make decisions is narrowed and delegation becomes essential.

(c) Centralisation places stress and responsibility onto senior management.

(d) Subordinates experience restricted opportunity for career development toward senior management positions.

(e) Decisions often take considerable time. This restricts the flexibility of the organisation, as well as using valuable time.

Slower decision making impairs effective communication. Such communication problems may affect industrial relations.

4.4 Organic and mechanistic structures

Burns and Stalker in *The Management of Innovation* looked at how management systems might change from being organised to handle stable conditions in response to the demands of changing market and technical conditions. They suggested that there were two distinctive 'ideal' types of management system - mechanistic and organic.

Mechanistic systems - are appropriate for conditions of stability, where the management of change is not seen to be an important factor. The features of the mechanistic system are summarised below.

- High degree of task specialisation.

- Responsibilities and authority clearly defined.

- Co-ordination and communication a specific responsibility of each management level.

- Selectivity in release of top-level information to subordinates.

- Great emphasis on the organisational hierarchy's ability to develop loyalty and obedience.

Organic systems - which are more responsive to change, and therefore recommended for organisations moving into periods of rapid changes in technology, market orientation or tasks. The features of the organic system are summarised below.

- Skills, experience and specialist knowledge recognised as valuable resources.

- Integration of efforts through lateral, vertical and diagonal communication channels.

- Leadership styles based on consultation and involvement are the order of the day in problem solving.

- Commitment to task achievement, survival and growth more important than loyalty and obedience.

These types of system were not seen as complete opposites, but as polar positions between which intermediate forms could exist. It was acknowledged that firms could well move from one system to the other as the external environment changed, and that some organisations could operate with both systems at once.

The type of environment that the organisation faces can range from 'Simple' and 'Static' to 'Complex' and 'Dynamic', in their polar positions, as shown in the diagram below:

	Static	**Dynamic**
Complex	Decentralised Mechanistic	Decentralised Organic
Simple	Centralised Mechanistic	Centralised Organic

The relative positions of organisations within these 'compartments' will depend on their external environment. Mintzberg, *The Structuring of Organisations*, suggests that where the environment for an organisation is simple and static, organisations standardise their operations and their management. Management styles tend to be centralised and mechanistic, eg, mass production.

Where the complexity increases this is dealt with by handing down decision responsibility to specialists. This means that organisations in complex environments tend to be more decentralised, whilst still being mechanistic. Universities are a good example of those organisations that have traditionally been in a static complex environment.

Where the conditions are constantly changing without increased complexity, a more organic style of management is likely to be adopted. Mintzberg calls this type of organisation centralised organic. Retailing is an example of this type. For a complex and dynamic environment, such as electronics, Mintzberg suggests that decentralised organic organisations will be found. The environment for these organisations will be changing so fast that they need the speed and flexibility of an organic management style. Also the level of complexity means that they must devolve responsibility and authority to specialists.

4.5 Contingency theory

The contingency approach can provide a useful guide for the structuring of modern enterprises. It implies that, within the same organisation, there may be a number of different structure types. Some areas will be bureaucratic and role-determined, others will display the features of an organic structure. The type of structure must be appropriate to task performance and individual/group satisfaction. Burns and Stalker argue that an organisation that is operating in stable conditions (eg, The Church) will have a more bureaucratic and tradition-based organisational structure than one that is operating in dynamic conditions (eg, computer manufacturer). The more dynamic the environment in which a business operates, the more flexible and contingency-minded the management of that business needs to be.

The variables identified below are seen as being important when determining the most appropriate organisational structure:

- Environment - according to contingency theory, different approaches to design are conducive to high performance, depending on whether or not the environment is dynamic and complex in nature or stable and simple.

- Complexity - with a diverse organisation (in terms of products, markets and locations), it is more likely that the most appropriate structure will be in decentralised divisions.

- Size - the larger the organisation, the more likely it is to have formalised structures allowing for delegation. Specialisation will also be a feature as will the tendency to be bureaucratic in respect of control structures.

- Technology used - Joan Woodward's studies suggest that when an organisation structures fit their technologies, they achieve a high level of performance.

- Human resource policies - the behavioural approach to management suggests that the more jobs are enriched, employees motivated and job satisfaction provided, the more likely it is that employees will perform effectively.

In conclusion, the flexibility and range of consideration that the contingency approach encourages, represents a very useful framework when structuring and re-structuring modern organisations.

4.6 The virtual organisation

The growth in computing power and networks has encouraged information to be distributed instantly within and beyond the organisation. This facility can be used to transform the organisation's structure, scope, reporting and control mechanisms, workflows, products and services.

Information systems can reduce the number of levels in an organisation by providing managers with information to manage and control larger numbers of workers spread over greater distances and by giving lower-level employees more decision-making authority. It is no longer necessary for these employees to work standard hours every day, nor work in an office or even the same country as their manager.

As well as reducing the numbers of middle managers in the organisation, information systems have been progressively replacing manual work procedures with automated procedures, workflows and processes. Redesigned workflows can have a dramatic effect on the efficiency within an organisation and can even lead to new organisational structures, products and services.

With the emergence of global networks, team members can collaborate closely even from distant locations. Information technology permits tight co-ordination of geographically dispersed workers across time zones and cultures.

Networked information systems are allowing organisations to link people, assets and ideas to create and distribute products and services and to co-ordinate with other organisations as virtual organisations without being limited by traditional boundaries or physical location.

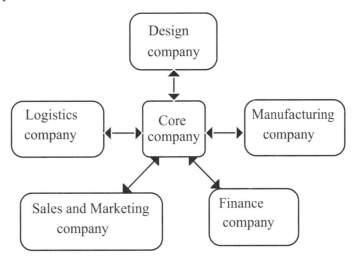

Different companies can join together to provide goods and services.

Information systems have been progressively replacing manual work procedures with automated workflows, work processes and work procedures. Electronic workflows have reduced the cost of operations by displacing paper and the manual routines that accompany it.

5 Mintzberg's organisational configurations

5.1 Building blocks

Mintzberg argues that the organisation structure exists to co-ordinate the activities of different individuals and work processes. The nature of co-ordination changes with the increasing size of an organisation. In small organisations, mutual adjustment is sufficient, but as organisations increase in size increased reliance is placed upon standardisation as a means of co-ordination.

Earlier in this chapter, we discussed the views of Mintzberg and outlined his ideas on the building blocks and co-ordinating mechanisms which make up the detailed configuration of the organisation (shown in the diagram below).

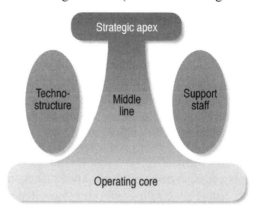

5.2   Configurations

The importance and relative size of these building blocks will vary with organisations, the configuration chosen to support the organisation's strategies depending on the mix of building block and co-ordinating mechanism. Mintzberg discusses six configurations, covering the environment, the type of work and the complexity of tasks facing the organisation. These are outlined below:

	Environment	Internal factors	Key building block	Key co-ordinating mechanism
Simple structure	Simple/ dynamic	Small Young Simple tasks	Strategic apex	Direct supervision
Machine bureaucracy	Simple/ static	Large Old Regulated tasks	Technostructure	Standardisation of work
Professional bureaucracy	Complex/ static	Professional control Simple systems	Operating core	Standardisation of skills
Divisionalised	Simple/static Diverse	Very large Old Divisible tasks	Middle line	Standardisation of outputs
Adhocracy	Complex/ dynamic	Young Complex tasks	Operating core Support staff	Mutual adjustment
Missionary	Simple/ static	Middle-aged Simple systems	Ideology	Standardisation of norms

Simple structure – corresponding to the entrepreneurial organisation. The strategic apex – possibly consisting of a single owner-manager in a small business – exercises direct control over the operating core, and other functions are pared down to a minimum. There is little or no middle line, and technostructure and support staff are also absent. The fact that co-ordination is achieved by direct supervision means that this structure is flexible, and suited to cope with dynamic environments.

Machine bureaucracy – just as the simple structure is based on predominance of the strategic apex, so the machine bureaucracy arises from the power of the technostructure. The emphasis is on regulation: bureaucratic processes govern all activities within the organisation. This means that speedy reaction to change is impracticable, and this arrangement is best suited to simple, static environments.

Professional bureaucracy – this organisational structure arises from the predominance of the operating core. The name is appropriate, because this type of structure commonly arises in organisations where many members of staff have a high degree of professional qualification (for example the medical staff in a hospital or the analysts and programmers in a software developer).

Divisionalised form – this is characterised by a powerful middle line in which a large class of middle managers each takes charge of a more or less autonomous division. Depending on the extent of their autonomy, managers will be able to restrict interference from the strategic apex to a minimum.

The '**adhocracy**' – refers to a complex and disorderly structure in which procedures and processes are not formalised and core activities are carried out by project teams. This structure is suited to a complex and dynamic environment.

Missionary organisations – are organisations formed on a basis of a common set of beliefs and values shared by all workers in the organisation. Firm belief in such norms implies an unwillingness to compromise or change, and this means that such organisations are only likely to prosper in simple, static environments.

5.3 Structure and systems

If we take a system that is a mass production process with a large work force, we can illustrate what the structure might look like using Mintzberg's structural configuration.

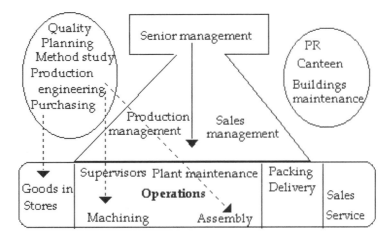

There are several layers of management and supervision connecting the strategic apex to the operating core. It is a structure that abounds with systems - production planning, job descriptions, quality assurance procedures, job cards, budgetary control, standard costing, induction, appraisal and disciplinary procedures etc. Because most of the work in the operating core is procedural and routine and controlled by systems developed by the technostructure, supervisors can be responsible for groups of up to fifty operatives. The support staff eg, cleaners, security, market research etc, differ from the analysts in the technostructure because their work can be done by outsiders. This makes them vulnerable and relatively lacking in political clout within the organisation.

6 Globalisation

Some years after writing *The Mind of the Strategist* which many people regarded as the bible of corporate strategy, Kenichi Ohmae shifted his attention to the changing shape of the business world. The titles that he gave to works such as *Beyond National Borders*, *The Borderless World* and *The End of the Nation State* clearly indicated the direction of his thinking. His thoughts on these issues are contained in the later work entitled *The Invisible Continent*. Ohmae contends that the world in which business now takes place is so vastly different from the past that it is analogous to the discovery of a new continent.

Ohmae suggests that there are four 'dimensions' to this 'new continent'.

The first is the **Visible Dimension** of this new invisible continent. Whilst products still need to be made and sold, not everything will happen in cyberspace. However what may change with the passage of time is the way things are made and distributed as the other dimensions of the new world have their impact. For example delivery trucks may be driverless, being controlled by satellite navigation systems or propelled by hydrogen.

The second of the four dimensions Ohmae cites is that of **The Borderless World**. E-commerce is a real business world phenomenon which knows no boundaries. In today's business world knowledge workers can and do work anywhere in any country as knowledge transcends geographical boundaries. Globalisation is inevitable and no country or organisation can shelter behind its own borders any longer.

The third dimension is the **Cyber Dimension**. The advent of the world wide web, the internet and mobile phone technology are, if they are not already, becoming a part of our everyday business lives as they become more accessible and cheaper and easier to use.

Arguably, the fourth dimension (which Ohmae refers to as the **Dimension of High Multiples**) is more questionable. Ohmae is referring to the manner in which the stock market in recent times has placed exaggerated values on some shares that have yet to produce their promised earnings. The very high valuation placed on such shares has enabled such new economy companies to buy out old economy companies that were larger than themselves in every respect.

The high multiples enabled the growth of what Ohmae referred to as Godzilla companies such as Microsoft, Oracle, Dell and Cisco. He further contends that the old 'Titans' like IBM, Hewlett Packard, Sony and Walmart will be unable to compete unless they try to enter the new continent and grow like the 'Godzilla' organisations.

6.1 Towards globalisation

Globalisation is a term that has become fashionable since the 1980s when it began to replace words like 'internationalisation' and 'transnationalisation' as a suitable term to denote the ever intensifying networks of cross border interaction in all areas of human activity: social, political, cultural, financial and economic. The concept covers an enormous variety of contemporary social change the connections between which are not yet clear.

An extreme view of globalisation means the dissolving of national economies into world markets, where in a sense there aren't countries any more, there aren't national firms, there aren't markets that are distinguished by their national characteristics.

So the financial markets and the markets for manufactured goods and services would become world markets. The driving force in these markets would be truly transnational companies, companies that operated across the world and basically thought in terms purely of world competitive strategies, that were no longer interested in maintaining themselves in one primary nation.

The ability of a business to become a global player depends on a number of factors. Some companies service niche markets, which are protected from global competition. In many cases, however, it is necessary to enter into strategic alliances of some sort in order to become a global operator.

Kenichi Ohmae suggests there are five stages to globalisation:

- The export-oriented company - a product is developed at home and perfected to global standards. It is designed to meet the needs of customers in the region we hope to market it in. We now export the product from a home production base using dealers, distributors and agents.

- Overseas branches - we have succeeded in exporting our products to different regions. We find that there are high levels of customer satisfaction in those markets and we now aim to set up our own sales, marketing and after-sales service in these foreign markets.

- Relocating production - we have created a large enough demand for the product to the point where export-related costs are blossoming to eat into profits. We scan our environment and find that it is feasible to set up production in the area or close to the area. So we relocate production to our key markets or close to them.

- Insiderisation - this is a crucial stage in globalisation. The company sets up a blueprint of its home operations and clones itself in its global markets. This enables a complete local response to local consumers by being able both to analyse consumers and tailor local products to their needs. It is important at this stage to identify innovation in each market and translate that innovation back home or to other production areas around the world.

The global company - Ohmae says that at this stage some common core functions consolidate back to the centre to provide the business with common shared values the global aspect while maintaining the ability to provide a specific local service. Operation remains dedicated to local management, but there is global control of areas such as research and development, brand development and so on.

Conclusion

This chapter has concentrated on structural and design implications of strategic change. It has been argued that strategy implementation is brought about through the people in an organisation, and the way those people are organised is of key importance.

The subdivision of control in a large company can provide the motivation to perform well as a division and thus improve the company performance as a whole. In order to structure an organisation, work needs to be reduced to manageable proportions. This can be done by separating into segments by function, by product or service and by location. Organisation charts may be used to define, in broad terms, an individual's duties and responsibilities.

In this chapter, Mintzberg's strategic types were introduced, as examples of how a strategic architecture might function. This model may also help to answer ACCA questions on corporate culture.

Different types of organisational structure

1   Give four ways that a strategy might influence a structure. (2.1)

2   What levels of planning are associated with the divisional structure? (2.5)

3   Explain the difference between a matrix structure and a holding company. (2.6, 2.7)

Transitional and adaptive structures

4   What structural difficulties are faced by multinational companies? (3.2)

Mintzberg's organisational configurations

5   Outline the key differences between Mintzberg's organisational configurations. (5.2)

Cole Pitt plc

Cole Pitt plc is an international company, with business interests in three broad areas, metals, industry and energy. The group's results last year were as follows.

Sector	Turnover £m	Profit £m
Metals	2,700	60
Industry	2,000	150
Energy	700	90
	5,400	300

Fifteen years ago, when group profits were £40 million, two-thirds of the profits came from metals, ie from mining interest. The main part of the mining profits came from Kannacoolie Mines, a 70%-owned Australian subsidiary. Since then, the Australian government has acquired a bigger stake in Kannacoolie Mines, so that Cole Pitt plc now owns only 40% of the equity.

Cole Pitt plc's pre-eminence in mining has been attributable to its success in running low cost mines, but mining is a cyclical business and the group survived the recession in the metals markets in the 1980s only because of its success in diversifying into other industries.

Most of the group's industrial interests are based in the UK, and there are three divisions, engineering, chemicals and construction. The importance of these industrial interests has been enhanced over the past ten years or so by a strategy of diversification by takeover.

The group's energy interests are mainly in North Sea oil and gas.

Sir Hector Grouse, the group's chairman until recently, has built up a more diversified company over recent years with a personalised style of leadership. The 28-man board of directors had little influence over the operations of each division, which were run by divisional chairmen (none of them directors of the group board of directors) each reporting directly to Sir Hector. Sir Hector has recently retired, and the new chairman believes that there should be a reorganisation of the group and a re-assessment of its corporate strategy.

Required:

(a) Suggest a form of organisation structure for the group, whereby more centralised authority is given to the group's board of directors, but at the same time an effective profit centre structure remains. **(12 marks)**

(b) Discuss the strategic problems for a group involved in the mining and energy businesses, and suggest whether Cole Pitt plc has taken effective measures to minimise these problems. **(4 marks)**

(c) Respond to the suggestion that if Cole Pitt plc is to grow, it should concentrate on diversification by acquisitions, and should not invest heavily in organic growth by incurring large capital expenditures in mining or energy ventures, which are high-risk cyclical business sectors. **(4 marks)**

(Total: 20 marks)

EXAM-TYPE
QUESTION **2**

Organic organisation

You are required to describe **five** features of an 'organic' organisation, explaining how these affect the operations of the organisation. **(20 marks)**

Chapter 20
COMPETING GLOBALLY

Many large commercial organisations choose to confine their operations to a single country. This is quite possible, especially in a large country like the United States. However, for most growing companies an entry into some form of international trade is an almost inevitable development.

This chapter examines the various ways in which companies can profit from global expansion and reviews the strategies that companies engaged in global competition can adopt. It also discusses the optimal choice of entry mode to serve a foreign market and explores the issue of managing a global company

Objectives

When you have studied this chapter you should be able to:

- discuss the effect of an international environment on organisations

- describe the alternative ways to enter foreign markets

- discuss the impact of the global market

- analyse the effects of cultural differences

- explain the emergence of international and global business

- outline the key aspects of an international business environment

- distinguish between global and international competition

- outline the nature of global and international competition.

1 Internationalisation of business

1.1 Reasons for internationalisation

Businesses are increasingly operating on a global scale. This may be in response to opportunities overseas or to threats in the home market.

For example, Coca-Cola has followed a strategy of exploiting any potential opportunities to sell its products abroad, even if they are unlikely to generate profits for some time. For this reason it was one of the first US companies to sell products to the Communist bloc in the early 1970s.

According to Whellan organisations commence international activities in order to gain:

- Increased sales and profits by absorbing extra capacity and thus reducing unit costs and spreading economic risks over a wider number of markets.

- Competitive advantages by seeking low cost production facilities in locations close to raw materials and/or cheap labour, obtaining wider channels of distribution and access to new technologies through joint ventures and supplies of raw material resources by engaging in their exploration, processing, transportation and marketing.

Other reasons for overseas expansion include the following.

- Exploiting overseas markets at an earlier stage in their product lifecycle than in the home country

- Exploitation of cheap local labour or other resources

- Economies of scale, particularly with regard to high-ticket items such as motor cars etc

- If a company decides to expand internationally, then its suppliers may also have to supply goods internationally.

Features of multinational companies include the following.

- Overseas subsidiaries are often guided by global corporate policies.

- Efficiencies arise from economies of scale.

- They are good at getting the best out of individual countries (sharing work over regions).

- International sourcing can lead to cost savings.

- Brand names are becoming global.

The following are some effects of operating in an international environment.

- More difficult communications (although technology such as e-mail etc is reducing this problem)

- Restrictions of host governments (eg China)

- Diverse range of cultures

- Exchange rate exposure

- Difficulty of deciding how much local autonomy to grant

In the exam, look for organisations operating internationally (or considering international operation) perhaps as a result of market development (Ansoff's grid).

1.2 The concept of globalisation

Globalisation, if it is a single thing at all, is a very complex thing. The term provides a collective label for a whole series of trends and changes related to the significance of geography in shaping organisations and the interactions between them. For example, many local markets are globalising as their governments reduce import restrictions and tariffs, or as other countries re-open trade relationships. This not only means that goods and services become available from other parts of the world, but that the nature of competition changes from local to global, in turn affecting the way that local firms must operate in order to survive and thrive.

A somewhat different type of globalisation concerns the homogenising of tastes across geographies. Food, once highly local in style, has become more global in many respects. This is not simply what has been called the culinary imperialism of America being rolled out across the world via Coca Cola and McDonalds. The changing economics of transportation and increased experience of foreign travel have enabled consumers to break away from largely national determinants of taste, and re-segment across countries on more individual lines. It is not that everyone is moving to a single global standard, but that shared tastes transcend national borders. Some consumers are moving towards a traditional Italian diet whether they live in London, Toronto or Stockholm, while others eat increasing quantities of Chinese style stir-fries, whether in New York, Adelaide or Madrid. In this context globalisation simply means that geographic location is no longer the key determinant of behaviour.

Other forms of globalisation can also be distinguished. More and more firms have a presence in multiple locations across the world, rather than simply exporting from a home base. But, perhaps more importantly, as such firms seek to standardise approaches or gain purchasing economies, they increasingly demand co-ordinated, multi-country support from their suppliers. This requires the suppliers not only to be present in different parts of the world, but also to manage the relationships between their local units in new ways.

Even without physical presence in more than one country, organisations, like individuals, are no longer isolated from economic events far away. The globalisation of capital markets and increasing international trade flows mean that local economies are heavily, and rapidly, affected by what is going on thousands of miles away, just as individuals are instantaneously linked, via CNN or BBC World, to events whose impact was once muted by distance and time.

1.3 Competitive advantage of nations

Within a multi-domestic industry, international business is really a collection of domestic industries, where competitive advantage in one country is more or less independent of competition in the others. For this type of industry, many of the activities involved in production, marketing and servicing need to be tailored to the particular requirements of the country. This tailoring is critical to competitive advantage.

In global industries the competitive advantage in one country is strongly influenced by its position in others. Rivals battle it out worldwide and competitive advantage may be gained by operating and organising on a global basis.

Japanese companies have tended to take a global strategy approach, which has resulted in a gradual challenge and displacement of market leaders and significant players in a number of countries. This can be seen in the UK in respect of motorbikes, cars and consumer electronics. The globalisation process was developed in line with market segmentation. Typically, Japanese companies entered the bottom end of the market, which was usually badly defended and by trading-up, displaced the significant players.

Some of the advantages of this global approach include:

- **Economies of scale,** which arise by offering standard products across many markets. This allows for the benefits of large-scale operations to be achieved.

- **Experience** and resources may be shared across countries giving rise to advantages.

- **Location**, where it may be cheaper to produce components in one country, assemble them in another and carry out the R&D in a third. The global company can choose the most advantageous locations for different parts of the business.

- **Differentiation** allows for organisation on a global scale to service multinational buyers. For example, accountancy practices go global to service their multinational clients.

1.4 Porter's determinants of national competitive advantage

Porter's Diamond, discussed in Chapter 4, is particularly useful in understanding how geographical location has contributed to competitive advantage.

1.5 Comparative advantage

The benefits of international trade are often quite clear. When a country, perhaps because of its climate, is unable to produce certain goods at home (or can do so only at a very high cost) it will have to import them from abroad and offer other goods which it produces cheaply in exchange. Britain, for instance, could produce bananas and pineapples, but only at a prohibitively high opportunity cost by growing them in hot houses. Similarly, countries like Japan with little or no natural endowment of resources such as oil, coal and other mineral deposits must buy their requirements from overseas. Nevertheless, the basis for trade is less obvious when, say, the USA, which can produce most goods more efficiently than the rest of the world, imports vast amounts of goods like motor cars, cameras, TVs and other electronic products from countries such as Japan, Taiwan and South Korea.

Take two countries, A and B, which can produce the following amounts of two goods, food (F) and clothing (C), with one unit of resources:

Output per unit of resources

	A	**B**
Food (units)	240	80
Clothing (units)	60	40

We can see immediately that country A is more effective than B in producing both goods. We say that A has an absolute advantage in both goods. Alternatively, if costs are measured in terms of the resources needed to produce a unit of either good, A can produce them absolutely more cheaply than B. There seems therefore to be no basis for trade between A and B as country A, we might think, will not import goods from B which it can produce more cheaply itself. However, the theory shows that a sufficient basis for trade is a difference, not in absolute costs, but in relative or comparative costs.

Thus, country A is absolutely superior in producing both goods but to a different degree. It is three times more productive in food but only one and a half times in clothing. A is therefore comparatively better at producing food - country A has a comparative advantage in food. Similarly, although B is absolutely inferior in both goods, the inferiority is less in clothing than in food - B has a comparative advantage in clothing.

Each country could gain (at least potentially) from specialising in the production of, and exporting to the other, the good in which it has a comparative advantage. In exchange, of course, it would import the good in which it has a comparative disadvantage. How the gains arise can more easily be seen if we use the modern notion of opportunity costs in place of comparative costs.

Suppose both countries have fully employed resources - extra output of either good can then only be achieved by diverting resources from production of the other - the opportunity cost of food is the sacrifice of clothing needed to produce one more unit of food. This can be calculated from our figures.

In country A an extra 60 units of clothing (60C) requires the switching of one unit of resources from food and thus a reduction of food output of 240 units *(240F)*. If 60C has an opportunity cost of 240F, 1C has an opportunity cost of 4F. Similarly 1F has an opportunity cost of ¼C. We can calculate the costs in country B in the same way. The opportunity cost ratios in both countries are:

Opportunity cost ratios

A	B
1C:4F	1C:2F
1F:¼C	1F:½C

Comparative advantage is now expressed in terms of opportunity cost. Country A can produce food with a lower opportunity cost than B; B can produce clothing with a lower opportunity cost than A. Imagine now that trade opens up and that the governments of the two countries agree on an international exchange ratio or **terms of trade** of 1C:3F *(1F:1/3C)*, halfway between the respective opportunity cost ratios. Consider the effect in country A. Food producers who have been giving up 4F to obtain each unit of clothing now find they have to sacrifice only 3F to do so by importing clothing from B. So the opportunity cost of clothing has fallen from 4F to 3F.

A's food producers will therefore cease to buy clothing from the domestic industry. In turn, clothing producers with no demand for their output will switch resources into food production. Country A will therefore become completely specialised in food and will import all its requirements for clothing from B at a lower opportunity cost. A's consumers will benefit from the reduction in the cost of clothing.

Exactly the reverse happens in country B, which becomes specialised in clothing and imports food more cheaply from A. Thus, both countries benefit so long as the terms of trade differ from their own domestic opportunity cost ratios. If so, they can each buy the imported good from the other at a lower cost in resources than producing it at home.

1.6   Gains from trade

International trade based on comparative or opportunity cost differences thus results in a more efficient division of labour between countries and an increase in world output and real income. What is in doubt is the division of the gains between countries. A country will gain more the greater the difference between the terms of trade and its own opportunity costs. If country B, for example, could trade at or close to A's domestic ratio of 1C:4F it will be able to buy food even more cheaply.

A country's gains can be illustrated diagrammatically as in diagram below. For simplicity, we have implicitly assumed constant internal opportunity costs in both countries

A country's production frontier can therefore be drawn as a straight line like *JK* which represents B's production possibilities on the assumption that it has a million units of resources available per day. At the extremes, it can produce either 40 (million) units of clothing (40*C*) at *J* or 80*F* at *K*. Before trade the production frontier is also B's consumption frontier - it cannot consume anywhere outside *JK*. Suppose it ends up halfway down *JK* at *E*, producing and consuming 20*C* and 40*F*.

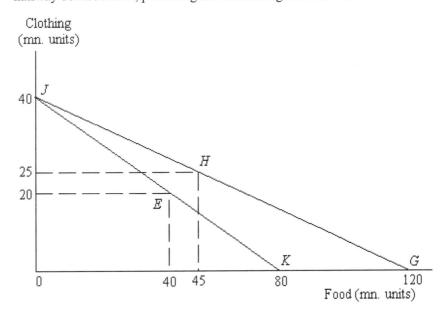

How country B gains from trade

When trade opens up with a terms of trade of 1*C*:3*F*, B's production shifts from *E to J* - all resources are moved into clothing to produce 40*C*. But B's residents can now buy food from A - every unit of clothing sacrificed by exporting it brings back in exchange three units of food. In principle, all 40 units of clothing could be exchanged for 120 units of food at *G*. *JG* is now country B's post-trade *consumption frontier*. B can consume any combination of goods along *JG* which (except for point J) lies outside the pre-trade consumption frontier. So B's residents can now have more of either good with no less of the other. If they end up at point H they now have 5 units more of each good than before trade. The basic gains from trade are shown by the outward shift of the consumption frontier and the corresponding expansion of B's consumption possibilities.

Students should draw for themselves a diagram for country A showing how A will become specialised in food production while obtaining clothing at a lower opportunity cost from B. This means a similar expansion in consumption possibilities in A with a shift outwards in the consumption frontier. So trade based on differences in comparative or opportunity costs is of mutual benefit to the participating countries even when one country has an absolute advantage in producing all goods.

1.7 Political environment

The problem facing strategic planners is how to plan for changes in the political environment. As change is not predictable, the planner needs to approach the problem by considering what type of political change could affect the enterprise rather than trying to estimate all the political changes that might occur.

The trend of political actions can be co-related to changes in social behaviour and values, economic activity, and problems arising from the physical infrastructure or environment. Additionally there are a number of indicators of possible, or intended, future government actions and policy. These indicators are obtained from:

- annual conferences of political parties;
- public utterances of party leaders and seniors;
- international events;
- directives from international trading groups (in the case of UK, the EC directives);
- political commentators and analysts;
- international summit meetings;
- staged legislation;
- efforts of public pressure groups (particularly with regard to local government policy);
- political manifesto.

Legislation and regulations - this is a complicated area covering the Companies Acts, employment legislation (determining the basic employment rights), health and safety regulations, consumer legislation (credit regulations, etc) and so on. There is an almost endless list of laws, or categories of legislation, that affect business enterprises, in domestic, national or international dimensions. The main categories are listed below:

- Labour legislation (safety at work, employee protection, redundancy payments etc).
- Trade union legislation.
- Consumer protection legislation.
- Company legislation.
- Taxation legislation.
- Anti-trust (monopolies) legislation and rulings.
- Trade legislation (countries restricted for export, etc).
- Business legislation (contract and agency law, etc).
- Social legislation (welfare benefits, etc).

The law constitutes a set of environmental factors that are increasingly affecting strategic decisions. Most of the nations of the world are, or are becoming, regulated economies. Government, or self, regulation of business has four principal aims.

(i)   To protect business entities from each other, such as laws putting limits on market dominance.

(ii) To protect consumers from business entities, with hosts of detailed consumer protection regulations covering packaging, labelling, food hygiene and advertising, and much more.

(iii) To protect employees from their employers, with laws that governs the recruitment of staff and health and safety legislation that regulates conditions of work.

(iv) To protect the larger interests of society against excessive business behaviour.

Also at the most basic level, perhaps, laws are passed that enable Government to levy taxes - whereas company law affects the corporate structure of the business, and prescribes the duties of company directors.

Strategic planners cannot plan intelligently without a good working knowledge of the laws and regulations that affect their own companies and the businesses they operate in. In addition to those laws, which apply generally to all companies, such as laws regulating Corporation Tax or Value added Tax, there are laws specifically used to deal with individual industries, like Petroleum Revenue Tax in the offshore oil and gas industry. As with taxation, there are special regulatory regimes for particular industries or sectors eg, nuclear energy or transport or broadcasting or food. Planners should also know the reasons for the laws, and how they are being interpreted in the courts. They also need to be aware of the many local government bye-laws affecting the conduct of their plans. The laws are numerous, most of which you would have studied at your earlier examination stages.

Legislation adapts slowly relative to some other environmental segments, with the exception of company legislation and self-regulation, which has seen lots of changes in recent years. In fact, particularly in respect to labour and consumer protection, organisations often pre-empt legislation by providing more than the statutory requirements. However legislation is becoming more complex, particularly for those companies that trade internationally where the interface, indeed probable conflict, between domestic laws, the host country's laws, and probably also the laws of the trading block of nations the host country belongs to, provides an extremely complicated legal scenario. The legislation associated with the Single European Market gives evidence to this kind of legal complexity. (In the White Paper set out to timetable the 1992 target, some 280 measures were needed to complete the internal market regulations.)

1.8   Single markets and trading blocs

A feature of the modern world economy is its division into three distinctive regions. This idea is referred to as the 'triad model' of the economy, and consists of the European Union, the Pacific Rim and the Americas. In most cases, each group tries to reduce trade barriers within the bloc, to form a single market, while erecting barriers to those outside it. This has further increased the pressure to internationalise, and much trade between triads is actually multinational companies moving products and services between subsidiaries.

A single market occurs when several countries reduce trade barriers to allow the benefits of competition to emerge. The benefits of this are said to be.

- undermining of national monopolies

- reduction of unnecessary costs to international traders greater choice to consumers

- increased competitive pressure on organisations to reduce costs and improve products a larger 'home' market for all companies.

The single market is often very effective at removing some kinds of trade barrier, but many inconsistencies remain. Laws concerning technical specification, packaging and so on, still obstruct the flow of goods and services, although these are much greater between blocs than within them.

1.9   The multinational corporation

The key strategic issues facing multinationals are substantially different from those facing the small business. Here the organisation is likely to be very diverse in terms of both products and geographic markets. It may be that the organisation is in a range of different types of business in the form of subsidiary companies within a holding company structure, or divisions within a multidivisional structure. Therefore issues of structure and control at the corporate level, and relationships between businesses and the corporate centre, are usually a major strategic issue for multinational organisations. At the business unit level, many of the competitive strategic issues will, perhaps, be similar to those faced by smaller organisations - though the strength of the multinational within a given geographical area may be greater than for any small firm. However, for the multinational parent company a significant issue will be how corporate business units should be allocated resources given their different, and often competing, demands for them; and how this is to be co-ordinated. Indeed the co-ordination of operational logistics across different business units and different countries may become especially important. For example, a multinational manufacturing company such as Ford or General Motors has to decide upon the most sensible configuration of plants for the manufacture of cars. Most have moved from manufacturing a particular car at a particular location, and now manufacture different parts of cars in different locations, bringing together such components for the assembly of a given car in a given location. The logistics problems of co-ordinating such operations are immense, requiring sophisticated control systems and management skills far removed from those in the smaller organisation. An important choice that a major multinational has to make is the extent to which it controls such logistics centrally, or devolves autonomy to operating units.

2   The development of the global business

2.1   Developments

'In tomorrow's world, managers will need to be truly global. Education, experience and international mobility will be among the qualities they require'. R Horton, BP (Managing Director)

One of the most significant developments to occur in business over the past quarter of a century has been its increasing internationalisation. International trade, has of course, always existed; what is new is its scale and penetration. This is evidenced by a number of factors.

- The standardisation and integration of operations between subsidiaries in different countries eg, car manufacturing.

- The growth and power of multinationals, so that today they form some of the largest economic units in the world.

- The interdependence of the world economy.

Companies often develop businesses in several international markets and get involved in overseas ventures. A company may export to one country, licence to another, own a subsidiary in a third and have a joint-ownership venture in a fourth. Sooner or later it will create an international division, and have one, or a number, of overseas subsidiary companies to handle its international activities. The international division will be organised according to particular needs, by geographical region, product-group or matrix. A major disadvantage of the international divisional concept is that the corporate management may regard it as just another division and never get involved enough to appreciate its cultural and economic differences, and plan for global marketing.

While it is not practical to attempt a definitive identikit of a modern multinational company (MNC) because of the variety of organisational structures, industries, products, management philosophies, investments, sales volumes, relationships between parent companies and host governments, it is possible to draw up a set of characteristics which most possess.

- They comprise overseas subsidiaries which are complete industrial and/or commercial organisations covering research and development, manufacturing, selling and after-sales activities.

- There is involvement in numerous countries, which may be at different stages of economic and political development.

- The formulation of a universally accepted and understood corporate policy for the guidance and direction of the overseas subsidiaries in pursuit of declared aims and objectives.

2.2 Motives of multinationals

The driving force behind the growth and expansion of MNCs is the belief that vertically integrated companies linked by a global strategic plan should possess a distinct competitive advantage over under-capitalised and technologically-backward local companies in the exploitation of any potentially profitable overseas markets. The reasons why MNCs possess this distinctive advantage are reasonably clear.

- Effectiveness in mobilising, directing and controlling the resources at their disposal.

- Better opportunities of achieving economies of scale because of their larger production base and market horizons.

- Able to draw on a wealth of corporate experience in strategic planning, forecasting, market research, finance, production and marketing (particularly in the fields of product positioning, pricing, advertising and promotional budgeting, and distribution).

- Ability to keep in close and constant touch with their overseas subsidiaries by the use of high capacity cable, distributed database systems, satellite communications, and efficient airline systems.

For example, Unilever have categorically stated that one of their prime objectives is to invest capital wherever profitable opportunities exist, and if these opportunities occur more frequently overseas, then so be it.

2.3 Effect of an international environment on organisations

Another motive for overseas investment has been the attempt to secure and protect supplies of key raw materials, prompted by the prominence given to the threats of worldwide shortage of natural resources, and/or their politicisation. Moves by MNCs have been counter-balanced since the early 1970s by host countries who have become increasingly reluctant to allow foreign countries to control the extraction and processing of their prized indigenous raw materials.

The comparatively lower labour costs of many overseas countries has also been an incentive to MNCs to transfer the manufacture of their products to selected areas of the world.

For example, in May 1990 Japanese car giant Toyota began building a £700 million assembly plant at Burnston, just outside Derby. It was planned that on completion the plant would cover 2 million square feet and produce 100,000 cars a year, at full capacity. The Toyota factory is significant, not just for the size of the investment, but for the way in which it highlights the plight of the British automotive industry over the past 25 years. While Ford, British Leyland and General Motors were putting their workers on short-time, the Japanese were investing heavily and planning their assault on Europe from the bastion of Britain.

Operational activities conducted on an international scale are far more complex than those confined to the domestic field.

- Communication with subsidiaries is more difficult; documentation procedures tend to lengthen the delivery chain; while the lack of immediate and close contact with overseas customers tends to escalate trivial complaints over such matters as quality and reliability into major issues.

- Where the MNC is a leader in its industry, the problems of the industry tend to hit the MNC more heavily than a smaller company. Industrial problems are often compounded by oil price rises, sluggish development of the home market, industrial disputes, inflation, high interest rates, and world recession.

- Restrictions are imposed by host governments. Whereas the MNC will be principally concerned with prospective return on its capital invested, the host government will be concerned with:

  (a)   number of local people employed, and wage rates paid;

  (b)   contribution of the MNC to the local GNP;

  (c)   percentage of control exercised by nationals;

  (d)   imposition of taxes, currency movement;

- transfer pricing;

- environmental pollution; and

- degree to which the MNC can assist in strengthening the home industrial base.

- The co-ordination and control of activities of a heterogeneous group of overseas companies operating in countries with a diverse range of cultures and languages; at different stages of industrial, commercial and social development; and with no apparent common purchasing behavioural patters; raises unique problems. There is no **folklore** to which companies can refer, and central management has to develop its own set of rules, procedures and principles. We discuss this problem more fully in the following sub-sections.

- Exchange rate fluctuations; transfer of capital into and out of subsidiaries; and cross border transfer pricing.

- The split between centralised and decentralised control ie, the degree of independence to be given (or taken by) overseas subsidiaries.

- Deployment of limited resources for investment, and the reconciliation of potentially divisive needs and demands of overseas companies and countries.

- Reconciliation of conflicting pressures from overseas markets which are subject to different cultures, political climates, language, geography, time zones, buying behaviour patterns, buying power and susceptibility to advertising and promotion campaigns.

- The growing complexity of the legal environments affecting MNCs. Basically, a government can only effectively legislate for the activities of those of its citizens and companies living or operating within its boundaries. At law, most countries appear to regard MNCs and their overseas affiliates as part of a unitary enterprise, but the plain fact is that the national governments accord anti-trust measures and restrictive practices different levels of priority. The regulations of the European Community are a minefield for MNCs.

2.4 Foreign exchange

Since most foreign exchanges are not fixed but are allowed to vary, rates are continually changing and each trader will offer new rates for customer enquiries according to how the currency dealers judge the market situation. Deals are settled immediately with currency being purchased on the same day or for a date in the future.

- Spot: for immediate delivery
- Forward: for delivery at a date in the future

Thus, a UK firm might receive US$150,000 from a US customer, and sell it spot to a bank, to receive sterling immediately (in practice normally two working days after the contract is made). If the exchange rate is $1.5000 to £1, the UK firm would receive £100,000.

If a firm knows that it is going to receive some foreign currency in the near future, which it will want to sell in exchange for domestic currency, it can make a forward exchange contract with a bank, at an exchange rate that is specified in the contract. Thus, if a firm knows that it is going to receive US$100,000 in 3 months' time, it can make a forward exchange contract now to sell the US dollars in 3 months' time at a specified exchange rate. If the spot rate is $1.5000 to £1, the forward rate may be higher or lower than $1.5000 (depending on comparative interest rates in the USA and the UK).

2.5 Factors influencing the exchange rate for a currency

The exchange rate between two currencies is determined primarily by supply and demand in the foreign exchange markets. Demand comes from individuals, firms and governments who want to buy a currency and supply comes from those who want to sell it.

Supply and demand in turn are subject to a number of influences-

- The rate of inflation, compared with the rate of inflation in other countries
- Interest rates, compared with interest rates in other countries
- The balance of payments
- Speculation
- Government policy on intervention to influence the exchange rate

Total income and expenditure (demand) in the domestic economy determines the demand for goods. This includes imported goods and demand for goods produced in the country, which would otherwise be exported if demand for them did not exist in the home markets. Output capacity and the level of employment in the domestic economy might influence the balance of payments, because if the domestic economy has full employment already, it will be unable to increase its volume of production for exports. The growth in the money supply influences interest rates and domestic inflation.

If the rate of inflation is higher in one country than in another country, the value of its currency will tend to weaken against the other country's currency.

2.6 Global competition

It is necessary to distinguish between global competition, global businesses and global companies.

- Global competition occurs when companies cross-subsidise national market share battles in pursuit of global brand and distribution positions.

- Global businesses - are those for which the minimum volume required for cost efficiency is not available in the company's home market.

- Global companies - are those, which have distribution systems in key foreign markets that enable cross-subsidisation, international retaliation and world scale volume.

In traditionally global businesses, protectionism and flexible manufacturing technologies are encouraging a shift back to local manufacturing. Yet competition remains global. Companies must distinguish between cost effectiveness based on off-shore sourcing and world-scale plants and competitive effectiveness based on the ability to retaliate in competitors' key markets.

Although the pattern of cross-subsidisation and retaliation describes the battle, world brand dominance is what the global war is all about. Japan has been winning this war, establishing worldwide reputations for Canon, Hitachi, Seiko and Honda equal to those of Ford, Kodak and Nestlé in less than 20 years. In consumer electronics, Japan is present in, or dominates, most product categories.

ACTIVITY 1

A large UK manufacturer of confectionery wishes to expand into European markets. However, the UK style of chocolate is not widely appreciated in Europe. What mode of entry would you suggest for the manufacturer?

Feedback to this activity is at the end of the chapter.

3 Global strategies

3.1 Market entry strategies

In a survey of international market entry, Young draw attention to the complexity of market entry decisions:

'The choice of foreign market entry and development strategy is a 'frontier issue' in international marketing, with the method of market servicing likely to have a major impact on a company's performance overseas, and indeed on overall corporate performance. Choosing the most effective market supply strategy, however, is one of the most complex decisions facing the international firm. Choosing the most appropriate strategy will involve trade-offs between objectives. A firm may have multiple objectives in entering and developing a new foreign market (including non-profit objectives) and these must be included in any model of entry strategy choice. Three different approaches have been applied to the entry and development mode decision, namely, the economic approach, the stages-of-development approach and the business strategy approach. 'Each of the three approaches identified by Young emphasises a specific aspect of corporate activity:

- **Economic entry.** This approach emphasises rational behaviour, comparing the costs and benefits of different opportunities.

- **Stages of development.** This approach emphasises the internationalisation of the firm over time.

- **Business strategy.** This approach emphasises the pragmatic nature of decision-making in most organisations, which arises from uncertainty and the need for consensus.

The complexity of the international market entry choice facing most organisations is best seen from a listing of the standard range of entry methods, shown below

Exporting	Transfer of goods/services across national boundaries via direct or indirect methods
Licensing	The licensor provides licensees abroad with access to technologies or know-how in return for financial compensation
Franchising	The franchisor provides the franchisee with a 'package' including not only trade marks and know-how but a range of management and other services in return for a fee.
Management contract	Control of an enterprise is provided by a separate enterprise in return for a fee.
Turnkey contract	A contractor has responsibility for a complete project up to commissioning for a fee.
Contract	A company in one country places an order manufacturing with a firm in another country. Usually limited to production.
International	Agreements between Western governments and their agencies, often with regard to countries in the former Eastern Bloc.
Joint ventures	Contractual arrangements formed for a project of contractual limited duration
Equity	Equity joint ventures involving the sharing of assets, risks and profits and participation in ownership of a particular enterprise or investment product by more than one firm
Wholly owned	Wholly owned 100 per cent owned operations abroad. May subsidiaries be manufacturing or sales/service ventures. May be formed through acquisitions or green field sites.

3.2 The concept of market entry

The concept of market entry relates to the ease or difficulty with which a firm can become a member of a group of competing firms by producing a close substitute for the products they are offering (Bradley, 1991). The firm must develop a set of products, assets, and management activities for the new markets it is entering. The success of the venture depends on how the firm

- uses information about opportunities for profitable market entry
- accesses productive resources
- accesses markets
- overcomes market entry barriers.

Established firms usually perform better than new firms on all four of the above factors because they are superior to new firms in their ability to overcome barriers to resources and markets, and to attain scale economies of operation. The firm in international markets, however, faces two generic market strategies:

- a market penetration strategy, concentrating on a few select markets
- a market skimming strategy, spreading effort over a large number of markets.

A market penetration strategy is based on a longer-term view of opportunities in international markets. In this case the firm needs to support its strategy with the commitment of significant amounts of resources in capital and labour. A market skimming strategy involves using resources in such a way that a relatively equal spread across many markets is achieved.

A market penetration strategy might involve setting up sales offices in a few countries or the establishment of a manufacturing plant. Market skimming, on the other hand, may only mean employing a network of agents to represent and sell the products of the company. Often these agents will represent a wide range of clients and may not achieve the same level of results as might a dedicated sales office.

3.3 Sequencing of market entry

Ayal and Zif identified two alternative penetration strategies for foreign markets:

- Enter a small number of promising markets initially; only after a 'presence' has been established in these markets and the potential of the product proved are new and less lucrative markets entered.

- Enter simultaneously as many markets as possible; initial wide penetration is followed by a period of consolidation where less profitable markets are abandoned.

There is no unique combination of product-market situation and entry strategy. It is therefore for organisations to decide how best to approach the whole problem of market entry. Often the best approach is to involve external expertise in the form of consultants who speak the language and specialise in international issues.

ACTIVITY 1

A large UK manufacturer of confectionery wishes to expand into European markets. However, the UK style of chocolate is not widely appreciated in Europe. What mode of entry would you suggest for the manufacturer?

Feedback to this activity is at the end of the chapter.

3.4 Standardisation versus customisation

A key issue in the development of a global strategy is the extent to which the strategy, particularly the marketing strategy, will be standardised across countries. The more standardisation, the more potential there is for scale economies. The vision of a single product sharing not only the R&D and manufacturing but also a common name, position, package and advertising drives some people's version of the ultimate global strategy; the assumption that it will lead to decisive efficiencies and scale economies.

Two strong motivations for a standardised global brand and position are the media spillover and cross-country customer travel, which can be extensive, especially in Europe. Brand awareness, in particular, can benefit from the exposure of a brand in a different country when customers travel between countries. When media coverage overlaps regions, a global brand can buy exposures much more efficiently. In particular, as the European common market matures, there is likely to be more and more media overlap and customer crossover and thus more payoff to a global brand strategy.

A third rationale for a standardised global marketing strategy is the associations that can result. The image of being a global player achieved by firms like IBM, Ford, and Canon can provide prestige and reassurance to customers. In other contexts, a 'home' country association can be the essence of a brand's positioning. For example, Levi's are U.S. jeans, Chanel is French perfume, Dewar's is Scotch whiskey, Kikkoman is Japanese soy sauce, and Bertolli is Italian olive oil. In each case, the brand is established in its home country and the country itself is central to the image of the brand. In such a context, a standardised strategy may pay off.

Standardisation provides	Customisation provides
Scale economies in the development of advertising, packaging, promotion etc	Names, associations and advertising that can be • developed locally • tailored to local market • selected without the constraints of standardisation
Exploitation of media overlap exposure to customers who travel	Reduced risk from 'buy local' sentiments
Associations of a global presence of the 'home' country	

However, the reality is that a standardised global product and marketing effort is not always desirable or even possible. In general, each element of a marketing program needs to be analysed to determine whether or not the advantages of standardisation outweigh the gains in effectiveness amassed in tailoring the program to local markets. It is very much like deciding whether or not to market the same soup in Texas and New York. There are times in which standardisation is not the answer and it makes sense to tailor the product and marketing program to a particular country.

3.5 The customisation option

To achieve standardisation for some aspects of a strategy can be difficult in the face of differences between countries and involve little potential for scale economies. For example, Kentucky Fried chicken has been successful in Japan, but only after they realised that the American model of free-standing units would not work in land-scarce Japanese cities. They also had to change its menu - making the coleslaw less sweet and also adopted Japanese training methods. Insisting on a US clone would have guaranteed failure in Japan.

Distribution and personal selling are two features that usually need to be adapted to the realities of a country mainly because distribution and selling organisations tend not to be standardised and there are only a few economies of scale involved and there is often a substantial fit problem.

However, if firms are willing to make the investment and commitment to a different distribution/selling system in Japan, it can result in attacking or creating competitive barriers. For example, Coca-Cola developed an in-house delivery system that has become an important advantage, leading to its domination in the Japanese soft-drink market. Xerox exported the U.S. system of extensive personal sales/service to Japan in the 1960s and is often regarded as a model of how to succeed in Japan. Kodak in 1985 broke the Fuji lock on the Japanese market only when it built its own distribution network. The Kodak approach not only gave the firm access to a market but also direct contact with its customers, providing better information on customer needs.

A study of Japanese firms found that a brand name and advertising theme are likely to be standardised across countries. The use of a common name for some Japanese firms like Canon, Yamaha, and Honda can work, but for other firms the constraint that the name be the same in all countries is very confining and can result in the use of bland choices and are neither memorable nor meaningful. Most names, especially names with useful associations, will have a dam- aging meaning (or will be pre-empted) in some countries. For example, Proctor and Gamble's Pert Plus, a very successful-combination shampoo and conditioner, is sold as Rejoy in Japan, Rejoice in much of the Far East, and Vidal Sassoon in the United Kingdom because the Pert Plus name (or something similar) was pre-empted. The Budweiser name is not available to Anheuser-Busch in most of Europe because it is owned by a small Czechoslovakian brewery.

A local brand can benefit from distinct associations that can be useful - even pivotal. Is there any tendency to 'buy home-grown' or any positive feeling toward local traditions or characteristics that can be integrated into a brand's positioning strategy? Or does the global brand have negative associations locally because it has an undesirable meaning in some countries or is tied to a country's politics and thus is subject to the ups and downs of international events?

A worldwide advertising theme may simply not be appropriate in some countries because of the competitive context. A British Airways globalisation effort involved the centralisation of advertising, which resulted in 'the world's favourite airline' theme. It featured a 90-second commercial that showed the Manhattan skyline rotating slowly though the sky. Even in the United States, where the campaign originated, managers wondered if the replaced campaign (which emphasised traditional British values with the theme 'we'll take good care of you') was not more effective. In countries where British Airways was an also-ran, the claim did not make much sense.

A decentralised approach to the development of marketing programs can generate a product or advertising campaign that can be used globally. Levi Strauss got its successful Dockers pants from a product development effort in its Brazilian operation. When Polaroid was repositioning from a 'party camera' platform to a more serious, utilitarian one, a campaign developed in Switzerland was the most effective. It promoted the functional use of instant photography as a way to communicate with family and friends-the 'learn to speak Polaroid' campaign. If local units had not been free to generate their own campaigns, this superior campaign would not have surfaced.

3.6   Creating a global brand

When a new product is developed, most firms will attempt to make it a global product with a common name and position. The pressure for standardisation is particularly strong in Europe, where there is considerable media overlap and fewer distinct distribution systems.

However, a more difficult issue is whether or not to create a global brand when regional brands are in place.

When a brand is established in a country, for example, it has an equity based on its awareness level and a set of associations that are often very valuable. Changing the name and/or position simply in order to conform to a standardised global brand may be extremely costly. The effort to change the Datsun name to the global brand Nissan in the United States in the early 1980s probably cost over $1 billion. As part of the effort, the effective 'Datsun, we are driven' campaign was replaced with the expensive but punch less one, 'the name is Nissan'. Five years after the name change, the Datsun name was still as strong as the Nissan name.

A new name also kills any associations that the old name might have developed. The VW Rabbit attempted to recapture some of the funkiness and magic of the manufacturer's earlier Beetle using imagery associated with the rabbit symbol. Although for many reasons the Rabbit was a poor substitute for the Beetle, it did develop some positive associations. It was later replaced with the global brand name, Golf, which was worse with respect to associations. Heinz is one firm that does not put its name on the products it acquires outside the United States because it wants to retain their associations.

If an existing name has weak associations, of course, it has little to lose by changing. In the late 1980s in the U.S. market, Mars successfully changed the name of its Kal Kan dog food to 'Pedigree' and its Kal Kan cat food to 'Whiskas' to create a worldwide name. In contrast to Kal Kan, which mainly was associated with cans, the name Pedigree was associated with a quality, expensive pet that would only be served the best food and the name Whiskas was feline-sounding and likable.

Some brands are positioned quite differently in different countries. For example, Heinz baby food and Levi's jeans both have a strong value position in the United States and a premium position in other markets. Clearly, it would be foolish to force a common position on such brands in order to achieve a standardised global brand.

The rush to standardised global branding is somewhat ironic as there is a strong move to regional marketing in the United States. Firms like P&G, Campbell Soup, and others are giving local marketing units responsibility for sales promotions and advertising that had previously been centralised.

4 Managing a global company

4.1 Factors determining choice of overseas market

According to Rowe the choice of an overseas market will depend on the preferred method of entry together with an assessment of the following five risk factors

Political stability	Attitudes regarding foreign investors, cost of social benefits, possibility of repatriation, preferential treatment of nationals.
Monetary considerations	Inflation and devaluation, balance of payments, currency convertibility, exchange rates.
Infrastructure	Possibility of bureaucratic delays, support available in professional services and construction, communication and transportation facilities.
Managerial considerations	Ability to enforce contracts, labour cost and productivity, level of sophistication of equipment, quality of local management talent, availability of skilled labour and raw materials.
Economic and tax considerations	Rate of long-term capital and venture capital, tax benefits. economic growth, availability of short term credit,

4.2 Stages of multinational development

Perlmutter recognised three stages in the development of multinationals

- **Ethnocentric** – here the company carries out its overseas operations for the benefit of the home, or source country and the ways of working in the home culture are imposed on the foreign subsidiaries. Many host countries are suspicious of such operations, believing that national assets are being used for the benefit of external investors. However, the multinational activities are tolerated, as the host country is anxious for direct foreign investment and the employment of its nationals, which accompanies such investment.

- **Polycentric** – as it becomes involved with more and more countries, a multinational tends to take less and less account of the home country's interests. Operations in the host country are left increasingly to local management, who are more affected by the host government and the host culture than the expatriates, but who are also absorbing the corporation's culture. Doz claims that up to the 1960s multinationals allowed their *autonomous national subsidiaries* to follow a national responsiveness strategy with only finance and treasury operations, technology transfers and possibly export coordination being centralised.

- **Geocentric** – if polycentric organisations are allowed to develop naturally all managers will begin to take on a supranational approach to objectives. Eventually, according to Paton *et al* ...' all considerations regarding growth and survival will be based wholly on the interests of the corporation itself – national pressures in any country (including the mother country) being regarded as a constraint like any other and not having prior status. By then it is more important to identify the manager as a member of the corporation than as any particular nationality, and positions in the global organisation can be reached by anyone regardless of nationality, according to merit. A corporation culture emerges and managers do not carry any constraints, including national cultural constraints, from one country to another.'

According to Doz such geocentric organisations can follow a strategy of global integration, which has the following advantages

- economies of scale and experience go beyond national markets – and for the resultant global industries there are higher barriers to entry

- the growing discrepancy between efficient market for goods (because of free trade) and imperfect labour markets can be exploited

- there are more opportunities to take advantage of the differences in tax and exchange rates through transfer pricing.

However, national disputes can disrupt such integrated strategies as was the case when a strike at Ford's Dagenham plant affected operations in Germany within twenty-four hours.

Moreover, according to Hofstede, American multinationals have been successful because their dominant home culture has resulted in a well-established frame of reference. There is a danger that geocentric organisations will become like the many international organisations such as UNESCO and the EEC whose members do not have a dominant culture to fall back on. These organisations can achieve political success but administratively they are inefficient.

4.3 Management strategy options

Market Products	Existing	Expanded	New
Present	Option 1	Option 4	Option 7
Improved	Option 2	Option 5	Option 8
New	Option 3	Option 6	Option 9

- **Option one**: Existing market/present products - to achieve growth, it is usual to try to gain market share. One option for share growth is to gain a better identification and preference for the brands of products. Another option is to price the product below that of the competitors.

One of the world's largest manufacturers, Warnaco, tried two different types of international involvement to increase their market share of existing products in the United States. Firstly, they sought lower cost foreign supplies in order to keep prices down and, secondly, gained rights to use some well known foreign brand names, such as Christian Dior, which was well known in the United States, although not for men's ties. Warnaco was already producing ties but reasoned that it would cost more to increase market share with its existing brands. By negotiating the right to use the Christian Dior name, Warnaco was able to gain an advantage of brand recognition, which incorporated a perceived quality and thus increased its tie sales in the United States.

- **Option two**: Existing market/improved products - the strategy for gaining share is to incorporate new product features or to make improvements to the product. This is a concentration rather than product diversity strategy. The improvements or new features may be the result of detailed research or by copying new ideas developed by other companies.

  A number of factors have led companies to look abroad for new ideas. One factor is the trend toward the diffusion of technological development. Another is that market segments increasingly cut across national boundaries; product characteristics are mainly internationally accepted. These factors also influence organisations to seek new ideas from abroad.

  In early 1970, Chrysler's top management decided to improve the lower priced car models by making them smaller and more fuel-efficient. Chrysler could do this either by using its own research and development methods or by acquiring new ideas from other organisations. Chrysler did the latter by establishing a joint venture with Mitsubishi in Japan, for Chrysler, this was the cheaper and faster of the alternatives and Mitsubishi gained car distribution in new areas.

- **Option three**: Existing market/new products - this strategy makes use of present distribution channels but adds or replaces products currently sold to customers. Sales staff may, for example, be able to sell additional products with little or no additional effort. This may also utilise capacity in areas such as warehousing.

  Organisations may look abroad for products to add to or replace their existing lines. They may either import the new product or produce it at home under a licensing or joint ownership arrangement. Whereas the preceding strategy was one of product concentration, this one is for product diversity. Companies such as American Home Products have cross-licensing arrangements with several foreign, pharmaceutical organisations and each has access to the others' new product.

- **Option four**: Expanded market/present products - the emphasis in this strategy is to increase sales market share. When a product is at its mature stage, an organisation may try to increase product usage by attracting new customers or by promoting new product uses. One way of determining if there is a usage gap, which could be exploited is to investigate the usage of similar products in a foreign country and if sales are high then an attempt can be made to copy some of the foreign product uses or marketing methods.

  Mitsubishi, in addition to producing the cars described in the second strategy section, has a large agricultural division. One of its agricultural products is broiler chickens and in Japan this market was mature. However, nearly all the chicken sold in Japan was sold for preparation at home and it was sold without bones. Mitsubishi investigated the US market and discovered that a large proportion of the market in the United States was sales of prepared chicken with bones; this was sold through fast food chains. They, therefore, approached Heublein's Kentucky Fried Chicken division and established a joint venture with them in Japan. In this way they successfully promoted new uses of chicken and the joint venture was able to expand sales in what had appeared to be a stable market.

- **Option five:** Expanded market/improved products - this strategy differs from strategy two as it introduces a new product as an addition rather than substituting it for the existing product. The addition enables the organisation to widen its market.

Gillette has long dominated the shaver market in the United States through its sales of razor blades. A large proportion of the market, however, was in electric shavers. Gillette decided to compete in the electric shaver field in order to grow and maintain or improve its share of the total shaving market. Rather than accepting the delay whilst developing an electric shaver Gillette acquired a German company, Braun, which included shavers and small electrical appliances.

- **Option six:** Expanded market/new products - the difference between this strategy and the third strategy is that the new products are intended for new customers. Option three nearly always involves horizontal moves into closely related products. This strategy, however, involves either vertical integration or unrelated lateral product diversification in order to serve the new customers. This strategy may be pursued through horizontal diversification by either acquiring products or the technology to make them from abroad. If a company seeks vertical diversification to reach an expanded market, it may acquire the technology from abroad by a licensing agreement or through some other association with a foreign company.

Group Industrial Alfa is one of Mexico's largest companies. During the late 1970s it was content to concentrate its sales almost entirely in the rapidly expanding Mexican market. Management, however, was concerned that sales of its existing products, such as beer and steel, would not grow as fast as the economy. The company expanded horizontally by seeking new products from abroad. Alfa diversified into manufacturing products such as televisions, electric motors, motorcycles, and artificial fibres, all of which were destined to reach some of the Mexican consumers who buy beer and steel and they did this through licensing or joint ventures with foreign companies.

- **Option seven**: New market/present products - under this strategy, a company attempts to grow by selling its products in an ever widening sphere. Foreign sales may be an evolutionary process after the company has expanded from a local to a regional or national market. If a company is successful in its pursuit of this strategy, it should be able to reduce unit production costs as it moves down the experience curve and may further build on its distinct product specific competencies.

As the French market was saturated with bottled water Source Perrier had difficulty sustaining its growth. It initially tried a type three strategy by producing soft drinks, milk and chocolate, which it already sold through its existing retail distribution. This strategy, however, did not succeed. Source Perrier decided to export the identical product to the US market but market it differently than in France. This strategy did succeed.

- **Option eight**: New market/improved products - this strategy differs from the preceding one in that, in this case, a company makes variations of its products in order to sell them in new geographic areas.

This is perhaps the most common strategy for companies selling in foreign markets. They take advantage of their product specific expertise but make variations to fit the new customers' orientations. An example of this is NCR, which dominates the world's markets for cash registers. In order to sell in some of the poorer countries, NCR designed crank operated machines as an alternative to its electric registers.

- **Option nine**: New market/new products - companies may stabilise sales and earnings by selling products, which move counter-cyclically. They may also do this by selling in markets, which are unlikely to move together in the same direction during business cycles. Option nine encompasses a simultaneous diversification by both means.

This strategy is not common and companies are usually hesitant to diversify simultaneously by product as well as location. It is often felt that such diversification may take the company too far afield of its established expertise, thus creating control problems. Companies that diversify in this dual manner are likely to do so as a by-product of an acquisition or merger. For example, Nestlé decided in the early 1970s to alter the geographic composition of its sales and profits. Management wanted the North American operatives to hold a larger portion of its worldwide operations. In order to achieve this, Nestlé acquired North American companies with similar food products to its own. As a by-product of its acquisition of Stouffer, a producer of frozen food, Nestlé also became the owner of a chain of hotels in the United States. This acquisition, therefore, not only produced a geographic diversification as was intended but also resulted in product diversification as well.

5 Reaching global customers

As in all commercial activity, much can be done to reduce risks and take the opportunities effectively by marketing research. In the case of an international business, the work has the additional problems of distance and interpretation of the results. Moreover, in many countries, the data one would like simply does not exist, and it would be expensive and time consuming to collect it oneself. For example, in the UK data concerning family budgets and purchasing decisions is usually obtained from women, but in Islamic countries there may be much reluctance by women to discuss these things – or anything else – with strangers.

The first stage in an international marketing research project is to use secondary sources to build up background material on the country under investigation. In general, this is not difficult and the problem may be that too much information is collected. The main points that should be uncovered are given in the table below:

Market information	Market size, projected market growth, location, key segments, sophistication and income of segments	Secondary sources, some primary sources if early investigation seems promising
Product information	Existing products, characteristics and marketing mix attributes. Standards of design, legal restrictions and standards	Secondary and primary if promising
Competitor information	Number and strategies of key producers, critical success factors and threat of new entrants	Secondary data limited primary
Distribution information	Availability of distributors, infrastructure, cultural preferences for distribution	Secondary

It can be seen that much of the early work can be done from secondary sources. These are widely available and include:

- official government statistics: from both the target country and the home country

- industry associations

- industry magazines and periodicals

- supranational bodies – United Nations, International Monetary Fund, World Bank, etc

- international press

- organisations of industrialists with an interest in trading in a particular region or country

- Chambers of Commerce.

However, when using secondary data there are risks that must be taken into account:

Aggregation: The level of data sought may not exist, and proxies taken might not be very close.

Comparability: Data is frequently classified inconsistently, or information put together in an arbitrary way. Such items as growth rates and income levels can be calculated in different ways, and the source might not give any details in this respect.

Validity: Many publishers collate information given to them but do not check its reliability. For example, income estimates drawn from taxation figures tend to underestimate actual income, by a great deal in some countries.

When trying to assess secondary data, it is always wise to err on the side of caution, particularly when the organisation has little experience. However, it is important to remember that the purpose is not to build up a comprehensive study of the country in question. The purpose is simply to answer some basic strategy and marketing questions:

- Is this market attractive to the organisation?

- Can the organisation develop an advantage in it?

It may be possible to answer these questions adequately with relatively little information, providing the information available is reliable.

5.1 International market segmentation

Within a country, a marketer attempts to find different market segments that can be reached by varying the marketing mix. Naturally, the same kind of approach is used when building a strong market position in a particular country. However, the international dimension raises a further possibility of systematically identifying similar market segments in different countries, so that the benefits of standardisation can be achieved without becoming too enmeshed in the necessity to compete in areas where the company has no particular advantage.

There are two stages to the segmentation process used in this way. Firstly, a macro level considers objective measures and acts as a first stage filter. The second level is a micro approach and is a more detailed analysis of lifestyle behaviour that may require primary investigation.

Macro segmentation

Five particular categories are used for this brand-based approach.

(a) *Language* is important because it reduces the difficulty of promotion strategy.

(b) *Religion* is an important influence on lifestyle and purchasing decisions. Often countries that share a strong religion will adopt similar lifestyle characteristics. Often, the categories of religion and language are combined in an ethnic segmentation, which may be less misleading than using either category alone in some cases.

(c) *Geography* – Cultural similarities are often seen between countries in close proximity. Thus expansion into a similar segment in a neighbouring country is often a strong possibility, although marketers should be aware that cultural similarities might be rather superficial. A great deal of research has gone into identifying the European consumer, but in general local conditions appear to influence market segments more than geographical ones.

Within Europe, three regions can be identified as sharing very broad consumption patterns:

(a) Spain, Italy and France

(b) Germany, Switzerland and Austria

(c) Scandinavia and the UK.

(d) *Technological capability* – The level of economic development in a country determines consumption patterns. Countries at a similar level of development usually demand similar products and services, and make similar demands upon the infrastructure.

(e) *Economic* – Countries with similar national income per head, or purchasing power parity, often share consumption habits. There is much similarity between segments of young people in USA and Japan.

These wide criteria are used to develop potential targets. However, the following three factors will need to be investigated before the firm commits its resources:

- behavioural characteristics – usage (heavy, occasional)

- lifestyles – attitudes to novelty and experimentation, use of surplus income, symbols and so on

- attitudes and taste – use of the product in the segment (is a mobile telephone used as a status good, a lifestyle option or a work necessity, for example).

Often the results of this macro and micro study of segmentation can be surprising. For example, many marketers have recently discovered that the size of the Indian middle class is huge and relatively concentrated in a few cities. This has opened markets in a wide range of quality and high technology products that would not normally be associated with a country that has a very low national income per head.

5.2 Sales force considerations

While segmentation issues are at the front end of the internationalisation decision, the success of the operation will ultimately come down to the ability to sell the product. In this section, we consider the range of sales force management decisions that a company will need to evaluate.

(a) *International level decisions* – Should the company use a locally recruited sales force, a sales agency or a mixture or both? Much depends upon the cultural specificity of the product, and the importance of the business. A key account will frequently expect to be able to deal directly with a senior executive in the home country, while smaller buyers may prefer to speak with a trusted agent.

(b) *National decisions* – Organisation of the sales force structure (regional, product, customer, etc), volume and share targets for the subsidiary.

(c) *Local actions* – Sales force training, corporate style, relationship with important customers, etc.

5.3 Global account management

Recent work has emphasised that, as large companies become global, they expect their suppliers to follow suit. Thus, in addition to the national and international sales force teams, there is also a requirement for Global Account Management (GAM). Marsden and Yip (1996) identified several themes that reoccur on successful GAM programmes:

- consistent world wide service

- single point of contact for buyer

- partnering customers

- outsourcing for customers

- GAM structure
- uniform purchasing and pricing
- GAM incentives and compensation.

However, many GAM projects are unsuccessful, in terms of both establishing the systems and making them profitable. Christoph Senn, writing for the Sales Research Trust, argues that there are three levels to effective GAM.

Strategic Level: Identifying suitable GAM partners. GAM is expensive, and quite difficult to do well, so only worth doing when there are substantial gains to both parties. The two organisations need to co-ordinate their activities and develop at the same pace.

Operational Level: Products and services need to be combined internationally. The most effective way of doing this is through customer demand. As the relationship between GAM partners grows, this will become less difficult as learning takes place, but there may well be significant errors in the early stages.

Tactical Level: The integration of management and information systems. This is difficult because there are potential conflicts of interest between the international management processes and GAM processes. Further, since GAM relationships are, by definition, internationally mobile, it is likely that personnel will need to be moved frequently, adding further disruption.

GAM is a developing technique. Even companies that have tried it and failed – such as Citicorp – have been forced to try again as important clients become more global.

6   Assessing opportunities and threats

6.1   Opportunities of global competition

The opportunities available to an international company arise from different sources, such as the following:

(a) an inherent national advantage used to gain comparative advantage abroad (e.g. low labour costs in Taiwan and Korea relative to other countries)

(b) production economies of scale. In some industries such as steel and car manufacture the minimum efficiency production unit is too great for solely national demand so exporting from a central base will out-compete national producers

(c) operating worldwide may allow necessarily high fixed costs incurred nationally for logistical needs to be recouped, e.g. specialised cargo ships

(d) marketing economies of scale

(e) choices in location. It may be cheaper to produce parts in one country and assemble them in another, and it may be more effective to locate fundamental R&D in a third country. The global company can choose the most advantageous locations for different parts of the business

(f) experience curve advantages. Organisations can gain opportunities from sharing resources and experiences across countries

(g) differentiate with multinational buyers. Where the organisation's customers are multinational, there may be opportunities to organise on a global scale to service them, e.g. consider the trend for accountancy practices to go global to give a better service to their multinational clients.

ACTIVITY 2

Describe an organisation or industry that chooses advantageous locations for different parts of its business.

Feedback to this activity is at the end of the chapter.

6.2 Threats to global competition

The scope for global competition is limited by the following factors:

(a) national tastes and needs can be markedly different, e.g. the German beer trade is strongly regionalised in taste, the opportunities for an imported or licence manufactured standardised beer being poor

(b) lead times may be critical and only a national company on the spot can provide the service dictated

(c) access to established distribution channels might be blocked

(d) terms of trading may require local ownership or provision of local sales and servicing organisations

(e) government impediments through tariffs, subsidies to national producers, tax regulations, etc.

6.3 Experiences

These threats can be very powerful and, in some industries, outweigh the general environmental factors that are encouraging globalisation. These factors include a narrowing of national differences in taste and culture, acceptance of free trade concept and reduced global distribution and communication costs.

There are companies who have tried to go 'global' and failed.

ITT (USA) went global in the 70s and found that various countries would not swap R&D information and the company was forced to withdraw from the market where it had been leader. There is a general comment that American companies are bad at international management and tend to compensate by strong centralisation. KAO (Japanese soap manufacturer) failed in its attempts to become global. The reason given for this failure was that while everything in Japan sold on performance and quality, which works well with high technology products, it fails with products sold on 'image', e.g. personal care products.

6.4 Strategic issues

Porter's strategic recommendations for the competitive organisation are:

- sell to the most sophisticated and demanding buyers because they will set a standard for the organisation

- seek out buyers with the most difficult needs which then become part of the firm's R&D programme

- establish norms of exceeding the toughest regulatory hurdles or product standards: these provide targets that will force improvement

- source from the most advanced and international home-based suppliers: those with competitive advantage already will challenge the firm to improve and upgrade

- treat employees as permanent instead of demoralising hire-and-fire approach

- establish outstanding competitors as motivators.

The challenge facing the global company is how to respond to the particular needs of individual countries whilst at the same time not jeopardising the advantages of being part of a global company. A small number of branded products are marketed in the same way across the world, e.g. Coca-Cola and Marlboro, but these tend to be the exceptions. Most global organisations adapt either the marketing approach or the product to the particular requirements of each country, e.g. Unilever's global shampoo brand, Timotei, is promoted with the same healthy image worldwide, but the product is changed to suit the different ways that nationalities wash their hair. Schweppes tonic water is marketed as a mixer for alcoholic drinks in the UK but as a soft drink in France.

Organisations need to develop global strategies in marketing but create local autonomy for managers to adopt strategies for local markets. International companies achieve their best success in using a country as a 'lead subsidiary', i.e. by specialising in that nation's strengths. For example:

(a) Phillips use Taiwan as lead company in everything related to black and white TVs.

(b) Ericsson use Australia as lead country globally for R&D.

Conclusion

In this chapter we have considered the internationalisation of the world economy.

SELF-TEST
QUESTIONS

Internationalisation of business

1   Outline two advantages of the global strategy approach. (1.3)

The development of global business

2   Describe spot and forward exchange rates. (2.4)

Global strategies

3   What are the three market entry strategies identified by Young? (3.1)

Managing a global company

4   Give three risk factors when determining the choice of overseas market. (4.1)

5   Describe any entry strategy available to an organisation. (4.3)

Assessing opportunities and threats

6   What are the difficulties associated with GAM? (6.3)

EXAM-TYPE
QUESTION 1

Multinational

The acquisition of a local company by a multinational conglomerate from abroad must take account, not only of differing tax regimes, currency controls and tariff and quota systems, but also of the cultural background developed within that local company.

Required:

(a) Discuss to what extent a foreign parent should permit a local subsidiary to retain its practices that are due to local cultural factors and which might conflict with group practices.   **(12 marks)**

(b) Discuss how the integration of expatriate and locally recruited personnel can be engendered.   **(8 marks)**

(Total: 20 marks)

EXAM-TYPE
QUESTION **2**

Protectionism

The principle of comparative costs shows that countries are likely to benefit from free trade. Why then is protectionism so prevalent in industrialised and developing countries alike? **(20 marks)**

For the answers to these questions, see the 'Answers' section at the end of the book.

FEEDBACK TO
ACTIVITY **1**

The company would probably manufacture overseas, maybe buying an overseas company with existing expertise and available brands.

FEEDBACK TO
ACTIVITY **2**

An example of an industry that locates different areas of its business to take advantage of particular skills or low wages is the computer industry. R&D may be concentrated in the US, the microchips and printed circuit boards are constructed in the Pacific Rim and the machines are assembled in various countries, such as the UK.

An example of an organisation is Ford. The components for car manufacture are made in many countries, e.g. gears in Germany, some models are assembled in Spain, others in the UK and the engine design is in the US.

Chapter 21

OUTCOMES OF THE STRATEGIC MANAGEMENT PROCESS

This chapter explores the outcome of the strategic management process. To monitor its own strategic performance, an organisation needs to establish a number of performance indicators, relevant to different aspects of the business. Over-reliance on financial results alone can mean that managers do not address the longer-term strategic issues - hence measures such as the balanced scorecard are used to redress the emphasis.

Corporate decline is a test of managerial skill, either to turn round an under-performing company or to pull out from a product market in permanent decline.

Objectives

When you have studied this chapter you should be able to:

- discriminate between corporate and business outcomes

- discuss market orientated and resource based approaches to sustainable competitive advantage

- outline the importance of organisational learning, and outline the nature of the learning organisation

- select appropriate financial and non-financial indicators to help monitor progress towards desirable strategic outcomes

- identify reasons why a firm may fail to adapt to its environment effectively.

1   Corporate and business performance

1.1   Sustaining a competitive advantage

A competitive advantage is difficult to achieve, and even harder to maintain. The problems associated with sustaining a competitive advantage have been a recurring theme throughout this text.

KEY POINT

Grant identifies appropriability, transparency, portability and replicability as factors that contribute to superior profits in the long run.

A competitive advantage might be temporary for many reasons. The most obvious is that there are few products and services that cannot be replicated by the market. Grant identifies *appropriability, transparency, portability and replicability* as the major factors that contribute to superior profits in the long run.

Appropriability

Even if a firm is capable of generating a large financial surplus, it is not always the case that they are able to enjoy it. For example, many professional football clubs can generate revenues from television rights, gate money and sponsorship. Yet the players who take advantage of legal restrictions on contracts appropriate much of this surplus. Similarly, much of the profit generated by the PC industry finds its way back to Intel and Microsoft.

Transparency

Before something can be copied, it is necessary to work out how the original works. At the product level this is often straightforward, but is less so at the organisational level. For example, why is Sony more innovative than other companies, or Proctor and Gamble better at brand management than many others? The answer lies somewhere in the organisational routines, but it is not easy to identify exactly what – even for the companies concerned. Consequently, it is difficult to work out exactly what to copy. Companies that try extensive benchmarking often run into difficulties as they copy the features that are most transparent, rather than most important.

ACTIVITY 1

A service sector firm began comparing financial ratios across the sector for the first time, and realised it was significantly more highly geared than the sector average. It quickly began to reschedule its investment programme, so that it could pay off debt and bring the figures back towards the sector mean. Comment on the quality of management thinking here.

Feedback to this activity is at the end of the chapter.

Replicability

Even when a routine or product is transparent, it is not always possible to copy. This may be because of protective patents, copyrights or the reputation and size of the existing market leader. There is a further problem that understanding how something works does not mean that it can be replicated; after all there is no secret to the skill of juggling with five balls at once, but few can actually do it.

In spite of these things, firms often overestimate the difficulties that a rival might have in replicating their competitive advantage, and are caught out when a smaller, or unknown company, finds alternative technologies and routines and undermines their dominant market position. This issue is dealt with below in discussing the resource based view.

Retaining competitive advantage, year after year, is exceptional in practice and the subject of much debate in the strategic management literature. There are two competing principles that suggest how it might be done:

- the *market orientation theory* – suggests that firms should aim to satisfy known customers effectively ('outside-in approach')

- the *resource based view* – development of resources and core competences will open a wide variety of product/market opportunities ('inside-out approach').

Both approaches agree that sustainable advantage is developed by organisational behaviour (or culture) rather than some transitory advantage in the product or its marketing. However, there is less agreement about what those successful behaviours might be.

1.2 Porter's competitive advantage - market orientation

A sustainable competitive advantage will have been achieved when a firm receives a return on investment that is greater than the norm for its competitors, and when this enhanced return persists for a period long enough to alter the relative standing of the firm among its rivals.

Porter argued that a firm's ability to outperform its competitors lay in its ability to translate its competitive strategy into a competitive advantage. Competitive strategy entails positioning the firm favourably in an industry relative to competitors. Positioning results from choosing one of four competitive strategies - differentiation, low cost leadership, focus differentiation, or focus low cost leadership. Competitive advantage, the achievement of above-average industry profitability, is garnered by differentiating (i.e., offering some uniqueness valued by customers), or by being the lowest cost producer in the industry. In making the choice of being a differentiator or low cost producer, a firm must consider five competitive forces - the bargaining power of customers, the bargaining power of suppliers, the intensity of rivalry amongst firms in the industry, the threat of substitute products, and the threat of new entrants into the industry.

In this traditional view, sustainability arises from the sources and number of cost or differentiation advantages. Cost advantages that are sustainable include entry or mobility barriers such as economies of scale and proprietary learning.

Sustainable differentiation advantages include a unique activity or product valued by customers that competitors cannot easily imitate. The competitive advantage is more sustainable the greater the number of sources of cost or differentiation advantages.

Thus, in this framework, gaining competitive advantage is determined primarily by responding effectively to industry-specific requirements.

However, when we look more carefully at the significance of costs we find that costs arise for a business because it acquires **resources** (people/ machines/buildings), builds an **organisation** to mobilise and co-ordinate them, creates **capabilities** and **competencies**, creates brand names, creates a **reputation**, establishes positions in markets, creates firm specific knowledge, acquires patents, creates supply networks, creates relationships, creates a portfolio of strategic actions/ policies and so on.

These **benefits** are the business's assets.

- Organisational assets
- Positional assets
- Knowledge assets
- Network assets
- Brand assets/ reputation assets
- Capabilities/competencies (such as for product development/ marketing/ innovation/cost management)
- Relational assets
- Patents

Low cost/differentiation may indeed be the proximate cause of competitive advantage but it cannot be the ultimate source. Low cost positions, superior quality, speed to market, or whatever, **must come from something or other the organisation has or does.** For example, Nokia's or Dell's superior returns come ultimately from something (scarce and hard to make more of) that allows them to do things which enable them to offer a better 'value for money' proposition to consumers. But what things exactly?

This question was answered in the 1990s when the **capabilities/competencies** approach emerged as a 'new orthodoxy' leading to a distinctive **'resource based view'** of the firm and approach to strategy.

1.3 The resource based view (RBV)

More recently, attention has shifted to focus on the organisation's capabilities and assets or resource endowments.

Barney outlines the popular RBV framework specifying the source and conditions of competitive advantage and sustainable competitive advantage. A firm's resources (e.g., assets, capabilities, competencies, processes) are considered the source of both competitive advantage and sustained competitive advantage. A firm possesses a competitive advantage if it has resources that are rare (i.e., are not possessed by many firms) and valuable (i.e., permit the firm to respond effectively or efficiently to environmental conditions). The competitive advantage is considered sustainable if those resources are also non-imitable (i.e., cannot be easily duplicated by competitors), non-substitutable (i.e., other resources cannot perform the same function), and non-transferable (i.e., cannot be acquired in the marketplace).

Thus, compared to the traditional view, the RBV shifts the locus of competitive advantage from external forces (i.e., the industry) to internal factors (i.e., a firm's resources).

Barney recognises that depending on the unit of analysis – the firm or the industry - competitive advantage can be defined differently. He prefers to view competitive advantage using the firm as the unit of analysis and offers two different definitions.

- ' ...a firm is said to have a competitive advantage when it is engaging in activities that increase its efficiency or effectiveness in ways that competing firms are not, regardless of whether those other firms are in a particular firm's industry'

' ....firms that generate higher returns than were expected by stockholders (at constant level of risk) have a competitive advantage. This definition of competitive advantage is often called an economic rent'

The main themes of resource based approaches are shown in the diagram below:

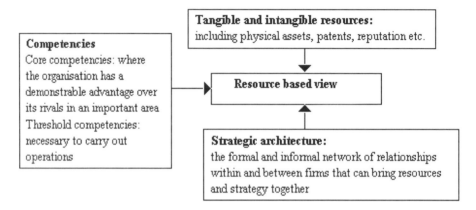

1.4 Critical success factors

Customers buy a product or service because they see the features it possesses as providing more value for money than alternatives on offer. Those features that must be present for an offer to appear credible and win sales are termed the critical offer features.

It is important to consider critical offer features, since competing well today provides the wherewithal to establish a strong future position. However, it is also vital to look beyond the critical offer features to the fundamentals of the organisation's operations - the sources of the critical offer features required in the future. All competitive arenas will have associated with them some or critical success factors that are very significant for doing business there. These significant operating factors will be different in different competitive arenas. For example, during the 1960s and 1970s economies of scale were critical in steel and shipbuilding; in the 1980s seating/fare management using computer reservation systems was vital for the airlines. Any organisation that was not strong in these critically important factors was competitively disadvantaged. The significant operating factors are the concern of all the organisations in the competitive arena. However, some businesses are better placed with regard to them than others.

An organisation's ability to achieve a strong competitive position hinges on how well its strategic resources support the offer features that are critical to success. These strategic resources are the source of the critical offer features, they are:

- Structural assets - the advantage an organisation enjoys because of the competitive arena eg, organisations located in one country may be beneficiaries of a benign government regime, while ones in other countries may be handicapped.

- Reputation - the way that the market deals with product/service features that customers cannot easily determine for themselves

- Internal architecture - the linkages between resources within an organisation

- External relationships - with its stakeholders eg, e-commerce between suppliers and buyers.

Critical offer features are associated with an offer and allow it to compete effectively. The critical offer features arise from the firm being strongly positioned with respect to the significant operating factors. Underpinning this strong positioning are the strategic resources that a business possesses. One important skill in strategic management is to align the firm's strategic resources with the significant operating factors, and thus be able to provide the necessary critical offer features.

Specific critical offer features will obviously depend on the characteristics of the particular customers being targeted. At the general level, however, critical offer features must provide value for money to customers and be based on an appropriate combination of value and price.

The achievement of the appropriate balance between features and costs is based on the strategic resources that the business has.

- There are only two main ways of providing greater than average offer features - through reputation and through innovation used to improve the product/service.

- There are two main routes to achieving lower than average costs - by using structural assets and through innovation when this is used to improve efficiency.

In the short term the main concern is not with the significant operating factors. These are taken as given because the concern is with providing appropriate critical features. The strategic resources will be able to provide the features if they match the characteristics of the operating environment In the longer term, however, the concerns are very different because the organisation has to consider the future significant operating factors and determine the strategic resources it needs to be successful in this future.

While the leader-manager has to be mindful of developing the strategic resources required for the future, it is also very necessary for them to consider the (present) critical offer features. It is success in the marketplace today that provides the wherewithal to build future assets. The tension between present and future performance is ever present within organisations.

From the point of view of a customer, there are two main dimensions to any offer: its value and its price. Value is not absolute; it is in the eye of the customer or potential customer. Thus value is always perceived value: how useful the customer thinks the offer will be to them

There are two types of feature in an offer that are critical to its acceptability in the market. There are order-qualifying features that must be present in the offer for it to be a credible one, and there are order-winning features that then achieve a sale. It is important to differentiate these two features, since they should be managed very differently.

1.5 Order-qualifying and order winning features

Order-qualifying features are the features of an offer that must be present or there will be no sale at all. A car must have doors that lock, windscreen wipers and lights or no one will buy it. A theatre must have seats and offer a warm environment or it would soon have no patrons.

Order-qualifying features are switches that, when set, prevent a potential customer from 'switching off'. A very important consideration with order-qualifying features is that it is against the interests of the business to supply more than the threshold amount. If the business provided more than the minimum required by the customer, it would cost the business more but with no corresponding extra value perceived by the customer. Providing an extra amount of an order-qualifying feature reduces a business's profits.

In contrast to order-qualifying features -where to be over the threshold is all that is required -order-winning features are such that customer value increases the greater the amount of a positive feature there is or the lower the amount of a negative one. For example, the greater the fuel economy, the more that many customers will value a car; the lower the road noise the greater the satisfaction.

One problem that all businesses have is that over time what were order-winning features become order-qualifying ones. For example, when you go to a supermarket you are provided with free plastic bags at the checkout. At one time this was an order-winning feature, but now you would only remark on the bags if they were not provided. In car manufacture the quality of cars has improved greatly over the last two decades, so much so that the Japanese advantage in quality is of much less significance now than previously; quality differences are no longer critical and other factors such as price have become more significant. This demonstrates the tendency as a market matures for quality to become an order-qualifying feature and for price to become an order-winning feature.

An important way in which an order-winning feature is converted into an order-qualifying feature is when new legislation is enacted or a new, widely acknowledged standard is established. If legislation forced all car manufacturers to put airbags in their cars, then simply having an airbag would not confer any competitive advantage.

Order-qualifying features are features that must be present for an offer to be credible in the marketplace. Yet to provide more of them than are required by the customer represents an unnecessary cost. Thus the management of order-qualifying features is aimed at providing them at the lowest cost and in this the business should seek efficiency. Ford has recognised that it has been providing 'needlessly unique' elements in its cars: for example, it has reduced the number of alternative car horns from 33 to 3, steering wheels from 50 to 3, batteries from 44 to 14 and cigarette lighters from 15 to one.

Order-winning features are very different. The business requirement is to identify the form of the relationship between value and amount that applies to each element of the bundle of features that the organisation is thinking of putting into its offer, and to seek an appropriate combination of the features that balance overall value against the costs of providing it.

2 Learning organisation

2.1 Shared vision and the learning organisation

A vision gives a general sense of direction to the organisation, even if there is not too much attention to detail. A vision enables flexibility to exist in the context of a guiding idea. It ensures that the values of the organisation are in tune with the personal values of the individuals working for it. A cohesive group is typified by having a clear sense of vision, purpose and identity.

A shared vision that is not so forceful as to discourage organisational learning nor filters knowledge which undermines learning was outlined by Peter Senge as one of the five disciplines that individuals and groups should be encouraged to learn to create a learning organisation. The other four are:

- Systems thinking - is the ability to see particular problems as part of a wider whole and to devise appropriate solutions to them.

- Personal learning and growth - individuals should be encouraged to acquire skills and knowledge.

- Mental models - are deeply ingrained assumptions that determine what people think eg, a marketing group may think that price is more important than quality. Learning organisations can use a number of group techniques to make these models explicit and to challenge them.

- Team learning - teams must be trained to learn because there are factors in group dynamics that impede learning.

Organisational learning is the process by which an organisation, like an individual, adapts its behaviour based on experience. For example, when new employees join the firm the formal induction procedures will incorporate previous understanding. Their supervisor, colleagues and subordinates will also give them additional information. This will represent more recent learning, which may become part of the formal knowledge of the firm.

The key features of this type of learning are where the organisation:

- encourages continuous learning and knowledge generation at all levels;

- can transform knowledge into actual behaviour;

- encourages questions and explicitly recognises mistakes as part of the learning process. It tries to resolve any immediate problems and learns from the process;

- practices self development and action-learning. As the organisation learns from its actions, so does the individual;

- recognises that failed answers are as important as successful ones, because they want to find new answers;

- has the processes to move the information/knowledge around; and

- encourages testing and experimentation.

The aim is to design an organisation, which is capable of adapting, changing, developing and transforming itself in response to the needs, wishes and aspirations of people, inside and outside. It is about developing knowledge that can be used perhaps to develop a distinctive competence.

2.2 Systems thinking - the holistic view

A prerequisite for learning is systems thinking. Much thinking in Europe and America has traditionally been reductionist, where an issue is broken down into its constituent parts and the characteristics of these smaller chunks are identified. The assumption is that the whole can be understood by combining the understanding of the parts.

Unfortunately, the whole is often more than the sum of the parts eg, a hand is more than the sum of bones, nerves, muscles and tissue of which it is composed. Surrounding and embedded within the parts are other factors such as organisation and control that make a hand so complex.

A similar situation exists in organisations. A more holistic view is that as well as the sum being greater than the parts, two other aspects of systems thinking are important:

- Interconnectivity - few processes are completely isolated from others around them so the managers must take into consideration the impact of their actions on others

- Feedback - the outputs of the processes at any one time will be affected by the residual influence of past outputs. This is very obvious in relationships - building up a good relationship in one period will result in a better reception for actions in a subsequent period.

2.3   Learning difficulties

According to Peter Senge, there are seven sources of learning disability in organisations which prevent them from attaining their potential - which trap them into 'mediocrity', for example, when they could be achieving 'excellence'.

- 'I am my position'. When asked what they do for a living, most people describe the tasks they perform, not the purposes they fulfil; thus they tend to see their responsibilities as limited to the boundaries of their position. As a result, individuals within departments can be performing efficiently, yet when you put the efforts of several departments together, the result is more poor quality and performance than would have been the case had the various departments pooled their efforts.

- The enemy is out there'. A by-product of 'I am my position', a result of over-identification with the job is the fact that if things go wrong it is all too easy to imagine that somebody else 'out there' was at fault.

- The illusion of taking charge. True learning should lead to proactivity, but too often being proactive can mean that the individual decides to be more active in fighting the enemy out there, trying to destroy rather than to build. Senge states that if we believe the enemy to be 'out there' and we are 'in here', then being proactive is really reactivity in overdrive: true proactive behaviour comes from seeing how our own actions contribute to our problems.

- The fixation on events. Conversations in organisations are dominated by concern about events (last month's sales, who's just been promoted, the new product from our competitor), and this focus inevitably distracts us from seeing the longer-term patterns of change. At one time, concentrating on events was essential to man's survival (you had to worry about whether you had a sabre-toothed tiger over your left shoulder) but today, according to Senge, 'the primary threats to our survival, both of our organisations and of our societies, come not from sudden events but from slow, gradual processes'.

- The parable of the boiled frog. Poor adaptation to gradually building threats to survival is so pervasive in systems studies of corporate failure that it has given rise to the parable of the boiled frog. If you place a frog in a pot of boiling water, it will immediately try to scramble out; but if you place the frog in room temperature water, he will stay put. If you heat the water gradually, the frog will do nothing until he boils: this is because 'the frog's internal apparatus for sensing threats to survival is geared to sudden changes in his environment, not to slow, gradual changes'.

- The delusion of learning from experience. We learn best from experience, but we never experience the results of our most important and significant decisions.

Indeed, we never know what the outcomes would have been had we done something else.

- The myth of the management team. All too often, the management 'team' is not a team at all, but is a collection of individuals competing for power and resources, forming short-term alliances when it suits them, looking for someone to blame when things go wrong. Chris Argyris believes that 'Most management teams break down under pressure. The team may function quite well with routine issues. But when they confront complex issues that may be embarrassing or threatening, the team spirit seems to go to pot.'

3 Alternative performance measures

3.1 Standards and control

Performance measurement aims to establish how well something or somebody is doing in relation to the planned activity and desired results. The 'something' may be a machine, a factory, a subsidiary company or an organisation as a whole. The 'somebody' may be an individual employee, a manager, or a group of people.

Performance measurement is a vital part of *control*: it generates the results which are fed back for comparison with objectives.

Any control system should have three main components:

- The establishment of standards or targets to express planned performance;
- The measurement of actual performance and comparison with target;
- Follow-up action to correct adverse results or exploit favourable variances.

Performance evaluation can be:

- quantitative, eg. reject work percentage, time delays, cost overruns, sales call ratios; or
- qualitative, ie. judgemental, eg. staff morale, organisational climate, environmental protection, product appeal.

Even with qualitative factors, attempts should be made to include quantitative measures where possible, even if these cover only part of the total. For example, staff morale may be indicated by labour turnover or absenteeism rates.

Although not exhaustive, the following Table illustrates how performance evaluation can be used to measure actual achievement against key strategic planning elements.

Key planning element	Performance indicator
Financial results	
Profitability	Ratio analysis
Cost structures	Cost variance analysis
Cash flow	Cost and revenue budgets
Investment returns	Capital budget and post-investment audit
Marketing results	
Marketing initiatives	New product acceptance, Portfolio analysis, Advertising response analysis
Competitive position	
Sales effectiveness	Market share, Market segment analysis, Position audit
Sales efficiency	Sales per head/call/invoice value
	Calls per day/cost per order
Research and development	Number and value of commercial viable new products, Quality standards

| *People factors* | Succession plans, Promotion success, Labour productivity, Labour turnover, absenteeism |
| *Resource usage* | Capacity fill statements, Down time, Materials usage and wastage |

3.2 Performance measures

One of the difficulties in strategic market management is developing performance indicators that convincingly represent the long-term prospects for the organisation. The temptation is to focus on the short-term profitability measures and to reduce investment in new products and brand image that have long-term

The concept of net present value does represent long-term profit stream, but often it is simply not very operational. It often provides neither a criterion for decision-making nor a useful performance measure. It is somewhat analogous to preferring £6 million to £4 million. The real question involves determining which strategic alternative will generate £6 million and which will generate £4 million.

Thus, it is necessary to develop performance measures that will reflect long-term viability and health. The focus should be on the assets and skills that underlie the current and future strategy and its critical success factors.

- What are the key assets and skills for a business during the planning horizon?

- What strategic dimensions are most crucial: to become more competitive with respect to product offerings, to develop new products, or to become more productive?

- These types of questions can help identify performance areas that a business should examine. Answers will vary depending on the situation but they will often include customer satisfaction/brand loyalty, product/service quality, brand/firm associations, relative cost, new product activity, manager/employee capability, and performance.

Market share - is often regarded by marketers as strategically significant, and perhaps more important than profits in the short term. Japanese companies, in particular, often build share rather than maximise profit (although they rarely, if ever, run on very low margins to achieve this result). There are several reasons why the indicator should be used in this way, the most significant is the relationship between relative market share and relative cost.

You will recall that the Boston Consulting Group Matrix relates cash generation to relative market share. The argument is that if costs are related to volumes, then the firm with the highest relative market share will have proportionally lower costs. The scale of the cost advantage will depend upon the experience curve effect and the size of the relative advantage.

A further reason for treating market share as a strategic target concerns its importance in establishing market presence. High market share enables a company to dominate partners, and promotional aspects will be easier with a well-established brand name.

Customer Satisfaction/Brand Loyalty - perhaps the most important asset of many firms is the loyalty of the customer base. Measures of sales and market share are useful but crude indicators of how customers really feel about a firm. Customer satisfaction and brand loyalty are much more sensitive and provide diagnostic value as well.

- First, problems and causes of dissatisfaction that may motivate customers to change brands or firms should be identified.

- Second, often the most sensitive and insightful information comes from those who have decided to leave a brand or firm. Thus, 'exit interviews' for customers who have 'left' a brand can be very productive.

- Third, there is a big difference between a brand or firm being liked and the absence of dissatisfaction. The size and intensity of the customer group that truly 'likes' a brand or firm should be known.

- Fourth, measures should be tracked over time and compared with those of competitors. It is the relative comparisons and changes that are most important.

Product and service quality - a product (or service) and its components should be critically and objectively compared both with competition and with customer expectation and needs. How good a value is it? Can it really deliver superior performance? How does it compare with competitor offerings? How will it compare with competitor offerings in the future given competitive innovations? One common failing is to avoid tough comparisons with a realistic as- assessment of competitors' offerings now and those that will likely be soon announced.

Product and service quality are usually based on several critical dimensions that should be identified and measured over time. For example, an automobile firm can have measures concerning defects, ability to perform to specifications, durability and ability to repair. A bank might be concerned with waiting time, accuracy of transactions, and making the customer experience friendly and positive. A computer manufacturer can examine relative performance specifications, and product reliability as reflected by repair data. A business that requires better marketing of a good product line is very different from one that has basic product deficiencies.

Measures of customer satisfaction and brand loyalty are much more sensitive and provide diagnostic value as well.

Brand/firm associations - an often overlooked asset of a brand or firm is what customers think of it - what are its associations? What is its perceived quality? Perceived quality, of course, can be very different from actual quality .It can be based on past experience with prior products or services and quality cues such as retailer types, pricing strategies, packaging, advertising, and a profile of the typical customer. Is a brand or firm regarded as expert in a product or technology area (such as designing and making sailboats)? Innovative? Expensive? For the country club set? Is it associated with a country, a user type, or an application area (like racing)? Such bases of positioning strategies can be key strategic assets for a brand or firm.

Associations can be monitored in a gross but effective way by talking to groups of customers informally on a regular basis. The identification of changes in important associations will likely emerge from such efforts. More structured tools are also available. A brand or firm can be scaled on its key dimensions using a representative sample of customers. Key dimensions can then be tracked over time.

Relative cost - a careful cost analysis of a product (or service) and its components, which can be critical when a strategy is dependent on achieving a cost advantage or cost parity, can involve tearing down competitors' products and preparing a detailed analysis of their systems.

If a component such as the braking system in a car or a bank's teller operation is both more expensive and inferior to that of the competition, a strategic problem requiring change may exist. An analysis could show, however, that the component is such a small item both in terms of cost and customer impact that it should be ignored. If the component is competitively superior, however, a cost-reduction program may not be the only appropriate strategy .A value analysis, in which the component's value to the customer is quantified, may suggest that the point of superiority could support a price increase or promotion campaign.

If, on the other hand, a component is less expensive than that of the competition but inferior, a value analysis might suggest that it be de- emphasize. Thus, for a car with a cost advantage but handling disadvantage, a company might de-emphasize its driving performance and position it as an economy car. An alternative is to upgrade the relative rating with respect to this component. Conversely, if a component is both less expensive and superior, a value analysis may suggest that the component be emphasized, perhaps playing a key role in positioning and promotion strategies.

3.3 Financial and non-financial indicators

A 'balanced scorecard' approach is required when evaluating performance in exam questions. You should recall from your previous studies that performance evaluation is required on the key success factors (KSFs – non-financial areas such as quality, flexibility and innovation) since these areas *ensure* success whereas performance evaluation on the financial areas simply *measures* success.

There are a number of key financial ratios, which the examiner uses for financial performance evaluation.

- Return on net assets (RONA)
- Return on sales (ROS)
- Gearing
- Gross profit margin
- Asset turnover
- Overheads as a percentage of sales
- Market value added

It is useful to memorise material by concentrating on key words and building a story around the key words. For example imagine going to a party to meet the two girls *Rona* and *Ros*. They wear strange *gear,* which makes them look *gross.* They have some attractive *assets* but are *expensive (overheads)* to take out and their company does not *add value* to the evening.

The financial ratios are calculated as follows.

$$RONA = \frac{\text{operating income}}{\text{net assets}}$$

$$ROS = \frac{\text{operating income}}{\text{sales revenue}}$$

$$Gearing = \frac{\text{debt}}{\text{equity}}$$

$$\text{Gross profit margin} = \frac{\text{gross profit}}{\text{sales revenue}}$$

$$\text{Asset turnover} = \frac{\text{sales}}{\text{net assets}}$$

$$\text{Overhead/expense margin} = \frac{\text{overheads}}{\text{sales revenue}}$$

$$\text{Market value added} = \frac{\text{market value}}{\text{net assets}} \text{ or net assets} - \text{market value}$$

The above ratios are used by strategists to make three critical comparisons.

1. Comparing the firm's performance over different time periods

2. Comparing the firm's performance with that of competitors

3. Comparing the firm's performance with industry averages.

Illustration

QA Design Limited (QA) – An example case study

QA Design Limited (QA) is a fast growing company specialising in the design, artwork, copywriting and production of high quality catalogues and brochures. The company was formed only ten years ago by Melissa Foret, a charismatic art and design graduate, and has grown largely as a direct result of her personal leadership. The business focus at QA has been constant throughout this period – quality, client responsiveness and innovation in both design and the use of associated information technology. When once asked for her view of the mission for QA, Melissa simply replied 'to win'.

QA has a staff of about 40, most of whom are graduates, and with an average age of about 30 years. The company operates through a very loose management structure which is essentially based on project design teams forming and reforming in response to the nature and flow of work received from clients. There are some dedicated functions, namely, the sales account executives who manage a portfolio of clients, and the buyers who commission print production when design has been completed.

QA's growth to date has been entirely organic, making use of high levels of profitability, high levels of retained profits and an extensive use of operating leases for design technology equipment. A summary of the 1994 financial results can be found in Table 1. About 70 per cent of turnover arises from sub-contracting out the printing work, which arises as a result of design, and about 30 per cent for the design work itself. QA aims to make about a 5 per cent operating profit on clients' print production. Print production is sub-contracted to a number of printing businesses based usually on the lowest tender price, subject to clear-cut quality and delivery guidelines.

Melissa Foret is of the view that the next stage in QA's development must be to move into the actual printing business itself, so integrating design and production completely and maximising value chain profitability. She believes that this process of vertical integration should be carried out by acquisition and has targeted Quick-Fix-Print Limited (QFP), a family-run printing business, as a prime candidate for takeover.

QFP has been in existence for over 40 years and the present managing director and majority shareholder has for some time been wishing to sell the business and retire. QFP has some 250 employees, mainly in operational areas such as stores, job layout and machine set-up, print machine operation, maintenance, packaging and dispatch. Employees are all trade union members. Current summarised financial results for QFP and average results for similar printing businesses are provided in Table 1. These results are typical of performance in recent years for this sector of the printing industry, although QFP's results have shown a steady deterioration over the last few years. About 5 per cent of QFP's turnover arises from print jobs already sub-contracted from QA.

A preliminary acquisition agreement has been reached which values QFP at a multiple of six times current pre-tax profits. QFP's balance sheet values are seen as broadly realistic, if a little over optimistic, and reflect a going concern situation. The fixed assets are largely represented by printing machinery, much of which was acquired some years ago. The acquisition price is to be paid as to 40 per cent on takeover and the remaining 60 per cent in equal instalments over the next six years. QA plans to meet 10 per cent of the initial 40 per cent payment through existing cash resources, and to raise the remaining 30 per cent through a medium-term bank loan secured against the assets of both QA and QFP. The remaining balance of the purchase price will be paid through operating cashflows generated by the amalgamated businesses.

You are a management consultant who has been approached by the auditors of QA. The auditors are a small five partner practice and are seeking your advice on the implications of the acquisition for their client. The auditors are concerned about a number of issues, not least of which is the risk to QA which would arise from such a major acquisition. Although QA is a very successful business, the auditors are not aware of any formalised strategy that has been either adopted or agreed by Melissa Foret and the management team at QA.

Table 1 Summary financial data (all figures in £ millions)

	QA	QFP	Printing industry average
Sales	10.5	20.3	30.5
Cost of sales	7.2	14.6	19.6
Gross profit	3.3	5.7	10.9
Expenses	2.2	4.9	7.5
Net profit	1.1	0.8	3.4
Fixed assets	1.2	8.4	17.2
Current assets	3.6	5.3	6.3
Current liabilities	1.3	2.2	3.3
Net assets	3.5	11.5	20.2

Refer to the case study QA Design to see how some of the financial ratios can be used in answering the question.

There will be alternative approaches to answering the question. The following illustration is only a suggested approach to using some of the financial data to support the points made.

The table below shows key financial ratios calculated from the data given in QA Design. The ratios illustrate the different financial characteristics of the design and printing industries. The design-based business operates on lower profit margins but has a high activity ratio (sales/fixed assets) giving a very high return on net assets (RONA). The printing industry is much more capital intensive and operates on higher margins but with a low activity ratio. It follows that expansion into or expansion of a business in the printing industry will require significant levels of new capital investment.

Key financial ratios

	QA Design	Quick-Fix-Print	Printing industry average
Gross margin	31.43%	28.08%	35.74%
Expenses ratio	20.95%	24.14%	24.59%
Net profit ratio	10.48%	3.94%	11.15%
Fixed asset turnover	8.75	2.42	1.77
Working capital turnover	4.57	6.55	10.17
Net asset turnover	3.0	1.77	1.51
Return on net assets	31.43%	6.96%	16.83%

The risk elements associated with the acquisition are considered under the categories of business risk and financial risk.

Business risk factors

- *Age of QFP technology* From the financial ratios (see table below) it would appear that QFP is operating with old technology showing a low balance sheet value (ie written down value). For example, QFP is operating an activity ratio on fixed assets of 2.42 compared to 1.77 for the printing industry average.

- *QFP turnaround strategy* QFP is suffering from low profitability (28.08% gross margin as against 35.74% industry average). To turnaround QFP will require substantial investment of finance and management time. The acquisition does not make sense if QFP's RONA of 6.96% cannot be substantially improved to a level approaching the industry average of 16.83%.

Financial risk factors

- *Gearing* At an agreed price of £4.8 million (six times pre-tax profits of £0.8 million) the long-term loan element of £1.44 million (30 per cent of purchase price) of the financing package will significantly increase the gearing ratio for the newly constituted business.

- *Financing payments* The current aggregate annual profits of QA and QPA (before tax and interest) are £1.9 million. The new business must generate sufficient net cashflows to meet six annual payments of £0.48 million each.

- *Capital expenditure* It is assumed that capital investment will be required to bring QFP's RONA closer to the industry average. If the required level of new investment reduces QFP's activity ratio to the industry average of 1.51 then this indicates a guideline figure of almost £2 million additional investment (increase in net assets from £11.5m to £13.4m).

- *Valuation* Although the acquisition price is significantly below balance sheet value there is always potential valuation risk when an unknown business is taken over. A clear view of asset and liability values is essential if a coherent financial plan is to be put into place.

Non-financial performance evaluation

The figure below provides a useful summary, which you should memorise.

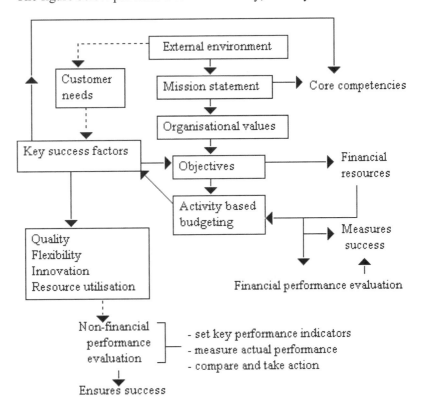

You know by now that an analysis of the external environment is a key aspect of the strategic planning process. The mission statement, organisational values and objectives will be determined and set as a result of this analysis.

The KSFs will also be identified from an analysis of the external environment. In particular, an analysis of customer needs will identify the activities, which the firm should concentrate on to ensure quality of product and flexibility of service.

Financial resource needs to be allocated into the key (value added) activities to ensure that the organisation is competent in its KSFs. Activity based budgeting (ABB) is a resource allocation system designed to achieve this aim.

To ensure that the organisation is performing at a high level (ie competent) in its KSFs, a (control) performance evaluation system needs to be designed and implemented on these areas. The following steps are therefore required.

- Set key non-financial performance indicator targets on the KSFs. This should involve 'benchmarking' the targets set with the competition.

- Measure the actual performance achieved against the target set.

- If actual performance is below the target set, strategies need to be implemented to bring actual performance in line with the targets.

The following illustration shows how non-financial performance measurement assists with the management of business units.

ZXP is a smaller family business, employing some 200 staff, making a limited range of farm animal vaccines. Until recently, its output was given entirely to 'own brand' products and the company never had any reason to develop or market its own products.

A change of generation at top management level led to a more ambitious programme, with limited research and development and manufacturing of foreign products under licence. Since the family did not wish to risk losing control of the company, the new ventures were funded by borrowing. This has raised gearing to a very high level for a company in its position, and the extra capital has not yet generated an increase in profits. A recent development in the industry has found a way to replace much of the company's existing product range with biotechnology-based products that are chemically equivalent. Some of the company's competitors have made the switch, and found it cheaper and more reliable to produce using biotechnology.

ACTIVITY 2

ZXP is a smaller family business, employing some 200 staff, making a limited range of farm animal vaccines. Until recently, its output was given entirely to 'own brand' products and the company never had any reason to develop or market its own products.

A change of generation at top management level led to a more ambitious programme, with limited research and development and manufacturing of foreign products under licence. Since the family did not wish to risk losing control of the company, the new ventures were funded by borrowing. This has raised gearing to a very high level for a company in its position, and the extra capital has not yet generated an increase in profits. A recent development in the industry has found a way to replace much of the company's existing product range with biotechnology-based products that are chemically equivalent. Some of the company's competitors have made the switch, and found it cheaper and more reliable to produce using biotechnology.

What will the performance indicators show?

What do you think happened to the company?

Feedback to this activity is at the end of the chapter.

Illustration

The CiniCentre

The CiniCentre was established in 1960 as a charitable trust to promote and increase public awareness of the cinema as an entertainment and cultural medium. The CiniCentre is managed through a part time board of governors drawn from representatives of the film industry, from government nominees and from elected nominees of the membership of the CiniCentre Film Institute. The board of governors delegate executive responsibility to a chief executive officer (CEO). CiniCentre has five major activity areas or operational divisions each of which has its own manager. These are as follows.

- The multi-screen Film Theatre (FT), which provides performances for the general public of new releases, classic films and minority interest films.

- The Museum of the Cinema (MoC), which provides a permanent exhibition of the history and development of the film industry.

- The Globe restaurant, bars and cafeteria, which are open to cinema goers and to the general public.

- The Film Archive Unit (FAU), which is, concerned with the transfer of old film archive material to video as a means of long-term preservation.

- The CiniCentre Film Institute (CFI), membership of which is open to members of the public by annual subscription. Members receive preferential bookings to events, seat discounts and a free copy of CiniCentre's monthly magazine *Film Fan*. The magazine and associated publishing activities also form part of the responsibilities of the film institute.

In addition to the five business units there are also three support units, which provide common support services as follows.

- Administration – office services, finance, personnel, computing.

- Buildings – building maintenance, cleaning, security, repairs and renewals.

- Maintenance – technical and technician support for the repair and maintenance of capital equipment. The three support units come under the control of a head of support services.

The CiniCentre is partly funded by government grant and partly funded from its own commercial activities. However, as part of government policy to reduce the contribution to the arts, the grant to the CiniCentre will, over the next three years, be reduced by 20 per cent. A financial summary of the current year's operations of the CiniCentre is provided in Table 3.5.

John Umbasa has recently taken over as chief executive officer of CiniCentre. He has been recruited from a senior position in an international media business. The board of governors at CiniCentre were directed by the Government to bring in an external CEO as a result of a series of management problems, which have attracted considerable adverse publicity. These have included the following.

- A failure to stay within government financial guidelines of not operating an annual financial deficit

- Press criticism about the loss of archive film due to the failure to speed up the transfer to video tape

- Further press criticism on the recent imposition of an admission charge to the Museum of the Cinema

- Reports of poor quality service and expensive food in the Globe restaurants

- Persistent labour relations problems with the public sector staff trade union which represents almost all the non-managerial museum, film theatre, clerical and catering staff

- Complaints from the CFI membership that the film season has concentrated too much on popular income earning mainstream films with a subsequent fall in the number of showings of classic and non-English language films.

John Umbasa realises that he faces major challenges in revitalising the CiniCentre organisation and dealing with the proposed sharp reduction in government funding. He believes that what the CiniCentre needs is a vision of its role and priorities plus management control systems which link performance to clear-cut divisional objectives. He has offered you a one-year management consultancy contract to assist him.

Summary financial data (all figures in £m)

	Commercial income	*Direct costs*	*Apportioned indirect costs*	*Surplus/ (Deficit)*
Film Theatre	1.20	1.70	0.86	(1.36)
Museum	0.25	2.20	1.11	(3.06)
Globe catering	1.70	0.90	0.45	0.35
Film Archive	0.00	3.20	1.62	(4.82)
CFI	2.30	1.90	0.96	(0.56)
	5.45	9.90	5.00	(9.45)
Government grant				9.00
Surplus/(Deficit)				(0.45)

Financial performance measurement is crucial in measuring efficiency (conversion of inputs to outputs) but is not sufficient on its own to measure outputs (relating outcomes to goals). There is a consensus that management need a range of performance assessment indicators to measure not simply financial health but also perspectives such as customers, business processes (where do we add value?) and organisational learning (innovation and improvement). The term 'balanced scorecard' has been used to describe this wider perspective of performance measurement.

Carefully selected performance measurement indicators (PMIs) could help deal with the problems at CiniCentre by setting division and support activities targets which link to the outcomes established through the strategic management process. Suitable examples for each of the divisions could be as follows.

- The multi-screen Film Theatre: percentage of minority films to overall showings, percentage of seat capacity filled for each film showing, number of showings per period.

- The Museum of the Cinema: visitor profiles (numbers, type), number of special exhibitions per period, visitor satisfaction measures.

- The Globe restaurant, bars and cafeteria: customer satisfaction indicators, quality indicators of food/meals, change/rotation of menus, comparative value for money surveys, time taken to serve in non self serve areas.

- The Film Archive Unit: feet of film archived per period, archive machine capacity utilisation, film archived per staff member, time taken between film receipt to film archived, loss of archived film, archive quality.

- The CiniCentre Film Institute: membership growth, response time to a member query (for post/fax/phone), member satisfaction survey data, advertising to editorial ratio for the magazine, editorial quality indicators.

4 Strategic failure

Strategic failure in a business occurs when a company cannot achieve a satisfactory return on capital over the longer term. The issue is more problematic in sectors, or economies, where profitability is not an issue. For example, in the former Soviet Bloc, the economy simply does not identify poorly performing companies. For not-for-profit organisations, the issue is usually one of funding, and failure is indicated by the inability to raise sufficient funds to carry out activities effectively.

Although stated in financial terms, the reasons behind such failure are rarely financial, but seem to have more to do with a firm's ability to adapt to changes in its environment. In this section, we are going to look at some commonly observed reasons for failure, and look at the cultural causes of such problems.

4.1 Causes of strategic failure

A major study (Grinyer, Mayes et al., 1988) examined reasons why firms experience decline. Chief among the reasons found (in order of frequency) in the study were:

- adverse changes in total market demand
- intensification of competition
- high cost structure
- poor financial controls
- weak management
- failure of a large project
- poor marketing effort
- poor acquisitions
- poor quality.

Clearly, some of these are not, in themselves, strategic issues. Much can be done, by strong management accounting, to reduce costs, improve financial information and controls, improve project management and quality control systems, without changing strategy. It is always worth repeating the adage that strategic management builds on good operations management. No strategy can compensate for operational inefficiency in the long run.

However, many of the items listed involve changes in the market place, and the way that competition is carried out. Strategy is chiefly about adapting the firm to such changes, and strategic failure results when the organisation does not change as quickly as the market.

4.2 Z scores – a financial technique for predicting failure

Z scores are an attempt to anticipate strategic and financial failures by examining company financial statements. The Z score is created by weighting several ratios depending upon industry sector, but commonly including measures of profitability, working capital, financial risk and liquidity. Many financial databases calculate the figure automatically, and display it with their company profiles.

The danger figure for the Z score is zero. Negative, or very low scores, might be taken to predict that the company concerned is in danger of strategic failure. Failure in this case would lead to insolvency, major financial changes (disposal of assets, restructuring, emergency rights issue) or take-over. In one study of 152 cases of corporate failure, only two had positive Z scores (and in one case at least, the financial information on which the Z score was based proved to be unreliable).

Z scores are therefore quite effective in forecasting failure. However, in a few cases the companies only reported a negative Z score immediately before the failure, while some companies with negative scores seemed to recover without drama.

The lesson, as with all such indicators, should be that a weak Z score should prompt further investigation into the cause of the low score and possible solutions. Actions based on Z scores alone are likely to be misguided in a significant number of cases.

4.3   Argenti's failure model

From historical data on a wide range of actual cases, J Argenti developed a model, which is intended to predict the likelihood of company failure. The model is based on calculating scores for a company based on

- defects of the company eg, autocratic chief executive, passive board and lack of budgetary control

- management mistakes eg, overtrading (expanding faster than cash funding), gearing - high bank overdrafts/loans, failure of large project jeopardises the company

- the symptoms of failure - deteriorating ratios, creative accounting - signs of window-dressing, declining morale and declining quality

For each of the scores there is a 'danger mark'.

4.4   Other indicators of financial difficulties

You should not think that ratio analysis of published accounts and score analysis are the only ways of spotting that a company might be running into financial difficulties. There are other possible indicators too. Some of this information might be given to you in an exam case study, so it is worth being on the alert.

- Information in the published accounts, for example:

    (i)   very large increases in intangible fixed assets;

    (ii)   a worsening cash and cash equivalents position shown by the cash flow statement;

    (iii)   very large contingent liabilities;

    (iv)   important post balance sheet events.

- Information in the chairman's report and the directors' report (including warnings, evasions, changes in the composition of the board since last year).

- Information in the press (about the industry and the company or its competitors).

- Information about environmental or external matter. You should have a good idea as to the type of environmental or competitive factors that affect firms.

4.5   Going concern evaluation

A useful source of guidance on the troubled company is available in the form of an auditing guideline formerly issued by the accountancy bodies and entitled *The auditor's considerations in respect of going concern*. (This document has been replaced by the Auditing Practices Board Statement of Auditing Standards 130, but is still valuable in this context).

Of particular practical assistance are the paragraphs identifying possible symptoms of going concern problems. Examples are outlined below. Again, if you come across any of these features in a case study the warning bells should start to sound.

- Symptoms indicating an inability to meet debts as they fall due eg, adverse financial figures or ratios, recurring operating losses, financing to a considerable extent out of overdue suppliers and other creditors (for example, VAT, PAYE, National Insurance), heavy dependence on short-term finance for long-term needs, working capital deficiencies, low liquidity rates, over-gearing, in the form of high or increasing debt to equity ratios and under-capitalisation, particularly if there is a deficiency of share capital

- Borrowings in excess of limits imposed by debenture trust deeds

- Default on loans or similar agreements

- Dividends in arrears

- Restrictions placed on usual trade terms

- Excessive or obsolete stock

- Long overdue debtors

- Non-compliance with statutory capital requirements

- Deterioration of relationship with bankers

- Necessity of seeking new sources or methods of obtaining finance

- Continuing use of old fixed assets as there are no funds available to replace them

- The size and content of the order book

- Potential losses on long-term contracts

Other factors not necessarily suggesting inability to meet debts

Internal matters

- loss of key management or staff

- significantly increasing stock levels

- work stoppages or other labour difficulties

- substantial dependence on the success of a particular project or particular asset

- excessive reliance on the success of a new product

- uneconomic long-term commitments

External matters

- legal proceedings that may put a company out of business

- loss of a key franchise or patent

- loss of a principal supplier or customer

- the undue influence of a market dominant competitor

- political risks

- technical developments which render a key product obsolete

- frequent financial failures of enterprises in the same industry

4.6 Reasons for failing to adapt - weak leadership

Reasons for failing to adapt include:

- complacency

- risk averse decision making

- economies of production and administration

- limited opportunities for innovation and diversification

- limited mental models.

Complacency is a charge frequently levelled at managers, and there are, no doubt, occasions when senior managers convince themselves that everything is fine, when it is not. However, the charge is frequently made with the benefit of hindsight, rather than observation of the efforts made by those managers at the time. There are several entirely sensible reasons why managers are reluctant to make large strategic changes.

Firstly, it is not possible to quantify the risks of making a major change. Several studies have shown that predicting changes in the environment and devising appropriate counter measures is among the most difficult things a manager is required to do. Only in hindsight are the dynamics clear. It is worth remembering that case studies are written backwards, where a known outcome is traced back to its origins. As Kierkegaard said, 'history proceeds forwards but it is understood'.

Faced with such difficulties, managers are reluctant to make large-scale changes that might risk increasing the problems, and might be very difficult to implement adequately anyway. Rather, they select options of relatively limited impact – a process referred to as logical incrementalism, introduced in an earlier chapter.

Secondly, changes to production can reduce the opportunities for economies of scale, and raise the firm's cost base. There is always a temptation to try to retain share, by reducing price, rather than make fundamental changes to a product of its method of production and risk escalating costs.

Thirdly, it may be that management is entirely aware that the strategic situation is worsening, but be unable to see opportunities to innovate or diversify out of trouble. It must be accepted that there are situations where there are no feasible solutions, and there might be better uses of the shareholders' funds than attempts to turn around the business.

Finally, a large part of the problem is caused by the mental models of those who have control of the strategy within an organisation. A mental model is the way that individuals think about problems and issues. In the next section, we look at Johnson's notion of strategic drift, where the firm's mental models stop the company from changing quickly enough to keep up with environmental change.

4.7   Strategic drift

Strategic drift is a term devised by Johnson (1988) to describe as a warning to those who champion the idea of strategy emerging as a series of logical, incremental steps. Johnson argues that this limits the rate of change to the speed at which management might feel comfortable, which has many advantages (particularly in implementation), but might be inappropriate in periods when the environment moves very quickly.

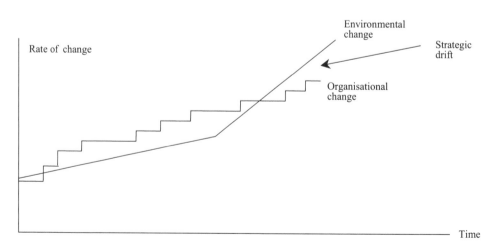

Strategic drift

In the figure above, the organisation takes a series of logical, incremental steps that enables it to change ahead of the market, developing a competitive advantage. However, the rate of change in the market place speeds up, and the firm's incrementalist approach is not enough to maintain its advantage, and it is left behind. At this point, the firm must abandon the approach, and adopt radical, discontinuous change in order to stay with the market leaders.

Johnson's main argument is that the reasons for failing to increase the tempo of change are largely cultural, rather than technical. He argues that the corporate paradigm, as revealed by its cultural web and described in an earlier chapter, is the biggest constraint on strategic thinking and action. It is important to see that management cannot change a corporate paradigm, partly because they are themselves caught up in it, and partly because some elements of it are not amenable to management techniques.

Logical incrementalism is successful because it does not challenge the underlying paradigm, allowing change to take place relatively smoothly. More revolutionary change must damage the paradigm before it can begin.

4.8 The Icarus paradox

Miller (1990) produced a study which suggested that outstanding companies often encountered difficulties even though the environmental change that they were facing was not especially severe.

His key conclusion was not that excellent firms became complacent or inattentive to what they were doing, as one might have thought. Rather, he observed that firms continued to improve and develop those things that made them excellent, but in ways that had little commercial value. This became known as the 'Icarus Paradox'.

In short, the mental models of the managers became focused on a limited range of activities, while other insufficient attention was paid to other activities. Miller identified four ideal types of such activity.

Craftsman to Tinkerer - in these companies, a firm builds upon its competences in producing quality products, but the abilities of the firm run ahead of what the market wants, or is willing to pay for.

An example of this can be found in the Scottish knitware industry, that initially dismissed the innovative, colourful and well marketed competitors from Europe on the grounds that the construction techniques used were inferior.

Pioneers are innovative companies that lose sight of the market and its requirements. Many companies in the IT sector invest in hardware innovation well in excess of the requirements of the software. By the time software has improved, and the innovative hardware become worth paying for, other hardware producers have caught up and are able to compete on cost.

Salesman to Drifter

Salesman firms have their competence in brand management. They usually offer a portfolio of respected products that are well managed and distributed. Corporate culture is usually strong, with great emphasis on customers and customer service. *However, they may concentrate overmuch on customer service and their own image, and fail to maintain the strength of the brand themselves.* That is, they will tend to use their marketing ability to overcome shortcomings in their products. Over time, competitor's products achieve recognition, and only those customers needing high levels of customer service will remain loyal.

Builder to Imperialist

In the fourth of Miller's Icarus models, a successful company expands beyond the abilities of management to monitor and control the activities that were used to grow the company in the first place. Senior managers retreat behind strategic plans, monitoring systems and 'management by pseudo science' instead of dealing directly with key aspects of business growth and development. Corporate attention moves from strengthening SBUs to corporate dealing in companies and shares, and the resulting conglomerate no longer adds value to its parts. There have been many promising business empires that have arisen impressively, and crashed overnight, in this way.

The important point to notice is that, in all of Miller's examples, managers are actively trying to improve their businesses and add value. They are not complacent or ignorant of the business environment. The problem is that they develop a paradigm, or mindset, that makes them take inappropriate actions with the best of intentions.

5 Inappropriate leadership

However, even when the skills are present, leadership may well act inappropriately. When leadership skills are absent, the organisation will only achieve adaptation successfully by chance.

For example, the hard headed, top down leadership that is requisite for turnaround management might be inappropriate for a highly innovative company, where informal styles and middle up management is generally more effective. A poor appointment at the higher levels can create havoc in an organisation functioning well.

When looking at Miller's four trajectories immediately above, it is observed that many firms run into difficulties because senior managers, and middle managers too, develop a mindset that makes it difficult for them to see problems in a wider context. It would be wrong to infer from this that leadership with a different orientation would be more effective. On many occasions, successful companies – such as Apple for example – have run into difficulty and investors have demanded that new leadership with greater financial or marketing orientation should be introduced. Although this is sometimes successful, it is more often the case that the improvements are short lived. It must be remembered that the skills and style that made Miller's excellent companies were craftsmanship, innovation, salesmanship and corporate parenting. These things need to draw upon marketing and financial expertise, but do not respond effectively when dominated by such expertise.

A further source of inappropriate leadership was identified by Kets de Vries and Miller, (1989) and their work on organisational neurosis. As with the Icarus paradox, the problems were not caused by sloppy management, but rather by the exaggeration of an otherwise entirely sensible managerial trait.

Five examples were identified in a study of poorly performing companies.

5.1 Paranoid organisation

The organisation has excellent environmental scanning systems, and takes the results of these very seriously. It can usually follow trends well once they have been clearly established in the market place. The weakness of leadership is that they move defensively, never building a strong market position or set of core competencies to compete with. Over time, the company may become too diversified as a legacy of following changes without its own sense of purpose or mission.

5.2 Compulsive organisation

This organisation develops a large number of rituals based upon conformance, standardisation and routinisation. A large number of effective monitoring and control systems exist, but these tend to be internally focused. Consequently, leaders can often develop superior skills in its operations management, but fail to deploy these effectively in the market place. Further, these strong control systems and codes of practice restrict the ability of the organisation to move quickly, or think creatively. Changes managers and entrepreneurs are severely restricted by the formal channels of communication and action that pass for effectiveness in such organisations.

5.3 Dramatic firm

The dramatic firm is dominated by its leader's flair for bold business activities. Such companies are frequently exciting and unpredictable. Power tends to be centralised, and is used to initiate projects and force them through by direct involvement from the top.

Although these firms attract wide publicity and can often dazzle investors, the decision-making style tends to be haphazard and based on plausibility rather than careful analysis and reflection. The actions taken may be inconsistent. Market entry and exit is often high, and risks are not effectively assessed. If allowed to develop too far, the leadership will often generate too many projects, and his or her vital energy will become too dissipated to be effective.

5.4 Depressive organisation

Depressive organisations can be found after organisational trauma, such as the departure of a dominant senior management team, or take-over. These organisations are often found in sheltered markets, where good organisation is all that is necessary to ensure survival in the short run. The firm tends to be hierarchical, but leaders do not exercise their power, leaving a leadership vacuum.

The firm is extremely conservative, and ambitious managers will move on rather than try to energise the business. Those remaining will continually formulate and reformulate strategies and organisational changes, and are rarely unable to identify the key problems and solutions. However, they lack the energy, confidence and leadership style to take the risks implied by their solutions.

5.5 Schizoid organisation

In the schizoid organisation, leaders share the passivity exhibited by the depressive organisation. The difference, however, is that middle managers are energetic and ambitious. Leadership's failure is not lack of delegation or listening to middle managers, but failure to set any long-term sense of purpose or arbitrate effectively. Senior management feel themselves helpless in the face of political obstacles, while middle management find themselves forced into perpetual political plays to achieve anything at all.

The effect is that strategies change incrementally, along with the shifting balance of alliances and power among middle managers. Product market strategy and orderly operations management wax and wane with currently popular solutions to politically-motivated problem analysis.

Again, it is important to see that these companies create their own problems by poor leadership, rather than fail to respond to changes in the environment. All five neurotic types perform poorly, even when the environment is stable and relatively benign.

Norman English – an example

Norman English was a mechanical engineer, who founded his own company in the early 1970s, producing automotive parts. His early successes enabled him to diversify into a wide range of component manufacturing, and eventually into assembly of unbranded products. Many households are entirely unaware that the product they identify by an expensive, foreign brand was actually made in Coventry by this British producer.

In the mid 1980s, the company was floated on the Unlisted Securities market and attracted favourable City opinion. New investment was used to launch into several new projects, and exporting. The latter was particularly well received and, with his forthright views, made Norman English a minor spokesperson for industry. Public speaking and committee work took a great part of his time. During the 1980s, company size increased by more than five times, and a full listing on the Stock Exchange was achieved in 1990.

By 1998, Norman was ageing, unwell, and thinking about retirement. For several years, his involvement as CEO had been somewhat peripheral, and he was aware that his middle managers spent some time fighting each other. In the past, he had seen off such problems with his forceful personality and understanding of the business. The geographical spread of the company, and the proliferation of information made it extremely hard for him to keep the issues clear in his mind.

Further, the company's financial performance was not good – dividends were low and the Z score had fallen to 4. Manufacturing plant was old, and needed replacement. Product design was also looking dated; the firm had been slow to incorporate microchip technology into its products and was increasingly forced into producing budget models with little margin.

A widely circulated report suggested that the export initiative had never been profitable, but had consumed a great deal of capital. Nonetheless, investors and lenders wanted to feel that Norman English was still in control.

ACTIVITY 3	Is this strategic failure (give reasons for your answer)? How has this arisen?

Feedback to this activity is at the end of the chapter.

Conclusion

This chapter has looked at the idea of strategic outcomes in terms of how they might be measured and the processes by which they might be obtained. Sustaining competitive advantage was discussed. The importance of this needs to be stressed - because only by doing so can an organisation ensure that customer value, shareholder value and future strategies are superior to industry rivals. Unfortunately, not all strategies are a success and we concluded the chapter by examining strategic failure.

SELF-TEST QUESTIONS

Corporate and business performance

1   What is the main difference between the market orientation and the resource based view? (1.2, 1.3)

Learning organisation

2   What are the elements of Senge's learning organisation? (2.3)

Alternative performance indicators

3   How can you link market share with the BCG? (3.2)

Strategic failure

4   What do Z scores measure, and how confident should the strategist be about using them? (4.2)

5   What are Miller's four trajectories in the Icarus Paradox? (4.8)

Non-financial indicators

Many writers propose the greater use of non-financial indicators to control organisations

(a) You are required to explain and discuss the advantages and disadvantages of using non-financial indicators in control. **(10 marks)**

In many industries long-term contracts for materials supply have to be entered into to ensure secure supplies over a period of years.

(b) You are required to explain whether, and if so how, entering into such contracts should be controlled, considering that the sums involved can easily exceed those that would require board authorisation of capital expenditure.

(10 marks)

(Total: 20 marks)

Structure and evaluation

Your company is reconsidering its organisational structure and is concerned that in the future some means of measuring departmental efficiency should be available.

(a) You are requested to list points for inclusion in a discussion paper for circulation to other members of the management team, setting out the problems of selecting appropriate measures of efficiency for departments of your company.

(10 marks)

A company which manufactures domestic electric appliances gives customers a 12 month warranty, so that if an appliance breaks down within 12 months of purchase, it will be repaired free (or replaced free of charge). The company employs service engineers to visit customers' premises to do the repair work.

(b) How should the performance of the service department be evaluated?

(10 marks)

(Total: 20 marks)

In this true account, the organisation cut back on its investment in premises. This was rather unfortunate as it had already stoked up demand by its marketing activities. Consequently, customers did not enjoy the service or return to the service provider, and the falling revenues reduced the surplus available to invest and pay off debt. Once profitability began to fall, investors began to worry about the high gearing, and the manager's anxieties became self-fulfilling prophecies.

Inappropriate benchmarking started the problem. As we have discussed in earlier chapters, benchmarking is effective when critical success factors have been identified, rather than some arbitrary ratios selected simply because the information was available.

Appraisal of the company's accounts will show the depressing effect of investment on ROCE. This may be the case for rivals that have invested in biotechnology production as well. However, these competitors will be reporting beneficial movements in margin and perhaps turnover per employee, while ZXP will not, and the latter may even be adverse.

Since only a few companies have switched to biotechnology, it is not too late for ZXP to follow and build a market presence. However, the high gearing implies that the company will have difficulty raising non-equity finance to pay for it.

This particular scenario – where the technological basis for an industry has changed – has been fatal for generations of companies. It is always a strategic risk to assume that the core market is stable while diversification is attempted. In this case, management stopped its development work and switched production to lines that were not under immediate threat from changing technology. In the short run, this has been successful, perhaps because the family seems content with lower returns than the industry average. However, the longer term looks much less comfortable.

FEEDBACK TO
ACTIVITY 3

Although the company has not yet failed, it would seem to be only a question of time. When we look back at the purpose of a strategy, we see that the company is under performing in most respects. The firm has failed to adapt to the environment – it is no longer producing goods that top firms wish to be associated with. It has failed to develop its resource base, both in terms of plant and learning about the capabilities of recent technologies. It no longer has a sense of purpose about the future, rather it seems that middle and senior managers cannot even agree on how to manage the business in its present state. Finally, it has confused a strategy – exporting – with the purpose of the strategy, to produce a return on investment.

The problem may have arisen in several ways, but the Kets de Vries and Miller picture of a depressed organisation seems quite convincing. A formerly dramatic leader has lost his touch, leaving an absence of strategic thinking and energy. There is the added problem that the obvious solution, succession planning, leading to replacement of the CEO, would not be well received by the City. Consequently, this situation has been allowed to continue for longer than usual.

Chapter 22

ETHICS AND CORPORATE RESPONSIBILITY

Large corporations are among the most powerful institutions in the world today, and are frequently more powerful in local situations than their host government. Consequently, serious thought must be given to the wider social responsibilities of these corporations and the effect on the people they contact, directly or indirectly. Even smaller businesses still consume a large proportion of these individuals' lives, and often have a disproportionate influence in the community.

Objectives

When you have studied this chapter you should be able to:

- outline the nature of social responsibility, and its relationship to corporate behaviour

- contrast the positions of leading commentators on the subject

- describe corporate governance and its relationship to stakeholder interests

- review the nature of ethical behaviour on national and global scales.

1   The meaning of social responsibility

For much of this course on strategy, we have examined the ways that an organisation can create value for its customers and shareholders. However, customers and shareholders are not the only ones to be affected by the organisation's behaviours, it is also necessary to consider the wider implications of business activity.

The term **social responsibility** is used to describe the duties an individual or an institution has towards the wider community or society. Naturally, there are usually rights and privileges associated with carrying out these duties of an individual or an institution, but the main concern in the present context is the scope and fulfilment of those duties.

Philosophers have argued about the nature of these duties for thousands of years, but the following consistencies emerge:

- It is wrong to treat others in ways that you would not wish them to treat you.

- Others should be treated with respect and allowed their dignity.

- It is wrong to withhold assistance where this would not harm the giver.

Naturally, these are rather simplistic, but carry the essence of the nature of social responsibility. They are not merely 'nice' things in themselves, but essential for the maintenance of a fair society overall.

1.1   Social responsibility of management

Whilst it is accepted that managers have a responsibility to their shareholders, we are still unsure whether they have a responsibility to others, particularly the community as a whole.

No management can ignore the environment in which it operates and the success of organisations may depend to a large extent upon their public image. The attitude of the organisation to its employees forms part of this image. Throughout history, management has been influenced by social concepts.

Management's attitude to labour is at the core of their social responsibility. Workers have become better protected eg, collective bargaining has given more security to workers. Management must give a lead in these matters and the government periodically 'exhorts' industry to do things, which would aid the country socially, for example the location of new companies in development areas.

Subscribers of capital eg, shareholders and debenture holders, have allowed their money to be used by a company, and the company is responsible to them as they are entitled to a fair reward for the use of their capital and the risk involved. If such obligations are not honoured, future capital would be harder to obtain and unemployment may result.

Consumers have a right not to be exploited by an organisation, which depends upon the community in many ways. The question then arises - should an organisation share its property with its customers eg, by lowering prices, because of reduced costs through mass production and increases in sales? Legislation eg, on resale price maintenance and monopolies, has shown that the government adopts the attitude that companies must act in the public interest. Management therefore cannot avoid the fact that its responsibility for industrial and commercial direction is mainly its responsibility to society.

Other social issues managers face upon which they have to decide policies are:

- marketing policies -should they avoid manufacturing products detrimental to health, eg, cigarettes, weapons;

- policies that imply social costs, e.g. pollution of rivers -the organisation reduces its costs by pumping waste into rivers and this involves social costs in clearing the rivers;

- the relations which an organisation should have with political parties; .

- whether or not to export to particular countries.

1.2 Corporate social responsibility

Corporate responsibility is the detailed issues on which an organisation exceeds the minimum obligations to stakeholders specified through regulation and corporate governance.

A good business is also a good citizen. As well as making a profit by supplying products or services that people want to buy, it can be a positive influence on the rest of society, including - in the case of multinationals - local communities spread across the globe. An enlightened business recognises that it is in its own interests to be socially responsible, since an enhanced public image is more likely to be attractive to investors, employees, customers, consumers, suppliers and host governments.

The modern business corporation has become a major source of power and influence and also a major force for social change. The corporation has become the predominant device for the transformation of science and technology into economically useful goods and services. In performing this economic role the corporation has created significant social changes.

A report on social responsibilities of business by the Committee for Economic Development suggests that the public wants business to contribute a good deal more to achieving the goals of a good society. Its expectations of business have broadened into what may be described as three concentric circles of responsibility.

- The *inner circle* includes the clear-cut basic responsibilities for the efficient execution of the economic function - products, jobs, and economic growth.

- The *intermediate circle* encompasses responsibility to exercise this economic function with a sensitive awareness of changing social values and priorities eg, with respect to environmental conservation, hiring and relations with employees and more rigorous expectations of customers for information, fair treatment, and protection from injury.

- The *outer circle* outlines newly emerging and still amorphous responsibilities that business should assume to become more broadly involved in actively improving the social environment. Society is beginning to turn to corporations for help with major social problems such as poverty and urban blight.

The public at large and many business people, particularly in larger corporations, are prepared to accept the social responsibilities indicated in the first two circles. However, when it comes to business responsibilities for solving broader social problems, the issues become blurred. Even the largest corporation can deal with only a limited range of activities and cannot respond to all social needs. Which broad social problems does it assume responsibility for? It must be selective, but what are the criteria for decision-making?

Although there are no easy solutions to this question of the extent of business responsibility, we can identify some broad guidelines. Where the corporation is clearly involved in the creation of social problems, such as air and water pollution, it should participate with other agencies in finding ways to ameliorate these harmful effects. On the other hand, some adverse consequences of economic activities are beyond the control of individual corporations. For example, product breakthroughs may make individual firms or entire industries obsolete. The social consequences of the resulting unemployment may be devastating to an entire community but the company involved may be unable to cope with the situation.

ACTIVITY 1

A visitor to a factory notices that a machine operator is using the machine without the safety guard in place. What are the social obligations?

Feedback to this activity is at the end of the chapter.

1.3 Areas of social responsibility

Three main areas of social responsibility can be identified, depending on the groups affected:

- **Environmental issues** - includes all forms of pollution

- **Exploitation** - is concerned with the treatment of people in poorer countries who typically have little power and who are not protected by health and safety legislation.

- **Sustainability** - is generally a longer-term concern. One highly publicised issue is the enhanced greenhouse effect with the warming of the earth due to the industrial production of carbon dioxide and other gases.

The nature of the pressure for social responsibility seems to depend on how close the organisation's activities are to the consumer. Those dealing with raw materials are open to charges of non-sustainability, those dealing with more refined products are open to charges of not considering the environment, while those near to the consumer are open to charges of human rights abuses.

1.4   The extent and boundaries of corporate social responsibility

A question that lies at the heart of any discussion of a company's corporate social responsibility is about the extent and boundaries of CSR. Defining what it is that a business is responsible for, and to whom it is responsible, is not an easy task. The right balance has to be struck between doing no more than the law requires and picking up responsibilities for which companies have neither the mandate nor the capacity.

Over the years, business has become engaged in areas outside its original sphere of influence, and some have taken for granted that companies should do more. As a result of this drifting borderline, the expectations of companies' social responsibilities have grown. At the same time, expectations of a company's or industry sector's responsibility for addressing a particular issue are likely to vary between different stakeholders depending on their country and culture. Setting the boundaries of a company's role and responsibility vis-à-vis government and civil society, is therefore often a question of dialogue and negotiation. Fixing such a line depends largely on the cultural context and the rate of development of the societies in which the company operates.

1.5   Social responsibility programmes

Most companies with social responsibility programmes are likely to operate them for enlightened self-interest. When it contributes to those activities that the state does not fund sufficiently, a firm can improve its reputation and visibility in society.

In earlier decades wealthy individuals were patrons of the arts and social welfare eg, The Tate and its sugar connections. In the nineteenth century a number of business owners saw their role in society as extending to the provision of public buildings, parks and so on. Their motives ranged from calculated self-interest to the highest levels of altruism and pride in their role in the local community.

Historically, owners of companies with Quaker beliefs in particular accepted a wide definition of the role of the business in society. Most firms did not have such a wide view but concentrated on the interests of their shareholders, seeing such matters as the responsibility of national and local government. Many companies have made donations to particular political parties, but their social responsibility role is seen to operate in other areas, typically:

* work creation and training programmes
* sponsorship of the arts and sport
* community welfare programmes
* support for educational institutions and links with business
* contributions to overseas aid.

1.6   The business case for corporate social responsibility

A growing body of evidence suggests that there is a compelling business case for corporate social responsibility (CSR). A fundamental premise of this business case is that businesses cannot remain aloof from what is happening around them. Rather, companies are an integral part of the societies and communities in which they operate, and business cannot continue to generate wealth if the society around it fails.

A coherent CSR strategy, based on integrity, sound values and a long-term approach, can offer clear business benefits including a better alignment of corporate goals with those of society; maintenance of the company's reputation; a continued licence to operate; and the reduction of its exposure to liabilities, risks and associated costs.

But more specifically, what is the business case for CSR?

- First, within the company, CSR represents a longer-term motivation, in which business seeks to extract returns for its social spending. There is a growing link between reputation and the ability of companies to command higher market prices for their products and stock offerings, lure more job applicants, raise clout with suppliers and reduce the risk of crises.

- Second, the communities, local or national, in which business operates are essential to a company's licence to operate. Building prosperous surrounding communities and a strong social fabric is required for market growth.

- Third, on a global level, a business behaving as a good corporate citizen can help any given society to accept the changes brought by globalisation. In this globalised and transparent world, managing a company's reputation thus becomes a central element in managing a corporation.

However, there are many writers who denigrate this point of view, including Friendman, Reidenbach and Carr; taken together, their arguments are quite compelling:

Business organisations are created and run in order to maximise returns to their owners. They have no social mandate to assert a moral code, or behave contrarily to their owner's best interests where this would conflict with some notion of ethical behaviour.

The ethics of doing business are not those of the wider society – taking advantage of a rival's mistake is perfectly fair in games and business, but not acceptable in, say, family life. Hence, adoption of ethical principles would weaken a firm's competitive performance.

Market capitalism is the most equitable society that has ever appeared, and, even if not perfect, does rather better than societies that aim to be fair above all other things.

Since much business strategy is of an emergent kind, it is not possible for a corporation to anticipate unethical behaviour in advance any more than it is able to anticipate profits and other prospects with much accuracy.

It is only required that organisations should keep to the law. In so far as the law is ethical and just, so organisations will be.

2 Business ethics

2.1 What is business ethics?

Business ethics is the application of ethical values to business behaviour. It applies to any and all aspects of business conduct, from boardroom strategies and how companies treat their suppliers to sales techniques and accounting practices. Ethics goes beyond the legal requirements for a company and is, therefore, discretionary. Business ethics applies to the conduct of individuals and to the conduct of the organisation as a whole. It is about how a company does its business, how it behaves intrinsically.

Business ethics relates to how any company conducts its business in order to make profit. Any company can seek to do business ethically. An ethical business, on the other hand, has a much broader agenda and focuses on making a positive contribution to the community. A mainstream bank, for example, may take ethics seriously by taking responsibility for its negative impacts on society and the environment and seeking to minimise those impacts. An ethical bank, such as The Co-operative Bank, states that it seeks to make the world a better place by taking a different approach to banking. In the case of this type of business, ethics becomes at least as high a priority as profitability.

2.2 Scope and importance of ethics

Ethical issues concerning business exist at three levels:

- Macro level - the role of business at national and international level and concerned with assessing the relative virtues of different political /social systems eg, centrally planned economies and free enterprise.

- Corporate level - focuses on the ethical issues facing individual companies when formulating and implementing strategies.

- Individual level - concerns the behaviour and actions of individuals within the organisation.

Business activity involves complex interactions between producers and consumers, employers and employees, managements and owners, business executives and members of the communities in which their firms operate. While these relationships are essentially economic in nature, they also have moral dimensions. Some of these dimensions include the work environment, the effects of pollution and depletion of natural resources, and the safety of consumers. Business is an economic institution, which has to be based upon a moral foundation if business relationships are to be reliable and predictable. Nonetheless, we hear and read of a variety of practices in business which most of us would judge to be unethical, among them bribery, embezzlement, breaking contracts, price fixing, collusion, deceptive advertising, falsification of expense accounts, underreporting of income or padding of expenses on tax returns, use of substandard materials, producing and selling products which fail to function as advertised, failing to divulge to consumers possible product dangers, and so on. Any of these behaviours may erode the moral foundation of business and make business activity both unreliable and unpredictable.

The pursuit of *profit* has traditionally been viewed as the chief motivation to engage in productive activity but this cannot be regarded as a morally neutral activity because the receipt of profit income may lead to inequality in the distribution of income between those who are entrepreneurially successful and those who are not or who do not choose to behave in an entrepreneurial fashion.

2.3 Ethical dilemmas

An ethical dilemma involves a situation that is morally problematic and makes a person question what is the 'right' or 'wrong' thing to do. Ethical dilemmas make individuals think about their obligations, duties or responsibilities. These dilemmas can be highly complex and difficult to resolve. Easier dilemmas involve a right versus wrong answer. The vast majority of people will agree, for example, that it is morally unacceptable to pretend that someone else's work is our own. However, the complex ethical dilemmas involve a decision between right and right. As example might be where you uncover a friend's misdemeanour. You have a duty to your employer to report it, but also a duty to be loyal to your friend in a situation that could lead to his or her dismissal

Ethical considerations pose many dilemmas. The following examples show the range of problems facing some managers in organisations.

- Should a manager break the law if he/she thinks it is morally right to do so? For example, the apartheid laws that used to be in place in South Africa caused a dilemma for some people. They can take the view that all laws should be obeyed and that effort should be made to change a law rather than disobey it. The dilemma is between obeying a 'legal' law or a 'moral' law.

- Trading with unsavoury governments can be seen as either contributing to the continuation of the regime or supporting economic growth that benefits all concerned.

- If a foreign subsidiary of a company is operating in a country in which it is legally permissible to employ slave labour, should your company take advantage of this facility?

- In order to protect the environment, should an organisation simply comply with the law or do more than is required to take due regard of the well being of future generations?

- What do people do when offered a bribe? The dilemma revolves around the size of the bribe and the influence that is being sought. In Europe, many managers receive a bottle of whisky from suppliers at Christmas. This may be the done thing but if bigger gifts are involved there might well be a conflict between personal and organisational interests. In countries where bribery is commonplace eg, baksheesh, you cannot do business there unless you pay. Should you necessarily judge others by your own standards? Is one set of ethics better than another?

- When there is a need to downsize and some people are to be made redundant, the dilemma is often between fairness and efficiency. Does a manager operate the 'last in first out' rule or retain a mix of employees that would be most cost-effective?

- If asked to falsify some data regarding the safety of a product or to be economical with the truth, there is a dilemma between going along with it and helping the organisation (and the boss) and refusing, although it may adversely affect the prospects of promotion.

ACTIVITY 2

How would you apply ethical considerations to the following dilemmas?

A rival company creates the legally permitted maximum of toxic waste. Your company has a range of expensive systems that keep waste to much lower levels. Not using these would reduce costs, and there is increasing pressure from industry analysts to increase the return on investment.

A young, talented and ambitious team leader wants you to dismiss a member of his team, who is much older than the rest and does not really fit in. However, the worker in question has worked at the company a long time with a good record of service.

You are forced to make redundancies in a department. The Human Resources manager has said, off the record, that it must not seem that gender or ethnicity is an issue, so you must make it look fair. However, this would require you to keep some weaker individuals, and lose some good ones.

Feedback to this activity is at the end of the chapter.

2.4 Attitudes to corporate ethics - Eric Reidenbach and Donald Robin

The diagram below shows how US academics Eric Reidenbach and Donald Robin have established a sort of moral pyramid to demonstrate the range of corporate attitudes to corporate ethics.

Although not apparent in the model, we can assume that a multi-divisional organisation may occupy several stages at the same time, and companies may also regress from higher to lower levels.

The Reidenbach and Robin Model

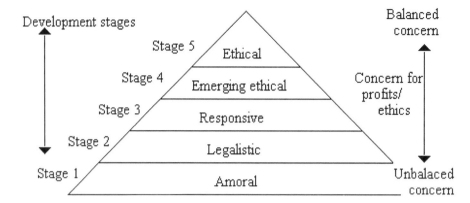

This model proposes a two dimensional form that considers four developmental stages that a company may grow through, tempered against a concern for profits and ethical standards.

Stage 1   Amoral

At the base are the amoral or ethically challenged companies. Amoral organisations are around strictly for the short term. They are prepared to condone any actions that contribute to the organisation's aims and pursue winning at any cost. Obedience is valued and rewarded and there is little concern for employees other than their value as an economic unit of production. The ethical climate of a stage one organisation can be summed up by phases like

- They'll never know
- Everybody does it
- We won't get caught

At the heart of this organisation is the philosophical conviction that business is not subject to the same rules as individuals and that there is no set of values other than greed.

Stage 2   Legalistic

Legalistic organisations obey the law, though ethical concerns are judged on the basis of adherence to the letter if not the spirit of it, if that conflicts with economic performance. They adopt codes of conduct that read like products of legal departments (which they are)

The argument goes that *'If its legal, its OK', 'and if we are not sure, have the lawyers check it out'* typifies the legalistic approach. Economic performance dominates evaluations and rewards. A legalistic company's code of ethics - if it exists - would be dominated by don't do anything to harm the organisation statements.

Some legalistic companies have no ethics code, and do not accept the necessity. Often they see little purpose in expressing explicit ethical standards, and indeed some feel any such statements could lead to difficulties and complication.

Stage 3   Responsive

Responsive organisations are those that take a view - perhaps cynically - that there is something to be gained from ethical behaviour. They are interested in being responsible corporate citizens, mainly because it is expedient and have codes of conduct that begin to look more like codes of ethics. Managers understand the value of not acting solely on legal basis, even though they believe they could win.

Although a reactive mentality may remain, it is coupled with a growing sense of balance between profits and ethics. Management begins to test and learn from more responsive actions. A responsive company's ethics code would reflect a concern for other stakeholders, but additional ethics support vehicles, such as hotlines, are less likely to be found.

Most stage three companies would leave ethical concerns aside until they become a problem only then would they consider remedial action.

Stage 4   Emerging Ethical

Emerging ethical (or ethically engaged) organisations take an active (rather than a reactive) interest in ethical issues. They recognise the existence of a social contract between business and society, and seek to instil that attitude throughout the corporation. Managers have an active concern for ethical outcomes and want to do the right thing. Values are shared across the organisation. Ethical perception has focus but may still lack organisation and long term planning.

Ethical values in such companies are part of the culture. Codes of ethics are action documents, and contain statements reflecting core values.

These organisations accept that their code of ethics is a starting point - any code not monitored and enforced rapidly becomes a dead letter. One leading UK bank has put in place a range of instruments for enlisting staff commitment to its code, including ethics hotlines and regular assessment of code effectiveness.

Stage 5   Ethical Companies

Ethical organisations have a 'total ethical profile' with carefully selected core values (and an approach to hiring, training, firing and rewarding) reflect it. They have a philosophy that informs everything that the company does and a commitment on the part of everyone to carefully select core values. They balance profits and ethics throughout their culture.

Although the concept of social responsibility may change from time to time, the pyramid model gives us a framework for understanding the evolving nature of the firm's economic, legal, ethical and philanthropic performance.

Reidenbach and Robin classify a growing number of organisations in the 'emergent' stage four, but say they cannot find any examples of the 'ideal' final stage, which starts off with a founding moral stance permeating the whole culture.

2.5   The Carroll Model of social responsibility

Carroll's 4-level model has a number of similarities to that of the Reidenbach and Robin model. The Carroll model has four levels, and a firm can be classified as being at different levels by looking at its behaviour and its actions in the market place. Carroll's pyramid of social responsibility model is outlined below.

Level 1 - Carroll describes this level as Economic. This he argues is fundamental to the firm, as the overriding need is to be profitable and to protect the longevity and success of the firm. However this does not preclude the firm from behaving in an ethical manner.

Economic components

- It is important to perform in a manner consistent with maximising earnings per share

- It is important to be committed to being as profitable as possible

- It is important to maintain a strong competitive position

- It is important to maintain a high level of operational efficiency

- It is important that a successful firm be defined as one that is consistently profitable.

Level 2 - Carroll describes this level as Legal, where the need is for the firm to be a law-abiding entity. The law, Carroll argues, offers society a codification of a set of standards to which firms and individuals are bound. The firm should respect both the letter and the spirit of the law.

Legal components

- It is important to perform in a manner consistent with expectations of government and the law.

- It is important to comply with various national and supra-national laws and regulations.

- It is important to be a law-abiding corporate citizen.

- It is important that a successful firm be defines as one that fulfils its legal obligations.

- It is important to provide goods and services that at least meet the minimal legal requirements.

Level 3 - Carroll describes this as Ethical, the onus on the firm is behave and act in an ethical manner and to avoid harm in its actions.

Ethical components

- It is important to perform in a manner that is consistent with the expectations of societal mores and ethical norms.

- It is important to recognise and respect new or evolving ethical/moral norms adopted by society.

- It is important to prevent ethical norms from being compromised in order to achieve corporate goals.

- It is important that good corporate citizenship be defined as doing what is expected morally or ethically.

- It is important to recognise that corporate integrity and ethical behaviour go beyond mere compliance with laws and regulations.

Level 4 - Carroll describes this level as Philanthropic. The firm, Carroll argues should behave as a good corporate citizen and make a contribution to the community in which it operates.

Philanthropic components

- It is important to perform in a manner consistent with the philanthropic and charitable expectations of society.

- It is important to assist the fine and performing arts.

- It is important that managers and employees participate in voluntary and charitable activities within their local communities.

- It is important to provide assistance to public and private educational institutions.

- It is important to assist voluntarily those projects that enhance a community's 'quality of life'.

Carroll also discusses three different manager typologies within the pyramid model - Immoral, Amoral and Moral. Briefly these manager types are described and characterised as follows:

Immoral managers - are managers whose decisions, actions and behaviour suggest an active opposition to what is deemed to be right and ethical. These managers care only about their or their organisation's profitability or success. Legal issues are there to be circumvented and loopholes in the law actively sought. Strategy is to exploit opportunities for personal or organisational gain at any cost.

Amoral managers - are neither immoral nor moral but are not sensitive to the fact that their everyday business decisions may have a deleterious effect on others. These managers may lack an ethical perspective in their organisational lives. Typically their orientation is to the 'letter of the law' as their ethical guide. Amoral managers may not consider a role for ethics in business.

The moral manager - in moral management, ethical norms that adhere to a high standard of right behaviour are employed. Moral managers not only conform to accepted and high levels of professional conduct, they also lead on issues of ethical behaviour.

The law is seen as giving a minimal guide to ethical behaviour. The 'spirit of the law' is more important than the 'letter of the law'. The objective is to operate well above what the law mandates the firm to do. Moral managers want to be profitable and ethical. Moral managers will use ethical principles to base their judgements upon - justice, rights, the Golden Rule, utilitarianism etc.

When ethical dilemmas arise, moral managers and moral companies will tend to assume leadership in their companies and industries.

2.6 The ethical stance

Johnson and Scholes define ethical stance as 'The extent to which an organisation will exceed its minimum obligations to stakeholders'.

There are four possible ethical stances:

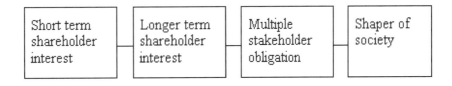

Short-term shareholder interest (STSI).

This ethical stance has a short-term focus in that it aims to maximise profits in the financial year. Organisations with this ethical stance believe that it is the role of governments to set the legal minimum standard, and anything delivered above this would be to the detriment of their taxpayers.

Longer term shareholder interest (LTSI)).

This ethical stance takes broadly the same approach as the short-term shareholder interest except that it takes a longer-term view. Hence it may be appropriate to incur additional cost now so as to achieve higher returns in the future. An example could be a public service donating some funds to a charity in the belief that it will save the taxpayer the costs associated with providing the entire service should the charity cease to work. Hence this ethical stance is aware of other stakeholders and their impact on long-term profit or cost.

Multiple stakeholder obligation (MSO).

This ethical stance accepts that the organisation exists for more than simply making a profit, or providing services at a minimal cost to taxpayers. It takes the view that all organisations have a role to play in society and so they must take account of all the stakeholders' interests. Hence they explicitly involve other stakeholders, and believe that they have a purpose beyond the financial.

Shaper of society

This ethical stance is ideologically driven and sees its vision as being the focus for all its actions. Financial and other stakeholder's interests are secondary to the over-riding purpose of the organisation.

2.7 Ethics at an international and national level

The problem is compounded by the fact that in a world of multinationals, where competition is now international, the standards of ethics vary from nation to nation.

Some countries have higher standards than those of the West, whilst others have standards that are very much lower. The payment of contributions to political parties is an interesting example. In England, it is allowed and it must be declared in the published accounts, but other than in the rare cases such as where the future of the organisation is threatened, it is not tax deductible. This practice is not permitted in the US. However, in several countries of the world, payments to government officials and other persons of influence to ensure the expedition or favourable handling of a business transaction are not regarded as unethical bribes, but rather as payment for services rendered. Indeed, in many cases such payments to ensure the landing of a particular contract are considered a desirable and acceptable way of doing business. There have been instances where foreign nationals have even threatened to close operations down if payments are not met.

This is a very difficult problem and a contentious and emotive area. In addition, standards vary from profession to profession. The student will be familiar with the crisis of ethics that frequently faces the medical profession, and the high ethical standards expected of the members. The famous Hedley Byrne case has enforced high standards of professional care upon the accounting profession and on any profession that gives advice, which people reasonably expect to be accurate. Furthermore, higher standards are expected higher up the social and corporate echelon. What might be considered acceptable among the lower echelons is considered totally unacceptable amongst those who are in the public eye. This may be the root cause of the problem. As democracy spreads, and there are more equal opportunities, the accepted standard of ethics has to be imposed upon people. It could be that they were originally and traditionally outside the scope of such standards of behaviour, and perhaps had a different understanding of what was acceptable. This may suggest that the law needs more frequent review or updating.

3 Corporate governance

3.1 Corporate conduct

Corporate governance is about the way in which organisations are run and who should control them - the chairman, the chief executive, and the board of directors, shareholders or other stakeholders such as employees. It is also about the process of governing - how decisions are to be taken and, if by vote, who has the right to vote.

Johnson and Scholes suggest that a governance framework determines whom the organisation is there to serve and how the purposes and priorities of the organisation should be decided.

Ethical issues also arise in the area of corporate governance and finance. An example is provided by the various Maxwell scandals and some accusations that companies are over zealous in their use of creative accounting techniques.

The principal problem of corporate governance is how the providers of capital can ensure that the directors act in their interests. The laws relating to company reporting and auditing have developed in order to answer this problem by delineating the relationships between the directors, the auditors and the shareholders. This started with the concept of the stewardship of the directors over the assets of the company, which they managed on behalf of the shareholders; they accounted for that stewardship to the shareholders in the annual report.

The three-way relationship between directors, auditors and shareholders has been developed and changed over time, often in response to events such as major corporate collapses due to fraud and other problems. Corporate law and regulation is now extremely complex, but fraud still takes place.

3.2 Aims of corporate governance

The broad aims of corporate governance at a political level include the following:

- Creating a framework for the control of large, powerful companies whose interests may not coincide with the national interest.

- Controlling multinationals, which can dominate the local economy.

- Ensuring that companies are answerable to all stakeholders, not just to shareholders.

- Ensuring that companies are run according to the laws and standards of the country and are not in effect states within states.

- Protecting investors who buy shares in the same way as investors are protected who buy any other financial investment product, such as insurance or a pension.

Increased disclosure has been seen as one of the main methods of increasing the interest of shareholders and thus encouraging them to act as a proper check on the managers of the company. Its effectiveness, however, depends on the willingness of shareholders to exercise their influence rather than selling their shares.

3.3 Principles of good corporate governance

In recent years, some high profile business frauds and questionable business practices in the UK, the US and other countries have led to doubt being cast on the integrity of business managers. Many large organisations are multinational or trans-national which means that they impact on citizens of several countries across the globe. If things go wrong, they will affect many countries, albeit some more severely than others. This has led to scrutiny of corporate governance and a desire for governments to tighten the regulation around corporate governance further.

Essentially, the pressure for improvements in corporate governance has been based on the view that senior executive directors have enormous powers, and in some cases these can be exercised to promote the self-interests of the director rather than in the interests of the company's shareholders (and other stakeholders).

The degree to which corporations observe basic principles of good corporate governance is an increasingly important factor in investment decisions. Of particular relevance is the relationship between corporate governance practices and the increasingly international character of investment. International capital markets enable corporations to access funds from a much larger pool of investors. Countries with high standards of corporate governance practices are more likely to attract international capital. Although there is no single model for good corporate governance, it is affected by the relationships among participants in the governance system, which are subject to law and regulation, market forces and voluntary adaptations.

The OECD (Organisation of Economic Co-operation and Development) has carried out work among member countries, and identified some common elements, which underlie good corporate governance.

The OECD Principles of Corporate Governance cover five sections:

1 **The rights of shareholders** - the corporate governance framework should protect and facilitate the exercise of shareholders' rights. By raising capital from shareholders, companies commit themselves to earning an investment return on that capital. The Board of that company must, therefore, be accountable to shareholders for the use of their money.

2 **The equitable treatment of shareholders** - the corporate governance framework should ensure the equitable treatment of all shareholders, including minority and foreign shareholders. All shareholders should have the opportunity to obtain effective redress for violation of their rights.

3 **The role of stakeholders** - the corporate governance framework should recognise the rights of stakeholders as established by law and encourage active co-operation between corporations and stakeholders in creating wealth, jobs, and the sustainability of financial sound enterprises.

4 **Disclosure and transparency** - the corporate governance framework should ensure that timely and accurate disclosure is made on all material matters regarding the corporation, including the financial situation, performance, ownership, and governance of the company.

5 **The responsibility of the board** - the corporate governance framework should ensure the strategic guidance of the company, the effective monitoring of management by the board, and the board's accountability to the company and the shareholders.

These principles can be used by a nation state to design its own corporate governance rules. Auditors may use them to assess the adequacy of any corporate governance regime in the absence of more immediate standards.

DEFINITION

The OECD Principles of Corporate Governance cover five sections: The rights of shareholders,

The equitable treatment of shareholders,

The role of stakeholders Disclosure and transparency and The responsibility of the board

3.4   The role of executive and non-executive directors

The powers of directors are given by the Companies Acts and by the company's articles of association. Public companies must also comply with the regulations of their stock exchange, and UK listed companies must comply with the UK Listing Rules (which are the responsibility of the UK Listing Authority, a department of the Financial Services Authority). Shareholders entrust the day-to-day management of their company to the directors and the directors generally set their own agenda to run the business. Shareholders may vote in general meeting to add to or curtail these powers, but in practice the board is seldom constrained by shareholders. If shareholders are unhappy with directors' actions, they tend to simply sell their shares rather than confront the directors.

The Cadbury Report stated the responsibilities of directors as including 'setting the company's strategic aims, providing the leadership to put them into effect, supervising the management of the business and reporting to shareholders on their stewardship'

The contribution of independent non-executive directors (NEDs) is an area receiving attention worldwide as a reaction to the corporate scandals currently destroying investor confidence. They seem likely to also become 'Key players' in corporate governance. This will see a move away from the view of independent NEDs as a 'necessary evil' and towards them having real power and influence.

This view of NEDs was prompted by many being seen as looking for a boardroom seat to provide 'a comfortable sinecure ahead of retirement'. Typically, they were drawn from the business and social networks of the senior managers in the company, seriously compromising their independence, power and willingness to raise difficult issues for the senior management team. Once again, issues of power and interest are raised. One area of particular concern is their role on audit committees of large corporations where their independence is essential for decisions on the appointment and remuneration of auditors. The audit committee's primary role 'is to ensure the integrity of the company's financial reporting'. This may involve them taking a more adversarial approach to management where things are clearly going wrong.

In an article (January 2003) in the ACCA's *Accounting and business* journal, a way forward for NEDs was suggested. The current view of NEDs as 'a mixture of policemen and guardians of shareholders' interests' was argued to be insufficient. NEDs were seen as having an important strategic role. NEDs may contribute valuable expertise not otherwise available to management; or they may act as mentors to relatively inexperienced executives. The role of the board, executive directors and NEDs and the chairman differ from country to country. ACCA supports the present unitary UK based structure where all directors have equal responsibility in law and work as a team. Clearly, reconciling the monitoring role of NEDs with their ability to contribute to the strategic thinking of a company may bring certain dilemmas.

ACCA sees NEDs' monitoring role as including:

- bringing external (and independent) influence to bear on the company's financial reporting.
- deciding the remuneration (and leaving packages) of the executive directors.
- effecting necessary changes in board composition.
- making recommendations to shareholders on the appointment of auditors.

NEDs also should act as the 'corporate conscience' in respect of corporate social responsibility issues. As the issue of corporate social responsibility (CSR) rises up the business agenda, it is appropriate for NEDs to accept a responsibility for ensuring that social, environmental and sustainability issues receive an appropriate degree of board level attention. This will become particularly significant if the proposed mandatory Operating and Financial Review Statement becomes law in the near future. NEDs should also be sensitive to the public interest issues inherent in balancing long-term sustainable growth with the short-term financial demands associated with the recruitment, retention, motivation and reward of the executive directors.

NEDs should exercise individual judgement, but they should act primarily through the board or in committees. NEDs should also prepare their own corporate governance report to the shareholders as part of the annual report.

Finally, through the audit committee, NEDs should give prior approval to any non-audit work to be carried out by the external auditors and they should regularly assess the independence of the auditors.

How would you apply ethical considerations to the following dilemmas?

A rival company creates the legally permitted maximum of toxic waste. Your company has a range of expensive systems that keep waste to much lower levels. Not using these would reduce costs, and there is increasing pressure from industry analysts to increase the return on investment.

A young, talented and ambitious team leader wants you to dismiss a member of his team, who is much older than the rest and does not really fit in. However, the worker in question has worked at the company a long time with a good record of service.

You are forced to make redundancies in a department. The Human Resources manager has said, off the record, that it must not seem that gender or ethnicity is an issue, so you must make it look fair. However, this would require you to keep some weaker individuals, and lose some good ones.

Feedback to this activity is at the end of the chapter.

3.5 Rights, duties and expectations of stakeholders

In this section, we consider the ethical position of several major stakeholders (principally shareholders, society as a whole, the finance sector and employees) and consider the ethical dilemmas that might arise.

Shareholders have a variety of rights in terms of receiving a dividend and appointing a managing director. It is not clear where their duties might lie. Since it is understood that buying shares is an investment, there is no reason why a shareholder should remain loyal to a company or its management team in any circumstances. It is thus entirely unreasonable for industrialists to accuse shareholders of short-termism when selling shares that have not performed to expectations. Neither is it incumbent upon shareholders to ensure that a company behaves to a particular ethical standard, although some minority shareholders have succeeded in exerting pressure on senior management by raising ethical issues at the company AGM.

This text has stressed the importance of developing strategies which will result in a sustainable comparative advantage and will thereby increase the long-term wealth of the shareholders. A wide range of views have been expressed on the extent to which the pursuit of wealth maximisation is ethically acceptable. Some of these views are summarised below.

Friedman argued that the search for profit is what motivates firms to respond to market needs, which in turn reflect the needs of society.

Stenberg stressed that business organisations are distinguished from others in society by their pursuit of shareholder wealth. If businesses become involved in social responsibility concepts they are changing their role and invading the domain of charities, governments, etc.

By contrast, the Social Contract Theory of Rawls argues that a business operates under a contract with society. The business enjoys rights (such as the right to carry on its business uninterrupted), but in return the business has duties expected of it – the primary duty being to behave responsibly towards society as a whole.

One area where these conflicts may become apparent is the role of the finance sector in the economy. Financiers are periodically criticised for not paying attention to the performance of a business when giving loans. High Street banks, in particular, are often criticised for supporting small business start-ups that have no real chance of success, and repossessing property used a security for the loans when they fail.

Conclusion

An organisation operates in a social and ethical environment which offers constraints over what to can do. However, the areas in which responsibilities must be exercised are not clear. The stakeholder view holds that there are many groups in society with an interest in the organisation's activities. Some organisations have objectives for stakeholders. Some argue, however, that an organisation's only objective should be to make money: the government, representing the public interest, can levy taxes to spend on socially desirable projects or can regulate organisational activities.

Organisations have to ensure they obey the law but they also face ethical concerns because their reputations depend on a good image and because employees need guidance in cases of uncertainty.

SELF-TEST QUESTIONS

The meaning of social responsibility

1   What are the three main elements of social responsibility? (1)

2   Give four criticisms of corporate social responsibility. (1.6)

Business ethics

3   What does the easier ethical dilemma involve? (2.3)

Corporate governance

4   Give two broad aims of corporate governance (3.2)

EXAM-TYPE QUESTION

Social responsibility

Social responsibility may be defined as the obligations that an organisation has towards society and the broad environment in which the organisation operates. Management should therefore concern itself with the way in which the organisation interacts with its environment

Required

Explain how and to what extent should management recognise social responsibility extending beyond the boundaries of the organisation.

(20 marks)

For the answer to this question, see the 'Answers' section at the end of the book

---

FEEDBACK TO ACTIVITY 1

There is no legal reason why the visitor should involve himself or herself. However, doing nothing would violate all three principles of social responsibility. In the first place, it is reasonable to suppose that the visitor would prefer to be told of an unsafe action were the position reversed. Bringing it to the operator's attention will not inconvenience or harm the visitor in any way. By acting politely, there is no reason why the affair should lead to embarrassment or loss of dignity.

Note that with a social obligation, there is no obvious penalty if no action is taken. However, society would be much the worse if everyone did so.

FEEDBACK TO
ACTIVITY 2

In all these examples, the dilemma cannot be resolved, but much can be done to defend the values that are creating the problem in the first place. For example, there may be some competitive advantage in asserting the cleanliness of the product, or supporting an older worker's experience that might be interpreted as dissent by a younger worker. Making redundancies based on the image of fairness, rather than rewarding ability and application, is poor business.

The answers are often legitimately found in steering between the two extremes of the dilemma.

Answers to exam-type questions

CHAPTER 1

EXAM-TYPE QUESTION

Corporate planning

Argenti argues that corporate planning should be distinguished from other forms of planning where managers make decisions *ad hoc*, i.e. as and when opportunities arise. With corporate planning, management select a strategic framework on which to evaluate and select individual strategies continuously. Corporate planning therefore takes a holistic and structured approach, which often affects the long-term direction of an organisation and is invariably complex in nature.

Corporate strategy consists of strategic planning at a corporate level and is not confined to one particular area – marketing, personnel, production/operational and financial implications are all taken into consideration. It is primarily concerned with the determination of ends such as what business or businesses the firm is in or should be in and how integrated these businesses should be with one another. It covers a longer time period and has a wider scope than the other levels of corporate planning.

Business strategy is concerned with how each business attempts to achieve its mission within its chosen area of activity. It includes corporate planning at the tactical level and consists of the allocation of resources for complete operations. It is means oriented and is mainly administrative and persuasive in its endeavours.

Functional strategy examines how the different functions of the business support the corporate and business strategies. Such corporate planning at the operational level is means oriented and most activities are concerned only with the ability to undertake directions.

However, despite the points evaluated above, the boundaries between the three categories are very indistinct and much depends upon the circumstances prevailing and the kind of organisation. Overall, corporate planning is concerned with the scope of an organisation's activities and the matching of these to the organisation's environment, its resource capabilities and the values and expectations of its various stakeholders.

All organisations, both large and small, should carry out some form of corporate planning activity. The need for involvement increases with the complexity of the organisation and with the uncertainty and turbulence of its environment.

An understanding of corporate planning is essential for all management because, through the means-end chain, lower level objectives are inexorably linked to higher-level strategies. An appreciation of these strategies and how they are formulated can be an effective guide to action. Moreover, whatever the level at which a manager operates within an organisation, he or she can have some influence over that organisation's corporate strategy.

CHAPTER 2	EXAM-TYPE QUESTIONS

Question 1: Long-term strategic planning

To: Managing director
From: Management accountant
Date: X.X.XXXX
Subject: Long-term strategic planning

As requested this report outlines the benefits of long-term strategic planning and examines the case for its abolition.

Long-term strategic planning can be defined as 'the formulation, evaluation and selection of strategies involving a review of the objectives of an organisation, the environment in which it is to operate, and an assessment of its strengths, weaknesses, opportunities and threats for the purpose of preparing a long-term strategic plan of action which will attain the objective set'.

The benefits of long-term strategic planning

(a)   Long-term planning enables an organisation to be more aware of its external environment so that managers can attempt to adapt the organisation to achieve a better fit with the environment. Without a system of strategic planning an organisation can become very inward-looking.

Encouraging managers to think strategically, with the full support of a strategic management accounting system to provide the information needed to make long-term decisions, can encourage a proactive rather than a reactive attitude to change within the organisation.

(b)   A long-term strategic plan gives managers a sense of long-term direction and provides a framework to guide them in short to medium-term planning. As a result the organisation's long-term, medium-term and short-term objectives, plans and controls can be made consistent with one another.

(c)   Long-term strategic planning helps to encourage creativity and initiative by tapping the ideas of the management team and showing their contribution to the operation of the plan. It can give a sense of purpose to the personnel in the organisation, leading to an improved quality of management.

(d)   Long range planning is particularly important and beneficial for capital intensive organisations that have a long lead time between deciding to invest in a new project and the investment coming to fruition and starting to earn money for the organisation. Organisations involved in extensive research and development such as pharmaceutical companies must also undertake long range planning because of their long lead times.

The case for the abolition of long-term strategic planning

This section of the report will review the arguments of those who believe that long-term strategic planning should be abolished.

(a)   Opponents argue that strategic planning and formal long-term plans can introduce rigidity and restrict an organisation's entrepreneurial flair. However, their preferred system of simply exploiting opportunities as they arise (freewheeling opportunism) has a number of disadvantages.

(i)   Without a cohesive objective companies are likely to under-utilise their resources and probably to duplicate them in some respects.

(ii)   The freewheeling opportunism approach cannot guarantee that all opportunities are identified and appraised. A well designed formal system should be more capable of identifying as many opportunities as possible. Strategic planning relies heavily on the creative thinking of its managers to design strategies, and a formal system is likely to be more thorough in exploiting this creativity to the full.

(iii) The freewheeling opportunism approach to strategic planning tends to emphasise the profit motive to the exclusion of all other considerations. A formal system of strategic planning ensures that all goals and objectives are consistent and focused.

(b)   Strategic planning can be a costly and time consuming exercise but even the advocates of long-term planning would accept the need to ensure that the benefits obtained from the system exceed the costs of running it.

(c)   The opponents also say that in today's rapidly changing environment it is not possible to carry out effective strategic planning because of the difficulty in producing reliable quantified forecasts. For this reason there is more emphasis on the need to consider qualitative factors in effective strategic planning. The inability to quantify all of the forecast variables does not invalidate the strategic planning exercise.

(d)   Another argument offered against long-term strategic planning is that it is not possible for some organisations, for example companies operating in the fashion industry, to plan long term. These companies with short lead times who need to respond to opportunities as they arise can, however, still benefit from long-term planning to ensure the future availability of the resources needed to achieve the short to medium-term plans.

In conclusion, long-term strategic planning is not obsolete and it does have a role to play in most firms. Many of the criticisms levelled at strategic planning stem from the inappropriate way in which it is sometimes carried out (for example the approach may be too quantitative) rather than from the concept itself.

Question 2: Proactive and reactive styles

(a)   Strategic planning is the pattern of decisions in an entity that determines and reveals its objectives, purposes or goals, produces the principal policies and plans for achieving these goals, and defines the range of business the company is to pursue, the kind of economic and human organisation it intends to be, and the nature of the economic and non-economic contribution it intends to make to its shareholders, employees, customers and communities. In other words, to paraphrase Hofer and Schendel, strategy 'involves matching organisational competence (internal resources and skills) with the opportunities and risks created by environmental change in ways that will be effective and efficient'. Put plainly, the 'rational' strategic planning model is one in which objectives determine strategy rather than the other way round.   The planning process involves a structured approach which entails systematic appraisals, the use of techniques and the interpretation and assimilation of business information.

The practice of *free-wheeling opportunism* essentially concentrates on finding, evaluating and exploiting short-term product-market opportunities instead of adhering to the rigidity of a predetermined strategy. It encourages a non-corporate philosophy, and managers who have vested interests will try to exert pressure for the acceptance of their own ideas even if they are incompatible with existing corporate aims. It is perceived by some managers to be dynamic, exciting and innovative. Furthermore because of its unstructured approach, strategy arising from it is seen to bear the stamp of individual managers.

Opponents of structured long-term strategic planning argue that in instigating explicit long-term strategy managers are putting their organisations into what is effectively a strait-jacket, resulting in a serious loss of flexibility rendering difficult the exploitation of opportunities on a more free-wheeling basis. The arguments imply certain weaknesses in the disciplined approach, such as its inflexibility, forecasting inaccuracy, complexity and bureaucratic nature.

Not withstanding these criticisms, planning long-term corporate strategy can be justified. Certain action which is fundamental to the corporate operations is irreversible in the short-term at least. It is difficult to imagine managers making decisions which have a degree of permanency without first going through some form of formalised strategic planning. Also the bigger an organisation grows the bigger are the risks involved in top management decisions. Strategic planning helps to identify these risks and either prevent or mitigate their effects. Large entities face dynamic and complex environments and an integral part of the strategic planning process is environmental appraisal which often uses sophisticated forecasting techniques requiring expert interpretation and evaluation of strategic options. The systematic survey of the corporate environment and of the company's internal strengths and weaknesses, acts as 'an early warning system'. The process will, hopefully, identify product/market threats and resource weaknesses in time for the company to bring in preventative or remedial measures.

Some companies have undoubtedly managed quite successfully without strategic planning. However it is probable that they could have performed much better. Even an upward sloping profit line can be criticised if it prevents the occurrence of an even steeper profit line. Strategic planning ensures that performance is targeted rather than merely assessed against loose expectations. In these terms strategic planning is concerned with the long-term, which is an essential dimension in the overall survival pattern of an entity. The planning disciplines concentrate management's attention on long-term matters, but not at the exclusion of short-term considerations. Freewheel planning is apt to focus only on the short-term and there is evidence to suggest that this is a dangerous policy.

Also, strategic planning requires the clarification of corporate objectives. The process aids in the formulation of organisational goals and objectives and the strategy formulation process can be used to evaluate whether or not the tentative objectives established are achievable, given the organisation's resources and the nature of the changes occurring in its environment, and, if not, what other objectives could be achieved. In this way strategic planning helps to integrate long, medium and short plans and to harmonise the activities of different departments and functions. The planning process results in people from different functions working together in teams, and the plan itself clarifies the contribution made by the different functions to the achievement of overall objectives. The emergent plan should reflect the 'corporate' nature of the entity, instead of merely being an aggregation of the plans of individual departments. The strategy spells out the responsibility and authority of each executive and management activity. This tends to boost morale, and produces improved results since most groups and individuals perform better if they know what is expected of them and how they contribute to the overall progress of the company.

Strategic planning demands a logical deliberation and analytical approach to decision making. It requires the generation of alternative strategies, and the evaluation of the probable results of their execution. The plans formulated can be used as yardsticks against which actual performance can be judged and remedial needs identified. The planning process is continuous and not conducted as a 'one-off' ad hoc exercise. The systematic approach requires the maintenance of an information system which will continuously provide up-to-date data for on-going decision making and control purposes. Strategic planning, when carried out imaginatively and conducted in the right atmosphere of communication, participation and incentive, helps to develop a climate conducive to creative thinking, initiative and innovation.

(b) The system of planning in any entity will depend on a mixture of factors.

- The size and nature of the company.

- The attitudes of the Board particularly the chief executive.

- The information systems in use in the company.

- The structure of the organisation.

- The general trading circumstances of the company.

- The ability of the individuals who occupy planning positions.

Many organisations are large, complex, diversified and geographically decentralised, and are based on formal organisation structures and bureaucracies. It is hard to imagine how these organisations could be managed effectively without imposing the discipline of long-term corporate strategic planning. A failure to impose this discipline would probably result in the fragmentation of the organisation into separate, uncoordinated management autonomies. (A distinction must be made here between a loose set of uncoordinated autonomies and a deliberate corporate policy to fragment the planning structure into strategic business units (SBUs), of the type used in a conglomerate group.)

'Freewheeling opportunism' is more likely to occur at the entrepreneurial stage of an enterprise's development, usually when one person (or at most a handful of people) dominates strategic thinking, and where strategy is seldom explicit. Senior management of the entity know the business environment and are in direct touch with it by visiting customers, dealing with bank managers, negotiating directly with suppliers and are knowledgeable about competitors and their activities. There is no need for information systems, sophisticated management techniques nor structured planning and evaluation. Consequently the planning system has to be seen in relatively simple ways. All companies, big or small, with simple or complex environments, diversified or concentrated product-market positions have to cope with environmental uncertainty. Uncertainty can best be managed if a disciplined approach is taken to cope with the future by using skills to identify and analyse trends, and forecast possible future events.

Managers at all levels possess attributes of creativity and innovation. However such attributes need to the encouraged, channelled and developed. The strategic planning system focuses attention, and creates a working environment suitable for creative management.

On balance it would seem that the arguments for formal strategic planning are strong. The distinctive and identifiable pressures of rapid growth, the rising cost of resources, accelerating technology, government fiscal policies, inflation, ethical, social and political considerations, matched with the development of techniques such as gap analysis, product-portfolio appraisal, sensitivity analysis, capital investment appraisal, computer database processing, forecasting and cost analysis, have provided the impetus and stimulus for the spread of strategic planning converts, even for those managers in small entrepreneurial organisations.

Question 1: J & T

Part (a)

Handy has defined culture as 'the way we do things around here'. This can be expressed more fully as the sum total of the belief, knowledge, attitudes, norms and customs that prevail in an organisation. J & T has deliberately set out to create a culture that is conducive to customer satisfaction and company growth. It operates in a stable environment, brought about by its dominance as a supplier to its customers for many years, and by vertical integration which ensures ready supplies at each stage (production, warehousing and delivery), and profits at each. Because J & T has operated in a stable environment, Dennison would describe the culture as one of internal 'consistency'.

With this consistency one would expect J & T internally to have a well-developed bureaucracy covering its major line activities, such as purchasing, stock control, production and distribution, perhaps each having internal efficiency ratios, standard costing and other management accounting techniques to help monitor efficiency.

Dennison also promoted the idea of a 'mission' culture for stable environments. This is prevalent in organisations such as J & T, where much emphasis is placed on the personal role of the partners. The extent to which it is customer-focused means that employees should know the 'mission' very well and co-operate to achieve corporate aims. This is often exemplified by their treatment of staff, with long-service awards and few disciplinary or dismissal cases, and a philanthropic or paternalistic management style based on trust, but with an underpinning of bureaucratic controls.

Part (b)

At the moment there are two separate cultures, those of J & T and its UK suppliers. When the merger takes place a different culture will emerge for IC plc.

The prevailing culture at J & T has been described above, and on merging it will be evident that the suppliers have a very different culture. The turbulent environment in which the suppliers have operated, perhaps with irregular supply patterns and less market dominance than J & T, have probably led them to a more outward-looking, even aggressive, stance. The merger idea itself is an example of that outlook.

Dennison would label its strategy 'adaptive'. This strategy would be seen as proactive, results-oriented, attentive to customer needs, and therefore perhaps also stronger on innovation (eg customer specifications used in the production of new products, demands for quick delivery leading to manufacturing process improvements like JIT).

Public ownership may encourage IC plc to be cautious in its decision-making style, allied to the larger number of managers involved. This tendency will need to be balanced strongly by the increased dynamism of departments outside the core. A newly floated company might engage a firm of PR professionals or even create a PR department to deal with the City and the media.

Merging the two cultures will be a difficult task, the biggest challenge being the integration of the different payments and benefits systems across IC plc, and the merging of the R&D departments, which cannot escape change. It may not be necessary for the operating cultures of the different divisions and departments to change significantly (differentiation), because most organisations of 2,000 people will tolerate different cultures in marketing and production environments.

Question 2: Cultures in 'excellent' organisations

Peters and Waterman identified the following core values that were associated with 'excellent' organisations:

(a) A bias for action – the excellent companies get on with it. They are analytical in their decision making but this does not paralyse them as it does with some companies.

(b) Close to the customer – they get to know their customers and provide them with quality, reliability and service.

(c) Autonomy and entrepreneurship – leaders and innovators are fostered and given scope.

(d) Productivity through people – they really believe that the basis for quality and productivity is the employee. They do not just pay lip service to the notion 'people are our most important asset', they do something about it by encouraging commitment and getting everyone involved.

(e) Hands-on, value driven – the people who run the organisation get close to those who work for them and ensure that the organisation's values are understood and acted upon.

(f) Stick to the knitting – the successful organisations stay reasonably close to the businesses they know.

(g) Simple form, lean staff – the organisation structure is simple and corporate staff are kept to the minimum.

(h) Simultaneous loose-tight properties – they are both centralised and decentralised. They push decisions and autonomy as far down the organisation as they can get, into individual units and profit centres. But, as Peters and Waterman state, 'they are fanatic centralists around the few core values they hold dear'.

Though Peters and Waterman stress the positive benefits of having a strong organisational culture there are also potential drawbacks:

(a) Strong cultures are difficult to change.

(b) Strong cultures may stress inappropriate values.

(c) Where two strong cultures come into contact, e.g. in a merger, then conflicts can arise.

(d) A strong culture may not be attuned to the environment, e.g. a strong innovative culture is only appropriate in a dynamic, shifting environment.

Despite these problems it is still possible to agree with Alan Sugar, Chairman of Amstrad, who said in 1987: 'It is essential to retain a strong corporate culture and philosophy, otherwise the business can drift and become confused and lost in direction'.

CHAPTER 4   EXAM-TYPE QUESTION

Organisations as open systems

(a) In the general systems approach, organisations are systems of inter-related activities. The organisation interacting with its environment is viewed as an open system made up of two aspects - the inputs and the outputs. The inputs or factors of production (people, finance, etc) are drawn from the environment and the outputs (the products or services) are offered to the environment. Closed systems, on the other hand, are systems which are self-supporting and do not interact with the environment outside the system. The interdependence of open systems is particularly important for a company because, if it is to flourish, it must respond to the changes, threats and opportunities in its environment.

Using concepts from open systems theory, we can describe CA as buying components, assembling them into computers, and marketing the completed product, raising money to continue buying inputs and generate outputs. CA makes computers using its own separate resources and identifiable management entity, whilst inter-acting with others outside itself. (For example suppliers who are developing new components, customers who want new features, and competitors who want to grab a larger share of the market.)

A model could be drawn to show this activity:

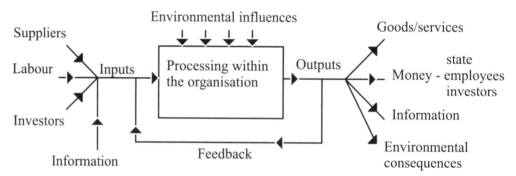

Open systems are composed of several subsystems. CA is not just one entity, but a combination of different departments and different sites. Management is the sub system that co-ordinates all of the other sub systems, by means of policies, plans and resolving conflicts, etc. The production sub system is the heart of the organisation but the quality control operation may be distinct from the rest of the production process. Each will have its own sense of identity, its own physical space and personnel, its own cost centre management, its own leader and its own ways of handling interaction with other parts of CA.

Each part of CA takes in its different inputs, adds value in its own way and generates its own different output. The maintenance sub system keeps the organisation functioning. It may repair and service the building. Alternatively, the human resource department can be seen as a maintenance sub system that recruits, retires and counsels employees. Yet, for the world outside CA, the cumulative effect of all their separate (but linked) efforts is the output generated by CA as a whole.

Open systems have a dynamic relationship with their environment and receive various inputs. They transfer these inputs into outputs, which they then export. Such systems are also open internally in that interactions between components affect the system as a whole. Feedback control enables a system to change itself, including its goals, so that it can survive in a changing environment.

(b) Whilst the Classical approach to organisations is impersonal and the Human Relations and Behavioural approaches stress the importance of individuals and informal groups, the Systems approach emphasises the need for correct decision making through the interaction of man and machines. Followers of the approach are interested in studying whole situations and relationships rather than segments of an organisation. They recognise the interactive effect of activities and functions upon each other and make efforts to harness the controlling influences.

We can use open systems theory to assist our understanding of the operation of organisations like CA because:

- It focuses on the activities, including aspects of the technology employed, the people in the company, their relationships and roles, as well as the interaction with the environment.

- It draws attention to the dynamic aspects of organisation and the factors influencing the growth and development of all its sub systems.

- It creates an awareness of sub systems, each with potentially conflicting goals that must be integrated. When sub systems pursue their own goals to the detriment of the system as a whole, it is called sub-optimisation.

- It focuses attention on inter-relationships between: aspects of the organisation; the organisation and its environment; and the needs of the system as a whole. Managers should not get so involved in detail and small political problems that they lose sight of the overall objectives and processes.

- It can highlight 'linear causality', showing managers that decisions intended to achieve result 'X' may inadvertently create unwanted side-effect 'Y' somewhere else in the system because of the unpredictability and uncontrollability of many inputs.

- It underlines the importance of sensitive but firm central co-ordination if the overall outcome of an organisation is to be greater than the sum of the outcomes of its constituent parts.

The systems approach expresses a manager's role as being co-ordinator of the elements of a system, of which people are only one part. A manager is encouraged to spend greater time and effort in improving, planning, controlling and operating systems rather than motivating staff, since this will lead to greater efficiency. Like any other approach, managers should take what they find useful in practice, without taking it to extremes.

| CHAPTER 5 | EXAM-TYPE QUESTION |

Market segmentation

(a) Market segmentation allows companies to treat similar customers in similar ways, whilst distinguishing between dissimilar customer groups. Each customer group has slightly different needs, which can be satisfied by offering each group, or segment, a slightly different marketing strategy. For example, the market for washing machines can be split up into a variety of different sub-markets - the family market, the elderly market, the young trendy market, the budget market etc. It would be virtually impossible to provide one single washing machine that would satisfy all people in the above markets. Because the people in the different sectors will have different needs and wants, the manufacturers have a choice in terms of their marketing approach. It can go for:

- *Niche or target marketing* - (sometimes referred to as concentrated marketing) specialising in one or two of the identified markets only, where a company knows it can compete successfully. It acquires a great deal of expertise in its market segment, which must be large enough to sustain profitability. Targeting makes it easier to analyse customers, gives a better understanding of the competition and allows for more effective market planning. It also helps the company to respond quickly to any changes in customer requirements. For example, Dyson offer brightly coloured, expensive machines that appeal to trendy young people who are technologically minded.

- *Differentiated marketing* - offers a variety of products to suit all of the needs. Companies like Hotpoint offer a variety of washing and drying machines to appeal to most markets. These machines may be at different prices, in different colours, with different wash loads and drying facilities. Unfortunately, catering for the different needs of every individual customer is costly and impractical for most organisations. Resources in all organisations are limited and the task of dealing with individual customers is too costly for most companies to contemplate.

- *Mass or undifferentiated marketing* - is the opposite of differentiated marketing, in that it treats all customers and potential customers as identical. In the washing machine sector, if a company offers just one type of machine hoping that it would appeal to the majority of people, it would be competing against all of its rivals, who have become specialists in their own areas. This approach is inefficient in many ways because much of the marketing effort is wasted on consumers who have no interest in purchasing the product and are unlikely to do so whatever the efforts of the marketing staff.

Market segmentation aids competitor analysis because it enables a company to develop an understanding of the nature of the competition they face. By focusing on particular segments, it is much easier for a company to identify whom its competitors are and at which segments it is targeting its products. It is very important for an organisation to know who their competitors are and how strong each of them is. In any market where there is more than one significant competitor, the marketing decisions will be based on what the competition has done or is about to do. An analysis of the competition should focus on identifying threats, opportunities or strategic questions raised by emerging or potential competitor strengths or weaknesses.

(b) There are different bases used to segment a market. The traditional method was segmentation on demographic grounds; but the use of lifestyle, motives and personality are used more to segment a market today. Market research studies are frequently broken down by age, income, social class, sex, geographical area, occupation, family unit, etc. This can be highly relevant with some products. For example, certain brands of breakfast cereals have regular sales to families where there are children aged under eight, whereas other brands such as Bran Flakes and Shredded Wheat sell almost entirely to adults. In other areas, demographic influences appear to have no effect - for instance, own label products are believed to sell equally to high and low incomes, to families and single people, and across age groups.

This is still the starting point for many segmentation exercises, though further investigation often finds that demographic influences are not the prime determining factors of purchase.

The variables that might be useful as a basis for segmenting the market for clothing include the following:

- Sex - the market for clothes, cosmetics, perfumes and facial care products are segmented by sex.

- Age - retail department stores can specialise in clothing for children, young teenagers, older teenagers, and young adults to mature adults.

- Size - specialist retailers sell clothes to suit short, tall, small and large people.

- Income/wealth - designer clothes are positioned with wealthier customers in mind

- Occupation/lifestyle - professional, managerial and administrative workers tend to wear formal attire to the office while other occupational groups tend to wear casual clothes.

- Purchasing characteristics - customers may be segmented by the volume they buy, by the outlet type they use, or by the pack size bought. A clothes manufacturer will approach supermarket chains very differently to the small independent retailer probably offering better prices, delivery terms, use different sales and delivery techniques. They might also supply own label product to the large chain but they are unlikely to be able to offer the same terms to the smaller retailer.

Segmentation based on industrial markets is not so broad because there are fewer buyers. Segmentation variables include geographical area, type of business, application, usage and size.

A paint manufacturer segmenting the market in paint sold to other businesses might use the following types of segmentation:

- Type of business - potential customers may be divided into several different groups such as paint wholesalers, do-it-yourself retail outlets, specialist decorating outlets, housing developers, contracting decorators, and vehicle manufacturers

- Usage, range and size are all means of segmenting the paint market. The size of container and packaging of the paint will vary according to the user needs of the customer. Contracting decorators may use large containers of a limited range of colours and not be particularly concerned about packaging, while do-it-yourself outlets and specialist stores may require a full range of colours and containers of various sizes with attractive decoration.

- Geographical area is an important segmentation variable for this type of industry. Customers may be domestic or overseas. Paint is exported to many different countries - each will need their own marketing strategies.

CHAPTER **6**   EXAM-TYPE QUESTIONS

Question 1: The product life cycle

Many products pass through a number of stages in their history until they eventually decline in the face of outside competition or a change in consumer tastes. As illustrated below, it is very important to consider carefully when to start developing new products in order to achieve a steady rate of growth in both turnover and profits for the whole company.

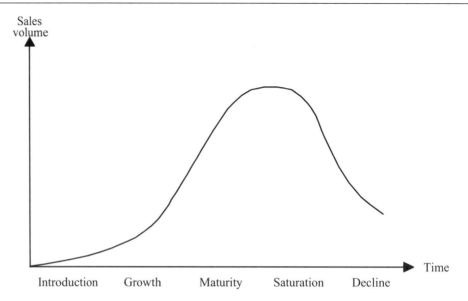

It should be noted that periods are only shown in the diagram as being of equal size for convenience. For example, product development may take three years but the product may be in decline for four years after market introduction. If this were the case, the product development of the second product would need to be started before market introduction of the first.

Some products have much longer life cycles than others – basic foodstuffs have much longer lives than more fashionable products such as clothes, although perhaps the days of the white loaf are numbered. The time required to develop a product also varies tremendously – 40 years so far have been spent developing the fast breeder nuclear reactor and it is still not commercially viable. Conversely, it now takes about four years to develop a new car although the Mini took 15 years.

It should also be realised that within an industry different products will have reached different stages that might not be typical of the industry as a whole. It is commonly believed that the electrical domestic appliance market has reached the maturity stage. However, although refrigerators are already in 90% of homes, microwave ovens have less than 15% ownership and it is consequently hardly surprising that the Japanese have decided to focus on this segment in order to enter the industry globally.

Marketing activities will change as a product passes through its life cycle. For example, strategic issues at the development stage of a grocery product would be concerned with such questions as 'What business are we in?' whilst marketing research would be concerned with new product testing. Marketing mix considerations would be at the planning stage although sales training would be taking place.

During the market introduction of the product the overall strategic decision would be whether to continue or to cancel. Marketing research would be directed at customer and consumer reactions which could lead to modifications to the product or to the pricing policy which could initially have been based on skimming or a penetration price. Promotion would be concentrating on the 'creation of demand' while the sales force would be dealing with unforeseen problems and gaining new distribution outlets.

In the growth stage the company can take risks with over-capacity and even with quality in order to establish a market position – profit margins will permit production inefficiencies. Strategic issues would include how to deal with private brands, and marketing research would be focusing on brand share information. Price falls are likely and new variants would be introduced as a result of new product development. Promotion would be building up brand loyalty as the sales force battled for shelf space. Distribution would have to cope with the surge of demand as new outlets stocked up.

During maturity and saturation, efficient use of plant and close attention to production costs become much more important. Strategy will be concerned with the introduction of new products and the relation of these to existing products. Marketing research will be looking for signs of market saturation and stagnation. Price will remain steady if no private brands exist; otherwise it will fall, particularly as large outlets pressure for special terms. 'Below the line' promotional expenditure will rise if private brands exist.

The decline stage will raise the question 'Do we wish to remain in business?' and how much will depend on the forecasts provided by marketing research. Prices would continue to fall and there would be greater promotional expenditure in an attempt to maintain sales.

It can therefore be seen that the product life cycle concept is not only a useful tool for analysing demand but is also valuable in managing the marketing mix during the introduction of a product and throughout its life cycle.

Question 2: Porter's strategies

(a)   Porter argues that the most crucial strategic aim of all companies is to obtain and maintain competitive advantage. He defines three generic strategies, and argues that only one of these may be employed at any time.

Overall cost leadership - companies usually achieve cost advantages by entering into efficient, high volume production, typically employing capital-intensive 'high-tech' equipment. The Japanese are the masters of this type of production. It is argued that this type of production results in industry's 'critical mass' (low volume, inefficient producers remain uncompetitive largely due to their small size). In the car industry, the high critical mass means that the market is virtually impenetrable for newcomers.

The economies of scale which result from large scale producers mean that certain activities, such as research and development, treasury management, and efficient distribution systems will only be possible for a sufficiently high volume producer.

The learning curve factor will be more applicable to the more automated production techniques of larger companies.

Differentiation - presents the product in a unique way, and in this way shields itself from competition by shedding (or hiding!) the product's commodity status. It is vital that potential buyers should be aware of the differentiating factors. Differentiating can be achieved by branding, or more substantially by improved quality, design, technological benefits, etc.

A focus strategy - involves concentration on particular products, well-defined demographic segments, and possibly distinct geographics. Success is achieved by specialising in providing a particularly efficient and effective product or service to a small market segment. Such products may be niche products. The Morgan sports car would fall into this category. The focus strategy enables an 'expert' image to be credibly relayed.

(b)   Given that a company has effective, reliable distribution channels and a comprehensive marketing apparatus to reach its customers, the cost leadership strategy critically hinges on the following resources:

(i)   *Capital* – As high volume production tends to be capital intensive in nature, companies have vast capital requirements to pay both for the equipment and for the vastly increased working capital requirement to support the increased sale of operations.

(ii) *Manpower* – The new computerised techniques will require well trained and committed employees, in large numbers. Thus an effective personnel department would typically be required.

(iii) *Product design and quality* – It is crucial that the product will be so apparently 'crammed' with added value as to prove irresistible to the end consumer. The product benefits should be obtained using efficient working practices. (For instance, Japanese car factories are able to make several different products on one production line.)

(iv) *Distribution channels* – These should be sufficiently comprehensive to cover consumers in as many countries as possible. The channels should be capable of carrying a high intensity of product, and should be as short as possible to achieve this end (with the minimum number of 'middle men').

(v) *Cost control* – This is crucial, and inefficiency should be able to be detected by a comprehensive budgetary control system.

(vi) *Sales and marketing* – Should be sufficiently expert, and employ enough talented resource, to steer the corporation towards new world markets (and service existing customers).

(c) The risks involved in attaining 'overall cost leadership' include the following.

(i) The low unit cost of product may result in compromising safety.

(ii) The larger organisational size may prove too complex for the current management.

(iii) There may be an over-emphasis on efficiency, not considering the market characteristics in enough detail.

(iv) Technological advances can quickly erode the competitive edge of large companies (when the transistor was invented, many producers were obliterated overnight).

(v) Larger companies will be less adaptable to other environmental changes, for instance violent swings in the economy.

(vi) Cost advantage may be achieved at the expense of maintaining a balanced portfolio of products.

CHAPTER 7	EXAM-TYPE QUESTIONS

Question 1: Strengths and Weaknesses

When conducting a survey of the strengths and weaknesses of an organisation, invariably there is a tendency for management to concentrate on certain aspects of the operation. This is not to say however, that the extent of the survey will be identical in each area on every occasion. Neither does it imply that other areas of investigation should automatically be eliminated. A strengths and weaknesses appraisal is part of the work of a position audit.

(a) **Financial resources**

As with internal appraisal, this consists of constructing a series of accounting ratios to measure profitability, growth and liquidity, and then comparing them with earlier results and also with results of other firms in similar circumstances. Such an exercise will indicate the firm's strengths and weaknesses both in terms of former occasions and current competitiveness.

(b) **Profitability**

This involves a series of analyses each with the aim of identifying the organisation's operational position. For example, it might include an analysis of sales and profit involving sales mix, pricing strategy, discount facilities, and an assessment of the returns on total assets employed. Costs obviously have important implications for profitability and therefore, determination of operational costs and internal efficiency is also required.

(c) **Effectiveness of functional departments within the organisation**

This is normally done by defining the specialist knowledge available, specialist activities undertaken, the significant factors on which the company depends, including the areas of vulnerability.

During the exercise these issues will be raised in connection with all the functional activities and in addition, it is necessary to ascertain specific details for each function. For example, the plant utilisation rate, the proportion of bad debts, the extent of production delays due to failure of supplies etc.

(d) **Product range**

Frequently companies have an extensive product range, which needs frequent reviewing to ensure that it is well balanced and relevant to current market needs. This involves the determination of the profit contribution of each product in relationship to the resources it utilises. It is also necessary to pay particular attention to market trends to ascertain whether in the product mix, certain products need upgrading whilst others require phasing out. In addition, there is the need to establish the position regarding the introduction of new products, both in terms of frequency and timing, to ensure the company's competitive position is maintained. All these various activities add up to an extensive marketing research assignment.

(e) **Human resources of the organisation**

Any such appraisal must ensure that personnel are suitably motivated and adequate facilities are available for appropriate staff development. One technique which many companies have adopted in one form or another, is management by objectives (MBO). This includes establishing key tasks for a job, agreed performance standards and providing suitable encouragement for such standards to be achieved and is followed by a subsequent stage in which a review is conducted involving the managers and their superiors to compare actual performance against the standards agreed. It also provides from time to time, an assessment of the potential of each manager.

Whatever form of management style the organisation uses it is essential that a thorough assessment of the human resources of the organisation is carried out with the main purpose of ensuring that the manpower resources of the company match both the current technical and social skills requirements, and also those that it is anticipated will be required in the future.

In addition, it is necessary to ensure that the organisational structure is the most suitable for present day needs. With rapid technological, economic, political and sociological changes, an organisation can rapidly become out of date. Conducting frequent organisational appraisals should avoid this happening.

Therefore, it can be seen that an appraisal of the firm's strengths and weaknesses is a considerable task with a notable contribution required from the accountant. The exercise involves considerable analysis and invariably leads to certain criticisms of the existing arrangements. Such criticisms, even if only implied, may not always be readily acceptable but must be carried out, and carried out authentically, if the company is to obtain the maximum benefit from an appraisal of its strengths and weaknesses.

Question 2: Cuddles

(a) Some of the general environmental forces that may impact on Cuddles Limited over the next few years can be considered under the headings of political, economic, social and technological factors (known as PEST analysis).

Political

The UK is becoming more closely integrated with the rest of Europe. European Community legislation has a strong influence on UK companies, for example, legislation and regulations relating to working conditions for employees and consumer rights for customers. These are constantly changing.

Economic

The UK presently enjoys a strong economy, with stable and low rates of interest, inflation and unemployment. This has made the pound sterling very strong in relation to other currencies.

Cuddles may find that its customers find it much cheaper to import its products rather than manufacture them. The strong pound will also make it very difficult to export its garments.

Social

The demographic trends are that generally UK's population is ageing and the birth rate is declining in spite of government efforts to encourage marriage, "the family" and having children.

Fashions are changing more rapidly and there is a growing need for fashionable clothes for children by their parents.

This will affect the demand for Cuddles' garments.

Technological

The technology of garment manufacture, particularly computer aided design and manufacture (CAD-CAM) as well as production methods are constantly changing.

Unless Cuddles keeps abreast of the changes and has a programme of updating the technologies it uses, it will fall behind its competitors.

These are just a few of the factors influencing Cuddles' strategic and operational position now and in the future that Richard has to take into account in achieving his ambitions.

(b) The competitive forces that are likely to impact on Cuddles Limited as a small player in the children's garment industry can be considered under the five forces categorised by Michael Porter.

Threats from potential entrants

There would be very few barriers to entry for another competitor entering the market to compete against Cuddles. The barriers to entry as a major player are significant as the established large manufacturers have established strong brands and major investments in modern technologies and distribution channels.

The major threat of entry is from overseas, particularly suppliers from the Far East on a low price approach.

Threats from substitutes

There are likely to be many alternative substitute fashions for Cuddles' garments. In the absence of developing a strong brand image, Cuddles will face severe competition and from alternative firms who have their own designs supported by strong brands. This will lower the price Cuddles can charge for its products.

Threats from the power of buyers

The retail outlets have many domestic and foreign suppliers they can buy from and with the large quantities they buy, Cuddles' margins will be squeezed.

Cuddles will be in a relatively weak position with buyers compared to rivals who have more fashionable garments supported by strong brand image.

Threats from the power of suppliers

Cuddles, as a small firm, is unlikely to be buying significant raw materials and services from suppliers relative to larger competitors. It is unlikely to be in a position of demanding lower prices, as it will not have the scale of operations to enjoy such economies.

Rivalry and Competition

Although Cuddles has decided to concentrate on garments for babies and infants, the market it is operating in is large and is dominated by several large firms. Cuddles is a very small player in this market.

The manufacturing industry for children's clothing is extremely competitive and the competition is intensified by the global nature of the market. Cuddles will be facing intense competition from both local and overseas firms.

The larger firms are often vertically integrated having their own retail outlets and their own manufacturing base.

Cuddles will find it difficult to compete with its limited resources to, for example, fight price reductions, introduce matching or better technologies or to market its products and develop a brand.

Overall, taking into account all five forces, Cuddles' position is weak relative to its competitors and its ambitions to grow will increase the intensity of competition and reduce or eliminate profitability.

(c) Michael Porter provides a range of strategic options that Cuddles can choose from in deciding how to compete in its market in order to grow and sustain competitive advantage.

Cuddles can choose from three generic strategies categorised as:

1. cost leadership

2. differentiation

3. focus

Cost leadership can be pursued through improved efficiency, low unit cost production, increased automation and generally achieving economies of scale. This approach would not be advisable for a small firm with limited resources such as Cuddles. It is an approach more suitable for the dominant firms in the market.

Differentiation would involve Cuddles in developing unique fashions, a strong brand based on quality with value and generally providing a distinctive service relative to its competitors. This is probably a better approach for a firm like

Cuddles that does not have the resources to achieve economies of scale. Developing a strong brand image based on quality will give Cuddles sustainable competitive advantage.

Focus relates to specialising in a segment of the market. The specialisation can be based on product features, customer type, quality or geographical location etc. Cuddles may be suited to a strategy of differentiation based on quality to focus on supplying a dedicated large customer, say a leading high street clothing retail chain.

This would give it a strong base for further growth at the risk of having a limited customer base.

CHAPTER 8	EXAM-TYPE QUESTIONS

Question 1: Firebridge Tyres Ltd

Tutorial note. This is a fairly straightforward question on the environment and how an organisation can ensure environmental fit.

Part (a)

Main factors in the external environment

The environment of an organisation is everything outside of its boundaries. Organisations are by definition open to the environment: it is the source of their inputs; it is the destination of their outputs; and it sets constraints over what the organisation can do. Some argue that the environment is increasingly a source of uncertainty for organisations, and that it is becoming harder to read. The degree of uncertainty it causes results from its complexity and the rate of change.

Hofer and Schendel argue that the very purpose of strategy is to secure some sort of environmental fit. This might be an extreme position, as it implies reaction to the environment rather than activity to shape environmental forces. However, any formal strategic planning process takes the environment into account.

As far as the general environment is concerned, we can analyse PEST and competitive factors.

Political and legal factors. Firebridge Tyres Ltd (FTL) operates in a stable political environment. Agreements between governments on the single European market and GATT have opened up international markets, not only to FTL but to its competitors: however GTC does not want FTL to increase its exports outside Europe. There is no shortage of car service stations, a fragmented industry, so political interference is unlikely. Local government might determine the siting of certain activities. FTL is indirectly affected by government transport policy, if this affects the demand for and use of cars.

Economic factors. In the UK, tyres must be checked annually, as part of the MOT testing process. The overall level of economic activity determines transport use, which influences wear and tear of tyres. However, in times of hardship, people will be less likely to buy the premium brand range preferring to go for the lower cost Freeway range, cheaper overseas tyres, or even retreads. The general level of prosperity also influences the number of people in the population who use cars; rising incomes and wealth mean rising numbers of cars purchased, hence greater demand for tyres. People will also move to lower cost service options in hard times: FTL does not want a service business lumbered with heavy overheads. The UK market is much smaller than the US:

GTC might be unrealistic in assuming that the same formula, which might depend on economies of scale, would work over in the UK.

Social factors influence demand indirectly, via political pressure for legislation or changing patterns of demand. For examples, governments are more concerned with ecological issues. There are disposal problems with used tyres. This might affect what they are made of. Some can be burnt as fuel, but with landfill taxes increasing, recyclable tyres may be preferred. The proposed service business depends on patterns of car use. It may be that many drivers and will prefer a garage.

Technological factors. Tyres are a fairly mature technology, although there are improvements to be made to increase their grip, their longevity, and their recyclability. Any changes in the plastics and materials industry might be relevant. Also, if cars become lighter, lighter tyres will be needed.

The main factor in the environment is competition, which is impinging directly on FTL

A number of service chains already exist in the UK, but otherwise the industry is fairly fragmented. Competition on price is important, but also on quality. However, FTL needs to assess how the competition will respond.

The competitive environment can be described using Porter's five forces model (barriers to entry-see below, substitute products, customer bargaining power, supplier bargaining power, competitive rivalry). There are few substitute products, but competitive rivalry is intense. Suppliers have low bargaining power probably.

Part (b)

Barriers to entry discourage new competitors to an industry. If they are low, it is easy to set up shop, but hard to discourage other people from doing so too. The main barriers to entry are described below.

Economies of scale. For some firms, a barrier to entry is the size of the operation needed to be profitable. Tyres are high volume, low margin products on the whole, and for most cases, the best way to make money is to manufacture in large quantities. A large plant implies high fixed costs and a high breakeven point. There is little evidence that significant economies of scale can be achieved in *servicing*. There are some service chains, but the industry seems fragmented.

Product differentiation. FTL already pursues this strategy by producing different tyres, directed at different segments. In service, differentiation might be achieved on the basis of FTL's brand name, and a promise of service quality. Advertising costs might be considerable, however, to build the brand.

Capital requirements. No new factories need to be built, of course, but FTL will have to acquire leases or freeholds of a number of properties in which to set up its service stations. Many of the prime spots might be taken over by petrol stations. Ideally FTL will be positioned near residential areas or near roads, to make them easy to find. The cost of this depends on the size of the operation that GTC is proposing.

Switching costs are minimal; new customers are easy to find, but hard to keep, unless service quality is better.

Distribution. The chain is basically a distribution outlet for FTL's tyres. The importance of choosing the right sites for distributing the service was identified in (iii) above.

Existing service providers know the market, but otherwise they have no special advantages.

Barriers to entry are fairly low. This will make it easy to set up business, but hard to make a profit perhaps, unless some unique lessons can be transferred from GTC, operating in a very different transport infrastructure.

Part (c)

Distinctive competences and critical success factors

A distinctive competence is those activities which a firm carries out uniquely or distinctly well. To be an enduring source of competitive advantage, a distinctive competence should be hard to imitate.

Critical success factors, on the other hand, are aspects of a business's performance which are essential to its success. Some of these relate to internal processes, others to the basic infrastructure of the business.

What is FTL's distinctive competence. FTL is a manufacturing business, making what is essentially a commodity products, tyres, with a stab at product differentiation. This competence is not truly distinctive, as there are other tyre manufacturers in the world, but FTL has built up a market presence in Europe. The distinctive competences in such a business might be the ability:

(a) To build a brand which customers recognise

(b) To make incremental technical innovations, to encourage new sales

(c) To keep costs under control, to support the brand, and to prevent its erosion by competition

(d) To win the support of distributors and garages for the tyres, as opposed to competitors

How do these relate to the service business? A key problem is that services are a very different proposition to products. There are several possible critical success factors for the service business.

(a) A brand which customers recognise (eg as with McDonald's for hamburgers) and choose, having realistic and satisfied expectations of what it offers

(b) A number of well chosen sites for people to choose and access easily, which make the experience not too unpleasant (eg by offering customers a lounge or coffee bar)

(c) Well trained staff who not only know how to change wheels and tyres, and do other repairs but who are able to demonstrate higher standards of customer care

(d) To be seen as preferable to the local garage in terms of the processes by which the service is provided

FTL's existing competences at best cover brand building. It has no experience in choosing and managing properties: US conditions are different, so a transfer of skills between the US and the UK firm may be hard to achieve. FTL runs a manufacturing business; a service business, based on a variety of intangibles such as staff courtesy, is a different proposition. The required cultures of the two businesses might conflict.

The firm might have to spend a lot of money on training, both technically and in terms of customer care. Also money would have to be spent on building the brand. However, GTC should be able to provide some expertise in building the service aspects.

In short, FTL's distinctive competences are not sufficient to make a go of this plan, given the fragmented nature of the industry. GTC may be able to provide some help, but GTC might end up investing more money and making short term losses, rather than the profits it is looking for.

FTL is in a difficult situation, because its managers are tied by the priorities of the US parent

Question 2: Value chain analysis

Value activities consist of all those activities a firm undertakes, from the moment of initial purchase of raw materials and other inputs, to the moment of final receipt of payment from the customer. Value Chain Analysis (VCA) looks at each of the processes that make up the chain of activity and asks both how important it is in a given company's production or service activity, and how the company compares in that respect to its competitors. The value chain model divides an organisation's activities into nine generic activities, five primary activities and four support activities.

To review the withdrawal rate of students from the University's courses a clear statement of the University's objectives and what they are trying to achieve needs to be drawn up by the management team. The management accountant will then analyse the primary and support activities in the University's value chain and identify areas that are causing the greatest level of concern (see diagram below).

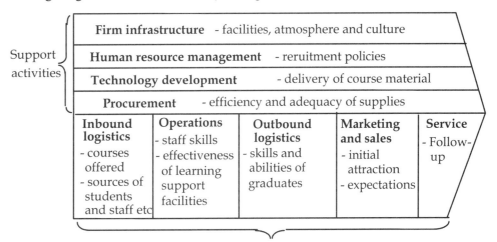

Primary activities

Primary activities - are concerned with converting the inputs into the finished product/service and its transfer to the customer and any after-sales service. They include the following five functions

Inbound logistics - are the activities concerned with handling the inputs. From the University's point of view the analysis will cover:

- The intake of students eg, whether entry requirements have changed. A lowering of standards may lead to students being unable to cope with the work, while a raising may find students' expectations of the course is not fulfilled. An increase in the intake could lead to more revenue but less individual attention for students with short-term problems.

- The courses offered and whether they have changed over the period of increased withdrawal.

- The sourcing of staff and support facilities. The University seems to be focusing on consultancy work and research and recruiting lecturers who have achieved success in these areas, rather than concentrating on its main purpose of education.

Operations - are concerned with the transformation of the inputs and will look in detail at:

- How the University compares with competitor institutions - do they have similar withdrawal rates in the first year? If not, then the University needs to determine what they are doing differently and what they must do to improve the service. A review of the students that leave might show a pattern to the transfers eg, students leaving to go to particular universities.

- The calibre of staff - are the lecturers able to communicate effectively and do they show an interest in helping the students in their studies? Also, does their treatment of students vary between the first year and subsequent years?

- The course content - is it comprehensible and challenging and are the academic standards being applied in an appropriate manner?

- The assessment structure on the courses with the highest withdrawal rate - analysis might show poor results from assessed coursework and little feedback to help students overcome difficulties. Alternatively, to achieve target pass rates, lecturers may be encouraging certain students to leave the course.

- The effectiveness of the learning support facilities.

Outbound logistics - are concerned with the finished product ie, the skills and abilities of the graduates after completing their courses and the perception of the customers - the government and employers

Marketing and sales - are responsible for communication with the customers eg, advertising and promotion. The analysis should assess what attracts the students and why an increasing number believe that the course is not living up to their expectations.

Service - covers all of the activities that occur after graduation and includes arranging milk rounds, job fairs and other links to potential employers. The management accountant should analyse the types of contact with the graduate and the retention rates for students moving on to other courses in the University?

Support activities

Each of the groups of primary activities is linked to support activities. These can be divided into four areas:

1   Procurement **-** is the process of purchasing inputs. Areas that will be analysed include the efficiency and adequacy of the supplies and the level of administrative support provided to the lecturers and students.

2   **Technology development** - covers not just machines and processes but know-how. Improved technology development may be employed in delivering course material to students. Technology may also be used in undertaking marketing research into the attractiveness of types of courses to prospective students.

3   **Human resource management** transcends all primary activities. It includes all the activities involved in the recruitment, training, development and remuneration of staff.

4   **Infrastructure -** which supports the entire value chain, includes the systems of planning, finance, quality control and estate management.

Managing the linkages

Having gathered information under all these headings, it is then essential to assess how they all fit together. There are three types of linkage:

Primary-primary   Inter-departmental co-operation between, say, inbound logistics and marketing to ensure that prospective students are given sufficient information about courses.

Support-primary   Computer-based operations, involving co-operation between information technology and lecturers. For example, teaching aids and course notes made available

Support-support   Computer-based information systems automatically monitoring recruitment policies.

CHAPTER **9**   EXAM-TYPE QUESTION

Balanced scorecard

Reference is increasingly made to the 'balanced scorecard' when performance measurement is discussed because, given an appropriate strategy, business success is dependent upon effective operational practices and processes. Some writers claim that traditional financial performance measures alone are of limited value and:

- are backward looking and reflect yesterday's decisions;

- are sometimes of doubtful validity due to the manipulation of figures;

- reinforce short-term thinking;

- can give misleading signals for continuous improvement and innovation - activities today's competitive environment demands.

Kaplan and Norton have advocated the balanced scorecard approach as a framework to translate a strategy into operational terms. This method deals with internal and external, current and future perspectives and uses financial and non-financial performance measures to put strategy and mission, and not control, as the centrepiece of a performance measurement system. It requires top management and each part of the organisation to look at itself from four different perspectives

Financial perspective - the performance indicators used, to assess whether the objectives are being achieved in both profit-motivated and not for profit organisations, highlight the observable financial results of past management actions and typically include, profit, sales, ROI, cash flow or economic value added (EVA). With profit-motivated organisations, the returns must be sufficient to keep the shareholders satisfied and loyal. With not-for-profit organisations, high levels of effectiveness and an economic use of resources must be achieved to add value to the members/clients and society.

Customer perspective - focuses on what the organisation must do to satisfy its customers and achieve its financial objectives. For all types of organisations, although especially the profit-motivated ones, managers must initially clarify the marketing objectives and identify the target market so that the measures chosen focus on the achievements of the organisation in reaching and satisfying its target market. Market research is used to measure market share, customer acquisition, retention, profitability and satisfaction. These can be sub-divided into measures relating to lead times, on-time delivery, product quality and product cost. For profit-motivated organisations, feedback from customers will identify what they like and dislike about the product or service and how this impacts on the organisation's image or reputation. However, the not for profit organisation also has an obligation to provide appropriate levels of service to its clients or members, which should be measured against established targets.

Internal business processes - linked to the customer perspective, the organisation should assess how it goes about delivering its products and services and identify the processes that have the most impact on customer satisfaction. The internal processes generate financial returns to the profit-orientated organisation and for both sectors this perspective is concerned with increasing efficiency and achieving improved effectiveness in the levels of product or service delivery

Innovation and learning - whilst the customer and internal process perspectives identify the current parameters for competitive success, the company needs to learn and to innovate to satisfy future needs. Both profit-orientated and not-for-profit organisations will want to measure how much the internal processes are improving over time. Measures of likely future success include:

- length of time to develop new products/services (compared to competition)

- percentage of revenue from new products

- investment in innovative products/services/materials and processes

- intellectual assets and organisational learning;

- employee satisfaction.

The measures for all four of the perspectives are linked and must be viewed as a whole eg, excess capacity can be a by-product of quality improvements. Increasing productivity may mean that fewer employees are required for a given level of output. Increasing sales may result in these improvements being exploited. A limited number of key measures for each perspective will be identified and monitored to ensure that the strategic direction of the organisation is maintained. The set of measures chosen will differ from organisation to organisation and will vary over time depending on the specific circumstances faced by the enterprise and its current vision and strategic objectives. The financial measurements remind management that improved quality, productivity and response time only benefits the organisation when it creates a sustainable competitive advantage or is translated into improved financial results or an increase in EVA.

Although the balanced scorecard provides an appropriate mechanism to achieve overall improvement in shareholder value or effectiveness within the not-for-profit sector, there are certain limitations:

There is no overall control measure, but an assortment of diverse measures.

The measures themselves may not always be consistent with each other and might give out conflicting signals to management.

Not all perspectives can be maximised at the same time ie, there are trade-offs between the perspectives

CHAPTER 10

EXAM-TYPE QUESTION

TDM plc

To: The Managing Director

From: Accountant

Subject: Corporate mission statements

The meaning of corporate mission

The corporate mission embodies the overall purposes of an organisation. A corporate mission statement is formulated to express the company's philosophy and should answer fundamental questions such as: Why does the company exist? Who will be served by and benefit from the company? What products or services will be provided? The majority of mission statements are presented using general, rather than detailed, concepts.

Corporate mission and strategic planning

In order to prepare an effective strategic plan, the management must first address the organisation's mission. There is a certain amount of controversy regarding the point in the planning process at which the mission statement is best formulated. One view is that the mission statement is of such a fundamental nature that the strategic plan cannot be prepared without reference to it. Another view, expressed by Argenti, is diametrically opposed. He postulates that the mission statement is the end result of the strategic planning process. These opinions demonstrate how difficult it can be to differentiate between an organisation's mission and its objectives. The *mission* is a wide-ranging statement that presents the organisation's *raison d'être* in terms of its ability to satisfy some of society's needs whilst its *objectives* are the company's broad goals.

Areas to be covered

The mission statement is likely to be formulated by the company's board of directors. Although it will not be quantitative in nature it will usually highlight several areas, such as:

(a) the kinds of products and services the company aims to provide

(b) the customers to be served

(c) the markets in which the company anticipates operating

(d) an overview of the company philosophy and the broad expression of its policies

(e) the company's attitude towards matters encompassing social obligations

(f) the manner in which management wishes the firm to be perceived by the public.

Benefits from developing a mission statement

The usefulness of a mission statement may be summarised as follows.

(a) All staff will gain an understanding of the firm's purpose and philosophy.

(b) Expectations and attitudes within the firm will be expressed in terms of a long-range vision.

(c) The organisation will benefit from unanimity of purpose, which should result in decisions advantageous to the purposes of the company.

(d) The boundaries within which the company operates will be clearly laid down. This will assist in developing co-ordinated plans.

(e) An unambiguous statement regarding the overall direction of the company should lead to enhanced allocation of resources.

Conclusion

The company would gain several benefits from the formulation of a mission statement. It would greatly assist the decision makers and those responsible for implementing the firm's policies. The mission statement also has an important role to play in helping management focus on fundamental issues in terms of strategic planning and will ensure that strategic plans do not conflict with the basic purpose of the organisation.

CHAPTER 11	EXAM-TYPE QUESTION

Strategic objectives

(a) The survival of the organisation is usually considered to be the prime objective of any business. It is a commonly held view, however, that if a company is not growing, then it is dying. If the total market is expanding, it is likely that most competitor companies are planning to grow and firms who remain static will be out-performed by other organisations in the industry. Therefore, many companies include a 'growth objective' in their strategic plan, considering this as a more aggressive policy which will help ensure the firm's survival.

There are a number of additional reasons why growth is seen as an attractive objective. Systems of taxation generally influence the owners of a firm to favour growth. As shareholders must pay tax on dividends they generally prefer the majority of profits to be reinvested, thus resulting in capital gains which will reduce the total liability of the shareholders as individuals. The management of a company will opt for growth as a means of enhancing their personal position. Association with a larger firm will be perceived as desirable and the managers' individual goals will play a part in the formulation of a strategic plan.

There are several definitions of the term *growth*. It may be viewed as an increase in sales or market share, or alternatively in terms of increased profitability and shareholders' returns. Another important factor is that growth should have a specific purpose; that is, as a means of achieving the stated objectives of management; and not be seen as an end in itself.

It is normally assumed that the objective of a company will be to maximise shareholders' wealth, and growth is one way of achieving this. Another view holds that each company has multiple objectives. One of these may be survival, with growth and profit maximisation seen as a means of achieving this aim.

The concept of growth must be placed within the context of the past performance of the company and the average for the particular industry. The strategy adopted by management will be influenced by an accurate view of the environment, the strategies adopted by competitor companies and the available resources.

(b) Management can consider several growth strategies as follows.

(i) *Market penetration* – This is increasing sales of present products in present markets and can be accomplished by inducing current customers to purchase more of the firm's products, attracting non-users or by persuading competitors' customers to purchase from the company.

(ii) *Market development* – This involves increasing sales in previously untried geographical locations or new market segments.

(iii) *Product development and diversification* – An important distinction must be drawn between these two strategies as they involve different levels of risk.

Product development entails providing the present market with a new product, whereas diversification involves both new products and new markets. In order to establish which strategy should be developed, it is important to draw up forecasts about present products. If the current market environment is favourable in terms of customers and products, then market penetration or market development and diversification will be suitable strategies to adopt. If, however, the current market environment is not viewed as favourable for growth, management would be advised to adopt a strategy of product development and diversification.

Of the possible strategies, diversification entails most risk as it involves the development of both new products and new markets. Means of minimising the risk should therefore be assessed by firms embarking upon this strategy. One method, defined by McNamee as an organisation acquiring 'totally, or in part, another organisation whose business is not related to the acquiring organisation's business', is that of *conglomerate diversification.*

Although conglomerate diversification can be adopted by a company as a means of achieving rapid growth with relative ease, the nature of the strategy as defined above necessarily means that the acquiring and acquired firms will be operating in different areas. This means that considerable risk is involved. Nevertheless, there are several reasons why management may opt for conglomerate diversification.

(i) Management may consider profit as the sole objective of the firm.

(ii) If the acquiring firm has a high level of specialisation, conglomerate diversification may be the only possible strategy for expansion.

(iii) If the threat of a decline in current markets is forecast, the position of the company may be jeopardised and conglomerate diversification may be seen as a solution.

CHAPTER 12	EXAM-TYPE QUESTION

Business environment

(a) (i) Strategic management concerns the determination of a general direction for the enterprise and the formulation of overall business policies. Examples of strategic decision are the markets in which it is to operate, how many divisions and departments the firm is to have, whether to acquire other businesses and how to finance operations. Strategy embraces all aspects of business policy, planning, organisation and control.

Within this process, environmental scanning is essential. This is the systematic examination of each firm's environments to identify opportunities and threats created by external exchange. Not all environmental factors can be investigated, so a handful of relevant external variables must be selected for research and forecasting. Normally, these variables concern:

- *marketing* - the activities of competitors, etc;

- *legislation* - government attitudes to the industry, etc;

- *technology* - production methods and their efficiency, etc.

Forecasting assists in producing a 'good fit' between an organisation's strategic management and its environment by allowing time in which the organisation can adapt and change in response to environment disturbances.

(ii) Gap analysis is where the planner sets targets based on what he or she believes to be attainable in the longer term and then compares these targets with forecasts of future achievement taken from projection of current activities, assuming that present circumstances continue. Divergences are then analysed and measures implemented to bridge the gaps. The process of gap analysis can be summarised in the following steps:

Step 1: *Goals or targets are set* - These are the performance levels, which are desired by the end of the planning period.

Step 2: *Current performance is extrapolated* - Using environmental data and internal revenue and cost data, the organisation's performance at the end of the planning period is forecast. These forecasts are based upon the existing strategy continuing with no substantial change, except for amendments to incorporate changed environmental or internal circumstances.

Step 3: *The forecast gap is measured* - Once the forecast has been made, the difference between it and the goal or target can be measured. The difference is an indication of the size of the strategic adjustments that will be necessary to achieve goals or targets.

Step 4: *Develop strategies to close the gap.*

Figure 1 shows a simple gap analysis and Figure 2 shows a continuous gap analysis.

Figure 1: Simple gap analysis

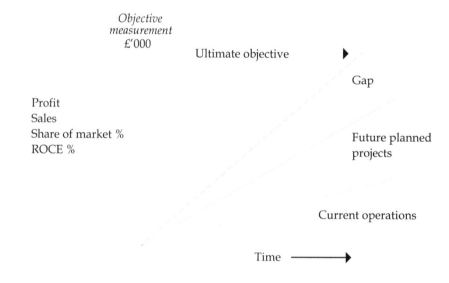

Figure 2: Continuous gap analysis

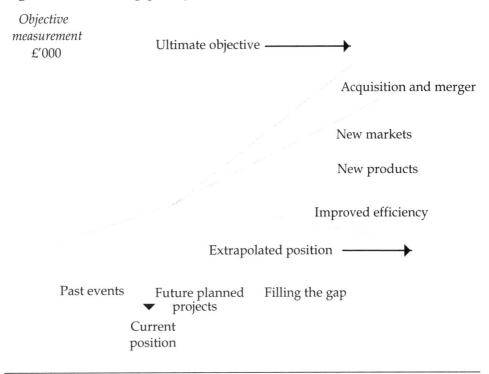

CHAPTER 13   EXAM-TYPE QUESTION

Market segmentation

Part (a)

The feasibility of market segmentation is affected by the following four factors.

Identification

The main task of marketing research is the identification of the sub-markets.

This entails identifying sectors of significant interest and analysis of trends within them, paying particular attention to resources used and requirements.

An in depth understanding of the market situation must be obtained, and hence qualitative data along with quantitative should be used.

Current competitive marketing activities should be analysed and a comparison made with the company's proposed strategies and products.

The company's brands must be evaluated to highlight their product appeal along with the estimated market share.

The analysis and comparison of advertising used by competitors should be identified to ensure that the company sustains its competitive advantage.

Each product market should be examined to highlight the nature of demand specific to that market (ie how far it is influenced by economic factors, such as price).

Accessibility

Particular sectors of the market should be accessed in terms of directing marketing effort.

Marketing objectives must be realised. This will be ensured by careful analysis, planning and control.

Sub-markets should be analysed in terms of how much media coverage is received, along with behavioural factors such as family lifestyles and their influence.

The most effective method of distributing products within each market segment requires attention, and the facilities available for doing so.

If marketing overseas, the entry into a market and trading restrictions should be examined.

Measurability

An estimation by objective research will measure the effective size of a sub-market.

Therefore, suitable data needs to be available to provide the information. The types of data which are required will be demographic and psychographic.

Appropriateness

The needs of each firm differ. For satisfactory operation the market needs to be larger for one company than for another.

The company's resources and needs will arise from the relationship borne by market opportunities.

Part (b)

When purchasing a car, you don't just buy transport. A car has a particular style and a certain performance.

The car will have different levels of associated safety, economy and comfort. It may also have individual added features such as air conditioning or a CD player.

Overall, the product will have to satisfy the customer needs, being feelings of individuality and power.

An Aston Martin is a sign of success and is a big status symbol; the owner would acquire prestige upon purchasing the vehicle.

However, a Skoda being an unusual and cheap vehicle gives the impression that the owners are socially inferior to the owners of more expensive cars.

Ferrero Rocher chocolates are presented and promoted in such a way as to give the impression of an up-market product, when in fact it is just a piece of chocolate.

Purchasers of Ferrero Rocher do not believe that they will be involved with expensive parties as portrayed in the TV advertisements. However, when offered to guests they will be welcomed more than, say, peanuts. This is due to the promotional aspect which gives the impression of high class associated with wealthy people. This opinion of the product is one which would have been sought by the organisation.

The analysis of all goods can be performed in a similar manner. The attitude of every potential customer must be scrutinised, so that their needs can be satisfied.

Possible strategies

The marketing management has a number of alternative strategies to evaluate if it wishes to regain the lost share of the market and improve its profitability. Basically, decisions must be taken in respect of product, place, price and promotion.

The term 'product' covers the quality, unique features and style of the cutlery that is sold. At the present time the board attaches great importance to the high quality of the product resulting from it being marked 'Made in Sheffield'. This, together with a premium price, indicates that the firm has opted for a high-quality image for its product. This will mean that the product should be well designed, and the packaging and the presentation must emphasise that it is a superior product. It will also be necessary to bear in mind the quality aspect in respect of each element of the marketing mix.

'Place' focuses on the channels of distribution and the target markets. If a strategy of differentiation is adopted and only high quality products are produced, then the products should be sold in exclusive outlets. This will reinforce the quality image of the product. This means that HB should concentrate on superior retail outlets and boutiques. This may be expensive, as several wholesalers and a relatively large sales force will be needed to cover these smaller outlets.

'Price' is an extremely important aspect of the competitive position of HB's products. The major UK competitor, BQ plc, is able to import cutlery from Korea at a lower cost and there has been increased competition from the countries of the Pacific Rim. At the present time the product is selling at a premium and it is possible that the price can be increased further if customers are willing to pay for the perceived extra quality.

The promotional activities and the amount to be spent are decisions that form an important part of the overall marketing strategy of the firm. The high-quality image will be enhanced by a promotional campaign that emphasises the quality and superior design of HB's products. The advertisements and the magazines used will be important in establishing the image of the product that is fundamental to the whole marketing strategy. The significance of the 'Made in Sheffield' marking should be investigated in order to see how important this is to the purchasers.

CHAPTER 14	EXAM-TYPE QUESTION

W Limited

Part (a)

Management accounting is primarily concerned with providing information to managers to enable them to make decisions and to exercise control in order to eliminate wastage and inefficiencies.

Currently, the reports presented to the managers of W Ltd focus on the monthly cost variances in direct materials, direct labour and both the variable and fixed production overheads. As these reports highlight the differences in cost within the factory, they provide a useful means of directing the attention of the management to inefficiencies, which have occurred. Although this is an important aspect of control for W Ltd, it is only one aspect of the information that is needed to manage the organisation efficiently and effectively.

W Ltd's current reporting system does not look forward: it ignores information needed to manage the strategic aspects of the company and it appears to be inadequate for decision-making.

Part (b)

In the initial stage of the strategic planning process it is necessary to review the external environment in which the company operates, and also to conduct a position audit of the firm. To be able to undertake these initial steps in the strategic planning process, it is essential that information is prepared regularly. This is in order to keep the managers informed about the firm's customers, its suppliers and the availability of resources. In W Ltd this type of information is not currently provided, but is essential if the company is to improve its strategic planning.

Regular reports should be prepared to provide both financial and non-financial information about a range of different factors (eg market share is important). This refers to the position of the firm in relation both to its competitors and the size of the total market. Forecasts of future market trends would be helpful.

Reports about customers would provide details of the size of each organisation, the type of industry and their cost structure. It is particularly important to know about the profit generated by each group of customers. It is essential to know the reason why customers prefer to buy from W Ltd and what makes the company's technology and skills unique. These factors are what gives W Ltd its competitive advantage.

A specific issue in W Ltd is the amount of business that is turned down because of the lack of adequate facilities. Details should be recorded of the extent of the business that is rejected.

It is advisable to calculate the profit margin of the different products, jobs and customers. This will assist the managers to make correct decisions. This information should also include competitors' pricing policies.

CHAPTER 15	EXAM-TYPE QUESTION

Competitive edge

The strategic and competitive value of information technology has advanced in recent years to be a critical factor in systems planning issues. The high capital expenditure that new systems command, together with the greatly enhanced information processing capacity provided by technological developments, has meant that organisations are reviewing in detail the positive commercial advantage that can accrue from an imaginative application of information technology to their activities as a whole.

Much depends on the organisation's perception of the future strategic and competitive value of its information systems and on the role of the current information systems. If management simply see the function of information systems as the provision of support for other production or managerial structures, then the strategic and competitive value of future systems will not be regarded as particularly important.

Alternatively, information systems might be viewed as a means to 'factory' produce its information to enable the organisation to produce its goods or services efficiently. The systems might be felt to be vital in providing a competitive edge in existing products or markets, and to make new kinds of products possible.

Michael Porter emphasises that tomorrow's successful organisation will be a collection of skills and capabilities that are ready to pounce on any market opportunity. Possessing competitive edge means having those factors that lead customers to consistently prefer your products. He has suggested three overall competitive strategies that an organisation can implement.

(i) **Overall cost leadership**

This means becoming the most efficient producer. The objective to achieve overall cost leadership in the market is generally held by organisations in very competitive price-sensitive markets, where any means of reducing costs, or maintaining margins on lower prices, can lead to price reductions in goods and services offered to clients or customers. Information systems can reduce staff time spent on clerical work, allowing more to be spent on business development. Information technology can help not only by mechanising production systems but also by making the planning of production more efficient and using effective accounting control systems, e.g. activity based costing (ABC). Cost containment measures can include detailed control of stock levels, and an information system might allow a company to tie up its purchasing services directly with its suppliers by the use of computerised just in time (JIT) systems, reducing stock-holding costs and delays in processing orders.

(ii) Product differentiation

This means having unique products or varying them in such a way that they appear to be different from those offered by competitors. IT can help in the design of products, e.g. computer-aided design. Information systems can enhance an organisation's ability to compete by providing it with up-to-the-minute information as to customer needs and in tailoring their products or services to a customer's specific requirements. IS can also be used to compare customer purchases of the organisation's goods with those of other suppliers, allowing an organisation to differentiate its products on factors other than price.

(iii) Market niche

A niche market is a relatively small section of the overall market where customer needs are not fully satisfied. Information technology may be used to identify or exploit such a market niche by the analysis of market research data and other sales statistics. An example of the competitive value of information technology is the introduction of automated teller machines.

Additional to the provision of competitive advantage in the market place, internal changes in an organisation's structure can enhance its competitive edge, by encouraging more effective use of its human and material resources. Sometimes changes can be radical, e.g. a distribution organisation may get rid of one of its warehouses and employ a more efficient computerised distribution system.

Information systems might be used to foster innovation, by encouraging a free flow of ideas in a large organisation. A computer conferencing system, where individuals communicate their ideas with relative informality, is an example of such a system.

Information technology does not guarantee an enhanced competitive ability for the simple reason that any advantage due to information technology alone is likely to by temporary as competitors can also use it. Moreover, improved information does not necessarily lead to better decision making.

CHAPTER 16	EXAM-TYPE QUESTIONS

Question 1: Installing a training and development system

(a) All firms, whatever their size and level of complexity, will need some form of training if staff resources are to be used properly. Even smaller firms who tend to recruit staff ready trained will need to train existing staff to cope with new systems and to teach new staff the finer details of their working practices. The main difference between the different types of firm is likely to be the degree of formality involved in the training system.

The steps that should be taken to set up a training system will depend on its formality, but would normally include:

(i) an analysis of the organisation's training needs, based on a comparison of the skills possessed by its employees with those needed for its smooth operation

(ii) a decision on the scale and type of training system needed, and whether it can best be provided by the organisation's own staff or by external consultants

(iii)   the allocation of responsibilities for training within the firm, including a co-ordinator for any external training

(iv)   planning specific training courses and ensuring that they are properly timed to allow normal operations to continue

(v)   reviewing the system on a regular basis to ensure that it is still satisfying the organisation's training needs.

(b) In particular, the most likely benefits of a training system for the accounting function of an organisation are:

(i)   more efficient use of staff resources as staff understand their duties more clearly, so that, for example, difficult accounting entries will be dealt with more intelligently

(ii)   greater flexibility of operation as more staff acquire more skills, allowing for replacement of those concerned with maintaining one set of records by those working on others if workload or absences demand it

(iii)   greater ease in introducing new techniques as a training system will exist to help with the changeover; particularly useful if the accounting records are being computerised

(iv)   greater capability for dealing with staff turnover as the training programme automatically provides for career succession

(v)   general improvements in efficiency and staff morale.

Question 2: Human resource planning

Human resource planning is ' a strategy for the acquisition, utilisation, improvement and retention of an organisation's human resources'. It attempts to predict how many and what types of people will be needed in the future and the extent to which these needs are likely to be met. It should take into account how existing conditions might change, both inside and outside the organisation, and devise appropriate policies to ensure that the demand for staff is met. Its purpose in both the short and the long term is therefore:

- to estimate the (uncertain) demand for each grade and skill of employee;

- to estimate the (uncertain) supply of labour of the appropriate grades and skills;

- where there is a discrepancy between demand and supply to take measures, which will reduce the demand or improve the supply.

In other words, have the right people in the right jobs at the right time.

The process that the organisation might use for human resource planning is shown below:

```
┌─────────────────────────────────────┐
│ Strategic analysis of:              │
│ - the environment                   │
│ - the strengths and weaknesses,     │
│   opportunities and threats         │
│ - the organisation's use of labour  │
│ - the organisation's objectives     │
└─────────────────────────────────────┘
              │
              ▼
┌─────────────────────────────────────┐
│ Forecasting of:                     │
│ - internal demand and supply        │
│ - external supply                   │
└─────────────────────────────────────┘
              │
              ▼
┌─────────────────────────────────────┐
│ Job analysis                        │
│ - investigating the tasks           │
│   performed in each job             │
│ - identifying the skills required   │
└─────────────────────────────────────┘
              │
              ▼
┌─────────────────────────────────────┐
│ Implementation                      │
│ - training and developing existing  │
│   staff                             │
│ - recruiting required staff         │
└─────────────────────────────────────┘
```

The human resource plan is prepared on the basis of the analysis of labour requirements and the implications for productivity and costs. The plan may consist of various elements, according to the circumstances. For example:

- The recruitment plan - numbers and types of people and when they are required, culminating in the recruitment programme.

- The training plan - numbers of trainees required and/or existing staff needing training, culminating in the training programme.

- The redevelopment plan - programmes for transferring and retraining employees.

- The productivity plan - where and when redundancies are to occur; policies for selection and declaration of redundancies; redevelopment, retraining or relocation of redundant employees; policy on redundancy payments etc.

- The retention plan - actions to reduce avoidable labour wastage.

The plan should include budgets, targets and standards. It should allocate responsibilities for implementation and control - reporting and monitoring achievement against the plan etc.

One of the most valuable assets owned by an organisation is its staff. They sit at the centre of strategic planning. Whilst strategic planning seeks to minimise the uncertainty of the enterprise's environment (within a given set of constraints on its actions), it is the employees that actually implement the strategy ands take the opportunities offered. They must be motivated and developed and this is of the greatest importance when the people under consideration are professionally qualified. This is for a number of reasons:

If the organisation seeks excellence, it must realise that high quality of product and service is crucially dependent on a similarly high quality of staff. Excellence and human resource planning are closely related.

Developing such staff is generally quite expensive, and there are therefore quite considerable investment implications for the medium to long term. This is emphasised by the relatively long lead-time required in such development. If this is combined further with the high level of uncertainty inherent in attempting to develop individuals to a very high level of expertise and performance, the potential investment in these employees is clear. The uncertainty arises because some will fail to reach the required standard if the standard is very high, and even those that do reach it may take their expertise elsewhere.

Since professional skills tend to be at a premium, the development of 'home grown' experts may well be desirable. The influence of competitive employment markets is reduced and it may well be that professional employees, that are developed in-house, will show greater commitment and loyalty to the organisation as a result.

Professional employees are highly important to an organisation because it is through them that vital skills are acquired for such processes as the management of innovation, change and development. If accountants are taken as an example, the management of cash flows from new product lines is crucial to the flow of funds for the continuing development and success of future products. They will also be necessary for the budgeting process and the analysis of variances from the budgeted figures.

Question 3: Appraisal systems

Report on Performance Appraisal Systems

For the attention of Accounts Manager

June 2006

1   Terms of reference

This report was requested to provide the following information:

(a)   The purpose of an appraisal system.

(b)   The objectives of appraisals from the viewpoint of:

(i)   The individual

(ii)   The organisation

(iii) The barriers to effective appraisal

2   The purpose of an appraisal system

The general purpose of any assessment or appraisal is to improve the efficiency of the organisation by ensuring that the individual employees are performing to the best of their ability and developing their potential for improvement. It enables a picture to be drawn up of the human 'stock' of an organisation - its strengths and weaknesses, enabling more effective personnel planning.

Staff appraisal is a procedure where the managers or supervisors in an organisation discuss the work of their subordinates. They see each person individually and consider the progress they have been making in their job, their strengths and weaknesses and their future needs as regards training and development and the employee's potential for promotion.

The purpose therefore is:

- to assess the level of reward payable for an individual's efforts by measuring the extent to which the individual may be awarded a salary or pay increase compared with his or her peers.

- to review the individual's performance, identify training needs and plan follow-up training and development. By encouraging two-way communication, it permits an evaluation of a subordinate's strengths and weaknesses and the reasons for them. Thus, for example, if a subordinate's failure to perform is due to some failure in the work system, corrective action can be taken quickly. This will help the individual to do his or her job better and assist the organisation to achieve its objectives.

- to review the individual's potential by attempting to predict the type and level of work that the individual is likely to be capable of in the future. At the organisational level, this permits career and succession planning. At the individual level, it permits superior and subordinate to assess the most effective development plans for the subordinate.

3 The objectives of appraisals from the viewpoint of the individual

An appraisal is a process where the progress, performance, results and sometimes personality of an employee are reviewed and assessed by his or her immediate superior. The objectives of an appraisal from the individual's point of view include the following:

- it compares the individual's performance against a set and established standard;
- it identifies work of particular merit done during the review period;
- it provides a basis for remuneration
- it establishes what the individual has to do, regarding the objectives of the organisation;
- it determines the future employment of the individual eg, to remain in the same job, be transferred, promoted or retired early.
- it determines whether the individual is in a job where proper use is being made of his or her skills and talents;
- it establishes key results which the individual needs to achieve in work within a set period of time
- it identifies training and development needs

4 The objectives of appraisals from the viewpoint of the organisation

An appraisal system is used by the organisation to review and change, to inform and monitor and to examine and evaluate employees. The objectives from the organisation's point of view include the following:

- it monitors human resource selection processes against results;
- it identifies candidates for promotion, early retirement etc;
- it helps to identify and provide a record of any special difficulties/hazards surrounding the job, perhaps not previously realised;
- it identifies areas for improvement;
- it provides a basis for human resource planning;
- it helps formulate the training plan;
- it improves communication between managers and the managed where the organisation adopts the joint problem solving approach in their appraisal system

5 The barriers to effective appraisal

There have been studies on the effects of performance appraisal that show some negative effects eg:

- criticism had a negative effect on goal achievement;
- subordinates generally reacted defensively to criticism during appraisal interviews;
- inferior performance resulted from defensive reactions to criticism;
- repeated criticism had the worst effect on subsequent performance of individuals who had little self confidence;

Too often appraisal is taken as a personal criticism session, and therefore staff become very suspicious and uncooperative as it may announce financial disadvantage or lost promotion opportunity. The superior might show bias towards certain employees or may be reluctant to 'play God' with the subordinate's future. Since its very basis is face to face meetings, it is subject to particular barriers, and may be seen as:

- confrontational because of a lack of agreement on performance, badly explained or subjective feedback performance based on recent events or disagreement on longer term activities;

- judgmental - where appraisal is seen as a one sided process based entirely on the manager's perspective;

- an informal, loosely constructed and badly managed conversation without purpose;

- a bureaucratic system based on forms, devised solely to satisfy the organisation's personnel department, which make no attempt to identify individual and organisation performance and improvement;

- unfinished business and not part of a continuing process of performance management;

- an annual event which sets targets that quickly become out of date.

| CHAPTER 17 | EXAM-TYPE QUESTION |

BPR

Business Process Re-engineering (BPR) is one of a number of techniques that have been advanced to overhaul existing business processes and practices with a view to improving organisational performance. It is an approach where management ask radical questions about why things are done in a particular way, and ask whether alternative methods could achieve better results. The aim is to reinvigorate a staid management structure and culture, and end up with a company better able to serve customers' wants at lower cost.

It seems as though the structural and cultural emphasis of the Dose Company has remained static over its whole existence. They probably exist in isolation from their suppliers and customers with each department handling different functions with no idea of their place in the value chain. Re-engineers are not constrained by existing methods, people or departments. They ask 'why' and 'what if' questions about everything that happens in the organisation and then begin to explore better ways of doing it. They start form the future and work backwards.

The first step for the management of Dose is to look at the customer interface and improve sensitivity to the customer needs. Unless Dose is providing the best quality at the best price, it will face extinction.

To achieve this it needs to address the primary processes and:

- re-develop the demand process of customer links, marketing and service;

- re-develop the product - looking at innovation in design;

- ensure that quality is built into the product from inception and not merely inspected in afterwards;

- re-design the order fulfilment process - investigate the acquisition of resources, reduce development and production costs and reduce the lead time between product inception and commercial sale and delivery

The secondary processes that may need re-engineering include the support services of administration, finance and personnel management.

After BPR the company should see itself as part of a longer value chain and organise along activity streams (or processes) running through the business

In this respect, there is a similarity to other management theories. Value Chain Analysis looks at the physically and technologically distinct activities that an organisation performs and looks for the sources of advantage that can be obtained form each stage. Activity Based Management also discards the old departmental approach of R&D, Finance, Marketing, Personnel, Purchasing, Production and Sales, and re-organises these activities along tightly-linked systems running through the business.

As a manufacturing company, the managing director of Dose will be able to find numerous examples of similar businesses that have tried BPR. Some have succeeded in adding profits by improving the processes and the efficiency of activity flows in the business. Others have failed at huge cost because it was either too late when they applied the re-engineering or the reforms were not suitable for the culture and structure of the company.

Dose, like other manufacturing companies, needs to examine radical change ideas as they come up, but healthy scepticism is also wise. Although outdated management techniques and manufacturing methods are a significant reason why new competitors are taking market share from established industrial groups, other reasons are also important. Manufacturers need to look at their fundamental cost structure (labour rates, automation, capital costs) and at their responsiveness and innovation in design, delivery, service etc.

Dose needs to appreciate the lessons learned by others over the last few years and, if the BPR path is chosen, it needs to be done with commitment and leadership from the top. The managing director should not rely too heavily on expensive and temporary external consultants. Top management need to understand the likely impact and thorough analysis of what the business is about with no preconceptions. Once plans for change are decided, management must ensure they implement the appropriate changes fully and carefully, guiding through any cultural change needed to match structural ones.

CHAPTER 18	EXAM-TYPE QUESTION

Managing change

Any four from the following six strategies will suffice.

(a) **Participation**

This approach seeks to involve employees in the decision-making process. There are cases where this has been extended to the designing of own jobs, payment systems, etc. This has proved successful, as the American Coch and French study of Harwood Manufacturing and the UK experience of Pirelli would suggest. The advantage of this method is that it enhances commitment to change, since the employees have developed their own change. In addition, the wider range of input into the change process will bring in an equally wide range of knowledge and experience.

However, there are a number of significant disadvantages. First of all, there must be the culture and climate to permit participation in change. RC Townsend boasted how change worked in Avis with the same people. However, the type of person who would work for a car-rental firm is likely to be different from, and probably more adaptable than, someone who is in a very highly programmed job with little scope for creativity. The cynic would view the Pirelli example in terms of what were the implications upon the shop floor.

Secondly, the greater number of people in the decision-making process can give rise to an extremely protracted decision-making process. Also, as is evidenced from the Japanese ringi approach, no one is responsible and hence accountable for the decision.

Thirdly, there is a need for a high degree of trust between the management and work people. Again, there may not be the culture and tradition of this, with the result that the invitation to participate will be treated with considerable suspicion.

Fourthly, participation must be honest. Pseudo-participation is always exposed for the sham that it is, and only serves to exacerbate the problem. This can easily happen, since with the wide variety of people being involved, there is a high risk that plans for change degenerate into a talking shop.

(b) **Education**

There is a mistaken view that if people are better educated and trained, then they will be receptive to change. While better education and training may make changes easier, and create an environment where people are prepared to participate in the change process, it will also raise the expectation of the individual. This could mean an increased turnover as people become more marketable, or an exacerbated hostility derived from frustration where enhanced expectations have not been met.

(c) **Communication**

This assumes that if the plans for change are effectively communicated, then people will understand the need for change and accept the changes. This would lay the foundations for change to be implemented fairly easily and painlessly.

Sadly, the communication of the plans for change is subject to misinterpretation and, if wrong medium is selected, manipulation into disinformation by self-seeking interests. In addition, communication can be a two-edged sword. People may learn of the need for change and morale may drop, exacerbating the current situation. Similarly, the more marketable people may move, and this will also create a situation where change is needed, but the best people to implement it have left.

(d) **Power**

This is where management exerts what is perceived as its 'right to manage' and imposes change unilaterally. Management has the formal authority to do this within the parameters of appropriate legislation, and the de facto situation in relation to the labour market. In periods of high unemployment, management may elect to take this option, knowing that if employees do not like the situation, then they should look very carefully at the alternatives. It is argued that this draconian method is a viable option only in times of high unemployment, but it could be argued that in times of full employment those who are not prepared to go along with the changes can be eased out less painfully.

Such a strategy has the obvious advantage of being easy and quick to implement, especially if the workforce is in a weak and demoralised position. However, there are two significant potential disadvantages. First, in the short term, there is the obvious problem identified by Etzioni that such a coercive strategy will fail to gain the wholehearted support of the workforce, with the result that the desired levels of motivation, morale and output will not be achieved. Secondly, in the long term the company may be building up further problems for itself. Unions have long memories, and a coerced, demoralised workforce provides a fertile area in which confrontation and antagonism will develop. As a result, when the time becomes ripe for a more co-operative approach, the management is unlikely to find the unions and the employees very helpful, or predisposed to comply with managerial wishes.

(e) **Manipulation**

This can be very similar to the power strategy. It is ostensibly less coercive. A management team may use the media of pseudo-participation and pseudo-effective communication to persuade the workforce about the need for change. Ideally it will be done through a mass meeting, similar to union meetings outside the factory gate. Agreement comes from position power and an unwillingness to step out of line. The benefits are the same as from the power strategy, as are the considerable disadvantages.

(f) **Negotiation**

This moves along the spectrum from autocratic styles to a more consultative approach, usually through the media of the unions. The objective is an acceptable compromise solution. Two possibilities exist. First, that one side wins and one loses. Compromises are often unsuccessful, so this approach may be the best way. Secondly, is there the possibility to work towards a compromise? This option may not exist or it may be very unpalatable. The obvious example is where rationalisation is required. The unions may resist the closures, but the future of the whole company or even the industry may be at stake. This may mean that the path towards a compromise is really not available. It also means that one party to the negotiations is fighting with a considerable handicap.

The obvious advantage of negotiation is that it recognises potential conflict and seeks a solution without running the risk of creating damaging industrial disputes. It has the further advantage that the resultant agreement will produce a commitment to the changes and maintains the morale of the workforce and the output that management requires. However, it can be a protracted process, and if it goes on too long patience may be lost on both sides. It also depends upon the level of confidence that exists in the union and the negotiating team. If there is a feeling that the unions have sold the employees out, if they could have got a better deal, and if they feel they have been the victims of cynical manipulation, then the whole process will fail.

CHAPTER **19**	EXAM-TYPE QUESTIONS

Question 1: Cole Pitt PLC

(a) The group's board of directors appears to have been deprived of authority in the past by the personalised style of leadership of Sir Hector Grouse. A key element in a new organisation strategy should be to centralise some authority.

- It might be a practical suggestion to cut the size of the board of directors to a smaller number which might be more efficient as a decision-making group.

- The board should not be allowed to make operational management decisions for any of its divisions, but divisional managers should be required to submit regular performance reports - possibly monthly - to the group board.

- The board should also consider strategic decisions for the group as a whole, and should formulate and approve a corporate plan at regular intervals - say once a year or one every two years. Divisional managers would then be expected to operate within the guidelines of the strategic plan, or ask the board for approval to pursue any unexpected opportunity which may subsequently emerge.

- The divisional chief executives should either be given seats on the group board, or should be formed into a chief executives' committee, chaired by a board member. This is to ensure that there is a continual and efficient *combination* flow between operation managers and the group board.

- Capital expenditures above a certain amount should be submitted to the group board for approval by the operating division concerned.

- At divisional level, the chief executives should be responsible for carrying out group strategy, setting divisional targets and budgets, and achieving the desired level of performance.

- It might also be worth considering a form of matrix structure, since Cole Pitt plc is an international company, with regional managers responsible for promoting the varied interests of the group in a particular region of the world, eg a UK manager, a European manager, a manager for the Americas and so on.

- The remaining interests in the Australian mine should be handled at board level, perhaps by the group chairman personally, because of the strong interest the Australian government has in the mine.

(b) The main problems are that as follows.

- Mining appears to be a cyclical business with metal prices on the world markets fluctuating between high peaks and low troughs. When prices are low, there may be loss-making activities.

- Energy costs (oil in particular) have also been shown to be very variable. A further problem is that energy resources in the North Sea are limited and the supply will eventually run out.

The group has taken effective measures to protect itself against the risks of its cyclical businesses by diversifying into industry, which now accounts for 50% of the group profits and over one third of turnover.

(c) When a company operates in a high risk industry, it should either invest to remain successful in the industry, or it should pull out of the industry altogether. If Cole Pitt plc considers that it should remain in mining and energy as a part of its corporate strategy, it must continue to invest. Given the group's long-standing expertise in mining, it would make sense to investigate through the group's own minor subsidiaries.

The suggestion in the question is that since mining and energy are high-risk business escorts, the group shouldn't invest in them. This suggestion ignores the points that although to some extent risk should be reduced by diversifying, a company investing in a high risk business sector should seek recompense by means of higher returns or a quicker payback.

Question 2: Organic organisation

Burns and Stalker in their book 'Management of Innovation' studied the relationship between management practices and characteristics of the external environments, in particular, ability to innovate. They defined two main management systems:

- mechanistic where formal communications and hierarchy existed;

- organic where the looser structure was more suitable for coping with unstable conditions and unpredictable problems.

Burns and Stalker discussed five main features that identified an 'organic' organisation.

1   The management style tended to be strongly participative wherein a manager would adopt a role of being a guide and counsellor rather than an issuer of instructions. The manager would talk through problems with staff members, eliciting their involvement by encouraging them to contribute their knowledge, ideas and experience. In such discussions the manager would be a provider of advice and information and seek to achieve a consensus decision. This open

approach would encourage staff to understand the difficulties facing the organisation and to adopt the solution as their own. In this way, staff members feel protected when volunteering their ideas and able to exercise initiative when faced with rapidly changing circumstances. Management encourage staff to think of themselves as tackling a task rather than fulfilling a company duty. This builds a greater sense of action and encourages initiative. Under such an approach, staff feel valued as individuals and their contribution increases. Harvey Jones commented that he never ceased to be surprised in ICI at the performance that young managers could achieve if they were given freedom and encouragement.

2   Inherent in any organic system is the presence of a control system, which is based on results to be achieved rather than the means of getting there. Whereas a mechanistic organisation would exercise tight control through detailed rules and procedures; an organic system relies on motivation to achieve an agreed result. An individual working in isolation cannot achieve many organisational tasks; the motivated efforts of a team of people is necessary. The organic approach encourages this by allowing freedom of action to members of a team to determine their own methods and pursue their own ideas to achieve results. Typically, a management by objectives system evolves whereby a manager will be closely involved in determining the parameter of the task, the obstacles that need to be overcome and the result expected. Once that stage is achieved, the manager will maintain a watching brief and may only become involved in detail, if the team members encounter a problem that is beyond their scope.

Control therefore is results based and is effected by means of a network of control rather than being formally exercised by an individual operating through a hierarchy.

3   One feature of an organic system, strongly emphasised by Burns and Stalker, was the nature of the communication system. In a mechanistic system, communication will flow in a vertical direction, as staff report strictly to their boss within their own function. The nature of such communications tends to be commands and decisions issued downwards and a statement of results achieved passing upwards. Such communication tends to be formalised between different status levels in the same function. Such a communication system would prevent a task centered control system and open style management. Therefore, an organic structure will ensure that staff at all levels feel involved in the issues and are kept informed of aspects that affect their operations. This cannot be restricted to vertical communication flows, since team tasks will require substantial horizontal communication. In addition, a formalised communication system cannot keep pace with rapid changes in environmental factors; it is important to develop a strong information communication system. The organic structure will achieve this by encouraging lateral communication links, whereby a member of staff could freely contact members of other departments, even where there is a difference in status.

4   An organic structure recognises that adapting to change will require flexibility in assigning work, whereas a mechanistic organisation would have clearly defined roles, this is discouraged in an organic structure where there is continual redefinition of tasks as a result of interaction between individuals. Fluid definitions of roles and tasks will enable individuals to respond to changes with minimum control. this is important where an organisation faces intense competition or rapid technological changes. In such circumstances, assessment and re-adjustment to the new order are clearly important. Tom Peters in his book 'Thriving on Chaos' points out that rapid changes in environmental factors (eg social demands, economic changes, customer patterns, etc) will intensify and require management to adopt ever more fluid approaches. Individuals will see

their contribution as being part of a team achieving a result, rather than fulfilling an individual role. This will mean redefinition of individual's tasks and a willingness to adopt to new demands.

5   An organic organisation will develop a management structure that enables lateral communication and rapid adjustment to change. The specialist knowledge of individuals will be recognised as contributing to achievement of team tasks and ultimately, organisation objectives. To bring together the line management and staff advisory functions, an organic organisation will develop a network structure. Here control, authority and communication will operate through networks, not through a strict, formal hierarchy. For example, control will be vested jointly in line managers and technical staff, requiring both parties to co-ordinate to achieve the final goal. A matrix organisation structure is likely to develop as joint ownership of tasks and objectives is defined.

Note: This is a straightforward question if you are familiar with the work of Burns and Stalker. The two main pitfalls to avoid are:

1   merging one aspect with another (eg management style with structure) so that the identity of each of the five aspects is lost;

2   contrasting organic and mechanistic systems to any great extent. This is not asked for in the question.

| CHAPTER 20 | EXAM-TYPE QUESTIONS |

Question 1: Multinational

(a) Most multinational conglomerates have their own 'international' culture that is adapted to the host country they are operating in. The overseas company should identify with the multinational and this is usually done through standardised policies, procedures and operating instructions, thus allowing for consistency of operation as far as possible around the world.

The multinational headquarters will usually carry out long-term strategic planning and decision making. These plans and decisions will then be reviewed by each country, which will adopt the most appropriate 'local' tactics to achieve the objectives formulated. This means in practice that multinationals build a degree of flexibility into their planning process to allow for local conditions.

Headquarters should remember that local cultures will produce attitudes, desires, expectations, beliefs and customs which may have a significant effect on the way the organisation is managed and functions. A country's nationals cannot change practices of a lifetime, nor would it be appropriate to do so, as the organisation would be 'out of step' with business practices in operation in the host country, which would cause trading problems.

For example, local management will be familiar with local customs, suppliers, customers, government regulations and employment practices, none of which can be ignored by the multinational.

Where an acquisition or a merger attempts radically to change the approach taken by the host country's management, serious problems can occur. Employees may feel resentment and concern, and communication barriers may be constructed. This can lead to demotivation and alienation.

It will take time and considerable effort to find the right balance between a multinational and local culture, but without this balance the operation will not be working at its most efficient and effective.

(b) The integration of expatriate and locally recruited personnel has always been a challenge to multinationals. Many multinationals appoint expatriate managers to senior positions in the overseas company, in order to ensure that the 'corporate' line is followed, and local managers are trained in the appropriate manner.

The selection of expatriate managers is a key feature, as they are required not only to have good technical skills but also to develop diplomatic and advanced social skills in order to avoid or resolve potential areas of conflict. Managers are encouraged to mix and live in an integrated fashion with the 'locals' in order to facilitate their understanding of the culture. Usually expatriate managers' appointments last a defined number of years and can be seen as part of their management development programme.

Multinationals have developed various programmes that are specifically designed to integrate expatriate and local personnel. These programmes can cover such topics as language training, skills training and international management courses. Often local management are trained at the multinational's headquarters in order to facilitate identification with the corporate culture.

Multinationals tend to use local personnel as far as possible through all levels of the organisation, providing training where required.

There is potential for unity providing that it is based upon the sharing of tactical and managerial knowledge, the development of human and material skills and equity of treatment.

(c) Subsidiaries can be encouraged to respond to local opportunities whilst having regard to the wider interests of their parent companies.

The subsidiary could be organised as a profit centre; employees would then be responsible for the subsidiary's performance. This should motivate staff to perform efficiently and effectively, as results will be directly linked to local effort rather than getting lost in the multinational's performance. This will make it an identifiable part of the organisation, and can encourage local pride in achievements.

In addition, pay could be linked to profit or another performance measure, with bonuses being paid or shares being issued to staff.

Locally generated profits could be used to the benefit of local employees and inhabitants, for example the provision of sports facilities.

It may be appropriate to exploit local opportunities by using the international expertise, as well as inputs from the appropriate resources of the multinational.

Question 2: Protectionism

The principle of comparative advantage is that countries can benefit from trade based on differences in their comparative or opportunity costs. Take an example of two countries, A and B. producing two goods, wheat (W) and cloth (C). Assume full employment and constant opportunity costs. Suppose productivity in the two industries is:-

Output per unit of resources

	A	*B*
Wheat (units)	300	600
Cloth (units)	60	300
Opportunity cost	5*W*:1*C*	2*W*:1*C*
ratios	1*W*:0.2*C*	1*W*:0.5*C*

Though Country B is absolutely superior in producing both goods it has a comparative advantage in cloth - the opportunity cost of one unit of cloth is only $2W$ compared with $5W$ in country A. Country A similarly has a comparative advantage in wheat, which it produces with a lower opportunity cost than B. If trade opens up at an intermediate 'terms of trade', say, $1C:4W$, each country can gain from importing the good in which it has a comparative disadvantage at a lower opportunity cost than it can produce it at home. Country A can now obtain a unit of cloth by exporting $4W$; domestic production of cloth requires a sacrifice of $5W$. Country B can import wheat at a unit opportunity cost of $0.25C$ compared with the domestic cost of $0.5C$.

If prices reflect opportunity costs, free trade leads to each country specialising in and exporting the good, which it produces with a lower opportunity cost and importing more cheaply the good it produces with a higher opportunity cost. The result is a more efficient division of labour between countries and greater real income.

Widespread protectionism, particularly by restriction of imports, is partly explained by failure of the full employment assumption in practice. At times of recession and unemployment governments often attempt to stimulate output and employment by import controls to switch spending away from foreign output. This may be followed by a multiplier expansion of domestic demand, production and employment. However, boosting employment in this way may lead to retaliation and to an escalation of protectionism as in the 1930s and more recently during the recessions since the 1970s.

Governments in any case are under continual pressure to grant protection to domestic industries. 'Producer interests' of employers and workers use a wide range of arguments to achieve protection. Apart from the employment argument, these include:

- *Dumping and unfair competition* - Industries may claim that foreign suppliers are dumping goods on the home market, that is, selling at prices below cost. But genuine dumping is difficult to prove and dumping is often used merely as a pretext for increased protection.

- *Low wages/cheap labour* - Industries in industrialised countries again often claim unfair competition from goods produced with cheap labour in less developed countries (LDCs). As a general argument it is invalid since low wages in LDCs reflect low absolute labour productivity. It is not unfair if they then export labour-intensive goods in which they have a comparative advantage based on low wages.

- *Revenue* - Some countries justify tariffs as a means of raising revenue but this is a good argument only when there is a narrow domestic tax base, as in some LDCs.

- Infant industries and economic development - LDCs often justify protection of new industries which face excess costs when they are first established. But, even when true, this is an argument only for temporary protection. Similarly, many LDCs protect domestic manufacturing and service industries to diversify out of primary production. However, the evidence suggests that protection actually retards rather than promotes economic development.

- Balance of payments - Imports may be restricted in order to reduce a payments deficit and save foreign exchange but this argument falls down if there is widespread retaliation.

- Non-economic arguments - Examples include: strategic (defence industries, agriculture); environment and conservation (agriculture, fisheries) and need to preserve national 'culture' (books, films, TV and arts).

The trouble with these arguments is that there are invariably more efficient and direct means of achieving these non-economic goals than protection.

These arguments anyway do not explain protection; rather they try to justify protection, the real reasons for which lie in politics. Protection is the outcome of bargaining in the political market place. Thus, protection is 'supplied' by governments, legislators and bureaucrats. The demand is from producer interests who will be more successful in lobbying for protection where they can promise significant political or financial advantage in return. For example, the success of agriculture in gaining protection in most countries is related to the disproportionate electoral importance of farming communities and to the wide range of appealing non-economic arguments for protection, which are available (preservation of the countryside, 'need' for self-sufficiency in food, and so on). Most important, though, is the concentration of land ownership among the 'ruling elite' itself which supplies protection.

So, although we can show that protection raises prices and denies consumers the benefits of cheaper imports, politicians and bureaucrats often see political or financial advantage from granting protection to producer interests which are much more powerful and better organised than diffused consumer interests.

CHAPTER 21	EXAM-TYPE QUESTIONS

Question 1: Non-financial indicators

(a) Management information can usefully be provided in non-monetary terms. Instead of valuing items such as output and stocks in financial terms, managers can be provided with information in the form of physical measures such as kilograms, tonnes or litres, or in terms of time or units of output.

The *advantages* of non-financial indicators include the following.

- They can be provided quickly, per shift, say, or on a daily or even an hourly basis as required. In terms of control, speed is of the essence.

- They are likely to be easy to calculate, or at least easier than traditional financial measures.

- They are expressed in terms that non-financial managers understand and they are therefore easier to use effectively: they will prompt the *correct* corrective action.

- They can be expressed in the form of ratios or percentages for comparative purposes (with other divisions or periods or with competitors).

- Arguably, NFIs are less likely to be manipulated than traditional profit-related measures and they should, therefore, offer a means of counteracting short-termism, since short-term profit is not the goal.

However NFIs do have certain disadvantages.

- There is a danger that too many such measures could be reported, overloading managers with information that is not truly useful, or that sends conflicting signals.

- NFIs may lead managers to pursue detailed operational goals and become blind to the overall strategy in which those goals are set.

A combination of financial and non-financial indicators is thus likely to be most successful.

(b) Basic control theory dictates that control is required because unpredictable disturbances arise and enter the system, so that actual results (outputs of the system) deviate from the expected results or goals. No aspect of an organisation's activities is immune from this and thus every aspect should be subject to some form of control.

Where long-term contracts are involved, the cost of the unexpected could be immense and thus very careful control is necessary. This could be achieved in the following ways.

- The potential suppliers should be assessed to determine their financial stability and the stability of their economic and political climate if applicable. Their ability to deliver materials of the required quality at the required times should also be taken into account. Conditions could be written into the contract to cover such matters if the purchasing business is in a position to dictate terms.

- Before committing itself to a long-term contract the purchasing business should be sure that it will need the materials to be purchased. This means that it needs to conduct research into its own market and perhaps enter into agreements with its own customers. The state of its own economy, inflation, and currency fluctuations must all be assessed to ensure that the use to which the materials will be put will remain a viable one for the length of the contract.

- The purchasing organisation should also consider its own ability to produce the end product. Is its workforce sufficiently well trained? Will its machines be able to process the materials as intended? Do the materials need special storage facilities? Are there other production factors to be taken into account?

- Once the information outlined in (i) to (iii) has been assembled it should be analysed, perhaps by using financial modelling techniques to assess the risk.

- Any avenues which could reduce risk should be explored. These might include insurance, using formal exchange contracts or futures, entering into risk sharing agreements with suppliers and/or customers, securing long-term sales contracts, obtaining government support and so on.

- Only then, if satisfied on all points, should a contract be drawn up by the respective lawyers of the purchaser and supplier. The contract may need board authorisation before it is finally signed.

- Control should be maintained throughout the period of the contract to ensure that its terms are being adhered to. This would include regular monitoring of the quality and timeliness of supplies and of the amount charged for them, and indeed of all of the matters considered before entering into the contract. Deviations from the contract should be drawn to the attention of the suppliers and any penalties on failure to comply with the terms should be exacted. The purchasing organisation should also have control procedures to ensure that it fulfils its part of the bargain.

Question 2: Structure and evaluation

(a) The points that might be raised in the discussion paper are as follows.

If the organisational structure is about to be changed, there must be a new look at:

- who is responsible for each aspect of operations;

- what level of efficiency might be required from them.

An O & M study might be needed to establish new standard procedures and times.

- Finding a measurement of output for a department. There will be few problems with production, selling and distribution, but measurements are not so obvious for administrative departments, such as personnel, accounts, data processing, research and development, engineering design and so on.

- Choosing the standard of efficiency against which to compare actual results, for example ideal, attainable, current or basic standards.

- The accuracy of measurements of actual output and actual times should be questioned. Might measurements of output and times by employees be recorded incorrectly, perhaps deliberately?

- Measuring efficiency tends to detract from the quality of work. Faster times are often feasible, but at the expense of poorer quality.

- Measures of performance must be selected and reported in such a way as to motivate controllers and their subordinates.

- Agreed control limits should be established so that investigation of efficiency variances would only be necessary if they exceeded the limit.

- One department might rely on other departments for work and support. For example, the accounts department can only achieve a high productivity per person employed if there are sufficient sales, purchases, cash transactions etc in a period to keep them fully occupied.

(b) The important areas for control are as follows.

- *Cost.* Costs will include travelling costs (vans, running costs, petrol and so on), wages or salaries of staff, cost of replacement parts or machines, and general administration costs of the repairs department.

- *Number of complaints and efficiency in dealing with them.* All complaints must be answered. Productivity of the service engineers will depend on how quickly they respond to service calls, how long it takes them to reach a customer's house, and how quickly they can complete the repair and the documentation that accompanies the job.

- *The effectiveness of repair work.* Do customers have to be re-visited because a repair job was not done properly the first time?

Possible measures of performance are as follows.

- Average repair cost per complaint dealt with

- Number of repairs per service engineer per month

- Average time per repair

- Average travelling time per repair visit

- Proportion of repair visits where subsequent re-visits are necessary

CHAPTER 22	EXAM-TYPE QUESTION

Social responsibility

Social responsibility is a hard term to define, but many would say it means acting with regard to social welfare. No organisation would ever admit to be socially irresponsible and many organisations claim to act responsibly on social issues.

For an organisation to act with social responsibility, it should align its goals with those of the wider society of which it is a part. Whether a society as such has easily defined goals is hard to assess: the purpose and direction of society, not to mention the means by which those goals are achieved, are generally political decisions rather than commercial ones. Is the wider society limited to the national economy or the world as a whole? The consequences of a global corporation acting with 'social responsibility' in one society may cause it to act without social responsibility in another. Moreover, a business almost certainly has its own objectives, which, in the long term, it claims will enhance social welfare, if only that the creation of wealth as a result of business activities is felt to be of benefit to society as a whole.

The managers of organisations, however, which seek to be socially responsible, rarely start off with a theoretical notion of social responsibility, which they then seek to implement. Rather, organisations that act responsibly do so in response to pressures from their various stakeholders. Some of these pressures are outlined below.

- **Employees** - are internal stakeholders. Their relationship with the organisation is twofold. Firstly, it is their labour that keeps the organisation in operational existence. Secondly, as citizens they are members of the wider society in which the organisation exists. Employees value the certainty and regularity of wages, in other words that the employing organisation will honour the contract of employment. To act with social responsibility also implies a concern and respect for safety in the workplace, whether this relates to equipment, building, or hours worked. The organisation's social responsibility includes adaptation to other pressures on employee's lifestyles. Workplace crèches, for example, are of great assistance to working mothers, but employers are unlikely to introduce them without any consequent commercial benefit. If, for example, the cost of labour turnover is higher than the cost of running workplace crèches and if labour turnover is reduced significantly by a workplace crèche, then the crèche can be justified (in financial terms).

  Management has a certain amount of discretion, but this is circumscribed by law. Health and safety for example is the subject of regulation, as it was felt that commercial imperatives would not justify the expense, and that employers are not necessarily altruistic. Other benefits are won as the result of the relationship between management and organised labour. The exercise of social responsibility towards the workforce is constrained by the law, by organised labour, and in some instances by the recognition that social responsibility can be of benefit in encouraging employee loyalty and skill.

- **Customers** - are stakeholders in that they pay for the organisation's output of goods and services. Here the situation is more complex. In some consumer goods sectors, public attitudes -with some direction from government and lobby groups have made the environmental impact of an organisation's activities open to public comment. This has led suppliers to reduce CFCs in aerosol cans, and to introduce ranges of goods, which are supposed to be friendly to the environment. Finally, it sometimes happen when a firm bids for a contract with a local authority, for example, that contract compliance, by which the contract is only awarded to a firm which operates an equal opportunities policy, will be required of any successful bidder.

- **Suppliers** - in multinational corporations, the exercise of social responsibility is distributed over several countries, but again, management will only let it override commercial objectives if it either is part of the inbuilt culture of the firm, or if the voice of public opinion in the market is strong. An example is the use of rainforest hardwoods: some consumer organisations are suggesting boycotting these products. A supplier may also make restrictions on the end-use of products a condition of sale. For example, a supplier of high-technology items may require that these are not re-exported to the enemies of the nation where the supplier is based.

- **Professional bodies** - control is exercised over certain members of management by their membership of professional bodies, which have standards of ethics and conduct.

- **Elected authorities** - society's elected political representatives are external stakeholders and can affect management in a number of ways, by legislation as has already been mentioned, by influencing the climate of public opinion, or by trying to persuade commercial organisations to follow a particular line or policy. An example is business sponsorship of the arts in the UK. (The tenor of government policy has been to reduce government funding and to encourage commercial organisations to avail themselves of the marketing opportunities thereby provided.)

- **Shareholders** - are connected stakeholders. The main interest of shareholders is profit, and they might have objections to money being spent on projects which are socially responsible but which reduce the return on the investment. As many shareholders are large institutions like pension funds, then their duties can be adversely affected by the use of organisational resources on activities, which do not make a profit. It is possible that some shareholders, and other commentators, would assert that the creation of wealth is the only desirable social objective of a business and anything, which intervenes in this objective is damaging in the long run.

- **Management issues** - social responsibility has costs and benefits for an organisation, and management have to weigh up the conflicting demands of different stakeholders. There is also the problem of managing social responsibility policies and activities so that the most effective use is made of the resources allocated for the purpose. This means:

    (a) monitoring the expectations people have of the organisation, as an enterprise which trumpets its environmental friendliness will be expected to live up to its claims in all areas;

    (b) achieving the maximum good publicity from the project;

    (c) selecting an appropriate choice of socially responsible activities which can be divided between:

        - ensuring that the firm's core activities are conducted in a socially responsible way;
        - subsidising, supporting or sponsoring those activities which are for public welfare

    (d) clearly distinguishing between what are the minimum acceptable standards in a particular situation, and what are additional to them.

Index

FTC Foulks Lynch
A **Kaplan Professional** Company

STUDY TEXT REVIEW FORM
ACCA Paper 3.5

Thank you for choosing this text for your ACCA professional qualification. As we are constantly striving to improve our products, we would be grateful if you could provide us with feedback about how useful you found this publication.

Name: ....

Address: ....

....

Email: ....

Why did you decide to purchase this Study Text?

Have used them in the past	☐
Recommended by lecturer	☐
Recommended by friend	☐
Saw advertising	☐
Other (please specify)..	

How do you study?

At a college	☐
On a distance learning course	☐
Home study	☐
Other (please specify)...	

Within our ACCA range we also offer Exam Kits and Pocket Notes. Is there any other type of service/publication that you would like to see as part of the range?

CD Rom with additional questions and answers	☐
A booklet that would help you master exam skills and techniques	☐
Space on our website that would answer your technical questions and queries	☐
Other (please specify)...	

During the past six month do you recall seeing/receiving any of the following?

Our advertisement in *Student Accountant* magazine?	☐
Our advertisement in any other magazine? (please specify)	☐
....	
Our leaflet/brochure or a letter through the post?	☐
Other (please specify)...	

Overall opinion of this Study Text

	Excellent	Adequate	Poor
Introductory pages	☐	☐	☐
Syllabus coverage	☐	☐	☐
Clarity of explanations	☐	☐	☐
Clarity of definitions and key terms	☐	☐	☐
Diagrams	☐	☐	☐
Activities	☐	☐	☐
Self-test questions	☐	☐	☐
Practice questions	☐	☐	☐
Answers to practice questions	☐	☐	☐
Layout	☐	☐	☐
Index	☐	☐	☐

If you have further comments/suggestions or have spotted any errors, please write them on the next page.

Please return this form to: The Publisher, FTC Foulks Lynch, FREEPOST NAT 17540, Wokingham RG40 1BR

Other comments/suggestions and errors

....
....
....
....
....
....
....
....
....
....
....
....
....
....
....
....
....
....
....
....
....
....
....
....
....
....
....
....
....
....
....
....
....

Other comments/suggestions and errors

....
....
....

FTC Foulks Lynch
A **Kaplan Professional** Company

ACCA Order Form

Swift House, Market Place, Wokingham, Berkshire RG40 1AP, UK
Tel: +44 (0) 118 989 0629   Fax: +44 (0) 118 979 7455

Order online: www.financial-training.com
Email: publishing@financial-training.com

Examination Date: Dec 05 ☐ Jun 06 ☐ (please tick the exam you intend to take)	Study Text £26.00	Exam Kit Dec 05 £13.00	Exam Kit Jun 06 £14.00	Pocket Notes £10.00	Drill & Practice £10.00
Part 1					
1.1 Preparing Financial Statements (UK)	☐	☐	☐	☐	☐
1.1 Preparing Financial Statements (International)	☐	☐	☐	☐	☐
1.2 Financial Information for Management	☐	☐	☐	☐	☐
1.3 Managing People	☐	☐	☐	☐	N/A
Part 2					
2.1 Information Systems	☐	☐	☐	☐	N/A
2.2 Corporate & Business Law (English)	☐	☐	☐	☐	N/A
2.2 Corporate & Business Law (Scottish)	☐	N/A	N/A	N/A	N/A
2.3 Business Taxation – FA 2004	☐	☐	N/A	☐	N/A
2.3 Business Taxation – FA 2005	☐	N/A	☐	☐	N/A
2.4 Financial Management & Control	☐	☐	☐	☐	N/A
2.5 Financial Reporting (UK)	☐	☐	☐	☐	N/A
2.5 Financial Reporting (International)	☐	☐	☐	☐	N/A
2.6 Audit & Internal Review (UK)	☐	☐	☐	☐	N/A
2.6 Audit & Internal Review (International)	☐	☐	☐	☐	N/A
Part 3					
3.1 Audit & Assurance Services (UK)	☐	☐	☐	☐	N/A
3.1 Audit & Assurance Services (International)	☐	☐	☐	☐	N/A
3.2 Advanced Taxation – FA 2004	☐	☐	N/A	☐	N/A
3.2 Advanced Taxation – FA 2005	☐	N/A	☐	☐	N/A
3.3 Performance Management	☐	☐	☐	☐	N/A
3.4 Business Information Management	☐	☐	☐	☐	N/A
3.5 Strategic Business Planning & Development	☐	☐	☐	☐	N/A
3.6 Advanced Corporate Reporting (UK)	☐	☐	☐	☐	N/A
3.6 Advanced Corporate Reporting (International)	☐	☐	☐	☐	N/A
3.7 Strategic Financial Management	☐	☐	☐	☐	N/A
Research and Analysis Project Guide (supporting Oxford Brookes University BSc (Hons) in Applied Accounting)	☐				
Postage, Packaging and Delivery (per item): **Note**: Maximum postage charged for UK orders is £15				**TOTAL**	

Study Texts and Exam Kits	First	Each Extra	Pocket Notes and Drill & Practice	First	Each Extra
UK	£5.00	£2.00	UK	£2.00	£1.00
Europe (incl Republic of Ireland and Channel Isles)	£7.00	£4.00	Europe (incl Republic of Ireland and Channel Isles)	£3.00	£2.00
Rest of World	£22.00	£8.00	Rest of World	£8.00	£5.00

Product Sub Total £...................	Postage & Packaging £.................	Order Total £....................	(Payments in UK £ Sterling)

Customer Details

☐ Mr   ☐ Mrs   ☐ Ms   ☐ Miss   Other ....

Initials:.................... Surname: ....

Address: ....

....

....

Postcode: ....

Delivery Address – if different from above

Address: ....

....

Postcode: ....

Telephone: ....

Email: ....

Fax: ....

Delivery please allow: United Kingdom   – 5 working days
                            Europe   – 8 working days
                            Rest of World   – 10 working days

Payment

1 I enclose Cheque/Postal Order/Bankers Draft for £....................................

    Please make cheques payable to '**The Financial Training Company Ltd**'.

2 Charge MasterCard/Visa/Switch/Delta no:

   ☐☐☐☐ ☐☐☐☐ ☐☐☐☐ ☐☐☐☐

   Valid from: ☐☐☐☐   Expiry date: ☐☐☐☐

   Issue no:

   (Switch only) ☐☐   Verification No. ☐☐☐

   Signature: .... Date: ....

Declaration

I agree to pay as indicated on this form and understand that The Financial
Training Company's Terms and Conditions apply (available on request).

Signature: .... Date: ....

Notes: All orders over 1kg will be fully tracked & insured. Signature required on receipt of order.
Delivery times subject to stock availability. A telephone number or email address is required for
orders that are to be delivered to a PO Box number.

ACCA
Approved Publisher

FTC Foulks Lynch
A **Kaplan Professional** Company

SPECIAL OFFER - Our Distance Learning Students consistently achieve pass rates above the ACCA global average. Increase your chances of success and upgrade your Official ACCA Study Text to a Distance Learning Course for only £88 per paper and gain

- Personal Tutor Support by telephone and email (local rate 0845 number for UK callers)
- The whole range of Official ACCA Publications including Exam Kits and Pocket Notes
- Work Programme
- Unique 5-Star-Guide written by a Specialist Tutor
- Two Progress Tests which you can send to us for marking and feedback
- Hints and Tips Audio CD on study skills and exam technique
- Student Handbook packed with practical information about your course
- 10% discount on any FTC revision course.

This offer is only available if you already own the Official FTC Foulks Lynch ACCA Study Text for the December 2005 or June 2006 Examinations.

ACCA Distance Learning Enrolment Form

Surname	First Name	Mr / Miss / Mrs / Ms

Home Address

Post Code	Country
Home Tel	Office Tel
Mobile	E-mail
Date of Birth	ACCA Registration Number

Exam sitting: ☐ CBE   ☐ December 2005   ☐ June 2006

EMPLOYER DETAILS (Sponsor must be UK based company)

Company Name

Manager's Name

Address

	Post Code	Country
Telephone	Email	

SPONSORED STUDENTS: EMPLOYER'S AUTHORISATION

If the above employer is responsible for the payment of fees, please complete the following:

As employer of the student for whom this form is completed, we are responsible for payment of fees due on receipt of the invoice in respect of the student named above and undertake to inform you in writing of any change to this arrangement. We understand that we are fully responsible for the payment of fees due in all circumstances including termination of employment or cancellation of course.

Purchase Order Number _____

Manager's Name _____

Manager's Signature _____ Date _____

DATA PROTECTION ACT:
Your sponsor can be informed of your test results unless we are otherwise notified.

HOW TO ENROL:

By phone:	If you are paying by credit card, please telephone +44 (0)113 200 6363
By post:	Complete this enrolment form and return to:
	FTC Foulks Lynch Distance Learning, 49 St Paul's Street, LEEDS LS1 2TE
By fax:	Fax both sides of your completed enrolment form to +44 (0)113 243 0133

Distance Learning Courses include VAT and all materials. Add postage & packing – applicable to both Distance Learning options (for rates see below).	Distance Learning		Distance Learning (excluding Official ACCA Study Text applicable for the December 2005 and June 2006 examinations sittings only)	
	£	✓	£	✓
Part 1				
1.1 Preparing Financial Statements (UK)	114		88	
1.1 Preparing Financial Statements (International)	114		88	
1.2 Financial Information for Management	114		88	
1.3 Managing People	114		88	
Part 2				
2.1 Information Systems	114		88	
2.2 Corporate & Business Law	114		88	
2.3 Business Taxation	114		88	
2.4 Financial Management and Control	114		88	
2.5 Financial Reporting (UK)	114		88	
2.5 Financial Reporting (International)	114		88	
2.6 Audit & Internal Review (UK)	114		88	
2.6 Audit & Internal Review (International)	114		88	
Part 3 Options				
3.1 Audit & Assurance Services (UK)	114		88	
3.1 Audit & Assurance Services (International)	114		88	
3.2 Advanced Taxation	114		88	
3.3 Performance Management	114		88	
3.4 Business Information Management	114		88	
Part 3 Core				
3.5 Strategic Business Planning & Development	114		88	
3.6 Advanced Corporate Reporting (UK)	114		88	
3.6 Advanced Corporate Reporting (International)	114		88	
3.7 Strategic Financial Management	114		88	

FEES	£
Postage & Packing	£
Total	£

POSTAGE & PACKING
Distance Learning (per paper):
UK & NI £6, Europe & Channel Islands £15, Rest of World £40

DISTANCE LEARNING TERMS AND CONDITIONS OF ENROLMENT:

1. A completed enrolment form must be accompanied by the full fee or employer's authorisation.
2. Where an employer's authorisation is received, the full fees are payable within 30 days of the invoice date. The employer is responsible for the payment of fees due in all circumstances including termination of employment or cancellation of course. FTC reserves the right to charge interest on overdue accounts.
3. A deferral can be processed to the following exam sitting subject to a deferral fee of £25 if notified in writing. If new study materials are required due to syllabus changes or changes in Finance Acts, they will have to be paid for in addition to the deferral fee.
4. Refunds are only available on study materials returned within 14 days in a saleable condition.
5. Courses are not transferable between students.
6. Distance Learning fees include VAT and all materials but exclude any taxes or duties imposed by countries outside the UK.

METHODS OF PAYMENT:

☐ Please invoice my employer (details completed overleaf).
☐ I enclose a cheque made payable to The Financial Training Company Ltd. for £ _____
Payments will only be accepted in UK Sterling.
☐ Please charge my Credit/Debit Card Number for the fees indicated above.

| Valid from | | | | | Expiry | | | | Solo/Switch Issue No | | | Security Code | | | |

I agree to the terms and conditions of enrolment which I have read.

Student Signature _____ Date _____